Hmong Refugees
in the New World

Hmong Refugees in the New World

Culture, Community and Opportunity

CHRISTOPHER THAO VANG

Foreword by GREGORY S. GOODMAN

McFarland & Company, Inc., Publishers

Jefferson, North Carolina

Library of Congress Cataloguing-in-Publication Data

Names: Vang, Christopher Thao.
Title: Hmong refugees in the new world : culture, community and opportunity /
Christopher Thao Vang ; foreword by Gregory S. Goodman.
Description: Jefferson, North Carolina : McFarland & Company, Inc.,
Publishers, [2016] | Includes bibliographical references and index.
Identifiers: LCCN 2015047830 | ISBN 9781476662169 (softcover : acid free paper) ∞
Subjects: LCSH: Hmong (Asian people)—Foreign countries. | Hmong (Asian
people)—History. | Hmong (Asian people)—Social life and customs. |
Political refugees—United States—History—20th century.
Classification: LCC DS509.5.H66 V35 2016 | DDC 305.8959/72073—dc23
LC record available at http://lccn.loc.gov/2015047830

British Library cataloguing data are available

ISBN (print) 978-1-4766-6216-9
ISBN (ebook) 978-1-4766-2262-0

Front cover: Hmong tapestry designed by Youa Xiong (used with permission)

Printed in the United States of America

McFarland & Company, Inc., Publishers
Box 611, Jefferson, North Carolina 28640
www.mcfarlandpub.com

To all Hmong refugees,
Hmong leader Major General Vang Pao,
and to the Hmong children
who need to learn about their heritage

Table of Contents

Acknowledgments

The year 2015 marked the fortieth year of my people living in the western nations. I am proud of my heritage and respect my history, people, culture, and traditions. I am also honored and privileged to be an American.

I am grateful for the opportunity to write this book about my history and people. I have poured my heart and soul into its contents because I want to retell the history, life, and migration of my people. I would like to share the remarkable progresses and successes my people have achieved in life in the new world since 1975.

This book is written about Hmong refugees who emigrated from China to Laos and then left Laos for the western nations since 1975. Their life-long sacrifices in search of freedom, social justice, equality, socioeconomic opportunities, and prosperity have never been forgotten by their children. Their life-long journey from the eastern world to the western nations will always remain in their children's hearts and souls forever.

This book is also written in honor of the leadership of the latest Hmong leader, Major General Vang Pao aka *Phagna Norapamok General Vang Pao*, who dedicated his entire life to serving Hmong people and who ruled Hmong sociopolitical leadership for nearly 67 years before his death in 2011. For the Laotian Kings, Major General Vang Pao was the Lord Protector of the Land, but in the Hmong world, he was the Father of Hmong refugees because he loved Hmong people with all his heart and soul and left behind an invaluable legacy for all Hmong to commem-orate. He was the honorable commander-in-chief who led the Hmong Special Guerrilla Unit (SGU) during the nearly 15-year-long "Secret War" in the Military Region II in Laos. Most importantly, Major General Vang Pao was the human bridge all western Hmong refugees had walked on to cross the Atlantic Ocean to find freedom, equality, social justice, democracy, and socioeconomic opportunities in the western nations. Therefore, Phagna Norapamok General Vang Pao is the most honored and revered Hmong leader of all time; his legacy will live in Hmong hearts and souls forever.

This book is intended to educate Hmong children who would like to learn, understand and study Hmong history, traditions, customs, values and beliefs. The contents of this book will guide them every step of the way and will provide them with the foundation needed for further research and studies to help them gain more insights into the sacrifices made by Hmong ancestors, forefathers, past leaders, soldiers and ordinary civilians who risked their lives to save themselves and others, endured brutal atrocities to avoid ethnic extirpation, and died in honor to pave the way for Hmong refugees to find freedom. The book is also intended to help Hmong children appreciate and remember the history, life, and migration of Hmong refugees who journeyed from the ancient world to the new world to save themselves and to start a new life.

I am honored to have known Gregory S. Goodman throughout my educational life. I am indebted to him for his sincere and invaluable encouragement of my work. This book could not have been attempted, much less written or published, without his expertise, scholarship, and countless hours of support. Goodman is the impetus behind the book. I am blessed to be a recipient of his kindness, friendship, mentoring, and scholarship, for these are what have made this book a reality. I thank him for all he has done for me.

I also want to thank Mr. Dar Xiong, for allowing me to use an artistic Hmong tapestry designed by his mother, Mrs. Youa Xiong, for the book cover.

Foreword

Gregory S. Goodman

Nyob Zoo.

Here is another brilliant book by Christopher Vang. This new book, *Hmong Refugees in the New World: Culture, Community and Opportunity*, was written to retell Hmong history and the remarkable journey of the Hmong people in seeking freedom and better opportunities in the western world. Vang is a Hmong American professor who has put his own history into a book that unfolds the migration of Hmong refugees from eastern countries to western nations. The content of this book is a great resource for multicultural educators who are interested in knowing and learning more about the Hmong refugees in diaspora.

I worked with many Hmong students and professionals from the 1990s through 2015 and learned much about Hmong families, traditions, and community. However, this book gave me information I did not previously have about the history of the Hmong people: their challenges, opportunities, and successes since arriving in the West. Vang has synthesized the topical issues in this book in a way that makes readers eager to delve deeper into Hmong history and culture. This book will add in-depth knowledge and enhance the inter-cultural skills of any professional who encounters Hmong refugees. During my tenure as a school psychologist in California, I came to know this beautiful culture and the traditions of the Hmong people. I believe the facts and insights in this new book will stir the same appreciation in other educators who are passionate about knowing and understanding the people they serve.

The Hmong are a unique group of war-displaced refugees who emigrated to the United States and other western nations since 1975. Over the last forty years, western sociologists have explored and written about the Hmong, but ignorance, myths, and misperceptions persist about their origin, their history, and their culture. Western scholars and researchers need a thorough and accurate picture of the Hmong, and Vang provides that in this book. Some Americans still think Hmong refugees are foreigners who immigrated to the United States purely in search of better economic opportunities. In fact, Hmong are refugees and not immigrants; they came to America to escape persecution, imprisonment, torture, oppression, and death. They came to start their lives over again. Today, Hmong children know their parents' recent past, but they know little about the great sacrifices their parents and grandparents made before arriving in the western world. Retaining oral history helps Hmong children use the past to navigate the present by passing down fables, folktales, folklore, stories, myths, epics, legends, and religious rites from forefathers to descendants from one generation to the next. In this new book, Vang has done scholarly research to piece together some of the major events of Hmong history, including their migration from ancient China to the West. Vang also provides clarification about the name *Hmong*, or *Mong,* explaining that Hmong are not Miao or Meo, as some western scholars have erroneously believed.

Hmong Americans are still relatively new in the United States compared to other Southeast Asian groups. The Vietnam War made the ethnic Hmong known around the world, primarily because of their role in the so-called "Secret War" in Laos. Americans have learned some things about the Hmong since their arrival in the West in the mid–1970s, but most Americans know little about them. The Hmong have been portrayed as indigenous to Laos or as montagnards and mountain dwellers. In this new book, Vang presents his research that demonstrates that the Hmong in the United States are freedom fighters and American patriots who played a vital role in assisting downed American pilots and furthering U.S. foreign policy in Southeast Asia during the Secret War.

As with many other refugee and immigrant groups, Hmong in America have experienced educational and sociopolitical successes. I have learned over the years that their successes have not been achieved easily; they came from a preliterate and mostly isolated society to one of the most complex and sophisticated societies in the world. Many had to struggle to overcome a variety of social barriers and cultural issues. Some remained stranded between two worlds and others took the opportunities in front of them and turned them into success. Tremendous socioeconomic challenges confronted them as they strove to make better lives for themselves in America and elsewhere in the western world. To live the American Dream, Hmong refugees made huge sacrifices as they went through the socialization process of repeated conflict and adaptation. They were unprepared for the obstacles in the West, beset as they were with family difficulties, low employment, ill preparation for western schools, physical and mental health problems, and difficult psycho-social adjustments. As a Hmong scholar, Vang uncovers and shares some remarkable examples of the success of Hmong Americans and describes how they cope with their new lives in a new world.

I am proud of Vang for writing this beautiful book, for sharing from his unique vantage point with other educators. Vang presents a compendium of scholarship and research in this book. It is my great honor and privilege to introduce his new book, *Hmong Refugees in the New World: Culture, Community and Opportunity,* to everyone who would like to learn more about the Hmong and their role in history. Vang has been my dear friend for many years; therefore, as both a friend and a professional educator, I am honored to recommend this book to prospective and current educators who are working with children from diverse backgrounds in schools and communities. Hmong Americans are part of the American fabric, and this book provides practical information that will benefit parents, teachers, students, and educators in multicultural settings.

Ua tsaug.

Gregory S. Goodman has worked with Hmong people and their communities for many years in California. He teaches multicultural classes at Clarion University.

Preface

This book presents Hmong history and describes the journey of the Hmong people from eastern to western countries. Its purpose is to enable prospective and current educators to understand *how* war-displaced Hmong refugees came to the United States instead of wondering *why* they are here or *what* brought them here in the first place. Prospective and current educators play a vital role in informing the general public about different groups of refugees, emigrants, and immigrants who come to the United States of America for survival as well as to find better economic opportunities and enjoy freedom and democracy. The Hmong are still relatively new refugees; they came here to survive, to save themselves, and to start their lives all over again.

The U.S. is known the world over as a land of great opportunity, a nation of many nationalities, and a country that welcomes refugees and immigrants. Thus understanding why people come to the U.S. is easy; however, respecting, appreciating, and celebrating those who come requires knowledge of the histories, cultures, and traditions of the different groups. This book gives prospective and current educators a foundation that will empower them to teach the American public what many do not know about Hmong refugees: their remarkable role in assisting the American government in implementing its foreign policy in Southeast Asia in the 1960s and 1970s, their part in fighting Communism in Vietnam, and their bravery and sacrifice in the so-called "Secret War" in Laos. This book answers some basic questions about Hmong refugees, such as who they are and why they are here.

What This Book Provides for Educators

This book provides prospective and current educators with clear approaches to learning about the history of the Hmong. The Chinese Hmong were war-displaced refugees and immigrants, but the Laotian Hmong are only war-displaced refugees, not immigrants. The Hmong in the West are war-displaced refugees from China and Laos. Over the last two centuries, misidentification has portrayed Hmong refugees as of an ethnic group other than Hmong. This mislabeling has caused massive confusion about Hmong history. They have been erroneously called *Miao, Meo, Miaozi, Meng, Mu,* or *San Miao.* The truth is they have a history and rich cultural traditions that have yet to be understood by the American public. Today, Hmong refugees are part of the fabric of America, but many Americans still wonder how and why the Hmong got here. This new book invites prospective and current educators to take a journey back in time to discover the nearly 6,000-year-old story of the Hmong.

The ethnic group called *Hmong* was not known in the western world until the late 20th century when the National Geographic Society put a picture of the Hmong people on the front cover of a special issue of *National Geographic* featuring a group of Southeast Asians that was allied with the Americans in the Vietnam War. Almost no one in the West had heard of the Hmong before the Vietnam War, and few knew of them before their arrival in the United States and other western countries in 1975. Centuries earlier, however, they existed as an ancient ethnic group in China. They were called by different names: *Miao, San Miao, Man, Meng, Yue, Ma, Mao, Meo*, and so on. Some of these names are derogatory, translating to a variety of negative meanings such as barbarians, people of the dirt, savages, slaves, women, poor, and rice stalks. The Hmong, of course, rejected these terms, always referring to themselves as *Hmong, Peb Hmoob, Neeg Hmoob*, or *Peb Haiv Hmoob*. However, some of the belittling names were assumed to be accurate and were therefore transliterated and scholars referred to the Hmong as *San Miao, Maozi, Miao*, or *Meo*, based on such blanket ethnic classifications imposed on the Hmong thousands of years ago. The information in this book invalidates these offensive terms and presents arguments that reclaim the true Hmong ethnic identity. Hmong will always be Hmong no matter where they reside.

The contents of this book cover a variety of topics that clarify some of the misconceptions about Hmong refugees and Hmong migration. For instance, some western researchers claim that the Hmong originated in Russia, Siberia, Mesopotamia, or Mongolia. Contrary to that assertion, Hmong legends, preserved in Hmong oral tradition, place Hmong ancestral origin in the central regions of China, near the Yangtze and Yellow River Basins. Over the centuries, the Hmong migrated to Southeast Asia and then emigrated to western countries after the fall of Laos in 1975.

The Hmong people comprise a number of distinct groups, each with its own culture and traditions. They speak several dialects and belong to different tribes. Although each tribe is unique, the different Hmong groups have many values and traditions in common, such as funeral rituals, ancestor worship, spiritual healing, marriage, and cultural customs. Today, the Hmong are divided into 18 distinct clans or tribes with legends and myths specific to each family group. In each Hmong

clan, members learn the family ancestry, evolution, and movement. Researchers have followed the various oral traditions to trace Hmong origin and history. The folktales chronicle nearly 6,000 years of Hmong history.

Once, long ago, the Hmong were able to read and write in their native tongue; they had written forms of their language, called *Kiashi, Dazi, Kaizi, Hanzi, Mongshu*, or *Xiaozi*. In the early days, Hmong were literate in Chinese official writings and could read an ancient textbook called *Zaishu*, a taboo book or a book of legal codes. According to Hmong Chinese legends, after the first written forms of their language, known as *Kaishu, Dazi, Hmongshi*, or *Hmongshu*, were lost, they had no writing system until French missionaries created one for them in the early 1950s. The French missionaries invented the Romanized Popular Alphabet (RPA) writing system for Hmong in Laos, and it has been used ever since. There are other systems for writing the Hmong language have also been developed, including the Lao-Hmong, Phaj Hauj (PaHawh), and Paj Ntaub systems, but the RPA remains the most prominent. It has enabled the Hmong people to read and write in their native language.

Most of today's Hmong Americans are war-displaced refugees who emigrated from Laos. The first group of Hmong refugees to resettle in the West consisted of former soldiers, civic leaders, and uneducated civilians. The U.S. government implemented a refugee resettlement policy that dispersed Hmong refugees across the fifty states, expecting that the new arrivals would assimilate quickly into the mainstream society. However, the dispersion was difficult for Hmong refugees because they resisted the drastic assimilation. Instead of assimilating in small groups, they relocated to metropolitan areas with other Hmong families and established Hmong communities around the nation. This relocation has been called the second Hmong migration in America.

Today, forty years after their initial arrival in the West, how are Hmong refugees doing in their new homelands? According to some scholars, the current world-wide Hmong population is approximately 12 million, with 9 million living in China, 2½ million in Southeast Asia, and the rest in western nations. The U.S. is home to about 300,000 Hmong. Of the 12 million, only 5 million call themselves Hmong; the remainder are classified under a blanket term that may mean *Miao, Miaozi, Man, Yao, Mien*, or *Meng*. These different names are imperial ethnic classifications used by Chinese warlords and other foreigners who conquered and enslaved the Hmong during the Spring and Autumn eras and the Warring States periods. This book helps prospective and current educators navigate the events of Hmong past and present to provide some responses to the many questions that are often raised about Hmong refugees and their progress in the U.S. since 1975.

My Motivation for Writing This Book

I am a Hmong refugee. I was born in Laos. My family left Laos for Thailand when I was about seven years old and my parents brought me to our new homeland when I was about twelve. I pretty much grew up in the U.S. Living here for thirty-five years, I have learned to be both Hmong and American. I am so proud to be Hmong and am honored to have become an American. I want to share what I know about my culture, my traditions, my history, and my people with other educators and with other Hmong people to help them better understand Hmong refugees, their challenges, their successes, and their role in history.

The Need to Learn About Hmong Refugees

Today, Hmong Americans constitute one of the fastest growing Asian American groups. Perhaps Hmong Americans are also among the most vibrant Asian groups in America. And yet, Hmong Americans are probably the least studied Asian group in the U.S. Since their arrival in the U.S. in 1975, Hmong refugees have made remarkable progress toward achieving self-sufficiency.

Like other refugee and immigrant groups, they have struggled from the beginning of their time here. Upon arrival, they engaged in blue-collar jobs in order to survive and raise their families. Those who could not work received public assistance. Hmong adults still face high unemployment because they do not have a good education and many still cannot read, write, or speak English well. Most Hmong adults are bilingual in Hmong and Lao, Thai, or English, but many are still illiterate in their native language. Lacking English skills, many Hmong parents are unable to provide adequate academic support for their children at home. Studies indicate that Hmong children are among the poorest socioeconomic student groups in the American educational system but are not the poorest performing student group. Despite the lack of parental support in academics, Hmong children work hard in school and are becoming model students in many metropolitan areas across this nation. Hmong academic achievement is remarkable after only four decades in the U.S.

Again as with other refugee and immigrant groups, Hmong Americans also face tough challenges within their own families and communities. Today's Hmong Americans are different from the first-generation refugees. Young Hmong Americans are westernized; they easily adopt the mainstream culture and traditions. The foreign-born children are referred to as the 1.5 generation and are much like the traditional, old-fashioned Hmong Americans. The U.S.-born Hmong children, however, are Americanized and would like to make drastic changes in their families. After four decades in the new homeland, Hmong children are losing their native tongue and prefer to speak English. Approximately 80 percent of Hmong-American children are illiterate in Hmong; they use "*Hmonglish*," a mix of Hmong and English, and they sometime use pidgin Hmong to communicate with their parents.

As assimilation progresses, the intergenerational gap between parents and children grows wider. In some families, as Hmong parents see it, the gap that separates the young and the old is a painful scar of division. Many parents have lost control over their children because of the clash of cultures. Over the years of difficult socialization, Hmong adults have encountered a number of social problems and have suffered tremendous health and social difficulties. The divorce rate among Hmong families has increased by 15 percent in some Hmong communities. Domestic violence is on the rise and abuse is becoming more common. There are several cases of spouse killing involving Hmong refugees. The number of single-head-of-household families has risen significantly in the last two decades. The Hmong way of life is changing, and fear of challenges is greater than excitement over opportunities for success.

In recent years, Hmong leaders, community-based organizations, social service agencies, and mental health specialists have intervened to assist troubled Hmong families in averting family breakup and spousal abuse. Many Hmong refugees are former soldiers who have suffered post-traumatic syndrome disorders (PTSD). In America, due to the high demands on their lives, some chronic mental health and psychological problems go untreated for years. As a result, middle-aged Hmong refugees experience great difficulties but are reluctant to seek professional assistance. In some cases, untreated conditions contribute to more serious health issues such as nervous breakdowns, psychotic episodes, and psychiatric ailments. As noted by Hmong researchers, the number of Hmong immigrants on Social Security Supplemental Income has increased significantly in the last several years. This indicates that the general wellness of Hmong families is still inadequate as compared to that of other refugee groups from similar backgrounds. However, the Hmong have made remarkable progress in many areas of life, such as education, economic development, and self-sufficiency.

The future for the Hmong in the field of education is promising, holding both challenges and opportunities. Hmong children should take advantage of any resources and services available to them to attain their academic goals. They should aim high and withstand social temptations. They should study their culture and traditions and learn how to speak and write Hmong while also learning English. Cultural preservation is highly important for future generations. Hmong students need to master the English language; otherwise, they will not be able to compete in the real world. America is the land of opportunity: the land in which they can make their dreams come true, the land in which they can live forever without having to emigrate again.

California has nearly 90,000 Hmong refugees, and approximately 36,000 Hmong-American students in its K–12 schools. Of that number, 80 percent are classified as limited English proficient (LEP) students; only 20 percent are fluent in English. In some school districts in the state, 80 percent of the Hmong students in grades K–6 are LEP students. Nationally, nearly 75,000 Hmong students are enrolled in K–12 schools, and Hmong students are over-represented as ELLs or LEP in some schools. Hmong students were once considered a model minority group, but now they are likely to be the delinquent group in inner-city schools. Even though the school dropout rate among Hmong children is at an all-time low as compared to that of other racial groups, Hmong students ought to do better in American schools because they are native born. Two decades ago, Hmong students were mostly foreign born, but today, nearly two-thirds of Hmong K–12 students are native born.

Studies show that Hmong children have special educational needs, specifically language skills, academic preparation, and curricular resources. Public schools need to have more Hmong teachers and better resources to help Hmong children excel academically. Special instructional approaches and curricular strategies are needed to deal with the multitude of problems Hmong children face today. One of the main problems in academia among Hmong children in grades K–12 is low scholastic achievement. If this problem persists, a large number of Hmong students will be at risk for school dropout. Studies reveal that Hmong students are unlikely to succeed beyond secondary education. In addition, early marriage is prevalent in the Hmong community and often sabotages the quality of life of Hmong children.

Despite all obstacles, Hmong-American students have achieved remarkable academic success. Many are now attending colleges and universities. Hundreds of Hmong Americans have received doctoral degrees in various fields and several thousands have earned master's degrees in education, business, counseling, social science, social work, and other fields. Moreover, tens of thousands of Hmong Americans have received bachelor's degrees across all academic disciplines. Education is the key to successes for the Hmong and both males and females are capitalizing on the education that is available to them in the U.S. One-third of Hmong professionals are women, and female Hmong teachers outnumber males in the public school system. Hmong businesses are booming, as is Hmong homeownership.

On the other hand, as a whole, the Hmong still lack community organization and development, leadership and shared governance, and a smooth acculturation process. They still struggle with matrilineal and patriarchal conflict. At the same time, they are experiencing gender and role changes at home and in the larger society. Hmong children are still facing tough challenges in American public schools. The progress that has been made and the problems that remain make it essential that educators understand Hmong refugees and their socioeconomic situation in America.

Limitations of This Book

Each and every Hmong family has its unique family history, ancestry, migration story, and journey from the eastern world to the western world. The contents of this book may not directly reflect the stories of all Hmong refugees and their struggles for survival.

The word *Hmong* is used in this book for both HMONG (*White Hmong*) and MONG (*Blue Mong*). Other words, like *Hmong Amer-*

icans, *Laotian Hmong*, *Hmong Lao*, *Hmong Chinese*, *Hmong Vietnamese*, *Hmong Thai*, *Hmong German*, *Hmong French*, *Hmong Canadian*, *Hmong Australian*, *Hmong Argentinean*, and *Hmong Guyanese*, may also be used to describe Hmong refugees living in different eastern and western countries.

It is impossible in a single book to cover every facet of Hmong refugees, their history, their commonalities and differences. The issues addressed and the information provided may not reflect all aspects of Hmong life, all the Hmong subgroups, or every nuance of the different traditions. The transliterations, translations, and connotations of some terms, cultural phenomena, and religious meanings may not accurately depict their true natures as perceived by some individuals whose traditions and belief systems need further research because each Hmong family has its own story to tell. Nevertheless, the contents of this book will give educators a clear and fairly comprehensive picture of Hmong refugees and their future challenges and opportunities.

My Desire for Writing This Book

Today, years since I left Laos, I still remember my native country in faded memories like a dream. I attended a Lao public school for two years prior to my emigration to Thailand after the fall of Laos in 1975. In Thailand, I attended a public school for refugees in the Ban Vinai refugee camp for three years before resettling in the United States. During my teen years in the early 1980s, I was part of a Hmong high school club. In the early 1980s, I was a member of the Hmong Student Association of Fresno, serving as its president from 1986 to 1989. I was a member of the Hmong Student Association at California State University, Fresno, in the mid–1980s to the late 1990s. I was a member of my family clan organization from the early 1980s to the late 1990s. I worked for Lao Family Community of Fresno from 1985 to 1987. From the late 1980s to the late 1990s, I served on the Fresno County Emergency Taskforce.

From the late 1980s to the early 2000s, I participated in many community events: student club-sponsored events, New Year's celebrations, higher education orientation and outreach, church activities, Hmong youth events, political campaigns, and fundraising events. I served as a board member, treasurer, and election chair for Lao Family Community of Fresno from 2004 to 2008. From 2007 to 2010, I served as an advisor for the Hmong-American Ad Hoc Committee. In 2008, I co-chaired and hosted the first Vang National Conference at CSU, Fresno. I was one of the co-founders of the Vang National Unity Foundation, Inc. I became a board member of the Vang National Unity Foundation, Inc., in 2009 and executive director of the foundation in 2010. From late 2010 to 2011, I was a consultant and advisor for Hmong United, Inc., in Fresno and became executive director of the organization in 2012.

From 1997 to 2011, I hosted radio talk show programs on stations KGED, KXEX, KQEQ, KBIF, and LCN. I played a prominent role in the community during my tenure on the radio. I interviewed many leaders, educators, and politicians and gained much knowledge from my research on issues and concerns regarding the Hmong people and their communal life. I covered topics such as human rights, AAA issues, political platforms and elections, the arrest of Hmong leaders, Hmong refugees in Thailand, Hmong issues in general, and Hmong New Year's celebrations.

From 2000 to 2010, I wrote and published thirteen newspaper editorial articles on a variety of topics related to Hmong issues in the Central Valley of California. From 2001 to 2011, I was active in community events such as fundraising for political campaigns, a monument fund drive, the Hmong media group, refugee fundraising, and educational events. I have written hundreds of online articles on Hmong issues and concerns. I have published articles in professional journals on the topics related to the Hmong. As a university professor, I have published three college textbooks and many research articles. I have spent time researching Hmong history and contemporary issues related to their challenges, opportunities, and successes in the western world.

Lastly, in 2010 Major General Vang Pao gave me a special assignment to assess the tribal split in the Hmong Council and to examine tribal conflicts over the Hmong New Year's celebration in Fresno. Similarly, in 2007 I received an urgent request from Major General Vang Pao to coordinate the first ever Hmong National Conference to be held at Concordia University in St. Paul, Minnesota. Currently, I am part of the Hmong National Unity Committee that is working to help Hmong Americans and their communities find a sensible approach to restore Hmong traditional leadership in honoring the legacy of Major General Vang Pao.

How This Book Is Organized

There are five main parts divided into fourteen chapters. Each chapter presents a variety of issues in a single domain. Headings and subheadings are used to guide readers to various topics. Part I has three chapters that provide an overview of the history of the Hmong people as they moved from China to the United States. Part II has five chapters that cover Hmong culture and traditions in western nations. The two chapters of Part III describe the oral traditions and written languages of the Hmong people. Part IV has two chapters that discuss the challenges, opportunities, and successes of Hmong Americans related to their educational attainments and academic progresses and the state of the Hmong community. Finally, the two chapters of Part V cover the history of Hmong leaders and leadership and the journey forward for Hmong Americans.

• ONE •

Brief History of the Hmong

Peb Hmoob lub neej tom qab tsis sib pab thooj siab koom ntsws...
Tsis sib fwm kho peb neej Hmoob peb thiaj poob puv thoob qab ntuj...
Tsis sim hlub thiab tsis tsim nqi.

Lyrics of a classic Hmong song

Introduction

Many books have been written about the Hmong and their history. Online resources are abundant. Among the many scholars who have dedicated much scholarship to researching the Hmong and their history are Francois M. Savina, Keith Quincy, Yves Bertrais, Jacques Lamone, Gary Yia Lee, Jean Mottin, William A. Smalley, Nicholas Tapp, Anne Fadiman, Lillian Faderman, Jane Hamilton–merit, Gayle L. Morrison, Yang Dao, Thomas Vang, Zhigiang Yang, and Taichiming Cha, to name just a few. To some researchers Hmong history remains a mystery; they see the Hmong as undocumented people who at one time lived in China and elsewhere. Some western researchers believe Hmong were once Caucasian people with light complexions and blue eyes. Such an assertion, however, is based on isolated cases that do not represent the majority of the Hmong people or the bulk of scholarship on the subject. Perhaps interracial marriages created some mixed racial profiles and some Caucasian genetic markers.

Some experts attempting to answer the question *"Who are the Hmong?"* have linked today's Hmong people to Hmong history through oral traditions, religious practices, shamanism, linguistic similarities, genetic markers, folktales, and embroidery textures.

Often Hmong people and their history are confused with other ethnic groups; they have been mischaracterized and mislabeled. The morphology of the name "Hmong" (used of White Hmong) or "Mong" (used of Blue Mong) is still relatively new to historians and researchers because the written form of the name Hmong use for themselves is unknown. Today, Hmong are called by imperialist names such as *Miao, Meo, Maozi, Man, Ahmao, Hmu,* and *San Miao* even though the correct ethnic names *Hmong* (for White Hmong) and *Mong* (for Blue Hmong) were coined in the mid–1970s.

This chapter takes a journey back in time to explore the history of the Hmong, retracing their origins and their whereabouts in the ancient world. It presents what is known of Hmong history in China as uncovered in Chinese historical events and Hmong oral tradition.

Hmong Origins

Where did the Hmong come from? This is a question many have asked. According to some western educators and scholars, the history of the Hmong can be traced to nearly 3000 BC, but the details remain largely unknown to Hmong themselves. More research is needed to verify the present speculations, assumptions, and beliefs about the earliest

Hmong history. Even though Hmong culture and traditions are nearly 6,000 years old, the ancient historical timeline of Hmong history is still sketchy and the different accounts provided through folktales, religious rites, oral histories, epics and legends, myths, and Chinese historical accounts are perplexing. However, for example, Hmong still use this old descriptive phrase, "*mab sua*," to refer to their past allies or enemies, meaning, "the Ma people and the Chinese." This could also mean that Hmong had involved with the Ma people and the Chinese in the ancient world, and perhaps, the Hmong, the Ma, and the Chinese were the three largest ethnic groups during the Autumn and Spring eras and the Warring States periods.

Navigating Hmong history to determine Hmong origins is an interesting venture. Scholars and educators have approached the study of Hmong origins in a variety of ways. Over the last 200 years some scholars have attempted to link Hmong origins to biblical events, mythical stories, shamanism, and folktales. They have tried to decipher Hmong history through their religious rites, genetic markers (somatoscopy, anthropometry, brachycephaly, hyperleptoproscopy, and mesorrhiny), and linguistic similarities with various eastern civilizations. The "*emic*" (insider's beliefs) and "*etic*" (outsider's beliefs) perspectives have been used in academic discourse for years in regards to Hmong history and ethnic identity. Some researchers have attempted to locate the Hmong somewhere in Chinese history, most commonly in the Spring and Autumn eras, the Warring States periods, the times of the 3 kingdoms or the 16 king-

doms, and somewhere in the shadow of all the imperial Chinese dynasties. Perhaps piecing together the different threads will give a clearer picture for both Hmong and non–Hmong of Hmong history and people.

One way to explore the origins of the Hmong is to examine the ancient world in which they lived. That world can be divided into five major geographic regions, which are, from north to south: the *Gobi Desert* (in the far north, toward Mongolia), the *Upper World* (located between the Gobi Desert and the Yellow River basin), the *Upper Yellow River Basin*, the *Lower World* (located between the upper and lower Yellow River basins), and the *Lower Yellow River Basin*, as illustrated in Figure 1.1. Centuries of Hmong oral tradition clearly indicate that the Hmong originated somewhere in central China—in present-day Guizhou, Sichuan, Chongqing, Shaanxi, Henan, Yunnan, and Hunan—and then moved elsewhere. Therefore, today's Hmong in Southeast Asia as well as in the

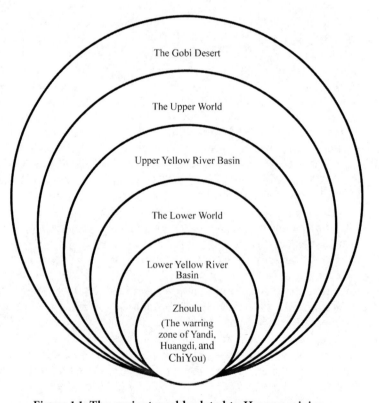

Figure 1.1. The ancient world related to Hmong origins.

West are descendants of Hmong Chinese refugees and emigrants. The term *Hmong Chinese refugee* is used to reflect Hmong origins in China as found in Hmong oral history.

Hmong origins may be hidden in Hmong culture and traditions, particularly in their funeral rites and rituals. Some scholars believe that Hmong death rituals, especially the verses used in the *Showing the Way* rite (*Qhuab Ke* in Hmong), mention places and events that have to do with the historical origins of Hmong Chinese refugees and emigrants. Because all Hmong recite these verses, it is reasonable to conclude that the death rituals and the religious rites associated with them were framed around the experiences of Hmong Chinese refugees. On the other hand, death rituals and religious rites may contain stories of fanciful places and imaginary events created by men to provide comfort and joy in times of sorrow. Whichever is the case, the rituals are important reminders to Hmong Chinese of their long-gone past.

Whether these verses appear relevant to particular individuals for whom they are said, Hmong use *Showing the Way* for every Hmong who passes away, regardless of where the person was born or where he or she traveled in life. Will the words of *Showing the Way* be changed a hundred years from now if a person born in a western nation should pass away? Maybe, maybe not, but they will be recited in the same manner as they are today.

The verses mention places such as the deadly freezing mountains, under a dry sky on brittle earth, the cold sky and dark earth, under a burning sky on the scorched earth, under an icy sky on the dark earth, summer hot desert sand, cold winter dark land, and through the barren land under a hot and dry sky (*Roob tuag no, ntuj qhua teb nkig, ntuj txias teb tsaus, ntuj kub teb qhuav, losi toj kab ntsuab dawm kab ntsig* in Hmong). Some scholars and educators link these places to the Gobi Desert, Mongolia, South China, North China, East China, West China, the Yellow River basin, or the Yangtze River basin. The verses may refer to areas where the Hmong originated or they may denote places where Hmong traveled, places they passed through, and places to and from which they migrated in the early days. Perhaps the verses are meant to recall hardships and tribulations Hmong Chinese refugees endured during migrations and settlements in various places so many years ago. These descriptions match the climate and weather conditions of the rugged mountains, barren hills, and desolate plateaus of Tibet, Nepal, and Himalaya.

Nothing in Hmong oral traditions, folktales, religious rites, legends, or mythological accounts state that Hmong once lived in Russia, Siberia, Mesopotamia, Mongolia, or anywhere other than China, and no historical discoveries indicate that Hmong ever had kingdoms in any of these places. However, it is possible that Hmong traveled through these locales in ancient times. The stories in Hmong oral traditions, myths, and epics that appear to refer to these places may simply be storytellers' creations, imaginations and duplications. Hmong do not retain records and detailed accounts of their families' origins; they cannot trace their histories further than the very first family member who emigrated from China and settled in Southeast Asia. Therefore, nearly all Hmong in Southeast Asian countries and in the western nations say their ancestors or great grandparents came from only one place: *China*. Hmong do not pay much attention to western research because they know where their ancestors (*pog suab thiab yawg suab* in Hmong) came from. Hmong usually refer China in their oral history as *Suav Tuam Tshoj Teb Chaws*, meaning, the land of resistance, chaos, and tribulations. They know without a doubt that the Hmong originated in central China near the Yellow and Yangtze River basins. Interestingly, Hmong family last names or surnames are similarly identical to Chinese last names or surnames, for example, *Vang-Wang, Yang-Yang, Lee-Lee, Hsiung-Xiong, Han-Hang, Fang-Fang, Cheng-Cheng, Lo-Loh*, and so son. As Hmong people always say in Hmong, "Hmoob pog suab thiab yawg suab tsiv tuam tshoj teb (*suav teb*) los tsim lub neej tshiab nyob rau xov tshoj teb chaws," in English, "Hmong ancestors left China for Southeast Asian countries to start new life over again."

Unless credible historical evidence surfaces to refute this claim, it should be concluded that Hmong origins are in China.

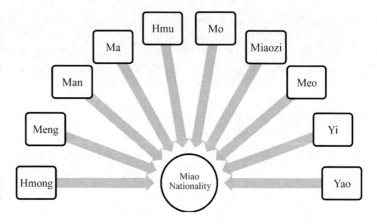

Figure 1.2. The composition of Miao nationality.

The Hmong and the Miao

Are Hmong Miao? Clarification is needed to reduce the mystery surrounding Hmong and Miao identity. For the last two centuries, massive confusion has attended this question because researchers and scholars have portrayed Hmong to be Miao and Miao to be Hmong. As some Hmong historians and Chinese scholars note, "de–Miao-ification" is necessary to reclaim Hmongness. Miao are not Hmong and Hmong are not Miao; they are two distinct ethnic groups with nearly identical histories.

The Hmong and the Miao were ancient peoples in China, perhaps closely related ethnic groups. The word *Chinese* is a very broad term used to denote all people living in China. It includes 56 identified nationalities and many other unidentified subgroups such as Hmong, Man, Ma, Yi, Chu, Han, Qin, Meng, Hmu, Wei, Zhou, Jin, Qi, Mo, and Mu. Some scholars have considered some of these groups' subsets of the Miao nationality, as shown in Figure 1.2. In fact, however, from ancient times to the present time the Hmong have never called themselves Miao. As Cha (2013) pointed out, Hmong people have always referred to themselves ethnically as Hmong, even while living with or among people of Miao nationality and people of other ethnic groups.

Unraveling some of the complex historical events in China may be helpful in explaining Hmong existence in the shadow of the Miao in the ancient world. Chinese scholars such as Taichiming Cha and Zhiqiang Yang, along with western scholars such as Nicholas Tapp, Jacques Lamoine, Gary Yia Lee, Keith Quincy, and Francois M. Savina, have written differ-

ent versions of Hmong history before their appearance in Southeast Asia. Their accounts are somewhat parallel to one another, but they contain a number of contradictions with the records of Hmong oral tradition. For instance, at no time did the ancestors of the Hmong claim to be Miao in China, nor do any Hmong remember their ancestors as being Miao prior to their migration to Southeast Asia. Interestingly, the Hmong and the Miao do not practice the same death rituals or religious rites, nor do they have the same family names. The name *Miao* is a political label put on ethnic minorities, especially poor, farming, working, and underserved groups. For example, the term *Miao Rebellion* suggests that all rebels were of Miao ethnicity, but according to Chinese historical records, people of many ethnic groups and subgroups supported the rebellion, including Mong, Hu, Yi, Ba, Ma, Mao, Meng, Chin, Han, Manchu, and Yin.

Despite the contradictions, scholars still confuse the Hmong name with the names for the Meo, Miao, Miaozi, Meng, Man, Ma, and San Miao. Perhaps one reason the confusion persists is that for some time the Hmong themselves did not totally deny the assertion that they and these groups were synonymous. According to Hmong legends, the Hmong tolerated the ethnic mislabeling for sociopolitical purposes. In times past, Hmong were often the main enemies of the Chinese because the Hmong revolted against them. The

Chinese persecuted, chased, and hunted them down, forcing the people to live in seclusion in rugged highland mountains. For centuries the Hmong had no political clout with which to rebut the false claim that their original name was Miao. They put up with the mischaracterization because they feared political retaliation and reprisals, including atrocities.

In modern times, however, Hmong have rejected the inaccurate names, insisting on the terms *Hmong* (White Hmong) or *Mong* (Blue Mong), labels they have always used. In the early 1950s and 1960s, Major General Vang Pao and other Hmong leaders told their western allies and royal Laotian government officials that they needed to call the Hmong "*Hmong,*" not "Meo" or "Miao." They denounced any reference to the Hmong as "Meo" or "Miao" as derogatory. Their objections were heard and usage gradually changed until the name "Hmong" was coined in written form in the early 1970s by Hmong educators and western scholars.

Another source of the misperceptions of the differences between Hmong and Miao has to do with the histories of the two groups in China. For many centuries, the Chinese ruling classes exploited ethnic minorities, using social stratification and racial classification of ethnic groups, lumping them together under broad definitions. Because the Hmong were not in the majority, they were either classified with the Meo, Miao, Maozi, Meng, Ma, or San Miao nationalities or not officially recognized as a distinct group by the Chinese rulers. In order to trace Hmong history to its beginnings, first and foremost, the idea that the Hmong are Miao, Meo, or San Miao must be rejected.

The Hmong Prior to the Imperial Xia

Where were the Hmong before the Xia, the dynasty that emerged in China sometime around 2070 BC? Hmong history in mainland China preceded the Xia occupation and domination by thousands of years. According to Hmong legends, the Hmong lived in the fertile land in the vicinity of the Yellow River basin long before the arrival of the Xia. The area was known as the *Jiuli kingdom*, but the legends are unclear about whether the Hmong were the ruling group. Eventually the Xia, presumably Han Chinese who lived in the Upper World, moved south from the northern regions (the Upper World and Upper Yellow River Basin) to conquer the Hmong kingdom and occupy the Yellow River basin.

While living among other racial groups, the Hmong were dominated politically and culturally by Chinese emperors and warlords for thousands of years. The Hmong were an independent ethnic group with an agrarian lifestyle. They cultivated crops, herded livestock, kept draft animals, and owned land. As a preliterate group, Hmong faced the same hardships and economic challenges as any other ethnic group. However, despite the difficulties they thrived, hunting, raising food and livestock, and conducting trade.

Then as now, self-sufficiency and independence were important to the Hmong. They valued freedom, community, dignity, and integrity. In central China, they wanted to live without imperial control, free of warlords, free from unjust laws and ethnic oppression. They were especially rankled by unfair taxation and land policies and government encroachment on their land. Some western Hmong educators contend that today's Hmong have the same values as their ancient ancestors, desiring to be free from external control. However, the 21st-century Hmong have learned to adjust to the western way of life.

Political oppression was inevitable for the Hmong in China because of their fierce love of freedom. For much of their time in China, everyday life was filled with formidable obstacles as people tried simply to make ends meet. Chinese rulers took over their land and imposed heavy taxes. Some Hmong detested the Chinese overlords and fought them politically; others envied their power and learned to behave like them. Because the Hmong as a group wavered between direct opposition to the ruthless emperors and merciless dictators and vying with them for position, they were vulnerable to political exploitation and financial enticements.

As a result, over time the Hmong underwent drastic social and cultural changes. They assimilated, practicing some of the traditions of the host culture. They adopted Chinese cultural values and sought social status and political power among the Chinese ruling classes. The hunger for power, status, and an assimilated lifestyle created internal and external conflicts. According to Hmong legends, some Hmong became traitors and defectors, hiring themselves as mercenary soldiers to the Chinese against the rulers of their own kingdom. This behavior marked a turning point for the Hmong in the ancient world. Eventually the Hmong kingdom was dissolved and Hmong became oppressed and persecuted throughout the remainder of their history in China.

The Hmong and ChiYou

Was there a Hmong king in China? Perhaps there was more than one king from whom the Hmong are descended. The most famous Hmong hero, *ChiYou*, was unknown to Hmong in the West until the early 1990s. Hmong travelers to China and Hmong Chinese visitors to the U.S. claimed that ChiYou was a Hmong king in ancient China. However, before the 1990s ChiYou was not mentioned in the oral history, folktales, legends, epics, or myths of Hmong in the U.S. ChiYou could have been an ordinary Chinese ruler of one of the many tribes or clans of ancient China. The Hmong who migrated to Southeast Asia from China did not reveal the names of Hmong kings or rulers in China. Therefore, whether ChiYou was a Hmong king or not has not been established.

ChiYou could have been a great leader, like Major General Vang Pao, Phagna Touby Ly-fong, Kiatong Lo Blia Yao, Tasseng Moua Chong Kai, and Tasseng Ly Chia Fong. However, other indigenous people, like the Puyi, Lue, Mien, Lahu, Kha, Khamu, and Yao, who lived with the Hmong in the Xieng Khouang and Sam Neu provinces, did not claim these Hmong leaders to be their kings, protectors,

rulers, or saviors in their histories as the western Hmong nationalists have claimed of ChiYou.

Hmong civilization and culture began nearly 6,000 years ago in central China in the Yangtze and Yellow River basins. As told in Hmong oral tradition and Chinese mythological accounts, Han Chinese, the descendants of Yandi and Huangdi, were emperors during the time the Hmong lived in the Yellow River basin. The Hmong occupied fertile land, beautiful with forests and mountains. Like other ethnic groups or clans, the Hmong lived independently and freely. The Chinese rulers classified Hmong as part of the Miao nationality, blending them with other ethnic groups during the time of the three kingdoms under ChiYou (as written in Hmong, *Txiv Yawg*), Yandi (as written in Hmong, *Yajtim*), and Huangdi (as written in Hmong, *Huajtim*).

Chinese historical accounts record that the Hmong and many other ethnic groups, tribes, or clans lived in a kingdom ruled by ChiYou. Under ChiYou, the Hmong enjoyed independence and peace. ChiYou was a powerful and magical ruler; he was known as the red cloud, a ferocious beast, and the creator of magical power. Yandi was a ruler of the northern region and was known as the virtue of fire, a destructive ruler. Huangdi, who reigned over the northeastern region, was known as the yellow emperor or yellow king. These three rulers governed their independent states for years.

One day, say the Hmong Chinese folktales, the Chinese of the northern countries, *Suav Liab*, wanted to invade Hmong land and take over the Hmong kingdom. The powerful ChiYou had no problem defending the Hmong kingdom. The Chinese in the north waged wars against the Hmong to the south of them for many years. ChiYou used his magical power to drive out the Chinese armies every time they invaded Hmong territory. After many defeats, the Chinese, *Suav Liab*, combined their military forces to mount major attacks against ChiYou and his army near the Yellow River basin. Many years of resisting brutal invasions weakened ChiYou and the

Hmong kingdom eventually fell to the Chinese. The Chinese enslaved and oppressed the Hmong and many fled to distant countries.

Another version of the Hmong Chinese legends has ChiYou as a Miao king or ruler who controlled nearly 80 different ethnic groups or clans in a kingdom called *Jiuli* (*Cuaj Hli Ntuj* in Hmong) in the Yellow River basin. Yandi and Huangdi ruled other groups. Racial tension built up between tribal groups of different languages, cultures, and customs. Ongoing altercations brought the three rulers into major conflicts on the battlefield. They fought lengthy wars against one another for many years. Fearing ChiYou's magical power, Yandi and Huangdi joined forces to overpower ChiYou and his armies. The yellow emperor (Huangdi) and the virtue of fire ruler (Yandi) managed to defeat and kill ChiYou in a battle near Zhuolu. The two northern rulers then took control of the Jiuli kingdom and formed a new regime that became known as Han Chinese. Thereafter, the survivors of the Jiuli people, including the Hmong, scattered and migrated from the Yellow River basin to the southern regions. The Hmong kingdom fell into the hands of the Han Chinese.

Some scholars have pointed out that although the Chinese legends call ChiYou a Miao king, he could have been Hmong. The Chinese Hmong continued to worship ChiYou after his death, as did the Miao and other ethnic groups including the Man, Meng, Mu, and Han. It is likely that ChiYou was the king of many or all tribes living in the Jiuli kingdom; he could have been Miao, Hmong, Mu, Mo, Wei, Meng, or Man because he was the ruler of 80 different tribes or clans. The Jiuli kingdom was undoubtedly composed of many different ethnic groups under ChiYou. The Hmong were thought of as part of the Miao nationality, and they could very well have been part of Miao, Man, Yi, Wei, Jin, Qin, SiMa, and Han Chu political movements.

After the death of ChiYou, his three sons, ChiPang, ChiFu, and ChiLi, continued to lead the Hmong until they established a new kingdom. The Hmong lived for another several hundred years in peace and prosperity before the Chinese cracked down on them again.

The Hmong and the San Miao

Were the San Miao and the Hmong the same people? Maybe they were. Hmong could have been part of the San Miao, but Hmong were not the rulers during the time of the San Miao. The San Miao were a mixed ethnic group; the name is a blanket term the Chinese used to refer to minorities. As the Jiuli kingdom dissolved with ChiYou's defeat, the Xia people of the north moved south to the Yellow River basin. The very first unified group after the Hmong kingdom was the Xia Dynasty (2070 BC–1600 BC), which was founded by the Yandi and Huangdi people who migrated southward to live in the lower Yellow River basin. They created a coalition of three sovereigns and five emperors. According to Chinese accounts of history, the Xia Empire was ruled by five emperors: Huangdi, Zhuanxu, King Ku, Yao, and Shun (Cha, 2013).

During the 470-year reign of the Xia people, also known as Han Chinese, ChiYou's followers underwent many tribulations. They lived in isolated and desolate regions in the south until they were able to establish a new regime, the *San Miao Kingdom*, in today's Hunan Province, near the Zi Shui River basin. Similar to the old Jiuli kingdom in the Yellow River basin, the San Miao Kingdom was made up of many tribes engaged in agriculture because of the fertility of the land. Once again the Hmong enjoyed a peaceful agrarian existence for a few hundred years. During this time, Hmong Chinese legends say, the Hmong were referred to as *Hmoob Sis Suav Sis*, which means a mixture of two or more ethnic identities living together. Over the many years of ruthless occupation of the Yellow River basin, the Xia king, known as King Jie, had numerous conflicts with the Tang tribal people. The conflicts got out of hand, and the Tang organized a series of rebellions to overthrow the Xia. The Hmong joined with other tribes and took part in the rebellion against the Xia. The rebels succeeded in ousting the Xia from power and exiling King Jie. The Tang created a new dynasty, the Shang Dynasty.

Some western Hmong believe the San Miao kingdom was a new Hmong kingdom also known as *Kuj Cuab Peb Hmoob*. However, it is unclear whether San Miao was made up of a single ethnic group or of multiple tribes. ChiYou's oldest son, ChiPang, was a prominent leader of this kingdom, which lasted for nearly 1,000 years before falling into the hands of the Chinese. Based on the fact that the Jiuli kingdom had been composed of many groups, it is reasonable to assume that the San Miao Kingdom contained more than one tribe or clan. According to Chinese myths, the southern region included Mo, Mu, Man, Miao, Dai, Yi, Min, Pu Yi, Yue, Shu, Ba, and other non–Han people. The region of the San Miao kingdom encompassed present-day Anhui, Chongqing, Guilin, Guizhou, Henan, Hubei, Hunan, Jiangsu, Jianxi, Schuan, and Yunnan. The fact that Hmong very likely once lived in the San Miao and Jiuli kingdoms supports the theory that the Hmong came from and probably originated in central China.

The Hmong and Chinese Dynasties

Were the Hmong Chinese? According to both Chinese and Hmong legends, the Hmong have always been part of Chinese history. The study of wars and tribal conflicts in ancient China provides insight into early Hmong civilization and perspective on the lives of the Hmong in the ancient world. To understand the Hmong history of migration and multiple rebellions in ancient China through the Spring and Autumn eras, the Warring States periods, and the various Chinese dynasties, one has to know the pain and suffering the Hmong endured as the result of brutal taxation, unjust takeover of land, forced labor, harsh slavery, ruthless persecution, and unrelenting political oppression. Examining the actions of the Hmong in the various Chinese dynasties sheds light on the whereabouts of the Hmong in ancient times and some of the historical mystery. Table 1.1 gives a chronology of the Chinese dynasties from 2070 BC to AD 1911.

Table 1.1. Chinese Dynasties, 2070 BC to AD 1911

Name of Dynasty	In Chinese	In Pinyin Chinese	Estimated Time Period	Estimated Years in Power
Xia	夏	Xia	2070 BC–1600 BC	470
Shang	商	Shang	1600 BC–1050 BC	571
Western Zhou	西周	Xi Zhou	1050 BC–770 BC	275
Eastern Zhou	東周 / 东周	Dong Zhou	770 BC–250 BC	514
Spring and Autumn period	春秋	Chun Qiu	770 BC–479 BC	295
Warring States era	戰國 / 战国	Zhan Guo	476 BC–221 BC	255
Qin	秦	Qin	221 BC–206 BC	15
Western Han	西漢 / 西汉	Xi Han	206 BC–AD 9	215
Xin	新	Xin	AD 9–23	14
Eastern Han	東漢 / 东汉	Dong Han	AD 25–220	195
Three Kingdoms	三國 / 三国	San Guo	AD 220–265	45
Western Jin	西晉 / 西晋	Xi Jin	AD 265–317	52
Eastern Jin	東晉 / 东晋	Dong Jin	AD 317–420	103
Southern and Northern	南北朝	Nan Bei Chao	AD 420–589	169
Sui	隋	Sui	AD 581–618	37
Tang	唐	Tang	AD 618–907	289
Five Dynasties and Ten Kingdoms	五代十國 / 五代十国	Wu Dai Shi Guo	AD 907–960	53

Name of Dynasty	In Chinese	In Pinyin Chinese	Estimated Time Period	Estimated Years in Power
Kingdom of Dali	大理国	Da Li Guo	AD 937–1253	316
Northern Song	北宋	Bei Song	AD 960–1127	167
Southern Song	南宋	Nan Song	AD 1127–1279	152
Liao	遼 / 辽	Liao	AD 907–1125	209
Jin	金	Jin	AD 1115–1234	119
Western Xia	西夏	Xi Xia	AD 1038–1227	189
Yuan	元	Yuan	AD 1271–1368	97
Ming	明	Ming	AD 1368–1662	276
Qing	清	Qing	AD 1638–1911	268

Note: *Information retrieved from http://en.wikipedia.org/wiki/Chinese_dynasties and from* Mong: China History and Heritage Preservation, *by Tachiming Cha, 2013, China: China Gold Printing Group.*

The Shang Dynasty and the Hmong

When the Xia kingdom disintegrated, the Tang people established the Shang Dynasty (1600 BC–1046 BC), which remained in control for about 570 years. According to Chinese accounts, the Shang Dynasty was actually a mixed Hmong Dynasty; Tang and Shang were Hmong descended from the Jiuli kingdom. In Hmong Chinese legends, the Hmong kingdom that was born again after the demise of Jiuli (San Miao) was ruled for nearly 1,000 years by two great Hmong rulers, Tao Tie and Huan Tuo, before the Han Chinese (the Xia) invaded. A series of wars between the San Miao and the Han Chinese resulted in many bloody years of deadly conflicts. The suffering and deaths caused many Hmong to leave the area; they migrated southeast, southwest, and northeast.

Conflicts grew among different states that made up the San Miao kingdom and wars followed, leaving the whole kingdom vulnerable to invasions from the north, south, and west. The Han Chinese took advantage of the tribal conflicts and mounted major attacks against Tang territory. Finally, the San Miao kingdom fell to the control of the Han Chinese, and the Hmong once again were persecuted harshly and forced into slavery. Hmong ancestors claim that the Chinese took away their kingdom and slaughtered them to near extinction. The overwhelming oppression and suffering of this time have been immortalized in Hmong songs, folktales, death rituals, religious rites, epics, legends, and myths. Even today, during the death rituals, the Hmong use a verse of warfare against *Suav*, known as "*tsa rog nrog Suav*," meaning, waging war against the Chinese.

The Zhou Dynasty and the Hmong

After the overthrow of the Shang Dynasty, under the Western and Eastern Zhou Dynasties (1029 BC–771 BC and 770 BC–256 BC), the surviving Hmong assimilated into the dominant culture. Some resisted acculturation and migrated southward and westward to find refuge in the rugged mountains. The two Zhou Dynasties lasted for nearly 790 years, the longest period in Chinese history, and throughout the Spring and Autumn era (771 BC–476 BC) and the Warring States period (475 BC–221 BC). Hmong Chinese legends tell of Han Chinese, or *Suav Liab*, setting up fortresses and city gates as barricades to prevent Hmong from escaping. Chinese domination was very tight and extremely brutal. To elude capture and persecution, Hmong families had to disguise their identities by wearing Chinese clothing and changing their family names to Chinese names. Those who could not escape were subjected to persecution, oppression, imprisonment, being tortured to death, or being made life-long slaves. As a result of Chinese draconian rule, Hmong men were hunted down for years and Hmong women were taken by the Chinese as wives or slaves. Some were sold into slavery. Hmong bore the Chinese oppression for many years, and many took great risks to escape the ethnic cleansing and ongoing persecution in China. Hmong oral tradition reveals that to elude Chinese authorities, families were broken up, husbands and wives were separated, children were in hiding, and relatives were dispersed into the woods. Chinese soldiers pitted Hmong against one another, hiring some to go after fleeing refugees. Those who could escape hid in the highland mountains and lived in seclusion. From that point on, the Hmong were not able to establish a new kingdom. Hmong survivors adopted a reclusive lifestyle.

The Qin Dynasty and the Hmong

As with previous dynasties, both Zhou kingdoms dissolved as the result of internal conflicts, struggles for power, and civil war. When the Qin Dynasty (221 BC–206 BC) rose to power and reigned for only 15 years, the Hmong had some peace and independence in the isolated regions where they lived. Hmong ancestors remember this period as the time certain literature was banned and religious writings destroyed. The Qin policy of destroying historical documents, books, and archives had a negative impact on Hmong literacy. This was the time, Hmong believe, when they lost their writing system. Qin emperors feared that literate minorities might rise up against them. The Hmong complied with the imperial orders to avoid political retaliation and either destroyed or hid their writing systems from the oppressive emperors.

According to Chinese historical accounts and Hmong Chinese legends, the Qin emperors were strict, issuing death sentence for any civil disobedience. Not only was punishment harsh, but it was also cruel. Sometimes people were ordered to commit suicide or to murder family members. Such brutality drove the Hmong farther away. Some fled northward while many continued to migrate southward and westward.

The trail of Hmong resistance went cold for many years after the Hmong lost their great leaders during the Zhou and Qin Dynasties. Chinese accounts about the activities and whereabouts of the Hmong during this period are sketchy and Hmong stories are largely silent about the time after the fall of the San Miao kingdom. Yet, Hmong ancestors insist, hiding from the Chinese brutal persecution and draconian oppression was the only way to live safely. As happened many times in the past, living in seclusion allowed the Hmong to regain their strength so they could reestablish themselves. Hmong Chinese legends suggest that between the fall of the San Miao kingdom to the first century, around the birth of Jesus Christ, the Hmong lived in peace in the southern and western regions without engaging the Chinese in serious conflicts. Hmong ancestors claim that not feuding with the Chinese was the right course of action, enabling them to avoid capture, imprisonment, and death. Otherwise, the Hmong legends say, the inhumane killing would have continued until the Hmong were nearly or totally annihilated. Moreover, according to Hmong oral history, the Hmong who remained within the warring states and engaged in battles suffered severely because Hmong fought on both sides. Like the Zhou, the Qin used some Hmong traitors and mercenaries to chase and hunt down Hmong rebels.

The Han Dynasty and the Hmong

Following the collapse of the Qin Empire, the Western Han Dynasty (206 BC–AD 9 and AD 23–25) ruled for more than 200 years. The Hmong became part of the Han Empire because both the Hmong and the Han revered ChiYou as a hero and an ancestral icon. For the Hmong, this time offered a great opportunity to recuperate from their losses and recover from the trauma they had endured under previous dynasties. As the Hmong Chinese legends tell, the Hmong maintained a mutually beneficial relationship with the Han. During this period, the Hmong had freedom to reestablish themselves as an agricultural people and reacquire social status. They lived in harmony with their neighbors, owned their own land, and built their communities. It was a nearly two-century period of recovery during which the Hmong lived in peace and tranquility.

However, the peace did not last. The empire had been divided into 18 states, and conflict arose among the states. Through the rebellions, corruption, and political turmoil, the Chu Han succeeded in overthrowing the ruling Han family. The Han Dynasty was replaced by the Xin.

The Xin Dynasty and the Hmong

The Xin Dynasty (AD 9–23) was short lived, lasting only 14 years and consisting of only one emperor. The problems and conflicts that troubled China under the Han rolled over to the Xin. During the brief Xin period, the states were in great turmoil, led by a young and inexperienced emperor who was incapable of ruling. As Hmong Chinese legends tell, the young emperor faced a number of political revolts and was unable to manage the wars against ethnic groups such as the Lulin, Chi Mei, and Liu people from the southern region. Hmong were among the revolting groups because they wanted to establish their own country to protect their land. With other ethnic groups, Hmong joined the rebellion in the Battle of Kunyang. The emperor built a feeble military force and was ineffective in combat. When the dynasty's military leaders were killed on the battlefield, its troops panicked and retreated. The rebels, especially the Liu from the southern region, rose up in force, took control of the warring states, and won the war, marking the political demise of the Xin.

The Second Han Dynasty and the Hmong

After the Xin Dynasty dissolved, the battle between ethnic groups continued until the Liu managed to overcome rival groups and formed the Eastern Han Dynasty (AD 25–220). The new dynasty controlled the states for 195 years. Hmong undoubtedly took part in the new regime because of their good relationship with the Western Han of the former regime. However, Hmong oral history records that in every battle Hmong fought on both sides. According to Hmong Chinese legends, for nearly three centuries before the Eastern Han Dynasty came into power the Hmong had ruled over the northern and northeastern regions. During the Han Dynasty, the Chu Han waged a political campaign against Hmong rule in the northern regions. Regional conflicts escalated into war as people migrated south to avoid the harsh environment of the Gobi Desert; the Hmong had to fight to maintain their territory. The Chu Han sided against the Hmong and war dragged on for many years. Hmong Chinese legends describe many battles such as the rebellion of the Yellow Scarf Bandits, the battle against the Black Mountain Bandits, the battle of White Wolf Mountain, the battle of Red Cliffs, and the battle of Pingyang. The fighting ended with the establishment of the three kingdoms (AD 220–265 or 280), a period known as the Era of the Three Divisions.

According to Hmong Chinese legends, when the Eastern Han Dynasty neared its dissolution, the Hmong and other ethnic groups organized themselves into separate states in the Yangtze and Yellow River regions. Hmong Chinese legends also record that the far northern tribes formed five major divisions: the Luanti, Hu Yan, XuBu, QiuLin, and Lan. Each had a unitary form of government. The HuYan and XuBu controlled the east region, the QiuLin and Lan dominated the west region, and the Luanti governed the central region. During this 45-year period, the Hmong returned to the Yellow River basin and attempted to slowly take control of the region in order to colonize the southern people. However, the attempt was cut short when another tribe rose to power and joined forces with northern allies to overthrow the Hmong. A new dynasty now emerged and ruled.

The Jin Dynasties and the Hmong

Chinese legends tell that both Eastern and Western Jin Dynasties (AD 265–317 and AD 317–420) were formed by the leadership of the SiMa family from the southeast region; they lasted 155 years. The Jin appeared to be family dynasties because they had many princes. Hmong folktales tell of eight princes who rose to power and ruled over the warring states: "*Huabtais yim leej tub txawm sawv los kav lub teb chaws nyob suav tuam tshoj, tiam sim kev sib txeeb noj sib txeeb haus ua rau yim tus tub huabtais tsis muaj kev sib haum xeeb. Huabtais laus tuag kiag tag nrho xwb ces kev sib ntau sib tua sawv ntsee, ces Hmoob tsis paub ua licas vim hais tias sab twg los puav leej yog huabtais tag nrho. Hmoob thiaj li tawg kev sib koom siab vim hais tias ib cos yuav tuaj sab xi* (joining the right group), *ib cos yuav tuaj sab laug* (joining the left group), *ces ib cos hos yuav tuaj pab nyob nrub nrab* (joining the neutral group) *thiab no lau. Lub sib hawm ntawd mam Hmoob ua lub neej nrog mab nrog suav, Hmoob kuj muaj hwj chim thiab...*" Politically, as told by Hmong oral history, Hmong became a tripartite ethnic group during this period.

As Hmong Chinese legends say, the time of the two Jin Dynasties was known as the Chaos of the Eight Princes; it was a chaotic period that followed the death of the well-known emperor SiMa Yan. The states were in great distress because of unrest and internal tribulations. A series of wars broke out among the ruling Jin princes, all after the throne. As in the past, Hmong were divided; Hmong fought against their Hmong brothers in many battles. The time of the Western Jin was an era of much bloodshed and great turmoil. Leaders rose to claim positions only to be toppled as princes fought for political power. Many generals, emperors, and leaders were betrayed and assassinated. The violence spread among the different ethnic groups. Every tribe—the KagHan, Wei, Rouran, Yan, Xia, Qin, Zhai, Liang, Mu Rong, Zhao, Liu, and others—was at war at some time and nearly all tribes took part in the many rebellions. According to Hmong Chinese accounts, many of these groups were Hmong. The rising and falling of the eight princes drove the whole country into a morass of instability, insurgency, and political coups. The fifth of the 15 Jin emperors moved southward to establish the Eastern Jin Dynasty. The move did not stop the warfare, which continued until the last emperor of the SiMa family was murdered by the Liu. His death marked the end of the Jin Dynasty, and a new regime under Liu people came to power and began to rule.

The Song Dynasty and the Hmong

The Song Dynasty (AD 420–479), formed by the Liu people, ruled for 59 years. By this time, according to Hmong Chinese legends, the Hmong had been scattered and some lived among the northern tribes, the Turks, TuJue, and BuMin Khan. Disagreements boiled up between the TueJue and Wei tribes and dragged the Hmong into a series of tribal wars and war with the Liu Song. As Hmong Chinese legends explain, the Hmong fought against the Liu Song, who were also Hmong, and drove them out of the region until the Liu people moved back to the Yellow River basin. There, the Liu Song joined aboriginal ethnic groups such as the Mong Ran, Mu Rong, Jie, WuHuan, Qi, and Qiang. Scandals, royal feuds, mistrust, and assassinations of Liu Song led to another series of bloody inter-tribal warfare.

The Liu rulers were ruthless dictators who turned against their own family members. Hmong oral folktales describe the Liu Song rule as a treasonous era: "*Suav thiab Hmoob sib tua tau ntau lub xyoo, ces muaj ib hnub ib tug nom tswv suav txawm ntxeev siab ua neeg tsa taw tuam ntuj, muab suav tus nom tua tuag, ces lub tebchaws thiaj li rov nchuav dua.*" The meaning is that betraying and killing your own leaders causes the country to dissolve. The Song Dynasty ended when a general conspired against and assassinated the last ruling prince. The Hmong migration continued.

The Northern and Southern Dynasties and the Hmong

During the Song period, the whole country had been divided into two halves, the northern world (*sab qaum teb* in Hmong) and the southern world (*sab qab teb* in Hmong). After Song rule dissolved, a series of Northern and Southern Dynasties (AD 420–589) controlled the states for nearly 170 years. According to Chinese historical accounts, each half, northern and southern, had four states, and each state had its own ruling classes, known as king families or dynasties. In the north, which encompassed the northern regions and the Yellow River basin, were the Xianbei, Qi, Zhou, Wei, and Yuan Wei tribes. They were ruled by four dynasties: the Eastern Wei (AD 534–550), Western Wei (AD 535–557), Northern Qi (AD 550–577), and Northern Zhou (AD 557–581). The four southern dynasties were the Liu Song Guo (AD 420–479), Southern Qi Guo (AD 479–502), Liang Guo (AD 502–557), and Chen Guo (AD 557–589).

Hmong Chinese legends tell that some people from the northern tribes migrated south to cohabit the land of the southern tribes. The Hmong played major roles in the colonization of both northern and southern areas. Those Hmong who lived off the land moved back to the fertile land of the Yangtze and Yellow River basins. Hmong lived in both northern and southern worlds under a variety of kings, some Hmong and some Chinese. The lives of the northern Hmong were hard because resources were scarce and weather extreme, either cold and icy or dry and hot. From the descriptions of the northern region in the Hmong folktales, scholars are unclear whether the area was the Gobi Desert, Mongolia, the vicinity of Beijing, or another place. For example, Hmong remember their ancestors talking about using cornstalks and rice stalks as firewood for cooking because they had no wood. The description fits the barren desert land of present-day Mongolia.

During the Northern and Southern Dynasties, the Hmong and other ethnic groups underwent sociopolitical changes. They coped with challenges, took advantage of opportunities, and experienced some successes in seeking government jobs, attempting to improve their living conditions, gaining social status, earning respect, becoming literate in the official language, assimilating, acculturating, and working as high ranking officials. As expressed in Hmong terms, "*Hmoob xav mus ua nom ua tswv, xav nrog mab sua sib txeeb hwj chim thiab tswv cheej, xav muaj kev ywj pheej, xav tau kev vaj huam loj sib luag, thiab tsis xav raug luag caij tsuj tsim txom.... Hmoob zwm haiv ua mab ua suav.*" Hmong adopted and assimilated ethnically and culturally.

Even though they enjoyed relative peace, the Hmong were not free of turmoil during the time of the eight states. As in the previous dynasties, each state experienced internal and external struggles for prosperity and survival. Political instability seemed always present, as civil revolts, ethnic rebellion, and coup attempts were common. Disputes over natural resources and land ownership as well as anger over taxation inflamed racial tensions. Corruption was widespread and the government was full of conspiracies, espionage, and betrayal. These crises and power struggles often erupted in civil wars and eventually dissolved the reign of the Northern and Southern Dynasties.

The Sui Dynasty and the Hmong

Following the death of its latest ruler, Emperor Xuan, the Northern Zhou created the Sui Dynasty (AD 581–618). The Sui ruled the states of both north and south for 37 years. They brought with them to the new dynasty the conflicts and instabilities that had plagued the Northern Zhou. According to Hmong Chinese accounts, at Emperor Xuan's death, a struggle for power immediately took place between the emperor's son and his father-in-law. At the same time, tensions between the southern tribes and the northern tribes were escalating into inter-tribal conflicts. The western tribes remained neutral and the eastern tribes played a role in the Sui political occupation of the southern region. When the Sui plotted to oust the TuJue from power, the western tribes refused to cooperate but the eastern tribes joined in the takeover. To crush revolts in the southern region, which was dominated by the Chen, the Sui deployed hundreds of thousands of troops to the Chen state near the Yangtze River basin and launched heavy assaults for many years until the region was finally captured.

The constant warfare around the Yellow and Yangtze River basins inspired the Hmong expression "*Tsis pom dej dag (daj) ces siab tsis nqig,*" meaning "If you do not see the Yellow River, you will not settle down or calm down." The expression implied that because they had engaged in so many wars in the area, if Hmong returned to the Yellow River basin, wars would displace them once again. The idea was that Hmong would be better off staying away from the area than returning to the old place to face old problems with the same enemies. On the other hand, the expression could also be translated something like this: "If you do not see it, you may not believe it."

The downfall of the Sui Dynasty was its inhumane and brutal public policy requiring people to engage in major projects. The projects, building grand canals and constructing and reconstructing the great wall, demanded hard labor. In addition to this cruel policy, a famine, freezing weather conditions, public resentment, ongoing rebellions and civil wars, and the division of military forces into multiple factions and placement in different regions that competed against one another for power sapped the central government of its ability to manage the country. Hmong Chinese legends tell of top government officials and generals trying to topple one another for personal gain, continued struggles for power, and a series of civil conflicts that brought the dynasty to its demise.

The Tang Dynasty and the Hmong

When the northern tribes defeated all the warlords in the southern regions, a former Sui general and his sons formed the Tang Dynasty (AD 618–907), which ruled for 289 years. As Hmong Chinese legends tell, the Tang rebuilt the country's economy, rebuilt the legal system, and instituted social welfare policies. Compared to previous dynasties, the Tang was a more powerful empire with international influence. The Tang promoted education and literature, allowed foreign trade to boost regional economic growth, improved legal codes and laws, and created a central government system. The relationship between northern and southern tribes improved under the Tang because people were allowed to migrate to the Yangtze and Yellow River basins. Local leaders and people were given freedom. The Tang Dynasty was a feudal period with rich and poor classes. Rich feudal lords owned property and extensive

tracts of land; poor people were servants, tenants, indentured workers, or sharecroppers.

Perhaps this was the time Hmong become profitable merchants, trading and selling goods. Hmong elders say the Hmong learned to sell, bargain, and negotiate like the Chinese. Many Hmong received informal education about business from wealthy Chinese. Capitalism was not a part of early Hmong life.

The freedom to migrate allowed the Hmong to seek fertile land for farming farther south, to leave central China for other parts of the country. Some scholars believe the Hmong migrated to Southeast Asian nations such as northern Vietnam, northern Burma, and northern Laos at this time; however, this contention cannot be verified. Nevertheless, during the Tang reign Hmong were able to move freely without fear of being hunted down, arrested, and persecuted. Under previous dynasties, most Hmong ancestors claim, Hmong who fled China departed alone or in pairs in order to elude capture, leaving family members and relatives behind. As Hmong folktales and fables say, "*Tom qab peb Hmoob tau raug kev tsim txom tau ntau lub xyoo, muaj ib lub sij hawm peb Hmoob khiav tawm suav teb los rau teb chaws xov tshoj teb coob heev. Lub caij ntawd nom tswv suav tsis cheem thiab tsis txwv vim tias neeg khiav qaum teb rau qab teb, thiab kev lag luam zoo.... Lub sij hawm ntawd, Hmoob tsiv tawm khiav uake coob heev, vim suav tsis soj qab taug lwg li thawj ob peb tiam ua ntej dhau los.*" These phrases tell the early exodus of Hmong Chinese refugees who migrated to the southwestern regions of China bordering Vietnam, Burma, and Laos in the early days.

Even though daily life was probably better during this period than previously, the Tang Dynasty had its share of problems. The downfall of the Tang Dynasty followed a familiar pattern. Its heavy taxation of the wealthy feudal lords caused trouble. Some tax collectors abused their power, crushing the poor by demanding higher payments, encroaching unjustly on Hmong land, and imprisoning tax evaders. The empire fell because it could not subdue the ongoing conflicts between tribal groups, it failed to defuse tensions between ethnic groups, and it was unable to prevent a series of civil wars. Rebellions, internal struggles, corruption, a weak central government, and clashes among political factions weakened the empire and ultimately brought it down.

The Liang Empire and the Hmong

The Huang Chao or Liang Empire that replaced the Tang ruled for nearly half a century (AD 907–960). According to Chinese historical accounts, the country was divided into 10 kingdoms and governed by a succession of five dynasties. The time is called the Five Dynasties and Ten Kingdoms period. The five dynasties were the Liang Gou (AD 907–923), also known as the Later Liang Dynasty; the Later Tang Guo (AD 923–936), sometimes called the Later Tang Dynasty; the Jin Guo (AD 936–947), or Later Jin Dynasty; the Han Guo (AD 947–982), known as the Later Han Dynasty; and the Zhou Guo (AD 951–960), or Later Zhou Dynasty. At the same time, 10 countries were established, most in the southern region: Wu (AD 902–937), Wu Yue (AD 907–978), Min (AD 909–945), Southern Han (AD 917–971), Chu (AD 927–951), Jing Nan (AD 924–923), Former Shu (AD 907–925), Later Shu (AD 935–965), Southern Tang (AD 937–975), and Northern Han (AD 951–979). During this period many nationalities reestablished use of their preferred tribal and nationality names. This was a revival period during which indigenous and unrecognized groups reclaimed their cultural identities by establishing their own kingdoms. Some of the indigenous and unrecognized groups had been dominated in the past by larger ethnic groups such as the San Miao, Man, Yi, and Xia. Some previous dynasties were able to continue to reform during this period. At the same time, some promoted acculturation, integration, and assimilation. As the Hmong folktales put it, *"Hmoob xyaum chais taub hau zoo li mab sua, zoo nkaus li lub mag qos."* This was the time in which Hmong began shaving their foreheads, adopting the bald forehead custom of the Chinese culture under the ruler Li Yuan Hao.

The Dali and the Hmong

As explained in the Chinese historical accounts, during the Kingdom of Dali (AD 937–1253), the Hmong could have been the dominant group in the northern regions. Two kingdoms, Qidan and Xianbei, were in different regions, but they were both Hmong kingdoms. In fact, the names of many states in the northern regions can be traced to the Hmong who moved back to the Yellow River basin. As Chinese legends tell, during the Northern Song Dynasty (AD 960–1127) and the Southern Song Dynasty (AD 937–1253), the Hmong established kingdoms in the central region and ruled over many regions of the north and northeast.

According to Hmong Chinese accounts, the Hmong found their own capital city, the Southern Heavenly City called Nan Jing Cheng (*Naj Ceeb Tsheej*). They began five other cities during this period also: Shang Jing (*Saum Ceeb Tsheej*); Dong Jing (eastern Jing Cheng, or *Toob Ceeb Tsheej*); Zhong Jing (central Jing Cheng, or *Tsoob Ceeb Tsheej*); Nan Jing (southern Jing Cheng, or *Naj Ceeb Tsheej*); and Xi Jing (western Jing Cheng, or *Xyib Ceeb Tsheej*). At this time, Hmong were able to practice their culture and traditions and they developed writing systems called *Dazi and Xiaozi*. Scholars and historians have not always linked Hmong to these historical events because at the time of the events the Hmong were not recognized by the name "Hmong"; they may have been thought of as belonging to groups such as the Xi, San Miao, Liu, Wu, Mo, Xianbei, Zhou, Li, Xia, Wei, or others.

The Yuan Dynasty and the Hmong

According to Hmong Chinese legends, the Hmong continued to rule in the northern regions and make progress throughout the Liao (AD 916–1125), Jin (AD 1115–1234), Western Xia (AD 1038–1227), and Yuan Dynasties (AD 1271–1368). The Yuan imperial government appeared to be led by Mongols; however, many believe the Hmong participated in it as well. Some speculate that Hmong joined forces with the Han Chinese to overthrow the Mongols. The Hmong ruler for part of that time was Kag Han Ku Blai. Under this ruler, Hmong were exposed to Islamic and Buddhist ideologies and Confucianism was restored to the Hmong kingdom. Ku Blai and his supporters also promoted the practice of shamanism (*kev ua neeb ua yaig* in Hmong) as a national religion of the Yuan Dynasty. This account explains and supports Hmong religious practices of the present day. The Hmong have multiple belief systems besides ancestor worship and animism. Shamanism (*ua neeb ua yaig*), *Basi Khite, saib kab teg, saib yaig, mus thov hauj sam saib*, reincarnation, and the Buddhist concepts of karma and nirvana have become part of Hmong culture and traditions.

During the Yuan Dynasty, the Hmong kingdom was divided into two states, south and north, as the result of a disputed election and a struggle for power. According to Hmong Chinese legends, the Hmong fought a series of civil wars between two brothers (Ku Blai and Ariq Buke) until the south defeated the north. Ku Blai then found the Yuan Dynasty, which ruled the Hmong kingdom for another century. He also ousted the Southern Song Dynasty from power in the Yangtze River basin. During this time, the Hmong were self-governed, ruled by Hmong brothers and BorJigin families. There were a total of 16 Yuan rulers in the 1,000 years of the dynasty, and the Hmong were widely spread throughout central China. However, the Hmong kingdom gradually declined. The Hmong folktales say, "*Hmoob sib txeeb nom ces Hmoob thiaj li poob teb chaws rau suav. Suav raws Hmoob tua thoob tebchaws. Hmoob tsis muaj chaw nyob chaw nkaum. Hmoob tawg ua pab ua pawg. Zaum no mas yog zaum ob losi yog zaum peb uas suav raws Hmoob tua kom tu noob. Hmoob thiaj li ua ib siab khiav los rau cov teb chaws nyob rau xov tshoj teb. Lub sij hawm Hmoob khiav los ntev li peb plaub tiam neeg* (300–400 years)." These phrases explain how Hmong kingdom became disintegrated as Hmong divided into different groups and immigrated to different regions, and subsequently, into Indo-china. The Hmong migratory process took nearly 300–400 years.

As with previous dynasties, the Yuan Empire experienced internal conflicts, political instability, and civil turmoil. Similarly to the Sui and Tang Dynasties, Yuan leaders were beset with corruption, assassinations, inexperience, lack of vision, and nepotism. Government policy was weak, central control was poor, and financial practices were bad. Famines, droughts, and floods strained resources. The inability of the Yuan rulers to stabilize the country and deal with the crises angered people. Some migrated to the north and others staged revolts to overthrow the central government. Numerous uprisings, such as that led by the White Lotus extremists and the Red Turban, Han, and Ming rebellions brought the Yuan Dynasty to an end. Once again, the Hmong lost their kingdom and the people scattered.

The Ming Dynasty and the Hmong

After the Yuan, the Ming Dynasty (AD 1368–1644) dominated for nearly 276 years. Like the previous Han dynasty, the Ming initially faced ethnic revolts from the southern regions. The leaders lacked a consistent policy for dealing with regional and ethnic groups, and they allowed the groups to govern themselves as long as the regional leaders collected taxes for the Ming central administration. This policy led to corruption among different ethnic groups. Conflicts and tensions built up and a series of revolts broke out. Hmong Chinese legends refer to this period as *grass bundle grass*, or *Miao manage Miao*, or *Yi manage Yi*, or *Hmong manage Hmong*. Like other groups, the Hmong revolted against the Ming draconian tax and land policies. Again, Hmong fought on both sides and suffered life-long consequences.

According to Hmong Chinese accounts, the Ming imperial government used trickery to entice Hmong to its side. Hmong who worked for the Ming Empire had to join the Ming armies in suppressing the revolts from the southern regions. Ming Empire officials treated Hmong defectors as criminals and killed them.

The ethnic unrest escalated and turned into a series of rebellions such as the Mia-Yao rebellion, also known as the Mien rebellion, and the Hmong rebellion. The Ming government came down harshly and ruthlessly on the Hmong; they considered the Hmong the main enemy and accused them of being behind all the major rebellions. The Hmong had little choice but to rebel; the Ming encroached on their land, confiscated their property, taxed them steeply and unfairly, denied them political power, and oppressed them culturally.

The Ming Empire bribed some Hmong to take part in its programs and rewarded them with a prestigious lifestyle. Such enticements damaged Hmong pride and destroyed relationships. Some Hmong were rich and some were poor, some were powerful and some were powerless, but all were victims of exploitation and extortion by the Ming. As Hmong oral tradition says, "*Hmoob sib tua nrog suav liab, tabsi Hmoob swb vim hais tias suav liab ntiav Hmoob rov qab tuaj tua Hmoob, thiaj ua rau Hmoob swb tebchaws.*" Undoubtedly many Hmong were Ming's subservients or mercenary soldiers during the ethnic rebellions. The Hmong were labeled "cooked" or "raw." "Cooked Hmong" (*Hmoob siav*) were those who were forced to assimilate, especially those who adopted Chinese culture and traditions; "raw Hmong" (*Hmoobnyoos*) were those who resisted such assimilation and lived isolated in desolate areas.

As the rebellions escalated into civil wars in the northern region and more people resisted Ming dominance, the Ming Empire showed signs of collapsing. The wars impacted local economies heavily as farmers were desperate for supplies and aid. The number of revolts increased, rebels took over cities and regions, and the dissolution of the Ming Dynasty was inevitable.

To prevent the collapse of Ming Empire, three groups—Hmong-Ming, Hmong Galah, and the Ming Empire—reached an accord to combine efforts and forces to stabilize the status quo, take over the other states, and form a new country. Not all Hmong supported the coalition since Hmong were on both sides. As Hmong folktales say, "*Suav tuaj txeeb Hmoob liaj teb, txeeb Hmoob teb Hmoob chaw, Hmoob tsis muaj av ua noj ua haus. Hmoob thiaj li khiav mus nrhiav chaw ua noj ua haus ... ib cov Hmoob khiav los rau tebchaws nplog, nyablaj, thiab thai teb ... ib cov nyob nrog suav, ua suav qhev ... ib cov khiav mus zwm haiv ua lwm yam neeg lawm...*" Basically, the confiscation of agricultural land, the ongoing persecution, the brutal oppression, and the very real threat of extermination caused Hmong to leave their villages.

The Qing Dynasty and the Hmong

After the Ming, the Qing Dynasty (1644–1911) ruled for the next 267 years. The coalition government began immediately to suppress the many rebellions throughout the country. It implemented strict, oppressive control over regions, towns, and villages. The Hmong were divided into two groups: the ones who supported Qing and Ming imperialism and the ones who were against it. Some western scholars and researchers noted that the Hmong once again became classified as either "cooked" or "raw."

Being cooked (*Shu Miaozu* in Chinese) meant having become half Chinese and half Hmong or having been assimilated to become fully Chinese. Politically, being cooked also implied having sold out, being a traitor, defecting, and devoid of ethnic pride. Remaining raw (*Sheng Miaozu* in Chinese) meant rejecting Chinese imperialism in order to continue being Hmong, and being raw implied resistance, rebellion, revenge, and the likelihood of future insurgency. People in the cooked group often became subservient to the Qing Empire, supporting the empire by going after their relatives who were raw. On the other hand, people in the raw group were insubordinate, unyielding, stubborn, and unassimilated Hmong who were fiercely opposed to the Qing Empire. The cooked Hmong, those who accepted Qing and Ming control, had political favor; they became soldiers or government officials and were regarded as Hmong-Chinese, as *Hmoob Suav* in Hmong. As for raw Hmong, those who chose not to join the new regime, the imperial Qing viewed them as savage people, barbarians, and enemies. The Qing considered raw Hmong its main enemy because Hmong had revolted against the Ming numerous times and Hmong were also the main rebels in the southern region. This political labeling by the Chinese could have earned the Hmong the derogatory name *Meo* or *Miao*.

Hmong legends record that the hardest and darkest period in Hmong history occurred under Qing imperial dominance. Qing officials treated the Hmong unjustly, took their land by force, refused to recognize them, and imposed hostile regulations in Hmong areas. The Hmong suffered from imperial corruption, bribe, distortion, extortion, exploitation, and abuse of authority. The Qing took Hmong wives, daughters, and sons for their slaves. They forced the Hmong to live on mountain slopes and barren hills where there was little good land to farm. Most raw Hmong became poor farmers who could neither read nor write. Hmong had no political clout whatsoever and were badly treated by local officials. In some cases, they were abused, bullied, chased, humiliated, and insulted by imperial policies and authorities. The mistreatment led the Hmong to organize what has been called the Crazy Miao Rebellion in the mid–1700s. Hmong folktales say the Hmong, taxed heavily and unfairly, especially by a food tax, were forced to be indentured farmers and sharecroppers under Qing imperialism.

The Qing oppressed not only the Hmong, but also aboriginal people such as the San Miao, Man, Li, Ama, and others. As Hmong folktales explain, Qing genocide against ethnic groups was prevalent in the southern regions. The typical method was to torture and murder people in the targeted group, set their villages on fire, revoke their right to own land, and seize their property and give it to others. Hmong oral history suggests that the Hmong had had enough of this type of atrocity by the late 1700s. At that time they united

under a Hmong leader known as Wu Ba Yue (*Vwj Paj Yias* in Hmong) in a series of rebellions against the brutal treatment of the Qing. Sadly, the leader was betrayed by some of his own people; he was captured and killed by the Chinese warlords.

The Chinese repressive domination continued. In the mid–1800s, during a food shortage, Hmong sought relief from local imperial officials from high taxes on food, especially on rice. Instead of receiving help, the Hmong leader submitting the plea was apprehended and murdered. Consequently, according to Hmong Chinese accounts, Hmong mounted several unsuccessful rebellions against Qing imperial rule from the mid–1800s to the early 1900s. For instance, Yan Da Wu and Bao Da Du led Hmong rebels against Chinese oppression and killed many Chinese soldiers in combat; Zhang Xiu Mei became a Hmong protector, similar to ChiYou, and led Hmong forces against Chinese oppressions; Yin Hua led the Crazy Miao rebellion; Xu Ting Jie led the Red Turbans rebellion; Huang Hao June led the Yellow Soldiers rebellion; and He De Sheng led the Yellow Turban rebels. These were Hmong leaders who made heroic sacrifices. Other Hmong leaders who fought valiantly for freedom were Tao Xin Chun, who led a Hmong rebellion; Zhang Ling Xiang, who led and commanded the White Flag soldiers; Yang Jiu, who led a group of Hmong rebels; Li Wen Mao, whose troops attacked Chinese forces in battle; and Hong Xiu Quan, who also led a rebellion. Major General Vang Pao observed that there were 32 Hmong kings or warlords in China prior to the Hmong emigration to Southeast Asia, and all 32 were referred to by Hmong as *vaj ntswv*, meaning kings or mighty protectors. These are examples of some of the historic revolts led by Hmong leaders during the Qing Empire. A sad character in this history was the Hmong traitor Li Wen Cai, who was bribed by the Qing to go after Hmong rebels (Cha, 2013).

As told by Hmong Chinese legends, the Hmong rebel groups disintegrated as the result of disunity, economic hardship, casualties, arrests, executions, and brutal persecution. In the early 1860s, out of the blue, European forces helped the Qing Empire retake control of Hangzhou, Suzhou, and some cities of the Yangtze River region. During two decades of rebellion, the casualties have been estimated at nearly 5 million people. The Qing government chased the Hmong rebels from the southern regions into Indochina and beyond. Hmong oral traditions say the Hmong fled the southern regions to the wilderness of the southern mountains and into Vietnam, Laos, and Thailand. They ran, hid, and fought to save themselves from being wiped out by the Chinese. The Hmong were told to run for their lives; otherwise, the Chinese would kill all their males, regardless of age. They would hunt and slaughter Hmong males without sparing any, to complete extinction. Hmong ancestors once shared with their Hmong offspring about the trail of tears and the trail of fears they traveled while being pursued by the Chinese. As recorded in Hmong oral history, "*Lub noob luaj taum daj ces suav yeej muab raws caum tua kom tuag tag, tsis pub dim. Hmoob thiaj ua ib siab khiav los rau cov tebchaws nyob rau xov tshoj teb.*" The meaning of these phrases is that the Chinese concocted ethnic cleansing against the Hmong rebels and would go after them to hunt them down to wipe out every identified Hmong males. This horrific fear still lingers in Hmong hearts and souls today because of the unhealed scars caused by the Chinese extirpation. How Hmong rebels survived the extinction still remains a mystery; however, Hmong great grandparents told Hmong offspring that Hmong Chinese used the Chinese camouflage to elude capture and to hide their loved ones from being arrested, imprisoned, and murdered.

The Hmong suffered attempts at ethnic cleansing and genocide for hundreds of years, and they made great sacrifices to save themselves as a people by emigrating from China to Southeast Asia and beyond. Sadly, as told in Hmong oral history, the cooked Hmong somewhat played a role, although very small, in this ethnic cleansing. It is time for Hmong to learn Hmong history and understand how and why their ancestors migrated from China to Southeast Asia and then to the West.

Hmong Settlement in Indochina

The French sent missionaries to India and Vietnam in the early 1600s. The imperial French call India, Laos, Vietnam, and Thailand *Indochina*, but Hmong call these countries *xov tshoj teb*, meaning smaller southern Chinese country. In China, Hmong call the ancient world *tuam tshoj teb*, meaning large northern Chinese country. Literally, in Hmong today, the word "*xov*" means small, little, tiny, or petite; and the word "*tuam*" means big, large, huge, gigantic, giant, or grand. The Hmong word "*tshoj*" means to make, to become, to regain, to retake, to incite, to provoke, to fight, to argue, to encourage, or to establish. Politically, "*tuam tshoj*" refers to the time Hmong Chinese underwent tribulations and turmoil during the Spring and Autumn eras and the Warring States periods at the Yellow River basin and "*xov tshoj*" refers to the different periods of Hmong Chinese migration and resettlement in Southeast Asia. Historically, according to the transliteration of Hmong Chinese legends, the phrase "*tuam tshoj*" means to resist, to rebel, to fight, to charge, to rise, to assemble, or to against; and similarly, the phrase "*xov tshoj*" means to leave, to migrate, to abandon, to disband, to disappear, to vanish, to flee, or to disperse (Cha, 2013). Interestingly, these historical phrases explain the early part of Hmong political history in the ancient world and the later part of Hmong migration from central China to Southeast Asia.

The term *Indochina* is broad and mainly refers to Vietnam, Laos, Cambodia, and Thailand. In the early part of French and British occupation and expedition, Indochina might have included Cambodia, Burma, and India as well; however, to be inclusive, the word Indochina was replaced with *Southeast Asian nations* in the mid–1900s. Hmong migration history started in central China and from there the Hmong gradually moved southward to the southwestern regions of

China, then, as Figures 1.3 and 1.4 illustrate, they settled in Southeast Asia, and then in early 1975 they left Laos for the western nations.

At the beginning of the 1800s, as most Hmong understand, the Hmong migrated on a large scale into Southeast Asia from the southwestern regions of China. They came to the Southeast Asian countries of Vietnam, Laos, and Thailand. However, some scholars believe that some Hmong had come to Indochina before the 1800s, prior to and during the Ming Dynasty and the early Qing Dynasty when they fled Chinese political oppression and persecution. This belief is supported by Hmong oral history, which suggests that Hmong families had been living in Southeast Asia, specifically in northern Vietnam bordering Laos, for a few generations before a new wave of Hmong refugees arrived in the early 1800s. Because they were oppressed by the Chinese government, the Hmong usually lived in secluded and rugged highland mountain regions where contacts by foreigners were virtually impossible. The refugees' choice of these areas is supported by western researchers who discovered Hmong families living at 4,000- to 5,000-foot elevations in the wilderness of northern Laos bordering Vietnam. The Hmong inhabited regions no one else wanted to occupy so they could be

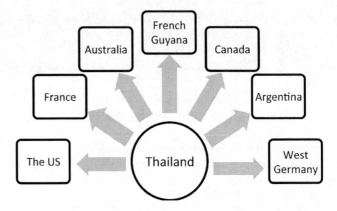

Figure 1.4. Hmong dispersion from Thailand to the western nations.

free. Hmong oral tradition affirms that the early Hmong were nomadic farmers who had an agrarian lifestyle, a way of life that enabled them to be free and independent.

As the Hmong reestablished themselves in a new life in the new countries, living off the land was challenging and often difficult. But the Hmong liked the life prospects the new countries offered. They built villages in secluded regions and raised cattle, goats, pigs, buffalos, horses, and chickens. They worked hard to become self-sufficient and independent. They cultivated vegetables, rice, corn, and herbs. The cool climate of the highland mountain slopes permitted them to grow opium to sell to the Chinese merchants. Opium was not only a cash crop for trade but was also a valuable commodity used to pay taxes to the imperial French and Laotian government officials. The Hmong also used opium as herbal medicine. The ongoing practice of reclusive lifestyle contributed to Hmong socioeconomic hardship.

For hundreds of years, the Hmong found refuge and safe haven in the wilderness of northern Vietnam, Laos, and Thailand. The governments of these nations neither officially recognized them nor denied them citizenship, and no law prohibited them from using and occupying the land. Some western scholars identified them as indigenous to Southeast Asia while others called them mon-

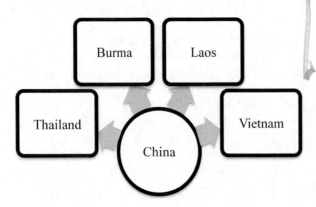

Figure 1.3. Hmong dispersion from China to Southeast Asia.

tagnards, mountaineers, or highland dwellers. The inhabitants of those nations referred to the Hmong as Miao, Meo, refugees, or immigrants. No matter what names foreigners used, Hmong always referred to themselves as "*Hmong*" or "*Mong*." To date, Hmong have not adopted any of these imperial labels or names to replace the Hmong original and only ethnic name. However, Hmong call highland dwellers "*neeg yaj sab*."

In the mid–1800s, the Hmong came into contact with foreigners from western countries, particularly the imperial French and British who were exploring and occupying Southeast Asia. When the French made expeditions to exploit the natural resources in northern Vietnam, which is located in the southwest region of China, they invaded the territory occupied by the aboriginal refugees who had fled China and resettled there. These refugee groups, including the Hmong, Ma, Man, Yi, Haw, and Yue, primarily came from Guangxi and Yunnan located in the southern regions of China. According to Hmong Chinese legends, Hmong refugees were part of the Black Flag Army and the Yellow Flag Army living in those regions. As Hmong oral tradition says, the Hmong first met Yue people, whom they referred to as Vietnamese; Buyi people, who were Man or Ma people from southern China; and the Khamu, whom they referred to as Lao Theung (*puab thawj* in Hmong). The refugees in Southeast Asia were of different ethnic groups, including the aboriginal Yue, Buyi, Hakka, Mien, Yao, Lahu, and Hmong. Because the Qing Chinese had been in contact with the refugee groups, especially the Black Flag Army, during the early years of rebellions, both the Qing Chinese and the refugees disliked imperial foreigners and wanted to dislodge the French and the British. The Qing Chinese sent the Black Flag Army to sabotage the French expedition by denying the French access to the northern Vietnam region and the southwestern regions of China. The conflict escalated into a war between the imperial French and the Qing Chinese on the border between Vietnam and China, and the Hmong fought on the side of the Qing armies. Eventually the Qing Chinese withdrew and left the Hmong to fend off the imperial French occupation in the region. Hmong gave the imperial French the ethnic name *Fabkis,* a derivative phrase from the Chinese word *Faguo* for French.

According to Hmong legends, the battles between the Hmong and the imperial French went on for some time but the French continued to occupy the land. The Hmong revolted when the French imposed a heavy tax on Hmong civilians in late 1890s. The French had created a central administration for collecting taxes from the Hmong and other ethnic groups living in northern Vietnam and northern Laos. As described by Hmong, the French government was as corrupt as that of the Chinese warlords. The French appointed local chieftains, known as *kiatongs* (*canton* in French and *kastoo* in Hmong), or little kings, clan leaders, or village chiefs, to take charge of the tax collection. For the Hmong, taxes on food, land, and people were not new because they had endured this unwelcome policy from the Chinese dynasties over the centuries. Neither were the Hmong afraid to rebel against the taxation if they could not afford to pay. Living off the land was hard and the people were poor. When Hmong civilians were unable to pay the heavy taxes, the French insisted the Hmong chiefs, or kiatongs, exact penalties and increase the taxes on the Hmong. The French ordered military forces to the region to force Hmong leaders to take action against tax evaders. The Hmong refugees had no choice but to revolt. The Hmong kiatongs sided with the rest of the Hmong in rebelling against the brutal French taxation policy. The French tried to arrest and kill the Hmong who were insubordinate. The ensuing gun fight between the Hmong and French soldiers lasted for several days and nights near the city Ban Ban.

The bloodshed finally stopped when the French entered diplomatic negotiations with the Hmong kiatongs and leaders. According to legends, to reach an accord with the imperial French, Hmong chiefs selected a representative of all the kiatongs to negotiate a resolution with the French. His name was

Moua Tong Zer or Moua Kiatong, also known in Hmong legends as Moua Chong Kai. The two sides reached an agreement and the fighting ceased. The Hmong call the clash the "French War," or "*Rog Fabkis*," because the French provoked the conflict. The peace lasted for nearly 25 years before another Hmong revolt took place in the early 1920s.

In return for arranging a settlement, Moua Chong Kai, aka Moua Tong Zer, was promoted by the French to become a tasseng (*toj xeem*), a representative leader of all Hmong kiatongs in the region. The French changed their governing strategy, making the Hmong kiatongs the leaders or chieftains of their villages, towns, and clans. Initially, this bureaucratic system allowed local chieftains, or kiatongs, to report to the tasseng, the regional leader who was appointed by the French, any problems that arose.

The establishment of Hmong leaders was relatively new under French control, and most Hmong Chinese refugees were not used to the western bureaucratic system of decentralized government. The shift in leadership paradigms drove Hmong leaders into more social conflicts within their own groups. For instance, the Hmong tribunal court system was flawed and corrupt to the point it was unjust to the poor. Basically, Hmong had adopted the culture of bribery and extortion they had learned from the Chinese feudal system. The system contaminated the Hmong leadership, fostering corruption, bias, prejudice, nepotism, favoritism, and struggles for power. In simple terms, the French oppressed the Hmong while Hmong loyalists to the French became aggressors and oppressed their own people. Hmong leaders carried these practices with them to Laos and beyond.

The French occupation in Southeast Asia had two major effects on the Hmong, one negative and one positive. First, the French draconian tax policy destroyed Hmong relationships; bonds of trust dissolved because the taxation spawned corruption and fraud. Laotian officials and village chieftains imposed double taxes on Hmong families in order to cover their expenses. Some Hmong

parents had to sell their own children and their livestock to pay the taxes. Hmong oral history notes, "*Fabkis (French) sau se loj heev, Hmoob them tsis taus. Tus txom nyem ces muab metub menyuam muag los them se. Tus muaj tsiaj txhuv ces muab tsiaj muab txhuv muag los them se. Tej tus ces them tsis taus se, nom tswv tuaj coj metub menyuam mus ua qhev li lawm ... peb Hmoob raug kev txom nyem heev, Hmoob thiaj li tawm tsam Fabkis.*" These phrases describe how Hmong struggled to pay high taxes imposed by the French and economic hardship led Hmong to revolt against the French colonial policy.

Second, the French helped some Hmong prosper academically and socioeconomically. They gave the Hmong access to French schools and many Hmong became literate in French and Lao. With French support, some Hmong became connected politically with the king and local Laotian officials. Academically, French missionaries supported the education of some Hmong children and enrolled them in French elementary and high schools. Hmong civilian soldiers were recruited to be trained by French officers. Last, but not least, some Hmong families converted their religious beliefs and practices to some forms of Christianity, especially Catholicism.

The Hmong and French Colonial Policy

The idea that the Hmong first settled in northern Vietnam bordering southwestern China before migrating to the northern region of Laos, Burma, and Thailand is only a theory. Some scholars and historians believe that most Hmong actually migrated straight to Laos from southern China because Hmong refugees had connections with Hmong settlers and prospectors who had resettled there prior to the 1800s or during the Ming and early Qing Dynasties. Most of the Hmong ancestors in Laos did not mention anything about living in Vietnam prior to settling in Laos; they spoke of their trek from China to Laos. However, they could not reach Laos, Thailand, or Burma without crossing the southwestern region bordering Burma, Laos, and Vietnam. Some Hmong families migrated from northern Vietnam to join family relatives in Laos during the 1900s. Some Hmong historians and western scholars believe Hmong refugees entered northern Vietnam from the southwestern region of China and then went into Sam Neu, the northwestern region of Laos. Or, they suggest, Hmong refugees could have followed the Nan Ong River into the Nong Het region, the northern region of Laos. Some believe that, following the Tokin War or the French War in Vietnam, Hmong refugees moved farther south across Vietnam into northern region of Laos. In Laos, according to Hmong oral history, the Hmong first resettled in the Nong Het highland mountains (*Looj Hej* in Hmong). In Lao, Nong Het literally means the *pond of rhinocerous*, or as in Hmong, it means *lub hawm twj kum.*

As the Hmong searched for fertile land for agriculture, according to Hmong legends, resettlement in the Nong Het region and elsewhere made a new beginning possible. A number of prominent Hmong leaders, or kiatongs, explored the area: Cher Li Cha Lo, Sai Sue Lo, Moua Chong Kai, Lo Pa See, Sai Kue Vue, Lo Xia Vue, Ly Nhia Vue, a Chinese prospector merchant Thong Ma (*Toos Mas* in Hmong), and many others. Table 1.2 lists

some of the early Hmong leaders in the Hmong resettlement in Nong Het (*Looj Hej*) from the mid–1800s to the early 1900s (Ly, 2013). As Hmong legends tell, these Hmong kiatongs played a major role in the transformation of the Hmong to their new life in the northern regions of Laos. The ruling Hmong clans of Hmong emigrants were the Ly, Lo, Yang, and Moua families.

The Hmong not only loved the dense forests and lush landscape, but they also believed the region would give them a safe haven in which to start life over again. However, they could not simply settle in the land without confronting people who were already living in the region. In Laos, the Hmong fought against the aboriginal Kha, also known as the Khamu, and had conflicts with other tribes such as the Puyi, Lue, Lahu, Yao, Ma (*Mab Qus* in Hmong), and Mien. According to Hmong legends, the Khamu tribes were the inhabitants of the land when the Hmong arrived. The battle to control the highland mountain between the Hmong and Khamu took place and became bloody conflicts until the Hmong finally defeated the Khamu. The Khamu people eventually ceded land to the Hmong as the Hmong population grew faster than that of the Khamu. The Khamu fled the region and gradually disappeared into the mountains of Luang Prabang province.

Table 1.2. Prominent Hmong Leaders Who Resettled in Laos

Name in Hmong	English Transliteration	Year of Public Service	Title and Duty in Hmong	English Transliteration
Txawj Lis Tsav Lauj	Cher Ly Chang Lo	1845 to 1850	Tus tuam thawj coj Hmoob khiav tawm Suab Teb los rau xov tshoj teb	Leading Hmong migration from China to Southeast Asia
Kiab Toom Paj Txhim Lauj	Kiatong Pa See Lo	1850 to 1870	Siv kev tuav xov xeeb tiv thaiv Hmoob zej zog	Issuing and forming civic ordinances, decrees, and edicts to protect Hmong
KiabToom Nyiaj Vws Lis	Kiatong Nhia Vue Ly	1870 to 1895	Caum cov tub rog chij daj chij dub tawm teb-chaws thiab nyom	Leading to oust the Yellow and Black Flag Bandits and rebel-

Name in Hmong	English Transliteration	Year of Public Service	Title and Duty in Hmong	English Transliteration
			tsis pub Hmong them se rau Fabkis thiab Nplog	ling against French tax policy
Kiab Toom Xaiv Xwm Lauj	Kiatong Sai Sue Lo	1880 to 1895	Nyom tsis pub Hmoob them se rau Fabkis	Supporting Hmong rebellion against French tax policy
Kiab Toom Tswv Lauv Yaj	Kiatong Chue Lau Yang	1880 to 1985	Coj Hmoob mus nyob rau av loj kom muaj kev ua noj ua haus	Leading Hmong refugees to find fertile land for agriculture
Toj Xeem Txoov Kaim Muas	Tasseng Chong Kai Moua	1895 to 1915	Thawj tug toj xeem Hmoob	First Hmong tasseng
Kiab Toom Npliaj Yob Lauj	Kiatong Blia Yao Lo	1910 to 1935	Coj Hmoob kom muaj kev sib haum xeeb nrog Nplog thiab Fabkis	Leading Hmong to find diplomatic relationship with Laotians and French allies
Toj Xeem Txoov Tub Lauj	Tasseng Chong Tou Lo	1915 to 1939	Tus toj xeem thib ob ntawm Hmoob tom qab toj xeem Ntxoov Kaim Muas	Second Hmong tasseng
Paj Cai Vwj	Pa Chay Vue	1918 to 1921	Nyom tsis pub Hmoob them se rau Nplog thiab Fabkis	Rebelling against French tax policy
Soob Ntxawg Lauj	Song Ger Lo	1918 to 1921	Nrog Paj Cai Vwj nyom tsis pub Hmoob them se rau Nplog thiab Fabkis	Supporting the rebellion against French tax policy

From the late 1800s to the mid–1900s, there were approximately 60 different ethnic groups in Laos, and each group had its own dialects, languages, cultures, and traditions; however, all diverse ethnic groups were classified into three major political groups in the 1950s. The Laotians who practice wet paddies farming and occupy the lowlands of the Mekong valley along the Lao-Thai border belong to the dominant group called *Lao Loum*, meaning Lao people of the lowlands. The Lao word "*loum*" means low, below, or valley. Most members of this group speak Thai-Lao dialects. The Laotians living in the highland mountains comprise of a mixed group called

Lao Theung, meaning Lao people of the mountain slopes. The Lao word "*theung*" means top, up, or above. This diverse group usually occupies the lower elevations and slopes and speaks Mon-Khmer (*Cambodian*) like dialects and languages. Another mixed group made up of different tribal people who speak dialects and languages belong to the Tibeto-Burman family belongs to a lumping group called *Lao Soung*, meaning Lao people of the mountain tops. The Lao word "*soung*" means far, high, or elevated. The Lao Soung people usually live at elevations above 3,000 feet. Ethnically, regardless of linguistic differences, one of the most dominant groups living on the mountain tops is the Hmong, follow by the Iu Mien and Khamu.

Being mountain dwellers, the Hmong lived quiet and reclusive lives in the northern regions of Laos, Vietnam, and Thailand; they were poor farmers and practiced a nomadic lifestyle. Hmong villages were located at 4,000- to 5,000-foot altitudes in the dense forests of the highland mountains. Regardless of the Hmong's seclusion, the French occupiers of Laos and Vietnam continued to impose heavy taxes on the Hmong refugees. In Laos, the French and the Hmong became uneasy allies because French colonial policy taxed the Hmong heavily. As noted in Quincy (1988), in the early 1900s, Moua Tong Zer retired from office and Lo Blia Yao, who was his assistant, took over the duty of collecting taxes for the French. However, as told in Hmong legends, Kiatong Moua Chong Kai was Lo Blia Yao's predecessor, not Tasseng Moua Tong Zer. It is possible that the name of the Moua kiatong was misspelled and mispronounced by western scholars and researchers.

As mentioned previously, the local Laotian officials and some of the kiatongs were corrupt, and they added taxes to the already high French demand. The heavy taxation created a semi-feudal system in which poor Hmong families were victims of wealthy tax collectors. Many poor families had to sell their children or livestock to pay the taxes. However, local kiatongs insisted that the French were the ones who required the Hmong to pay the high taxes. Tax collection under Lo Blia Yao was quite burdensome for all Hmong in the region because the French enforced a strict tax policy, which caused local Laotian tax collectors to abuse their power. Many struggled to pay their taxes; most Hmong families could not make ends meet. The colonial taxes made life unbearable, yet the French continued to order the Hmong kiatongs to collect taxes with penalties or ask the Hmong kiatongs to identify tax evaders. As had happened so many times, the Hmong felt they had no choice but to rebel against the unfair and brutal colonial practices.

In the late 1910s, a Hmong messianic leader, Pa Chai (*Pachay*) Vue, led a rebellion to liberate the Hmong from French control and heavy taxation. Pa Chai was a mysterious man; the people knew little or nothing of his background. According to Hmong legends, Pa Chai had married a daughter of the Vue clan and become a member of that clan; however, no one knew his actual family name. Pa Chai became enraged and organized a rebellion against the colonial tax policy and other forms of social injustice after a local Puyi leader confiscated his only horse. Pa Chai summoned God, the spirits of heaven and earth, and magical powers to protect his soldiers and led a few thousands Hmong soldiers against the French forces and the Hmong loyalists who sided with them. The Hmong were split into two groups; one group sided with the French and Lo Blia Yao and the other was with Pa Chai Vue. The French recruited Hmong from northern Vietnam to help them suppress the revolt. Lo Blia Yao was a Hmong who was a French loyalist. Under the imperial French command, he recruited fellow Hmong to go after the rebels. The revolt of Pa Chai Vue against the French lasted three years.

As Hmong legends tell the story, Pa Chai Vue and his forces were successful at first; they destroyed French forces throughout the region near Lao Chai (Chay), a small town. His victories attracted more Hmong rebels. One day, however, Pa Chai was not able to summon the magical power he had relied on to protect him from French bullets; he was injured on the battlefield. He immediately knew that something had gone terribly wrong. Pa Chai questioned his team leaders and learned that a crew leader had committed a sinful act on the battlefield; he attributed the loss of his magical power to this sin. Losing his magical power meant the end of the rebellion for his army. Pa Chai ordered his soldiers to surrender to the French and ask the French to spare their lives. Many refused to follow his order and insisted on continuing the fight. As a result, his soldiers suffered heavy casualties and fled with their families into the wilderness. Many of the soldiers were subsequently captured and killed. As Hmong oral history records, Pa Chai eluded capture; however, a bounty was placed on his head and he was killed by the French. According to Hmong legends, the French became outraged and hired Khamu mercenary soldiers and Hmong tribesmen to track him down. The rebellion has become known as the "Mad Man's War," the "War of the Insane," or "Pa Chai's War." This unsuccessful messianic revolt had caused Hmong not only a strained sociopolitical relationship with the French but was also the turning point in imperial government control of the Hmong in Laos. As told by Hmong legends, right after the war, the French began scrutinizing Hmong clan leaders and issued civic ordinances to censor Hmong political movements in the region in order to prevent potential insurgency and revolt.

In the end, the imperialist French enacted new colonial policies and guidelines to control Hmong immigrants and warned them of harsh political punishments and consequences if they should create war against the French again. For instance, as cited in Cha (2013), the French warned:

> Hmong shall not ever create war, if any Hmong intended to up rise, there would be severe punishment. Hmong revolt would not intimidate the French government; it only creates chaos among the country and the punishment will not be pardoned [333].

Once the revolt fizzled, the French promoted *Lo Blia Yao* to the position of tasseng because he and his fellow Hmong helped the French suppress the rebellion. Initially, Lo Blia Yao refused to assume the leadership of tasseng (*toj xeem* in Hmong) and later became known as Lo Kiatong in Hmong history. According to Hmong oral history, Lo Blia Yao's unofficial kiatong leadership was based on imperialist control and became repressive toward certain Hmong groups because most of the local leaders and appointed officers either belonged to White Hmong clans or were closely related to members of the clans. As requested by Lo Blia Yao, his son, *Chong Tou Lo* aka *Song Tou Lo*, was appointed by the imperialist French and Laotian officials to the

tasseng post (*toj xeem*). Even though Lo Blia Yao tried to build strong diplomatic relationships between the Laotians, French, and Hmong, his political platform was somewhat culturally unfavorable toward the Blue Hmong clans, especially in deciding civil disputes. Conflicts among Hmong clans festered through the region. Then, Ly Fong, who was literate in Lao and French, from the Ly Clan was recruited to become personal secretary to Lo Blia Yao. Ly Fong was Lo Blia Yao's nephew and Lo Blia Yao was his maternal uncle. Culturally, to maintain his official rank with the dominant Lo family and clan, Ly Fong later married Lo Blia Yao's daughter, becoming his son-in-law. Politically, Ly Fong seized the moment to be closer to his maternal uncle because he knew he could ascend to the imperial throne (tasseng or kiatong, as in Hmong *toj xeem losi kiab toom*). Ly Fong foresaw his political potential because he was one of the few educated Hmong at that time. As for the Lo family and clan, Lo Blia Yao and his biological sons had the upper hand since they had strong political ties with the imperial French officials. As for kiatong Lo Blia Yao, the matrimonial and marital kinship between Ly Fong and his family forged a solid alliance and family bond that would help him maintain his leadership reign for a long time. However, such personal hopes and political aspirations were short lived because his daughter's marriage soon became a political firestorm between Ly Fong and him. According to Hmong legends, as commonly practiced by Hmong leaders then, Ly Fong took a second wife and his first wife then committed suicide by taking an overdose of opium.

Her unexpected death marked one of the darkest moments in Hmong imperial politics not only for Ly Fong and Lo Blia Yao but for all Hmong refugees living in the region of Nong Het. Such a family loss led Hmong leaders and clans into tumultuous tribulations and everlasting tribal bickering throughout Hmong history. As Hmong family legends account, her death created a rift between the Ly and Lo families and a great divide between Ly Fong and Lo Blia Yao. Lo Blia Yao became angrily unsettled and filed civil and criminal complaints with the French authorities. Eventually, in 1922, Lo Blia Yao became politically antagonistic and dismissed Ly Fong from his post as his personal secretary. However, the French had done nothing about the complaints and nothing was resolved between the two men before Lo Blia Yao's death in 1935. Upon his death, according to Hmong legends, his kiatong position was passed on to his son, Lo Song Tou, aka Chong Tou Lo. Familial inheritance of such a title was considered a great and prestigious honor. However, Song Tou somehow was unable to fulfill his imperial leadership role of collecting taxes and thus failed to perform his duties to the satisfaction of the imperial French and local Laotian masters. The French were desperate for taxes and officially revoked his title and gave it to Ly Fong because Ly Fong was willingly to make up for the lost tax from his own money. Upon his appointment, Ly Fong immediately appointed his own son, Ly Bi (*Touby*), to the tasseng (*toj xeem*) post of a sub-district. With the French on its side, the Ly family became the ruling monarchy to control imperial tax collection levied on all Hmong living in the Nong Het region. However, the practice of family nepotism somewhat contributed to the short lived of Hmong political dominance.

As bitter feud between families continued, Ly Fong and Lo Blia Yao's sons wrangled over the imperial throne. It marked the rise and fall (as in Chinese, like the *spring and autumn* season) of Hmong dominant classes in the Nong Het region. As described by past Hmong leaders, the region became Hmong sociocultural warring state. According to Hmong legends, Song Tou felt disgraced and accused Ly Fong of conspiring to have his official title stripped from him. The deceit of the Lo family was intolerable to Ly Fong, but conspiracy was never proven. The Lo loss of the position of kiatong deepened the rift between the two families. The Lo family was furious with the Ly family. Song Tou's brother, Fay Dang Lo, lodged a personal complaint with the Laotian king and asked for assistance. The king could not reverse the actions of the French, but he vowed to return the position of tasseng of the

sub-district to Fay Dang Lo upon Ly Fong's death. Less than a year later, Ly Fong died unexpectedly. Under French rules the kiatong position became vacant, but the tasseng position needed to be filled. Under French colonial policy, the Laotian king had no authority to appoint a member of the Lo family as tasseng or kiatong; the French decided who would become the next kiatong or tasseng of the Hmong.

Following the death of the two rival fathers, Ly Bi, Ly Fong's son, and Lo Fay Dang, Lo Blia Yao's son, both sought the title and fought for the title politically and culturally. According to Hmong oral history, the competition became so heated and it culminated in a tribal war between the two families and their clans. The Hmong entered another period of corruption, bribery, distortion, and extortion created by continual infighting over imperial titles. In the end, the French awarded the title tasseng (*toj xeem*) to Ly Bi, who later became known as Touby Lyfong. Being dishonored by the French created a third rift between the two families and it was a political blow for the Lo family. Based on western values, Ly Bi was better qualified for the position because he had more education. The Hmong legends say Lo Fay Dang had ruling class experience but lacked a relationship with the French, although he did have ties to the king of Laos. However, Laos was under French occupation and the king had little or no political power.

The fight for the post not only widened the separation between the two families, but also generated hatred and a tribal grudge between the Ly and Lo families that is still in place today. This incident was not only the turning point in Hmong sociopolitical leadership but also marked the birth of Hmong communist leaders and Hmong democratic leaders in Southeast Asia. The Lo family moved back to northern Vietnam to start over while the Ly family remained in Nong Het to continue working with and for the French. According to Hmong oral history, these political rifts resulted in the Lo family vowing to do the opposite of anything the Ly family did in all future political and civil matters. Simply, in

Hmong, the vow was a vindictive curse of revenge. Eventually, Fay Dang had his chance to meet Touby Lyfong for the last time after the fall of Laos in 1975. The verbal exchange between the two giants is still a mystery to this day.

The Hmong and the Japanese War

Shortly after Germany began what would become World War II, Japan occupied Southeast Asia (1940) and remained in control until the war ended (1945). Hmong still remember the Japanese occupation as the Japanese War, or "*Rog Yiv Pooj*" in Hmong. The Hmong in Laos also know and refer World War II as the "Japanese War." The Japanese invaded Laos and attempted to drive the French from Indochina. Hmong legends tell of Japanese arresting French soldiers and lining them up like cattle in Hmong villages.

Most conflicts between the French and the Japanese took place in the lowland regions. The Hmong were not directly involved in the Japanese War in Laos but did help some French soldiers elude capture by the Japanese. According to Hmong legends, Touby Lyfong was arrested by the Japanese for his role in hiding and harboring French soldiers. As a prisoner, he was in grave danger but most Hmong were afraid to do anything to rescue Touby. Perhaps because of his strong ties with the French throughout his public service, a French bishop stepped in to save him. The bishop convinced the Japanese that a Hmong uprising was inevitable if something should happen to him. Ironically, Hmong elders say, Touby was targeted by Hmong oppositional force for revenge because of the old family feud. His enemies plotted his arrest to fulfill their vow of revenge. But the Japanese spared his life and, upon his release from captivity, he resumed working for the French. Touby, Lo Blia Yao, Major General Vang Pao, and other Hmong kiatongs and tassengs were pro–French.

According to Hmong oral history, the French soldiers tried to run away and hide from the Japanese soldiers. The Japanese came looking for them in Hmong villages and towns. Some French soldiers hid under Hmong roofs and some Hmong took French soldiers to the jungle to hide them from the Japanese. Without the Hmong, all the French soldiers might have been captured, and if Hmong had not lived in the highland mountains, the Japanese soldiers might have search all the Hmong villages and towns for the French. The Hmong and the French remained allies as a result of the role of so many Hmong in assisting the French during the Japanese War. Moreover, according to some Hmong, the Japanese burned Hmong villages down after learning that the Hmong concealed the French soldiers. The Hmong way of engaging in dual politics made them suspect and vulnerable to political reprisals. Nevertheless, the Hmong remained loyal in their support of the French throughout the Japanese invasion and beyond.

As in any other warfare, not all Hmong supported the French during the Japanese occupation. For instance, Fay Dang Lo and his followers sided with the Japanese and Vietminh and hunted down French commandos in Hmong villages and towns. His political ambitions were evident later in the Vietnam War and the Secret War in Laos. In the mid–1970s, Fay Dang became a high ranking communist official and was the only Laotian Hmong to be honored with such a rank in Hmong history.

The Hmong and the French War

When the Japanese soldiers withdrew from the area at the end of World War II, the French wasted no time in resuming their occupation of Southeast Asia. Besides South Vietnam and Cambodia, Laos was one of the dominos in Southeast Asia to become communist after World War II. In 1950, the French and the Vietminh, also known as the Viet Cong or communist Vietnamese, collided head-on in northern Vietnam near Dien Bien Phu. This marked the beginning of the fall of Tonkin, known as the "*French War.*" The French were at war with the Vietminh and communist Chinese.

As the conflict escalated, the Hmong under Touby supported the French in suppressing the incursion of the Vietminh into northern Laos. The French suffered heavy casualties on the battlefield and the Vietminh took over most of the northern region of Tonkin. Even with the help of Hmong guerrilla units, the French soldiers could not stop the advance of the Vietminh because the communist Chinese supplied the Vietminh, enabling them to mount a major offensive against the French and Hmong. The support of communist China for the Vietminh sent a clear message to the western nations that all of Southeast Asia would soon fall into the hands of communist Vietnam and communist China. To try to forestall this from happening, the United States joined the French for the next few years, trying to prevent Laos from becoming a communist state.

The French knew that retaking the lost territory from the Vietminh would not be easy. Their strategy was to recruit and train Hmong guerrilla forces to retake the border territory and towns and then cut off the enemy's supply line. To achieve these ends, the French recruited and trained Touby in 1951 and sent him to Laos to organize Hmong guerrilla forces in the northern regions, in Phong Saly, Xieng Khouang, and Sam Neu provinces and Pha Thi. Touby and the French were about to plunge the Hmong into another war in Laos.

As noted by historians and researchers, the French also sought help from another Hmong chieftain, *Chao Quang Lo* from Lao Chai, a town near the Vietnam-China border in the southwestern region. Chao Quang Lo, unlike Touby, was an extraordinary Hmong person who possessed great strength and natural abilities. He was a good marksman and a fearless warrior. His tactical skills made him a good guerrilla leader. The Hmong elders say that Chao Quang Lo was a Hmong-Vietnamese who was not well-known to many Hmong leaders and kiatongs at that time. Some Hmong believe his real name was Chong Koua Lo (*Txooj Kuam Lauj*), not Chao Quang Lo; Chao Quang Lo could be a Hmong-Vietnamese name, or the way the French wrote his name in the Roman alphabet. Oth-

ers believe his real Hmong name was Qhua Txos Lauj, or Kuan Chao Lo in English. With French supplies and support, Chao Quang Lo led his Hmong guerrilla forces in a major offensive and regained the territory lost to the Vietminh. Within a few months, the guerrilla forces led by Lo chased the Vietminh forces across the border into China. As noted in Quincy (1988), this success earned Chao Quang Lo the name "Terrestrial Dragon." However, his victory was short lived.

As the Hmong legends record, in 1953 Chao Quang Lo and his men ran out of ammunition and supplies while fighting the Chinese in the highland mountains. The Chinese chased the Terrestrial Dragon and his soldiers and hunted them down like animals. For months he and his men received no assistance; the French had failed to supply his troops. Chao Quang Lo did all he could to fend off the enemy. However, they not only ran out of artillery supplies, but they also ran out of food. They had to run for their lives. The guerrilla force reached a dead end and hid in a deep cave.

As told by Hmong oral history, Chao Quang Lo hoped the enemy would abandon them while hiding in the deep cave, but that was not to be. The search for his head continued throughout the region. The capture of one of Chao Quang Lo's family members marked the turning point in his demise. The brutal interrogation and inhumane torture led the enemy to his hiding place. The communist Chinese forces encircled the cave. The defenseless guerrillas had nowhere to go. The unit was trapped inside the cave for many days without food. Some tried to escape but they were unsuccessful. The Terrestrial Dragon was killed together with all his soldiers.

The Hmong legends have different accounts of just how the brave guerrilla force met its tragic end. Some believe that the enemy enticed some Hmong traitors to call to the guerrillas, claiming that the French had brought them food, ammunition, and supplies. The Hmong traitors thought they could capture Chao Quang Lo alive, but fighting began when Chao Quang Lo learned it was a trap. The fighting continued day and night until Chao Quang Lo and his soldiers were all killed. Others believe the Chinese used some kind of chemical weapon to weaken the guerrilla force hiding in the cave. They think the tear gas or chemicals forced Chao Quang Lo and his soldiers to come out of the cave.

Another theory, according to Hmong legends, a group of mercenary soldiers was hired to track down the guerrilla force hiding in the cave. Like the former messianic leader Pa Chai Vue, a bounty was placed on Chao Quang Lo's head by the communist Vietminh and the Chinese. There was no escape route because the surrounding area outside the cave was heavily guarded. Ultimately, after several days and nights of continuous engagement in gunfighting, Chao Quang Lo and his soldiers were ambushed and killed in action by the communist soldiers. As narrated in Quincy (1988), the Chinese forces claimed victory and paraded Chao Quang Lo's body before villagers in Hmong towns before transporting it to China to celebrate their triumph over the French Terrestrial Dragon. Upon his death, the French honored him with the Legion of Honor award. His was a heroic story of a brave Hmong leader who made great sacrifices to save his people.

The Hmong and the American Secret War

Following the death of Chao Quang Lo in 1953, the Cold War began in Southeast Asia. In 1954, the Geneva Accords were signed and Laos became a neutral and newly-formed democratic nation. However, Laos struggled to maintain its neutrality and became the political buffer zone and unofficial fighting ground between the eastern and western nations, such as China, Vietnam, Germany, Russia, French, England, and the United States of America. Some of the events of the Cold War in Southeast Asia are listed in Table 1.3. The communist Vietminh's next target was Laos. The goal was to invade and capture Laos to fulfill Vietnam's lust to rule all Indochina, as had France and Great Britain. In the 1800s, the French and British had similar

designs in occupying Southeast Asia. The Vietminh's short-term goal was to drive the French out of Indochina. In 1953, the Vietminh invaded the northern regions of Laos and advanced all the way to the Luang Prabang provinces. The western nations feared that Laos would fall to communism like a domino if they failed to intervene. Learning from the French defeat in 1954, they reasoned that an international coalition might be needed to stabilize the situation in Laos and Vietnam. At this time, Laos was politically unstable and in turmoil because of chaotic internal tripartite conflict between the two half-brother Laotian princes. By 1959, Laos had three political factions: the neutral group, the right group, and the left group. The neutral group (*proponents of neutrality*) belonged to the reigning prince Souvannaphouma of Laos and Captain Kong Le. The right group (*proponents of democracy*) was headed by a Laotian prince from the southern region (Boun Oumnachampasak) and a Laotian general (Phouminoksavanh). The left group (*proponents of socialism and communism*) was a coalition of Vietminh and Patheth Lao, aka the communist regime, led by Chao Souphanouvong, Nouhak Phoumsavanh, and Kaysone Phomvihane. Apparently, the West supported the right group for its political movement inside Laos. However, by 1961, the Pathet Lao forces and the neutral forces were the dominant political machines inside Laos.

Table 1.3. Chronology of Major Political and Military events in Laos, 1955–1975

Year	Political Event
Before 1955	Laos was a state in Indochina under French occupation.
1955	French left Indochina and Laos became a neutral and sovereign state. North and South Vietnam were divided.
1955	The U.S. Central Intelligence Agency (CIA) established a network in Laos to provide economic and military assistance.
1959	War broke out between Pathet Lao and Royal Lao Army on the Plain of Jars. U.S. sent aid to Laos.

1960	Captain Kong Le led the neutralist group. U.S. backed the anticommunist movement in Laos.
1960	U.S. worried about the fall of Lao based on the domino theory because the Soviet Union supported communist invasion of Laos.
1960	Vang Pao was promoted to lieutenant colonel in the Royal Lao Army for his role in anticommunist invasion.
1961	U.S. launched covert military operation in Laos. General Bill Lair arrived in Laos to train Hmong guerrilla forces. Vang Pao became full colonel in Royal Lao Army.
1961	Colonel Vang Pao recruited nearly 10,000 Hmong soldiers. U.S. clandestinely supplied arms and ammunition for the Secret War in Laos.
1961	Jerry Daniels arrived in Laos as a cargo-kicker.
1961	U.S. supplied aid to war-displaced Hmong villagers.
1962	Colonel Vang Pao was promoted to brigadier general in the Royal Lao Army. Declaration on the Neutrality of Laos was signed in Geneva.
1962	Laos needed a new coalition government. All foreign troops were to leave Laos. U.S. stopped its clandestine supplies. The communist regime remained to occupy Laos.
1962	Construction of U.S. air base in Long Cheng began.
1963	Communist regime occupied Laos. U.S. increased Hmong guerrilla force to nearly 20,000 to fight the civil war (Secret War) in Laos.
1964	Communist regime occupied northern region of Laos. U.S. trained and supplied Royal Lao Army to defend Laos.
1964	Brigadier General Vang Pao was promoted to Major General in the Royal Lao Army. Construction of U.S. air base in Long Cheng was completed.
1965	The civil war in Laos became the U.S. Secret War. Laos faced full-scale war with the communist regime. Long Cheng became the stronghold of Hmong guerrilla forces through MR2. The Special Guerrilla Unit (SGU) was formed.
1965–1966	Major General Vang Pao led the SGU (Hmong guerrilla forces) in rescue of downed American pilots and safeguarded the Ho Chi Minh Trail. Hmong were at war. Heavy in Laos.
1966–1967	Heavy fighting between Hmong guerrilla forces and the communist regime in northern Laos during wet and dry seasons. Hmong suffered heavy casualties. More communist troops came to Laos. U.S. sent no troop to Laos.
1967–1968	Bombing continued. The war got worse. More Hmong soldiers died. Communists increased their troops to over 100,000. In U.S., unrest and antiwar movement grew.
1969	Heavy bombing continued. Hmong guerrilla forces took control of the Plain of Jars. More Hmong soldiers died.
1969	Major General Vang Pao's house was built. Jerry Daniels became chief of operations of Secret War at Long Cheng. More Hmong villagers became war-displaced refugees. Communist regime increased its troops in Laos.
1970	Secret War deteriorated. U.S. launched more bombing in Laos. Northern cities and villages fell to the communists. Hmong guerrilla forces suffered heavy casualties. Thai volunteer troops were recruited to fight the war. More Hmong fled their towns and villages.
1970	U.S. began withdrawing its troops from Vietnam. U.S. sought to leave the war and began secret peace talks in Paris with the communist regime leader.
1970–1971	Half of the U.S. troops left Vietnam. Heavy fighting continued and the communists regained control of most of the northern regions near Long Cheng. Hmong forces continued to suffer losses. Heavy bombing continued. More Hmong villagers scattered.
1972–1973	U.S. reached an agreement with the communist regime leader to

cease firing and withdraw its troops from the region. Prime minister of Laos negotiated cease fire agreement with the communist regime leader. U.S. started to withdraw. Hmong guerrilla forces continued to fight and suffered more losses.

1973   Laos and North Vietnam signed a peace agreement in Paris. Laos began formation of a new coalition government to take control the country. The war continued in parts of Laos. Hmong forces continued to fight. Bombing stopped. U.S. withdrew its troops from Laos and Vietnam.

1974   In April, a new coalition government was formed. All U.S. personnel and all clandestine military planes left Laos. The communist regime invaded and occupied Laos. Hmong forces continued to fight in MR2. Laos was under Pathet Lao control. The communist regime invaded South Vietnam to expand its occupation.

1975   South Vietnam fell. U.S. refused to be involved. Cambodia fell to the Khmer Rouge. Hmong forces continued to fight in northern regions. In April, U.S. conducted massive air evacuation in Saigon. Major General Vang Pao was summoned to Vientiane. The Secret War was over. Laos fell to the communist regime. In May, U.S. conducted three-day massive evacuation at Long Cheng. Major General Vang was airlifted to safety in Thailand.

In the mid–1950s, an agreement was reached to remove the French presence in Indochina, mandating France to withdraw all its military forces from Laos and North Vietnam. The agreement also required the communist Vietminh to withdraw its forces from Laos and North Vietnam. As cited in Vang (2008), the Vientiane Agreement, dated November 2, 1957, contained six political conditions as follows:

1. The formation of a national coalition government, including the Pathet Lao, the Pathet Lao Combat Units were now recognized as a political organization under the name of Neo Lao Hak Sat, the National Political Front, enjoying the same rights as other political parties. They agreed to restore the two Northern provinces on the day when the coalition government was formed.

2. No party was to make any military alliance with any foreign country, and there were to be no foreign military bases on Laotian soil.

3. The Pathet Lao Combat Units were to be integrated into the national army as far as the budget allowed, and any remaining units were to be demobilized.

4. The Pathet Lao Combat Units must surrender all war materials to the royal government.

5. The new political party, Neo Lao Hak Sat, was to be established in Vientiane immediately, replacing the Pathet Lao.

6. Sam Neu province was to receive a royal Laotian governor and a Pathet Lao deputy; and Phong Saly, a Pathet Lao governor and a royal Laotian deputy.

Instead, the communist Vietminh dishonored the agreement and kept its troops in Laos to help build up the new regime, the Pathet Lao, which was the Laotian Communist party, or Neo Lao Hak Sat. The Vietminh's opposition to the agreement frustrated the Laotian loyalists and the king of Laos in their attempts to rule the country. The western nations condemned the Pathet Lao's actions, decrying the fact that its forces remained in Laos. The United States knew Laos was likely to fall into the hands of the communist party and protested the dishonoring of the agreement. Meanwhile a coalition government was formed that included representatives from both Laotian loyalists and communists. However, the new government disintegrated in just a few months as the result of the Vietminh's occupation of the Ho Chi Minh Trail that runs across northern Laos to South Vietnam. Laos was in political turmoil since its king was incapable of controlling the incursions of the Vietminh throughout the country.

The situation intensified when the Royal

Laotian party regained political power and imprisoned Pathet Lao representatives for plotting a political coup inside Laos. The hasty imprisonment prompted the Vietminh to supply military support to the Laotian Communist party, the Neo Lao Hak Sat. The conflict escalated quickly and the government started to disintegrate. In 1959, a fight broke out between the Royal Laotian Army and the Neo Lao Hak Sat, plunging Laos into a civil war. The Hmong had no direct role in this royal tripartite war until the Americans approached them for help. The civil war in Laos was magnified by the involvement and support of foreign powers such as the United States, France, and Britain. Clandestinely, the U.S. supplied the Royal Lao Army and the Vietminh and communist China backed the Pathet Lao with arms and personnel.

In mid–1959, CIA operatives of the U.S. government came to Hmong villages looking for Hmong military leaders. They spoke to some Hmong soldiers who had been trained for combat, but the trained Hmong soldiers the CIA approached could not undertake the responsibilities of a war because they did not have any civilian soldiers or military equipment. Someone suggested that Sergeant Vang Pao could handle the covert military operation. The CIA operatives flew to Xieng Khouang province to meet with Vang Pao, and that meeting was the turning point for the CIA in Laos. The CIA operatives and advisors who worked closely with the Hmong SGU and Major General Vang Pao were Captain James W. (Bill) Lair (1961 to 1967), Pat Landry (1967 to 1969), Dick Johnson (1969 to 1971), Vince Shields (1971 to 1972), and Jerry Daniels (1972 to 1975). Of the five operatives, Jerry Daniels became a close friend to Major General Vang Pao and the Hmong Special Guerrilla Unit (SGU) and was the only CIA operative who continued to lobby the international community in support of Hmong refugees after the fall of Laos in 1975.

In the early 1960s, the U.S. and the Royal Laotian Army sought out Hmong guerrilla forces to help suppress the communists' supply line coming from North Vietnam over the Ho Chi Minh Trail in northern Laos. According to the agreement signed earlier, the U.S. could not engage in another war in Southeast Asia after the Vietnam War. To prevent Laos from falling, the U.S. conducted a covert operation, helping to train the Royal Laotian Army and the Hmong guerrilla forces known as the Special Guerrilla Unit (SGU). The operation was known as the Central Intelligence Agency's "Secret War" in Laos. It was financed by the U.S. CIA. Hmong were recruited and trained to fight the U.S. Secret War in support of the Royal Laotian Army and the U.S. foreign policy in Southeast Asia. The U.S. covert military operation for the Hmong SGU was (1) to stop the infiltration of the North Vietnamese ground troops and supplies through the Ho Chi Minh Trail into Laos on their way to attack the U.S. pro-democracy Vietnamese troops in South Vietnam; (2) to help rescue any down American pilot along the Lao-Vietnamese border; and (3) to protect the U.S. Air Force Navigation Radar installed on the top of the Phou Pha Thi that guided the U.S. B-52s bomber and military jets to bomb the enemy's military targets and strongholds in North Vietnam.

The U.S. channeled supplies and arms through the central Laotian government; however, getting those supplies to the guerrilla forces on the frontline took time. Major General Vang Pao demanded that the U.S. bypass the central office and send the supplies and arms directly to his base. The U.S. granted his request. U.S. personnel helped train Hmong guerrillas, but no U.S. armed forces were involved in fighting the war. It was left to the Royal Laotian Army and the Hmong to fend off the communist invasion. Hmong guerrilla forces fought in all regions in northern Laos. Like the French, the U.S. and the Royal Laotian Army knew the Hmong would be the best forces to fight the communist Vietminh in the rugged highland mountain terrain of the northern regions. However, a shortage of Hmong adult males led Major General Vang Pao and other military leaders to recruit and train Hmong adolescents to fight the Secret War. According to survivors, thousands of Hmong children soldiers died in the war and hundreds were wounded. By the late 1960s, an estimated 40,000 Hmong soldiers had died in the war and 30,000 others were wounded although the actual number of casualties is still known.

To halt the communist advance, Major General Vang Pao, a well-known, charismatic, skilled, and fearless warrior, was the right person for the job. Under the CIA's field supervision, he led the Hmong SGU and mounted major offensives throughout Military Region II. Major General Vang Pao and his fellow Hmong were effective fighters, and both the U.S. and the Royal Laotian government commended them for their successful operations. The main objectives for the Hmong guerrilla forces were to rescue downed American pilots and guard the Ho Chi Minh Trail so as to cut off the enemy's supply line. Like Chao Quang Lo and Touby, Major General Vang Pao relied heavily on his fellow Hmong and he recruited many to join him. Sadly, safeguarding the Ho Chi Minh Trail caused many Hmong lives. The military operation became desperate for new soldiers. Major General Vang Pao had no choice but to recruit young Hmong males for the cause, and many Hmong males, some as young as 13 years old, were drafted to fight the war. Major General Vang Pao fought the war for 14 years, and for the Hmong, this war was their war after so many lives had been sacrificed and lost. Hmong suffered heavy casualties; thousands were wounded, including Major General Vang Pao. Many Hmong women became widows and children became fatherless because of the war. Nearly 35,000 Hmong lives were lost, about half of the Hmong male population in Laos. As Major General Vang Pao proclaimed, if had not been for the Hmong protecting the Ho Chi Minh Trail, Laos would have fallen into the hands of the communists within the first two years or sooner. He further asserted that Hmong guerrilla forces provided the Americans with a superb defense by sabotaging the communist invasion. As Quincy (1988) eloquently wrote,

> Actually, Laos could have fallen to the communists much earlier if it had not been for

the Laotian Hmong who did most of the fighting for a free Laos and, one must add, most of the dying. Nearly one third of the Laotian Hmong perished during the conflict, which included close to half of all males over the age of fifteen. All through the struggle the Laotian Hmong placed their fate in the hands of one man, General Vang Pao, the first and only Hmong to rise through the ranks of the Royal Laotian Army and achieve the rank of General [163–164].

Toward the end, in late 1972, according to Major General Vang Pao, the U.S. changed its political interests in Laos and decided to settle the war with North Vietnam without careful consideration of the implications. The ceasefire agreement between the U.S. and North Vietnam was concluded without the direct involvement of the Royal Laotian Army or the Hmong guerrilla forces until the last minute. While the agreement was being finalized, the U.S. informed the Laotian prime minister of its intention to end the war and urged both sides to come to a peaceful accord before the U.S. withdrew from the region. Without careful consideration, the prime minister blindly negotiated with the enemy and hastily conceded everything in order to end the war. Initially, when the agreement was signed, Major General Vang Pao was not informed of the decision to end the war; he continued to fight incursions in northern Laos until an order came to stop about two years later.

The Vietminh refused to withdraw its troops from Laos. In the two years following the proposed peace agreement, the communist Vietminh kept its forces intact and continued to mount sporadic attacks in Laos. In early 1974, a revolutionary committee was established to oversee a new government structure for Laos. A cease-fire agreement among all political factions known as the Vientiane Accord was reached. Early in 1975, while fighting the enemy on the battlefield, Major General Vang Pao was ordered by the Laotian prime minister to cease his attacks against the communist forces. Later he was summoned to meet the prime minister in Vientiane to discuss the war. There, Major General Vang Pao confronted the prime minister about the ceasefire orders, but the prime minister had secretly appointed a Laotian general to replace the Hmong general. Technically, the purpose of the meeting was to inform the Hmong general that his military duty was over. The two exchanged heated words, and Major General Vang Pao ripped off his five stars that identified him as a general, placed them on the prime minister's desk, and left to board a plane back to Long Cheng (Quincy, 1988). That was the end of the Hmong war, the end of so much sacrifice, the end of Royal Laotian regime, and the end of Laos.

According to Hmong soldiers, enemy troops secretly invaded the northern regions and gradually moved toward Long Cheng. When Major General Vang Pao was briefed on the urgency of the invasion, he ordered T-28 pilots to bombard the regions with bombs. He also ordered ground troops to retrieve the enemy flag that marked the territory as occupied. While the general commanded this mission to deter the enemies' advance, the prime minister issued an executive order demanding a stop to the bombing. The order was unexpected and led Major General Vang Pao to believe the prime minister had changed his position on the war and Laos would fall when the enemy reached the outskirts of the Plain of Jar. Shortly after the order to cease firing, Major General Vang Pao flew to the capital and was advised to leave for Thailand for his own safety. Within a week, the communists declared victory and took over Laos. Laos fell as Major General Vang Pao had predicted.

As the Hmong soldiers who survived say, Hmong history repeats itself. During the Secret War, the Hmong fought against the Vietminh, the Chinese, and some Hmong. Hmong settlers in northern Vietnam had been recruited and trained as communist soldiers to fight against the Hmong guerrilla forces in Laos. For instance, Fay Dang Lo joined the northern Vietminh and fought against Touby and Major General Vang Pao's guerrilla forces. This pitting of Hmong against Hmong was similar to what had happened to Hmong in China. The imperial Chinese dictators had recruited and trained Hmong soldiers to go after Hmong to crack down on Hmong rebellions and annihilate the Hmong. Throughout their history Hmong soldiers have fought on opposite sides against one another. Both cooked and raw Hmong have made political sacrifices for China, Laos, France, and the United States of America.

Just days before leaving for Thailand, Major General Vang Pao was still devising strategies for defending his country and stopping the invasion of communist forces. In Long Cheng, he concocted a military strategic action plan involving a major attack against the enemy once they reach the outskirts of Military Region II. However, when Yang Dao flew to Long Cheng to consult with Major General Vang Pao about the political factions in Vientiane and to brief him on the Vientiane Accord, Major Vang Pao abandoned the plan in order to avoid a useless bloodbath and save his people from annihilation. He prepared to say farewell to fellow Hmong leaders, combat soldiers, and civilians. Major General Vang Pao's final words encouraged Hmong civilians to live quiet lives after his departure and to put all the blame on him if the new regime ever questioned their loyalty.

Finally, in May 1975, Laos fell to the Vietminh and became a communist state. In December 1976, the Pathet Lao formed a coalition government, the Lao People's Democratic Republic. May 14, 1975, was the day the sky fell on the Hmong. Shortly after Major General Vang Pao was airlifted to safety in Thailand, thousands of Hmong rushed to Long Cheng to board U.S. planes and were airlifted to safe haven in Thailand, following the Hmong general. The country was in chaos and the exodus of Hmong refugees began.

Summing Up

This chapter gave highlights of Hmong origins and Hmong history from ancient times to the present. Hmong Chinese refugees migrated from eastern countries to western countries over a period of centuries. Hmong were known as Miao throughout the 19th and 20th centuries. Western scholars have studied Miao history and believe the Miao and the Hmong are the same people. However, Hmong have always referred to themselves as Hmong, not Miao. Hmong ancestors were known to be Hmong, not Miao. Eastern scholars believe that de-miao-ification of Hmong is necessary to understand Hmongness, the true Hmong. In fact, the Hmong have not totally denied or accepted claims to be Miao. Hmong have always known their ethnic identity regardless of what names they have been called.

Scholars argue about whether the Hmong originated in Russia, Siberia, Mesopotamia, Mongolia, or China. Without a doubt Hmong migration history places them in different locations. The Hmong have migrated since the Warring States period and the Spring and Autumn era in Chinese history. The lack of clear information about their historical roots in the ancient world has fueled an ongoing dispute among scholars, including some Hmong scholars. The origins of the Hmong are obscure because the Hmong were not well known to the western world until 200 years ago.

It is time to rediscover Hmong history; otherwise, the Hmong will be inaccurately portrayed based on the histories of other peoples. The Hmong and Miao are two distinct people with different cultures and traditions. The Hmong are ancient people who originated in central China. They have moved to several places throughout the world not as conquerors, but as refugees. Although a freedom loving, agrarian people, they have shown themselves to be brave and able warriors when their freedom is threatened.

• TWO •

The Hmong Refugees in Diaspora

Hnub twg txoj kev sib pab ciaj vaj peb lub yaj ceeb tseem yuav tshiab kaj...
Ua Neej sib hlub thiaj tau ntuj ntoo sawv daws sib pab thiaj yuav tau zoo...
Lyrics of a classic Hmong song

Introduction

The Hmong are a diaspora—a population of war-displaced refugees scattered over many lands. They came from the ancient world to the new world, from eastern lands to western countries, from Southeast Asia to the West. Today's Hmong are sometimes labeled as refugees, sometimes as immigrants. Like their predecessors—Hmong Chinese refugees from China—Laotian Hmong refugees emigrated from their native country, Laos, to find safe haven and to start all over again, not just to seek better economic opportunities. From the mid–1970s to the present, the Hmong in the West have been refugees displaced by the Secret War they fought in Laos. When the war ended in 1975, the Hmong had no place to go. If had not been for the U.S. resettling Hmong refugees, all of them would have been left behind and the communist soldiers from North Vietnam would have slaughtered them as did the Chinese centuries earlier. As promised, the United States and other western nations gave the Hmong the chance of a lifetime to save themselves. The Hmong have resettled in the United States, France, French Guinea, Canada, Argentina, and Australia. Today, Hmong are found in many countries, are mixed with other ethnic groups, and have become known in the eastern and western world. This chapter revisits the Laotian Hmong refugees' struggles for survival after the fall of Laos in 1975. It describes how they found their way out and how they escaped the communist regime.

The Final Rescue

In early May 1975, Laos fell to a communist regime that was one of three in Asia: China, North Vietnam, and the Pathet Lao, or Neo Lao Hak Sat. This began the darkest moment in the lives of Laotian Hmong. People scattered in different directions, most going south to cross the Mekong River to Thailand. They walked, marched, and trekked through jungle. Some were airlifted and others found their own ways of escape. Laotian Hmong all across the country fled. It was the only way to save themselves from death at the hands of the communists.

At one point, Major General Vang Pao pondered whether to flee or continue to fight. With guidance from CIA operatives, he saw that victory was unattainable in the near future. Moreover, he knew that without the support of the U.S., the Hmong would not be able to stand against the communist regime for another decade, and U.S. support was being withdrawn. His final farewell message to his military officials and civic leaders liberated them from their duties and asked them to put all the blame on him if the communist regime should question them. As a leader, the Hmong general took upon himself the responsibility for anything the communist regime might accuse his people of. He exonerated the people, directing them to accuse him of whatever crimes the communist regime wanted to charge them with. His final farewell speech still lives in the hearts of his loyal followers. A prominent Hmong civic leader still remembers his final farewell speech in 1975, and here is an excerpt from Major General Pao's last words about the end of the secret war:

> Cov kwvtij Hmoob sawv daws, hnub no yog ib hnub tu siab kawg nkaus vim hais tias kam teb kam chaw tsis mus raws li lub siab xav … kuv xav hais tias kuv yuav nrog nej sawv daws nyob sib puag ncaj dab kom mus txog hnub kawg, tabsi yuav ua tsis tau li siab nyiam vim kam teb kam chaw tsis mus li peb txoj kev xav tau … yog kuv nyob lub teb lub chaw yuav nyuaj zuj zus ntxiv … txawm licas los, ib hnub tom ntej, yog muaj txoj hmoov, kuv tseem yuav rov qab los coj peb cov Hmoob ib zaug ntxiv… [In English, *all my fellow Hmong brothers, today was one of the saddest days because the political situations were not moving our way.… I thought I would stay with you all until the last minute, however, could not do as wanted because the political climates did not fall in our favor … if I stayed the country would become tumultuous … despite of all, one day in the future, if fortunate, I will return to lead the Hmong one more time…*]

The very first Hmong the U.S. wanted to safeguard was Major General Vang Pao, the CIA general in the Royal Laotian Army and the mighty commander-in-chief of Hmong special guerrilla forces in northern Laos. Once Major General Vang Pao was safely out of Laos, the U.S. began evacuating other Hmong refugees from Long Cheng. As mentioned previously, May 12, 13, and 14, 1975, were historic days for Hmong refugees. Without Major General Vang Pao, the sky was not only falling on them but was crushing down on them from above and the earth was rising to shatter them from beneath; that is, pain and suffering were everywhere they turned. They had to find a way out of the country.

The final rescue was initially planned to save only the elites and high military officials. The U.S. conducted a three-day emergency evacuation operation at Long Cheng, the military base of Military Region II. It was the most panicked, chaotic time in Hmong history. People left everything behind and rushed to Long Cheng to board the planes. As Figure 2.1 illustrates, they came from all the cities and villages near the base. There was no time to prepare, no time to pack. Every Hmong was in total shock; their world was in disarray and their lives were in great danger. As Morrison (1999) described the scene, Hmong civilians came in like a colony of ants, marching like a colony of ants. News of the rescue operation came via telegraph and military radio, rocking Hmong towns and villages like roaring thunder and flashing lightning. People who lived far from Long Cheng could not make it in time. The base was jammed with people, and those who did not make it aboard the first planes stayed overnight waiting for the planes to return. The third day was horribly congested; everyone wanted to get on the planes. Families were separated and the planes were overloaded. Every flight from Long Cheng to

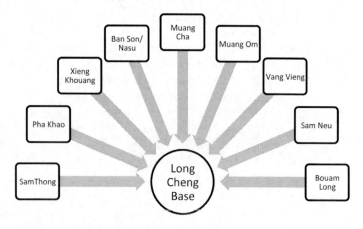

Figure 2.1. Hmong cities surrounding the Long Cheng base.

Thailand was a mission of hope over fear. The flights were all about saving as many Hmong lives as possible.

Although the pilots were originally to take only military officials, no one could stop the Laotian Hmong civilians from coming to board the planes. Over three days, nearly 2000 Hmong refugees were airlifted to safe haven in Thailand. But hundreds of thousands of former Laotian Hmong soldiers and civilians were left behind. When the planes were gone, a frantic aftershock set in; numb Hmong feared for their lives. The fear worsened when the communist government announced its intention to eradicate the Hmong, destroying them down to the roots. This death threat reminded the Hmong of the brutal treatment they had received from the Chinese dictators years ago.

The abandoned Laotian Hmong refugees had two choices after Major General Vang Pao left. Choice One: they could remain in Laos and join the communist party. Choice Two: they could leave Laos for Thailand as quickly as possible, before the communist regime saturated the country and closed the border. The Hmong chieftains and leaders feared for their lives and left without taking their followers. In villages and towns, Hmong civilians gathered to assemble plans. Every family was on its own. Those who took the first choice suffered severely. Those who decided to follow Major General Vang Pao in fleeing took the challenging and dangerous journey to refugee detention centers or refugee camps in Thailand. The Hmong refugees were divided into two main groups: the fleeing group and the staying group.

Staying Under the Communist Regime

The Choice One group basically chose fear over hope. Their decision to stay had cruel and inhumane consequences. Those who had been government officials, civic leaders, soldiers, and educators were oppressed, persecuted, imprisoned, and extirpated.

When the country fell into the hands of the communist regime and the emergency rescue was over, the Hmong knew life would be different and difficult, but they did not expect to be butchered like animals. Those who decided to stay in Laos had various reasons. For one, some of the high officials believed the new regime would give them an opportunity to be part of the newly formed government; they thought they could reconcile their differences and rule the country again. Second, many Hmong families lived far from Vientiane and were unable to finance their escape. Third, some families owned land and livestock and could not bear the thought of leaving everything behind. Fourth, some believed they could adjust to the new regime and hoped they could become part of the country through accommodation and acculturation without assimilating. Fifth, many did not know their way to Vientiane. Many Hmong had not set foot in the capital or any lowland city prior to the fall of Laos. Heading to a new place raised fears of sickness, disease, and death caused by the warmer weather of the lowlands. And sixth, some feared capture or arrest by the communist regime. If caught fleeing, they would be sent to a facility in northern Laos or Vietnam known as a reeducation camp. There, "reeducation" for Hmong meant receiving a death sentence. These were the primary reasons Hmong refugees decided not to flee Laos. However, their decision meant that their lives would be forever changed.

Those who decided to remain returned to their towns and villages to continue their normal daily lives and wait for the new communist government to determine their fate. Most resumed their agrarian lifestyle and acquiesced to the new regime's policies as they came along. Others waited for the opportunity to reestablish themselves to join and accommodate the new regime; they would not try to retake the country by force but would adjust and adapt to the new reality.

Shortly after the emergency evacuation in Long Cheng, many former guerrilla soldiers, Royal Laotian officials, and family members of the king were arrested by the new regime. They were sent to the reeducation camps located in northern Laos and Vietnam for political indoctrination. There the Laotian officials and Hmong civilians were severely tortured and psychiatrically brainwashed to spew out heinous political propaganda against the former regime. This is known because it was reported by prisoners who escaped the communist indoctrination in the reeducation camps and returned to their families. Very few were able to escape to tell of the brainwashing; most of those arrested died in the reeducation prisons.

The escapees told of harsh and inhumane conditions. Most of the prisoners were starved to death. For food, the communist guards gave prisoners rice mixed with sand and gravel. The prisoners ate and slept like animals. Each day they were brainwashed for several hours and had to perform hard physical labor. The camps were surrounded by landmines and heavily guarded. Only those willing to speak the communist propaganda and rail against the former government would be spared the daily torture and death; the completely indoctrinated would be allowed to return to society. Each day a prisoner had to answer a series of questions about the former regime. Failing to properly answer or failing to properly recite the indoctrination verses would result in death. Realizing that this is what awaited them if captured, former soldiers and other Hmong hid in the jungle and eventually organized a resistance force to protect themselves and their loved ones. To fight the communist regime, Hmong formed the Chao Fa guerrilla force, sometimes called the Soldiers of the Sky or God's Disciples of War. Hmong resistance started in late 1975 and is still going on today.

Some observers claim the Hmong Chao Fa guerrillas are insurgents making war on the communist regime; this is not the case. The guerrilla force came into being in reaction to the brutal and inhumane treatment of former supporters and loyalists to the U.S., Major General Vang Pao, and the Royal Laotian Army. Its purpose was not war, but protection of families and loved ones from capture, imprisonment, and death.

The fear of being arrested and sent to the reeducation camps or of being killed by the new regime was well founded. Hmong towns and villages were overrun with communist soldiers. The communist regime would send pairs of communist soldiers as informants to visit Hmong families frequently. The informants were communist Hmong. This undercover spying made Hmong very insecure. They fled their villages with their families and took to the dense forests and mountains. They went back to the old military bases to dig out buried guns, ammunition, grenades, bombs, dynamite, and artillery equipment. Many unearthed rifles and ammunition they had buried in their towns and villages. They organized a national resistance movement throughout the northern regions, especially in the MRII regions such as Long Cheng, Ban Sorn, Moung Cha, Moung Kassi, Phong Sai, Moung O, Ban Done, Pha Khao, and Phu Bia. They depended heavily on God's grace and magical power for their military actions.

A messianic Hmong leader, *Zong Youa Her* (Zoov Zuag Hawj in Hmong), was among the first group of Hmong resistance forces. In late 1975 his force ambushed communist truck convoys and blasted bridges to sabotage the enemy's ability to transport supplies. Prisoners who either were released or had escaped from the reeducation camps joined him. One prominent figure in the resistance was the Hmong rebel leader *Sai Shoua Yang* (Xaiv Suav Yaj in Hmong). Another prominent Hmong rebel leader was *Pa Kao Her* (Paj Kaub Hawj in Hmong). The Chao Fa guerrilla forces grew to nearly 50,000 in the late 1970s; however, only about 10,000 were combat soldiers. Most were women and children.

According to former soldiers, *Sai Shoua Yang* (Xaiv Suav Yaj in Hmong) was in the very first group of Laotian Hmong leaders, high officials, and educated individuals to be taken deceptively to the reeducation camps in northern Laos and Vietnam in mid–1975. Having been brainwashed by the communist regime, Sai Shoua Yang agreed to carry out a political propaganda action against the supporters of the Royal Laotian Army and former Hmong leader Major General Vang Pao. He was to persuade the Laotian Hmong not to flee but rather to comply with the dictates of the new regime. The communists released him from the camp on this condition. However, when he returned to his village and his family, he refused to carry out the propaganda mission. Instead, he fled to the forest and hid in the highland mountains. There he devised a plan to recruit his fellow Hmong to resist the cruel and inhumane practices of the regime.

In late 1975, Hmong rebels mounted many attacks around the country. Sai Shoua and his force managed to retake some Hmong towns and villages. He actually liberated his own village from communist control. Such successful attacks inspired other Hmong to join the force. Before the end of 1975, the popularity of the Chao Fa guerrilla forces had grown nationally and internationally, especially in the community of Hmong refugees in Thailand. Because Hmong refugees living in the refugee camps in Thailand still had family members and relatives trapped in Laos, they supported the resistance without any hesitation. Thousands of Hmong refugees in Thailand were eager to lend a hand to their comrades who had been left behind; however, there was not much they could do because they could not conduct transnational warfare.

Because Hmong were familiar with the jungle and highland terrain, most major Hmong resistance forces were concentrated in the Phu Bia Mountain region located on the southern side of the Plain of Jars. This location provided an impregnable refuge for Hmong rebels as they launched attacks on the towns and villages occupied by the communist regime. The rebels also attacked the enemy supply line and ambushed tanks and trucks transporting military artillery into the region. Heavy fighting continued for about two and a half years with the Hmong rebels mounting effective offensives and enjoying victories over the communist regime.

Calling themselves the *Disciples of God* aka the *Soldiers of the Sky*, the Hmong resisters felt they were magically protected in combat and could not be wounded. Then in 1978, the Vietminh changed its combat strategy and began using chemical warfare to crush the rebels' strongholds. Survivors describe rockets exploding in the air over the forest and reddish and yellowish chemicals flying in the air above the ground like smoke. They called the chemicals "red and yellow rain." As the chemicals permeated the towns, villages, rice fields, and forests, people started to get sick. Many fled their hideouts. As the survivors recall, the chemical warfare and napalm brought immediate nausea-like symptoms and people eventually died from exposure to the red and yellow rain. Women and children were affected by the chemical warfare. The Hmong rebels were not able to find any antidotes for the chemicals and they gradually surrendered to the enemy. In 1979, the communist regime launched heavy artillery attacks on the Phu Bia slopes and bombarded the region with bombs and chemicals. The rebel groups disintegrated. The communists ambushed the escape routes and most of the rebels were killed. The messianic leaders barely escaped the heavy attacks and the force dissolved into the wilderness of northern Laos.

In early 1979, the Phu Bia stronghold fell into the hands of the communist regime. The Chao Fa guerrilla forces nearly came to an end. Zong Youa Her and his men barely eluded captured but perished in the jungles of Laos. Sai Shoua Yang managed to escape the death trap and left Laos for Thailand. Pa Kao Her barely escaped to Thailand to continue his rebel movement in the northeastern region of Thailand. After visiting the U.S., Pa Kao was assassinated in 2002 in Thailand. Only a skeleton of Chao Fa remained in secluded locations in Thailand and Laos; it is still there today. Still today, survivors claim, the communist regime hunts the remainder of the Chao Fa rebels.

How many rebels actually died from the exposure to the red and yellow chemicals is unknown, but Hmong rebels claimed the number to be in the thousands. Perhaps malnutrition and starvation contributed to the death toll as well. During the years of heavy fighting, women and children suffered severe malnutrition and hundreds of thousands were starved to death because the rebels had no time to cultivate crops. Also, corn and rice fields were destroyed by the enemy. Massive starvation not only weakened the rebels, but also forced them to disintegrate and migrate. Many trekked through the jungles to join their families and relatives in Thailand. Others left the resistance and resumed civilian life. The survivors claim that many of those who returned to a normal life were arrested and imprisoned by the communist regime and hundreds of thousands of Hmong refugees were brutally oppressed and inhumanely persecuted.

Thousands of Hmong rebels did not survive the journey through the jungle to Thailand. They either died of starvation or were shot by communist soldiers before reaching the banks of the Mekong River. Small children were drugged with an opiate to keep them quiet during the escape and some did not wake up. In addition, thousands of sick and starving children died along the way. The elderly Hmong faced the same plight as the young ones. Many elderly Hmong were left to be slaughtered by the communist regime; only a few made it to the Mekong River.

Reaching the river was not the end of their struggle. The swift current made crossing the river extremely dangerous. Thousands of Hmong refugees drowned while attempting to cross at night and thousands were shot at and killed on both sides of the Mekong River by communist soldiers and Thai pirates. Hmong refugees were robbed at gunpoint and Hmong women were raped by Thai pirates. Hmong men were imprisoned and beaten badly. Sadly, Thai pirates threw some Hmong into the water and forced them to swim back across the river to Laos. Most drowned, and survivors were captured and imprisoned until they died. Only a very few eluded capture and returned to live in the wilderness.

A very small number of Hmong retreated to different parts of the country and continued to rebel against the communist rule, even to the present time. As of today, survivors say, Hmong rebels are still being hunted down like animals. When the bloodshed will end, no one really knows.

Fleeing the Communist Regime

The Choice Two group did not believe the communist regime's propaganda. Despite the regime's attempts to court Hmong civilians to stay in Laos, most Hmong knew that their lives would be in jeopardy if they did not leave. Their decision to flee enabled them to escape the cruel oppression and outright slaughter that befell those who stayed. However, their escape was not easy. The flight was a long journey; the destination was Thailand. To make it to Thailand, they had to find their own way out. They had four options for escape:

1. March on foot from their villages to Vientiane.
2. Charter a taxi to transport family members to Vientiane.
3. Trek through the jungle in search of an escape route.
4. Cross the Mekong River by air or by boat.

Any Hmong who was fortunate enough to be studying or living abroad was told not to return. Whichever option they selected, they had to act immediately, before it was too late.

In early May 1975, the trail of tears began for Hmong refugees. The first and largest group of Hmong refugees marched on foot on Road 13 to Vientiane. According to survivors, hundreds of people marched together—men, women, and children. Some draft animals accompanied them. When they reached the outskirts of the small village of Hin Her (*Heem Hawj*, in Hmong), they found the road closed; the security checkpoint was blocked for some unknown purpose. The leaders escorting the group tried to remove the barriers in order to proceed to the narrow bridge ahead. All of sudden communist soldiers hollered at them out of nowhere not to touch anything and not to remove the barriers. The Hmong refugees refused to stop; they continued to march past the barricaded gate. Suddenly the communist soldiers fired into the crowd. People fell to the ground and the group dispersed, out of control. The soldiers rushed toward the unarmed civilians and started beating them with their gun barrels. Some were shot and killed instantly, and many fell to the ground in piles. People panicked and ran, stumbling over one another in their haste to get away. As the innocent people scurried in all directions, crying out for help, the soldiers yelled to crush the crowd with machines. Armored tanks and trucks plowed into the group, pushing men, women, and children onto the narrow bridge. On the bridge, many marchers, fearing for their lives, jumped into the water below. Some swam downstream but many drowned. Some managed to flee on foot. Others dashed into the nearby woods. Many were stranded on the bridge. The communist soldiers beat the marchers and tossed people into the river even as the helpless people begged for their lives. Those who could not get away were detained and later released because the public decried the evil attack. One survivor remembered the incident as a massacre. Innocent refugees, even young children, were shot, gunned down in front of their loved ones, killed in front of their family members. Many children were terrorized and traumatized by the killings of family members. The communist soldiers chased, shot, bludgeoned, and murdered the marchers before and on the bridge. Some of the refugees were run over by armored trucks and tanks. Many were arrested. Some escaped and hid in the nearby jungle and others were sent to prison.

This massacre marked a turning point in the brutal takeover by the communist regime. The killing helped boost the resistance forces because the Hmong people realized what political repression and retaliation would come in the near future. Nearly all capable Hmong males took to the jungle and joined some kind of resistance. Others made decisions and plans to flee Laos. The exodus took place all over the country. However, there would be no more marching. From this point on, fearful Hmong refugees concocted escape plans in secret.

Those who had been arrested at the massacre site were interrogated repeatedly and tortured by the authorities. They were accused of being loyalists to the West, Major General Vang Pao, and the Royal Laotian Army. The ones who were spared an immediate death sentence were sent to reeducation camps in northern Laos and Vietnam. Most died in incarceration; only a few survived and returned to reunite with their families. The Hin Her Massacre still lives in the hearts and souls of many Hmong families and individuals now living in western nations.

One cautionary note, the Hin Her Massacre is still remained a highly sensitive issue in the Hmong community today because some Hmong have falsely ingrained that members and leaders of the Ly Clan were somewhat involved in the sabotage by supporting the communist regime's action; however, such a belief is based on survivors' speculations because many Laotian Hmong refugees then lacked the understanding of the political roles played by different members and leaders of the Ly Clan. It is fair to say that members and leaders of the Ly Clan did have political roles in the peace negotiation process during the time of the establishment of the new government coalition in Laos, and when the incident happened in Hin Her, the communist regime sought assistance from members and leaders of the Ly Clan to help intervene the exodus of Laotian Hmong refugees to prevent potential fleeing since they were working as government officials at that time. This diplomatic intervention had triggered a massive confusion in the Hmong community, and such a misperception had labeled members and leaders of the Ly Clan as red Hmong, meaning communist supporters. Presumably, the unsubstantiated allegations against members and leaders of Ly Clan were based on false assumptions in association with Hmong political adversaries and cultural mistrust and betrayal of the past.

According to Hmong survivors' accounts, leaders of the Ly Clan and Lo Clan showed up at the scene to tell Hmong refugees not to flee the country and made political statements that Hmong refugees would be protected under the new regime. However, Hmong refugees were leery of Hmong leaders who sided with the new regime. Shortly after the incident, some prominent Laotian-Hmong civic leaders and former military officials were arrested and taken to reeducation camps. Other civic leaders and government officials were frantically shocked by the arrest and became concerned for their safety, and most went into hiding or fled Laos to Thailand to find safe haven. Hmong refugees who were amenable to the political appeasement at that time finally learned the opposite and felt betrayed by such disingenuous political manipulations.

In May 1975, Thailand became a host country for Laotian Hmong refugees. From May to August 1975, the Thai government expected the influx of war-displaced refugees, so they welcomed the escapees kindly, but after August the border was closed and later escapees were mistreated. Thailand had to comply with the wishes of the regime in Laos or Thailand would be accused of harboring Laotian Hmong, whom the Laotian government considered criminals, and would be held responsible for the resistance activities of the guerrilla forces inside Laos. This change in border policy negatively impacted the flow of Laotian Hmong refugees.

Nevertheless, Hmong refugees found ways to escape the communist regime. People trekked through the jungle and made their way to the Mekong River. They hid, waited, built makeshift rafts, and crossed the river at night to Thailand. Some bribed taxi drivers to transport their family members to Vientiane and then hired Laotian Hmong smugglers to transport their families crossing the Mekong River. Others obtained permission from local authorities to travel on business trips or to visit family members living in different towns in order to make it safely to Vientiane, and there they hired smugglers to take them to Thailand. In some cases, relatives resettling in Thailand hired transporters to go back to Laos to retrieve their loved ones and smuggle them across the border to Thailand. According to Hmong leaders' visual calculations while they were in the refugee camps, from 1975 to the early 1990s, nearly 100,000 Laotian Hmong refugees escaped Laos and came to live in the refugee camps in Thailand. A very small number of Laotian Hmong refugees in Thailand did not settle in the camps. From the 1990s to 2005, the number of Laotian Hmong refugees in Thailand increased to approximately 150,000 because sociopolitical conditions inside Laos worsened. The number of refugee camps in Thailand rose to nearly a dozen, located in the north and northwestern regions of Thailand.

The continued exodus of Laotian Hmong refugees was the result of a number of issues:

- Push factors associated with the arresting and reeducating policy.
- Arrests, repression, persecution, and suppression of officials who had served in the Royal Laotian Army or under Major General Vang Pao.
- Economic factors associated with deteriorating trade, scarcity of natural resources, and anti-capitalistic policy.
- The disintegration of the guerrilla forces.
- Discontent with the totalitarian policy toward Laotian Hmong refugees.
- Enforce brutal and inhumane reeducation camp policy against former soldiers had connection with the West.

The closure of refugee camps in the mid–1990s reduced the number of Laotian Hmong refugees but it did not completely stop the flow. In fact, Laotian Hmong continue to flee Laos for the northern regions of Thailand today.

Crossing the Mekong River

The border between Laos and Thailand is the treacherous Mekong River, as shown in Figure 2.2. The Laotian Hmong refugees got across the river to find safe haven in Thailand in a number of different ways. The first wave of refugees was airlifted from Long Cheng to Thailand. In the early escape those who lived close to large cities, especially Vientiane, boarded commercial planes or boats to cross the Mekong River to Thailand. Well-off Laotian Hmong refugees were able to charter taxis from their villages or towns to transport their families to Vientiane; from there they hired private transporters to take their families to Thailand. From May to October 1975, thousands of Laotian Hmong city dwellers crossed the Lao-Thai border to settle in the refugee camps of Nong Khai and Nam Phong. In early 1976, two new camps were built to house the influx of Hmong refugees: Ban Vinai and the new Nong Khai camp located near the site of the old military base.

Poor families and less fortunate individuals struggled to find their way out. They had to either march on foot through towns or trek through the jungle to reach the Mekong River and then use makeshift rafts or swim across the

Figure 2.2. The Mekong River forms the border between Laos and Thailand.

deadly, swift, and treacherous currents at night. Some of the escape routes, such as the one near Luang Prabang in northern Laos, were easier in the first few months after the takeover. But following the massacre at Hin Her in May 1975, the border between Laos and Thailand was heavily guarded. In late 1975, many poor families had to bribe local authorities to give them permission to travel from town to town because anyone caught fleeing would be sent to a reeducation camp. Laotian Hmong refugees would do anything to keep out of the camp because the camp meant death.

The escape had to be carefully planned, and it was usually costly. Transporters and smugglers were plentiful, but the refugees did not know who they could trust. Many families were robbed and some were killed by the smugglers during the escape attempt. Both refugee and smuggler had to agree on all conditions and a third party was generally used to hold the money paid by the refugee; the transporters would return to reclaim the money once the refugees were safely in Thailand.

Refugee smuggling was a hot issue and was banned by the communist regime. Later escapees were sometimes betrayed or had money extorted from them by undercover agents and informants. Many families were turned over to the authorities and punished. The prospect of betrayal terrified the Hmong refugees and most decided to find their own way to Thailand without the help of smugglers or transporters. From 1976 to the early 1990s, thousands of Laotian Hmong refugees spent months trekking through the jungle toward the Mekong River. Along the way, many died of starvation and malnutrition. Communist soldiers ambushed and killed tens of thousands of escapees. As mentioned earlier, some of the children who were drugged to prevent them from crying died. The elderly and the sick were left to die along the way without proper burial.

Once at the river bank, crew leaders or heads of household made bamboo rafts and waited until nightfall or the early morning hours to cross the Mekong River. The desperate refugees used any floating devices they could find to help them across the river—balloons, water bottles, pieces of bamboo, and dried logs. The success of the crossing often depended on the lead swimmer, usually a trusted family member, sometimes a hired smuggler. Usually the fathers acted as the lead swimmers.

Of those who survived the journey to the Mekong River, many did not live through the crossing. Tens of thousands drowned in the river. From 1976 to the early 1990s, thousands of Hmong refugees were shot and killed by communist soldiers along the banks of the Mekong River, and thousands were robbed, beaten, and imprisoned once they reached Thailand.

Childhood Memories

The 1.5 generation Hmong children (Asian-born children of Hmong refugee parents) experienced these and other traumatic events during the Secret War and after the fall of Laos in 1975. Their childhood memories of these events are now personal narratives of struggles, pain, survival, and triumph. Every Hmong refugee child who was born in Laos has a personal story to share with the world, a heartfelt narrative that rekindles painful memories of the past. Non-refugee Hmong children should listen to these stories and appreciate the hardship the 1.5 children and their refugee parents endured in order to survive the brutal and heinous oppression, persecution, and exploitation of Hmong refugees after the fall of Laos in 1975. Escaping from the communist regime was not only a

choice and not only a quest for freedom, but also a vicious struggle to save oneself and one's family from being bludgeoned to death, from being extirpated down to the roots.

Below are two personal narratives from Hmong college students who wrote their childhood memories of how their family members escaped from Laos, survived the trek, crossed the deadly Mekong River, and saved themselves. These stories were collected from Hmong students by Juan Flores and Christopher Vang. The names of the students have been changed to protect their privacy.

"A Forever Memory"

As I was going back through time, I stumbled upon some old memories and thought to myself as I began to reminisce about my past. I remember one morning in the spring of 1975 in Laos, and I was only six years old. It was a morning that I will never forget. For some reason, that morning everyone in the village went wild. People were running around as though they were lost and others were crying as if someone had died. For that morning was a new day that would change everybody's life. It was my family's last morning in a beautiful little village called Kiav Haib (Kia Hai). That morning I saw my grandparents cry for the first time in my life. My grandfather said that my dad had gone to the other side of the world; he's either dead or alive for he left no clues. My father was the younger of two sons. My father was a soldier fighting in the Secret War of Laos for the CIA of the United States Government. He had fled with General Vang Pao to Thailand and left his family (wife and four children) behind, including his parents and a younger sister.

Around nine o'clock that morning we got news from my uncle living in Na Sou (*Na Sue*). He told the family to go and meet him in Na Sou because he made some connections. A plane would pick us up there and take us to Thailand. My grandparents and my mom were all crying while they packed what they could, leaving the livestock behind. I guess it was hardest for my mom. She had four children to care for, and the oldest was six, the next child was four, a toddler who was two years old, and the youngest was only eight months old. She had to make sure she got all her children to safety. Also, she alone had to carry all our belongings because the children were too little to help out. For example, she had to carry money, jewelry, food, and personal items along. The journey to Na Sou was long and arduous. We were one of the many frightened and shocked Hmong families that decided to flee the communist regime, and our only form of transportation was walking by foot.

When we got half way to Na Sou, we got news that the plane was now picking us up at the village (Kiav Haib). We then walked back up to the village. We had a lot of belongings so my mom had to stash some suitcases in the bushes; just in case we didn't make it to Thailand, we could always pick them up later. When we got to the village the people there told us that the plane had left and was not coming back. Therefore, we had wasted the whole day running around not knowing anything about the rescue. We spent the night back in our village. The next day, early in the morning around seven o'clock, the family got up and started heading toward Na Sou once again.

When we arrived there, my grandparents told my uncle that he had to make sure he got us to my dad in Thailand. My mom pleaded to him, "If we do get there and my dad is no longer living that he promises to take care of us." When I heard this, I felt something was wrong. Well, my grandparents decided not to go because they were old and the journey would be too difficult for them. Also, they wouldn't let their youngest daughter, my aunt, come with us; she needed to stay with them and take care of them. That was the last time I saw my grandparents, standing in the doorway crying and saying good-bye to us as we headed toward Na Sou with my uncle early that morning. It took us approximately one full day to get to Na Sou. When we arrived there, my uncle had arranged for a bus to take us to Vientiane, the capital of Laos. The bus trip was difficult because everyone wanted to get on the bus. Everyone wanted their people and family relatives to go, and there was only one bus. I remembered some adults pushed us, my sisters and my two cousins, off the bus through the windows because we were small. When my mom, aunt, and uncle got on the bus we were still outside. They had to get off and put us back on the bus. They were furious with the people and told them that they shouldn't do that

because they had already paid for our places on the bus.

During the journey we experienced many hardships. The worst catastrophe was when we got caught by the communist Pathet Lao soldiers. They put us in some kind of detention camp. They separated us. They put all the women and children in small groups and then booked them into small cells. I recall the bars were made out of bamboo sticks. They had us repeat what they were saying. For example, things like "I will not try to escape or I'm not trying to leave Laos." Well, they released the women and children around late afternoon, but not the men. My aunt was very worried because she didn't know where the communist soldiers had taken my uncle—whether he was alive or dead. As we were praying for his safety, my uncle finally showed up late that evening. My aunt and uncle told my mom to watch the children and to cook dinner for everyone while they were going to find a way to Thailand. So, they left.

When they got back it was around midnight and all the children were asleep. I still remember vividly about the night event. Everyone was getting into a taxi and getting off it when we reached the bank of the Mekong River. Also, I remember, everyone was getting into a small fishing boat and was told to be quiet and to stay under the cover. Then the next thing I knew was when the daylight came upon us and we were told to get off the boat as quick as possible because we were stepping on Thailand's soil. There were Thai policeman who demanded to check us. Everyone passed, except for one male escapee. He had brought some opium with him. The Thai officials demanded that he give up his opium or everyone was going back to Laos. He took out a gun and said, "If you take my opium from me, then I will kill myself." Everyone was very frightened because they had come a long way and now everything seemed to be going down the tubes: no one wanted to return to Laos. As he resisted, the Thai officials finally pinned the man down and put him in jail. The Thai officials escorted us to a big, long room; there was where we waited to see my father.

Just a short time later, as I saw my dad approaching us, I ran to greet him. My heart was beating faster and faster as I got closer to him; I was overwhelmed by elation. I was so happy and excited to see him that tears started rolling down my cheeks. Everyone was so happy to see each other and they all cried, too. We then got on a bus and headed towards the refugee camp called Nang Phong—the camp where my dad stayed. We were pretty lucky because my dad was there and we had a place where we could reside. There were food and rooms for us. I felt that we were more fortunate than other families. It took us no more than four days to get to Thailand. Even though we encountered many tragedies, we still made it easily compared to the later arrivals of Hmong refugees who faced many obstacles along the way. It's because we were the few people who arrived early and the Thai people were still lenient towards us as refugees.

While in the camp, my sister and I got really sick. My parents tried to give us shots and medicine. My sister and I didn't want the shots, and we cried and fussed. The adults pinned us down so that my parents could give us the shots. I was small and, being sick, I had no strength so they were able to give me the shots. However, my sister, on the other hand, was bigger and they had a hard time giving her the shots. My dad got really mad and struck her and she was unconscious. Everyone thought that she was not going to make it. My mom would pray hoping that she will get well again. She was hospitalized for four weeks and then was released. We stayed in the camp for several months. During those months, my dad went to Ban Vinai camp to help build the new camp, where we soon followed him to live when the camp was completed. Life in the camp was not the same as it was back in Laos. We didn't have the freedom to do what we wanted unless we had permission from Thai officials. We were stuck in the camps for almost a year before we came to the United States on August 10, 1976. My family finally resettled in the US to start our new life all over again.

"My Family Struggle and Survival"

Let me take a journey back in time to retell my childhood story how my family escaped from Laos and struggled to save everyone from being killed by the hands of the communist regime. My story is about my family's struggle and survival.

A barrage of bullets could be heard from afar as people ran for their lives. Families had to duck down and hide just to stay alive. We were told by our mother to hold each other's hands tightly, so that we would not be separated. This was a devastating catastrophe that will never be forgotten by any of my family members. Today, as a resident of the United States and a victim of the Vietnam War, I find myself pondering about my childhood past—a memory I will never forget.

The Vietnam War, also known as the Secret War of Laos, has been a tragic memory for many people, and I was one among them. I often find myself thinking of the things that happened to my family during the war. The Vietnam War started in the 1950s in North Vietnam and escalated to Laos in the 1960s when the Central Intelligence Agency (CIA) established its headquarter in Thailand. The CIA needed pilots so they recruited young Hmong men from Laos; my father was one of the CIA recruits. He was sent to Thailand for air pilot training. After he completed his T-28 training in Thailand, his mission was to return to Laos to carry out bombing assignments to sabotage the communist military bases and advancement into northern Laos. During his mission in December of 1971, my father's plane was shot down by the communist regime; however, his body was never found. To this day, my family still does not know whether he is dead or still alive. I was very young and therefore I have no recollection of my father.

In May of 1975 the war was over and the CIA pulled out of Laos. There were five people in my family; my three sisters, my mother, and me. The oldest sister, Kelly, was twelve; the second sister, Karen, was ten; I, Jenny, was six; and the youngest, Donna, was only two. We lived in a small city called Ban Xao. Everything was fine until the communist soldiers came to villages, towns, and cities and took all the educated men and former soldiers who served in the army to what they called re-education camp. One of my uncles was among these men. From that day on, he was never heard from or seen again. Because we were afraid of what the communist regime would do, we had two choices, to move to the rural area or to flee to Thailand. My mother did not want to go to a new country, so we moved to the rural area with the clan members of my father's side of the family. Life in the rural area was hard for us because we had never lived in the rural area before.

We moved to live in the province of

Moueng Pheng located in the northern region of Laos. Shortly after we settled down there, men and young boys formed groups to organize the guerrilla forces and called themselves "COB FAB," (in Hmong) aka Chao Fa (in Lao), meaning the soldiers of the sky or the disciples of God. COB FAB was formed to protect us against the communist regime and its brutality and atrocities. The guerrilla forces guarded the people and villages and went out daily to fend off the communist soldiers. Sometimes the forces searched for communist soldiers to kill before they could arrest more Hmong men. In the process of their daily missions, many men lost their lives. Some lost their lives because they stepped on buried grenades and hidden land minds; unlucky ones encountered communist soldiers in combat, and others fell into traps. As the days passed, the situation became worse. We lost more men and young boys. So many young boys had to join COB FAB to help safeguard their families. Simultaneously, life was difficult. Everyone was living in starvation because there were no men to help out in the field. As for our family, we struggled to survive because of the loss of our father. Our mother was the only one who worked in our field. She took my little sister, Donna, to the field with her every day. Kelly stayed home and did chores around the house. She fed the chickens and pigs, watered the garden, and made lunch to send to my mother and Donna. Karen and I went looking for other types of food in the forest. We dug up turnips for food because that was the most edible food we could find. Since there were not many turnips available, we were always competing with others who were also searching for the turnips. When there were not enough turnips we substituted other edible roots for food. The roots had a very bitter taste, so we had to soak them in water overnight and wash them many times before we actually cooked them. We lived like this for nearly a year.

One afternoon in 1976, our village was bombed heavily. Karen and I were in the forest digging turnips when all of a sudden we heard loud noise coming from the village. We dropped everything and rushed back to the village. In order to get to the village we had to walk through our field. When we got to our field, we saw my little sister, Donna, sitting inside an old-hollow-rotten tree stump. My mother and Kelly had already left to the village to get our valuable belongings. Karen left me with Donna and went after my mother and Kelly. I was trembling with fear but knew I had to be braved. Overwhelming thoughts came to my mind, "What if my mother and sisters got killed? How are we going to take care of each other?" and "Who would want to take us in?" I tried not to show Donna that I was scared, but my heart was pounding faster and faster. I could hear the sounds and explosions of gun shots and bombings coming from the village. People ran to and from the village trying to get their things. Missiles were flying all over our heads and exploding everywhere. It seemed forever before my mother and my sisters finally returned.

They took us to my grandparents' field because it was further away from the village so it was safer there. Around five o'clock, the shooting and bombing stopped, so my mother and sisters went back to the village to get some more things. Donna and I stayed with two of our cousins inside our grandparents' field. After they left, black clouds began to form in the sky and the evening became gloomy. The winds were blowing very hard everywhere as thunder roared loudly in the sky, and lightening flashed above us. It was almost as bad as the war. I had never been so frightened in my life because we were standing in the field with nothing to cover us as the rain started pouring down. Donna and I didn't have anything to cover up. My two cousins, on the other hand, had a plastic cover over them. I begged them to share it with us, but they would not let us. Instead, they let a goat get inside the cover. We were soaking wet; Donna was as cold as ice, and I watched her shivering all over. Her lips started to turn blue and her teeth were tittering against each other. I put my arms around her, and we held each other as close as we could to keep warm as we stood in the rain.

After the rain stopped, my mom and sisters came back, and we went to meet the rest of the people from the village. That night, everybody moved out of the village and left all of their domestic animals behind. We could only flee at night because we did not want the enemy to spot us. All the people trekked at night and it was very dark. I couldn't see anything so I held to a rope tied to the basket Kelly carried on her back. I carried my father's briefcase which contained a pair of his clothes and important documents about our family. It was difficult for me to walk in the dark because the briefcase was very heavy. The journey was long and weary because there were no trails to walk on. I was physically exhausted and did not want to continue the journey, but unfortunately I had no choice. We walked in the dark all night.

Day after day, week after week, we kept moving. We walked approximately three months before we reached our destination, the province of Moueng Ong. This was where my uncle, Charlie Toua Moua, lived. My uncle's family came to meet us at half way and helped carry our belongings. As soon as my mother and uncle set eyes on each other, she broke down and cried. This was the first time I saw my mother cry. She was crying so much that she couldn't say anything. The situation made me sad because I thought she should be happy that we have reached our destination.

My uncle took us to live with his family in the village. He gave us chickens and pigs to raise so that we could start a new life in the new village. After eight months in the village, life began to feel normal. Beautiful flowers bloomed everywhere, rice and corn were ripe and ready to be harvested, and families and relatives were interacting with one another as life was perfectly peaceful. Everyone was getting ready for the New Year. Families gathered rice to store away, and mothers sewed new clothes for family members to wear. Everyone was so happy until the village was bombed again. Thus, we had to run for our lives once again. I remember that Karen was very angry with my mother because she had asked my mother a couple times to kill one of the pigs so we all would have some meat to eat. But my mother said, "It's almost New Year, let's wait until then." When the village was bombed, we fled and left all of the animals behind again.

We could not stay in the village anymore because the communist soldiers were coming to the village. It seemed like the communist regime was after us. We had two choices: to surrender and join the communist regime, or go join the COB FAB. My uncle refused to surrender so we ended up joining the COB FAB. In order to join COB FAB, we needed a great leader. This person needed to be someone who knew the way around the jungles and who had courage and patience to lead the people. People in the village were separated into different groups. We went up to hide in the tallest mountain called Phu Bia. That was where all the COB FAB stayed in hiding. It rained most of the time because the area consists of mostly tropical rainforest. The path was slippery and muddy, like slough and wetland. I remember, after walking a whole day and at the end of the day, my little sister was completely covered with mud. All we could see was her two little blinking eyes.

Unfortunately, the mud infected the scratches on my feet. They became swollen and turned red. I prayed for the rain to stop, and my mother told me that it was good that God made it rain so it would cover our footprints. Thus, the enemy would not find us. We kept on going no matter how tired we were. Many people were abandoned along the way. These people included children and adults who were sick, hurt, or too weak to keep up with the trekking. They were left behind to die. When we got to Phu Bia, all the people had to spread out so it would be harder for the enemy to find us. We were careful not to leave traces behind for the enemy to follow. We could not pick any fruit or break branches from trees, not even a leaf, to leave traces. We could only whisper and whistle so the enemy would not hear us. I had a hard time with this kind of communication because I could not whistle, yet. Children were not allowed to play together; we had to be with our families and ready to run at any time. We the children were conditioned so well to control our emotions. When we cried, tears would only roll down our cheeks, and there would be no sound. As for the babies, parents gave them opiate substance to keep them quiet and to make them fall asleep so they wouldn't cry. Many times the babies died because they were accidentally overdosed.

There was no food or water up high in the mountain, so the men had to go steal rice from nearby fields for their families. These fields belonged to people who surrendered and stayed behind in the villages. My mother and Kelly were the ones who went out to find food for my family. Every morning, we had to go down to get water from the creek in the canyon. It took about an hour to go back and forth. It was cold and foggy all the time on the top and the slopes of the Phu Bia Mountain. The ground was covered with mostly "bia." Bia were large trees that grow on the mountain, and that's why the mountain was called "Phu Bia," meaning mountain of bia. The floor of the forest was so soft, and every step I walked I felt like I was going to sink in. We were only allowed to cook at night so the enemies wouldn't see the smoke. Each time we cooked, we would prepare enough for dinner and breakfast for a day or two. After a couple of nights at one place, we fled to a new location. We moved from place to place not knowing what the next day would be like. I remember being wakened up in the middle of the night to move because the adults thought that we might be in danger. "The communists are getting close, so we have to find another hiding place," my mother usually told us. We hid in the mountain for nearly two years. These were the longest years in my life because I thought I would never see the bright side of life again.

After two long years of hiding in the jungle, my uncle realized that the war was not going to end anytime soon, so he sent some men to find a way to Thailand. The following year, three of the men returned from Thailand for their families. These three men left their families with us so that they would come back for them. At this point, my uncle decided that we should go to Thailand. The adults talked about the trip among themselves, and they concluded that it might take about three weeks to get to Thailand because of the women and children. Therefore, the escape plan was set. Each family would have to carry enough food to last for three weeks or longer. In addition, we would need tools to dig for other food along the way in case we ever ran out of food. Also, we would need weapons to protect us in case we got ambushed along the way. In preparation, the women gathered enough rice for the trip while the men made their weapons.

Since our group was too big, we had to divide into two groups. The men that returned from Thailand would lead the way. Two of them took charge of the first group, and one man stayed with us. The first group left a month earlier in February 1979. We stayed behind until we heard from the first group that they had made it to Thailand safely. About a month later, the news came and we started our formidable journey to Thailand. Each of us had to carry something. My mother carried 50 pounds of rice, Kelly carried about 30 pounds of rice, and Karen carried 10 pounds of rice along with some blankets, clothes, and tools. I still carried my dad's briefcase, and Donna carried a bag of lunch and a bottle of water for herself.

Our journey to Thailand was long and there were many afflictions along the way. It took us longer than we originally anticipated because we were ambushed twice. On the way to Thailand, we saw graves of people who had died recently along the route. There were threatening notes pinned on trees everywhere stating, "Anyone who walks this route will die." It was very creepy and spooky as we walked past these graves. Most of the time, we made our own trail to walk on. We practiced swimming whenever there was water so everyone would get used to it. As we got closer to the bank of the Mekong River, families made bamboo rafts to carry with them to use to cross the river. We could only cross the Mekong River at night because we didn't want to be spotted by the Thai soldiers or the communist soldiers on either side. Therefore, we had to get as close to the bank of the river as possible during the day and wait patiently. When night came, we would be able to cross it. Before dark, my uncle would name a place where we could all come back to meet if something should go wrong. The first time we tried to cross the river, we got ambushed. It was because we took the wrong direction and ended up on the property of some Laotians. They chased us back to the jungle. Luckily, nobody got hurt.

The next day, we found another route at a different section of the Mekong River to cross. During the night, we made another attempt to cross the river. However, to reach the bank of the river, we had to cross a rice paddy field surrounded by a fence before we could get to the river. The rice paddy field was all dried up so it was difficult to walk on due to the many animal foot holes made by the water buffalo in it. Once we got to the fence, we had to climb over it in order to get to the river. Karen and Donna were already on the other side of the fence. They could see the river from where they were standing. My mother was just about to the climb over the fence. Kelly and I were right behind our mother. All of a sudden, there were gun shots coming from the other side of the fence. Kelly grabbed my hand and we started running back. I heard my little sister say, "Mom, wait for me." My mother ran back to get her. We kept running until we were in the jungle and out of sight. Once we got to a safer place, my mother checked to see if we were all there. Luckily, Karen made it back too. It all happened so quickly that on the way back, we did not remember walking through the animal foot holes in the rice paddy field. During this second ambush, two men got killed. My uncle, his wife, and two of his children made it across the Mekong River to Thailand.

The next day, we met at the location where we were supposed to meet. Seven of my uncle's children were left behind with us plus the rest of the group. We did not know what to do anymore, so we went up to hide in the jungle again. When my uncle got to the camp in Thailand, he hired four men to come back to get us. We stayed for ten days in the jungle. On the eleventh day, the four men got to us and told us that my uncle had sent them to rescue us. These men told us that they had hired two fishermen to take us across the river at night.

Later that night, the four men took us to the two fishermen. The section of the Mekong River where we were supposed to cross this time was divided into two channels. Therefore, we had to cross the first section of the river by foot before we could get to the second section where the fishermen would be waiting for us. I didn't know how deep the first section of the river was; all I know was that as we went into the river I felt the water coming up to my neck, but we still kept going. I thought that I was going to drown until one of the men pulled me up. At last, we made it to where the two fishermen were waiting for us. The minute we got there, they put us in two canoes and took us across the river. They made several trips before they could get all of us across. We finally reach Thailand in April of 1979.

It was sad when we got to Thailand because all our possessions were taken away by the Thai officers—we were robbed. There was nothing we could do because we were on their land. We were happy that they did not deport us back to Laos. We realized that as soon as we stepped on the ground of Thailand, we would have to face new struggles and to conquer whatever would come our way. Even if we were broke and had nothing to live on, we felt at ease because we survived and had escaped the communist regime. For my family, this journey of life would always be remembered as a memoir in our lives.

Today, it is still sad to look back at this part of my life and I still remember all the terrible things that happened as a result of the Vietnam War. Many lives have been shattered by it, and even though the war is over, the scars continue to torment the people who lived through it. Thank God that my family survived and is still alive today.

Hmong childhood memories are very similar to Hmong family stories of life struggles, pain, and triumphs. Today, 40 years after the events, the memories and the stories still live in Hmong refugees' hearts and souls because so many lives were lost to pave the way, so many sacrifices were made in order for some to survive, so many atrocities took place against Hmong refugees, and so many soldiers and their families who were left behind still face political persecution today.

Two Case Studies of Hmong Families

Every Hmong family has a unique story to share with the world about its history, its migration, and its struggle for survival in its journey from the eastern world to the western world. The two stories presented here, those of the True Vang and the Ker Her families, are different. One family initially chose to stay in Laos; the other chose to flee. Thousands of other family stories could be shared to help readers understand the sorrow and misery and the sacrifices that all Hmong refugees endured. These two represent but a very small part of the whole story.

The True Vang Family Story

When Laos fell, very early in 1975, the True Vang family (TVF), living in Phakhet, a town in the southern region near Long Cheng, planned its escape. The immediate family consisted of eight people, but they coordinated their escape plans with relatives. First, all the relatives had to find a way to Nam Sou, the closest commercial town, located a few hours away. There all the family leaders— that is, all the parents—would meet and decide together how to get to Vientiane, the capital city.

The TVF left Phakhet on a taxi heading south to Nam Sou. There, all the relatives from the different towns and villages converged. For about one week, the parents met and discussed escape possibilities. It turned out that the TVF did not have enough money to pay transporters and smugglers to take its eight members to Vientiane and then to Thailand. The amount needed was about 1,000,000 kibs (Laotian currency). The other relatives could afford the trip, so they left for Vientiane and abandoned the TVF at Nam Sou. Two weeks later, the TVF returned to its old town and continued living there for another five months.

In early December 1975, after being told by the communist regime to dig a tunnel at the back of their house so they would have a hiding place in the event the Chao Fa guerrillas attacked at night, the TVF made a second plan of escape. Within a week, the predicted attack did occur in the middle of the night. The assault lasted for several hours. The morning light revealed that the communist regime had suffered heavy casualties. A few days later, the TVF parents approached the town chief to ask for permission to travel to Nam Sou to visit a sick family member. The request was granted. The town chief whispered to the father not to return unless he absolutely had to.

The next day, in the early evening hours, the TVF marched on foot across a hill to bypass a security checkpoint located between Phakhet and an adjacent town. They bribed a taxi driver to transport the entire family to Nam Sou. Within a week, the TVF found a Hmong couple who would be traveling from Nam Sou to Vientiane. The TVF parents paid the couple to take four of their children with them to Vientiane while they and the remaining children hoped to join them in two weeks. The couple agreed to help. In Vientiane, the four children stayed with family acquaintances of the couple's relatives until the rest of the family arrived. During this time, the communist regime set up facilities in every town in an attempt to apprehend supporters and loyalists of the former regime who might be fleeing illegally. It took a full

month for the TVF parents to make it to Vientiane with the rest of the family. They had bribed taxi drivers to transport them from town to town. They had spent the days in the towns and the nights marching on foot to elude detection and bypass the search facilities. Finally, the whole family was reunited in Vientiane. The next step was to cross the Mekong River to Thailand. Speed was critical and money was essential to survival.

In about two weeks the TVF located a group of smugglers and transporters who agreed to take the family across the border. The cost was nearly 2,500,000 kibs. That was more than the TVF had, but they were able to borrow 1,000,000 kibs from a close relative. They deposited the money with a third party and obtained a receipt. Once the family was transported across the border to Thailand, the TVF would give the receipt to the smugglers so they could claim the funds from the third party. This type of plan was very common and also very risky.

On the day of the escape, the family members were separated and taken to a secluded location near the river bank. They were hidden in the brush near a launching dock. The plan was for the transporters to ferry all the family members across the Mekong River in a motored fishing boat in the early morning hours in four round trips. Everyone was nervous, knowing that if they were caught by the communist soldiers they would be sent to prison for the rest of their lives ... which were likely to be short. Also, many families had been murdered by smugglers and transporters for money. Some had drowned when the boats capsized. Others were shot at and killed in the middle of the river. Thai pirates had robbed Hmong refugees when they reached the border. They were tense, but the hope of freedom overrode their fear.

Finally the moment came when the transporters signaled the TVF to come out of the brush, slowly make their way to the launching dock, and get into the boat. One by one, they did so and sat down quietly. The smugglers gave each a straw hat to make them appear to be farmers. They were told not to speak a word in Hmong. Only the smugglers were allowed to speak; they spoke Lao or Thai. The captain of the smugglers gave a hand signal to the boat driver, who started the engine. Within 30 minutes, all the TVF reached the Thai side of the Mekong River. Immediately after unloading the family, the transporters asked for the receipt. The father reached into his backpack, took out the receipt, and handed it to the transporters. They took off to return to Laos.

The TVF walked from the river bank to a dirt walkway above. There, a Thai farmer approached and asked where they were heading. The father told him that they were going to the Nong Khai refugee camp.

Before leaving Laos, the TVF had offered a cow to its ancestors for protection and guidance (in Hmong, *fiv ib lub yeem nyuj*); now they were counting on that protection and guidance. The Thai farmer told the family to rest while he walked to the highway nearby to find a taxi. About 45 minutes later, the farmer returned to the group and told the father that he had flagged down a taxi to take the whole family to the camp. It would take several hours to get there. When the taxi arrived, the driver wanted 15,000 kibs. The father insisted that the driver ensure the family's safety. The driver promised to avoid all Thai security checkpoints in every town in order to safely transport the family directly to the camp. Finally, the two agreed and sealed the deal. The TVF thanked the Thai farmer for all his kindness and rewarded him with some money.

Everyone got into the car and the final leg of the journey began. The taxi driver did indeed keep away from all checkpoints and transported the TVF directly to the camp. After seven long hours, the family finally reached the main entrance of the camp. There, the Hmong refugee officers guarding the entrance came to the car and asked the father to identify his leaders and any family relatives living in the camp. The father mentioned a prominent leader and immediately the officer sent a message about the new arrivals over the camp intercom. Within two hours the leader arrived at the main entrance to greet the family and welcome them into the camp. It was two days before Christmas 1975. The TVF was very fortunate. Today, they thank God, their ancestors, and all people who played a role in their survival story.

The Ker Her Family Story

The story of the Ker Her family (KHF) took different twists and turns before the family got to Thailand. When Laos fell and Major General Vang Pao was airlifted to Thailand, the KHF of six people decided not to flee the country. The family left their village, Ban Sorn, to live with relatives in Pha Khao. The father of KHF was an elementary school teacher. When he heard about the summoning of all former supporters and loyalists and the communist regime's plan to send former officials to the reeducation camps in northern Laos and Vietnam, the father decided to go into hiding in the woods. A few months later, he learned that his former colleagues had been captured and sent to the reeducation camps. Terrified, he immediately took his family to join the Chao Fa guerrilla forces.

The KHF lived in the wilderness near the Phu Bia slopes. They moved constantly from place to place to continue their agrarian lifestyle. Communist soldiers assaulted their towns and villages and chased them away many times. On numerous occasions, the family was encircled and trapped, barely able to slip through the enemy's net. Between 1975 and 1980, the three oldest children were killed by the communist soldiers in combat. Only the youngest son survived. The KHF moved southward after the red and yellow rain chemical bombs dropped on the region where they were living. The KHF feared exposure to the chemicals and fled along with other families.

According to the KHF, life in the jungle was miserable; they lived in fear day and night and rationed their meals and drinks just to survive. They saw many elders die of starvation and malnutrition. Young children survived with great difficulty; many infants died because their mothers could not enough nourishment to breastfeed them. They stayed alive by eating leaves, sprouts, roots, and berries. After a time, everything in the wilderness that was edible became scarce because so many people had depended on the plants for their survival. The Hmong refugees in hiding were starving to death. There was hardly any food at all after the chemical spill. Rivers and streams were also tainted. The people had to steal rice from the field to feed their families. During winter, they ran out of food and dug up and ate roots. Salt became the most valuable food. Without it, everyone became weak and exhausted. They had to beg villagers for salt. Coming to a town or village to ask for salt or anything else was to risk their lives. If spotted, they would be chased and shot at by the communist soldiers. Life in seclusion was a living hell. Sometimes, they travelled long distances to buy or steal salt. Confrontations with villagers were inevitable, but usually they resulted in only minor quarrels.

In early 1981, the KHF decided to join other families going through the jungle to escape to Thailand. Nearly a thousand people marched on foot day and night for months. Along the way, hunger struck because they ran out of food. The leaders, typically the fathers, decided to go to nearby towns to steal rice and livestock to save the group from starvation. The fathers descended from the hills and mountain slopes to the outskirts of the towns and waited in the woods until nightfall. Slowly, they made their way into the towns, looking for farm houses with livestock. They crept through the dark and stole whatever they could before retreating back into the woods at dawn. These were dangerous ventures, but they had no other way to stay alive.

After trekking through the woods for several months, the group of one thousand people had shrunk to 350. Many of the older people, women, and young children had died of starvation or exhaustion. Some had stepped on landmines and some had been killed when the communist soldiers ambushed them. There was not enough time to bury all the dead bodies. The group had to keep marching or the enemy would catch up with them.

By the time they reached the Mekong River, many children were fatherless and motherless and some women no longer had husbands. So everyone relied on the leaders and other male adults in the group. The group spent two weeks at the river bank preparing for the crossing. The men lashed together rafts from bamboo logs for the women and children. They tied vines to the rafts. The plan was to cross the river in groups of 10 to 20 people, each group with an assigned leader. The men would swim, pulling the rafts behind them. They estimated it would take several days for the entire group to make it to the Thai side. As each small group reached the Thai side, they were to hide in the woods and wait for the arrival of the rest of the group. If anyone was caught by Thai soldiers or pirates, they were not to tell about the rest of the group.

It was September. The water level was low in some areas, but the current was swift. Crossing, particularly in groups, would not be easy. In their fear, the leader of each group called upon God and the spirits of Heaven and Earth and offered a cow to their ancestors for protection and guidance during the crossing (in Hmong, *fiv yeem ntuj thiab fiv yeem nyuj*). The people were separated into 15 groups with each group leader determining when to cross the river.

The KHF made it safely across the Mekong River to Thailand. However, nearly 50 of the 350 who reached the river lost their lives during the crossing. Some drowned because the vines broke when the group leaders tried to pull them. A couple of group leaders perished because they became physically exhausted, possible suffering from hypothermia or muscle cramps. One entire group disappeared in the swift current.

After reaching the Thai side, a few groups were robbed by Thai pirates but their lives were spared. The pirates beat one group leader for bringing more refugees to Thailand. Most of the refugees were rescued by Thai soldiers and civilians. They were transported to detention centers and later taken to the Ban Vinai refugee camp. Although the KHF survived the trek and the river crossing and made it to the camp, they lost three children and witnessed many deaths. Today, the KHF is living in the U.S. Their struggle for survival will always live in their hearts and souls.

For the TVF and the KHF as for all the Laotian Hmong refugees, the struggles and suffering did not end when they left Laos. In Thailand they were free of their communist oppressors and they had the hope for a better life, a chance to start all over again. But that hope had to be kept alive in the confines of refugee camps.

The Refugee Camps

Just days before Laos fell, right before the final rescue and evacuation took place in Long Cheng, the U.S. had no place to take Hmong refugees. No arrangements had been made to provide safe haven for them. The only place Hmong could go to was the old U.S. airbase in Thailand known as Nam Phong. That is why Major General Vang Pao told his soldiers, civil leaders, and followers that the U.S. might take only 2000 to 3000 Laotian Hmong refugees when Laos fell. In fact, Major General Vang Pao wanted all

Hmong evacuated by the U.S. Many were unaware of the limitations and felt betrayed by Major General Vang Pao, the U.S., and the Royal Laotian government.

The first wave of airlifted refugees resettled temporarily in the Nam Phong camp. From 1975 to 2005, as illustrated in Figure 2.2, the major Laotian Hmong refugee camps were Nam Phong, Nong Khai, Ban Vinai, Napho, Chiang Kham, Houei Yot, Ban Tong, Ban Nam Yao, SopTuang, Ubon, Sikhui, Phanat Nikhom, Wat Thakrabok monastery (1992–2005), and Ban Huay Nam Khao (2004–present). Nam Phong was the first temporary detention center for refugees. Several months after it was built, refugees were transferred to Nong Khai and Ban Vinai. The first Nong Khai camp was overcrowded to the point it was not sanitary for the swollen refugee population. A new Nong Khai camp was built and divided into two main sections in 1976. One section was occupied by Hmong refugees and the other section belonged to non–Hmong Laotian refugees. Ban Vinai had four main sections and housed mostly Hmong refugees until the early 1980s. Nong Khai closed in 1979 and its refugees were transferred to Ban Vinai and other detention cen-

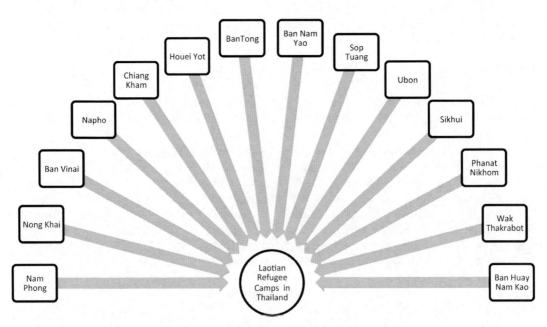

Figure 2.3. Major refugee camps in Thailand.

ters. The Hmong refugees joined other Hmong refugees already in Ban Vinai and non–Hmong Laotian refugees were moved from Ubon, Napho, and Nong Khai to Ban Vinai. Some of these camps were used for temporary shelters, detention centers, transitional facilities, and processing centers for transferring Laotian Hmong refugees and other refugee groups (Laotian, Cambodian, and Vietnamese) to other camps and to the western nations. For instance, Phanat Nikhom was the main transitional center for Laotian refugees resettling in the western nations.

As a result of camp closures and the brutal repatriation policy against Laotian Hmong refugees, in the early 2000s many displaced war refugees living in Thailand sought refuge at Wat Thakrabot and Ban Huay Nam Kao; they had nowhere else to go. These sites were not official refugee camps designated for refugee sanctuary or resettlement. In 2005, the international community decried the living conditions in these camps, and most inhabitants were subsequently resettled in the West.

The sheer number of Laotian Hmong refugees created political pressure between communist Laos and Thailand. By the 1990s, over 100,000 refugees had arrived in Thailand. As a result, Thailand implemented a repatriation policy against Laotian refugees known as the *policy of refugee deterrence*. The country gradually closed existing camps and enforced strict border controls to reduce the entrance of refugees. However, the policy had little impact on the rate at which war refugees fled Laos. Even the reduction in food assistance did not deter refugees from coming. The ongoing oppression and persecution inside Laos prompted refugees to leave for Thailand despite the closure of refugee camps that started in the early 1980s.

In 1982, the Soptung camp closed. Two years later, in 1984, the Nam Yao camp shut down and all refugees were transferred to other camps. The Chiang Kham camp was converted to a detention center as was the Napho Camp. In 1983, Nong Khai was shut down by the Thai government and Laotian

Hmong refugees were transferred to Ban Vinai and Napho. Then in 1992, the Ban Vinai camp was ordered to be closed. The remaining refugees faced tough choices: going to the western nations, going back to Laos, resettling in China, or relocating to other camps such as Nam Yao, Ban Huay Nam Khao, and Wat ThaKrabok. The closure of the camps and the brutal repatriation policy left Laotian Hmong refugees stranded and hopeless, especially those who had missed resettlement opportunities.

For Hmong refugees, life in the camps had not been easy. Living in refugee enclaves gave them few options: resettling in the West, being deported to Laos, leaving the camp to live in the wilderness, or looking for refuge in nearby towns and villages. On the other hand, camp life was better than living under the communist regime. Most camps were enclosed and fenced with barbed wire. Refugees were told by Thai officials guarding the camps not to sneak out or leave without permission. Anyone caught leaving the camp could be arrested and fined, sometimes sent to jail. In the early years, life in the camps was bearable because humanitarian aid programs were adequate and refugees were permitted some flexibility. For instance, refugees in Ban Vinai were allowed to cultivate crops outside the camp. As time went on, however, food rations were cut to the bare minimum for survival. Thai officials wanted to deter Laotian Hmong refugees from emigrating from Laos. Large families had difficulty making ends meet.

As the population of the camps continued to increase, social problems skyrocketed. Camp residents were vulnerable to diseases and sicknesses because of the humid and hot weather conditions. Most refugees were extremely poor. Hungry and needy people are prone to illegal activities. Destitution drove many refugees to exit the camp at night to work outside or to seek odd jobs and temporary employment in the nearby towns, villages, and farmlands. Young women who disobeyed rules and sneaked out were raped by Thai pirates. Wood for cooking was scarce. Buying charcoal and burning wood was expensive. Some Hmong were caught stealing wood outside the camps; they were jailed and fined. Water wells inside the camps dried up because the underground supply was depleted. In the early 1980s, Thai soldiers and police raided the dwellings of many families inside Ban Vinai for drug trafficking and illegal gambling. Some were arrested and sent to prison. Death rate soared because of the lack of medical care; only scarce life-saving medical care was available. Despite the hardships, the Hmong refugees were able to manage what resources they had.

By the late 1990s, most of the refugee camps had been shut down. Newly arrived refugees were considered illegal immigrants and denied political asylum or temporary shelter. From the 1990s to the mid–2000s, many were repatriated to Laos, where they were subjected to harsh punishment and imprisonment. By this time, most resettlement programs had ceased. Refugees feared having no place to live. Thai soldiers used force to repatriate refugees who had been living in the camps. On numerous occasions, refugee families were forced into military trucks and sent back to Laos. These actions prompted camp inmates to flee. As the camps began to close, some Hmong refugees chose to abandon them before facing repatriation *en masse*. Many joined relatives living in the jungles of northern Thailand. Some Laotian refugees blended in with the Thai people and disappeared among them. Some were able to become Thai citizens. Some made the choice to return to Laos to face their "crimes" and punishment. Many others, especially those living in the Wat Thakrabot monastery and Ban Huay Nam Kao, decided to resettle in the western nations. In 2005, the last few thousand Laotian Hmong refugees who sought refuge at Wat ThaKrabok were resettled in the U.S. Today, although the camps are closed, refugees are still living in northern Thailand.

Coming to the West

In late 1975, Major General Vang Pao, under political pressure from the Thai government, resettled in the U.S. When he came to the U.S. with his family, he left the Hmong refugees behind at the Nam Phong camp. Hmong leaders said the Thai government and the communist regime became concerned that Major General Vang Pao's presence in Thailand might indirectly influence the Chao Fa guerrillas to intensify their activities inside Laos. Also, the U.S. and Thai governments were concerned for his safety if he should continue to live in Thailand. These were legitimate reasons for the U.S. to grant political asylum to him and his family and enable them to start over again in the West.

His departure to the West upset the Hmong refugees. They felt that without Major General Vang Pao, their plight would be more difficult and their fate was uncertain. Most Laotian Hmong refugees chose to follow their leader, Major General Vang Pao, to the West rather than remain in close proximity to the communist regime. Perhaps more importantly, Hmong refugees feared the communists might invade the camp to arrest them and take them as prisoners of war. Shortly after Major General Vang Pao left, a resettlement program was initiated. It offered Laotian refugees the opportunity to come to the western nations. Many refugees were reluctant to accept the offer of resettlement because they hoped to return to Laos one day. Others decided to come to the western nations to start over again. Some Hmong families were willing to resettle but had difficulty deciding to which host nation they wanted to go. First, Hmong refugees were granted political asylum to settle in France, France Guyana, Australia, Canada, and the U.S. Then, in early 1990s, Hmong refugees were allowed to settle in Argentina and West Germany, as shown in Figure 2.3. Some former Hmong students and high ranking officials chose to go to France because they were familiar with the French from the French occupation of Laos. Some selected Canada and Australia as their new homeland. Most chose the U.S. because that is where Major General Vang Pao was.

The very first group of Hmong refugees to resettle in the West arrived in late 1975. The first few groups went to France, the U.S., and Australia. As the influx of refugees from Laos continued, the refugee resettlement programs were expanded. The resettlement processes had several steps:

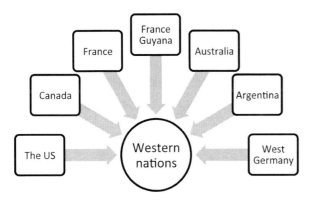

Figure 2.3. Hmong resettlement in Western nations.

1. Refugees desiring to resettle had to register and apply for one of the programs.

2. Applicants were screened and interviewed.

3. Applicants were examined.

4. Applicants had to meet eligibility requirements and be accepted for resettlement.

5. Applicants had to undergo a routine medical examination.

6. Applicants had to be cleared for resettlement.

7. Sponsors had to be found in the host nation.

8. The details of the sponsorship process had to be confirmed.

9. Temporary visas and other travel documents had to be processed.

10. Specific arrangements had to be made.

The resettlement programs required documentation and interviews of refugee families demonstrating their direct involvement in the Secret War in Laos. The interviewers usually asked the refugees about their past military leaders, governors, mayors, council members, and place of residence in Laos. Sometimes interviewers asked the refugees to identify pictures of former leaders or to name their former leaders who worked under the command of Major General Vang Pao. Some applicants failed the test and were not permitted to resettle. Those who failed either (1) lacked proper documents; (2) could not establish ties to the U.S. Secret War; (3) gave conflicting statements; (4) could not identify military leaders or official figures; (5) were involved in communist activities or had political affiliations with other nations; (6) had not been admitted into the camps with refugee status; (7) failed to establish a relationship with the sponsor's family; (8) were rejected by camp officials; (9) did not emigrate to Thailand on time; or (10) were consider to be illegal immigrants or outsiders. Those who passed went through at least three interviews before being accepted for resettlement. The name of each eligible family was posted on the resettlement schedules. Once the name of a family appeared on the list for resettlement, a date was set for transfer to a temporary center such as Phanat Nikhom camp for processing before the family could board an international flight to come to the western nations.

Medical teams conducted routine medical exams in the camps on all individuals eligible for resettlement. Each family member had to have a blood test, urine analysis, TB screening, physical exam, vision test, hearing test, and chest x-ray. These were standard procedures. If any family member failed the medical exam or had a medical condition, the whole family had to wait until the condition had been treated and cleared by the doctor. Sometimes families were stranded for months or years before resettling in the western nations. Very rarely was a family rejected because of a medical condition.

Coming to the western nations was referred to by Hmong refugees as traveling to the third world. The experience reminded Hmong of their emigrating from China to Southeast Asia; however, this move was different because most Hmong refugees had little or no understanding about western cultures, traditions, or way of life. Language was also a challenge. Some Hmong refugees could speak French, but almost none knew a word of English. The Hmong refugees knew they were going to face great challenges and uncertain opportunities in the western nations, but they desperately wanted to be free and they could not be free living in the refugee camps.

The first Laotian Hmong refugees arrived in the West in late 1975. This group included military families, government officials, civil leaders, educators, young couples, and single individuals. The resettlement processes gave Hmong refugees new hope; however, it also separated families and loved ones. Teenage lovers had to part because they were resettled in different countries. Single young adults accompanied close family members to the West and left their parents behind in the camps. Large families had to be broken into two families in order to resettle in the West. Sometimes families and loved ones were able to reunite in the western nations years after arrival. At other times the separation was permanent. The process of Western resettlement put Hmong refugees through another time of chaos and turmoil, but at least this time life was better when the turbulence ended.

It should be noted that not all the people who were resettled were real Laotian Hmong refugees. Some illegal immigrants took advantage of the plight of the real Laotian Hmong refugees and seized the chance to come to the West. Illegal immigrants from Thailand and Laos sneaked into the refugee camps in Thailand in the mid–1980s to the late 1990s, pretending to be war-displaced refugees from Laos. They claimed to have ties to Major General Vang Pao and the Royal Laotian Army when, in fact, they were impostors who acted as con artists. They lied to the representatives of the United Nations High Commissioner on Refugees about their roles in the Secret War in order to be eligible for resettlement in the West. Such people should be ashamed of themselves for using the suffering and sacrifice of the true war-displaced Laotian Hmong refugees for selfish ends. Today there are plenty of these fake refugees living in the western nations.

From 1975 to 1980, a few thousand Hmong refugees went to France. A few hundred Hmong families chose to resettle in Australia and Canada. Most came to the U.S. The second wave of Hmong refugees included immediate family members of the first wave as well as new families. Western sponsors of the first group of refugees included church members, individual citizens, private organizations, and a few family members. The second wave was sponsored primarily by many family members who had come to the West in the first wave. Subsequent groups were sponsored mostly by immediate family members.

From 1980 to the mid–1990s, thousands of Laotian Hmong refugees resettled in the western nations. The U.S. was home to approximately 75,000 refugee families. In the West, Hmong refugees experienced culture shock and unfamiliar events. In the mid–1980s, the Hmong settlers living in the West reported back to the camps their unexpected encounters and culture clashes; they warned prospective newcomers about the western culture and traditions. As soon as Hmong refugees arrived in the West, they faced cultural differences right away. Some of the unusual social phenomena were troubling, even frightening to them. For example, some Hmong refugees who arrived in late October unexpectedly experienced Trick or Treat traditions at their doorstep and believed ghosts were returning from the graveyard.

No formal orientation was given to prepare the Hmong refugees for resettlement in the West. Most found out about life in the new homeland the hard way. For example, their inability to speak English or French was a major difficulty for all refugees. Serious miscommunication was common and was especially frustrating when a refugee attempted to ask for help when a family member was sick or when a mother had labor contractions. Seeking medical help or calling 911 for an emergency was something unheard of in Laos. The refugees had plenty of food in their new countries, but drinking milk or eating dairy products gave them severe diarrhea and stomach problems. New settlers warned the incoming refugees to watch out for milk.

Also, family separation was a terrifying experience for newcomers. Some fathers and mothers had to take jobs just a few days after arrival to support their families. Sometimes fathers worked during the days and mothers worked at nights. Parents did not see each other for days, nights, or weeks. The swing shift and graveyard shift disrupted Hmong customary life. Some parents became agonizingly depressed and distraught, but they did not know how to ask for help. In the late 1970s, some community-based organizations were established to help the newly arrived refugees adjust.

Newcomers faced tremendous stresses while struggling to adjust. In the late 1970s to early 1980s, a series of sudden-death incidents struck the Hmong refugee communities. Presumably healthy individuals, usually middle-aged males, died in their sleep. The cause was mysterious but the problem was eventually attributed to a variety of factors: (1) life related stress, anxiety, and pressure; (2) insufficient diet or lack of dietary supplements; (3) post-traumatic stress disorders; (4) lack of proper medical care; (5) poor body immune system; (6) untreated and undetected heart conditions such as cardiac abnormality, cardiac arrhythmia, abnormal cardiac dysfunction, ventricular fibrillation, and genetic heart disease; (7) sleep apnea; (8) psychological trauma and psychiatric stress; and (9) physical and environmental stresses. These are examples of the many cultural and social pressures faced by Hmong refugees in the West. Some refugee families were deterred by these challenges and refused to resettle in the West. Others welcomed or at least accepted the challenges and took advantage of opportunities afforded them in the West that would not have been possible for them in Laos or Thailand.

From the mid–1970s to 2005, nearly 140,000 Laotian Hmong refugees resettled in the U.S., Canada, France, French Guyana, Australia, Argentina, and West Germany. Most made the U.S. their new homeland. The U.S. has resettled over 100,000 Laotian Hmong refugees. The last Hmong refugee group came to the U.S. in 2005 from Wat Thakrabot. Now, four decades after the fall of Laos, the U.S. Hmong population is near 300,000; the majority live in the states of California, Minnesota, and Wisconsin. France has several thousand. Canada has a few hundred and Australia has another two thousand. A few hundred live in Argentina and West Germany. The estimated distribution of the current Hmong population throughout the world is shown in Table 2.1, and it is projected that the actual number of Hmong people in each country could be higher by 2030.

Hmong refugees were allowed to come to the western countries following the fall of Laos in 1975 to save themselves and to start their lives over again. They fought the U.S. Secret War in Laos from 1960 to 1974 and became war-displaced refugees in 1975. The 14 years of sacrifices changed their lives forever, taking nearly everything from them. For the most part, their resettlement in the West has given them a golden opportunity to make a fresh start. Even though the opportunity comes with challenging obstacles, it has great possibilities and many are taking advantage of those possibilities. However, the resettlement processes has not been smooth for a great number of Laotian Hmong refugees.

Table 2.1. Geographic Distribution of Hmong Population Worldwide

Country	Estimated Population in 2014	Projected Population in 2030
China	4,000,000	5,000,000
Laos	400,000	460,000
Vietnam	1,000,000	1,200,000
Thailand	155,000	170,000
Burma	4,500	10,000
USA	260,000	300,000
France	15,000	16,000
French Guyana	3,000	3,500
Canada	500	650
Australia	2,000	2,100
Argentina	300	400
West Germany	450	500

Second Migration in the West

What to do with the Laotian Hmong refugees was a political and social pressure for western nations. Western governments had a covert dispersion policy for resettling the refugees. The western resettlement programs and policies expected Laotian Hmong refugees to assimilate quickly into the mainstream culture. Western nations wanted Hmong refugees to blend in and live among other races; they planned to disperse the Hmong families throughout the country to avoid refugee clusters and ghettos. The U.S. scattered Hmong refugee families throughout the 50 states and expected them to fit in quickly without any time for transition. These hidden social policy expectations backfired; they worked against Hmong adjustment to their new homeland. The dispersion policy resulted in Laotian Hmong refugees moving within the first few years after their arrival in the western nations. This movement is known as the *second migration* of Laotian Hmong refugees in the western nations. Even Major General Vang Pao decided to relocate his family during this period. Fleeing the first resettlement helped colonize Hmong families, clans, leaders, and communities in Fresno, Sacramento, St. Paul, Milwaukee, Madison, and elsewhere.

Despite the fact that cross-cultural trainings were supposed to take place in the transitional centers in Thailand, Laotian Hmong refugees were not properly prepared by resettlement personnel for adjusting and adapting to the new homeland. The training offered—multiple levels of English classes, a series of cultural orientations, and basic skills for work orientations—was poorly implemented and wholly inadequate to help the refugees resettle in the West. Only those considered capable, educated, and employable were assigned to take these trainings before coming to the West. Old parents and uneducated individuals were excluded from the trainings. None of the refugee children received any information about the western cultures and traditions. The Preparation for American Secondary Schools (PASS) training was not used to prepare Laotian Hmong teenage children for public schools prior to their arrival in the West even though the program was available. Moreover, most Laotian Hmong refugee families did not receive any American culture orientation workshops or training prior to their arrival in the West until the establishment of a chain of Laotian Hmong community-based organizations, even though, again, such resources were available.

As Hmong refugees continued to resettle in the western nations, in early 1977, Major General Vang Pao left his 454-acre cattle ranch in the mountains of Montana for southern California. The relocation of his family to California drew the attention of Hmong refugees worldwide. No one knew why he moved to California, but some believed he had a plan to reorganize Hmong refugees and Hmong communities that would ease their adjustment difficulties and help them navigate the cultural and social changes taking place in their families as they underwent the resettlement process. Because he was a highly respected former leader, Hmong refugees looked up to him for guidance and support. Many put great faith in his leadership, believing he could help them obtain assistance from the U.S. government. As the refugees expected, Major General Vang Pao and his fellow Hmong leaders founded Lao Family Community, Inc., a non-profit organization, to help southern California Hmong refugees adjust to the American way of life. Within a few years, the organization had branched out to serve many Hmong communities across the U.S. It was a great achievement under Major General Vang Pao's leadership; many branches still exist today.

In early 1980, news of Major General Vang Pao's relocation and his founding of the new organization began to draw Hmong refugees worldwide to the U.S. A few thousand Hmong settlers in France started to migrate to the U.S. Their reasons included culture clashes, problems assimilating, the absence of a Hmong clan system and community, and the desire for educational and socioeconomic opportunities. Vang (2008) identified some of the things the immigrants of the second wave hoped to find in the U.S.:

- freedom from culture clashes and social problems associated with clan clubs and clan religion
- socioeconomic opportunities
- clan system relationships and social organizations
- the ability to enjoy the Hmong communal way of life associated with familial values and sociopolitical needs.

In France, the opportunities open to Hmong refugees were very limited compared to what was possible for those in the U.S. In French Guyana, however, the Hmong refugees who resettled in 1977 had a great deal of freedom. They were allowed to clear the forests as they had done in Laos and build their own houses, live an agrarian lifestyle, and create their own community. However, the land was remote and did not permit involvement in modern life. Although their seclusion allowed the Hmong refugees to avoid assimilation into any new culture, it relegated them to isolation from western civilization in the 21st century.

In the U.S., Canada, and Australia, Hmong refugees relocated their families so they could live close to one another, and they formed mutual assistance organizations to help the community adjust to the host culture. For the most part, the first Hmong refugees were helpful in sponsoring newcomers to the West. Hmong mutual assistance entities and church groups played a major role in assisting and sponsoring Hmong refugees from Thailand and elsewhere to the U.S., Canada, and Australia. From 1980 to mid–1986, thousands of Hmong refugees in the U.S. relocated their families, concentrating in the three states of California, Minnesota, and Wisconsin. In the late 1980s to the early

1990s, Hmong families moved to other states—North Carolina, South Carolina, Texas, Colorado, and Alaska. Today, large Hmong populations can be found in major metropolitan areas, specifically St. Paul, Minnesota; Fresno and Sacramento, California; Milwaukee and Madison, Wisconsin; and Boulder, Colorado.

In the early part of the second migration, newcomers feared losing their culture and traditions in the process of adapting to the new society. As Vang (2010) explained, newcomers to America go through 10 stages of cross-cultural adjustment: arrival, family reunification, cultural shock, blaming, coping, accommodation, mixture, acceptance, rejection, and maintenance. Refugee families do not necessarily go through these stages in an orderly fashion; the order and pace of the progress depends on the family's educational level, socioeconomic status, and willingness to adapt to the host culture. For instance, Vang observed that in the maintenance stage, even without full assimilation, parents and children can enrich, accommodate, and integrate the mainstream society's values to a large extent at the same time they preserve their own culture and traditions.

As for the offspring of the Hmong refugees, Figure 2.4 illustrates the socialization forces that have direct impact on their lives and development. These forces are develop-

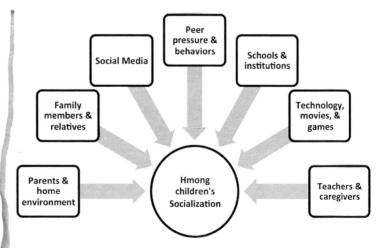

Figure 2.4. Developmental milieus in which Hmong children are socialized.

mental milieus in which Hmong children are socialized into the ways of the host culture without distinguishing between Hmong and non–Hmong. Table 2.2 lists some of the material and non-material elements of culture that are shaped in the developmental milieus.

Hmong children as well as their parents suffered culture shock and experienced social problems within the first several years of their arrival in the western nations. From the mid–1970s to the late 1980s, a large number of Hmong children became involved in gangs, substance abuse, and other criminal activities. These delinquent behaviors and attitudes not only shocked their Hmong parents, but also degraded Hmong pride and dignity, besmirching Hmong values, customs, and traditions. Some Hmong parents complained that their irresponsible and uncaring children were unworthy of the sacri-

Table 2.2. Material and Hmong Non-Material Elements of Culture

Material Elements	*Non-Material Elements*
Things that children can see, hear, and experience in daily life:	Things that are invisible to the naked eye but are perceived through social interactions and emulations:
1. Language and speaking—accents, intonations, emphatics, phonemics, slang, idioms, and so on	1. Ideas—of cleanliness, rationality, the past, the future, insanity, diseases, and so on
2. Dress and clothes—colors, designs, materials, dress codes, and so on	2. Values—customs, norms, formalities, protocols, time factors, culture, traditions, respect, birthright, and so on
3. Food and dining—cooking, food preparation, eating habits, ingredients, seasonings, and so on	3. Beliefs—religions, superstitions, taboos, bans, restrictions, fasting, sacrificial practices, offerings, and so on
4. Personal and body decorations—body odors, jewelry, earrings, bracelets, tattoos, head dresses, and so on	4. Feelings—guilty, embarrassed, shy, timid, reserved, outspoken, refrained, private, public, open-minded, close-minded, expressive, internalized, attitudes, personalities, and so on
5. Tools and utensils—cooking, cleaning, eating, brushing, polishing, scrubbing, cutting, sawing, and so on	5. Emotions—hidden, stern, mean, caring, composed, well-mannered, assertive, opinionated, controlled, impulsive, and so on
6. Artwork and artistic designs—styles, forms, colors, materials, folk art, embroidery, crafts, and so on	6. Childrearing practices—large family, small family, male and female offspring, extended family, nuclear family, and so on
7. Music and songs—lyrics, instruments, rapping, styles, practices, sounds, dances, and so on	7. Courtship practices—dating, engagement, sexuality, marriage, wedding, and so on
8. Building and construction—home, decorations, roads, buildings, parks, and so on	8. Notions of love—open-minded, close-minded, overt expression, covert expression, private, public, secretive, public display of affection, hidden, and so on
9. Talking and conversation—speed, loudness, personal space, eye contact, gestures, and so on	9. Gender roles—male roles, female roles, household responsibilities, religious practices, disciplinary actions, authority, decision making, and so on
10. Social greetings and manners—handshake, hugging, kissing, embracing, thank you, praising, introductions, and so on	10. Death rituals and rites—ceremonies, funeral services, wailing, crying, honoring, cremation, burial, and so on
11. Ownership—cars, houses, animals, tools, property, boats, bikes, and so on	11. Child raising practices, family structures, parental roles, family norms, gender roles, gender constraints, and so on
12. New Year's Celebration, cultural show, community events, social gathering, and so on	12. Decision-making processes and practices, patriarchal and patrilineal values, matrilineal roles, and so on

fices they had made in bringing them to the West. Many Hmong families were caught in the net of a dual society and parents worried that they were losing their children.

One of the factors contributing to the juvenile delinquency came from the low socioeconomic status of so many Hmong families. Most Hmong parents could not afford to live in good neighborhoods where their children could maintain their heritage and stay away from drugs, gangs, and criminal activities. Hmong families were concentrated in areas where housing was affordable. In these poor areas, the Hmong put their children at risk of exposure to violence and criminal behaviors. Hmong parents were new to the inner-city lifestyle and had no way of knowing the negative impact on their children's lives until they witnessed the change in their children.

To save their children, Hmong parents made sacrifices to relocate their families to different parts of the country where they could live near their relatives. The clan system and family ancestry are very important to Hmong. Living in close proximity to relatives gave Hmong parents and children a sense of security and belonging.

Hmong refugees migrated from one state to another also in search of better social and economic opportunities. In the late 1980s to the early 1990s, a large group of Hmong families moved from Fresno, California, to the Midwest to venture into chicken farming enterprises. Many Hmong families moved from the inner cities of large metropolises to smaller cities to farm. Some moved for better educational opportunities for their children. The cultural collectivism and familial structure of their communities facilitated cultural preservation; preserved the Hmong clan system and religious practices, especially the death rituals; and provided a support system in times of loss. During the 1990s, Hmong communities were booming in St. Paul, Minnesota; Fresno, Chico, and Sacramento, California; Milwaukee, Madison, and Wausau, Wisconsin; and Boulder, Colorado. Some Hmong refugee families did not move during the second migration; however, a decade later many Hmong relocated their families to U.S. cities with large Hmong populations. They were looking not only for better education, employment, and public assistance, but for the Hmong communal way of life.

Today, Hmong refugees appear to have settled into certain states and metropolitan areas. After nearly four decades in western countries, Hmong refugees have make remarkable progress toward prosperity and self-sufficiency. They have achieved great successes. Their socialization process has continued to evolve; Hmong refugees are becoming more and more Americanized, and nearly half of the current Hmong U.S. population is native born.

Summing Up

Laotian Hmong refugees have come a long way. As this chapter demonstrated, the majority of Hmong in the western nations are war-displaced refugees who emigrated from Laos. After the fall of Laos in 1975, Laotian Hmong refugees fled to Thailand and later resettled in several western nations. The exodus of Hmong refugees from Laos has been met with some confusion and misunderstanding. The refugees have been mislabeled as immigrants, undocumented people, or illegal aliens. In fact, after the Secret War in Laos, western nations granted them political asylum to save their lives and enable them to start over again.

Hmong refugees have made many sacrifices to save themselves and their families. Finding their own way out of Laos was not easy; escaping from the communist regime was fraught with dangers. They endured horrid struggles in the jungles just to stay alive. Many did not survive the trek through the wilderness, but died of starvation and malnutrition. Thousands were killed by soldiers or drowned in the Mekong River. Many who survived were robbed and raped by pirates. Many were tortured, beat, and imprisoned. The Hmong soldiers and civilians abandoned in Laos were subjected to brutal and inhumane treatment. The reeducation policy of the communist Laotian government indoctrinated

Hmong refugees to turn against their own. In response, the Hmong formed the Chao Fa guerrilla forces to protect their families and loved ones. Today, many war-displaced Laotian Hmong refugees are still being chased like animals in Laos.

Coming to the western nations was hard for most Hmong refugees. They went through a wringer of culture shock and difficult adjustments. Mysterious incidents of sudden death terrorized Hmong refugees. Once re-settled, the Hmong refugees began a second migration, moving from one country to another, from one state to another, and from one location to another. Today, Hmong refugees are found in the U.S., Canada, France, French Guyana, Australia, West Germany, and Argentina. Large Hmong refugee communities are concentrated in Minnesota, California, and Wisconsin. The current western Hmong refugee population is approximately 300,000 and growing.

• THREE •

The Hmong Today

Hnub twg txoj kev sib pab ciaj vaj... tsav lub yaj ceeb mus rau ghov kaj...
Peb mam sawv tsa kom cawv zoo xeeb... haus lawm lub neej nyob mus thaj yeeb...
Tsoom hluas yuav sawv txhij mus kawm ci... xav lub npe Hmoob lawm niaj ntav hli...
Lyrics of a classic Hmong song

Introduction

Hmong migration took place in both the ancient world and modern times ... in the ancient world from one part of China to another and to Indochina; in modern times from Laos to the West. Even though the historical events of early Hmong history are somewhat sketchy, the Hmong have a rich culture and traditions that they brought with them from the old world to the new world, from the East to the West. The cultural values and heritage they have treasured for so long can help people today make connections between their history in the ancient world and their lives now in the modern world.

Sometime in the 1800s the Hmong migrated to the Southeast Asian nations of Laos, Thailand, Burma, and Vietnam. As they had done in China, the Hmong in Southeast Asia lived agrarian lives in the rugged highland mountains and dense forests. As nomadic, tribal people, living off the land was hard, but the Hmong were resilient survivors. Living in seclusion presented the Hmong with both challenges and opportunities to be free from oppression and persecution. The Hmong's longing to find peace and freedom has contributed to their progress, accomplishments, and successes over the last 200 years.

Beginning in 1975, Hmong refugees resettled in the western nations of the U.S., Canada, France, French Guyana, Australia, Argentina, and West Germany. This chapter gives an overview of today's Laotian Hmong refugees living in different parts of the world and describes how they have dealt with the sociopolitical realities of their current situation in both eastern and western nations.

Identifying Today's Hmong

Who are the Hmong refugees? The Hmong are war refugees displaced from Laos. In the U.S., they are referred to as *Laotian Hmong refugees, Hmong,* or *Hmong Americans.* In other western nations, they are called *Hmong, Hmong French, Hmong Australian, Hmong Argentinean, Hmong Guyanese, Hmong German,* or *Hmong Canadian.* In the eastern countries, the Hmong are known as *Miao-Hmong, Hmong Chinese, Hmong Thai, Hmong Lao* aka *Laotian Hmong,* and *Hmong Vietnamese.* These names are used interchangeably with great flexibility. As Major General Vang Pao often said, all Hmong belong to one big family. Hmong families form tribes and tribes form clans. Their family surnames, or last names, serve for purposes of tribal intermarriage only. Most Hmong are bound by their matrimonial and marital kinship.

Hmong refugees living in the West comprise *18* prominent clan systems with familial subgroups, as indicated in Table 3.1. Of the 18 family clan systems, *12* are original and distinct families and 6 have been created out of family conflicts, marital taboos, religious fallacies, and cultural mutations (see Figure 3.1). Ethnically, Hmong in the western nations are divided into two main groups: the White Hmong and the Blue Hmong. The White and Blue categories are used to designate the two most common language dialects, *Hmoob Dawb* (White Hmong) and *Hmoob Lee* (Blue Hmong). Each Hmong family has its own history, ancestry, and genealogy with its own culture and traditions. However, most of the traditional religious rites are very similar from one family to another. For instance, Hmong traditional death rituals and the *Showing the Way* rite are identical in all clans. Hmong believe that familial subgroups were created by warfare and the migration from China to Southeast Asia, and

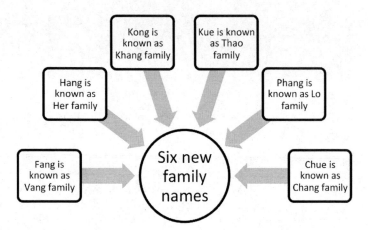

Figure 3.1. Six Hmong family clans added to the original 12 families.

familial separations caused families to alter their religious rites and rituals. During migrations, there was no spiritual leader over all the families, and once the clans settled in different parts of the world each family did its best to maintain proper religious practices. However, separation inevitably created divergences.

The colors used to classify Hmong refugees into two groups have nothing to do with any family's true ethnic identity. White and Blue refer to the two main dialects spoken by

Table 3.1. Western Hmong Family Surnames

Family or Clan Name	As spelled in Hmong(White/Blue)	Dialects
Cha, Chang	Tsab/Tsaab	White* and Blue
Cheng, Chiang	Txheej/Txheej	White* and Blue
Cheu, Chu	Tswb/Tswb	White and Blue
Fang, Feng	Faj/Faaj	Blue
Her, Heu, Hue, Herr	Hawj/Hawj	White and Blue
Hang, Han	Ham/Ham	Blue
Li, Ly, Lee,	Lis/Lis	White* and Blue
Lo, Lao, Lor	Lauj/Lauj	White* and Blue
Khang, Khan, Kha	Khab/Khaab	Blue
Kue, Ku,	Kwm/Kwm	Blue
Kong, Khong, Kon	Koo/Koo	White* and Blue
Moua, Mua	Muas/Muas	White and Blue
Phang, Phan	Phab/Phaab	White* and Blue
Thao, Thor, Tho	Thoj/Thoj	White and Blue
Vang, Wang, Va	Vaj/Vaaj	White and Blue
Vue, Vu, Wu	Vwj/Vwj	White
Yang, Ya	Yaj/Yaaj	White and Blue
Xiong, Song	Xyooj/Xyooj	White and Blue

*Note: *indicates the group predominantly speaks the White dialect*

Hmong individuals and the traditional costumes associated with each. However, linguistic variations exist among subgroups that help differentiate Hmong family groups and subgroups. For instance, in the large White Hmong group, there are family groups that speak Red Hmong, Black Hmong, Flower Hmong, Striped Hmong, and other slightly different dialects. In the smaller Blue Hmong group, families speak Green Hmong, Blue Hmong, Hmong Shi, Hmong Leng, and other very similar dialects. Speakers of each dialect have a distinct family ancestry and genealogical relationships.

There are more White Hmong dialects than Blue Hmong. As an example of the differences and similarities, the expression for "the future" in White Hmong is "*yam tom ntej*"; in Blue Hmong, it is "*yam pem suab.*" Linguistic differences and dialectical variations help identify specific regions of ethnic settlement in Laos. For instance, the expression for "broken" or "out of order" in White Hmong with different regional dialects is "*puas, piam, dam, tawg, ntsoog,*" or "*tsis ua hauj lwm lawm.*" All of these expressions are understood by all White Hmong, but the word "*piam*" is used mostly by White Hmong from the northern and northeastern regions of Laos.

The same word, "broken," in the Blue Hmong group is "*luv,*" "*puas,*" "*tawg,*" or "*tsis zoo lawm.*" Blue Hmong words for "butcher knife" illustrate use of dialect to identify regional subgroups. Some call a *butcher knife* "*rag*" and some call it "*tsag.*" These dialect variations pinpoint where the speaker's family settled in Laos; however, all members of Blue Hmong group use the same word for "knife": "*raab chais.*" Blue Hmong from different regions have different words for "father"—"*txiv*" or "*txwv*"—whereas most White Hmong use the same word, "*txiv.*" In everyday life, these dialectical variations do not cause communication problems and are not important; however, they are significant in identifying specific familial roots and genealogical kinship in Hmong culture and traditions. The various Hmong dialects are intelligible to all Hmong, except for the use of pragmatics in social contexts, situational registers, and dialectical slang and idioms.

From the past to the present time, Hmong have also been identified by their traditional costumes and embroidery textures. Traditional clothing is an extremely important part of Hmong life because cultural preservation is about learning, continuation, sharing, struggling for survival, and manifestation (Lessow-Hurley, 2000). Hmong manifest their culture and traditions through clothing, decoration, embroidery, songs, values, beliefs, and housing. Today, however, Hmong mix the textures and designs of their clothing so the outfits of an individual Hmong may not identify his or her true ethnic background or familial genealogy. White Hmong sometimes wear Blue Hmong skirts, pants, and shirts and vice versa.

According to Hmong legends, 12 clans of Hmong once lived in different parts of ancient China, as shown in Table 3.2. Each clan had its own tribal names, linguistic dialect, costumes, and customs, and each was concentrated in a specific geographic region (see Table 3.2). Similarly, Hmong in the West and East can be identified by the colors and designs of their clothes, their language variations, and how they refer to themselves.

As Table 3.2 indicates, the Chinese have considered the Hmong to be part of the Miao nationality according to their embroidery designs and clothing costumes. The colors used to refer to their dialects may not reflect the colors of their outfits or of their skin. In fact, many Hmong are bilingual and trilingual, speaking, for example, Chinese, White Hmong, and Blue Hmong. The Chinese habit of calling Hmong by colors such as *Hong, Hua, Bai, Hei, Huang, Han,* and *Qin* may also not reflect their true ethnic identities. The Chinese customarily use descriptive adjectives to refer to people groups. For instance, the Chinese at one time labeled Hmong as either "cooked" or "raw." The Chinese described their dynasties as *Qing* (pure), *Ming* (bright), *Yuan* (great), *Jin* (gold), *Liao* (vast), and so on in similar fashion to the way they classified the country's 56 ethnic minorities. The adjectives red, yellow, black, flowery,

Table 3.2. Eastern Hmong Clans in China

Name in Color	Name in Hmong	Tribal/Family Dialect	Self-reference	Chinese Classification	Geographic Areas
Black Hmong	Hmoob Dub	White Hmong and Blue Hmong	Black Hmong or dark skin	Hei Miao or Bai Miao	Guizhou, Guangxi, Yunan, and vicinity
Black Mu	Hmu Dub	White Mu, Black Mu, or Mu	Flower Miao, Hmong Shan	Hei Miao	Southeast Guizhou region
White Hmong	Hmoob Dawb	White Hmong and Black Hmong	White Hmong or light skin	Hei Miao and Bai Miao	West Guizhou, West Guangxi, Southeast Yunnan, and Vietnam
Yellow Hmong	Hmoob Daj	White Hmong, Yellow Hmong, and Blue Hmong	Hmong Chinese, White Hmong, Yellow Hmong	Han Miao, Huang Miao, or Pian Miao	West Guizhou, West Guangxi, Southeast Yunnan, and vicinity
Striped Hmong	Hmoob Txaij	White Hmong	White Hmong, Black Hmong, and Striped Hmong	Hei Miao	West Guizhou, Guangxi, Yunnan, and vicinity
Flower Hmong	Hmoob Phuam Paj	White Hmong and Blue Hmong	White Hmong and Blue Hmong	Hua Miao	West Guizhou, Yunnan, and vicinity
Hmong Sao	Hmoob Xauv	White Hmong and Blue Hmong	Flower Hmong, Hmong Sao	Hua Miao	Southeast Yunnan, Wenshan, and vicinity
Hmong Bia	Hmoob Npiab	White Hmong and Blue Hmong	Hmong Bia, White Hmong, and Blue Hmong	Hua Miao	Central Guizhou and vicinity
Hmong Rang	Hmoob Zag	White and Blue Hmong	Hmong Ran	Hua Miao	Central Guizhou and vicinity
Green Hmong	Hmoob Ntsuab (Qos Nom)	Blue Hmong	Blue Hmong, Hmong Sa	Qin Miao	East Guizhou and vicinity
Blue Hmong	Hmoob Lee los si Hmoob xiav (Qos Xyoob)	Blue Hmong	Blue Hmong, Hmong Sa	Qin Miao	West Huna and vicinity
Red Hmong	Hmoob Liab	White Hmong	White Hmong or white skin	Hong Tou Miao, Huang Miao, Hua Miao, Hong Miao	Guizhou, Sichuan, and vicinity

Note: Information from Mong: China History and Heritage Preservation, by Tachimeng Cha, 2013, China: China Gold Printing Group.

white, blue, and green used before the ethnic name *Miao* are merely descriptors, surface classifications, and visual identifications. Each Hmong clan had an ethnic name it used to refer to itself. Hmong have never called themselves Miao, Miaozi, or Meo.

Today in China, Hmong fall under one of these major groups: Black Hmong (*Hmoob Dub*), Red Hmong (*Hmoob Liab*), White Hmong (*Hmoob Dawb*), Green Hmong (*Hmoob Ntsuab*), and Flower Hmong (*Hmoob Paj*). Simply, in western Hmong terms, these groups are called *Hmoob Dawb, Hmoob Sib, Hmoob Peg, Hmoob Sua, Hmoob Ntsuab, Hmoob Pua*, and *Hmoob Xau*. These are broad classifications. The Green Hmong and the Blue Hmong are not religiously the same group. In the West, most Green Hmong have become Blue Hmong, and Green and Blue subgroups may speak slightly different dialects and practice different religious rites and death rituals.

The Hmong are not part of the Miao nationality; they were considered Miao by the Chinese entirely for political purposes. The Chinese lumped the Hmong in with the Miao because after civil warfare, tribal conflicts, and ethnic revolts, they wanted to eliminate the ethnonym Hmong. Therefore, any Chinese descriptive label for Hmong may be ethnically biased. The Hmong claim that originally they did not have last names but simply identified themselves by their tribal names; however, the Chinese gave them last names in an attempt to break Hmongs' ethnic bond of trust and solidarity. Whether this is true or not, the Hmong have always referred to themselves as Hmong no matter where they resided.

Impact of Wars on the Hmong

Why are there "cooked" and "raw" Hmong in history? All the domestic warfare and tribal revolts in ancient China had long-term effects on Hmong refugees and their migration history. Under the various Chinese dynasties, the Hmong fought in wars from nearly 3000 BC to the mid–1800s AD. The cooked and raw

labels were spiteful political descriptions given to Hmong by the Chinese emperors, warlords, and dictators, especially during the Ming and Qing Dynasties. They were used to distinguish between those Hmong who persisted in rebellion against the repressive Chinese rule (raw, meaning hard and resistance) and those who could be forced to assimilate into the dominant culture (cooked, suggesting softness and compliance).

In the 1600s, Hmong Chinese started migrating southward to Southeast Asia and settled in northern Vietnam, Laos, Burma, and Thailand, where they remained for a couple of centuries. Then in the late 1800s to mid–1900s, Hmong Chinese engaged in a series of civil wars in Southeast Asia, notably the French War, the Japanese War, and the Pa Chai Rebellion. From the late 1960s to the early 1970s, Hmong Chinese, known by this point as Laotian Hmong, were recruited by the U.S. to fight the communist Cold War in Laos, known as the U.S. Secret War. Under Major General Vang Pao, the Laotian Hmong constituted the Hmong special guerrilla units (SGU) in Military Region II and fought against the invasions of the communist Vietminh, the Pathet Lao or Neo Lao Hak Sat, and communist Chinese divisions in northern Laos. Hmong soldiers were trained by the Americans to fight the communist incursions and to cut off the enemy's supply line coming over the Ho Chi Minh Trail in northern Laos. The Hmong guerrillas also engaged in covert operations to help rescue downed American pilots along the Ho Chi Minh Trail.

In late 1972, the communist Vietminh concocted a plan to deceive the U.S. and enter into a peace settlement to end the fighting in Laos. The U.S. urged the prime minister of Laos to come to terms to settle the conflict pending negotiation. Once the deal was finalized, the U.S. pulled its military aid from Laos and left the Hmong guerrilla forces and the Royal Laotian Army in the hands of the communist Vietminh. In early 1973, the Laotian prime minister hastily negotiated a settlement with the communist Vietminh and blindly ordered a halt to all military actions against the enemies inside Laos. Despite the terms of the ceasefire, the communist Viet-minh continued to assist the Pathet Lao in its takeover of the country and maneuvered to overthrow the ruling Laotian king.

While communist forces were consolidating in Laos, fighting broke out in the northern regions of Laos and drove the country into more civil warfare through 1974 and 1975. Early in 1975, the prime minister of Laos ordered Major General Vang Pao, who was in the midst of fighting the communist forces, to stop his attacks against the communists in northern Laos and meet with him in Vientiane. In accordance with the terms and conditions of the settlement between Laos and the communist Vietminh, the Hmong general was replaced by a Laotian general appointed by the prime minister. The general and the prime minister got into a heated political discussion but the war was over. Laos fell into the hands of the Vietminh, the Pathet Lao, and communist China. Shortly thereafter, a new coalition government was established and chaos reigned. Because of Hmong involvement in the Secret War and their established alliance with the U.S., the communist regime vowed revenge on the Hmong, promising to extirpate the Hmong people down to their roots.

The aftermath of the wars had devastating direct impact on Laotian Hmong. Their role in the 14 years of fighting the U.S. Central Intelligence Agency's Secret War in Laos traumatically altered their sociopolitical status just as the fighting of so many civil wars and tribal revolts in ancient China had done. Both in China and in Laos, wars resulted in migration for the Hmong and periods of conflict and profound changes. The drastic changes caused by warfare created formidable obstacles, new challenges, the possibility of freedom, and opportunities for improving the quality of life. For instance, after the fall of Laos in 1975, migration to the western nations gave Laotian Hmong refugees better socioeconomic standing, challenges in adjusting to new homelands, and many opportunities for personal successes. Without the many sacrifices Hmong ancestors made over the centuries, modern Hmong would not have been in the West, realizing their hopes and pursuing the dreams their ancestors prayed and longed for thousands of years ago. Today, Hmong in the western nations are doing extremely well compared to Hmong who are still living in eastern countries. All the wars displaced the Hmong, allowing refugees to start over again, giving them the chance to save themselves, and providing them with new opportunities. Throughout Hmong history, in each episode the Hmong seem to improve their circumstances; this is especially true today of the Hmong in the western world.

Hmong in Western Nations

After the fall of Laos in 1975, nearly 140,000 Laotian Hmong refugees fled Laos to Thailand and nearly 100,000 resettled in the U.S., Canada, France, French Guyana, Australia, Argentina, and West Germany, as shown in Figure 3.2. Some reports of Laotian Hmong refugees may include some Laotian refugees (ethnic Lao, non–Hmong) as well; however, the overwhelming majority are ethnic Hmong. From 1975 to the early 1990s, most Laotian Hmong refugees resettled in the U.S., France, French Guyana, Canada, and Australia. However, as refugee camps closed

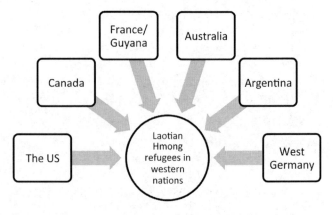

Figure 3.2. Western nations in which Laotian Hmong refugees resettled.

in the 1990s, some Laotian Hmong refugees chose to resettle in Argentina and West Germany. The exact sizes of the Hmong population in the West and the East are unknown due to a lack of statistical data and in-depth research. What is presented here is based on the best available estimates. Today, the western Hmong refugee population is growing substantially and, if the current trend continues, the Hmong population will be nearly triple its current size in the next 20 years.

Hmong in West Germany

In the 1990s, the plight of Hmong refugees became uncertain because Thailand was closing its refugee camps. Pressure was mounting on camp inmates to find places to go. A very small number of Laotian Hmong refugees had chosen to resettle in West Germany in the late 1980s and early 1990s and presumably they are still living in that country today. In the early 1990s fewer than 10 Laotian Hmong families, about 25 people in total, went to West Germany. Some believe these families left West Germany to join other Hmong refugees in France, the U.S., and elsewhere in the late 1990s to early 2000s. Based on information gathered in 2010, the best estimate of the number of Laotian Hmong refugees living in West Germany is fewer than 450 people.

Hmong in Argentina

Similarly, in the early 1990s, another very small group of Laotian Hmong refugees, facing imminent deportation due to Thailand's repatriation policy, chose to move to Argentina as their new homeland. According to relatives of these people in the West, about eight families resettled in Argentina and in the early 2000s some of them moved again to join other Hmong refugees in the U.S., France, or French Guyana. Recent Hmong refugees coming from France say that most Hmong families in Argentina who migrated to French Guyana did so because they wanted the freedom to engage in an agrarian lifestyle. Some of the families still living in Argentina say they plan to relocate to either France or the U.S. in the near future. Today the Hmong refugee population in Argentina is about 350.

Hmong in Australia

At the fall of Laos in 1975, nearly a dozen Laotian students were studying in Australia; only a few were Hmong. When Laos fell into the hands of the communist Vietminh, those Laotian Hmong students remained abroad and later reunited with their families and loved ones. From 1975 to the mid–1980s, a very small number of Laotian Hmong refugees in Thailand chose to go to Australia. Today the Hmong refugee population in Australia is relatively small as compared to the Laotian refugee population. In 1988, there were about 400 Hmong refugees in Australia. In 2013, the number was approximately 2,000 and growing.

Hmong in Canada

From 1975 to the mid–1990s, a small group of Laotian Hmong refugees resettled in Canada. The Hmong refugees chose Canada because its people speak French as well as English. In the early 1990s, the Hmong population in Canada was 700; however, in the mid–1990s some families migrated to the U.S. In the late 1980s to the early 1990s, a few Hmong families came from France to live in Canada temporarily before resettling in the U.S. Today, there are approximately 500 Hmong refugees living in Canada.

Hmong in France and French Guyana

The Hmong call the French *Fab Kis*. Throughout their history in Indochina, the French and the Hmong were uneasy allies. Between 1975 and 1990, the second largest group of Laotian Hmong refugees resettled in France and French Guyana. Prior to the fall of Laos in 1975, a few Hmong students were studying in France and they remained there after the war. The French resettlement program helped reunite them with their families and loved ones. Former Hmong students trained by French missionaries in Laos and former military and high ranking Laotian Hmong officials who had worked with the French chose France as their new homeland because of their familiarity with the French from the French occupation of Indochina.

In the early 1990s, there were approximately 7,000 Hmong refugees living in France and French Guyana. Of that number, a few hundred people lived in the villages of Javouley and Cacao in French Guyana. Today the Hmong refugee population in France has grown to approximately 15,000 and about 3,000 Hmong refugees live in the solitude of French Guyana. Before the second migration in the western nations, the number of Hmong refugees in France and French Guyana was much higher than at present. In the late 1980s to the late 1990s, a substantial number of Hmong refugees migrated from France to the U.S. for sociopolitical and socioeconomic reasons; however, a few Hmong French families returned to France.

Hmong in the United States of America

Of all the western nations, the country with the largest group of Laotian Hmong refugees is the United States. In the late 1980s, approximately 75,000 Hmong refugees arrived in the U.S. and by the mid–1990s, nearly 100,000 Hmong refugees made the U.S. their new homeland. In the early 2000s, the Hmong population increased to nearly 120,000. In 2005, the last group of nearly 15,000 Hmong refugees was resettled in the U.S. Today, census figures show that approximately 260,000 Hmong live in the U.S. However, some educators believe the actual number of Hmong refugees in the U.S. is nearly 300,000 because many Hmong refugees did not take part in the national censuses in 2000 and 2010. If that number is correct, the number of U.S. Hmong refugees has nearly tripled in just four decades. The U.S. Hmong population is concentrated in three states: California, Minnesota, and Wisconsin. The largest Hmong

communities are located in 12 metropolitan areas: St. Paul, Minnesota; Fresno, Sacramento, Merced, Chico, and Stockton, California; Milwaukee, Wausau, and Madison, Wisconsin; and Hickory, Lenoir, and Morganton, North Carolina. The U.S. not only has the largest Hmong population in the West but also has the most prosperous Hmong individuals and communities in the world. If it had not been for their involvement in the U.S. Secret War in Laos, Hmong refugees would not be in the U.S. As promised, the U.S. gave the Hmong a chance to save themselves and start life over again.

Hmong refugees in western nations strive for sociopolitical and socioeconomic successes. However, the different western nations do not offer the same opportunities to Hmong refugees. Of all, the U.S. offers the best opportunities for Hmong refugees. The availability of socioeconomic opportunities in the U.S. has attracted thousands of Hmong refugees worldwide. During the second migration in the West, the vast majority of Hmong refugees moved to the U.S., primarily seeking the advantages of public education and the possibilities of economic advancement in private businesses, farming, home ownership, and blue-collar jobs. If current trends hold, the number of Hmong in the western nations will nearly double in 10 years (see Figure 3.3). Although the total Hmong

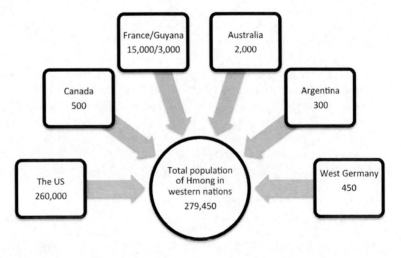

Figure 3.3. Numbers of Hmong refugees in Western nations.

population in the western nations is approximately 280,000, this figure is relatively small compared to the total number of Hmong living in eastern countries.

Hmong in Eastern Countries

As mentioned earlier, the Hmong originated in China; their history can be traced to about 3000 BC. Over the last two centuries the Hmong have been confused with other ethnic groups such as Miao, Meo, Miaozi, Meng, Mu, Man, and Hmu, largely because China did not recognize the Hmong as a distinct ethnic group. Nevertheless, as Cha (2013) explained, the Hmong are not Miao although the two groups may be closely related ethnically. The Hmong migrated from China prior to and during the Spring and Autumn era (770–476 BC) and the Warring States period (575–221 BC). After each civil war of those times, the Hmong dispersed in different directions, scattered throughout the warring regions, and migrated southward toward Southeast Asia. As of today, the world's largest concentrations of Hmong remain in the eastern nations of China, Vietnam, Laos, Thailand, and Myanmar (formerly Burma), as shown in Figure 3.4. The eastern Hmong population would be considerably larger than its current size if not for heavy Hmong casualties in the many wars in China and Southeast Asia and the continual political persecutions inflicted by Chinese and communist regimes.

Over several centuries of their residence in China, the Hmong took part in many civil wars and tribal revolts, and after each war or uprising ended, the Hmong were oppressed and persecuted by the imperial Chinese rulers and dictators. The Chinese vowed to go after Hmong rebels, and they hunted them down and slaughtered them to near extinction. In Hmong oral history, the Red Chinese (*Suav Liab*) were their worst enemies. Fear of the Chinese caused the Hmong to scatter over the various Chinese states and eventually to migrate southward in search of new land and freedom. As early as the 1600s, Hmong Chinese were slipping through the southern regions of China into the Southeast Asian countries of Burma, Vietnam, Laos, and Thailand. In some parts of Southeast Asia, the Hmong are not considered war-displaced refugees because they have been living in those lands for hundreds of years; they have enjoyed independence and freedom and have become part of those countries. In other parts, however, the Hmong have not been officially recognized as natural citizens and are therefore considered indigenous tribal people.

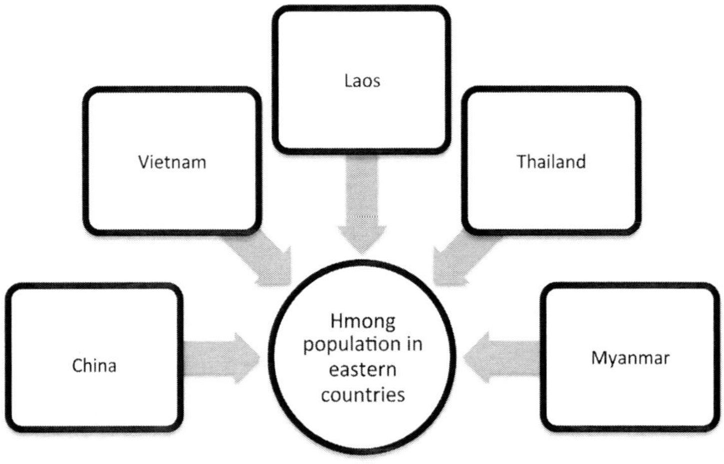

Hmong in Myanmar (Formerly Burma)

A small group of Hmong live in Myanmar, formerly known as Burma. As nomadic tribal people, Hmong Chinese refugees from the regions of Yunnan, Sichuan, Guizhou, and Guangxi found refuge in the highlands of Burma in the early 1700s; their descendants have continued to live in the north and northeastern regions bordering southwestern China and northwestern

Figure 3.4. Eastern countries with large Hmong populations.

Vietnam. The Hmong Burmese population is relatively small because the majority of Hmong people continued to migrate to Vietnam, Laos, and elsewhere. According to Hmong legends, some early settlers in northern Burma returned to live in the southern regions of China and others adopted the host culture and assimilated into Burmese society. Today, an estimated 4,500 Hmong live in Burma; this is the smallest Hmong population in Southeast Asia. Some scholars believe the Hmong Burmese population is larger than the estimated number, closer to 10,000 people or more.

Hmong in Vietnam

Like Burma, Vietnam is located on the south and southwestern border of China. Hmong Chinese fleeing the central and southern regions of China—Yunnan, Guangxi, Guangdong, Hunan, Guizhou, Sichuan, Hubei, and Shaanxi—could have made it to northern Vietnam in the 1600s and found refuge in the mountains bordering China, Burma, and Laos. According to Hmong legends, Hmong Chinese lived there for a few centuries before gradually migrating to Laos and Thailand in the late 1700s. Some actually returned to south China years later. Hmong ancestors say that some Hmong Chinese settled in the northern regions of Vietnam bordering Burma and Laos before moving into northern Laos. Various accounts of Hmong migration history from China suggest that pioneer groups of Hmong Chinese refugees first settled in northern Vietnam and from there migrated westward to Burma and southward to northern Laos in search of good farmland instead of the cold, rainy, foggy, and misty weather conditions of the highland regions.

Today, north and northwestern Vietnam are home to nearly 1,000,000 Hmong Vietnamese, the second largest Hmong population in Southeast Asia. Hmong Vietnamese spread over the region and are found in the cities of Lai Chau, Lao Cai, Lao Pachy, Hoang Su Phi, Ha Giang, Cao Bang, and Dong Khe. Some Laotian Hmong and Hmong Vietnamese share bloodline kinship and family relatives. In 1975, some Laotian Hmong families reunited with long lost relatives in Vietnam. Also, many Hmong Vietnamese communist soldiers found their blood relatives in Laos.

Hmong in Laos

Along with Burma and Vietnam, Laos became the new homeland for Hmong Chinese refugees from south and central China. In the 1700s, Hmong Chinese refugees migrated from China, Burma, and northern Vietnam and settled in the northern region of Laos. The very first region of settlement was Nong Het (*Looj Hej*). According to Hmong legends, Hmong loved the dense forests and beautiful highland mountains in the Nong Het region because they believed the weather and soil there would be good for farming.

Once Hmong chieftains and kiatongs discovered northern Laos, thousands of Hmong Chinese refugees poured into the region. By the mid–1800s or early 1900s, Hmong Chinese occupied many areas in northern Laos including Nong Het, Sam Neu, Viengsay, Bouam Long, Luang Prabang, Xieng Khouang, Phonsavan, and the Plain of Jars. During the second Indochina civil war, between 1960 and 1975, these regions became Military Regions I and II for the Hmong guerrilla forces. By the mid–1900s, Hmong also lived in regions farther south: Sam Thong, Long Cheng, Pha Khao, Muang Cha, Muang Om, Muang Kassi, Nasu, and Ban Sorn. After the fall of Laos in 1975, nearly 120,000 Hmong left communist Laos for Thailand and later resettled in the western nations.

Today, Laos has the third largest Hmong population in Southeast Asia; the best available estimate is approximately 400,000. If ongoing political oppression of ethnic Hmong had not driven them out, the Laotian Hmong population in Laos would be much larger than the present number. After the Secret War ended in 1975, Hmong were spread throughout the country. Some large Laotian Hmong villages and communities are located in northern cities such as Bokeo, Phongsaly, Sam Neu, Xieng Khouang, Oudomxay, Luang Prabang, Sayaboury, Vientiane, Muang Kassi, and Borikhamxay. However, many Hmong farming families still live in small towns and villages in secluded areas in the highlands. The migration from Laos to Thailand after 1975 has reduced the size of the Laotian Hmong population in Laos.

Hmong in Thailand

The last country in Southeast Asia to have a sizable Hmong population is Thailand. In the mid–1700s to the early 1800s, some Hmong Chinese migrated across Burma, Vietnam, and Laos to settle in the northern regions of Thailand. The pioneer groups of Hmong appeared to be relatively small as compared to those that settled in Vietnam and Laos. However, during the first and second Indochina wars more Hmong Chinese refugees migrated from Burma, Vietnam, and Laos to Thailand. By the early 1900s, thousands of Hmong lived along the northwestern region of Thailand bordering southwestern Laos. Hmong living in Sayaboury and Luang Prabang often migrated across the Thai-Lao border before and after the fall of Laos in 1975. The Hmong population in Thailand increased dramatically after 1975 because Laotian Hmong refugees crossed the Mekong River to join their relatives in secluded regions instead of settling in the refugee camps.

By the late 1900s, Thailand had nearly 80,000 Hmong living in the northern highland mountains, especially in Chiang Mai Province. During the closure and demolition of the refugee camps in the 1990s, some Hmong sought refuge in Hmong Thai villages. Others went to Wat Thamkrabot and later resettled in the West. Today, the Hmong Thai population is estimated at approximately 155,000, making Thailand home to the fourth largest Hmong population in Southeast Asia. Hmong Thai are concentrated in northern and northeastern regions, in cities such as Chiang Mai, Chiang Rai, Nan, Loei, Tak, and Phetchabun. The Hmong Thai population will continue to include Laotian Hmong refugees until the political oppression and persecution inside Laos ends; until then, Laotian Hmong will continue to flee the communist regime in Laos, coming to Thailand for safe haven.

Hmong in China

The country with the world's largest Hmong population is China. The Hmong originated in central China near the Yangtze and Yellow River basins at least as early as 3000 BC. The Hmong were a people in central China before the Xia Dynasty; they lived in the Jiuli Kingdom ruled by ChiYou, also known as the Red Cloud, the Beast, the Magical Warrior, the Hmong King, and the King of Many Tribes. After the Han Chinese defeated and assassinated ChiYou, the Hmong scattered throughout the warring states and eventually migrated southward. The Hmong lived in desolate and barren hills and were persecuted and oppressed by the imperial Chinese warlords. After about 1,000 years, the Hmong reestablished themselves and found the San Miao Kingdom. However, they continued to struggle for freedom in the midst of many wars. Historically, because the Hmong were poor, oppressed, and persecuted, they longed for freedom and fought many civil wars in China all the way into the late Ming and Qing Dynasties. As Hmong Chinese legends relate, the Hmong were hunted down by the Chinese, marked for extinction. On more than one occasion, the Hmong came close to extermination.

But they survived in China as they would survive later in Laos. Today, an estimated 4 million Hmong live in China. Taking the Miao and Hmong together, the total population of these two closely related groups in China is about 8 million people. Large Hmong Chinese communities can be found in Yunnan, Guangxi, Guangdong, Hunan, Guizhou, Sichuan, Hubei, and Shaanxi. The Hmong have a long and deep history in China even though the ethnonym Hmong is still unrecognized by the Chinese.

Nearly four decades after the Secret War in Laos, the number of Hmong in the world has grown substantially. According to the best available estimates, as shown in Figure 3.5, the number of Hmong in Southeast Asia and China is over 5.3 million people. Moreover, adding western and eastern Hmong populations together yields a total of approximately 6.1 million Hmong in the world today without counting the Miao population. If the Miao are included, the worldwide Miao-Hmong population is nearly 9 million people.

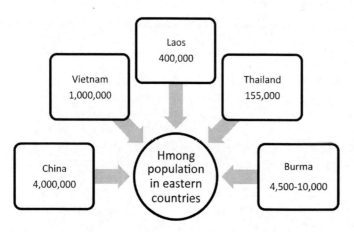

Figure 3.5. Hmong populations in Eastern countries.

Hmong Adjustment to Resettlement

A Chinese fortune cookie says, "Versatility is one of your outstanding traits." This is true for Hmong refugees. The struggle for survival has always been part of Hmong life, in the ancient world and in the modern world. Today, millions of Hmong refugees living in western and eastern nations are still struggling with cultural and social changes. The traditional nomadic way of Hmong life encompasses trials and tribulations through transitions and transformations. Change is always accompanied by conflict, disappointment, rejection, acceptance, challenges, opportunities, and progress; ultimately it can end in success. Hmong leaders in Laos, notably Chao Quang Lo, Pa Chai Vue, Moua Chong Kai, Lo Blia Yao, Ly Chia Fong, Touby Lyfong, and Major General Vang Pao, sacrificed much to transform the lives and sociopolitical status of the Hmong. Some circumstances, such as living in a new environment, not only gave Hmong challenges, but also

made them vulnerable to retaliation, insults, humiliation, and shame. After the fall of Laos, attempts were made to completely annihilate the Hmong.

As migrant war-displaced refugees, Hmong have learned to adapt to the world around them and they are resilient; they have survived in different environments in different parts of the world. Understanding the versatility that has made Hmong survival possible, the resiliency of the Hmong, and their sociopolitical adaptations requires an appreciation of the many struggles Hmong refugees endured over centuries. The Hmong have made great sacrifices to secure a better future for their offspring. As Hmong say in their language, *"Muab roj muab ntsav tiv thaiv lub teb lub chaw kom tau txais kev muaj yeej thiab vammeej."* Simply, Hmong made life sacrifices because Hmong always want to be free and independent.

Throughout Hmong history, dating back to around 3000 BC, Hmong refugees were often oppressed and persecuted. Both enemies and allies sought to destroy and exploit them because Hmong oftentimes were on both sides of conflicts; some Hmong fought against particular governments and others served as mercenary soldiers for those same governments. In diaspora, Hmong faced a myriad of hardships, including mistreatment, malnutrition, starvation, imprisonment, torture, brutality, rape, and murder. Hmong refugees have internalized their resentments, pain, and suffering and continue to hope for a better future. Their resettlement in the West came with new challenges of adaptation and survival amid chaos, crises, hopes, dreams, and fears.

In addition to more pressing issues of survival, Hmong refugees resettling in the eastern and western nations face language and cultural barriers. Today, many Hmong refugees living in different parts of the world cannot speak the language of the host nation fluently, although their children born in the host countries who have been acculturated can. Prior to 1975, approximately 10 percent of the Hmong population could read and write in the Hmong language or another language such as Lao, Thai, French, or English. In the western nations, hundreds of thousands of Hmong refugees have had to learn a new language at their new jobs. U.S. Hmong refugees of the first and second waves learned survival English through on-the-job training in English skills. Like many other war refugee groups, the Hmong have managed to overcome cultural pressures and social predicaments through hard work, perseverance, adaptation, acculturation, integration, tolerance, and patience. A versatile attitude has enabled Hmong refugees to adapt well to their resettlements in different environments. In Laos, at first many Hmong feared living in lowland regions because they did not know if their immune systems could fight the diseases (malaria, pneumonia, hepatitis, measles, chicken pox, cancer, and so on) and viruses (flu, cold, fever, cough, sinus, allergy, and so on) they would encounter there. However, since 1975 Hmong refugees have learned to survive in any inhabitable environment. Even in French Guyana, where the land was considered inhospitable due to infertility, insects, plagues, and bad weather, Hmong refugees were able to clear the thick rainforest, build houses, and coax crops from the fields. The relatively isolated setting allowed Hmong to continue their agrarian pursuits, their culture and traditions, and their traditional way of life without being expected to assimilate into western culture.

Adapting to a new environment is not easy and developing skills for living cross-culturally takes time. The Hmong refugees had to work hard and overcome many obstacles to achieve success in their new homelands. They had to navigate the 10 common stages of the socialization processes Vang (2010) described that most newcomers experience when making cultural and social adaptations as they adjust to life in a new country. These stages do not always follow the same order—they vary according to individual persons and

families and the degree of difference between old and new cultures—but they are typical of all people moving from one society to another.

First is the *arrival* stage. When they came to their new environment, Hmong refugees went through a honeymoon period but also experienced shock and flashbacks. Hmong refugee parents and children explored, discovered, and learned about their new environment, its culture, traditions, and people. At the arrival stage, newcomers are either pleased or unhappy to be in the new place. They have come for different reasons, some for refuge from persecution and oppression and some for personal ambitions; they all adjust differently and accordingly. Conflicts are inevitable, but tolerance and patience have helped the Hmong survive for centuries and tolerance and endurance have given them the courage to adapt to the new environment.

The second stage is the *family reunification* stage, which is actually part of the arrival stage. This stage gives the arrival stage a different feeling for those who have family members already in the new country. The new arrivals are usually happy to see their parents, children, or other family members after a time of separation; they want to enjoy one another and start celebrating. For many, there is no family already in the country with which to reunite. Of course, adults and children experience this stage differently. Some adults have more difficulty adjusting to the new environment than children. Children adapt to a new way of life much more quickly. Sometimes children adjust without expressing or exhibiting any personal feelings. Young people become integrated into the host nation and assimilated into the host culture much more easily than older people. Hmong refugees are almost never alone as one person or even one family. Hmong have always believed that one living in solitude may not survive, but even a few, if together, can survive anything. For the most part, family reunification strengthens the resettlement process and eases the adjustment to the new environment. The strength that is in the group is the rationale behind the second migration in the West;

Hmong refugees prefer to live in villages or communities with other Hmong.

The third stage is the *culture shock* stage. Upon arrival, Hmong refugee parents and children almost immediately encounter both positive and negative events as they learn and misunderstand, like and dislike, trust and mistrust what they see in the new environment. Culture shock can result in feelings of discomfort, personal guilt, embarrassment, shame, humiliation, and devastation. Some of the new events appear as serious threats. For example, the U.S. Hmong refugees who experienced Halloween with its practice of trick or treating were terrified. They had not been told about the custom, and it led them to believe there were ghosts in America. On the other hand, those who arrived in the month of December were very happy when they received many gifts from friends, family members, and of course, the American Santa Claus. In Southeast Asia, Hmong refugees and immigrants had experienced rejection, hatred, stereotyping, and opposition from tribal people who occupied the land before they arrived. In the West, Hmong refugees also encountered racism, stereotyping, prejudice, bias, discrimination, and rejection. However, overt expressions of these social injustices were limited because they were prohibited by law in the West.

Fourth comes the *blaming* stage. Hmong refugees came to their new homelands because of warfare. It is common to assign blame for the loss of lives, land, country, family members, homes, livestock, and family wealth. The Hmong refugees had plenty of places to lay the blame: the Chinese rulers and dictators, the French brutal colonial policy, the Secret War in Laos, and the bloodthirsty Laotian communists. The Hmong refugees could also blame themselves for not helping one another as they fought their enemies or for their disunity and betrayal. The feeling of blame that accompanies learning to cope with social and cultural pressures is a gut feeling. Parents must figure out how to deal with the clash of values, seeing their children become assimilated, the inability to communicate in the host nation's language, and

health problems related to post-traumatic stress disorders. The blaming stage sometimes lasts a long time. Today, Hmong refugees still use blame to ease their frustrations, anxieties, and discontent when they face challenges in the new environment.

The fifth stage is the *coping* stage. Once situated in a new homeland, newcomers must learn to deal with new situations, adjusting, accommodating, and adapting. In the western nations, unlike in Laos, both parents often have to work outside the home to provide financial support for the family. Gender roles are different from what they were traditionally, and children are enrolled in school to learn a new language. Issues that surfaced in the first four stages are now reality, and Hmong refugee parents must cope with these realities in everyday life. Children emulate their parents at home while imitating their peers outside the home. Communication between parents and children can be strained as younger children lose their native language and older children attempt to balance two cultures simultaneously. Even if some mixture of languages, values, and communication were possible, maintaining a dual rather than a divided life is quite challenging for young people. For instance, some Latino children speak "Spanglish" (a mixture of Spanish and English) and some Hmong children speak "Hmonglish" (a mixture of Hmong and English). In reality, parents must learn the host country's language as well as possible to maintain warm communication between family members. However, some parents are unable to learn the new language and adapt to the new environment accordingly because of their ages, stubborn attitudes, or unwillingness to change. In the eastern countries where Hmong refugees have resettled, most of the refugees have continued their nomadic and agrarian lifestyle without being integrated and acculturated, and for the most part, they live in seclusion in the highland mountains where accessibility to the modern world is virtually impossible. In order to gain access to the quality of life that is available through the education and employment opportunities of the new homeland, Hmong

children must learn how to cope with the realities of the new country.

After coping is the *accommodation* stage.
To survive in the new homeland, Hmong
refugees learn to accommodate the differences in the two cultures and parents and
children figure out how to adapt to differences between them caused by different levels of acceptance of the new culture. The
accommodations must be made by both children and parents. However, accommodation
can be made voluntarily or involuntarily. For
instance, the U.S. Hmong parents may slowly
change the food menu at home to accommodate their native-born children who are used
to the food served at school and are less inclined to eat traditional Hmong dishes at
home. Hmong parents learn to hug, kiss, and
comfort their children physically and publicly. They find that celebration of birthdays,
Mother's Day, Father's Day, and Christmas,
for example, brings joy to all the family members. In the accommodation stage, newcomers appreciate and embrace aspects of the
new culture. Other aspects, however, Hmong
refugees may completely reject based on personal values and religious beliefs. For example, some U.S. Hmong refugees refuse to send
their single daughters away to attend college,
and some Hmong refuse to accept interracial
marriage between certain races. In eastern
countries, Hmong refugees learn to accommodate imperial rule and colonial control;
in the West, Hmong learn to accommodate
the law and the court system. Therefore, in
the new environment, Hmong refugees gradually learn to modify their life situations to
accommodate the new influences and changes
such as working, schooling, childrearing,
parenting, socializing, adapting, and accepting.

The seventh stage is the *mixture* stage.
Hmong refugee parents and children let go
of some cultural practices and retain others
as they learn to accept some of the ideals and
values of the new environment. Parents want
their children to preserve the family's values
embodied in marriage customs, funeral services, religious rituals, cultural ceremonies,
and social structures such as a clan system,

group cohesiveness, collectivism, and respect
for elders. Children want their parents to understand the new social phenomena, including curfews, expectations of others on them,
social temptations, and adolescent courtship.
Most parents realize their children will fall
behind if they are expected to fulfill some of
their traditional roles, which may involve
strict performance of household chores, heavy
family responsibilities, and limited parent/
child interaction at home. Both parents and
children acculturate at home first before ven-
turing to live in the new culture outside the
home. However, each family is different, and
acculturation occurs at different paces. As
expressed in Hmong terms, "*Nyob luag ntuj
ces yoog luag txuj, nyob luag av ces yoog luag
kav, nyob luag chaw ces yoog kom luag tsawg.*"
This implies that Hmong must adjust to the
new environment, to the rules of the land,
and to the model fitted that of the host culture. In some instances, interracial marriage
may take place, but Hmong refugees have
been intentional in relocating their families
to be in a Hmong community where Hmong
children are likely to marry their Hmong
friends. Becoming assimilated is part of
everyday life, and drastic changes occur each
and every day, such as being involved in
gangs, having a dual-life approach, becoming
bilingual, and understanding cultural diversity.

The eighth stage is *acceptance*. Resettling
in a new homeland, Hmong refugees face a
tough choice: Love it or leave it. Most accept
the reality of their plight and learn to survive.
Especially in the West, Hmong refugee parents and children eventually enter a comfort
zone. Open communication is likely to take
place at home. Some of the traditional barriers between parents and children are removed although certain limitations and restrictions remain. But for the most part,
parents and children embrace new views and
new family roles. The new value system
brought home by the children is not viewed
as odd or as an external pressure. Many U.S.
Hmong Americans acknowledge that learning to adjust to the values of the mainstream
society brings economic as well as educa-

tional opportunities. They see education as the key to success. Parents who stubbornly demand adherence to old ways see their children lagging behind or moving away from them. In this stage, parents show more interest in their children's education, social development, and goals. As Vang (2010) noted, many parents encourage their children to aim high to achieve their personal goals and some of the characteristics of this stage are presented in Figure 3.6. Acceptance helps Hmong refugees cope with the new environment through understanding, appreciation, and accommodation.

Positive Interdependence	Promotive Interaction	Positive Relationships
Having feeling toward others	Promoting self-pride, self-concept, self-image, self-esteem	Realistic expectations and objectives, attainable goals
⇩	⇩	⇩
Engaging in frequent and open communication	Empowering productivity, success, and achievement	Maintaining positive communication with others
⇩	⇩	⇩
Understanding different perspectives	Aware of bias, prejudice, racism, stereotypes	Embracing differences through accommodation
⇩	⇩	⇩
Interpersonal attraction	Pluralism	Cultural diversity

Figure 3.6. Characteristics of acceptance.

The ninth stage is the *rejection* stage in which newcomers decide which elements of their past they no longer wish to retain. Like any other people, Hmong refugees reject some of their traditions as unworkable in the new environment. Hmong parents and children compromise, rejecting certain attitudes, traits, social norms, and customs they view as inappropriate in the new homeland. For instance, the U.S. Hmong Americans reject the traditional method of determining the value of daughters and sons expressed in the old cliché "Nine moons will equal a sun" (which means nine daughters are equal in value to one son), or as expressed in the Hmong language, "*Cuaj lub hli tsis zoo npaum li ib lub hnub, cuaj leeg ntxhais tsis zoo npaum li ib leeg tub.*" This rejection fosters a positive attitude toward both female and male children, declaring they deserve equal economic opportunities and success. Similarly, Hmong children reject the traditional view that females should get married young and stay home to rear their children. Instead, Hmong girls break away from their traditional gender roles to pursue higher education and become professionals who work outside the home. In some families, wives are the primary wage earners. However, regardless of status or educational level, most Hmong still adamantly reject the notion of a gay or lesbian lifestyle. Why? They believe this lifestyle is the worst curse a person could have. However, this belief may change in time. According to Vang (2010), Hmong parents initially resisted drastic change and some of the characteristics of the rejection stage are shown in Figure 3.7. Rejection could be based on personal values and religious beliefs as well as ignorance, such as personal bias or prejudice toward others. Sometimes rejection plays a part in the quality of a person's life. For example, subscribing to the same religious faith for all family members to practice instead of allowing different members to adopt different religions helps keep the family structure intact.

The final stage is the *maintenance* stage, which refers to maintenance of cultural identity. Throughout the centuries, Hmong refugees have adjusted to new environments and new countries by adapting and acculturating, but not assimilating. The Hmong have kept their culture and traditions alive, without full assimilation, enriching and accom-

No Interdependence		Oppositional Interaction		Negative Relationships
Little or no communication		Monopolistic views		Unrealistic expectations
⇩		⇩		⇩
Egocentric attitudes		Low self-concept and self-esteem		Lack of communication
⇩		⇩		⇩
Resistance to influence		Lack of cross-cultural experience		Blaming and scapegoating

Figure 3.7. Characteristics of rejection.

modating the mainstream society's values to a large extent while at the same time preserving their own culture and traditions. In a diverse society, each cultural group can maintain its own cultural heritage in a number of ways. People of a cultural group who share a common belief system can congregate to worship in a well-established setting. Cultural groups can hold commemorative celebrations, honor special holidays, and organize family gatherings.

For the most part, Hmong refugees who are now living in about a dozen nations on earth have successfully gone through these socialization stages more than once in their migration journeys. However, in some environments some Hmong are no longer holding in the maintenance state because they do not have a cultural center to educate their Hmong offspring about their heritage. The U.S. Hmong refugees have found ways to maintain their culture and traditions in their children. They believe teaching the native language is one way of maintaining culture. Hmong Americans offer special classes to young children that explain Hmong traditional rituals and customs. In church, Hmong parents and children learn how to read and write the Hmong language as part of their Bible study. The Hmong community holds New Year's celebrations each year to expose the young generation to Hmong traditional values and customs. Each cultural group has its own way of maintaining itself. Maintaining a culture requires persistent effort in order to keep up with social changes

and to bridge the generation gap. Cultural maintenance has global implications for all Hmong refugees living in different countries.

In some Eastern countries, the war-displaced Hmong refugees are still oppressed and persecuted, but their resilience has been remarkable. In China, the largest concentration of Hmong is still thriving and increasing in the desolate highland mountains and barren hills. In the West, the Hmong population has grown exponentially in nearly four decades despite difficult challenges and obstacles. At present, the Hmong are transforming themselves socioeconomically while living in two separate worlds, the East and the West. The two groups do not have the same challenges or face the same obstacles, nor do they have the same opportunities. However, they are connected culturally, and the Hmong refugees are likely to continue to struggle as they turn their current socioeconomic opportunities into successes today and beyond. Hmong refugees have come a long way and will continue to make progress throughout the 21st century.

Hmong Today and Beyond

Today's Hmong are making remarkable progress in the Western nations as well as in other parts of the world. Many have become more or less self-sufficient and the current socioeconomic trends look promising. Generally, Hmong now can be classified into three-tier stratum: *The college-educated, the high school–educated, and the non-educated or traditional.* Hmong refugees long for the day when their children can fulfill the parents' dreams, honoring all the sacrifices their parents, grandparents, and great grandpar-

ents made for them. They look forward to
the day Hmong children are living in prosperity and peace with the pride and freedom
their ancestors hoped for so long ago. Resettlement in the West has enabled the Hmong
to transform themselves into an industrial
society. Although life is very different for the
Hmong living in the East and the Hmong living in the West, modern Hmong life is far
more advanced in both worlds than four
decades ago. Still, Hmong continue to cope
with complex cultural and social changes in
employment, family structure, home ownership, economic growth, and education.

Hmong Social Classes

Hmong families have gone through at least
four major periods of socioeconomic transformation since they first arrived in the West.
The first is called the *resettlement and entitlement* period (1975 to 1985). As newly arrived refugees, Hmong were extremely poor
and went through a series of culture shock
while they resettled in different western nations to start a new life all over again. In the
U.S., Hmong had to scrimp to make ends
meet. Most were recipients of entitlement
programs and depended on the pittance of
public assistance for socioeconomic survival.
The second is called the *emergent and incipient* period (1986 to 1995). After the first ten
years, Hmong refugees adjusted slowly but
accordingly and realized about their socioeconomic challenges and opportunities in the
West. In the U.S., most started searching for
alternatives to help them make socioeconomic adjustments to accommodate their
needs and wants in order to achieve progresses and successes. Hmong parents employed in blue-collar jobs to provide financial
support for their large families. Only few educated Hmong worked in white-collar jobs.
During this time, a large numbers of Hmong
refugee children enrolled in public schools.
Fresno had one of the largest groups of
Hmong refugee children in its schools. Many
Hmong children also graduated from high
schools and colleges. The working class
Hmong families emerged during this period.
The third is called the *transitional and*

transformational period (1996 to 2005). At-
taining high school diplomas and college degrees, Hmong were able to secure good-paying blue-collar and white-collar jobs in the
public and private sectors. Hmong adults
learned and improved their survival English
skills and many became self-employed and
small business entrepreneurs in the community. Working Hmong families were qualified
to purchase their first homes and moved
their families from the ghettos to the middle
and upper class neighborhoods. By the mid–
2000s, Hmong have not only been accustomed to the western values and ideals but
have become westernized in some ways. This
period was the turning point in Hmong socioeconomic progresses and also marked the
improvement of Hmong socioeconomic status because of the growth of Hmong home
ownership. More importantly, it was a socioeconomic transitional period for Hmong
in the West, especially in the U.S., because
a great number of Hmong professionals
emerged and entered various professional
fields such as law, business, social work,
teaching profession, medical, auto mechanics, and agriculture. Educational attainments
played a pivotal role in Hmong socioeconomic growth and helped transform Hmong
way of life socioeconomically.

The last is the *advanced and mainstream*
period (2006 to beyond), or the current socioeconomic status of Hmong refugees in the
West, especially in the U.S. At present, Hmong
are making remarkable progresses in many
areas but still need help in other aspects of
life. Hmong are now native-born Americans.
Many Hmong parents are naturalized citizens. As new Americans, most embrace and
believe in American values and ideals and
are working diligently hard to pursue the
American Dream. With good education,
Hmong-Americans believe they can enhance
and advance their current life situations. The
number of Hmong college students continues to climb, so does the number of Hmong
college graduates. Hmong professionals are
increasingly growing, so do Hmong businesses in general. Overall, Hmong refugees
have achieved remarkable socioeconomic

successes in life since 1975. Like other Americans, socioeconomic opportunities also shape Hmong way of life. Some are enculturated while others are assimilated into American society. Many still undergo acculturation and integration without assimilation processes. Elders and Hmong parents are stranded between the two worlds. Hmong-Americans are divided along socioeconomic lines and belong to different social classes.

In the West, there is still limited research data on Hmong social classes; however, in the U.S., Hmong families can be categorized and classified socioeconomically based on their different social lifestyles in the Hmong communities. Like other American immigrants and refugees, typically, Hmong have upper, middle, and poor classes. Ethnically, Hmong-Americans can be stratified into three major classes: The *professional class* (Hmong families work in white-collar jobs), the *working poor class* (Hmong families work in blue-collar jobs), and the *unemployed class* (Hmong families depend on public assistance programs). Back in 1975, Hmong refugees belonged to the underclass because they had no asset. Today, four decades later, the family income gap between Hmong families is rising and wide; however, their lifestyles are similarly identical even if their levels of self-sufficiency may be different.

These broad categories may not be inclusive representation of all western Hmong but provide some insights into the understanding of their current socioeconomic status. Hmong communities and social classes are complex in nature because of their organizations and structures. In the U.S., Hmong are living among other ethnic groups in metropolitan areas. The saturated living situations scatter Hmong social classes throughout the city and county. Hmong clan systems play a major role in Hmong social classes and sociocultural structures that keep Hmong families together as a community. Hmong communities are made of different Hmong families, groups, tribes, or clans. Therefore, traditionally, Hmong social classes can be recognized or identified through familial structures: The family leader (*tus coj tsev neeg* in Hmong),

the group leader (*tus coj pawg kwvtij* in Hmong), the clan club leader (*tus coj pab kwvtij* in Hmong), the clan leader (*tus nre xeem* in Hmong), and the leader of clan elders (*tus thawj coj sawv daws* in Hmong). In the Hmong world, the title, rank, fame, reputation, or socioeconomic status of the family leader also represents the group's social class. For example, Hmong families led by a business owner or an educator would be recognized and regarded as rich, prosperous, sufficient, capable, and mature group; and Hmong families led by a former military official would be treated with great respect and honor because of his leadership, reputation, fame, and status in the community. Often times, Hmong would recognize a family or a clan by its leader or his social status, for example, Major General Vang Pao's family or group, Christopher's family or group, and the Bingo Market's family or group.

Moreover, another way to know Hmong social classes is to understand the socialization processes of each family group. Socially, Hmong families can be stratified into three groups: The *traditional* families (Hmong parents who speak little or no English), the *semi–Americanized* families (Hmong parents who were foreign-born and are bilingual in Hmong and English), and the *Americanized* families (Hmong parents who are native-born citizens and speak little or no Hmong). Today, Hmong social classes are not only socioeconomically intricate but are also linguistically diverse.

Typically, in the U.S., the location of a family residence may help determine its social status. For example, in Fresno, the upper class Hmong families live among other upper class Americans, the middle class Hmong families reside in the inner-city areas, and the poor Hmong families concentrate in poor and westside neighborhoods. Some underclass Hmong families are still living in the ghetto. However, this does not mean that there is no poor Hmong family living in the upper and middle class neighborhoods and vice versa. Most affluent Hmong families usually do not live among poor Hmong families and are solitary units. For instance, in

Fresno, the upper class Hmong families live in the east and north neighborhoods while the middle and poor class Hmong families reside in the south and west neighborhoods where they can find affordable housing for their large families. In the Hmong community, family income or employment alone is not the sole indicator or predictor of socioeconomic success and social class. Hmong would look at success in life and social status of an individual based on his family structure, marital status, employment, children, wealth, fame, reputation, legacy, leadership, public service, contribution, honesty, wisdom, integrity, interpersonal relationship, and character. These are sociocultural attributes and life qualities used to determine Hmong social classes and socioeconomic status. Simply, it is not about *what* one has in life, but it is more about *how* one lives his life in the Hmong community.

Employment

The current employment status of Hmong refugees in the West appears positive and rising although it is still low, as presented in Table 3.3. No current data are available for the employment of eastern Hmong, although they are known to still be in extreme difficulty socioeconomically. To compare Hmong life in the eastern countries with that in the western nations would be totally unfair because Hmong in the East live mostly in developing nations whereas Hmong in the West have resettled mostly in developed nations. Many western Hmong refugees work in blue-collar or white-collar jobs in different professions while many eastern Hmong refugees work as small farmers, making only enough to provide for their immediate families. In the West, Hmong families depend on wages and salaries for economic stability whereas in the East, most Hmong families depend entirely on family farming and livestock raising for economic survival.

Economically, the western Hmong refugees are far better off than the eastern Hmong refugees because most western nations have offered them plenty of educational and economic opportunities to start over since their arrival in the mid–1970s. In the eastern world, most Hmong refugees still have very limited educational and economic opportunities and face a myriad of social injustices. Since the fall of Laos in 1975, very few eastern Hmong refugees have attained anything but a rudimentary education and very few are working in professional occupations because the communist regimes of East Asia have imposed sociopolitical quotas and other forms of restrictions to control the advancement of Hmong refugees. Moreover, only affluent Hmong families can afford to send their children to high schools, colleges, or universities at home or abroad. The lack of opportunity and the limited resources available to eastern Hmong refugees have severely hindered their employment and their overall socioeconomic status.

In the West, many Hmong refugees have not taken the economic opportunities available to them seriously. After 40 years, as shown in Table 3.3, the employment status of Hmong refugees in many states in the U.S. is lower than expected. For instance, of California's approximately 91,000 Hmong refugees, only about 50 percent are employed. Minnesota is home to nearly 66,000 Hmong refugees and approximately 57 percent hold jobs. Wisconsin has about 49,000 Hmong refugees and 63 percent are working. According to these numbers, the largest Hmong communities have lower employment rates than smaller Hmong communities in the U.S. The states with the highest employment rates of Hmong refugees are Colorado, with 75 percent of its 3,800 Hmong refugees employed; Georgia, with 71 percent employed; Arkansas, with 68 percent employed; and North Carolina, with 67 percent employed. However, the Hmong refugee population in these smaller Hmong communities is just a fraction of the Hmong refugee population of the large Hmong communities. California's Hmong population is 24 times the size of Colorado's, Minnesota's is 17 times the size, and Wisconsin's is 13 times the size. Therefore, it is reasonable to conclude that large Hmong communities are doing relatively well even though the employment rates are lower than those of smaller Hmong communities. However, the level of self-sufficiency of Hmong individual families is different in these states. For example, more Hmong families living in St. Paul, Minnesota, own their first homes more than Hmong families living in California.

Table 3.3. Percent of Hmong Employed in Selected States

State	Total Hmong Population	Percent Employed
Arkansas	2,143	68.2
Arizona	229	59.7
California	91,224	49.6
Colorado	3,859	75.2
Georgia	3,623	71.4
Michigan	5,924	54.9
Minnesota	66,181	57.3
North Carolina	10,864	66.9
Oklahoma	3,369	55.8
Oregon	2,920	52.8
Washington	2,404	53.1
Wisconsin	49,240	62.5

Note: Data from The State of the Hmong American Community, *by M. E. Pfeifer & B. K. Thao (eds.), 2013, Washington, D.C.: Hmong National Development.*

Home Ownership

Home ownership among U.S. Hmong has also increased significantly over the last 10 years (see Table 3.4). During that time, the housing market in the U.S. in general was booming. However, in 2008 the housing market crashed and many Hmong home owners lost their primary residences. Currently, the Hmong home ownership is increasing slowly in metropolitan areas in different states.

Historically, most Hmong refugees did not buy their primary residences until the early 1990s because most Hmong families were unemployed, could not afford to buy their first homes, were not eligible to qualify for mortgage loans, and had little or no credit. In the 1990s, higher Hmong employment created new opportunities and Hmong families started purchasing homes as personal investment and to provide a sense of security for their families. Hmong refugees have learned over the years that having a stable home environment for their family members is the very first step toward better educational and socioeconomic opportunities. When Hmong first arrived in the U.S., most Hmong families were poor and lived in inner-city neighborhoods. Nearly all Hmong families rented apartments. At first, Hmong refugees knew little or nothing about life in the ghetto, but Hmong parents eventually saw the negative influences on their children. In the 1980s to the mid–1990s, many Hmong children became juvenile delinquents because of gangs, drugs, violence, peer pressure, and social temptations. Hmong refugee parents became seriously concerned about their children's delinquent behaviors and attitudes. One of the ways to help minimize the impact on Hmong children was to move their families to different neighborhoods, sometimes even different cities or states, where their children could enroll in good schools and stay away from the ghetto. For Hmong refugees, home ownership is a top priority because the location of the residence can make a big difference on the overall social welfare of their families.

As with employment, rates of home ownership are lower in the largest Hmong communities—in California (33 percent), Minnesota (49 percent), and Wisconsin (55 percent)—than in smaller Hmong communities such as Arizona (81 percent), Michigan (76 percent), Georgia (71 percent), Oklahoma (66 percent), and North Carolina (64 percent) (see Table 3.4). Again, however, the variances are not statistically significant because the Hmong populations in the largest Hmong communities are incredibly large when compared to those in smaller Hmong communities. The rate of Hmong home ownership is likely to increase in all parts of the U.S. in the next few years as the recession fades, unemployment decreases, the mortgage interest rates remain constant, and housing prices rise slowly.

Table 3.4. Hmong Home Ownership and Employment in Selected States, 2010

State	Total Hmong Population	Percent Employed	Percent Owning a Home
Arkansas	2,143	68.2	45.1
Arizona	229	59.7	80.7
California	91,224	49.6	33.4
Colorado	3,859	75.2	51.6
Georgia	3,623	71.4	71.2
Michigan	5,924	54.9	76.4
Minnesota	66,181	57.3	49.2
North Carolina	10,864	66.9	63.5
Oklahoma	3,369	55.8	65.5
Oregon	2,920	52.8	32.4
Washington	2,404	53.1	37.6
Wisconsin	49,240	62.5	54.9

Note: Data from The State of the Hmong American Community, by M. E. Pfeifer & B. K. Thao (eds.), 2013, Washington, D.C.: Hmong National Development.

For four decades, Hmong refugees have improved their new lives with remarkable progress and success. It is important to remember that these and other measures of progress and success may mean something entirely different in non-western cultures and in non-western parts of the world. For instance, having high credit debt may suggest wealth in the West, but in the East, owing lots of money means someone is poor and owing nothing to others means someone is rich. Modern life is often defined by socioeconomic indicators such as employment and home ownership. However, these are not the only measures of quality of life Hmong use. So, socioeconomic success should not necessarily be assessed solely on western values of materialism, acquisitive power, and individualism; Hmong and others may prefer to measure success on the values of peace, freedom, and choices.

Marital Status

If western values are the primary measures, one may conclude that eastern Hmong lag behind western Hmong in many areas. However, if debts, stress, depression, and social problems are to be examined, it would be apparent that western Hmong are likely to have more complex life problems than eastern Hmong and perhaps be less successful. For instance, the divorce rate among

Hmong has increased in the western nations over the last 10 years and the number of Hmong single-parent household has risen at the same time, as indicated in Table 3.5. Moreover, there are more uxoricidal (spouse killing) incidents involving Hmong in the U.S. than among all Hmong anywhere else.

Family structure is the backbone of the Hmong community, and parents and children are the core of Hmong family structure. Most Hmong firmly believe in the importance of good family structure, responsible parents, and forever marital status. Practically all Hmong refugees want to see marriage between a man and a woman and only one father and one mother living in the home. However, some Hmong families have more than one wife or mother. Some western Hmong live in families either without a mother or without a father, and a very few Hmong families have gay or lesbian parents. Single-parent households, headed by either females or males, are on the rise.

As Table 3.5 shows, in the three states with the largest Hmong populations, nearly half of Hmong 15 years and older are never married; fewer than half are married. This means that western Hmong refugees are moving away from the practice of early marriage or under-age marriage. Moreover, it appears that people have become accepting of unmarried women because many Hmong women have become less concerned with marriage than with their educational attainments, professional careers, and future stability and security. Also, rates of divorce, separation, and widowhood have increased significantly over the last 15 years. The overall improvement in the socioeconomic status of western Hmong may have something to do with these figures because, generally speaking, the higher the educational attainment of Hmong women and men, the higher the divorce rate; the higher the acculturation and assimilation, the higher the rate of separation; and the higher the incidence of family dysfunction (domestic violence, polygamy, substance

women were married to non–Hmong, but this trend has been reversed in the U.S. The rise in socioeconomic status of Hmong individuals has contributed to the increase in Hmong interracial marriages. In general, the higher the educational level, the more likely a Hmong man or woman is to marry outside the race. Highly educated Hmong women are three times more likely to marry a non–Hmong husband than less educated Hmong women. Even though Hmong who marry outside the race are still considered somewhat as outcasts, some Hmong individuals disregard the traditional mindset and cultural perceptions.

Table 3.5. Marital Status of Hmong 15 Years and Older in Selected States, 2010

State	Total Population 15 Years and Older	Never Married (%)	Married (%)	Divorced (%)	Separated (%)	Widowed (%)
California	62,120	49.4	43.2	2.8	0.9	3.7
Minnesota	40,486	49.6	40.2	4.3	2.3	3.6
Wisconsin	30,933	45.1	46.9	3.0	2.1	3.0

Note: Data from The State of the Hmong American Community, *by M. E. Pfeifer & B. K. Thao (eds.), 2013, Washington, D.C.: Hmong National Development.*

abuse, incarceration, divorce, separation, and mental problems), the higher the rate of widowhood.

In addition, some Hmong have domestic partners; they live together as husbands and wives without marrying legally or culturally. Some Hmong domestic partners have children together; however, these children may not know who their real fathers are because some fathers do not want to have their names appear on the birth certificates as biological fathers for socioeconomic reasons. Hmong marital practices are obviously changing. The new trends in Hmong marital status are likely to continue, and the only thing that will stop them is to convince individuals to conform to their traditional values, beliefs, norms, and customs.

Hmong interracial marriage is also on the rise. Currently, more Hmong women than Hmong men are married to non–Hmong. In the past, more Hmong men than Hmong

Educational Attainment

In nearly four decades in the West, Hmong have made remarkable progress academically; thousands of children of Hmong refugees are graduating from high school and college each year. Thousands have received bachelor degrees, several thousands have earned master's degrees, and a few hundred can boast of doctorate degrees in a variety of fields. As Tables 3.6 and 3.7 illustrate, Hmong refugees place a high value on education; they know education is the key to socioeconomic success and stability in the West.

The educational attainment of Hmong is directly related to Hmong attitudes toward the opportunities provided by the U.S. educational system. Prior to coming to the West, Hmong parents and children were extremely hungry for public education. One of the main reasons Hmong refugees made life-long sacrifices to pave the way for their children to come to the new homeland was public education. Hmong parents refer to education as gold and silver because they know education is the key to success. To stress how important education is, Hmong parents liken education to having a seeing eye versus a blind eye. The educated can see and the uneducated cannot see. In their loving hearts, all Hmong parents want their children to receive a formal education because they believe that knowledge is power and will last throughout a life time. Education is top priority in most Hmong families because in the past only a few Hmong had formal schooling in the old country. Even after years of living in the U.S., Hmong refugees still have positive attitudes toward schooling and toward the opportunities provided by the U.S. educational system. In the eastern world, very few Hmong refugees have educational opportunities. As of now, sadly, back in war-torn Laos, very few Hmong children are able to attend any school; only the affluent can afford education.

Occupations

The educational attainments of the Hmong refugees have led to successes in business and other professions. Today, thousands of Hmong businesses are flourishing in the U.S. and multiplied thousands of Hmong workers and professionals are employed in different capacities, as indicated in Tables 3.8 and 3.9. Western Hmong are experiencing success as they strive for a better life.

When Hmong refugees first arrived in the western world in 1975, most lacked English skills and employment histories from the old country, so the able and employable Hmong adults were employed as blue-collar workers. Working for hourly wages and monthly incomes was relatively new to Hmong refugees. Right away, sponsors of Hmong refugees put Hmong fathers and mothers to work as production workers, custodians, dairy workers, busboys, construction workers, food servers, kitchen aids, shelf stockers, electronic workers, and so on. Those Hmong refugees who had education from the old country and suf-

Table 3.6. Numbers of U.S. Hmong with Various Educational Attainments, 2010

High School Diploma	Four-year College Degree (BA/BS)	Master's Degree (MA/MS)	Doctorate Degree (PhD/Ed. D)
185,000	9,500	6,500	495

Note: Data from The State of the Hmong American Community, by M. E. Pfeifer & B. K. Thao (eds.), 2013, Washington, D.C.: Hmong National Development and Christopher Vang's estimated data on Hmong educational attainments from 2000 to 2013.

Table 3.7. Educational Attainment of Hmong in Selected States, 2010

State	Total Hmong Population	High School or Higher (%)	Bachelor or Higher (%)
Arkansas	2,143	37.0	00.0
Arizona	229	50.4	12.4
California	91,224	57.5	14.9
Colorado	3,859	73.4	8.4
Georgia	3,623	85.7	18.5
Michigan	5,924	65.5	19.1
Minnesota	66,181	63.1	14.7
North Carolina	10,864	59.7	9.8
Oklahoma	3,369	79.2	10.7
Oregon	2,920	72.6	10.5
Washington	2,404	64.9	14.0
Wisconsin	49,240	62.4	12.8

Note: Data from The State of the Hmong American Community, by M. E. Pfeifer & B. K. Thao (eds.), 2013, Washington, D.C.: Hmong National Development.

Table 3.8. Occupational Distribution of U.S. Hmong, by Gender

Gender	Production, Transportation, Material Moving	Natural Resources, Construction, Maintenance	Sales and Office	Services	Management, Business, Science, Arts
Male	38%	7%	20%	16%	19%
Female	22%	2%	32%	23%	21%

Note: Data from The State of the Hmong American Community, *by M. E. Pfeifer & B. K. Thao (eds.), 2013, Washington, D.C.: Hmong National Development.*

Table 3.9. Distribution of U.S. Hmong in Occupations and Specializations

Profession/Specialization	Percentage
Agriculture, forestry, fishing, mining, hunting,	1.5
Arts, entertainment, recreation, accommodations, food services	11.9
Construction	1.2
Educational services, healthcare, social assistance	19.4
Finance, insurance, real estate, rental, leasing	4.4
Information	1.9
Manufacturing	28.7
Other services	3.6
Professional managers, science, management and administration, waste management	6.3
Public administration	2.8
Retail sales	12.6
Transportation, warehousing, utilities	3.5
Wholesale trade	2.3

Note: Data from The State of the Hmong American Community, *by M. E. Pfeifer & B. K. Thao (eds.), 2013, Washington, D.C.: Hmong National Development.*

ficient English skills could work in white-collar jobs as bilingual translators, medical interpreters, classroom assistants, community workers, cultural brokers, liaisons, refugee program directors, case workers, and tutors. These are the typical jobs held by Hmong refugees from 1975 to the late 1980s.

Then in the early 1990s, Hmong employment started to change because of Hmong educational attainments. The first wave of Hmong college graduates emerged and the socioeconomic status of Hmong increased substantially. Today, Hmong refugee are employed as university professors, college instructors, K–12 teachers, lawyers, judges, peace officers, business owners, elected officials, school counselors, school principals, academic advisors, therapists, dentists, medical doctors, psychiatrists, psychologists, chiropractors, optometrists, pastors, priests, and specialists in many other professions. Incredibly, Hmong refugees have made remarkable progress. As Hmong educators and scholars predicted, if the current trends in educational attainment continue, the number of Hmong refugees in professional occupations will double in 20 years.

Still, many Hmong working families remain financially poor because the families are large and the hourly wages are low. Some Hmong families still depend on the pittance of public assistance they receive and they have not been able to get out of the welfare system. The high cost of living also plays a role in the poverty of Hmong refugees. Many struggle to make ends meet because of their personal difficulties related to cross-cultural adjustments and the process of socialization. Typically, large families and less educated Hmong refugee parents face difficult adjustments and are unable to secure long-term employment to stay off welfare. The lack of good-paying jobs limits Hmong parents' ability to provide financially for their children.

Some older Hmong parents are concerned about their inability to provide and their level of family poverty; they feel that the lack of financial support directly impacts their children's future. However, most Hmong refugee children are eligible for state and federal financial aid programs.

Government Assistance

Prior to coming to the U.S., Hmong refugees did not know that they would be able to receive government assistance. When Hmong refugees first arrived, they were told to apply for various government services because they were legally eligible for benefits. For the most part, these social services have helped Hmong refugees survived financially. Without the assistance, the plight of Hmong refugees could have been worse than what they experienced in the refugee camps in Thailand.

The socioeconomic achievements of the western Hmong refugees were made possible by a safety net of government assistance. Although the number of Hmong receiving public assistance has declined gradually and substantially since 1975, a high percentage of western Hmong refugees continue to depend on government programs. Unfortunately, no safety net is available for the Hmong living in the eastern countries. No public assistance has been available for the poor in Laos, Thailand, Burma, Vietnam, or China. Like all other poor people in those countries, Hmong have to work the fields, seek out opportunities, and scrimp to make ends meet. This reality is reminiscent of Hmong ancestors making sacrifices to provide better opportunities for themselves and their children. Developing countries have few if any policies or programs that help their needy. Sometimes emergency aid may be available for urgent purposes such as temporary subsidized housing for repatriated refugees, temporary aid for farmers, and limited assistance for students studying abroad. But such aid is scarce. More commonly, poor people, including Hmong, are left to fend for themselves. By contrast, in the western nations, Hmong refugees receive government assistance in the forms of medical care, food stamps, welfare benefits, social security benefits, housing, and various types of assistance at the state and local levels. They can take advantage of food banks, emergency care for needy people, social services programs, and temporary shelters.

Some Hmong refugees in the West do not take the available opportunities to pursue their dreams; they remain on the public assistance rosters and merely survive. But in the East, because opportunities are so limited, Hmong have to work the fields to feed their family; that is the only way they can survive. However, despite the extreme difficulty of Hmong life in the East, some eastern Hmong have gained some socioeconomic independence and improved their lives by achieving a higher level of education. Thus in the East as well as the West the only way for Hmong to advance beyond the status quo in modern society is to have access to and take advantage of the instruments of sociopolitical advancement: education, employment, and technological infrastructure. These instruments can be used to train Hmong to meet the demands of the 21st century. In 40 years of living in the West, some Hmong refugees have achieved great success. They have done so through formal education, which is the key to socioeconomic progress. Vang (2005) described in the *Fresno Bee* some of the successes of Hmong in the U.S.:

> They (Hmong refugees) have gone from welfare recipients to small farming or business operators. These transitions are remarkable and should not be overlooked. Hmong small business entrepreneurs are flourishing in Fresno and elsewhere. Hmong children are graduating from colleges and universities and entering professions. The Hmong community is rising in the political arena as a significant voting bloc, and Hmong people are emerging as a sizable minority group in metropolitan economics.

The current progress and success of Hmong refugees will enable them to continue their quest for better educational and socioeconomic opportunities in the U.S. and elsewhere. In the meantime, Hmong refugees should bear in mind that although life in the western world is abundant compared to life in the eastern world, that abundance may not include the best quality of life. In order to go beyond the status quo, western Hmong refugees have to advocate for the things they need and want in order to preserve their cultural heritage, their freedom, their independence, and most importantly, their way of life in a pluralistic society.

Summing Up

Since the Hmong migration to the West, sociologists as well as the general public have a better understanding of Hmong history and culture. Centuries ago, the Hmong migrated from ancient China and settled in the Southeast Asian countries of Vietnam, Laos, Thailand, and Burma. In the early 1970s, Laos fell into the hands of a communist regime and the Hmong left Laos for safe haven in Thailand. In the mid–1970s, Laotian Hmong refugees resettled in the western nations of the U.S., France, French Guyana, Canada, Australia, Argentina, and West Germany. The current Hmong population in the West is nearly 300,000 as compared to the 5.3 million Hmong living in the East. If Miao are also considered to be Hmong, the worldwide Hmong population is now nearly 9 million.

The Chinese called Hmong by many names such as Miao, Meo, Ma, Man, Meng, Wei, Yi, Liu, Qi, Ma, Mo, Xia, Zhou, Han, Chu, San Miao, Miaozi, and others. However, the Hmong have never recognized these names and have always called themselves Hmong. Today, the Hmong are divided into two major groups according to dialect, White Hmong and Blue Hmong. The groups are further divided into 18 clan systems—each clan is a family or tribe with its own surname—and divided still further into subgroups. Specific practices and traditions vary among the families and clans, but all Hmong share a common larger culture and traditions.

Western and eastern Hmong have made remarkable progress in modern society. However, some eastern Hmong still face political oppression and persecution. Western Hmong have abundant socioeconomic opportunities to enable them to reach their dreams. In 40 years, Hmong refugees have achieved many successes in the areas of education, employment, and home ownership. Many western Hmong are still poor, and poverty will continue for those who do not take advantage of the opportunities available to them. Eastern Hmong, whose opportunities are severely limited, are striving for socioeconomic success. They hope that circumstances and government policies will change to allow them access to the education and jobs that will enable them to rise above their subsistence lifestyles.

• FOUR •

Hmong Family Structure

Ua qoob ua loo los npaj tshaib, tu tub tu kiv los npaj laus...
vim ua neej nyob tsuas paub hnub nyob xwb tsis paub hnub yuav tuag...
A Hmong Proverb

Introduction

Since 1975, family structure for Hmong families living in the West has changed. The structure has gone from the extended family to the nuclear family and from the predominance of the two-parent household to a growing number of single-parent households. Western pop culture has influenced Hmong family structure in many ways. The children of Hmong refugees have all kinds of families although most are still headed by a father and a mother. Some families have only a mother or a father as the head of the household. Other families have a stepmother or a stepfather. A few families have more than one mother. Parents are divorced, separated, or single. A very few families have gay/lesbian parents. Some Hmong families have a Hmong mother and a non–Hmong father or vice versa. Hmong interracial marriage has increased over the last two decades. Hmong children are living in these non-traditional families. The non-traditional life situations appear odd but they are becoming more common.

Many young Hmong parents were born in the U.S. and have become Americanized, as have many children. Hmong families have to deal with two or more sets of values, cultures, and traditions at home. The number of households headed by single, divorced, separated, or widowed parents is on the rise in a number of metropolitan areas. Siblings are sometimes living in separate homes under court orders and have supervised visits with their parents. These are typical familial matters in the western countries, but they were not typical of Hmong in the past. This chapter describes the traditional and contemporary Hmong family structures and the values, customs, practices, gender roles, and religions of Hmong families.

Family Composition

Hmong family structure has evolved over time and has transformed from traditional model to neo-traditional and kaleidoscopic patterns. Some have strong family structure while others have fragile family structure. The collapse of Hmong traditional family hit the first and second generation families the hardest. This anarchic change has become evident when a large number of Hmong families entered the three-tier (*college-educated, high school–educated, and non-educated parents*) pattern of family structure in the mid 1990s. Basically, in the US, Hmong now have traditional, high school–educated, and college-educated families. Socially, the high-school educated and college-educated families are better recognized by most non–Hmong and educators; however, in the Hmong community, the traditional families play a more significant role in the Hmong social capital. Hmong family structure and community usually depend on the social connectedness of all Hmong families, including their informal and formal ties to family, relatives, friends, civic associations, religious adherence, and tribal affairs.

The typical Hmong family is comprised of a mother and a father with or without children. From the Hmong cultural perspective, a family denotes the civil union between a man and a woman, not a civil union between a man and a man or a woman and a woman. This is not to say that Hmong people condemn the gay/lesbian lifestyle choice, but such a lifestyle does not exist in their long-standing matrimonial traditions regarding marriage. This traditional view that may seem to some to be biased against gay/lesbian families does not preclude anyone from choosing his or her family structure. The gay/lesbian movement is quite popular in the West. In the U.S., gay marriages are legal in several states. Undoubtedly this phenomenon will have an impact on Hmong traditional values and customs, but it has had little effect to date.

Very few Hmong families do not include children. Family size varies from parents with one child to parents with several children. The typical family size is six people although the preferred family size is four. Most Hmong families have four or more children. Children are seen as the continuation of familial roots, so offspring are highly valued among Hmong. Culturally, the preferred structure of a Hmong family has a father, a mother, and children; and the extended structure includes grandparents, uncles, and aunts living with the family, as shown in Figure 4.1. However, today some Hmong families have either a mother or a father and children, and some Americanized couples have no children.

The increase in interracial marriage is adding new ingredients to the Hmong family structure. Grandparents, uncles, and aunts may be non–Hmong, and the family relatives are both Hmong and non–Hmong. Hmong

refer to this Hmong-American family structure as the western non-traditional Hmong family structure, or Hmong-American families. Nowadays, Hmong have blended families. Hmong children in these families may appear White, Black, Hispanic, Chinese, Korean, Vietnamese, Cambodian, Thai, Punjabi, Pacific Islander, or some other ethnicity. Remarriage, especially interracial remarriage, creates further complexities. Children in a Hmong-American family may have step siblings who are of a completely different ethnicity.

Despite the presence of interracial marriage in Hmong communities in the U.S. and elsewhere, most Hmong still prefer to have the traditional family illustrated in Figure 4.2. Hmong depend heavily on marital kinship relationships for everyday survival and cultural reciprocity within the family. Hmong have learned over the years that some interracial marriages have disrupted the family support and cohesiveness on which they rely. Of course, not all interracial marriages are unsettling to the family structure; some interracial marriages actually create stronger families than Hmong traditional marriages. The structure of a Hmong family may be different from the structure of the past and still

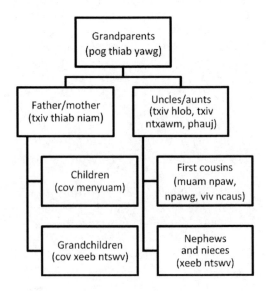

Figure 4.1. Typical Hmong extended family structure.

be positive as long as the family retains Hmong family values and practices Hmong traditional customs. Whether the family is traditional or non-traditional, purely Hmong or interracial, adherence to Hmong values and customs is what makes the family structure congruent with Hmong culture and traditions.

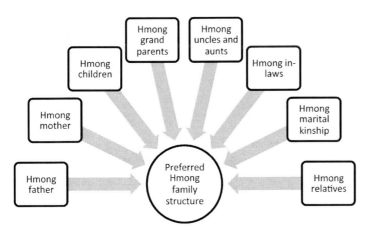

Figure 4.2. Preferred Hmong family structure.

Hmong Marriage

Marital and matrimonial practices are varied among Hmong college-educated, high school–educated, and traditional Hmong individuals. For instance, the age of the college-educated mothers appears to be between mid twenties and early thirties while the age of the high school–educated mothers is between late teen and early twenties. By contrast, the age of the traditional mothers could be as young as 13. Besides the age of the mothers, Hmong also face unexpected and unintended births, nonmarital births, divorce, cohabitation, and multi-partner family pattern. Of all marital issues and complexities, nonmarital cohabitation has become a common practice among westernized Hmong individuals and is one of the most despicable sociocultural stigmas that most Hmong parents would disapprove their children of adopting because such a nonmarital living arrangement disrespects and dishonors Hmong culture and traditions, especially for Hmong parents, Hmong elders, and Hmong clan leaders.

The marital and matrimonial status of Hmong families in the U.S. and in the three states with the largest Hmong population is shown in Table 4.1. The divorce rate among Hmong families is low compared to that of other ethnic groups with similar backgrounds. However, in the Hmong culture, the current divorce rate of just over 3 percent is considered high and unacceptable. The current trends in Hmong marital status illustrated in Table 4.1 and Hmong household characteristics depicted in Table 4.2 reflect the socialization of Hmong to the point of acculturation and integration without assimilation. There are more divorced and widowed Hmong females than Hmong males. More females are separated than males. This could mean that more males remarried shortly after being divorced, separated, or widowed whereas females remained single longer after marital dissolution or the death of their husbands. In recent years, Hmong families have battled domestic violence and uxoricidal incidents (spouse killing). These problems have contributed to the rise in the number of Hmong family dissolutions and of single-male and single-female households. The marital status figures of U.S. Hmong are alarming. National data show that divorce and separation among Hmong families has risen substantially since the 2000 U.S. census and suggest the trends are likely to persist.

Over the last two decades, interracial marriage involving Hmong has increased significantly because of a number of socioeconomic factors:

1. Hmong with educational achievements and professional occupations are increasingly in contact with non–Hmong of similar achievements and occupations.
2. Hmong have adopted western attitudes, values, and social norms.

Table 4.1. Marital Status of Hmong in the U.S. and in Three States, 2010

Marital Status	U.S. Hmong 15 Years and Older	Hmong Males	Hmong Females	Hmong in California	Hmong in Minnesota	Hmong in Wisconsin
Total population	166,906	83,249	83,657	62,120	40,486	30,933
A. Never married	47.8%	52.1%	43.5%	49.4%	49.6%	45.1%
B. Married	44.3%	43.6%	45.1%	43.2%	40.2%	46.9%
C. Divorced	3.1%	2.0%	4.2%	2.8%	4.3%	3.0%
D. Separated	1.5%	1.3%	1.7%	0.9%	2.3%	2.1%
E. Widowed	3.2%	1.0%	5.5%	3.7%	3.6%	3.0%

Note: Data from U.S. Census Bureau, 2008–2010 American Community Survey 3-Year Estimates and The State of the Hmong American Community, by M. E. Pfeifer & B. K. Thao (eds.), 2013, Washington, D.C.: Hmong National Development.

Table 4.2. Characteristics of U.S. Hmong Households in 2000 and 2010

Type of households	U.S. Households in 2000	U.S. Households in 2010
Total households	29,725	46,986
A. Family households	93.4%	89.6%
B. Married couples	75.%	61.6%
C. Female household without a male or spouse present	11.9%	15.4%
Non-family households	6.6%	10.4%
A. Male householder	3.5%	6.2%
B. Male householder, living alone	2.2%	3.4%
C. Female householder	3.2%	4.2%
D. Female household, living alone	2.2%	2.2%
Household size	6.3 people	5.4 people
U.S. family size	6.5 people	5.6 people

Note: Data from U.S. Census Bureau, 2008–2010 American Community Survey 3-Year Estimates and The State of the Hmong American Community, by M. E. Pfeifer & B. K. Thao (eds.), 2013, Washington, D.C.: Hmong National Development.

3. More Hmong tolerate or accept acculturation, assimilation, and integration.

4. Some Hmong prefer the ideology of individualism over that of collectivism.

5. Cultural and traditional barriers toward older single Hmong females have been broken down.

6. More Hmong are exercising personal choice over simple acceptance of traditional values.

7. Some Hmong lack true understanding of American culture, ideals, and values.

8. Some Hmong are unable to speak the Hmong language and lack true understanding of Hmong culture and traditions.

9. The acculturation and socialization process places Hmong increasingly in contact with non–Hmong.

10. Hmong feminism has risen in connection with the rise in educational, social, sociopolitical, and socioeconomic status.

11. Gender roles have changed and concepts of social equity between genders have been introduced.

12. Patriarchal dominance is less tolerated.

Interracial marriage is still relatively low among Hmong; however, it will increase in the next two decades if current trends continue. The numbers of interracial marriages involving Hmong in Fresno County, California, are presented in Table 4.3. Comparing the success of interracial families and traditional Hmong families is difficult because all marriages and all families undergo ups and downs. Regardless of choice, the Hmong marriage vow says, "*Ua lub neej sib sib hlub kom txog hnub laus es ob leeg cov plaub hau dawb paug zoo nkaus li cov ncag dos mas thiaj li yuav xav tau.*" This Hmong matrimony implies that a married Hmong couple has marital commitment to live together with love, happiness, and romance until the strands of their hairs turn white as the roots to the green onions; this also means they are husband and wife until they have lived to the ripe of age of 120.

Table 4.3. Numbers of Hmong Interracial Marriages in Fresno County, by Ethnicity of Partner

Race/Nationality	Males	Females
White	3	7
Hispanic	2	4
French	1	2
Canadian	0	1
Pacific Islanders or Samoa	0	3
Chinese	3	3
Hmong Chinese	4	0
Vietnamese	2	3
East Indian or Hindi	0	2
Black	0	3
Laotian	3	3
Thai	1	3
Cambodian	0	4

Note: Data compiled by Christopher Vang from 2000 to 2013.

As mentioned earlier, a Hmong interracial family is a family in which the mother or father is Hmong and the marriage partner is non–Hmong. In the traditional Hmong family, both parents are Hmong. According to Table 4.3, presently, Hmong females in Fresno County married outside the race more than did Hmong males. Hmong males married Hmong Chinese more than women of any other races and Hmong females married Caucasians more often than men of any other race. The number of Hmong interracial marriages could be higher in other cities but figures for other areas were not available. The numbers cited here may be underreported because people involved in interracial marriages are sometimes considered to be outcasts. Despite such attitudes, some interracial marriages are quite successful. However, in the Hmong world, Hmong strongly believe that traditional marriages will outlast most interracial marriages.

The overwhelming majority of Hmong marriages are between Hmong. This is likely to change as more and more Hmong in the U.S. are native born. The U.S.-born Hmong children are twice as likely to marry outside their race as foreign-born Hmong children. Regardless of birthplace, however, most Hmong marriages in the near future will take place between Hmong family clans. The new families may not be as traditional as those of the past. One cautionary note: Hmong females who marry outside the Hmong race and divorce are three times more likely to be unable to become remarried to a Hmong male. However, Hmong males who marry outside the Hmong race and subsequently divorce are likely to be able to marry a Hmong female. Culturally, nearly all Hmong men still prefer to have Hmong women as their wives because of Hmong family structure, marital kinship relationship, genealogical lineage, mutual reciprocity, and most importantly, family values, beliefs, norms, customs, gender roles, and religions.

Family Roles

Typically, Hmong family roles are different in college-educated, high school–educated, and non-educated or traditional households. For instance, the college-educated families are referred to as neo-traditional families that practice egalitarian principles in the gender roles and division of domestic duties, delay marriage and childbearing until their careers are under way, and work outside the home to provide financial support for the family. By contrast, the high school–educated parents practice childbearing early, build fragile families, and are subjected to have weak matrimonial ties that often lead towards complex family dissolution. This pattern causes the rise of Hmong single-family families, including step-parents and step-siblings. Similarly, the non-educated or traditional parents preserve traditional values, adhere to Hmong communal way of life, and honor the patriarchal social system. Of the three, the traditional households appear to be the predominant families in the Hmong community.

Most Hmong parents still prefer traditional roles and parenthood regardless of their children's socioeconomic status in the western nations. For instance, the traditional roles of father, mother, and children in the traditional Hmong family structure are as follows:

- The father is the head of the household regardless of his educational level or socioeconomic status.
- The mother is the caretaker of the household regardless of her educational level or socioeconomic status.
- The father maintains the supreme position in the family and is responsible for family matters.
- The mother supports her husband's position in the family and is responsible for the welfare of all family members.
- The father must be consulted on all decisions involving his family members and all family matters.
- The mother supports her husband in his position as consultant in all decisions involving her family members and all family matters.
- The father is the sole religious authority in the family and conducts all family and religious rites and rituals except rites in modern religious faiths.
- The mother is the sole preparer, coordinator, and supporter of all family and religious rites and rituals.
- The father bears the family name, root, social status, and reputation and preserves the family's culture and traditions in accordance with his familial ancestry.
- The mother adopts the familial culture and traditions of her husband and is honored according to the family name, root, social status, and reputation of her husband.
- The father is the role model for his children, especially his sons, and provides guidance to them until the children reach adulthood or become mothers and fathers.
- The mother is the role model for her children, especially her daughters, and provides guidance to them until they reach adulthood and become mothers and fathers.
- All children have to respect and adhere to the family's structure, rules, values, customs, religious practices, and norms.
- Children are the strongest ties between parents and they must conform to familial expectations and aspirations to bring honor to the family.
- Children, especially sons, bear the family name, root, social status, and reputation and continue the genealogical bloodline.
- Children are the means of continuing the life and the future of the family.

Above all, in traditional Hmong families, the father is the owner (*tswv tsev*) and fatherhood authority (*txiv tsev*) whereas the mother is the motherhood authority (*niam tsev*); however, both mother and father own and share the family deed of trust equally. These are typical basic beliefs and practices in traditional Hmong families, although variations exist as some fathers and mothers play different roles in the family. Capable mothers can fill their husbands' roles and duties except for the responsibilities regarding religious rites and rituals. For example, the mother may be a better disciplinarian for the children and the father may be a better enforcer of expectations. The educational level of a parent may make a difference in dealing with young children. Better educated parents, for example, may be able to provide stronger academic discipline and be better equipped to help children with their homework assignments.

Today, the fathers do not necessarily have to be the primary breadwinner in the Hmong family. Mothers are primary wage earners and the financial backbone of many Hmong families. Most young and middle-aged mothers work outside the home to support their families whereas older and elderly mothers who lack education and professional abilities do not work. In older families, the fathers may be the only wage earners because the mothers are homemakers. Some older Hmong parents are farmers and work in the field together.

Hmong people value the extended family and maintain strong ties with extended family members such as adult siblings, cousins, nieces, nephews, uncles, aunts, parents, grandparents, great grandparents, clan members, and other relatives. The Hmong family structure includes all these parties because they depend on and support one another in a variety of ways, as illustrated in Figure 4.3. Today, Hmong may live together in either an extended family or a nuclear family. Either way, the larger family and clan structure keeps members of different but related families attached at the core of family ancestry. Family ancestry plays a significant role in marriage, death, and clan system recognition; therefore, the ties of family ancestry keep all close and distant members in relationship regardless of their individual family lifestyles.

Hmong cultural values and beliefs. The U.S. Hmong have all kinds of families such as rich and poor, upper and middle class, low and under class, and traditional and westernized families.

Socioeconomic Status

Today Hmong college-educated, high school–educated, and non-educated have different lifestyles and live in different neighborhoods. When Hmong refugees first arrived in the U.S. and other western nations in the mid–1970s, the majority of Hmong families depended on public assistance to meet their immediate needs. Four decades later, the number of Hmong families on public assistance has decreased gradually in some states and dramatically in others. However, the number of Hmong families on public assistance is still significantly high in some metropolitan areas. According to Hmong National Development, Inc., nearly 3 percent of the U.S. population receives some kind of cash public assistance as compared to 12 percent of the U.S. Hmong population. This comparison indicates that many U.S. Hmong still struggle to meet basic needs. Tables 4.4 and 4.5 present the income of Hmong families in selected states and

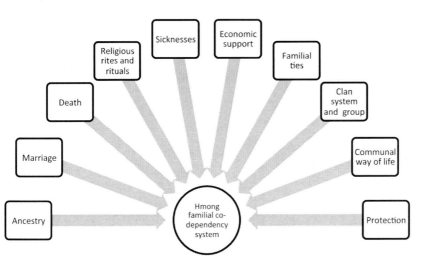

Figure 4.3. Co-dependency in the Hmong family.

There are only 18 Hmong families with 18 distinct family surnames, or clan systems or tribes. Each family has its own sets of beliefs, values, customs, and norms. However, the cultural values and traditions of the different families are very similar with only slight differences. Keep in mind that Hmong languages and dialects are intelligible so do

the percentages of Hmong families and children living below the federal poverty line in those states. In the western nations, income is used as the most common measurement of family wealth. However, in the Hmong world, income may not reflect the quality of life of an individual or a family. Other elements should be considered when measuring wealth or poverty or Hmong families might be judged to be extremely poor based only on western values and perspectives.

Table 4.4. Per Capita, Household, and Family Income of Hmong in Selected States, 2010

State	Per Capita Income	Household Income	Family Income
California	$9,800	$41,500	$40,900
Michigan	$11,600	$47,500	$47,500
Minnesota	$11,200	$48,700	$46,700
North Carolina	$10,800	$45,500	$44,500
Washington	$8,700	$40,300	$33,700
Wisconsin	$11,400	$48,000	$50,500

Note: Data from U.S. Census Bureau, 2008–2010 American Community Survey 3-Year Estimates and The State of the Hmong American Community, by M. E. Pfeifer & B. K. Thao (eds.), 2013, Washington, D.C.: Hmong National Development.

Table 4.5. Hmong Families and Children in Poverty in Selected States

State	Families (%)	Under 18 Years of Age (%)
California	30.7	41.9
Michigan	16.0	17.5
Minnesota	26.2	34.6
North Carolina	20.0	21.5
Washington	34.0	50.2
Wisconsin	20.3	21.0

Note: Data from U.S. Census Bureau, 2008–2010 American Community Survey 3-Year Estimates and The State of the Hmong American Community, by M. E. Pfeifer & B. K. Thao (eds.), 2013, Washington, D.C.: Hmong National Development.

Hmong families remain strong; families are integral parts of Hmong everyday life. The cultural ties among Hmong families foster maintenance of Hmong culture and traditions as well as Hmong marital kinship. Hmong children appreciate Hmong family values and customs because they understand that a solid family with a mother and a father present is a most precious gift. Bigamy and polygamy are not part of Hmong culture; the Hmong traditional marriage customs (kab tshoob kev kos) have never included any lyrics related to the practice of polygamy or bigamy.

Instead, the customary Hmong marriage rites and ceremonial rituals condemn such practices because they contribute to gender inequity, parental divorce and separation, single-person households, and interracial marriage. In the old days, some exceptions were permitted. For example, multiple wives were allowed when a wife could not conceive a child due to biological or genetic infertility, when a wife suffered long-term disabilities or illnesses, or when a wife could not conceive a male child to continue the family line of the father. However, Hmong women are not allowed to marry a second husband if the husband is infertile; in such rare cases, the marriage may be dissolved by the family.

Traditionally, in order to withstand social temptations and external influences, Hmong fathers and mothers consider their offspring to be their families' strongest ties. Children are the bonds that keep the family intact forever. In the old days, having equal number of sons and daughters played major roles in Hmong family socioeconomic status, especially the Hmong agrarian lifestyle.

Hmong Parents and Their Children

In the West, Hmong parents and their children live in a world with two distinct cultures and many sometimes conflicting traditions. Often Hmong families live dual lives in a dual society. In school Hmong children learn values, customs, and traditions that are different from those of their family. Their classmates are not all Hmong and their neighbors are a mixture of different people. Hmong children are part of the cultural diversity of America. At home, Hmong parents expect their children to conform to the traditional Hmong way of life. Many Hmong parents are traditional, some are semi-westernized, and others are completely westernized. Hmong families have struggled and changed over the decades to maintain their Hmong heritage while seeking a sensible balance between western and eastern ways of life. More importantly, college-educated, high school–educated, and traditional parents raise their children differently and, in some cases, cross-culturally and unexpectedly. In spite of having different family structures, the Hmong filial piety system still exists in most Hmong families. Both adults and children are expected to develop good behaviors and responsible attitudes, and moreover, most Hmong individuals are taught to practice the values of self-effacement, such as avoiding self-humiliation, losing face, displaying impatience, or being impolite around elders.

Hmong Family Lifestyles

As mentioned earlier, children are extensions of a family's life. Nearly all Hmong families have offspring. Traditional Hmong families want to have children, but modern Hmong families sometimes think differently about children. Today's parents may choose not to have children because of their professional careers and busy lives. For young Hmong couples, raising children is cumbersome because of the familial responsibilities and obligations involved. In the eastern countries, having children is challenging because of the high demands and low resources of the agrarian lifestyle; in the western nations, raising children is less challenging but costly. Daycare is quite expensive and many cannot afford it. Most Hmong parents depend on immediate family members to provide daycare for their offspring. For many couples, unplanned births disrupt education, careers, and work routines. Some young Hmong families have only one or two children as opposed to the four or more children common in the older Hmong families. Some couples simply do not want to have children. Traditional Hmong people think of couples who have no children as odd because childless Hmong families are rare. However, having no children is becoming less unusual.

Today, when Hmong couples think about having children, they often consider the quality of family life of having several children will bring. Most young Hmong adults in the U.S. have learned from their parents'

experience that raising multiple children is a struggle financially. By and large, Hmong teenage females have rejected the custom of early marriage in favor of concentrating on their education and professional careers. The marriage age used to be 13 or 14 for Hmong women; now it is 18, 19, or over. Whether life with or without children is better cannot be judged on the basis of a family's wealth, educational level, professional career, time, or desired lifestyle; rather, the choice can be evaluated by the happiness of an individual family and their thoughts about parenting. As a professional Hmong couple observed, regardless of a family's socioeconomic status, life is not free of struggles, sacrifices, changes, responsibilities, and disappointments, but families can learn to adjust to all that life brings. Furthermore, the couple said, there is so much to be enjoyed, including children, and if families are flexible they will be resilient. Hmong believe that children are the future; therefore, parents have to plant the seeds of the future. Otherwise, as Hmong elders are concerned about the increase of childless family structure, the Hmong family's posterity is at risk of becoming extinct.

The Core of Hmong Families

Social hierarchy and patriarchy, as shown in Figure 4.4, play major roles in Hmong family foundations and structure. The core of traditional Hmong families is the smaller unit of parents and children; this is the unit that maintains the genealogical bloodline.

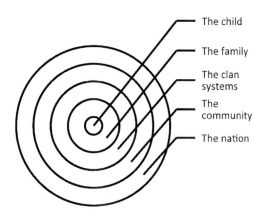

The child

The family

The clan systems

The community

The nation

Figure 4.4. Hmong social hierarchy.

Hmong family structure is a trinity of father, mother, and children. Children not only constitute the ties between parents, but they also provide the strength that makes a marriage work and makes it worthwhile. This may sound odd to those who do not wish to have children, but those who have children understand how important their children are to them.

Building a family requires a life-long commitment. Today, some Hmong parents do not seem to understand their parental obligation to raise their children to adulthood. Some parents have abandoned their biological children for personal greed. These irresponsible individuals see children as disrupting their social life. They leave their children to be raised by stepparents, grandparents, foster parents, the court system, relatives, and strangers. Others mistreat their own children. These are larger societal issues and Hmong parents are not excluded from them. However, most Hmong families are doing incredibly well at taking care of their children.

All children are born as innocent beings and want to be loved by whoever brought them into this chaotic world. Hmong parents see children as gifts from God and Heaven, and they want to have children who will care for them when they can no longer care for themselves. As an elderly Hmong put it, Hmong parents want to see their children and grandchildren sitting next to them before they leave this earth (the physical world) for heaven (the spiritual world). This wish is not always fulfilled because some Hmong children today lack familial values and do not see the importance of compensating their parents for their love and caring. Some parents do not wish their children to care for them in their old age because they have pensions, social security benefits, and retirement monies that enable them to care for themselves. Some adult children are not able to provide the kind of care their elderly parents may need because they have to work.

In the western nations, these and other socioeconomic factors have influenced the relationship between Hmong parents and their children. However, in the eastern countries, parents do not have avenues of financial security for their old age, so raising children to prepare for the responsibilities of parental decline is extremely important. A good son who cares for the needs of his parents is an honorable gift. As Hmong legends say, children who love their parents will achieve more in life than children who despise their parents and disregard them before death. For Hmong people, caring for elderly parents is not a curse, but a part of the cycle of altruism in life; once Hmong parents took care of their children and their children take care of their parents when they are old. For Hmong parents and children, cultural reciprocity is invaluable part of life.

Hmong Parents Today

Most Hmong parents in the U.S. are authoritative. Some are authoritarian and others are permissive. Many are traditional and some are Americanized. Some, called sandwich parents, are partly traditional and partly westernized. As Figure 4.5 illustrates, Hmong parents can be classified into three groups on the basis of acculturation: the elder and old group, the middle-aged and semi-traditional group, and the young and westernized group. Hmong parents place their children in one of three major categories: traditional, semi-westernized (*sandwich children*), and westernized. Hmong parents classify their children in this way based on their perceptions of the children's attitudes, behaviors, social lives, obedience, respect, and devotion to Hmong culture and traditions.

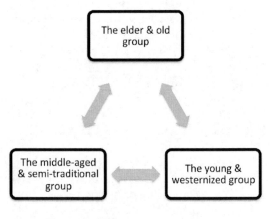

Figure 4.5. Hmong parent types.

The elder and old group is comprised mostly of refugee parents who emigrated to the West. Most in the U.S. speak no English although some have learned a little English. Nearly all have large families. Even though their literacy is low, many are bilingual, speaking Lao, Thai, English, or French as well as Hmong. They are very traditional and maintain their culture and traditions while adjusting to the mainstream society as much as possible. In this group are former soldiers, civil leaders, and former educators. Some are farmers and civilians without professional training. Old Hmong parents help their communities preserve their clan structure and Hmong culture and traditions, such as customary marriages, death rituals, religious ceremonies, shamanism, and herbal medicines and treatments.

The middle-age and semi-traditional group consists mostly of refugee children who were born in the Southeast Asian countries and grew up in the West; they are sometimes referred to as the 1.5 generation. These parents have been to school in the West and are bilingual in Hmong and English. Like their parents, some speak more than two languages, perhaps Lao, Thai, or French as well as English and Hmong. Although they speak English, they may not be fluent in that language. Most of the 1.5 generation parents appear to be semi-traditional and semi-westernized; the degree of westernization depending on socioeconomic status. Some have become Americanized because of their educational levels and occupations. Adhering to values learned from their parents, they hold good jobs so they can support their families and their parents. They are family-oriented. Interestingly, this group has achieved the highest level of self-actualization of the three groups and contains most of the Hmong professionals—teachers, counselors, social workers, medical doctors, lawyers, professors, pastors, business owners and entrepreneurs, politicians, judges, insurance agents, and so on. Many have overcome the language barrier and become self-sufficient. In social settings, they are the sandwich people who are caught between western culture and their traditional culture. As one Hmong educator explained, the1.5 generation children are the true culture brokers who build bridges between home and the outside world.

The young and westernized group consists mostly of U.S.-born parents. They are referred to as first-generation parents. Most in this group are not fluent in Hmong but speak English well. Their attitudes and behaviors are compatible with those of western culture because they grew up in the West; most are acculturated. Both the 1.5 and the first-generation parents speak *Hmonglish*, a hybrid of English and Hmong with bilingual code switching. They often use code switching to communicate with their parents and older relatives. Some are monolingual in English. Sometimes, people in this group require translators and interpreters because they do not fully understand Hmong languages. Some in this group have become self-sufficient and reached self-actualization; however, they trail the 1.5 generation. Unlike the 1.5 generation and elder and older generation, parents in the young and westernized group live and parent their offspring in ways that are based on western values and ideals. Westernized parents may or may not keep Hmong culture and traditions because they lack the Hmong language that supports the practice of Hmong traditional values and customs, such as religious rites, death rituals, and soul calling ceremonies. Many in this group have converted to Christianity and other western religious faiths.

Hmong Children Today

Hmong children in the West today can be classified into three groups according to their acculturation, as indicated in Figure 4.6. The groups are similar to the parent groups: traditional, semi-westernized, and westernized. Hmong children in the western nations adjust, integrate, acculturate, and assimilate to western culture differently from their parents. For Hmong parents, the socialization process is governed largely by place of birth; for Hmong children, personal attitudes, behaviors, and manners do not seem related to birth in the East or the West.

Traditional Hmong children maintain

their cultural values and familial heritages. They speak Hmong and English even though they may struggle with Hmong more than English. Of course, code switching is quite common, a necessary part of everyday life. For example, *kuv tsis* care *koj; noj daim* bread no; *mus* take shower; *hu 911; hu* police; *mus nram* court; *ua* homework; and *mus* school. In their daily lives, traditional Hmong children listen, emulate, and respect their parents and Hmong cultural perspectives. They follow the social order and cultural etiquette when they are around their elders and parents. They may adapt and acculturate with reservations. For instance, they may perform household chores in accordance with their parents' expectations even though they are professionals. Most traditional Hmong parents raise and want traditional children.

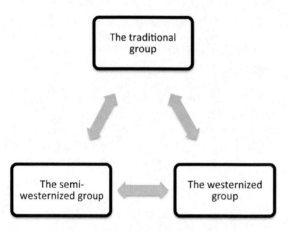

Figure 4.6. Hmong children types.

The semi-westernized group of children is known as the sandwich group; children so classified are caught between two or more cultures and traditions. Most are good children, but some are quite opinionated, cranky, defiant, and rebellious. Others are out of control and have become extremely rude. Most seem to like the western culture more than the Hmong culture. They may feel odd when talking about traditional Hmong values and customs. Some are proficient in Hmong and English, but many speak little and limited Hmong; these are the real Hmonglish speakers. Westernized children are considered at

risk for social problems; some tend to adopt extreme attitudes and go into gangs and abuse alcohol and other substances. Hmong parents have difficulty handling the sandwich children because the children cannot understand when the parents tell them the difference between right or wrong in Hmong, and when the conversation is in English, the parents do not understand where their children are coming from because the children show little or no respect for authority.

Semi-westernized children often present themselves as children of a new era. Most talk, eat, behave, and socialize as western children. Some are belligerent toward their parents and talk back to them while others ignore their parents. One Hmong mother described her frustration with her angry teenage children:

> They refuse to listen or to do anything at home, and when asked, they slam the door behind them and use the "F" word. … They turn the volume of their music to high and lie down on their beds. … They refuse to come out when called for dinner. I feel like the house is going to explode because the music is too loud. Sometimes, I feel like they are not my own children because they do not behave as Hmong children—showing respect and listening to parents.

This group of children may not follow social norms and cultural etiquette around elders and older parents or emulate their elders. They often do not accept Hmong traditional values or exhibit the attitudes and behaviors of traditional children. Many will not perform household chores as their parents expect them to. Some view parental controls as spiteful and parental expectations as unreasonable, especially those regarding courtship and dating. Having said all this, it is important to note that not all sandwich children behave in this manner. There are many good, decent sandwich children who love, respect, listen to, and care for their parents. Much depends on the family's lifestyle. Many semi-westernized children are family oriented and embrace Hmong culture and traditions.

The westernized group consists of enculturated children who were born and grew up in the western culture and traditions. Keep in mind that western culture is not monolithic; it is an amalgam of many different beliefs, values, customs, and traditions. Similarly to the semi–Americanized group, most westernized children speak little or no Hmong. Neither are they Hmonglish speakers; English or French is their primary language. Their communication with their parents has to be in English. English speaking Hmong parents have little or no problems communicating with them, but for those who speak little or no English, communication is challenging. Most of these children expect their parents to defer to them and what they like instead of complying with their parents' expectations. For instance, they may prefer American food over traditional Hmong food, they want to choose their own friends rather than have their parents dictate to them, and they want to dress and groom themselves without any input from their parents. Most want to conform to the behaviors and styles of their friends. For example, boys may want to wear baggy pants and girls may want to wear tight "skinny jeans." One Hmong mother expressed her frustration with her adolescent daughter:

> This American child is not my child because she is looking at me like I am not her mother. … She talks to me like I am a child and she is the mother. … I wanted her to do some household chores and she told me she is busy. … I told her to clean her room and she said she will do it later when she has the time. … I asked her to wash her clothes and she said she will do it on the weekend. … Finally, I asked her to put her cell phone down and concentrate on her homework and she said it is none of my business.

Similarly, a Hmong father shared his concerns about his teenage son:

> My son stays up late and gets up late most days. … I talked to him about my concerns. He said he is tired and told me to go away. I asked if he is sick. He said no. I asked why he is not going to school. He said it is fine. I confronted him with his poor grades. He said he will do the work to make the grades. The next day, I dropped him off at school. About one hour later, the school called saying my son is not in class. I called his cell phone. He told me he is at a friend's house and will come home later and hung up. I just do not know what to do with this Hmong-American.

These kinds of frustrations are not unique to the Hmong community. They are typical of many American families, but they are new to Hmong parents. Most westernized children are good children. Hmong parents of westernized children may become frustrated with their children because of communication difficulties and high expectations, but in most cases Hmong parents retain their parental authority. Problems occur when Hmong parents expect their westernized children to adjust to their ways without making any adjustments to the ways their children are learning in the western environment in which they are immersed. For instance, westernized children like to be hugged, kissed on the cheek, stroked, and praised frequently, but they seldom are treated this way in the traditional Hmong home.

Children: The Seed of the Future

Typical Hmong families have at least one or two children. Hmong have learned over the years that having many children makes life difficult. Sons have always been highly regarded because they are considered the familial roots, but that old-fashioned concept does not seem as important to Hmong in the western nations because all children can be part of the familial roots regardless of gender. Traditionally, the son bears the financial responsibility of caring for their parents and continuing the family's roots, perpetuating the family surname, culture, traditions, and religious rites. However, in the West today, a daughter can do as much as a son except she does not retain her family surname once she is married and she may not practice familial religious rites. For Christian Hmong families, these concerns are obsolete. Besides, many sons are unable to fulfill their traditional obligations. In the old days, sons were more valuable than daughters because of their familial roles and responsibilities. As a Hmong proverb says, "*Cuaj lub hli tsis zoo npaum li ib lub hnub, cuaj leeg ntxhais tsis zoo npaum li ib leeg tub.*" English translation: "*Nine moons will not be as good as a sun, nine daughters will not equal the value of a son.*" Such beliefs have changed over time and today sons and daughters have equal value in Hmong families.

Hmong parents love their offspring dearly. Hmong parents participate in the marriages of their sons regardless of their ages, who they are, and what they have become. Hmong parents are responsible for their daughters until the daughters marry regardless of their ages and socioeconomic status. Customarily, Hmong parents allow their children to live with them as long as they are unmarried. Regardless of age, single adult Hmong children remain with their parents until they have their own families. These are inextricable bonds between parents and children. When adult Hmong children move out of their parents' house and rent their own apartments, they are considered culturally disobedient. However, in the West, the door is wide open when children reach their 18th birthday and they are free to leave home. Such a thought has not been accepted by Hmong families.

For Hmong parents, children are essential to life. A Hmong elder listed several reasons why having children is so important:

- Children are the primary blessings of life.
- Children are the family bond between parents.
- Children complete the family and are the fulfillment of marital obligations.
- Children continue the bloodline and genealogical kinship.
- Children keep the family's roots alive and well.
- Children provide security in later life.
- Children are life's prosperity.

Some people see children as a burden. For Hmong, children are both a life-long burden and a gift from God. Without children, life has gaps that are never filled. Therefore, in Hmong life, parents and their children are the inner core of the familial structure. One Hmong elder explained that without children the family structure is incomplete, weak, un-

fulfilled, and cannot be continued; with children, the structure can be preserved, repaired, improved, restored, and reinvigorated to become better and stronger. As he said in Hmong, "*Ua neeg nyob yog tsis muaj tub muaj ki los npaj thaum laus, txawm hais tias ua lub neej muaj txiag nplua nuj npaum licas los yeej tseem tsis zoo lub siab tag, vim hais tias ua neej ib zaug xwb yus tsis nrog luag muaj tub muaj ki.*" For Hmong families, children are the continuity between the present and the future, whereas parents are the continuity between the past and the present.

Motherhood, Fatherhood and Childhood

Each family has its own way of raising children, managing tasks, and disciplining its members. Hmong parents establish the structure for their families. In some families the structure is loose and in others there is no structure at all. Some Hmong families have no rules, curfews, expectations, or guidance. Some families function well whereas others are dysfunctional. The family structure defines parental roles and responsibilities as well as children's roles and responsibilities. Typically, a Hmong family divides responsibilities among three familial roles: motherhood, fatherhood, and childhood (Figure 4.7).

However, in the Hmong community, college-educated, high school–educated, and traditional parents practice different parental involvements and have different expectations for their children. For instance, some parents use *concerted cultivation* to prepare their children to navigate life processes while others apply *natural growth* to expect their children to become well-bred and well-mannered individuals in adult life. In Hmong way of life, the process of concerted cultivation refers to the way parents teach, train, foster, support, guide, and involve in their children's early life; and the process of natural growth explains the way parents culturally and socioeconomically expect their children to become in their adult life. Educated Hmong parents appear to practice childrearing investments that help them foster their children's cognitive, social, emotional, psychological, and cultural skills needed for navigating everyday life events. Less-educated parents seem to lack proper guidance and allow their children to develop their own devices, and for the most part, they focus more on strict rules and discipline. In some households, parents rely less on scheduling, encouragement, monitoring, reasoning, communication, negotiation, and child-parent relationship. For instance, well-educated Hmong parents plan to raise opinionated, autonomous, independent, curious, self-directed, self-disciplined, and self-propelled children with high expectations, self-esteem, and inquisitive mind to promote their ability to make good choices whereas less-educated Hmong parents appear to focus more on traditional values, rules, discipline, obedience, social conformity, and family norms. Simply, less-educated parents seem to endorse social conformity and obedience over self-reliance, self-propelled, and self-esteem.

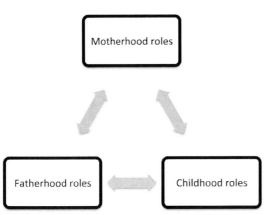

Figure 4.7. Hmong family roles.

Hmong Motherhood

In the West, Mother's Day is quite special, indicating the importance of motherhood. The occasion was celebrated for hundreds of years before being recognized officially nearly a hundred years ago. In good Hmong families, everyday functioning depends on a responsible, caring, nurturing, protective, dutiful mother. A good mother knows her roles and responsibilities without being told because she has learned them from her parents or after marrying her husband. As Hmong elders explain, everything in the house belongs to the mother; she is the house manager and has to know where things are.

In Hmong culture, the basic responsibilities of motherhood are housekeeping (cleaning, washing, organizing, cooking, decorating, grocery shopping...), childrearing (caring, nurturing, disciplining), managing everyday routines, preparing children for school, planning family activities and events (family gatherings, birthday parties, entertaining guests...), preparing for religious rituals, attending church, and supporting her husband in carrying out his responsibilities. Of course, these tasks are too much for one person to handle, but a good mother tells others that these are her normal responsibilities. Today, these responsibilities are often shared between wives and husbands because many mothers have duties other than those of homemaker. Most mothers hold jobs so they can provide financial support to the family, and many are professionals. In families in which the mother is not working outside the home, she handles most of these tasks. In a few families, the husbands are the homemakers because they do not hold jobs, they are willing to perform these tasks, or they have wives who are incapable of or unwilling to fill these responsibilities. In traditional Hmong life, a family without a good-nurturing mother is socioeconomically unstable and dysfunctional regardless of the father's socioeconomic standing.

Hmong Fatherhood

In traditional Hmong families, healthy functioning requires a responsible, caring, dutiful, protective, supportive, nurturing, understanding, appreciative, knowledge, and skillful father just as much as it needs a good mother. The father is the leader, captain, protector, and owner of the family. A good father knows his responsibilities without being told because he has learned them from his parents, especially his father, or he has learned to become a good father after marrying his wife. Hmong elders point out that every family has to have a father to lead the family and protect family members from disrespect and mistreatment by others, and a father is the authority figure who holds the family unit together. In a Hmong family, both mother and father are highly respected but the father holds a higher and more prestigious position because he is the guardian of all family members.

In Hmong culture, the basic responsibilities of fatherhood are leading the family, making decisions, solving and resolving conflicts, mediating disputes, conducting religious practices (offering, worshiping, soul calling, shamanism, summoning spirits for help, regular rituals, ceremonies, funeral and death rituals, praying...), honoring the family surname, belonging to the family clan, maintaining warm and close relationships with family and clan members, practicing marriage customs, maintaining the family unit, performing physical labor and handyman tasks, maintaining patriarchal character and integrity, and maintaining a good socioeconomic status for the family. These are typical responsibilities the father has to at least know how to perform; they are expected of him regardless of his occupation outside the home. In today's society, a father cannot perform all these responsibilities alone and he may share some with his wife. In Christian families, fathers have less to do because the traditional religious practices require quite a bit of time. In traditional Hmong families without a father, spiritual and religious practices are absent because the mother is not allowed to perform religious rites and rituals. In Christian families the mother can pray with her children. In regards to the father's position in the family, as simply explained by Hmong elders, without the father the family is like a body without the head. This concept indicates that fatherhood is far more important than a matter of roles and responsibilities.

As important as parental responsibilities are, not all parents fulfill their responsibilities well and not all are good role models for their children. Parents are their children's very first teachers who nurture and protect, but not all parents are good teachers. Good Hmong parents normally teach and train their offspring, helping them learn the basic functions, the knowledge, and the life skills necessary to become good parents themselves.

Hmong Childhood

The childhood of Hmong children today is quite different from that of their parents. However, gender role differences are still prevalent in Hmong families even though some tasks are now shared by father and mother. Hmong children learn the expected gender responsibilities from their parents over the course of their childhood. According to Hmong family traditions, daughters emulate their mothers to gain the maternal skills and knowledge they will need to raise their families and sons emulate their fathers to acquire paternal skills and knowledge they will need to build strong families.

Hmong daughters are expected to learn all the motherhood responsibilities described above. Symbolically, Hmong daughters are referred to as guest children (*ntxhais qhua* in Hmong) who will leave their families one day to start a new life and Hmong sons are considered as root children (*tub cag* in Hmong) who will continue the genealogical bloodline of their families. A good Hmong mother gradually teaches her daughters from a very young age the basic household tasks and responsibilities. In the old days, a mother would teach her daughters to fetch water from a well or stream, to cultivate and harvest crops, to make fire early in the morning and at night, to pound rice grains, to grind corn, to feed domestic animals, to cut and collect vegetation for draft animals, to plow the land for planting, to learn embroidery crafts, and to weed the crops. Today, the mother teaches personal grooming, dressing, cleaning, sewing and needle work, cooking rice and preparing meals, serving food and clearing tables, washing and sweeping, talking and responding, handling private and personal issues, making friends and dealing with social issues, dating and courtship, designated roles and assigned responsibilities, and specific household chores. Mothers begin their instruction in the various tasks at different stages in the children's development as illustrated in Table 4.6. Hmong believe that a daughter who has mastered domestic chores will become a better wife regardless of her educational level, professional occupation, and socioeconomic status. Westernized Hmong children often do not see these responsibilities as important values until they have to manage their own lives. A verse in the Hmong traditional marriage customs prompts Hmong brides to become good mothers: "*Cheb qab vaj kom to txhuav qab yia kom qawj.*" In English: "Sweep the bottom of the bamboo rice basket until there is a hole in it, wash the bottom of a steel pan with your hands until it is worn." The verse means to work hard in life to achieve success.

Most traditional Hmong fathers do not engage in the basic social and cultural teaching and training until several years into the life of a male child. The learning of a son is a mixture of their mother's consistent guidance and their father's sporadic reinforcements until the child reaches adolescence and understands his masculine roles and responsibilities. In some families, sons are taught how to behave and talk at an early age but these instances are rare. In most cases, sons and daughters are taught by their mothers in the early stages of their lives. Typically, Hmong

Table 4.6. Apprenticeship in Maternal Tasks According to Child's Age

Task Taught	Age 1–3	Age 3–5	Age 5–7	Age 7–9	Age 9–11	Age 11–13	Age 13–15	Age 15–17	Age 17–19
Personal grooming	x								
Dressing and changing	x								
Cleaning/putting away		x							
Sharing/playing	x								
Sewing/needle work			x						
Cooking rice/meals				x					
Serving/clearing tables					x				
Washing/cleaning				x					
Talking/responding			x						
Private/personal issues					x				
Friends/social issues						x			
Dating/courtship						x			
Designated roles and assigned responsibilities						x			
Maintain specific chores							x		
Learn new skills in needed areas								x	
Become responsible for most household chores									x

Note: X indicates the approximate starting age. A child may start a little earlier or later, depending on the child's developmental stage and cognitive maturity.

mothers play a bigger role in family matters such as grooming, bathing, cleaning, changing, feeding, playing, bringing up children, and so on. For traditional Hmong sons, expectations of masculinity include being tough and strong; emulating their fathers; knowing how to use tools; knowing how to hunt, fish, and trap; doing physical labor; learning religious rites and rituals; learning paternal values, roles, and responsibilities; being courageous; preserving the family surname, bloodline, and reputation; being the familial root and benefactor; understanding the functions of the clan system; being responsible for the family; and taking over the father's place in the family. Hmong sons can learn these values in any order depending on the lifestyle of their parents. Table 4.7 presents the typical ages at which each type of instruction begins.

In most families the responsibilities for children are divided into feminine and masculine duties. For example, cooking is traditionally the responsibility of females and chopping firewood belongs to males. But in families with no female child in the home, sons must meet all familial expectations just as daughters are expected to perform whatever tasks are necessary in families without sons. Typically, Hmong sons are given more freedom in traditional Hmong families simply because they are males, not because they are better children. This practice allows the male children to dodge basic household chores. That is why nearly 80 percent of traditional Hmong daughters know how to cook in comparison to only 20 percent of Hmong sons. Consequently, in adulthood, many Hmong men barely know how to cook and clean. Female Hmong children handle household chores far better than most male children because their training started young. In modern times, it is imperative that Hmong sons learn all familial responsibilities even if they do not customarily perform them all; otherwise, as owners of their families, they will lack the values that should enable them to build strong family foundations. Training both sons and daughters in gender role expectations for everyday life is an invaluable benefit Hmong children can pass on to their families.

In Hmong families, older children are expected to take care of their younger siblings.

Table 4.7. Apprenticeship in Paternal Tasks According to Child's Age

Task Taught	Age 1–3	Age 3–5	Age 5–7	Age 7–9	Age 9–11	Age 11–13	Age 13–15	Age 15–17	Age 17–19
Be tough/strong	x								
Emulate male model		x							
Use tools		x							
Hunt, fish, and trap			x						
Physical labor			x						
Religious rites and rituals						x			
Paternal values/roles					x				
Brave and courageous				x					
Talking/responding			x						
Maintain bloodline, etc...							x		
Friends/social issues				x					
Family root/benefactor						x			
Know clan system						x			
Responsible for family								x	
Take over father's role									x
Become responsible adult									x

Note: X indicates the approximate starting age. A child may start a little earlier or later, depending on the child's developmental stage and cognitive maturity.

In the old days, Hmong parents had to leave early in the morning to go to farms far away, and they left their older children to care for the young ones at home. Today, Hmong parents still expect their older children to shoulder this responsibility. However, western law prohibits children under the age of 14 from babysitting younger children at home. Nevertheless, Hmong parents rely on the older children to take good of the younger children during their absence. If a child gets hurt while the parents are away, the older children are blamed for being irresponsible.

In Hmong tradition, birthright plays a role in familial responsibility. Older children usually have to work harder, perform more family chores, and help parents more often than younger children. Sometimes Hmong children squabble over birthright and birth order because male children are treated more favorably than female children regardless of birth order. Despite all these gender and cultural roles, Hmong children are regarded as the seeds of the future and, to keep the familial roots alive, all Hmong parents plant and re-plant them with hope of better life and future.

Gender Norms

In the family circle, playing gender roles properly can be tricky. Fathers and mothers know their respective masculine and feminine roles but family responsibilities often overlap. For example, either the mother or the father may cook, clean, wash, discipline, drive, shop, and sweep. In some families, these and other tasks are clearly assigned to either males or females. In some families, all males eat before the females eat; in some families, daughters-in-law and fathers-in-law may not dine at the same table. Westernized Hmong children often misunderstand these gender norms. They do not understand why, for example, Hmong daughters have daily household chores but Hmong sons do not. They do not realize that, in accordance with family traditions, the girls are being trained in domestic responsibilities in preparation for their later roles as mothers. The norms involving gender roles may seem unfair, but they have remained intact for thousands of years.

Perhaps they will continue in traditional Hmong families. And, believe it or not, Hmong people prefer that Hmong females know how to perform domestic tasks, and dutiful mothers are regarded highly by Hmong people because they are knowledgeable and skillful to fulfill their feminine roles and responsibilities.

Hmong Social Norms

Every culture has its own social norms. Forms of greeting, eating customs, ways of demonstrating respect, decision-making and problem-solving processes, communication conventions, and many other social behaviors that are culturally determined. As a people living in two cultures, the U.S. Hmong have had to decide between Hmong and western social norms or figure out how to adapt the social behaviors expected in the West to the traditional norms of their Hmong heritage. Most, especially those of the older generation, still maintain Hmong culture and traditions regarding social behavior. Nowadays, Hmong not only have blended families but also have mixed family values, norms, and customs. For instance, the *Hmonglish culture* is present in most Hmong families and affects the way both Hmong parents and children communicate with one another. Also, the family food menu has changed to accommodate Americanized and native-born Hmong children who are fussy eaters when it comes to Hmong traditional food and dishes.

Social Greeting

Hmong greet one another in social settings cordially and politely based on matrimonial bloodline and generational order. Traditionally, Hmong women do not shake hands, hug, kiss, or embrace. They greet one another verbally or wave at one another unless they are addressing immediate family members or close friends. Today these once-forbidden forms of greeting have become acceptable and Hmong women can shake hands, hug, kiss, and embrace one another. However, they greet non–Hmong only verbally, occasionally shaking their hands in a formal setting. On the other hand, masculine greetings include handshakes, verbal acknowledgement, waving, and making eye contact. Hmong men shake hands with one another regardless of their relationship just to show respect for one another in public.

The greeting between married Hmong women is quite respectful and kind because they greet one another in the name of their very first child. For example, a typical exchange of greetings in the Hmong language would be as follows:

> "*Koj tuaj thiab los Maiv Kub Niam*" [You came, too, May Kue's mom].
> "*Aw kuv tuaj thiab os Yeej Niam*" [Yes, I came, too, Yeng's mom].
> "*Hais, Nyob zoo Huab Niam*" [Hi, Hua's mom].
> "*Aw nyob zoo os Mai Xis Niam*" [Yes, hi, May See's mom].

These special greetings are exchanged only between Hmong married women, not between married Hmong men. Usually, Hmong men greet one another by acknowledging their generational order and family rank, such as grandparent, parent, uncle, nephew, brother, cousin, and in-law. Culturally, the use of a person's first name is rare in Hmong greetings; however, professional titles are often applied to show respect. For example, Major General Vang Pao, Chris, Colonel Vang Fong, Chao Moueng Tou Chia, Nai Kong Say Long, and so on. Keep in mind that greeting may not be the same as addressing. Hmong grandparents and parents usually address their sons and daughters by the names of their first child instead of using their first names. For example, they refer to sons and daughters by using Melissa's father, Emilee's mother, Michael's father and mother, or Kevin's parents. Moreover, Hmong parents also use marital status to address their sons-in-law and daughters-in-law. For a son-in-law, Hmong parents use his marital status plus his first name, like son-in-law Christopher, as in Hmong, *vauv* Christopher; for a daughter-in-law, they apply her marital status plus her husband's first name, like daughter-in-law of Michael, as in Hmong, *nyab* Michael.

Traditionally, married Hmong women refrain from greeting people, especially males who are not immediate family members or relatives, because such greeting could cause misunderstanding about their marital fidelity, perhaps implying flirtation. Once they are married, Hmong women are expected to stay away from their male friends. Today, however, many married Hmong women maintain professional friendships. However, Hmong social norms do not support such social relationships unless the husbands are fully aware of the involvements. Similar norms apply to Hmong married men but laxity in men's social greetings appears to be more tolerable because of their machismo. In other words, standards regarding personal interchanges between married Hmong men are not as strict as those of married Hmong women.

Hmong tradition is that children should not greet their parents, family relatives, or in-laws by their first names, but by their familial rank and status such as aunt, uncle, or in-law and their leadership title. Hmong children also introduce their parents, relatives, and in-laws by their familial status except on rare occasions when they introduce them by first and last name to friends and neighbors. The proper way to introduce these individuals is to include their familial status along with their first names; for example, my uncle Chris, my aunt Nancy, my father-in-law Charles, and my mother-in-law Mary. Last names are optional in both informal and formal social settings. For people in leadership positions, the proper social greeting is to address people with their titles before their full names; for example, "*Nyob zoo yawg hlob nais phoo Vaj Pov*" (Hello, honorable Major General Vang Pao) or "*Nyob zoo txiv hlob nais phoo Vaj Pov*" (Hello, honorable Major General Vang Pao). The Hmong way of greeting people with official and academic titles is to use the first name followed by the title; for example, "Hello, Chris, Kay, and Bee" or "Hi, President John, Director Vang, and Pastor Mark." This is unlike the western custom, which is to introduce people with official and academic titles with the last name following the titles, such as Vang, Lee, and Yang or President Obama, Secretary of State Clinton, and Senator Rodriguez.

Hmong children are increasingly using westernized social greetings. Most children embrace, hug, kiss, and shake hands when they meet. They also greet one another with "Hello, hi, what's up, how are you?" instead of "*Nyob zoo, koj tuaj los, losi zoo siab tau ntsib koj, sib ntsib dua, mus koj os,*" and so on. This form of greeting is acceptable for non–Hmong and other children. The issue for Hmong youth is that they do not know how to greet Hmong elders, old parents, and family relatives in accordance with Hmong norms. For instance, to show politeness to a person, the Hmong standard is to say "hello, aunt, uncle, father-in-law, mother-in-law," or whatever the relationship is. The greeting word (hello) has to be used in conjunction with the status of the person. Hmong language expressions would be "*Nyob zoo niam tais, nyob zoo yawm txiv, nyob zoo phauj, nyob zoo yawg laus, nyob zoo txiv ntxawm, nyob zoo niam ntxawm*, and so on. Hmong parents and elders also use this form of social greeting for their offspring, saying, for example, "*Nyob zoo me nkauj ntxawm, nyob zoo tub ntxawg, nyob zoo metub, nyob zoo me ntxhais,*" and so on. The social greeting an individual uses reflects the individual's attitude and manner regarding the relationship; therefore, greeting Hmong people the right way is very important.

Manners

Hmong expect all Hmong people—fathers, mothers, and children—to exhibit good and polite manners. Manners—the ways one controls his or her actions, words, reactions, and emotions—are extremely important. Manners involve the exchanging of information. The two main ingredients of good manners are respect (*hwm*) for others and saving face (*tsis pub poob ntsej muag*). Hmong also expect personal politeness and consideration (*paub kev cai thiab paub xav* in Hmong). In the Hmong world, proper social manners are known as unpretentious behaviors, hiding one's needs and wants to show respect.

Manners involving communication among females are particularly important in Hmong culture. Hmong mothers are trained to control their emotions at all times, not voicing disagreements or showing disapproval in public. Any Hmong woman who violates this norm is considered rude, impolite, immature, and unstable because she has caused embarrassment and insult to her husband and other immediate family members. Hmong people prefer patient, passive, and submissive Hmong women who are considerate of others at all times. Even though these expectations are imposed on Hmong mothers and daughters alike, these norms are violated every day because many Hmong women and girls are opinionated, vocal, argumentative, and vindictive. Hmong women are permitted to vent their anger and frustration, but they are expected to do so politely and not in public.

Hmong men are also expected to control the expressions of their feelings. However, Hmong males are allowed to express contempt and disapproval. They are permitted to show their emotions, even at times with outbursts of anger. This does not mean that Hmong males can yell at Hmong women anytime they want or can explode any time in any place. It means that male aggression is culturally tolerated but not always accepted.

Manners used in one-on-one interactions contribute to social manners, and Hmong people highly regard patience, consideration, and politeness in social settings. Hmong, especially Hmong women, are expected to keep a low profile regardless of educational level or socioeconomic or professional status. For instance, talking about one's achievements is seen as showing off, arrogant, and boastful; bragging and asking for praise is not considered good manners. Hmong people do praise others; however, the person who is being praised is expected to respond passively and humbly. For example, upon being praised a Hmong might say, "Oh, that is nothing, don't mention it. … I just did what I could and thank you. … It's nothing, it is my duty. … Thank you, no problem. … I've tried my best and it is still not good enough. … (*tsis ua licas os, kuv twb tsis txawj es lam ua dog ua dig xwb os...*), or something similar." These are modest expressions, manners that Hmong people appreciate and respect. Hmong people seldom give praise or compliments, but when they do, a simple and modest reply is the acceptable response. Comparatively, for western Hmong, attitude is everything; for Hmong traditions, manner is the core of attitude.

Family Decision Making

When decisions must be made in Hmong families, mothers and fathers consult with each other and decide what is in the best interests of their loved ones. Traditionally, the Hmong father, as the head of the household, is the decision maker for the family and his wife supports his decisions. The decisions are not always wise or good, but within the family circle father and mother have full authority to decide for the family. For matters that are outside the family, the father has to consult with other male relatives before reaching a decision. Hmong fathers bear the burden of making decisions, solving problems, resolving issues, and mediating family concerns or social problems involving their immediate family members. Each Hmong family has its own way of making decision for its family members. Normally, the father has the final say because it is his family. In his absence, the mother takes his place in deciding for the family. A traditional Hmong woman will not render a decision before talking to her husband because he holds the highest position in the family regardless of his educational level, socioeconomic status, or career. No one can take his place except his mature son who is designated to be responsible for the welfare of the family.

Normally, Hmong males get together to resolve socio-cultural conflicts between family members, clan members, and outsiders. To mediate conflicts, Hmong families normally maintain a hierarchal system of male leaders for consultation and support. Traditionally, the process of involving Hmong family and cultural advisors to mediate conflicts helps Hmong parents maintain good relationships within their immediate family and with other clan members. Keep in mind that Hmong elders decide and resolve family conflicts and problems based on logic based on cultural norms, not legal codes. Sometimes a decision is culturally right but illegal; at other times, a decision may be legal but not culturally appropriate.

Children and Parent Relationship

The relationship between Hmong parents and their children is close, but most Hmong mothers generally have a closer relationship with their children than most Hmong fathers. Mothers usually manage the household, so children are around them more often than around their fathers. Hmong fathers are busy with activities outside the home such as problem solving, supervision, decision making, and protection of the whole family. Still, some fathers have very close connections with their children. Hmong fathers often distance themselves from their daughters, relying on the mothers to guide them to become responsible and well behaved adults. If the daughters get in trouble—if they misbehave, loiter, break curfew, or fail in school—the fathers blame the mothers for not doing enough to discipline their daughters. In some cases, it is necessary for the fathers to talk to their daughters in person or to confront them. This is rare because fathers typically convey information to their daughters through the mothers as messengers. This particular family norm does not mean that daughters cannot speak to their fathers. It is simply a way fathers defer to show respect for their daughters.

Just as they care for and guide their daughters, Hmong mothers are also strong supporters of their sons. But when it comes to explaining matters related to masculinity, mothers leave the instruction and guidance to the fathers. Fathers usually maintain closer relationships with their sons than with their daughters. Nowadays, a good and warm children and parent relationship is somewhat a mixture of understanding gender roles, having open communication, and sharing family responsibilities because they all belong to the trinity of a household—father, mother, and children.

Family Communication

Communication between Hmong parents and children has grown tremendously since the Hmong refugees have lived in the U.S. In the old days, Hmong fathers refrained from talking to their daughters to show respect, so communication was conducted through the mothers. Hmong mothers had open communication with all their children regardless of gender. For difficult problems or issues, they consulted their husbands or referred the children to talk to the fathers directly with the mothers present. Today, Hmong children, female as well as male, can talk to their parents directly or indirectly, depending on the situation. Mothers are always the go-between, keeping the communication warm and connected.

Some Hmong children respect this system of family communication and use it when communicating with their parents. They talk to their mothers before talking to their fathers, or they ask their mothers for suggestions and advice before sharing with their fathers. In some cases, Hmong children use the process in reverse, communicating with their mothers through their fathers. In rare situations, the mothers scold the children because the fathers will become upset over the children's actions. Sometimes, both parents attempt to mitigate the issues at hand in order to ease tension. Covering up misdeeds is not allowed but it does happen; however, the deeds nearly always come to light later. It is best to be honest with one another in dealing with family problems.

Today some Hmong parents have open communication with their children. They listen to what their children have to say instead of merely demanding their children do what the parents tell them. Direct communication between parents and children does not always happen because Hmong parents either do not have time to listen to their children or do not care about their children's concerns. In most cases, family communication occurs because there is a problem. Some Hmong fathers talk to their daughters or sons only when there are problems in school or at home. It is very important for traditional Hmong families to have healthy communication with their children. Interaction and discussion between parents and children should take place each and every day to keep family relationships warm and close and family ties strong.

Respect in the Family

Relationships and communication are at their best when family members have great respect for one another. Respect is a significant ingredient in Hmong families. Mothers and fathers show respect to their children and expect their children to honor and respect them in return. Reciprocal respect is extremely important for Hmong parents. Respect is shown by asking, talking, responding, sharing, caring, and understanding; it requires compassion, sympathy, honesty, loyalty, and empathy. Hmong parents expect their children to respect them as parents who have roles and responsibilities in the family, not as government officials who issue orders and make demands. Some children disrespect their parents because the parents cannot speak English, talk funny, and cannot understand what the children want. Some westernized children show little or no respect for their parents because the parents do not have good educations, are illiterate, and lack western values. Disrespectful children often use foul language toward their parents, speak to them directly and indirectly with slang, and sneer at them behind their backs. Respect is a two-way street; parents and children need to work together to achieve and exhibit mutual respect.

Familial respect is shown in a proper demeanor toward all immediate family members such as in-laws, grandparents, family relatives, children, grandchildren, uncles, aunts, nieces, and nephews. Hmong mothers are trained to show respect to all immediate family members by recognizing their cultural roles and familial status. Hmong children are to follow the same path when speaking to or about immediate family members, referring to their well-deserved status in the family. Addressing any immediate family member inappropriately, without properly mentioning their cultural and familial status, is considered impolite and insulting. Hmong parents immediately correct their children if they observe such behavior from them. If Hmong parents are guilty of such a breach, they apologize and ask for forgiveness because they have been intrusive and rude by mistakenly referring to someone inappropriately or by failing to recognize the individual's familial status.

Keep in mind that the purpose of properly greeting and addressing someone is to show respect in accordance with Hmong traditional values and customs. If one is unsure of the status of an individual, it is wise to address that person by a higher familial status before learning the actual status. For example, a man whose status is unknown should be addressed as brother, uncle, in-law, grandfather, or elder to show respect. Calling a woman sister, aunt, in-law, grandmother, or elder is appropriate. To show politeness, it is important for Hmong youth to follow these social norms when courting and dating someone's daughter or son.

Courtship and Dating

In Hmong culture, courtship and dating are conducted as secretive meetings between suitors. In the old days, Hmong youth went out at night to court and date their potential spouses. They talked through bamboo walls, sat around bonfires, or met at private location designated for their romantic affairs. Most Hmong parents did not meet or see their children's suitors until the day they got married. In some cases, Hmong parents selected potential suitors for their sons and daughters.

Today, Hmong children behave like western youths in matters of young romance. They hug, kiss, hold hands, spend time together at each other's houses, socialize every day, and live together as a married couple although unwed. When Hmong parents first observed these behaviors in the U.S., they were shocked. They thought western children were crazy and disrespectful to do such shameful things. Now, however, they see

these behaviors in their own children. Some Hmong parents have adapted to this reality, some are adamantly against it, and others do not care about it anymore.

In some Hmong families, parents are permissive and their children are out of control in their courtship and dating; however, the majority of Hmong families take the courtship and dating of their offspring as serious family matters. Hmong look down on the practice of bearing children out of wedlock. Hmong daughters are told about the dangers of fornication and the difficulties of unplanned pregnancy because Hmong families do not allow unmarried women to give birth at home. Some western scholars erroneously claim that Hmong people give their children freedom to engage in sexual activities irresponsibly; the truth is that Hmong parents do not condone their offspring being sexually promiscuous. On the contrary, Hmong people expect their children to court and date in accordance with their cultural norms.

Some Hmong children still honor the traditional norms of courtship and dating. Hmong parents dislike western courtship and dating practices because they want to save face. Hmong parents never want to lose face because of their children's inappropriate behaviors and actions, especially promiscuity and having children out of wedlock. Saving face is a big part of Hmong culture. Therefore, Hmong children should consider the practice of saving face for their parents when they decide to court and date their suitors; otherwise, Hmong parents would regard such precarious courtship and dating as intolerable and irresponsible acts.

To minimize the cultural shame and embarrassment in association with dating and courtship, Hmong parents should find quality time to discuss with their teenage children about their religious beliefs and values, puberty issues, human reproduction, masturbation, birth control, sexually transmitted diseases, homosexuality, personal responsibilities, and parental legal rights. Often times, there is little or no open communication between Hmong parents and children in regards to these topics. As of today, trying to save face alone is not good enough, and having little or no explicit expectations for teen children to refrain from promiscuity will not work well with westernized children because of peer pressure and external influences. For Hmong parents, having a good family name and keeping an esteemed reputation are an integral part of social status and Hmong traditions; however, in order to preserve such familial integrity, Hmong parents must be willing to educate their children early in life before it is too late.

Family Name Designations

The social courtesy name by which a Hmong person is recognized is of major importance in Hmong culture. Hmong are given hierarchical designations, something like family titles indicating seniority, birth orders, leadership role, and religious role, to indicate their position in the family structure. The designation has little to do with personal traits or socioeconomic achievements; it has everything to do with family relationships. It is used when referring to, addressing, and greeting people. Name designations do not supersede the bloodline and generational order when recognizing or addressing someone formally. For instance, Hmong men of the same clan usually recognize one another by the generational order of birth of their fathers, grandfathers, and great grandfathers. The generational orders help designate proper familial position, and social courtesy names such as paternal uncle (*txiv hlob*), young paternal uncle (*txiv ntxawm*), cousin (*npawg, muam npaw, losi viv ncaus*), son (*tub*), nephew (*tub xeeb ntswv*), and grand nephew (*tub xeeb ntswv yau*) refine the designation. Similarly, Hmong women address one another in accordance with the generational order of birth of their mothers, grandmothers, and great grandmothers, such as maternal grandmother (*niam tais laus*), maternal aunt (*niam tais*), cousin (*nus losi viv ncaus*), daughter (*ntxhais*), niece (*ntxhais xeeb ntswv*), and grandniece (*nthxais xeeb ntswv yau*).

These familial designations are appropriate for addressing people of the opposite gender. For example, Hmong children can address their paternal and maternal in-laws and relatives almost the same way with very slight differences in Hmong, as shown in Figure 4.8. Remember, Hmong children recognize their in-laws and relatives in accordance with the generational order of birth of their biological parents or the generational orders of their own births. For instance, a male child of the family can recognize his in-laws and family relatives according to the ranking of all family members:

1. The rank of ancestors (phaj pog suab thiab yawg suab)
2. The rank of great grandparents (phaj pog koob thiab yawg koob)
3. The rank of grandparents (phaj pog thiab yawg)
4. The rank of parents (phaj txiv thiab phaj niam)
5. The rank of son or daughter (phaj tub losi phaj ntxhais)
6. The rank of first cousins (ib phaj losi npawg, muam npaw, losi viv ncaus)
7. The rank of nephew or niece (phaj xeeb ntswv)

When a Hmong woman marries, she is no long called by her maiden name except by members of her biological family. Hmong people call her by her husband's first name and immediate family members address her in the name of her very first child. This cultural norm reminds Hmong women of their traditional status in the family. Even after the death of her husband, she is still remembered as his wife, called by his first name, until she is remarried. Today, married Hmong women are recognized by their socioeconomic status and educational level instead of their husbands' first names. For some that is perfectly all right, but many believe that a woman who prefers to be recognized by her title instead of her relationship with her husband is inconsiderate of her husband. Hmong husbands struggle with their public images when people address their wives by their professional titles rather than their husbands' names. Recognizing a married woman by her title suggests the woman is single, too Americanized, disrespectful, arrogant, self-centered, or not married to a Hmong man. In some cases, it is appropriate; however, in most cases, it makes the Hmong husbands feel uncomfortable and unrecognized.

When a Hmong woman is married to a professional, she is called by her husband's professional title; for example, *niam doctor Christopher*, wife of the doctor Christopher. However, when the situation is reversed and a Hmong man is married to a professional, Hmong people are hesitant to call him by her professional title such as *txiv doctor*, the husband of the doctor. Name designations are a sensitive issue in Hmong culture and both males and females must sometimes adjust their familial norms to accommodate their social status.

After a man becomes father to one or two children, his birth name is changed to a new name. His father-in-law and mother-in-law give him a social courtesy name, or a mature family name. This name replaces his initial first name and his wife is called by his new name. This is a gradual process; the initial first name fades away until it is not recognized by family members and relatives. The father's name can be changed as many times as the family

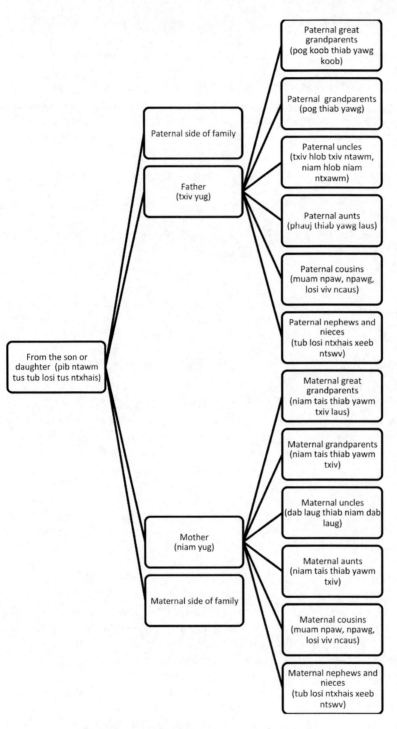

Figure 4.8. Relationships among Hmong family in-laws and relatives.

wants to reflect his health and social status. However, according to Hmong customs, if the name is changed more than three times, the change indicates a pattern of name change instead of a search for an appropriate social courtesy name. Families must be wise about name changing because the change involves religious rituals and approval by family members, especially the in-laws.

Furthermore, family name designation can add a new name to a distinguished family member. For instance, a Hmong person can have different names, like Tou Chia Vang, Nhia Chia Vang, Nao Chia Vang, Chai Chia Vang, or Cher Sia Vang, besides his legal name and professional title (Christopher Vang) because Hmong social courtesy name is only used in the Hmong family circle and community. Therefore, sometimes, Christopher Vang can be called and recognized by these unofficial names, like Tou Chia Vang, Nhia Chia Vang, Nao Chia Vang, Chai Chia Vang, or Cher Sia Vang in the Hmong community.

Family Religions

Hmong families today are diverse in their religious beliefs and practices. Apparently, college-educated individuals tend to adopt new religious values faster than do less-educated parents. This means that educated Hmong parents are more likely than tradtionalHmong parents to convert from an old religious practice to a new form of religious adherence. The majority of Hmong families still adhere to the old belief system of ancestor worship and animism associated with Taoism, Confucianism, Hinduism, and Buddhism (*teev hawm kev cai dab niam dab txiv losi coj kev cai dab qhuas qub*). The second most common religious system among U.S. Hmong is Christianity (*teev hawm kev cai ntseeg ntuj losi coj kev cai tshiab*). Some Hmong subscribe to a faith practiced by Hmong forefathers and foremothers known as *Poj Koob Yawg Ntxwv Niam Looj Tsav*. Others follow the Cha Fa faith, Islam, Taoism, and other religious sects. Very few have no religious faith at all. Religiously, Hmong traditional religious and spiritual leaders are called *txiv muam*, and practically, most Hmong religious and spiritual leaders are males. One newest group of western Hmong religious group is the *Temple of Hmongism*, the sensible mixture and condensation of old and new religious values, beliefs, and practices. Generally, Hmong family religious adherence, diversity, and practices can be explained in five broad categories, as shown in figure 4.9. However, nearly all Hmong family religious rites and rituals are religiously com-

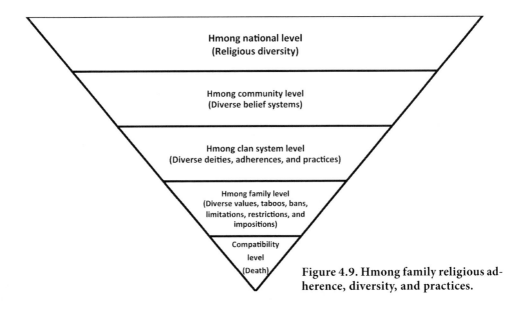

Figure 4.9. Hmong family religious adherence, diversity, and practices.

patible in some way in the celebration of the end of life with some slight differences in making sacrificial offerings to the souls and spirits of the deceased. For instance, the singing of the verses of the *Showing the Way* is done in the same way for all traditional rites and rituals, the player of the reed bamboo pipe plays the same dead song in the same way for all deceased, and death drum is played the same way throughout the funeral service; therefore, the slight difference of practices has to do with the specific religious impositions, bans, restrictions, taboos, and limitations that all surviving family members have to adhere to during the death rituals. For example, in some Hmong families, the surviving family members cannot eat the meat of any sacrificial animals during the funeral service, or the casket of the dead has to be hung on the north wall instead of putting it on top of a raised platform.

Traditionally, adult males are responsible for family religious practices. A family and its members have a family religion, and the father is in charge of all religious rituals and rites. But not all clan members share the same religious practices. Each family of a common ancestry has its own religious values and customs. For example, the Vang clans or Vang families share a common religion but have variations in religious practices. One Vang family uses a single bowl of offering and worship (*Vaj ib taig laig*) during the main religious ritual called *Nyuj Dab*. Another Vang family with a different ancestry uses 33 bowls of offering and three additional piles of special offering for the same ritual (*peb caug peb [33] txig thiab peb [3] ntsau*). In other Hmong families, the offering for the same ritual is five piles (5 *txig*), seven piles (7 *txig*), or nine piles (9 *txig*). According to Hmong legends, the standard practice became 13 bowls of offering plus 3 bowls of special treats in the late 1800s and then further changed to 10 bowls of offering with 3 bowls of special treats in the mid–1900s to clear up inconsistencies. It is unknown if all Hmong used the same religious offering before the mid–1900s; it appears that families had different religious practices and offerings. The

variations help identify the ancestry of a family, kinship, and genealogical bloodline and relationships. In some families, the father-in-law can never enter his daughter-in-law's bedroom regardless of his reasons. If he disobeys, he will suffer the ultimate consequence—the curse of blindness, spiritual sicknesses, and possible death. In Hmong, the pain and suffering are referred to as *npam*, meaning the final outcome of disobedience.

Mistakably, this religious disobedience has misled some to believe that Hmong worship the devils. Actually, Hmong only worship benovolent and holy spirits in order to cast away the evil spirits and devils. Religiously, each Hmong clan or family has its own ritual name and connection to the spiritual world for practice. Here, for example, *nrig* for Chang clan, *vug* for Cheng clan, *vug* for Fang clan, *tag* for Hang clan, *duag* for Her clan, *nkug* for Kue clan, *pluag* for Khang clan, *cai* for Lee clan, *cai* for Lo clan, *pluag* for Phang clan, *zag* for Moua clan, *dub* forThao clan, *vug* for Vang clan, *vug* for Vue clan, *mob* for Xiong clan, and *yawg* for Yang clan. As presented here, several clans do share the same ritual names and connections; therefore, they are religiously related based on their family ancestries and religious origins. Only Hmong religious and spiritual leaders can tell what these ritual names and connections really mean in religious practices. In fact, today most families have already forgotten about these ancient ritual names and conections and for that matter, more research would be needed to bring back the actual and true meaning of each ritual for future followers.

In Hmong tradition, the father is the religious and spiritual leader of the family. He performs most of the rites and rituals unless he is too young and inexperienced, in which case his father or other male relative fulfills the role for him until he is ready to carry out the practices. The mother is the organizer and coordinator of religious practices in support of the father. She helps prepare the altar and offerings. Even though she may be knowledgeable about the family religion, she is not allowed to perform religious rites and rituals except for minor ceremonies such as soul calling (*hu plig*). If the mother is a shaman, she can perform some limited rites and rituals in accordance with her spiritual capabilities. Otherwise, Hmong religious practices have always been paternal responsibilities.

Traditional religious preaching and teaching is limited to the paternal side of the family. In Christianity, however, both paternal and maternal sides are taught and trained according to the biblical scriptures. Very few old belief systems have scriptures to follow. Normally, familial religious rites and rituals are learned by emulation, oral recitation, and rote memorization. Some traditional Hmong religious rites and rituals cannot be taught at home. Even recorded rituals and verses have to be listened to outside the home or away from home. Failing to adhere to basic rules may cause harm to family members. Some Hmong religious rituals require absolute accuracy; otherwise, curses such as sickness could befall family members.

Today, different members of the same family may believe in and follow different faiths. Respect is the key to embracing different faiths and religious values and customs. The majority of Hmong people still practice the old belief systems, and hopefully, Hmong religious and spiritual leaders will find ways to help improve and modernize Hmong religious practices. Otherwise, it is foreseeable that Hmong will gradually convert to other forms of belief systems in the near future.

Summing Up

This chapter gave highlights of Hmong traditional family structure and other family matters. The Hmong people have all kinds of families: extended, nuclear, divorced, separated, two-parent, single-parent, and gay/lesbian. Since 1975, Hmong families have undergone a process of socialization. The proportion of Hmong couples who are married remains high and steady even though the divorce rate among Hmong is rising and the number of gay/lesbian families has increased gradually over the last 10 years. Nearly all Hmong families have children and Hmong family size has decreased dramatically over the last 15 years. The average family size is six. Family relationships and kinship are very important to Hmong.

Many Hmong still abide by traditional family norms but Hmong children are abandoning the traditional practices because they have to learn two or more sets of values and customs. Traditional Hmong children grasp and follow the traditional values and customs better than semi-westernized and westernized Hmong children. Hmong parents fall into three major categories: old, middle-aged, and young. Hmong children can be classified into three major categories: traditional, semi-westernized, and westernized. The sociopolitical changes that accompanied resettlement continue to impose challenges on Hmong families and parents. Gender inequity is still common in Hmong families. The preference for sons over daughters is considered old-fashioned. Maternal and paternal roles and responsibilities may appear to be unfair because they are uneven; however, they allow Hmong males and females to define their familial roles and responsibilities.

Hmong are religiously diverse, subscribing to a variety of belief systems. Family members may profess different religious faiths. Even family clans that adhere to the same belief system may practice slightly different rituals. Among Hmong, the largest faith group consists of those Hmong who follow the old belief system of ancestor worship and animism associated with Confucianism and Buddhism. The second largest group believes in Christianity. The rest adhere to different faiths and religious denominations. Hmong religious practices continue to evolve.

FIVE

Hmong Cultural Values and Customs

Nyob luag ntuj yoog luag txuj...
Nyob luag av yoog luag kav...
A Hmong proverb

Introduction

Hmong will always be Hmong no matter where they live. The Hmong brought their rich cultural values and customs with them when they came to the western nations. Their family norms and values have developed into social values and customs. After years in the West, Hmong have gone through the socialization process, making adaptations and dealing with conflict, experiencing acculturation and integration without assimilation, and now have become enculturated. Hmong still cherish and practice their traditional customs while living in a pluralistic society. Having become part of the fabric of America, Hmong are now included in the cultural diversity of the country with the motto "*e pluribus unum*"—one out of many.

Hmong families have had values and customs different from their own brought into their families because their offspring have learned and adopted new sets of norms, values, and customs. Today, a mixture of cultural practices is found in many Hmong families. This chapter presents the heritage of Hmong cultural values and customs that most Hmong still hold dear.

Values, Norms, and Customs

The unique and beautiful Hmong culture encompasses behaviors, attitudes, beliefs, practices, social norms, customs, reservations, modesties, humbleness, and characteristics that Hmong cherish, practice, nurture, and adhere to. The culture is based on the practice of a filial piety system that requires deep ethnic roots and mutual respect, especially self-effacement. Hmong culture is quite broad and varies somewhat from tribe to tribe or family to family because Hmong families came from different geographical regions in Laos and developed independently. The tribal or family differences are simply variations of the same general Hmong values, customs, and practices. Some of the cultural norms, religious rites, and formal procedures may be different, but the underlying values are the same for all Hmong.

Culturally, Hmong *values* are those abstract concepts that Hmong regard as sound, right, and of great worth. They are the principles and ideas Hmong deem to be acceptable, desirable, and compatible with Hmong cultural views. Hmong *norms* are the basic standards, models, patterns, attitudes, characteristics, behaviors, conducts, manners, and practices expected of each person of Hmong ethnicity. Hmong norms are the standards by which Hmong show respect and honor the Hmong communal way of life. Hmong *customs* are the habitual practices of Hmong cultural and traditional norms.

Hmong cultural values, norms, and customs have evolved over time. They are continuing to evolve as Hmong decide whether to adopt other cultural values and practice other cultural customs while living in the western nations. Cross-cultural adaption can make daily life in a new country easier, but acculturation may alter Hmong cultural values and customs; the effect could be positive or negative. For instance, exposure to more egalitarian gender roles in the West has had a direct impact on Hmong families, and equality of opportunity to receive an education has improved the overall socioeconomic status of Hmong families. At the same time, living as a minority in another culture has made it difficult for Hmong to maintain their traditional family lifestyles and preserve Hmong cultural values and customs for future generations.

The Patriarchal System

Presently, Hmong are not living in a patriarchal world, but the way Hmong practice, conduct, behave, and socialize is based on the old patriarchal system they used to practice for hundreds of years in the old country. The majority of Hmong still follow the centuries-old patriarchal system of societal hierarchy. The Hmong have great respect for the hierarchical system of societal stratification in their family and their community. Table 5.1 displays the order in the Hmong patriarchal system and compares it to that of other Southeast Asian and Asian groups that share similar hierarchies.

Hmong masculine figures dominate and control cultural values and customs in most parts of life. For example, Hmong women take the last names of their husbands without compromise, automatically and without question. If any Hmong woman should complain about this marital custom, the criticism would be heard faster than the roar of thunder in the sky. Very few Hmong women retain their biological family names after getting married: Mrs. Mayer Lee-Vang, Mrs. Song Xiong-Lee, or Mrs. Patty Vang-Lor. These dual last names are acceptable in western culture, but in Hmong culture, such names are odd and generally inappropriate. A married Hmong woman has to carry her husband's family name; a dual last name would signify her contempt for fully accepting her new family's name.

Some Hmong are disinclined to acknowledge their acceptance of the Hmong patriarchal system and patrilineal dominance in the practice of Hmong customs. However, Hmong behavioral and attitudinal expectations are deeply rooted in patriarchal approaches because masculinity is still the dominant force in everyday Hmong life. Some enculturated individuals have alienated themselves from this value for personal and socioeconomic reasons and espouse that Hmong men and women should be treated equally as they are under American values. This view appears to be politically correct; however, the majority of Hmong have not adopted this way of thinking. In some families, the patriarchal system is defunct but in

Table 5.1. Comparison of Hmong Patriarchal System with Selected Hierarchical Systems

Hmong	Vietnamese	Cambodian	Lao	Thai	Asian Indian
King	Scholar	King	King	King	King
Shaman/healer	farmer	monk	monk	monk	Scholar
military leader	fisherman	administrator	administrator	administrator	civic leader
civic leader	laborer	technician	technician	technician	businessman
clan leader	businessman	businessman	businessman	businessman	clan leader
teacher	teacher	teacher	teacher	teacher	teacher
farmer	farmer	farmer	farmer	farmer	farmer
laborer	laborer	laborer	laborer	laborer	laborer
parent	parent	other	parent	parent	parent
other	other		other	other	other

most families it is a primary principle of Hmong cultural life.

In the old days, following Hmong values and customs was a one-way street; today, acculturation and integration have made values and customs a two-way street. Hmong males understand the need for some flexibility and accommodation in continuing Hmong customary practices in order to promote equal rights for both sexes. But being equal under the law does not mean being equal under Hmong traditional values and customs. Some misunderstand male accommodation to the egalitarian system of the West. Gender equality does not fit with the Hmong way of life. Egalitarianism may work well in the public arena, but it does not work well in the family and the community where Hmong cultural values and customs are highly regarded and adherence to them is expected.

The Hmong patriarchal system lacks direct and consistent paternal apprenticeship and depends heavily on mothers to train the children in Hmong cultural values and customs. This does not mean the men are irresponsible, but it does place a burden on the women to preserve the Hmong cultural values and customs at home. As Figure 5.1 shows, the paternal domain of the patriarchal system is unilateral and limited to masculine values and customs whereas the maternal domain is bilateral, accommodating the needs of both male and female offspring. In other words, Hmong mothers are more practical in everyday matters than fathers because most Hmong mothers model cultural values to their offspring considerably more often than do Hmong fathers. Therefore, although all components of Hmong values and customs are part of the patriarchal system, the maternal domain of that system is the cultural training center in which children learn all components of expected behaviors and attitudes.

As Figure 5.1 illustrates, the paternal and maternal domains have a narrow scope regarding maintaining Hmong cultural customs and values. This limitation has contributed to cultural ignorance in western Hmong males; these males do not know Hmong customs and values and they expect

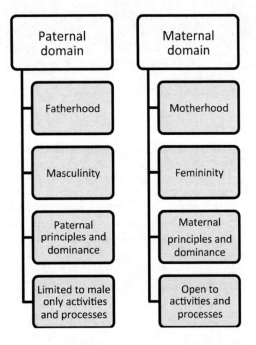

Figure 5.1. Paternal and maternal domains of hmong patriarchal system.

their wives or other Hmong females to perform all the traditional practices and domestic chores in order to be considered good Hmong women. Furthermore, even though Hmong males are in charge of the Hmong family clans, not all Hmong males are well educated in Hmong customs and values. Some Hmong women are much more knowledgeable about Hmong culture and traditions, but because of Hmong patriarchy and male dominance, they cannot perform certain cultural functions. Hmong females who overstep the cultural boundary of feminine roles are considered outcasts.

Despite the imperfections of the Hmong patriarchal system, most Hmong continue to rely on males for resolving social, societal, and cultural matters. All clan representatives are males; there has never been a female clan representative in Hmong history with a voice in Hmong cultural matters and family issues. The Hmong tribunal court system is strictly designed for Hmong males, and Hmong cultural matters are resolved by Hmong males. Marital disputes between a husband and a wife can be heard only by family members and close relatives who are male. Hmong females play no role in settling marital disputes; the involved individual is the only female allowed to be part of the process. The practice of male dominance has remained consistent across the 18 family clans for thousands of years.

Family Ancestral Origins

The inner core of every Hmong family is the family origin, the family ancestry. Hmong use family ancestry to identify genealogical lineage and bloodline, family roots and relationships, religious rites and rituals, family forefathers, family backgrounds, and past migratory histories. Hmong ancestries are what link today's Hmong to Hmong values, norms, and customs, including superstitions, taboos, restrictions, and bans. Hmong family ancestral values, norms, customs, and taboos are very important in Hmong funeral rites and rituals, traditional marriage and wedding ceremonies, major religious sacrifices and offerings, and everyday religious restrictions and bans.

Each family has a family tree and each clan is comprised of the family trees of the clan families. Each Hmong clan has its own group of family ancestries and is bound to its own sets of diverse cultural and religious taboos that originated in its past. Individual families have different requirements and restrictions because they have different ancestries. For instance, some Vang families cannot mix fruits with foods, cannot allow fathers-in-law to enter the bedrooms of their daughters-in-law and vice versa, cannot eat the meat of sacrificial animals during funeral rituals, cannot have fathers-in-law and daughters-in-law dining at the same table, cannot sit around the south side of the family cooking pit or stove, and cannot comment about the sacrificial animals and religious procedures during certain religious rituals and offerings to the souls and spirits of deceased parents. All members of the Yang clan are banned from eating the hearts of any animals killed for food or for sacrificial rituals due to ancestral prohibitions and spiritual curses.

Some Xiong families cannot wear red outfits, own red cars, or wear red hats because of ancestral restrictions that arose from the tragic death of a family member who was burned with fire. Similarly, some Vang families are forbidden to own red cars, houses, tools, and clothing.

These religious restrictions are permanent and cannot be changed or overridden. Every Hmong clan has to maintain the purity of its family ancestral taboos and restrictions for the wellbeing of clan members. All family members have to adhere to the ancestral obligations unless they have converted to new forms of religious practices such as Christianity, Islam, Buddhism, Confucianism, or Hinduism. Failure to observe the restrictions can bring spiritual imbalance and curses. Hmong people do not dare to disregard the ancestral bans unless they are willing to risk their lives.

Hmong children, especially male offspring, are taught about their family ancestries early in life so they will understand the religious practices of certain family taboos because the male children are the family roots that are responsible for carrying on the family traditions. Normally, Hmong children learn their family ancestries from their biological parents and elders who are in charge of religious rites and rituals. Each clan has different family groups and subgroups with different family ancestries, and parents and elders have to teach their children about their particular family ancestry. A Hmong family ancestry is identified by *four elements* of the family's origin: family ancestral story associated with the family traditions; the name of the first family ancestor who emigrated from China to Laos; ancestral restrictions and bans; and the cow sacrificial ritual and offering.

Here is an example of the elements that identify family ancestry from a Vang family:

FAMILY ANCESTRAL STORY

A long, long time ago, the ancestor of this Vang family married a beautiful Hmong woman. The couple built their life together and had children. They appeared to have a normal life, living happily together for many years. However, the wife had a dishonest heart and could not let go of her former boyfriend. She continued to have extramarital relations with him. No one knew about the wife's extramarital affair until after the husband died and his sister discovered the cause of his death.

He had become sick and lay in bed to recover from his illness. The wife, instead of taking good care of him, sought an opportunity to get rid of him. Taking advantage of his frail condition, she plotted to kill him in order to continue her adultery with her lover. For days and nights, she and her lover concocted an evil scheme and premeditated the murder of her husband. One night while the husband was asleep, she drove a steel chisel into his skull, killing him instantly. The next morning she relayed the sad news to her family members that she had found her husband dead in bed. She then consulted with her family members to help organize his funeral service.

The husband's family members assumed that he had died of natural causes; they had no suspicion of any foul play. The Hmong traditional funeral was held and members of his side of the family were invited as funeral head guests. His oldest sister was the most important head guest of all. About midway through the funeral service, the oldest sister became extremely sad. She was heartbroken and spent a lot of time weeping and crying next to her brother's corpse. She cried for long hours.

On the day before his burial, the distraught, depressed, and mournful sister searched the deceased brother's outfits, shrouds, and dead horse gurney to make sure everything was intact. When she gently rubbed her hand over his hair and head, she felt a hard spot on the right side of his skull above the ear. She wondered what it was and explored the area with her fingers. She discovered a steel chisel being pushed outward by the decay inside the skull. The oldest sister was shocked and stopped crying immediately. She called family members to the casket and showed them what she had found. Everyone was in total shock. The family notified the funeral directors, crew members, family clan leaders, and relatives from both families about this unexpected and unprecedented discovery. The family clan leaders, the dead man's sons, the elders, and the funeral directors verified that a steel chisel was embedded in the skull and determined that the chisel was the cause of death.

Now they had a murder case to solve. Family members gathered to sort out all the possibilities. They could think of no one else who could have done it besides his wife. So, family clan leaders, elders, and funeral directors brought the unfaithful wife in for questioning. No law enforcement agency was involved in the investigation; only Hmong elders, clan leaders, funeral crew members, and immediate family members. The investigation focused entirely on the wife as the prime suspect because she was the last person who saw him alive.

First the wife adamantly denied any involvement in her husband's death, but she was the person who slept next to him and the only person who provided care for him. The wife could not provide any credible alibi or evidence to clear her of guilt or prove her innocence. Family leaders, the man's sons and daughters, funeral directors, and relatives searched for any enemies who might have wanted the man dead, but they found none. Everyone insisted that the wife had to tell the whole truth about his death. Her family members, especially her brothers, threatened that if she did not tell the truth about the manner of his death she would face harsh consequences. Her brothers refused to defend her unless she told the truth. Finally, after long hours of interrogation, the unfaithful wife broke down emotionally and told them what had happened. She admitted killing him, but said she did it for the sake of her extramarital affair and she did not act alone.

When she revealed the scheme, she implicated her lover, who was the reed bamboo pipe player for the husband's funeral. He was brought in for questioning but denied knowing anything about the man's death. However, he admitted having an affair with the wife. The wife continued to insist that he was involved in the planning of the murder. The investigators concluded that her lover was involved in the death because of their extramarital affair. She admitted driving the steel chisel into his skull during his sleep and she also admitted committing adultery while he was still alive. After all the evidence was gathered, the investigative crew agreed that the only righteous sentence for both culprits was death.

On the day of the husband's burial, both murderers were taken to the graveside. There they received their sentence: they were to be buried alive under his casket.

They pleaded for their lives but no leniency was granted. The wife and her lover were thrown into the grave with their hands and feet bound and the husband's casket was lowered on top of them. All three were buried together in the same grave.

About a year later, the grave was found to be covered with bushes and shrubs and a bulky, thorny three was growing from the center of the gravesite. According to family descriptions, the tree flourished, growing to be big with beautiful blossoms. From that point onward, according to family descendants, this Vang family prospered.

Any Vang clan members, families, or subgroups that share this ancestral story have the same familial roots and ancestral origin.

FAMILY ANCESTOR AND FOREFATHER

This Vang family can identify its forefather who came from China to start life anew in Southeast Asia, specifically Laos. The great grandfather was Mr. Blia Sue Vang. He had two sons, Chong Kao Vang and Qia Pao Vang. The three became the ancestors for this Vang family. Any Vang families or subgroups that can link their family ancestry to these three individuals belong to the same familial roots and ancestral origin.

ANCESTRAL RESTRICTIONS AND BANS

Initially, this Vang family was banned from eating the meat of sacrificial animals during funeral services, but the ban was lifted after many years. Therefore, currently this Vang family has two sets of family ancestral origins: some families that still practice the old ban and other families that are free of the ban.

SACRIFICIAL RITUAL AND OFFERINGS

The biggest religious offering, the most solemn religious ritual, is the cow sacrifice and ritual (*ua nyuj dab* in Hmong), which is an offering to the benevolent spirits of deceased parents or grandparents or a compensation for curses from the spirits and souls of deceased parents. For this Vang family, the cow sacrificial offering can be done with a single bowl containing cooked internal organs combined with certain parts of the sacrificial cow (*Vaj ib taig laig*). Any Vang families or subgroups that practice this same sacrificial rite has the same familial roots and ancestral origin.

The sacrificial rituals of all Hmong are very similar, but the religious protocols of the sacrificial offerings are specific to each family with the same ancestry. The offerings must be made according to the family protocols. Differentiating Hmong family ancestries can be tricky because many Hmong families practice identical sacrificial rites and rituals and religious offerings. For instance, in the cow sacrifice and ritual, many family clans practice 33 piles of offerings plus 3 piles of special treats. Some family clans use 5 piles of offerings, some use 7 piles, some use 9 piles, some use 13, and some have no special treats. The way the rite is performed is determined by the family's ancestry.

In identifying a family's ancestral origin, Hmong people use *two* guiding phrases: *tug qhaib tug qhab tses*, meaning sharing the same household spirits, rites, and rituals; *tug tua tug tsev tau*, meaning one can die in other's house; and *thooj dab koom qhua*, meaning having the same religious practices and funeral rites and rituals. The phrase "*tug qhaib tus qhab tses*" implies that a member of the same family clan can die in the home of another family member because they have the same household spirits, rites, and rituals; the phrase "*thooj dab koom qhua*" means that the funeral service and death rituals of a deceased Hmong can be administered by different members of the same clan without causing any religious harm to the families of the dead and the living because the families share the same family ancestral rites and rituals. If the families did not share the same rituals, religious restrictions and bans would need to be applied. Hmong families are distinct entities when it comes to religious practices, sacrifices, and offerings.

Some family clans can identify their ancestral origins in other ways. The Vue clan can identify its genealogical lineage and bloodline through the special tree called ntseej (*coj ntseej* in Hmong) or the special bush called tauj (*coj tauj* in Hmong) used during the funeral rituals. Many Hmong family clans identify their family ancestries by the sun exposure ritual (*Hmoob tshwm tshav* in Hmong) or the covered ritual (*Hmoob pos* in Hmong) that is part of their funeral rituals. Other family clans identify their family ancestries by the way the casket of the dead sits on a raised platform (*Hmoob txawb* in Hmong) inside the house or the way the casket of the dead hangs on the north wall (*Hmoob dais* in Hmong) inside the house during the funeral rituals. Hmong family ancestral origins are an integral of the Hmong clan system.

Hmong Clans

The origin of the Hmong clan system is a mystery because Hmong do not know for certain how each tribe got its family name (*surname*) in the first place. Many Hmong think that the Chinese gave Hmong their family names during the Spring and Autumn eras and Warring States periods. They believe that a long time ago, Hmong recognized one another by family groups and tribes, but not by family names. Hmong used to live as a close group. When the Chinese conquered Hmong land, Hmong were introduced to the idea of different family clans with different last names. When the Chinese oppressed and persecuted the Hmong, Hmong had to use the family names given by the Chinese or face even more harsh and inhumane political reprisals.

Another version of how Hmong received their family names has the names originating with the Hmong themselves. According to this version, Hmong had no choice but to adopt the Chinese way of life because the Chinese oppressors carried out atrocities and ethnic cleansing. To survive, the Hmong assimilated into the dominant culture, creating family names similar to the Chinese to save themselves from being wiped out.

Since Hmong keep no record of their ancestors, any information about their origins and their distant past can be learned only from oral traditions. Today, Hmong still talk about how their ancestors emigrated from China. One Hmong elder related that his great grandfather told him that his forefather adopted the Chinese values, customs, and norms just to elude capture and imprisonment. Because the Chinese were after Hmong

rebels, this elder's forefather and many other Hmong changed their names to Chinese names and blended into the dominant culture in order to be spared by the Chinese. The Chinese spared the lives of Hmong who had the same last names as Chinese and looked like Chinese; therefore, Hmong voluntarily adopted Chinese family names. This claim is supported by the similarities between Hmong and Chinese last names: *Wang-Vang, Yang-Yang, Chan-Chang, Lee-Lee (Ly-Ly, Li-Li), Lo-Lo, Han-Hang, Khan-Khang, Mou-Moua, Hsiung-Xiong, Tao-Thao, Wu-Vue, Hue-Her, Ku-Kue, Kon-Kong, Chu-Chue, Cheng-Cheng, Pang-Pha,* and *Feng-Fang.* However, Chinese have nearly 100 family surnames and Hmong have only 18. This is another mystery: Why do Hmong not have other Chinese last names such as *Huang, Man, Mao, Yee, Ng, Teng, Gao, Jin, Tong, Ho, Tian, Yin, Sun, Gong, Dong, Lu,* and so on? Perhaps, the twelve original Hmong tribes are the sole survivors of the brutal ethnic extirpation taking place during the Ming and Qing Dynasties from the 1300s to the early 1900s.

Whatever the reason, the forced adoption of Chinese surnames severely damaged Hmong group solidarity because families from one tribe or family group could end up with different last names during the migration process. For instance, Vang and Fang are brothers, Thao and Kue are distant cousins, Phang and Lo share a common ancestry, Chue and Chang are one family, Kong and Khang are brothers, and Her and Hang are distant brothers. Having different last names means belonging to different groups, and grouping contributes to division, separation, and territorial sovereignty. Grouping erodes cooperation, bonds, trust, unity, and support. As Hmong still believe, the Chinese successfully exploited Hmong people by giving them family surnames. Ever since, Hmong have become solitary groups, families, clans, and tribes.

All Hmong families today belong to the complex clan system; each family is a clan or a tribe. Altogether, the Hmong have 18 different clans or tribes, each with its own family name, or surname. At one time there were more than 18 clans. In the present clan system, clans were consolidated and reduced to 18. Although there are 18 clans, there are only 12 main or original Hmong families or tribes. Inappropriate cultural practices involving family taboos and restrictions resulted in the creation of six new families, as indicated in the earlier Figure 3.1.

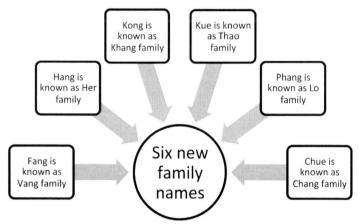

Figure 5.2. Six families added to the 12 original families.

The Hmong clan system plays a major role in shaping Hmong cultural values and customs because each clan has its own family leaders, religious practices, and social norms and customs. As mentioned earlier, each Hmong family has its own ancestors and migration history from China. The division of the Hmong into clans has at times divided and at times unified Hmong in the sociopolitical arena. In some ways, Hmong are their own worst enemies in the political arena because Hmong have betrayed their own leaders in the past. On the other hand, when unified Hmong are staunch allies and true freedom fighters, they become saviors who would sacrifice their lives to save others.

Despite the separation into clans, Hmong consider themselves part of the larger group of Hmong who share common cultural values and customs. The cultural bond as well as marital kinship keeps Hmong clans and families inextricably related. Some Hmong think of the clan system or family last names

for marital purposes only. All Hmong belong to one big family because of intertribal marriages, kinship, and common ancestors. Even though the clan system divides Hmong somewhat in accordance with family lineage, ancestral bloodline, and tribal sovereignty, marital kinship unifies Hmong families and clans.

The Hmong clan system serves several valuable functions:

1. It enables individual Hmong families to maintain their genealogy.

2. It perpetuates Hmong marital practices.

3. It identifies and separates Hmong families and subgroups for cultural purposes.

4. It facilitates the functioning of Hmong families and community.

5. It allows individual Hmong families to have cultural and religious sovereignty.

Overall, Hmong families and communities function well in the Hmong clan systems because family leaders provide leadership and adherence to religious practices that keep the bonds in Hmong families tight. If the clan system were to disintegrate, Hmong families would lose their genealogies, marital practices would become complex, and Hmong culture and traditions would be destroyed.

In recent years, some Hmong have advocated the dissolution of the clan system and the elimination of Hmong family names. They have done so in order to allow Hmong individuals who have the same last names to marry. Most Hmong have rejected this proposal as an insult to Hmong cultural values, customs, and traditions. Had such a petition been granted, Hmong marital practices would have been a devastating and tragic mess. The Hmong clan system is the foundation of Hmong socio-cultural wellbeing, and maintaining long-standing traditions benefits all Hmong.

Hmong Ecological System

In Hmong culture, the family is the foundation of social structure and stability. The family unit is part of a social network that includes other relatives in the community. A Hmong child learns Hmong cultural values and customs in an ecological system made up of his or her parents, siblings, immediately family members, and familial relatives, as shown in Figure 5.3. Cultural learning takes place mostly at home, not in a well-established or formalized process. Most mothers and fathers model to their offspring how to behave based on Hmong familial and traditional values and customs. The biological and social habitat of a Hmong child helps determine his or her understanding and appreciation of Hmong cultural values and customs. Traditional Hmong parents train their children in the basic Hmong cultural norms and practices such as greeting people, welcoming others, entertaining guests, cooking, cleaning, serving, and controlling their behaviors and attitudes in different social situations. In westernized Hmong families, these norms and practices may be absent because children adopt American values or because the traditional practices are considered old-fashioned.

Figure 5.3 depicts the general Hmong cultural ecology but the cultural specifics vary from family to family. What is appropriate for one Hmong family may not necessarily be accepted or workable in other Hmong families. Even though most Hmong share similar if not identical cultural values and customs, cultural variations still exist. Hmong children can become confused when other Hmong families' values and customs are different from their own. Some Hmong families do not embrace Hmong cultural values and do not practice Hmong customs. Some Hmong families have standards and expectations for their offspring that are incompatible with those of other Hmong families. For instance, White Hmong families expect their daughters-in-law to perform household chores differently from Blue Hmong families, and older Hmong households expect their children to know more about Hmong cultural values and customs than younger Hmong households. These particular expressions of Hmong cultural values and customs are determined by the Hmong family ecological system that is comprised of the father, the mother, and the children (See Figure 5.4).

Respecting Parents and Elders

Hmong expect their children to honor and show great respect for Hmong eld-

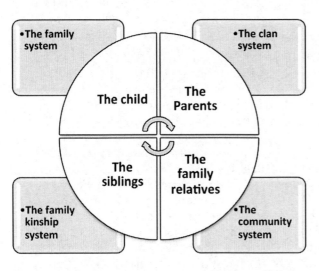

Figure 5.3. The Hmong ecological system.

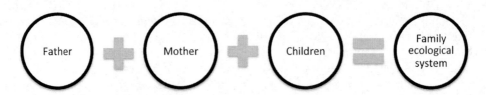

Figure 5.4. Hmong family ecological system.

ers and Hmong parents regardless of their social and professional status. Elders and parents are considered guardians of young people because Hmong believe that without the elders and parents the young people would not survive. An old Hmong saying illustrates this thought: "*Pub laus noj ces laus nco tshav ntuj, pub menyuam yaus noj ces menyuam yaus zov nruj.*" The meaning is: "Feed the old people and they will remember the kindness; feed the children and they will stay close by." Metaphorically, this saying means that respecting the elders and parents brings blessings and fortune, and caring for the children results in mutual benefit.

Hmong elders and parents play a vital role in Hmong cultural life. They are needed in all the traditional rituals and ceremonies such as weddings, funerals, family feasts, and the practices of shamanism. Their presence brings honor to the families hosting the cultural events. Moreover, blessings from elders and parents can uplift the host families, establish a peaceful state, and bring tranquility and harmony to those in attendance. In other words, the presence of the elders and parents bestows worth and meaning on cultural events.

Hmong employ symbolic and metaphorical sayings to convey messages that honor Hmong elders and parents. For example, "*Hlub niam hlub txiv thiaj tau ntuj ntoo, hlub pog hlub yawg thiaj tau qhov chaw zoo*" means "Love mom and dad to receive blessings; love grandmother and grandfather to earn a peaceful resting place." This saying tells children that if they care and provide for their biological parents they will receive blessings in life and if they care and provide for their grandparents they will have a peaceful resting place upon death. Hmong believe that showing kindness to their elders and parents yields a life-long reward of greatness and success. The ancestral and parental spirits will bless the children of the family, giving them fortune in life. Nowadays, this Hmong family value is known as *social and cultural contigent reciprocity*, or simply, the *serve-and-return* favor and exchange throughout life between parents and children. As expressed conjecturally in Hmong, "*Ua qoob ua loo los npaj tshaib, tu tub tu kiv los npaj laus,*" meaning, "Grow crops to prevent hunger, raise children to prepare for old age."

Sayings such as this may seem meaningless to people who think that working hard to earn academic degrees and good jobs is more important than respecting and honoring elders and parents. This belief, however, is culturally nearsighted because Hmong firmly believe that one's successes in the present life are predetermined by the goodness of one's behaviors, attitudes, and conduct in one's previous life as well as in the present life. Hmong who disrespect and dishonor their elders and parents will receive little or no blessings, and they may be cursed by the ancestral and parental spirits. Respecting and honoring Hmong elders and parents remains a most important fundamental Hmong value.

Hmong Social Behaviors

Culturally, Hmong expect one another to be well-bred and well-mannered at all times. But being considerate of others is one of the highest Hmong social values. It is also true for girls or females to develop coy attitudes and personality in order to gain respect from elders. Hmong people are somewhat conservative, have a strong sense of formality with one another, and exhibit extreme politeness and gratitude. Mature Hmong individuals (*yog neeg paub cai*) are unpretentious. Hmong adolescents can be unpretentious as well, depending on their level of apprenticeship in Hmong cultural values and customs. Take as an example an offer of an apple. An unpretentious Hmong may say at first that he does not want the apple. If the giver insists, the person will take the apple as a true offer rather than a tease. Most Hmong adults are unpretentious. In their social encounters, Hmong are humble, modest, considerate, understanding, compassionate, sympathetic, and empathetic. These behaviors are characteristic of Hmong regardless of their socioeconomic status, educational level, or profession.

In Hmong culture, humility and modesty

go hand in hand. Bragging about oneself is not acceptable. One must maintain an attitude of ordinariness and let others boast about his or her attractiveness, skill, knowledgeable, or other qualities or achievements. A mature Hmong person who is being complimented will react with a modest response. For instance, a Hmong shaman who has been commended for his wonderful performance in helping cure a sick person might say, "The performance was not as good as you deserve; I am not particularly good, so please forgive me" or "It was nothing; do not mention it." The shaman does not merely say "thank you"; he responds humbly because he does not want a compliment to override his performance.

In the old days, Hmong people gave compliments very rarely. Only subordinates thanked their superiors and leaders and children thanked their parents. Giving praise was considered unproductive because it would lead to failure. Instead of giving compliments, the older generation used words like "okay, not bad, right on," or "practice harder." The old way of thinking is still present, so compliments and thanks are not given liberally. However, most Hmong understand that expressing appreciation and gratitude is socially appropriate and quite common today in the West.

The way Hmong people express appreciation is quite different from western ways. Hmong give compliments indirectly and in negative ways. For instance, a Hmong may tease a toddler, saying the child is unlovable or ugly (*cas yuav zoo tau niag tsis txim hlub tsis txim nyiam kiag li lau...*). A Hmong would understand this as a compliment whereas a western person would take it as a direct insult to the toddler. The rationale behind the indirect and negative nature of the praise is that it tells the toddler (the object of the compliment) that no one will take him or her away from the child's parents. Moreover, giving a truthful and direct compliment makes the child vulnerable to sickness and evil spirits. Even more importantly, the soul of the toddler may be harm by sincere, truthful, and direct complimentary words.

The Hmong way of giving thanks presupposes a deep understanding of the situation that warrants the gratitude. Mature appreciation begins with consideration of others; it demonstrates a profound understanding of what the person to whom the thanks is directed has done. For instance, a Hmong who has been a guest in someone's house must express appreciation for such an act subtly, considering the sacrifice, hard work, time, preparation, and expense the person has put into the act of housing him. In return for the expression of thanks, the one who was a guest receives a humble and modest acknowledgement with indirect expressions to the effect that the benefactor regrets having been unable to render the hospitality in a way that better accommodated the needs and wants of the guest. In Hmong, the exchange might be as follows:

Ua tsaug os mos yij Bee thiab phauj Mai, neb tsis cia li os, neb tseem npaj zaub npaj mov rau peb sawv daws tau no ib pluag uake thiab, neb siv nyiaj siv txiaj thiab caij nyoog los ua tau ib pluag mov zoo txim qab kawg nkaus, kuv ua neb ob leeg tsaug ntau ntau nawb, peb noj ib pluag lawm los yuav tseg txhiab txhiab pluag mov rau neb kom neb noj tsis paub tag nawb... [In English, *thank you, brother-in-law Bee and sister Mai. You two did not let us pass by. You two have prepared a meal so we could all feast together. You two spent money and time preparing this delicious meal. I thank you so very much. We ate one meal to leave you thousands of meals for you two to dine in the near future...*]

Lus teb, Ua tsaug ntau ntau lau, dab laug, rau koj cov lus nyiaj lus kub... [In English response, *thank you so very much, brother-in-law, for your words of blessing...*]

Hmong social behaviors demonstrate compassion, sympathy, and empathy. Hmong people will not show up at a family meal without an invitation. But if a family experiences a tragedy such as a death or a catastrophe, Hmong people chip in voluntarily without asking. At any Hmong funeral service, thousands of Hmong people donate money to help the deceased's family. In return, the relatives of the deceased thank the donors with a promise to return the favor in the near future if they are able to and if not, to remember the kind and generous donation forever, as typically expressed in Hmong:

> Ua tsaug os mos … koj tsis cia li, koj saib neej saib tsav, saib duab saib ze … koj tuaj nrog peb saib peb xyuas ua rau peb twb zoo siab tsis txawj tag … koj npaj nyiaj npaj txiaj tuaj pab peb xyom cuab nta dab nta qhua puav tam li ncej txhawb … yog peb txawj ua lub neej xws luag ces peb yuav pauj tau koj tus txiaj tsha txiaj ntsim … yog peb tsis txawj ua lub neej ces peb yuav nco koj tus txiaj tsha txiaj ntsim mus tag ib sim mos…
> [In English, *thank you. … You would not forget us. You consider family kinship, family relatedness. … Your joining us makes us ever so happy. … You bring money to help our devastated family offer rituals on a temporary basis. … If we can make a living like others, then we can return your generous assistance. … If we cannot make a living like others, then we will remember your generous assistance forever…*]

These are just a few examples of the social behaviors that are characteristic in Hmong culture. There are many other behaviors that are specific to different life situations such as marriage, death rituals, award ceremonies, certain social events, and cultural celebrations. To describe them all would take considerable time and space. These few are given here to acquaint westerners with Hmong thinking and customs so they can develop a greater understanding of their interactions with Hmong people.

Hmong Humility and Proper Manners

Proper Hmong manners requires mastery of a few important phrases: losing face (*poob ntsej muag*), showing off (*muaj plhus*), knowing one's manners (*paub kev cai*), public disgrace (*nrhuav ntsej muag*), and self-control (*tswj tus kheej*). The essence of good manners is to always be in control of one's verbal communications by following the basic principles of thinking before acting and speaking with respect, civility, humility, and modesty. One must think carefully before speaking because it is not *what* one is going to say that matters,

but it is *how* one says it. The importance of thinking before speaking in order to show courtesy and respect is found in the Hmong expression "*Ntov ntoo yuav tsum saib ceg qhuav,*" meaning, "Watch for the dried branches before chopping down a tree." Reckless speech and actions that hurt someone's feelings can cause offenses, intentionally or unintentionally, and such actions are considered rude and impolite or, in some cases, immature.

Westernized Hmong view traditional manners as old-fashioned, but most Hmong still have great respect for proper manners. Hmong generally favor collectivism over individualism. That means that children learn and practice proper manners not for their own benefit, but because acting in polite ways brings honor and praise not only to the child, but also to all his or her family members and the entire clan. Traditionally, Hmong parents choose their daughters-in-law carefully according to their display of proper manners. They want their sons to marry women who understand cultural expectations such as doing household chores, being courteous and respectful, knowing right from wrong, and demonstrating a willingness to be subjugated to the family structure.

Hmong children who are well-mannered are frequently recognized and commended for their behavior outside the family circle and Hmong parents refer to these children as *ntxhais nquag thiab tub nquag*—dutiful daughters and sons. Dutiful Hmong children understand their cultural values, customs, and expectations regardless of their age and education. In the family, dutiful children relieve their parents of the responsibility of performing household tasks, and for Hmong parents, having such children is an enjoyment and a reward for the sacrifices they make in raising children. The Hmong expression is *ua qoob ua loos los npaj tshaib, tu tub tu kiv los npaj laus*. The meaning is: growing crops to prevent hunger, raising children to prepare for old age.

Proper manners come into play when a Hmong wants to seek help from someone who is in a higher position in the family or of a higher authority in the community. Even children questioning or asking something from their parents should convey the request in a manner that is not intrusive or impolite. Similarly, Hmong who wish to ask something of a person in authority must find the right way to do so. Hmong children are taught not to argue with someone who is older than they, but rather to show respect. They are instructed not to look at people directly in the eyes when addressing them or talking with them. Today, westernized Hmong cannot refrain from making requests of their parents or authority figures because they want answers to their questions. Some parents and people in authority accept this but others consider the questioning rude and impolite. If the questions imply criticism, the offense is greater; most Hmong do not appreciate direct criticism even if it is justified.

Proper manners dictate how Hmong conduct themselves around family members and other people. Hmong children as well as adults are expected to wear appropriate clothes, groom themselves properly, engage in proper conversations, and entertain guests properly. Wearing tight clothes around Hmong parents is not good manners because tight clothes show off body parts and revealing oneself through clothing is not only embarrassing but also immature. Poor grooming is an indication of laziness. Having voluntary conversations with different women or men is considered immature and discussing people's personal business is considered hot-headed and intrusive. For married women, tattling and gossiping are not only bad manners but also cause humiliation and insults to family members, especially to husbands and the responsible males of the household. An old Hmong saying states, "*Poj niam ua qaib qua, txiv neej sawv sib tua,*" meaning, "Women are the roosters who crow to wake up men to go to war." This suggests that men may respond to women's gossiping words and wage war against one another based on the women's information that may not be true.

Social conduct is extremely important for all married Hmong individuals regardless of gender. Hmong expect their daughters-in-law to wear clothing that covers their body loosely and avoid tight outfits, shorts, short skirts, tank tops, tube tops, spaghetti straps, and swimsuits unless such clothing is appropriate for a particular occasion. Sons-in-law are expected to wear appropriate clothes, to have good grooming, to have a courteous and respectful demeanor, and to accommodate others with humility, modesty, and understanding. Simply, well-mannered individuals are always mindful of what they wear, how they talk, what they share, and how they act. Ill-mannered individuals over expose themselves and are not considerate of others. Today, Hmong people accommodate western views in order to adapt to different situations. Nevertheless, Hmong still practice traditional manners.

Hmong Kinship and Relatives

Normally, a Hmong family has three sets of family kinship and relatives. Hmong kinship and relatives are bound with marital and intertribal ties. The first set consists of the immediate family members (*kwv tij koom niam koom txiv yug*), the second set includes most members of the clan or the clanmates (*pawg kwvtij koom ib lub xeem*), and the third set is made of blood relatives of the in-laws (*neejtsa*). The first two sets are connected by blood kinship, the third by marital kinship. Socially, Hmong families have a fourth set of family members: members of the community at large. These are called relative guests (*qhua*) and include distant relatives, acquaintances, friends, and all significant others. The relationships among various family members are what enable Hmong to know how to address one another with proper respect and honor. Hmong often use an umbrella term to include all kinship and relatives: *Kwv tij neej tsa*, meaning all Hmong brothers and relatives.

Blood kinship and marital kinship place individual Hmong in a generational order. Hmong generational order has nothing to do with age, but with birth order of family ancestry. The highest generational order is that of a person's ancestors and great grandparents. The next order is that of grandparents, then of parents, then of the child. So a person's generational order is determined by who his or her parents are. Children of the same parents—and children of those parents' siblings—are in the same generational order in the clan regardless of age. Hmong generational order is illustrated in Figures 5.5 and 5.6.

Hmong refer to one another by their po-

sition in the generational order and their relationship to the mother's or father's side of the family. So a maternal uncle and his wife are *dab laug niam dab laug*; a young paternal uncle and his wife, *niam ntxawm txiv ntxawm*; an older paternal uncle and his wife, *niam hlob txiv hlob*; a paternal aunt and her husband, *phauj thiab yawg laus*; a maternal aunt and her husband, *niam tais thiab yawm txiv*; and so on. Personal names are not used unless one is introducing a person to some-

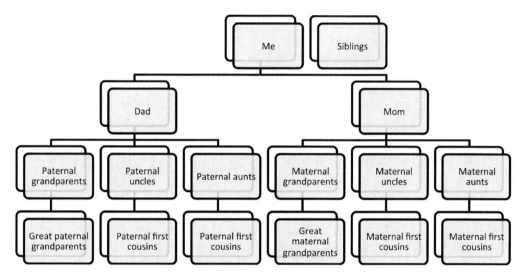

Figure 5.5. Generational order for paternal and maternal bloodlines.

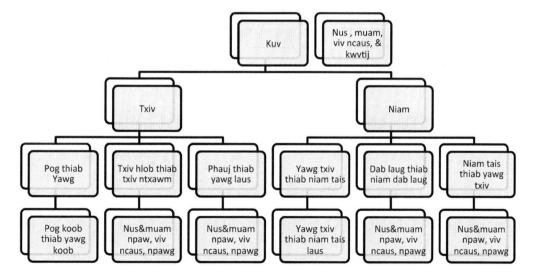

Figure 5.6. Generational order for paternal and maternal bloodlines in Hmong.

one. In that case, instead of presenting Mary and John as "my aunt and uncle," the person making the introduction would say, "These are my Aunt Mary and Uncle John." Typically, Hmong children do not know the first names of most of their relatives because they do not call them by their names.

When a Hmong marries and has children, the names used for relatives change. At this point, the newly married Hmong, when he or she has children, addresses all relatives in the way his or her children should address them. For instance, the father addresses his own sister as aunt (*phauj*) instead of sister (*muam*) on behalf of his children, and the father addresses his own parents as grandmother and grandfather (*pog thiab yawg*) instead of mother and father (*niam thiab txiv*) on his children's behalf. The reason for the change is to enable the children to learn the proper manner of referring to their relatives by recognizing their rank in the generational order of the family.

Whether an individual Hmong embraces Hmong values and customs or not, he or she has to know that marital kinship is extremely important in everyday Hmong life. Kinship is involved in all Hmong cultural customs. It plays a significant role in Hmong death rituals and marriage traditions. For instance, during the kneeling down ceremony (*pe*) in a Hmong wedding, the groom and his best man are required to kneel to pay respect to all relatives of the family in accordance with their generational order. Sometimes westernized Hmong dishonor Hmong marriage customs and celebrate their weddings in the western manner. In other cases, westernized or semi-westernized Hmong hold two wedding ceremonies, one to celebrate their civil union and one to preserve and honor Hmong culture and traditions.

Hmong Social Greetings

As mentioned earlier, today, Hmong practice a variety of social greetings; however, traditional Hmong still follow the old ways of addressing, acknowledging, and recognizing one another. Hmong have learned the social greetings of different cultures such as the Chinese, Lao, Thai, French, American, Australian, Canadian, and German. Typically, they greet one another by shaking hands, embracing, hugging, and waving. Generally, Hmong women do not shake hands and Hmong men do not hug one another. Giving a Hmong woman a high five is appropriate today and although kissing is not a traditional Hmong social greeting, it has become quite common between children and adults.

Knowing how to address people with their proper names and status is very important. Hmong people greet one another according to their kinship rank based on generational order. For instance, a girl greets an older brother as *tij laug*, an older sister as *niam laus*, the older brother of her father as *txiv hlob*, the younger brother of her father as *txiv ntxawm*, the sister of her mother as *niam tais*, and the sister of her father as *phauj*. Even two perfect strangers establish a temporary likely kinship in order to address each other politely; later they take the time to determine the accurate kinship relationship. For example, a young Hmong may call an older Hmong a big brother (*tij laug*), or the younger one may call the older "uncle" (*yawm txiv losi txiv ntxawm*) or "aunt" (*niam tais losi phauj*) just to show respect. The pseudo kinship could last a long time and even become permanent; however, most Hmong are related and are able to trace their actual kinship. Pseudo kinship may be based on the marriage of a niece, nephew, or family relative. For example, an individual may address a friend whose relationship is unknown but who has the same last name as a brother-in-law as "brother-in-law." Sometimes these Hmong social greetings appear peculiar, but for the most part, they are acceptable because they are given and received in politeness and humility.

Remember that Hmong refer to and therefore greet others according to the way their children refer to them. For instance, a brother and sister may address each other as aunt (*phauj*) and uncle (*dab laug*) because those are the terms their children use for them.

Sometimes people are called in accordance with the distant marital kinship relationship of a well known family or individual person. For example, a person who shares the same generational order as his prominent clan leader may be greeted according to that generational order. As another example, one may ask a person he is meeting for the first time if he knows a particular relative, says Kevin Kasiab Vang. If he does, then one should inquire further how they address each other. If it turns out that they share the same generational order, then the one may call that person according to Vang's social status and generational order. This entire system of greeting may seem complicated to non–Hmong, but it is actually easy for Hmong, who use it every day.

Hand waving is common in most cultures. However, in Hmong culture, hand waving is not used to call out to another person. Hand signals and other gestures are used for specific purposes. Hmong people move their hands with all fingers facing down to call out to someone or to tell someone to come to them. Using the hand with all fingers facing up to call to someone indicates contempt; it is considered impolite and suggests trouble or anger. Table 5.2 compares some of the common hand signals and gestures Hmong use with similar gestures of other Southeast Asian and Asian groups. Learning these and other Hmong greeting conventions will go a long way toward extending welcoming and hospitality to Hmong in the U.S.

Hmong Hospitality

Hospitality is a big part of everyday Hmong life, especially hospitality toward immediate family members. Although some Hmong today would rather spend the night in a hotel than impose on their relatives and many busy working families do not have time to prepare for and entertain guests properly, most Hmong people are very social and they enjoy having guests in their homes. Ordinary Hmong families do whatever they can to welcome family relatives. There are specific ways to cordially and properly treat guests and visitors to make them feel welcome. Whether one is the host or the guest, humility, modesty, and courtesy are the core ingredients that make a house a welcoming place.

Whether the visit is planned or unplanned, guests are received in a way that does not permit them to feel intrusive or unwanted. The host receives the guests at the door with a warm greeting. The host immediately invites the guests into the house and gently invites them to sit down. Engaging the guests in conversation keeps the atmosphere warm and receptive. The host need not ask what brought the guests to the house; an unexpected guest normally volunteers the reasons for stopping by. Expected guests converse freely and easily, talking at length about the travel that prompted the visit. When unexpected guests are ready to leave, the host may suggest they stay longer or come back again.

Planned visits involve lavish hospitality because the host has had time to prepare. The host generally has developed a plan to keep guests occupied and entertained during their visit. The host serves a meal following the guests' arrival, asks the guests about their immediate plans, and offers assistance to meet guests' needs and wants.

In Hmong culture, single female householders do not receive guests as do married householders. Guests are not boyfriends or girlfriends, but family relatives. Male visitors may feel uncomfortable being alone in the home of a single woman who does not have a husband because there is no male figure with whom to socialize and visiting a single woman is not appropriate unless the visitor is an immediate family member, a child, or a female sibling. A male visitor should not be in the home of a female and vice versa, especially when the guest is not a member of the host's immediate family.

These traditional restrictions are not always enforced today, but some reservations remain in practice. Normally, the mother of the house directs any male guest to the man of the house and the father directs to the mother any female guests coming to the home. Keeping the genders separate helps ease tensions between the opposite sexes. Hmong people perceive guests and hosts who are closely related to be more compatible

Table 5.2. Gestures Used in Selected Cultures

Gesture or Purpose	Vietnamese	Cambodian	Lao	Thai	Hmong	Asian Indian
Show respect	Bow head	Bow head	Bow head	Bow head	Bow head	Bow head
Pass object to another	Use both hands	Use both hands	Use both hands	Use both hands	Use both hands	Use both hands
Salute person of bow	Join hands at chest	4 levels: equal status, join hands at chest; older status, join hands at chin; higher status, join hands at nose; authority or royalty, join hands over head	Same as Cambodian	Same as Cambodian	Shake hands or bow head. To show higher respect, left hand touches right wrist when shaking hands	Shake hands, head, or hug, kiss on the cheeks (varied)
Making eye contact while talking to	No direct eye contact	No direct eye contact	No direct eye contact	No direct eye contact	No direct eye contact	No direct eye contact
Touching the head of a child	Considered rude	Considered rude	Considered rude	Considered rude	Considered rude	Considered rude
Use hand to call someone	Use all fingers, facing down	Use all fingers, facing down	Use all fingers, facing down	Use all fingers, facing down	Use all fingers, facing down	Use all fingers, facing down
Putting feet on desk while talking	Rude or impolite	Rude or impolite	Rude or impolite	Rude or impolite	Rude or impolite	Rude or impolite
Writing with left hand	Not allowed	Not allowed	Not allowed	Not allowed	No limitation	Not allowed, religious interpretation
Time orientation and punctuality	Time is flexible, no hurry, punctuality not necessary unless extremely important situation	Same as Vietnamese	Same as Vietnamese	Same as Vietnamese	Same as Vietnamese	Same as Vietnamese

than unrelated parties and therefore better able to engage in friendly conversation and entertain each other.

Hmong hospitality is concerned with lodging, meals, transportation, visiting relatives, and engaging in social activities. Hosts generally ask their guests what they want during their visit. Hosts accompany their guests as much as possible. The key to being a hospitable host is to know how to make guests feel comfortable and welcome during their visits. When guests leave, the host has to pack them a lunch to send them away well provided for whether the guests need the lunch or not. The lunch usually consists of boiled chicken with rice, salt, and black ground pepper. Providing a lunch keeps the bond between guest and host strong. The guest returns the favor to the host when the roles are reversed in the future. Thus Hmong hospitality is an expression of reciprocity that is part of Hmong culture.

Hmong Courtship and Dating in the U.S.

As stated earlier, Hmong practices regarding courtship and dating have changed drastically since Hmong began arriving in America in 1975. At first, Hmong parents encountered a huge culture shock when they observed western children kissing and embracing one another in public. Now, westernized Hmong teenage children no longer act like Hmong traditional children but behave like the typical American teenagers who shocked their parents. Many believe that Hmong teenagers are not only adopting the western views of courtship and dating but have actually lost their cultural values and norms regarding male and female interactions. Today's Hmong parents are angry and frustrated about the courtship and dating practices of their westernized Hmong children because the behaviors are completely unacceptable based on Hmong cultural values.

Despite their frustration, Hmong parents cannot explain to their children what is culturally acceptable and what is not in regard to courtship. The real problem is that Hmong parents rarely talk about sexuality with their teenage children. Courtship and dating are learned social behaviors. Most children learn these behaviors from their peers, social media, and of course, movies. Little or no formal education is involved. In the past, Hmong adolescents could get married as young as age 13, but this practice, too, has changed.

Hmong parents prefer that their teenage children interact with one another socially but not romantically or sexually until they are married. Hmong parents refrain from talking about premarital sex because courtship and sexuality are considered personal matters. They expect their children to learn how to preserve their virginity as long as possible and to hide any romantic involvement from their parents and peers until the involvement has become a committed relationship that will last—in which case marriage is the next step. Displaying any form of sexuality is culturally inappropriate and shameful. Christian Hmong families generally prohibit their children from engaging in sexual activities; however, controlling teenage children who live in a dual society is challenging.

In the old days, Hmong teenage children did not have sexual freedom or open courtship as they do today. Dating usually took place at night while parents were asleep; dating individuals hardly ever met face to face during the day. They talked to each other through walls and saw each other only in the early morning hours before dawn or in the late evening hours after dusk. They might catch a glimpse of each other while working on the farm or on the way to or from the farm.

This type of courtship is no longer relevant or possible in today's circumstances. Dating partners see each other day and night, behave like husband and wife, act romantically, embrace sexually, and sometimes live together like married couples. Girls and boys visit one another and their families without any shyness or reservation. They pick one another up for lunch and dinner and spend weekends together away from home. Sometimes, they travel together and go out freely without asking for parental permission. In some cases, they disobey their parents to be together. These kinds of dating behaviors are not consistent with Hmong cultural values and customs.

Sometimes, boys are disrespectful toward their girlfriends' parents or vice versa. Some Hmong teenage children get married without following the traditional Hmong wedding customs. At times, unexpected and unplanned pregnancies happen and children are born out of wedlock. These behaviors often result in single-parent households, custody battles, child support struggles, and low incomes. These behaviors also mean that divorce and family separation will continue to rise in the Hmong community as Hmong enter the second and third generation in the U.S.

At the very least, westernized Hmong children need to learn basic Hmong values and customs regarding courtship and dating in order to show respect for the norms of Hmong culture and to honor their parents. Americans have differing cultural values and what Hmong teenage children see in their American friends and the American media may not be the only true American values. Even if Hmong teenagers insist on making their own choices, they should learn how to choose wisely and carefully when it comes to courtship and dating. The important thing is not *who* they should date, but *how* they should go about it.

Roles of Daughters-in-Law

Daughters-in-law have always played a major role in Hmong family life. Today, however, that role has changed because many daughters-in-law do not live with their in-laws. In the old days, daughters-in-law had to get up early every morning to make a fire, to cook and clean, to carry firewood, and to fetch water from a well. Of course they do not need to carry firewood or fetch water in the U.S. cities; their chores are much easier today. Still, many daughters-in-law do not know how to do basic domestic chores.

Traditionally, the very first daughter-in-law to enter the family, usually the one who is married to the oldest son, has a full plate of responsibilities because she is considered the oldest daughter of the family. Besides her household chores, she is expected to take care of the whole family. The specifics of these tasks vary from family to family. In some cases, the daughter-in-law not only becomes the family servant, but also works as hard as a slave, performing every function for the family. Dutiful daughters-in-law never complain about their responsibilities or any of the household chores. Hmong parents usually consider daughters-in-law good if they are patient, passionate, and dutiful, having been well-trained by their biological parents.

Today, Hmong daughters-in-law attend college, work outside the home, or have professional careers. They may or may not perform the basic household chores on a daily basis. Hmong parents still prefer to have traditional daughters-in-law who know how to clean, wash, cook, maintain the house, and take care of family needs regardless of their careers and professional status. Above all, in the Hmong world, a daughter-in-law should not go over her husband's head even if he has less education and lower status and she is the breadwinner. Some affluent Hmong women have difficulty accepting the traditional role, particularly subjugating themselves to their husbands, but the Hmong patriarchal hierarchy requires it.

Hmong daughters-in-law who can maintain Hmong cultural values and customs are regarded as mature, dutiful, and understanding; they are good role models for the other daughters in the family because they honor their traditional roles, take care of family members, and place the family before their personal desires. Hmong parents appreciate daughters-in-law who can fulfill their traditional roles at home. Nothing can replace the kindness of heart of daughters-in-law who can provide for their families and their in-laws. Most Hmong expect daughters-in-law to be full-time mothers, dutiful domestic workers, and responsible providers for the entire family while holding highly demanding professional positions outside the home.

This may sound unfair to Hmong women; however, these values make Hmong women some of the best wives and mothers of all time.

Roles of Sons-in-Law

Hmong sons-in-law have responsibilities to three sets of family members: their immediate family members (*kwv tij koom niam koom txiv yug*), their clanmates (*pawg kwvtij*), and their in-law relatives (*neejtsa*). Sometimes friends and co-workers are added to this list, but most Hmong sons-in-law feel compelled to serve the three sets of family members throughout their life.

For the immediate in-laws, Hmong sons-in-law must be available for family gatherings and feasts and are responsible to chip in whenever they can to help out family members. In the old days, Hmong sons-in-laws were required to cut firewood for their in-laws every once in awhile, but this task is no longer needed. Also, Hmong sons-in-laws were expected to help cultivate and harvest crops whenever they could. Their in-laws could summon them for help at any time. In fact, in-laws still summon their sons-in-law when they have a family need and still expect them to respond.

The obligations of marital kinship are part of Hmong life. Some of these obligations require the son-in-law's service at funeral services and other death rituals, weddings, family feasts, religious rituals, sicknesses and hospitalizations, and family celebrations and ceremonies. Sons-in-law are expected to maintain cordial relationships, be part of the family support system, and make family visits. Marital kinship means maintaining connections with the entire family clan or tribe, and Hmong sons-in-law are responsible to know all blood relatives.

Hmong parents want sons-in-law who are considerate, dutiful, patient, understanding, caring, supportive, and kind. Today, many Hmong sons-in-law do not know or follow the traditional Hmong roles and customs. They cannot perform their responsibilities adequately because they are ignorant of the expectations of Hmong culture and tradition. Many Hmong sons-in-law cannot even express appreciation in the traditional Hmong way because they cannot speak Hmong well enough to recite the verses or because they do not know the cultural norms.

Regardless of career and professional status, Hmong sons-in-law should at least maintain basic Hmong values and customs in order to fulfill their parents' expectations. What matters in Hmong culture is not *what* you know, but *who* you know and *who* knows you.

Hmong Dining Etiquette

Hmong families do not have standards for formal dining, but they do have rules for basic table manners for family dining and dining at events. Families generally have three meals a day: breakfast, lunch, and dinner. Normally, the mother is the main cook for the family; she prepares all dishes for each meal. In time past, Hmong had little in the way of plates and utensils. A wooden or bamboo table was used as the dining table. Meals typically consisted of a bowl of rice (*tais mov*), a bowl with the main dish (*tais zaub qab ntsev*), a small bowl of hot sauce (*kuav txob, dos, txuj lom, ntsev*), and a bowl of plain vegetables (*tais zaub tshuag*). Family members gathered around the dining table, seated on wooden or bamboo stools, and ate together. Each had a spoon, but not a dinner plate or proper silverware. Each diner ate by dipping his or her spoon into the community bowls on the table. Everyone tried to avoid crossing over or colliding with others as they spooned food from the various bowls. The family seating arrangement started with the father then went to the mother, then the children from youngest to oldest. When everyone was finished, they left their spoons on the table.

This method of dining could be uncomfortable for a new daughter-in-law. She might be shy about eating with the family and hesitant to fetch her food from all the community bowls on the table. Her husband must recognize her dilemma and help her adjust when she is still new to the family. Keep in mind that in some Hmong families the daughter-in-law is prohibited from dining at the same table with her father-in-law, so she has to eat in a separate location or wait until the father-in-law has finished dining before she can join the rest of the family members.

Seating at the dining table is arranged in specific patterns to avoid insecure personal space and uncomfortable situations. Seating the father next to a daughter-in-law or the mother next to a son-in-law would be inappropriate and unacceptable unless the occasion is a family event. At a circular table, the seating order is male-female-female-male-male-female-female-male, and so on; or husband-wife-wife-husband-husband-wife-wife-husband, and so on. Simply put, a married woman does not sit between two married men and a married man does not sit between two married women at a social gathering. No woman, regardless of her professional status, sits at the head or the tail of the table. The women are the ones who serve the food. Men can order more food to be served, but no man gets up to serve food. The only time male servers are used is during Hmong funeral service; that is because funeral functions belong to men in accordance with Hmong religious traditions.

Family dining today is much easier for all family members than in times past. Plenty of utensils are available. Hmong always prepare large amounts of food. Each person has his or her own silverware, plate, and napkin. Seating patterns are still important at the dining table. At a circular table the pattern, starting from the father of the house and going to the left, is son, daughter-in-law, daughter, son, daughter, and so on. To the father's right the pattern is wife (the mother), daughter, daughter-in-law, son, son, daughter, and so on, as illustrated in Figures 5.7 and 5.8. This pattern applies to all married couples dining together: a man sits next to his wife, another wife sits next to her and

then her husband, another husband and his wife are next, and so on. The easiest arrangement is the parallel seating pattern at a rectangular table: family members are seated across from each other with all males on one side of the table and all females on the other side. When the meal has ended, everyone takes his or her dirty plates and silverware from the dining table and places them in the sink or, in a formal setting, everyone leaves plates and utensils on the table and the mother and daughter collect them.

Hmong table manners are unwritten conventions and they vary from family to family. As people eat with different relatives and in different settings, they have to adjust to the situation at hand or simply go with the flow. At religious rituals, weddings, and shamanistic offerings, dining cannot take place before certain traditional formalities are observed. The formalities may be brief or lengthy, depending on the event. For instance, at a shamanistic ritual two steps must be taken before everyone can eat. First, to give special respect and thanks to the shaman, the family prepares some pre-dining dishes for all men present. Only adult males and young adult males are invited to sit at the table for this step; children and women are excluded. The men can eat whatever is on the table except rice. During this pre-dining event, a few

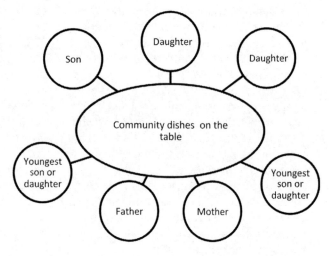

Figure 5.7. Typical seating arrangement of a Hmong family without in-laws.

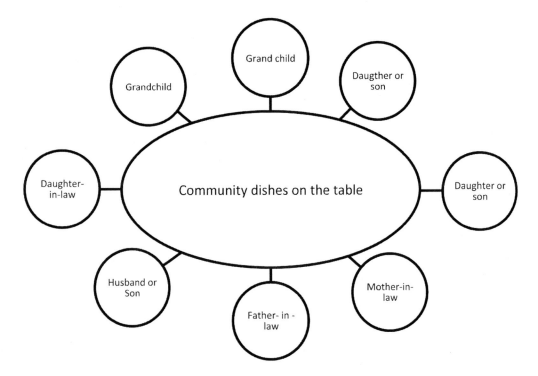

Figure 5.8. Typical seating arrangement of a Hmong family with in-laws.

rounds of drinks are offered to the shaman, guests, and the involved family members. When these formalities are completed, the leading male directs the family to bring rice and more food to the table for formal dining. At this point, he invites the rest of the family members, including children and women, and other guests to dine at a separate table. In some cases, children and women have to wait until all the men have finished eating at the main table before they can eat, and they eat at the same table.

The formalities of Hmong rituals can be tricky for young people who lack basic understanding of Hmong customs and traditions. At large gatherings such as weddings, death rituals, basi khite, and courtesy naming ceremonies, only mature males are invited to sit at the table for specific functions. Usually, individuals are seated properly in designated spots in the right locations so they can perform their particular functions. For instance, the basic table norm for parallel seating for the traditional wedding ritual starts with the groom. To his left are the best man, the

bridesmaid, the brother of the bride, the first cousin of the bride, the father of the groom, the father of the bride, and so on. To his right are the uncle of the bride, the father of the family, the brother of the family, and so on. This pattern may be altered in accordance with the tradition of each individual Hmong family; however, it is consistent in most Hmong traditional weddings.

Hmong table formalities are not as much about how one should conduct oneself during dining as about the cultural value that strongly emphasizes conformity to social norms. The protocols of formal dining are about honoring and respecting the various events and people.

Hmong Social Drinking

Despite having unpretentious attitudes and manners, Hmong are sociable and friendship-oriented. In the old days, drinking among Hmong was somewhat restricted to special occasions. Consumption of alcohol was limited because the supply was scarce and expensive.

Hmong did know how to brew their own tasty and refreshing alcoholic beverages for celebrating different occasions; they made hard liquor from rice, wheat, and other herbal ingredients.

The old custom of limiting alcohol to special times has been broken and Hmong social drinking today is at times out of control. Some Hmong believe a celebration without alcohol is not a worthy occasion. Like every ethnic group, Hmong have drinking customs. Hmong have drinking traditions for religious rituals (shamanistic ceremonies, death rites, soul calling, special offerings, and so on), weddings, New Year's celebrations, and major social gatherings.

In the western nations, Hmong drinking is not always related to Hmong customs, but is a matter of personal indulgence. Most Hmong adults can afford to buy beer and hard liquor for less important events not connected with traditional drinking such as birthday parties, seasonal occasions (Mother's Day, Father's Day, Christmas, Thanksgiving, the birth of a child, and so on), graduations, and other achievements. Apart from the traditional rituals and ceremonies, many Hmong men use alcohol as the main source of entertainment for guests and the sole purpose for

having social gatherings. Social drinking has become so common that some Hmong feel that hosts dishonor them or regard them as unworthy guests if the host does not serve alcohol. They see being intoxicated with friends as a sign of respect for the friendship and they think that drinking together strengthens friendships. Furthermore, some believe that one's tolerance for alcohol is a measure of one's machismo and bravery.

These are the points of view of drinkers. However, in reality, drinking is a matter of personal responsibility. When out of control, alcohol consumption leads to addiction and other negative health consequences. As Figure 5.9 shows, the intensity of hangovers decreases with age after age 30, but what the figure fails to show is that health problems increase rather than decrease. In their teen years and early 20s and 30s, people who drink to excess may not necessarily feel negative effects. However, starting in the 30s, hangover intensity declines and some health problems become noticeable. The good news for Hmong is that even though many Hmong men like to drink heavily on a regular basis, only a very few Hmong are addicted to alcohol or have serious drinking problems.

In those Hmong traditions in which

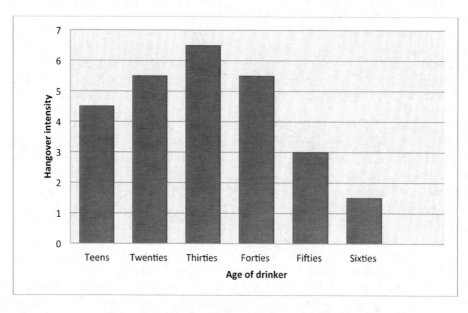

Figure 5.9. Hangover intensity, by age of drinker.

drinking is a part, people who prefer not to drink are still expected to participate. Because of the Hmong value of saving face, nondrinkers and people with medical conditions place themselves at risk of undesirable consequences by having to drink beer and other forms of alcohol in order to take part in the formalities of various traditions. Sometimes the host family may waive the requirement of drinking for guests who have life-threatening medical conditions. At other times, the nondrinkers and unhealthy individuals may decide not to join in the rituals.

Another danger in cultural drinking is seen when intoxicated Hmong are arrested, fined, and jailed for driving under the influence of alcohol or are involved in alcohol-related auto accidents. Hmong have learned the hard way about the dangers of alcohol consumption because many healthy individuals have developed alcohol-related illnesses such as gout, renal failure, kidney problems, hypertension, diabetes, heart diseases, strokes, liver cancer, throat cancer, ulcers, internal bleeding, mental impairment, obesity, and birth defects. In some cases, the drinking formalities contribute to the spread of communicable diseases. Hmong women and teenagers have picked up the habit of drinking and excessive use of alcohol has contaminated Hmong rituals and traditions.

Having said all this, retaining the Hmong drinking formalities is essential to the practice of some Hmong customs. However, the continuation of irresponsible drinking endangers the Hmong patriarchal system not only because intoxication leads to various health problems, but also because out-of-control drinking is destroying the foundations of Hmong family structure, marital relationships, and the integrity of parenthood. Alcohol should be consumed sparingly and responsibly during rituals instead of being used freely at any unimportant celebration.

Limiting one's alcohol intake is difficult because refusal to drink may be considered rude. However, one may leave the table without causing any cultural infraction or any disrespect to the formalities. As expressed in Hmong, "*Khiav lwm yam mas yuav txaum cai mentsi, tabsi khiav dej caw mas tsis txaum cai.*" English translation: "Running away from any other thing may cause an infraction, but running away from alcohol violates no rule." The Hmong perspective on alcohol consumption is contained in another Hmong saying: "*Dej caw tsis yog leej twg kwvtij.*" In English: "Alcohol is not anyone's brother."

Hmong Cultural Maintenance

Throughout their four decades in the western nations, Hmong have faced constant clashes of cultures in a dual society, and their children have learned to mix the values and customs of two cultures. Retaining Hmong cultural values and traditions is challenging because Hmong do not have a place where their offspring can learn Hmong heritage formally. Relying on emulation without formal instruction has not been totally effective.

Many traditional Hmong parents today find themselves at odds with their native-born children who are westernized and speak very little or no Hmong at all. Some Hmong parents have lost their heritage as well and do not practice it in everyday life. If Hmong parents expect their children to retain Hmong cultural values and customs, the parents must educate their children carefully and thoroughly; otherwise, their expectation that their children will follow and pass on the values and traditions of their Hmong heritage may just fade away because Hmong children have become enculturated in western ways.

Traditionally, the Hmong way of learning Hmong cultural values and customs is through observation and emulation with little or no formalized teaching. Learning Hmong culture is not like learning Christianity. Christianity can be learned through reading and studying the written Gospels, but the Hmong do not have written materials that would help Hmong children learn Hmong values and customs. The only way Hmong children can learn their heritage is through the informal apprenticeship process, which is unavailable to many Hmong children. Hmong parents cannot just preach Hmong values and customs; they have to practice them with their offspring. Parents are their children's first teachers. Hmong parents can model good manners at home and teach their children how to maintain Hmong values and customs at the same time they learn about the culture and traditions of other people in school.

One aspect of Hmong culture that is very difficult to maintain in the West is its gender inequality. Men retain their superior patriarchal positions in the family and the community and women retain their maternal roles with all their duties and responsibilities. Confrontation with the egalitarian societies of western nations has brought about some reduction in gender inequity among Hmong. However, embracing gender equality erodes cultural maintenance because it weakens both the paternal and the maternal domains as well as the Hmong family ecological system. It disrupts the traditional Hmong family, which is the foundation of social structure and stability.

Formal education can help Hmong men and women adapt to the new way of life in a dual society without giving up their traditional values and customs. Hmong have distinct cultural values and customs no matter where they live, and these values and customs are worth preserving. Hmong in the West will retain their culture and traditions because the resiliency they have demonstrate for centuries will be the driving force that will enable them to preserve their Hmong heritage for future generations.

Summing Up

This chapter described Hmong cultural values and customs in order to provide an overview of Hmong culture today. The Hmong patriarchal system of social hierarchy is still in practice today. The Hmong family ecological system is made up of the trinity of fatherhood, motherhood, and childhood. Hmong children learn Hmong cultural values and customs through the family ecological system. They learn the cultural attitudes and behaviors that are essential to everyday situations as well as special occasions.

In their social behaviors, Hmong are unpretentious. They do not boast or put themselves forward. They rarely issue compliments or praise, and when they receive praise from another they respond passively and humbly. Kinship relationships—not only biological, but also those formed by marriage—are extremely important in everyday Hmong life. These relationships together with generational order are essential in properly addressing and referring to people. Hmong use generational order to identify people rather than their names.

Social greetings are a big part of Hmong life because Hmong are social people. Traditionally, Hmong women do not shake hands, but that has changed over the years Hmong have been in the West. Hmong men traditionally do not hug or embrace in public, but this, too, has changed. Social kissing is still taboo except between young children and immediate adult family members. Hmong have always entertained in their homes, and they still provide lodging, food, and practical help to fellow Hmong who are traveling.

Hmong have basic dining rules and protocols for rituals and other events. At some events, men eat first, before women and children. Table manners at the rituals and events are not concerned with how individuals comport themselves; they are concerned with waiting for and showing respect to others.

Hmong in the West continue to adjust the expressions of their cultural values to the society in which they live. In that society, maintaining Hmong culture is challenging but possible. Hmong will always retain their cultural values and customs no matter where they live. Hmong resiliency has enabled them to preserve Hmong culture and traditions for nearly 6,000 years.

• SIX •

Hmong Traditions and Religious Practices

Kev ua noj ua haus ... kev ua tshoob ua kos...
Yoog tau luag thiab ua li luag ua los tau...
Tabsi kev ua dab ua qhua yuav yoog luag tsis tau...
A Hmong religious riddle

Introduction

Hmong traditions that started nearly 6,000 years ago in the ancient world have continued to the present day. Throughout the centuries, in China, Laos, and now in several western nations, Hmong culture has undergone some changes as the Hmong people underwent struggles, tribulations, triumphs, and reforms. Hmong adopted some practices from Christianity, Islam, Buddhism, Taoism, and Confucianism, integrating whatever was consistent with their traditional beliefs. For instance, in the mid–1950s a large number of Hmong in Laos, Vietnam, and Thailand converted to Christianity for practical reasons, namely because some groups and subgroups of Hmong people had been observing religious practices that were very burdensome and they did not wish to continue those practices. Hmong are able to accept new beliefs while at the same time retaining the core of religious practices that originated with their Hmong ancestors. This chapter presents an overview of contemporary Hmong traditions and practices including religious beliefs, religious rituals, traditional customs, and spiritual curses and taboos. The chapter also describes ongoing adaptations Hmong in the West make to their traditions.

Belief Systems

What do Hmong believe? Hmong beliefs include aspects of a variety of belief systems: ancestral spirits, animism, Taoism, Confucianism, Buddhism, Hinduism, and different forms of Christianity. Hmong have no written texts or scriptures to guide the practice of such broad and mixed religious beliefs. Although Hmong beliefs were influenced by different religious systems over thousands of years in China and Laos, most Hmong still believe in the spirituality of their ancestors and the spiritual benevolence of animism. Most traditional Hmong families are devoted to rituals associated with ancestral spirits and animism whereas a minority of Hmong families follows some kind of Christianity.

For Hmong, a personal *belief* is the acceptance of something they know to be true or real because of direct experience or family traditions. For example, if a Hmong refuses to obey the request of benevolent spirits for a sacrifice, the disobedience will result in a consequential curse (*kev khaum, kev looj koov, losi kev muaj mob muaj nkeeg* in Hmong). The person experiences the reality of the curse and therefore accepts as true that such a curse will continue if he or she continues to disobey. Most Hmong firmly believe in

157

spiritual benevolence and religious curses. For example, Hmong still believe that the cursing words *sub* and *fam* can help determine foreseeable events in life. Literally, *sub* and *fam* in Hmong mean sign of warning, bad lucks, misfortunes, omens, evils, devils, and demons. Therefore, Hmong beliefs are more than matters of religion; they are personally and privately held convictions about the benevolent spirits of their deceased family members and ancestors. Hmong who have the same beliefs may worship and make offerings in entirely different ways. As mentioned earlier, each clan has its own ritual name and connection to the spiritual world; however, those clans that share the same ritual name and connection may practice ritualistic symbols, chants, blessings, and sacrificial offerings differently.

One of the earliest influences on Hmong beliefs was *Taoism*. Practically, *Tao* means "the way" or "the natural course of nature." Taoists believe "the way" that is best is the way of non-aggression and non-competitiveness. The three jewels or three principles of Taoism are non-aggressive: compassion, moderation, and humility. What Hmong took from Taoism is the concept of the *Yin* and *Yan*, the simplicity and naturalness of life in harmony with nature and spirits. Yin is the black, feminine, and passive—qualities of the moon; Yan is the white, masculine, and active—qualities of the sun. Hmong faith is similarly based on the harmony between Yin Paradise (*Yeeb Ceeb*) and Yan Paradise (*Yaj Ceeb*), or the spiritual world and the physical world.

Traditionally, Hmong are firm believers in the existence of a spiritual world, but not heaven. Hmong believe the house is a sacred place and is safeguarded by different spirits. Hmong believe the body is guided by the soul and different spirits. Hmong use the soul calling ritual (*hu plig*) for almost all religious practices. The Hmong way of connecting with nature is based on the existence of benevolent spirits. Hmong summon Heaven and Earth spirits (*fiv yeem*) for guidance and protection when facing any dangerous plight.

Hmong religious values also have elements of *Confucianism*. As in Confucianism, Hmong emphasize a love for humanity, practice ancestral worship, stress the showing of respect and honor for parents and elders, and guard their thoughts and conduct in the present life in order to achieve greatness in the next life. The influence of Confucianism may explain why Hmong believe in a relationship between the spiritual world and the physical world, or between the dead and the living. The Hmong communal way of life is in keeping with the basic principles of Confucianism that include an emphasis on the relationships of ruler to subject, father to son, husband to wife, elder brother to younger brother, and friend to friend. Interestingly, the way Hmong practice their beliefs more or less incorporates the five constant virtues of Confucianism in regard to humility and relationship: benevolence, propriety, loyalty, intellect, and trust. These virtues are fundamental values seen in the religious rituals of the Hmong blood oath and justice water that strengthen bonds between people and honor justice and wisdom.

Practically, *Hinduism* also has beliefs and religious principles very similar to Hmong values: *Dharma*, the observation of moral law and spiritual discipline; *artha*, obtaining economic prosperity; *kama*, gratifying the senses; *samsara*, the cycle of reincarnation; and *moksha*, liberation from that cycle. Practicing dharma in Hinduism means applying moral and ethical restraints and observing certain religious practices. The personal *yammas*, or restraints, include patience, honesty, sexual purity, integrity, and character—all values that are part of Hmong culture. The *miyamas*, or observances, involve modesty, humbleness, charity, worship, and cooperation. In Hmong life, these suggest the code of conduct that one has to follow in the physical world in order to achieve joy and supreme happiness in the spiritual world with their family ancestors.

Hmong somehow believe that predestined scripts that can foretell life are inscribed on both *palms* of every individual. Basically, for a Hmong man, the left palm contains the life inscription, predetermination, and predestination for him and the right palm registers the detailed information about the life of his marital partner brought along from the spiritual world into the physical world. Simply, the right palm is for the man and the left palm is for the woman. For a Hmong woman, the right palm is for her and the left palm is for her spouse or him. These hidden life inscriptions and predestinations can be read by Hmong psychic analysts and shamans. However, the accuracy of reading these messages is subjected to different interpretations that may negatively or positively affect the life cycle of an individual. Therefore, Hmong do not accept palm reading completely and always consider its accuracy carefully when they apply the predestined inscriptions to their everyday life. The practice of shamanism is tied to animism because it has to do with the love, life, and relationships of all living beings, including animals that are sacrificed for religious purposes. Hmong believe that all living beings possess spirits and souls; therefore, the belief in animism helps Hmong know the relationship between the physical world and the spiritual world when they are offering animal sacrifices to the benevolent spirits. Moreover, Hmong believe that intentional cruelty to animals can produce long-life curses, even the curse of death, because the souls and spirits of animals that have been cruelly treated cannot be reincarnated in the spiritual world. To avoid such cruelty, Hmong healers and shamans ask the spirits of the sacrificial animals for forgiveness before killing them for all religious and ritual offerings to the benevolent spirits. Spiritual atonement is referred to as *ncwm* in Hmong, meaning to ask sacrificial animals for forgiveness and for being willing to fulfill the request.This belief has echoes of *Buddhism.*

Religiously, Hmong were introduced to the practice of *Buddhism* thousands of years ago; however, Hmong did not teach Buddhism to their children. Instead, they incorporated elements of Buddhism into Hmong religious rites, rituals, beliefs, values, and doctrines. The four noble truths of Buddhism are:

1. To exist is to suffer (pain, disappointment, fear, anxiety, depression, sicknesses, death, and so on).

2. To suffer is to crave or desire things that have no permanence (passion, love, wealth, prestige, status, power, sexuality, and so on).

3. To end suffering is to give up the craving and desiring (free oneself of a burden, let go of one's ego, stop coveting, stop being jealous, stop having personal greed, and so on).

4. To eliminate is to release oneself from these cravings and desires in order to reach *Nirvana.*

Hmong believe that hard work will overcome destitution, fortune is predestined before birth, suffering is part of the process of life, and saving will enable one to reach one's life objectives. These beliefs fall under the guiding principles of *Nirvana,* the eight-fold path, which are right view, right thought, right speech, right action, right livelihood, right effort, right mindfulness, and right concentration and focus. Considering Taoism, Confucianism, Hinduism, and Buddhism, the Hmong belief systems appear to incorporate guiding principles from all these ancient religions.

Hmong have faith in their religious practices because they believe they are meaningful to their lives; *faith* is confidence that does not require physical proof, but spiritual connections, interpretations, and meanings. Hmong know that religious faith is trust in something that cannot be seen, but something that is nevertheless a spiritually reality. Hmong depend on the benevolent spirits to help them live rightly in the present life so they will not only achieve good things now, but also successfully reincarnate, or come back to life after death. In the Hmong world, religious consequences are severe, sometimes matters of life and death. Some religious sanctions are spiritually permanent. For instance, the prohibition against eating the heart (*caiv plawv* in Hmong) of any animal is a permanent religious ban and breaching the ban has serious consequences. Admittedly, Hmong are more inclined to submit to spiritual restrictions and spiritual control than to follow man-made laws and rules because the spiritual world is the real and ultimate object of Hmong faith and religious practices.

Once a religious vow or ban is made, no one can alter it except through death rituals and funeral rites or religious conversion and relinquishment of one's own religious practices. In other words, Hmong funeral rites, death rituals, and marital practices have direct influence on Hmong spiritual reality—and thus physical reality—because these practices allow Hmong to positively enforce and/or negatively alter religious vows, adherence, restrictions, bans, and devotion.

Hmong religious rituals have evolved over time. Exposure to *Christianity* brought new views to Hmong traditional beliefs. Some Hmong converted to the new religious doctrines and embraced Christianity in order to avoid some religious bans and sacrificial obligations. By 1957, the largest group of Laotian Hmong had converted to the practices of Christianity. They rejected the traditional mindset and began to learn the principles of Christianity. Christian Hmong families were introduced to new religious concepts such as heaven (*ntuj ceeb tsheej*), hell (*ntuj cub tawg losi pas dej kub dej npau*), God (*yawg saub, vaj tswv, losi dab ruam ntuj*), the Bible (*phau ntawv vaj lus kub*), and disciples (*thwj tim*). Hmong believers describe the Bible better than any other Christian groups in the world. The Hmong phrase "*Phau Ntawv Vaj Lug Kub*" means "*The Book of Golden Words*," not the book of the four Gospels, because Hmong believers believe that every word in that book is as precious as gold. Prior to the introduction of Christianity, most Hmong firmly believed in ancestral spirits and family deities (*dab niam dab txiv*). Traditionally, Hmong somewhat believe in creationism but religiously reject fasting and resurrection. Today, the majority of Hmong still hold the old religious beliefs (*dab niam dab txiv losi kev cai qub*); only a minority adhere to Christianity (*kev cai tshiab losi kev cai ntseeg ntuj*). Some practice the new *Poj Koob Yawm Ntxwv Niam Looj Tsav* or Chao Fa faith. The newest religious practice is known as the *Temple of Hmongism*. Despite the diverse religious beliefs and practices in the Hmong community, most Hmong still maintain Hmong values and traditions in their everyday lives.

Traditional New Year's Celebrations

The origin of Hmong New Year is still unknown to most Hmong. In the old days, Hmong celebrated very few holidays and festive events. In the early 1900s, Hmong in Southeast Asia established that their New Year would be celebrated on the 30th day of the last month of the Hmong lunar calendar. They called the ceremony and celebration they held on the 30th day the Hmong Dining Festival (*noj tsiab*). The word *peb caug* is confusing; it has never been translated as "30-day festival." It actually means "the 30th day of celebration in December." Prior to the early 1900s, Hmong did not celebrate the New Year the way they do today. Hmong settlers in Laos and elsewhere became accustomed to the lifestyles of the native people of Laos and adopted local and regional festivities such as the *Basi Khi Te, Tuam Choj* ritual, *Noj Txhooj*, and so on.

The traditional Hmong family feasting festival (*noj tsiab*) is still the biggest national holiday for all Hmong in the world. Today, Hmong living in the western nations and those in the eastern countries celebrate the New Year on different days and at different times in different months of the year. Other festivities include regional holidays and familial religious events such as the Hmong Totem Pole Ceremony (*tsa hauv toj losi tsa ncej txheb ncej ntxhoo*), the Hmong township annual commemoration (*noj txhooj*), religious observances and house restrictions (*hnub caiv*), soul callings (*hu plig*), traditional wedding ceremonies (*noj tshoob*), the courtesy name ceremony (*ti npe laus*), and funeral and burial ceremonies (*kev ruam sim losi kab ke pam tuag*). In the past, when the Hmong had an agrarian lifestyle, harvest and cultivation seasons were major focuses of Hmong everyday life and celebrations were connected with those times. But today, most Hmong work outside the home to provide financial support for their families. As life has changed, so have Hmong cultural practices.

Celebrating Hmong New Year is a longstanding tradition; it is the only occasion observed as a holiday by all Hmong. Although elaborate ceremonies did not begin until the 1900s, the tradition of celebrating the New Year has been in practice for nearly 6,000 years. To properly celebrate Hmong New Year, Hmong have to make preparation all year long because the New Year is preceded by a series of religious rituals and cultural ceremonies on the 30th day of the 12th month of the Hmong lunar calendar (*hli Hmoob*), which is also the French lunar calendar (*hli Fab Kis*). The Hmong monthly calendar is different from western monthly calendars. In the Hmong calendar, each month has exactly 30 days, and each moon phase or cycle has exactly 15 days. The Hmong believe the moon waxes for 15 days and wanes for 15 days each month. The Hmong name their New Year's celebration *Tsiab Peb Caug*, the 30th day just before the very first day of the New Year according to the Hmong monthly calendar. According to the western calendar, the Hmong traditional New Year falls between the 25th of November (the 11th month) and the 25th of December (the 12th month). In the mid–1980s, in California, a state proclamation recognized the official Hmong New Year celebration as occurring from the 26th day of December of each year to the first day of the coming year. However, Hmong in California begin their celebration of Hmong New Year in November each year.

The Progression of Festivity

The Hmong New Year's celebration has three main components. The first part is the family feast (*noj tsiab*). Families gather together and celebrate with a festive meal. This part of the holiday is not as big as it used to be, but it is important for the family to feast together once a year.

The second portion of the New Year's celebration involves religious rituals and spiritual offerings (*kev ua dab ua qhua losi kev teev dab qhuas*). Each family has its own way of worshiping and giving offerings to its familial deities and benevolent spirits. The rituals and offerings are often performed at the time of the family feast. The last part is a communal festival and social gathering (*lub tshav pob peb caug*). The social-communal festival is the longest cultural celebration the Hmong observe; it has been known as the Hmong New Year's celebration since the mid–1900s. However, the family feasting and religious rituals and offerings have been the integral parts of Hmong life for thousands of years.

The Hmong New Year's celebration traditionally lasted three to seven days, depending on the number of days set by village leaders and allowed by the harvesting season. In the old days, the New Year's celebration was delayed in some regions and villages to accommodate the harvest priorities and seasonal cultivation. Typically, once all preparations were made and the crop cultivation was over, families settled down for the New Year. In traditional Hmong families, parents selected a day on which to perform the opening ritual (*lwm qaib, lwm sub, losi lwm tsiab*) in the afternoon hours to chant away all bad luck, curses, omens, misfortunes, and unwanted hardships and welcome good luck, fortune, successes, and prosperity for the new year.

The phrase *lwm qaib* is also applied to the very first ritual of the Hmong traditional wedding, used to tie together a man and a woman in marriage and validate their union. *Lwm qaib* is used here because it is easy for children who lack Hmong traditions to understand the ritual. The word *lwm* means spinning and the word *qaib* means chicken; therefore, spinning a chicken over the people is called *lwm qaib* in Hmong. The phrase *lwm tsiab* is an alternate expression; it means to religiously solemnize the New Year's spirits with the discarding of old ones. Of the three possible phrases, *lwm sub* appears to be most appropriate because it means to get rid of bad luck, misfortunes, omens, evils, devils, and demons. The word *sub* means omens, curses, and dangers; and also, as expressed in the phrase "*vij sub vij sw*" in Hmong, meaning bad luck, misfortunes, evils, and demons. These ritual phrases are used interchangeably and sometimes cause westernized children confusion. In Hmong traditions, the same ritual may be used for different purposes with different chantings and religious elaborations.

For instance, the soul calling ritual (*hu plig*) is widely used in many religious ceremonies such as the birth of a newborn, shamanistic rituals, reclaiming the soul from traumatic event or sickness, and other successful events in life (achievement, graduation, courtesy name, promotion, marriage, and so on).

Traditionally, the best part of the Hmong New Year festivities is on the evening of the first day when the celebration happens from dusk until dawn. After that, the celebration consists of cultural and social gatherings, including the traditional courtship and ball tossing activity. The nocturnal festivity that takes place from dusk to dawn is known as *noj tsiab*, meaning family feasting.

Just before dusk the father, mother, grandparents, or an individual selected by the family performs the soul calling ritual (*hu plig*). The purpose of calling the souls of all living beings of all family members is to welcome them back home to the family regardless of their whereabouts, their happiness or sadness, or their state of plenty or deprivation. The renewal of the household spirit altar, or shrine (*txi xwm kab losi seej khab*), also takes place. Of course, chickens and pigs are slaughtered for the rituals and feasting. Then, when all dishes have been prepared, the father makes another religious offering (*laig dab losi ntov pob ntoos*) to pay respect to all deceased family members, including his parents, grandparents, and all relatives of different generations. He invites all departed souls and spirits to join the family in the New Year's feast, to accept the family offering of spiritual monies to help them live in the spiritual world, and to bless and protect all the family members in the New Year.

The big family feast goes on into the night, with immediate family and close relatives dining together, remembering the old year and welcoming the new one. A light is placed on the altar overnight along with the offering meal, which might be a cooked chicken and rice; holy water; rice grains; and burning incense. The property ownership ritual (*foob yeem*) is performed to claim and reclaim all family property and all household items. After these ceremonies, the parents caution their children not to spend their money for at least three days. The reason for this restriction is not clearly taught to Hmong children, but it is assumed that saving money during the three days is a sign of future good earnings and prosperity. If pressed for the reason, parents vaguely explain that it is to help them learn that they need to earn money before spending it, or simply, possession is better than repossession of money.

For Hmong, the New Year's cultural event (*lub paj tsiab peb caug*) begins on the following day, which is the first day of the New Year. The New Year is to be celebrated with joy and friendships. Hmong parents seldom sleep on the night before the actual New Year because they are eager to participate in the new water ritual (*huas dej ntshiab*) and to be awakened before dawn by the noises of animals as the new sign of the New Year. In the old days, the animal sounds would foreshadow what the New Year would be like. As Table 6.1 illustrates, the sounds of different domestic and wild animals signified the types of situations they could expect in the New Year. Culturally, hearing the sounds of domestic animals was a better sign than the noises made by wild animals.

Different Hmong elders, monks, and shamans interpret animal signs differently.

Table 6.1. Expectations Hmong Associate with Pre-Dawn Sounds of Different Animals

Animal	Sounds	Associated Expectations
Rooster	Crowing, clucking, cackling, bocking, chirping, screeching, peeping, cockadoodledooing	Blessing, good, cheerfulness, welcoming, peace, minimal conflicts, ease, friendliness, caution
Pig	Oinking, snorting, grunting, squealing, grunting, panting	Good, fruitfulness, blessing, welcoming, peace, friendliness, abundance, cheerfulness, restfulness

Animal	Sounds	Associated Expectations
Horse	Neighing, snorting, whinnying, nickering, sputtering	Friendliness, good, fruitfulness, abundance, welcoming, peace, productivity, health
Cow	Mooing, lowing, bawling, bellowing, grunting	Good, fruitfulness, blessing, help, productivity, peace, minimal conflict, friendliness, hard work
Buffalo	Bellowing, lowing, moaning, grunting	Good, blessing, ease, hard work, productivity, rain, fruitfulness
Goat	Bleating, baaing, moaning, grunting	Good, blessing, health, friendliness, cheerfulness, ease, peace
Dog	Barking, woofing, baying, bow-wowing, yapping, howling	Violence, aggression, friendship, caution, spite, territoriality, sharing, grouping, hierarchy, ownership
Tiger	Roaring, growling, snarling, grunting, groaning, panting	Bad, wildness, violence, aggression, difficulty, bad luck, grouping, pride, power, territoriality, struggle
Wolves and foxes	Howling, barking, yelping, simpering, crying, yelling, grunting	Group strength, group power, group struggle, group conflict, unlucky, territorial conflict, wildness, solitude, violence, anger, aggression
Deer	Bellowing, grunting, kicking	Migration, leaving, abandonment, grouping, seclusion, solitude, health, friendship, wildness, violence, conflicting

Sometimes these signs have religious significance in predicting the futures of individuals, but at other times, the animal omens may not necessarily foretell life situations and events or they might portend the opposite of what one expects. Most Hmong believe the sounds of domestic animals predict good and blessing. They do not believe hearing the sounds of wild animals before dawn will bring certain things into their lives because Hmong have a poor animistic relationship with wild animals. Today, belief in the predictive power of animal sounds has become largely irrelevant to the Hmong celebration of their New Year. Hmong in the West are more likely to believe that education is the predictor of socioeconomic successes and job security.

New Year Kowtowing Tradition

In Hmong New Year's traditions, a formal kowtowing ceremony (*pe tshiab*) takes place to show respect to elders and leaders. The Hmong word *pe* means kowtowing, or kneeling down on both knees to pay respect. *Pe* is widely used for many occasions, and its meaning differs according to the occasion. The Hmong word *mom xyom* should not be confused with *pe* because *mom xyom*, which also means kneeling down or kowtowing, is used only during Hmong funeral rituals and rites. The Hmong word *xyom* alone means paying respect and honor to the deceased, and to do that one has to kneel on both knees, hold three joss sticks in both hands, and bow one's head twice when guided to do so by the dead song singer, the bamboo reed piper player, or the blessing singer during the funeral service.

In the New Year's ceremony, special individuals are asked to bestow blessings during the New Year's celebration and beyond. Clan members select an elder or a leader to honor in this ceremony. Individual families and clans can use the kowtowing ceremony to honor family and clan members as well. An elder could be a man or a woman, but a leader is usually male. A couple is also appropriate for this tradition. Following the family feast (*noj tsiab*), a public forum open to all in the community is held to pay respect and honor to the selected individual.

The process of planning the kowtowing event is relatively brief. First, a group representing the clans meets and decides who should be the honoree. Second, the group leaders and representatives notify the individual that he or she has been selected. Third, the group sets the day and time for the event and announces the schedule to the public via interpersonal communication and social media. Fourth, the group makes preparations for the event and plans the ceremony and rituals accordingly. Traditionally, light refreshment, wine, and hard liquor are included. And fifth, the group collects monetary contributions to be given to the person who is being honored.

On the day of the event, the selected individual is brought to the scene with great respect and honor. For a family event, members of the family go to the home of the honoree to conduct the kowtowing ceremony. A special seating arrangement is made to accommodate the physical needs of various individuals. The honoree usually sits on a stage or other raised platform facing the crowd, but if the honoree feels uncomfortable being honored in public he or she can sit at the event table. The leader of the group takes charge of the ritual and starts the ceremony by formally telling the honoree why he or she has been brought to the forum to be honored. Everyone is on their knees while the leader addresses the honoree. The group gives the honoree special thanks, respect, and blessings. Then the group asks the honoree to bless everyone who is present in front of him or her.

Remember, the main purpose of this ceremony is to ask the honoree to give everyone his or her blessings during the New Year's celebration and beyond. The blessings include fortune, good luck, good health, peace, freedom, prosperity, and respect. Once the leader has addressed the honoree formally, the honoree is presented with special offerings such as drinks, toasts, or the financial gift that was collected. The honoree either sits down or stands up to address the crowd, blessing all attendees with special blessings. Usually, the honoree casts away all bad omens and welcomes all good spirits to wish everyone the very best of luck during the New Year and beyond. When the honoree finishes blessing the people, everyone kowtows to the honoree and thanks him or her

for the blessings. The honoree then instructs the leader to distribute the blessing drinks to all attendees. Drinking the blessing wine or hard liquor symbolizes the reception of the blessings and spirits from the New Year's kowtowing.

The blessings received in this kowtowing tradition are different for different individuals. One person may wish for a child and others may wish for good health. Some may wish for good luck and others may wish for love and romance. The blessings have infinite possibilities depending on the needs and beliefs of the individual persons during the New Year's celebration. The kowtowing ceremony also provides benefits to the honorees. The honor and respect given to them are meant to uplift them and bestow spiritual wellbeing and health during the New Year and beyond.

Hmong New Year in the West

Since they have been in the West, Hmong refugees have celebrated Hmong New Year on different days from July to December because of differing weather conditions in different metropolitan areas and difficulty finding places and facilities suitable for the magnitude of the annual celebration that gathers all Hmong communities in one location. Wherever Hmong live, they can perform all the family and household rituals and ceremonies that precede the New Year on the 30th day of the 12th month of the Hmong lunar calendar and they can hold the Hmong New Year's celebration (*lub tshav pob noj peb caug losi lub tshav dhia qaib*) between the 25th of December and the 1st of the New Year. However, Hmong in the West choose not to do this for sociopolitical reasons (Vang 2010). Vang wrote about issues involving one of the largest Hmong New Year celebrations, the one in Fresno, California, in an editorial for that city's newspaper, the *Fresno Bee*:

> From the early 1980s, local Hmong put on the New Year festivities as a joint community effort and public celebration. In the mid to late 1980s, the annual event seemed prof-

itable, and some believed it could generate substantial revenues that might fund non-profit organizations that would help the Hmong community grow and thrive; thus it began to be privately organized. Ironically, the private organizers incurred tremendous financial debts and the event became a political firestorm as bitter disputes arose over finances and unequal distribution of power, privilege, and social esteem.

The original purpose of the New Year celebration was to preserve Hmong culture and traditions and so pass on Hmong values, customs, and beliefs to younger generations. In other words, it was and still is a pluralistic event that keeps Hmong culture alive in a diverse society. Moreover, the annual celebration educates both non–Hmong and Hmong Americans, especially Hmong-American children, about the richness and beauty of the Hmong culture. It is a focal point for cultural identity, pride, and practices.

The multiple celebrations of Hmong New Year in Western nations have portrayed the traditional Hmong New Year as a privatized socioeconomic event rather than a traditional festival supported by the public that honors, celebrates, respects, preserves, and continues Hmong culture and traditions. Some Hmong communities have been divided by the organizers of these annual events who have politicized the Hmong New Year. In some major cities with large Hmong populations, at least two New Year's celebrations are held at the same time and compete with each other. Hmong hold nearly ten New Year celebrations each year throughout the state of California. The practice of dual celebrations has caused massive confusion about the true cultural identity and integrity of Hmong New Year. The controversy over New Year's will probably not end anytime soon and more celebrations will probably take place. At the very least, Hmong ought to think about who they really are as an ethnic group rather than following the ideas of a minority of Hmong who have little or no passion to do what is best for the greater good of the people.

Western Hmong are more prosperous than eastern Hmong and are therefore better able

to celebrate the New Year in ways that preserve Hmong heritage, but the current public bickering and tribal squabbling has prevented western Hmong from continuing true Hmong culture. Western Hmong have failed to celebrate their holiday as other ethnic groups in America do. Other groups neither allow weather conditions to interfere with their traditions nor hold multiple celebrations of the same cultural event. In the case of Hmong New Year, Hmong feel they have every right to celebrate as many different times as they want because of weather conditions; however, these month-long and week-long celebrations do not represent the Hmong heritage, and the ongoing conflicts tarnish the meaning and integrity of Hmong New Year.

The Hmong have a rich culture and traditions that deserve to be honored, respected, celebrated, and at the same time preserved so they can be passed down to younger generations. Hmong must find right ways to commemorate their heritage; otherwise, as is happening now, complex sociopolitical circumstances will place them at odds with one another in the celebration of their culture and traditions. In other words, Hmong must be able to compromise with one another and settle their differences so they can organize the celebration of Hmong New Year in a way that is somewhat in conformity with the celebrations of the other people's cultures in the western nations. Even though Hmong have some customs, especially religious rituals that cannot be conformed to any western customs, they can find a sensible way to stop the multiple New Year's celebrations to be more in line with western practices and still retain the event's unique Hmong values and flavor.

Traditional Religious Practices

Hmong have preserved their religious practices for thousands of years. Most Hmong religious practices are based on familial deities, ancestral spirits, and benevolent divinity. As the result of the complexity of Hmong cultural traditions and religious practices, a mass conversion to Christianity took place in 1957 in Laos. Today, Hmong follow diverse religions and faiths; however, most are not religious people. They accommodate the practices of different religious faiths. Many traditional Hmong families practice the rituals and ceremonies of more than one religion. The term *Hmong traditional beliefs* is used of ancestor worship (*kev cai qub*) and animism (*spirits of all living*) in association with tenets of Islam, Buddhism, Hinduism, Confucianism, and Taoism. The term *traditional ritual* denotes old beliefs and practices.

Hmong traditional rituals and practices (*Hmoob kev cai dab qhua*) have been misinterpreted as ghost or devil worship. Therefore, an understanding of some religious and spiritual terms in Hmong language is in order. The word *kev cai* means "the way, the system, the protocol, the formality, the guidelines, the policies, the procedures, or the process of"; the word *dab* means "spirits, guardian angels, or benevolent spirits"; and *qhua* stands for supporting, promoting, encouraging, empowering, enabling, or entrusting. A phrase that can be used in place of *kev cai* is *txheej txheem*, meaning "the processes, procedures, guidelines, policies, protocols, and regulations." When Hmong combine these words and phrases properly, the way Hmong practice their religious rituals makes sense. When the words are not used correctly, *dab* is easily assumed to mean "ghost, devil, evil, or demon." Moreover, the phrases *teev dab* and *coj dab* can be confusing. In Hmong traditional religious practices, the phrase *teev dab* means "worship, practice, control, honor, pray, or pay respect to spirits, guardian angels, or benevolent spirits"; the phrase *coj dab* means exactly the same plus "belief, leading, showing, and guidance." If not said carefully, these phrases can be easily misunderstood as "worshiping ghosts, evil, devils, or demons."

The old Hmong religious practices are often referred to as ancestor worship, meaning worshiping the ancestral spirits (*teev dab niam dab txiv*). The Hmong phrase *teev dab niam dab txiv* simply means "honoring, wor-shiping, and respecting the ancestral spirits in association with the familial deities and household spirits." Hmong are animists; they believe that all living things have souls, spirits, and supernatural connections and interrelationships. Basically, Hmong believe in the combination of supernatural power, spiritual worship, ancestor worship, superstition, and taboos and the divinity of the soul. For instance, summoning the Heaven and Earth Spirits (*fiv yeem ntuj*) for protection and guidance is a common religious practice. As stated earlier, Hmong do not believe the existence of heaven; however, the word heaven is used here to refer to the highest God in the sky. So, too, is the summoning of the supernatural power and spiritual force for protection and guidance in the Blood Oath, Justice Water, Drinking Spiritual Water, and Blood Vow rituals. These rituals are performed to reinforce the religious bonds between comrades, assuring their commitment, loyalty, and willingness to make the ultimate sacrifice.

In the old days, Hmong used to summon the Heaven and Earth Spirits while using hot oil sentence (*siv roj kub*) to decide civil matters. Hmong honor (*hwm losi saib muaj nqis*), offer (*laig*), and worship (*teev hawm*) these benevolent spirits. They summon the heavenly spirits and supernatural forces for a number of practical purposes: making magical water for healing, calling the thunder to roar and the lighting to strike, calling the sky to pour down rain and fill the atmosphere with clouds, having the magical power to hold a red-hot iron, stopping the flow of blood, possessing the Godly verses and psalms of spirits and divinity, safeguarding and protecting the body, and foretelling future events.

The Hmong word *laig* means offering to spirits or consuming by the spirits. *Laig dab* is the ritual process of offering something to specific benevolent spirits and having the spirits consume the offering. The Hmong word *xym* typically means ghost-like spirits or evil spirits that may cause harm or may curse the soul and the benevolent spirits, making them ill. Hmong often use the ghost-like phrase *tej nyuag vij sub vij sw*, meaning all the bad, evil, dangerous, conflicting, infighting, or vindictive acts caused by curses and evil spirits. The Hmong phrase for demons or evil spirits is *ntxwg nyoog*, meaning notorious and monstrous demons that cause serious spiritual harm to human beings. Hmong are also concerned with religious demons from Laotian Buddhism: the fast, evil-calling, demanding satanic spirits called *phis nyuj vais*. Both *ntxwg nyoog* and *phis nyuj vais* are wild, animal-like demons, fierce and ferocious beings. The word *nyav* also means demons, monstrous, and devil.

Spiritually, Hmong identify all spirits and put them into two main categories: the domestic spirits (*dab nyeg*) and the wild spirits (*dab qus*). Hmong believe domestic spirits are benevolent beings and protect them from all the omens, curses, and harms caused by the wild spirits. Hmong believe the wild spirits are unfriendly, dangerous, intrusive, and deadly beings.

The way Hmong shamans and magicians cast away demons, omens, evil spirits, devils, and curses is based on this religious word phrase: "*Xa mus rau hnub coog hli kawg kom ntsej tsis hnov muag tsis pom*," meaning "To the end of the sunlight and moonlight where ears cannot hear and eyes cannot see." Religiously, Hmong believe this is the farthest place for all evils, demons, curses, and omens should belong in. Symbolically, this farthest place could be a refuge like hell; however, Hmong do not practice such a belief in the existence of hell.

As alluded to earlier, today, most Hmong still believe in and practice the traditional religion, called *dab niam dab txiv*, or *kev cai qub*, meaning "worshiping mother's spirits and soul and father's spirits and soul." The second largest belief system among Hmong is Christianity (*kev cai tshiab losi cov ntseeg ntuj*). Some families follow a new faith called *Poj Koob Yam Ntxwv Niam Looj Tsav*, meaning "the ancestor's spirits and soul of the heavenly mother." Others are devoted to the practice of *Chao Fa* and worship the protector in the sky, meaning the divine power given to the Disciples of God. Very few

Hmong have no adherence to any particular religion.

Hmong religious rituals involve animal sacrifices and offerings. Many Hmong families practice their traditional beliefs with some modest modifications to accommodate western views on animal rights. Hmong have stopped using the sacrificial offerings involving cats, dogs, and baby animals by substituting these offerings with man-made objects or by eliminating such practices for good.

Most importantly, Hmong are not ghost worshipers or devil worshipers but are firm believers in benevolent spirits and guardian angels. As stated earlier, Hmong classify spirits into two main groups: domestic spirits (*dab nyeg*) and wild spirits (*dab qus*). Hmong worship domestic spirits mainly—guardian angels and deities—but not wild spirits. However, Hmong believe there is a connection between all spirits.

As an influence of *Taoism*, in which spirits are ubiquitous, Hmong believe that life on earth is safeguarded by benevolent spirits and such spiritual beings live in different places. Some are in heavenly places (*saum ntuj ceeb tsheej*) and some are on earthly locations (*hauv ntiaj teb*). The virtuous being (*saub*) can tell Hmong what is right and wrong in regard to their spiritual wellbeing. Spirits in heavenly places give Hmong eyes in the highest place; they see everything on earth. The earth is vast and the spirits there can hear and see everything Hmong say and do. One of the sayings Hmong use to describe heavenly places and earthly locations of the spirits that dwell in the two places is: "Heavenly sky is above and earth is below (*ntuj nyob saud av nyob hauv*)." They use the saying "Heavenly sky is above and heavenly eyes see all (*ntuj nyob saud ntuj pom*)" to warn people that their good deeds as well as their bad deeds do not go unnoticed. As explained earlier, Hmong like to summon the Heaven and Earth Spirits (*fiv yeem ntuj*) for help in times of great fear or impending death, and Hmong can also call for the ancestral spirits (*fiv niam fiv txiv pab*) to provide benevolent assistance in times of need; they do so especially when people are sick or facing a serious threat. Hmong Christian families, on the other hand, believe God, as revealed in his son, Jesus Christ, is the only Holy Spirit they need, so whenever they need help or spiritual guidance they pray in his name.

Hmong believe that each body has only one main soul (*plig*) but many soul spirits (*ntsuj plig*). They believe three groups of soul spirits live near the body: the shadows of the soul (*ntsuj duab ntsuj hlauv*), the soul of feet and hands (*ntsuj te ntsuj taw*), and the soul of the body (*ntsuj xub zeb hlauv xub ntoos*). The Hmong word *plig* means the living soul in the body, or the main soul. The Hmong word *ntsuj* means the lesser soul, or the spirit of the main soul living in the body. The phrase *ntsuj plig* is used to refer to both beings in the body. In Hmong traditional religious practices, the *ntsuj* can foretell the well-being of the body's mini souls. For instance, the soul may be lost or wondering (*poob plig*), scared or spooked (*poob siab*), afraid or intimidated (*ntshai*), shocked or surprised (*ceeb*), being curses upon (*raug*), or being reincarnated (*mus thawj thiab*). These are terms used to describe the state of mind of the *ntsuj* and *plig* in the body.

To call the soul and its spirits or to initiate an offering to the benevolent spirits of the soul, Hmong usually use joss sticks, incense, paper money (*yaj khaum ceeb khaum*), a bundle of cut paper (*xav tsheej*), a mini bundle of spiritual paper (*ntshuas ntawv*), and two split animal horns (*kuam*) along with chicken eggs, chickens, a bowl of uncooked rice, and spiritual figures (*moj zeej*). These are the items commonly used in most Hmong spiritual and religious rituals and practices. Animals are used as sacrificial offerings when the need is particularly serious.

The terminology associated with various Hmong rituals and rites is complex and may seem strange to westerners. The phrases and the practices themselves are rooted in ancient religious foundations. Learning to understand Hmong traditional rituals and practices takes time and diligent effort because not everything is visible to the naked eyes. Despite the fact that many rituals are intricate and demanding, most Hmong still adhere to them.

Spiritual and Ritual Communications

For all Hmong traditional religious practices, there are only two main super highways Hmong religious practitioners use to communicate with all living and nonliving souls and spirits of human and animals in the spiritual world. The first way is through the use of a pair of two halves of a cut-split animal horn, called *txwm kuam* in Hmong, to communicate with all living souls and spirits before, during, and after making sacrificial offerings. In Hmong, *txwm kuam* means a pair of cut-split horns from a bull or a water buffalo, and the two halves are about six inches long. Hmong also refer to the pair as religious instruments or spiritual pointers. The healer, chanter, or shaman can use the *txwm kuam* to accurately determine the acceptance or rejection of the sacrificial offerings by the specific souls and spirits. For instance, when a shaman tosses the pointers to the ground by hand, one half faces down and the other half faces up to acknowledge acceptance, or in Hmong, it means yes. When both halves either face up or down, it means no. Sometimes, it is depending on the request made by the practitioner.

Similarly, for the souls and spirits of the deceased, Hmong use a small pair of two halves of a cut-split bamboo pipe in place of the *txwm kuam*, called *ob tug txhib ntawg* in Hmong, to communicate with all living and nonliving souls and spirits in association with the dead in the spiritual world. The pair is about three inches long. Practically, the process of tossing both sets of spiritual pointers by hand is similarly identical; however, the chanting of religious verses is different for each request, sacrifice, or offering during shamanistic rituals, soul calling rituals, funeral rites, and dead rituals. For example, in Hmong death rituals, when the souls and spirits of the dead accept the offering is called *Seem Kuam* (one half faces up and the other half faces down), and a rejection is known as *Yaj Kuam* or *Yeeb Kuam* (both sides either face up or down). In Hmong facing up is called *qhib or ntxeev*, meaning open; and facing down is known as *qos or khwb*, meaning closed. Therefore, *txwm kuam* and *ob tug txhib ntawg* are instrumental tools or spiritual pointers used in nearly all religious sacrificial and ritual communications between the spiritual world and the physical world.

New Year Opening Ritual

Hmong New Year begins with an opening ritual. Before or on the 30th day of the 12th month of the Hmong lunar calendar, the opening ritual ceremony (*lwm qaib, lwm sub, losi lwm tsiab*) takes place at the home of a clan member. The purpose of this opening ceremony is to get rid of all bad luck, omens, evils, devils, demons, and negative forces that may interfere with the life of the family in the New Year. The core value of the ceremony is to protect all living beings in the family from evil spirits. A house or other location is designated for the opening ceremony. The ceremony is open to all tribes, clans, and Hmong people. All clan members gather at the prearranged location. The ceremony takes place in the early afternoon hours before dusk. An elderly individual is designated to conduct the ceremony. The conductor needs to have a seven-foot tall cut green tree with some leaves at the top, a long rope made of straw grass, some straw grass rings, some red cloth strips or red fabric strings, and a live rooster. The rope made of straw grass is formed into a gigantic loop. One end is tied to the top of the tree and the other end to the bottom. The middle of the rope is stretched out to make the loop. A person usually holds the middle part of the rope to keep the loop open during the ritual. The conductor holds the tree with one hand (unless it is securely grounded so it stands upright) and the rooster in the other.

The ceremony begins with the crowd walking in a circular motion, passing through the loop several times. Usually, the crowd would march 3, 4, or 5 times clockwise and 2, 3, or 4 times counterclock to complete the ritual cycle. The conductor chants the verses required for the ceremony while waving the rooster over the participants in the same direction each time. The verses send any evil spirits, curses, omens, and misfortunes off with the old year. Before the conductor blesses all the participants with fortune, good health, joy, prosperity, luck, hope, and good wishes for the coming year and beyond, the crowd walks through the loop several times again, this time in the opposite direction, while the conductor chants and waves the rooster. Before the crowd disperses, a substitute takes the conductor's place and repeats the ceremony with the conductor walking through the loop so the conductor can also participate in the ceremony. Then, the rooster is killed and its blood is offered in the place of the sins of all the participants. All the materials used in the ritual except the rooster are tossed away and burned later. Usually, the conductor keeps the rooster for dinner that night. This marks the end of the opening ceremony. All participants go to their respective homes.

New Year Sweeping Ritual

Following the opening ceremony, families perform other New Year's rituals in their homes. One of the first rituals is the ceiling sweeping ceremony (*cheb qhab thab*). The purpose of this ceremony is to sweep away any evil spirits hidden inside the house and keep only the good spirits for the New Year's celebration and the coming year. This ceremony is quite short. The performer, usually the father, sweeps the house, starting from the bedrooms, proceeding to all the other rooms, and then to the front door. Today, this ceremony is optional.

Rice Patty Ritual

In the old days, the rice patty ceremony (*tuav ncuav*) took place either a day before or on the same day as the opening ceremony. The rice patty is similar to today's rice cake, except it has a natural flavor. Usually, sweet sticky rice or purple sticky rice is soaked in water for a few hours and then is steam cooked. The cooked rice is poured into a wooden rice patty trough (*dab tuav ncuav*) made specifically for this ceremony. The rice is pounded into mash in the trough, a job that requires the strength of two men. Each man has a pounding stick or pestle (*dauj tuav ncuav*) made of wood. It takes two men pounding at least 30 minutes to completely mash the rice. During the pounding, the two men push and pull the mashed rice to make it smooth. Hmong rice patties are used for eating, for offering to spirits, as an offering to the deceased, and in the soul re-visitation ritual after death and burial (*tso plig*).

Soul Calling Ritual

The soul calling ritual (*hu plig*) is the most commonly used ritual; it is used for a variety of purposes on different occasions throughout the year. Soul calling either precedes or follows any religious ritual, and it is part of most rituals and ceremonies. It is performed at the birth of a newborn, in shamanistic rituals, at graduations, at traditional weddings, as part of the social courtesy naming ceremony, for mild sicknesses, for traumatic fear and frightening experiences, and many other times. Soul calling is combined with most religious rituals because it determines the general health, plight, and fate of the individuals or of family members.

For two or more people, soul calling requires two live chickens, a male chicken for the female family members and a female chicken for the male family members. A bowl of uncooked rice, a joss stick, and some eggs are needed. The number of eggs used represents the number of people for the ritual. For one person, a live chicken is required. Following the first phase of the soul calling, the sacrificial chickens are slaughtered and steam cooked to prepare for the second, or final, phase of the ritual. Once the soul calling is done, the two cooked chickens are read in accordance with Hmong spiritual interpretations of signs, symbols, logic, and psychic analysis. The tongues of the chickens tell of the family's willingness to have the souls return and be welcomed; two pieces from the skulls of the chickens reaffirm the soul calling and spiritual wellness of family members; the eyes of the chickens foretell the general health, blessing, and fortune of the family; the wings of the chickens explain the close and warm relationship between the children

and their parents; the feet of the chickens tell of the future situation of a person, such as security, fortune, or triumph, and predict unexpected events the person will need to overcome such as health issues, omens, and bad luck. The readings of the different parts of the two cooked chickens are significant if one believes them; however, the interpretations are sometimes ambiguous, exaggerated, or out of context. The warning signs help Hmong prepare to overcome obstacles that occur in their lives because sometimes the omen of the soul calling is quite accurate.

Following the soul calling ritual, the property ownership ritual (*foob yeem*) takes place. The father of the family uses a stack of paper money to mark all his property, his tools, and his household items to show his ownership. The rationale behind this ritual is that as the father proclaims ownership of these items, the household spirits are asked to protect family members while they use the items, especially during harvest and cultivation seasons.

Household Shrine Ritual

Every traditional Hmong house, except for houses of families without fathers or sons, has an altar or shrine (*xwm kab losi seej khab*) as a place where family members can worship all the spirits related to the family's spirituality. This sacred shrine is the place of the household spirits that protect and safeguard the family spirits and souls and meet daily spiritual needs. According to Hmong legends, this household shrine has several important spirits: the spirits of wealth, the spirits of ancestors and deceased individuals, the spirits of offspring, the spirits of crops and cultivation, the spirits of guardian angels and protectors, the spirits of employment and earning, the spirits of abundant life, the spirits of saving life, the spirits of health and wellness, and the spirits of peace and tranquility. Some Hmong shamans can communicate with the spiritual world at times through the household shrine spirits. On every altar or shrine, spiritual objects are displayed in honor of the benevolent spirits (*cov cwj losi cov twj*). The objects might be a pair of split animal horns (*kuam*), a small bowl of rice, a few small cups of fresh water, some rice grains, a bowl of rice for joss sticks, a stack of paper money, cutout spiritual figures, chicken feathers, chicken blood, folded spiritual paper, and so on.

At least once a year, the shrine is renewed with new meals, spiritual papers, burning incense, and holy water. To start the renewal, the father burns incense to alert the house spirits living on the altar or shrine that because of the New Year's celebration a new offering will be given to them and their shelter will be taken down, renewed, and reconstructed for the New Year. Once that is done, the ritual takes place. Everything on the altar is replaced with new items. Usually a rooster is required for sacrificial purposes. The father first offers the live rooster to the altar spirits and asks all spirits to cast away all back luck, omens, and any unforeseeable events in life. Then, the father offers the rooster as a new meal and asks for blessing, good luck, fortune, health, wealth, and prosperity for the New Year. Once the initial offering is done, the rooster is slaughtered. Its blood and feathers are pasted on the altar to honor its resting place with the spirits. The whole rooster is steam cooked. When it is done, a new meal (a cooked rooster with some rice) is offered to the household spirits and their newly reconstructed shelter. The father chants and asks for protection for all family members during the New Year celebration and in the incoming year. The offering reaffirms the family's commitment to have these guardian spirits protect them at all times.

The sacrificial rooster is sacred and in some Hmong families, the female family members are prohibited from consuming it; it is to be consumed only by the male family members. This religious and ritual taboo is not significant today; however, it used to be a religious restriction observed by female family members.

Today, some religious shrines are temporary and others are permanent, depending on the father of the family and the spiritual wellbeing of the family. It is unnecessary to change the spiritual shelter every year as long as the offering continues throughout the year or worship takes place on a regular basis to keep the spirits informed of the family's commitment to the spirits. Sometimes the renewal is necessary because of bad luck, curses, or problematic life situations. Spiritual worship is a very private matter and one has to understand *how* to interact with the spirits; otherwise, the shrine will be meaningless. Moreover, the religious spirits are very sensitive and one has to be very careful about the fine line between being spiritually fit and being psychotic. Sometimes, the shaman can recognize wrong practices and offerings and tell if the spiritual world has been violated or if the worshipper has refused to comply with the request of specific spirits for specific offerings to the spiritual world. Overall, the household shrine spirits not only protect the family and the house, but also alert the family of any impending catastrophe, danger, or illnesses.

Shaman Spirits Release Ritual

Each year, right before or shortly after the opening ritual of the year, most Hmong shamans pay special tribute to their shamanistic spirits that give them the magical power to cure and heal sick people. They conduct a shamanistic spirit release ritual (*xav dab neeb, tso qhua neeb, losi xa qhua neeb*), offering the spirits meals, stacks of paper money, incense, and holy water. This ritual shows the shamans' commitment by releasing the spirits of Neeb (*Leej Nkaub* in Hmong) and the souls and spirits of all sacrificial animals slaughtered for the year back to the spiritual world (*yeeb ceeb*) for a few weeks during the New Year's celebration. The release ritual gives the spirits of Neeb a break and also provides a break for the shamans. As for the sacrificial animals, the release offers them new opportunities for reincarnation in the spiritual world. During this release, the shaman cannot perform any shamanistic rituals. He must perform a shamanistic retrieval ritual to retrieve (*ua neeb to qhua*) the spirits from the spiritual world before he can shamanistic rituals. The process of sending and retrieving spirits is tedious, and that is why shamans need to have spiritually strong wives who understand all these religious rituals. Besides depending on their wives, shamans also rely on trained individuals who understand the messages they send back to the people during the shamanistic rituals; these individuals provide them with spiritual support. Some of the details of the release ritual varies from shaman to shaman, but the ritual must include the release of all animals sacrificed throughout the year along with the spirits to allow both the animals and the spirits to be redeemed in accordance with the atonement of soul reincarnation in the spiritual world.

During this release ritual, the shamanistic shrine or altar (*thaj neeb*) can be renewed or reconstructed as well. Some shamans choose not to amend the shrine unless they feel it is necessary. When shamans do replace the shrine, they do so while the spirits are away. Each shaman has his or her own way of entertaining and worshiping these spirits. If for some reason, the shaman fails to fulfill his spiritual commitments, the spirits can depart from the shaman's altar or, in some cases, bring curses on the shaman and the shaman's family. There have been cases in which the shaman has lost all his magical power, spiritual intuition, and guiding spirits because of his neglect and poor commitment.

Hmong Shamanistic Rituals

Over the last 50 years, some western scholars and researchers have studied the rituals and practices of Hmong shamanism and have reported that the main spirit of the shaman is *leej nkaub*, or the *Neeb Spirit*. These scholars have described the trances of Hmong shamans as merely powerful psychotherapeutic treatments of unbalanced psychosomatic body images. Body images are the many souls in a person. Hmong, however, believe that a person has only one soul with many soul spirits (*ntsuj plig*). Shamans may possess several different spirits for different purposes. Moreover, shamanistic spirits (*dab neeb*) give the shaman magical powers to cure and revive the sick individuals' spirits from the spiritual world; this is not psychosomatic. Remember, the Hmong word *dab*

has been misinterpreted as ghost, evil, or devil; it really refers to benevolent *spirits* in rituals. Because Hmong people cannot see the spirits, they call them *dab*, meaning invisible to the naked eyes.

To become a shaman, one has to chosen by the Neeb Spirits. There is a process new shamans have to undergo. First, the chosen one becomes mildly sick with spiritual symptoms; he or she is being haunted by the shamanistic spirits (*dab neeb los tshoj*). Second, a veteran shaman is called to determine the cause of the symptoms. Third, if it is determined that the Neeb Spirits have chosen him or her to become a new shaman, the shaman will set a timeline (*teem caij kom zoo*) in which the sick individual should get well and promises to make an offering to the Neeb Spirits in return. Fourth, if the sick person gets well as predicted by the shaman, the ritual takes place in which an offering is given to the Neeb Spirits for their choosing of the individual. Fifth, the chosen one starts the process of becoming a shaman with the guidance of his or her chosen master. Any shaman can be the master who installs a new shaman (*tsa thaj neeb*). If for some reason the chosen one is not ready to become a real shaman, he or she can delay the worship of Neeb Spirits for a time. Whenever he or she is ready, the master shaman will be called again to perform a shamanistic ritual to install (*tsa thaj neeb*) the new shaman.

Hmong shamans perform a variety of acts to communicate between the human world (*yaj ceeb*) and the spiritual world (*yeeb ceeb*). During the spiritual trance, the *Shee Yee*, or the shamanistic healer, rides a magical horse and travels into the spiritual world to trace the soul and spirits of a sick person. The shaman can send messages back to the people to make sacrifices or offerings in accordance with the negotiation and agreement the shaman has made with the evil beings and the devil. Shamans cannot cure infections caused by bacteria and viruses or medical conditions caused by diseases such as kidney stones, diabetes, hypertension, gout, heart problems, and so on. Shamans heal only those sicknesses related to soul and spirits.

Shamanism can be classified into different types: the original ancestral shaman (*neeb txwv feej*), the Shee Yee shaman (*neeb siv yis*), the worship shaman (*neeb teev sam*), and the maid shaman, or female shaman (*neeb poj qhe losi neeb xua nplej*). Shamans use benches during their rituals, and the different types of shamans use benches of different sizes and types. The original ancestral shaman uses a flying horse bench (*nees huab cua*) that is about one foot tall; it is wide, rigid, and sturdy. The Shee Yee shaman uses an air ship bench (*nkoj huab nkoj cua*) that is a little bit taller (about two feet tall), narrower, more flexible, and longer. This bench is designed to allow the shaman to jump on and off with ease during the rituals. His feet may dangle on the ground as well. The maid shaman can use any kind of bench as long as it is sturdy enough for her to sit on.

Hmong choose from among several shamanistic rituals depending on the need at hand. Sometimes, the shaman prescribes the best ritual for the situation. Shamanistic rituals and practices include, but are not limited to the following:

- Spiritual diagnostic and predetermination calling (*txhij qhua saib*)
- Formal determination ritual (*ua neeb saib*)
- Formal replacement and offering ritual (*ua neeb kho*)
- Buried soul and grave replacement ritual (*ua neeb theej txhoj*)
- Wandering of soul and depression of spirits ritual (*ua neeb fab laj*)
- Unexpected and recurrent visitation of the dead ritual (*ua neeb phaug ntee*)
- Deadly soul revival and resurrection ritual (*ua neeb hloov ntsuj plig*)
- Retrieval of soul and swapping of soul ritual (*ua neeb hloov ntsuj losi ua neeb nqi hiav*)
- Separating the life between two people (*ua neeb faib thiab*)
- Extending the declaration of life or life span (*ua neeb ntxiv ntawv*)
- Safeguarding the family fortune and prosperity (*ua neeb tsa txhiaj meej*)
- Sending away omens, curses, and misfortunes (*ua neeb xa xyob txhiaj*)
- Driving away the curse and arresting the curse (*ua neeb kho cua*)
- Safeguarding the house and household spirits (*ua neeb kho tsev*)

The primary objective of the shaman is to save the human soul. While falling into a spiritual trance, an ordinary shaman travels from the physical world into the spiritual world through different levels, gates, or doors. The entrance into the spiritual world is referred to as the threads of the shamanistic journey, or the processes of spiritual voyage (*sab neeb*). The shaman travels through at least nine levels, or spiritual realms, before reaching the center and inner core of the spiritual world, the realm of heavenly places. The first three levels are the supernatural realm (*nyuj vab thawj tom*), the central pillar realm (*nyuj vab lwm tom*), and the doorstep realm into the spiritual world (*nyuj vab xab tom*). Some shamans are more capable than others, and the ability to go beyond the third level depends on the individual shaman's spiritual power, shamanistic magic, prowess, and authenticity since there are different realms and paths the shaman has to pass through in order to reach the spiritual destination. For instance, after the third level, the shaman enters the path of the shaman cliff, or the highest level of the Neeb Spirits, known as the rocky mountains of Leej Nkaub (*tsuas neeb*). Then comes the realm of the ancestors and great ancestors of the sick (*poj yawm txwv txoob*); the path of all the dead, or the valley of the death (*kev ploj kev tuag*); and the path of the genesis of life, or the originator of life (*niam nkauj kab yeeb tsim noob neej*). Shamans of good quality enter these places, but some shamans shun their spiritual obligations and refuse to enter these spiritual realms during the rituals.

Today, some rituals are easy and cheap and others are costly, requiring large amounts of time, preparation, and spiritual sacrifices and offerings. Not all shamans can perform all the rituals and practices. Some shun the heavy-duty rituals because of health related issues and spiritual incapability or because of the limitation of their *Leej Nkaub, or Neeb* Spirits. Older Hmong still practice shamanism along with herbal medicine for everyday healing of minor ailments related to the soul and spiritual being. Hmong shamanism is a good treatment option for Hmong people, especially the elders who are opposed to western medicine and those who are afraid of becoming victims of western medical malpractice and experimentation.

Hmong Herbal Ritual

In the old days, when there were no medical doctors, Hmong relied on herbal medicine and spiritual healing for illnesses related to spiritual matters. Western medicine was not available to Hmong until the mid–1950s. Hmong have practiced herbal medicine and spiritual healing for many centuries dating back to nearly 6,000 years. Today, there are very few Hmong who are specialized in such practices because of the availability of western medicine. Hmong herbalists and spiritualists worship the spirits of herbal medicine and believe in the power of psychic intuition and extraordinary magical knowledge connected with an altar or shrine (*thaj dab tshuaj losi yum vaj*). Hmong believe that true, quality herbal medicines have spiritual connections. The Hmong magical and powerful prophet (*saub*) can prescribe both herbal treatments and spiritual healings for some rare illnesses that may not be cured by western medicine. Hmong traditional healings and treatments include cupping, rubbing, spooning, massaging, twisting and turning to reposition an unborn child, egging with coins, dropping an egg in water, cupping holy water, pulling and measuring incense, and reading palms. Spiritual healings are part of religious rituals such as shamanism, magical chanting, soul calling, funeral and burial services, house restrictions, barring and banning activities, and so on. Most Hmong believe that herbal medicine is a natural treatment that has no side effects whatsoever. No one really knows for sure because no study has been done on Hmong herbal medicine. Western medical experts believe that 30 per-

cent of herbal-medical remedies are effective treatments for mild ailments.

Each year Hmong herbalists and spiritualists pay tribute and respect to the spirits of herbal medicine. They make offerings to them in thanks for and to secure their commitment to cure the sick. The altars or shrines to these spirits, unlike the altars of household spirits and shaman spirits, do not require yearly renewal and reconstruction. However, most practitioners renew their spiritual power during the New Year's celebration. They make offerings ranging from a simple meal to a major animal sacrifice. Believers treat the spirits of herbal medicine like any other spirit, honoring them, confident that intentional improprieties may result in spiritual curses and ineffectiveness. They worship the spirits in order to maintain the spiritual potency of the herbal medicine they use.

Heaven and Earth Spirits Ritual

When facing fears, life-threatening situations, or death, Hmong usually turn to the Heaven and Earth Spirits ritual (*fiv yeem ntuj*) for protection and guidance. Remember, the word heaven is used here to refer to the heavenly God in the highest place in the sky. Heaven and Earth Spirits can be summoned throughout the year and the ritual can be conducted any time as long as it falls within the timeline the requester set for completion of the ritual. For instance, if the requester summons the Heaven and Earth Spirits for protection and guidance and makes vows to pay the spirits for the services within six months, the ritual offering has to take place within the six-month period. If the requester fails to make the offering within the time promised, the spirits may curse him for not fulfilling his spiritual obligation and the curse may be disastrous.

The requester can summon the Heaven and Earth Spirits in one of two ways. He can establish a temporary altar or shrine (*lub thaj fiv yeem thiab pauj yeem*) outside the home as a location from which to call for the spirits. He can place ritual items on the altar such as a bowl of rice, an egg, a cup of water, some burning incense, a gong, a pair of split animal horns (*kuam*), or a stack of paper money. Or the requester can just stand up with burning incense in his hands and summon the spirits for protection and guidance. After chanting, he can place the burning incense in the ground and leave it to burn down to ashes.

Either way he chooses for the ritual, the requester must fulfill his vow within the timeline of promise. If he made an altar, he has to return to the location of the altar to pay the spirits for their services unless a shaman is called to perform a special rite requesting permission from the spiritual world to make the offering at a different location. If the requester did not make an altar, he can pay for the service at any location. Payment for the spiritual services has to match the original request or the spirits may not accept the offering. That is, if the requester promised to pay the spiritual debt with a cow, a cow has to be sacrificed for an offering, not a pig, goat, sheep, or chicken. If the requester promised a white cow for a special request, he has to find a white cow for the offering, not any cow.

Hmong summon Heaven and Earth Spirits for a variety of purposes, such as for the protection of soldiers and loved ones during war, for guidance in escaping and crossing the swift Mekong River, for protection and safety for lost individuals, for the recovery of a very sick or dying person, for protection during a traumatic experience or surgery, for protection in complicated births and labor, for help in uncertain plights. The Heaven and Earth Spirits are the almighty protectors and saviors for all of life's circumstances as long as one is loyal to the principles of commitment and adheres to its guiding commandments. Intentional infractions of the rules may result in poor services and a call to re-summon the spirits may not be effective. Hmong always say, "Neej ruam tabsi dab tsis ruam; dag neej tau tabsi dag dab tsis tau," meaning, "People are ignorant, but not spirits; lie to people is alright, but not the spirits."

All spiritual sacrifices are for protection, guidance, and assistance in times of need and suffering and not for the purposes of satisfying greed, revenge, or plotting to harm some-

one. Any worship and practice of the spirits of black magic would pose a serious threat to society, and a practitioner of black magic has to be rooted out and eliminated. According to Hmong legends, both the Chinese and the Hmong fought against black magicians and Hmong did not know how to cast evil spells. Hmong were sometimes victims of evil spells before they learned about black magic from tribal people such as the Khamu, Lu Mien, Laotian, and Thai. Evil spells comes in different forms: cow interwoven spells (*nyuj ciab nyuj ncau*), quo shee spells (*kua si*), cow hide and flint stone spells (*tawv nyuj zeb ntais*), spells of death spirits and deadly curses (*dab phim pauj*), and black magic spells (*khawv koob, tso pob zeb, losis tso dab tom*). Hmong refer to these evil spells as calling the ghost to kill someone (*tso dab tom*). Today, knowing and using these evil spells and black magic is considered a crime against humanity.

Parental Spirits Protection Ritual

When facing difficult and life-threatening situations, Hmong can call for their ancestors' spirits, or parental spirits (*fiv yeem thov niam thov txiv pab losi fiv yeem thov pog yawg pab*) for protection and guidance. The requester can summon two types of familial spirits. First, he can request protection and guidance from his deceased grandparents—only the parents of his parents, not further up the generational order. Second, he can summon the spirits of his deceased biological parents, either mom or dad or both, for protection and guidance. If his parents are still alive, he cannot summon their spirits, but the spirits of the grandparents. For either request, the promise to pay for the services must be kept as strictly as when summoning the Heaven and Earth Spirits. If he does not pay the spiritual vow as promised, harmful curses may fall on the requester or his family members. If one makes the payment in a timely manner, no curse occurs, but if one ignores the vow and disregards the requirement for payment, the results are likely to be costly and could even be deadly. Therefore, religiously, for every spiritual summon,

Hmong have to honor sacrificial offerings to compensate the benevolent spirits for their fulfillment of the request, or in rare cases, Hmong can repudiate the request or vow by offering nothing for the unfulfillment of the benevolent spirits. Spiritual repudiation, cancelation, or refusal is referred to as *thum yeem losi fij yeem*, having disagreement to offer restitution as the result of unfulfillment by the spirits. Basically, the refusal ritual is to inform the benevolent spirits not to expect any sacrificial offerings from the requester and therefore to friendly remind them of their unfulfilled role in such a request or vow in order to send them back to the spiritual world until a new summon is issued upon them again.

Parental spirits can be summoned for protection and guidance in two ways. One is to voluntary call for the spirits (*fiv losi hu tuaj*) in time of need or suffering. The requester can ask as many times as he or she wants as long as he or she is committed to offering the promised sacrifices to the spirits. The second way is to search for spiritual restitution and retribution (*tuaj yuav nyuj losi tuaj nrhiav noj*) from the parental spirits and souls. This way of summoning parental spirits is occasioned by a curse on one of the family members of the oldest or youngest son. It can be done only once in a lifetime, and if it is done right, the effects of the ritual last a lifetime. However, if it is done wrong, the ritual has to be repeated until it achieves the desired result.

To pay for the services in the voluntary calling, one has to find a close family member who knows the religious verses and chants to conduct the ritual, offering the specific sacrifice within the timeline promised by the requester. The ritual may take a half day, and no shamanistic ritual is required. For the search for spiritual restitution, the targeted family member, usually the oldest son, has to seek out a shaman to perform a shamanistic ritual to retrieve the parental spirits and souls from the grave and guide them back into the family in order for the spirits and souls to be in position to receive the offering before the actual restitution ritual can be performed by a close family relative. For both rituals, the items used in Hmong traditional funeral and burial rites are required: a performer of the reed bamboo pipe instrument (*txiv qeej*), Hmong burial costumes for all spirits, a drum, a bottle of wine, an egg cooked in a can, a pair of split bamboo pointers (*kuam xyoob losi txhib ntawg*), a rooster, a makeshift house, or others depending on the family's traditions.

Restitution to the parental spirits and souls is referred to as the spiritual and sacrificial cow offering (*ua nyuj dab losi txhaw qhov tsev*), or symbolically, sealing a hole in the wall. Keep in mind that the word *dab* is used for all benevolent spirits and the cow is the sacrificial animal. The animal cannot be an evil cow, devil cow, or ghost cow. This offering entails one of the biggest religious rituals, and it can be extremely sensitive spiritually. If the offering is done wrong, the cursed individual may suffer severe life-threatening consequences. Sometimes, the curse results in permanent damage or death. Most Hmong regard this as the most serious request made of the deceased parents' spirits and souls. In some family traditions, human sacrifice was used to fulfill this request in the past; the spirits accepted the human sacrifice and left the rest of the family members alone. If a person knows how to conduct the search or has a close family member who knows how to conduct the ritual, the event is not particularly difficult. However, if the person is young and does not have a family member who can perform this religious ritual, that person's life could be in danger unless he or she can find an alternative way to resolve the matter.

It is fair to say that fear of this cow sacrificial ritual (*nyuj dab*), especially the human sacrifice associated with it, is what has led some Hmong to convert to other religious practices over the last 75 years. In some tribes, the long-standing tradition of human sacrifice led a sister of the father (*muam phauj*) to take a stand during the Hmong traditional funeral services to amend the request by the spiritual world in an attempt to lessen the obligation to fulfill the offering. Human sacrifice has become a religious taboo. Some families bar their members from eating certain parts of the sacrificial animals or any slaughtered animal during funeral service.

Some Hmong religious rituals and practices are extremely sensitive and procedures must be followed very carefully. Deliberate violations of proper procedures could be fatal as they render the sacrifice unacceptable by the spiritual world. For instance, during a ritual, no one can comment or say anything about the sacrificial animal and the ritual's process; such comments immediately deter the needy spirits' and souls' acceptance of the offering. Recklessly made offerings could be deadly to the conductor of the ritual and to other family members. Many Hmong are afraid to be the family member who performs the rituals because of the seriousness of the consequences of performing them poorly. However, Hmong religious practices are not that different from many other religious sacrifices in the world.

Seldom-Used Rituals and Antiquated Practices

Hmong have tried to keep nearly all the traditional religious rituals, but some are rarely practiced because Hmong life has changed and many of the practices are no longer needed in the western nations. Some of the antiquated rituals and practices are not relevant today. For instance, most Hmong have stopped using the protection of Taoism and animism ritual (*npua dab roog*) to safeguard their livestock, draft animals, herds, or domesticated animals because Hmong do not raise these types of animals anymore. This ritual is known as the *family mother's ritual*. In the old days, protection was summoned by the mother of the family to safeguard all the animals that belonged to the family. *Npua Dab Roog* means the offering of a pig to the Heaven and Earth Spirits for the protection of all animals. *Npua* is the pig, *Dab* means benevolent spirits, and *Roog* means protection, or safeguarding.

Similarly, the ritual called *npua cawv* has likewise been abandoned by most Hmong families and tribes. *Npua cawv* is an offering of a pig that is a prelude to the major offering of a cow to the ancestors and their spirits. Hmong have consolidated some of their religious practices, folding this one into the parental spirits protection ritual (*nyuj dab*).

Besides the parental spirits protection ritual (*ua nyuj dab*), Hmong have an old practice called the great ancestors' spirits protection ritual (*ua npua tai losi tus npua laus; ua nyuj tai losi nyuj laus*). This is rarely used today although there are some families that still conduct the ritual. This ritual is strictly for males; no female should see or participate in it for their safety and spiritual wellbeing. However, if any woman refuses to follow the spiritual guidelines and principles disclosed in the ritual she will suffer immediate consequences such as having a bent mouth with bent lips, bent cheeks, or a bent facial appearance. These consequences are not curses, but the result of the fact that Tai Spirits are attractive to women and will take them to the spiritual world by making them look physically different for violating the ritual. Without proper treatment by the right religious and spiritual leader, their condition could be permanent.

The great ancestors' spirits protection ritual can be conducted only at night without the presence of any children or women. The leading performer calls for the Tai Spirits to come by tapping on an object such as a pan, pot, bowl, or bucket with spiritual chanting. Once the spirits have arrived according to the chanted words, the ritual begins. Usually a pig is sacrificed. Throughout the night, all males present consume the sacrificial pig, leaving none for the other family members. The performer reserves specific parts of the sacrificial pig (legs or feet) to make a final offering before dawn to send the Tai Spirits back to the spiritual world. Before preparing for this ritual and calling for the Tai Spirits, a shaman must determine that it is necessary for a specific reason. The ritual is restricted to specific purposes.

Old Rituals and Practices

In the old days, right before or during the New Year, Hmong villagers gathered at the top of a hill to perform the Hmong totem pole ritual (*tsa hauv toj losi tsa ncej txheb ncej ntxhoo*). The ritual signified the erection of the Hmong spiritual flag and renewed the spiritual vow for protection by the Heaven and Earth Spirits. This ritual was performed annually, offering sacrificial animals to the spiritual world for blessings during the New Year and in the coming year. Blessings included good crops, healthy livestock, personal health, protection, guidance, atonement, forgiveness, pardon, leniency, peace, prosperity, and conflict resolution. To signify strength and courage, spiritual leaders tied red ribbons or red strings to the totem pole. The conductor uttered a special chant throughout the ritual. Usually a few draft animals were slaughtered for the purpose because all villagers were invited to join in the ritual and dine together. This was a public ritual.

Most Hmong in western nations forgot that the totem pole ritual was part of the New Year's celebration until 2010, when the United Hmong Council included the ritual in the New Year's celebration. The *ncej txheb ncej ntxhoo* ritual has less meaning in the West, but it is still commonly practiced in China, especially in the cities, towns, and villages of Hmong people. According to Hmong legends, the ritual signifies the importance of the past history and civilization of the Hmong, Hmong origins, the Hmong kingdom, the Hmong in conflict and war with the Chinese, the Hmong struggle for freedom and independence, Hmong migration, Hmong unity and disunity, the encroachment of others onto Hmong land, political oppression and persecution against Hmong, and the Hmong king and ruling power. Perhaps, as some Hmong claim, the totem pole ritual belongs to the Hmong because Hmong ancestors started it centuries ago.

The religious decorations and designs on the totem pole vary from place to place. In the U.S., Hmong decorate the pole with ribbons, silver and gold wrap, and two layers of metal plates. In China, the Chinese Hmong use poles of different sizes and heights made of steel, concrete, wood, or pine (red, white, or fir pine) and the religious decorations and signs of each pole are different. They might have straight pines with silk cloths flags tied to the very top or they might make the poles look like trees with leaves at the top. They might be black, dark blue, or navy in color and decorated with swords or sun and moon signs. Poles might even have steps for climbing. The pole are erected on hilltops, flat ground, in open fields, and in public arenas. These variations demonstrate the uniqueness of religious practices of each Hmong ethnic group.

One old practice that has been obsolete is the annual political assembly ritual (*noj txhooj*) organized by leaders and elected officials. This is a day-long ceremony for all local leaders and villagers. Usually a few draft animals are slaughtered to feed all participants. The ritual signifies collaborative efforts in administrative power, shared governance, and political cohesiveness among the local leaders. In the old days, this annual assembly included a review and renewal of the political agenda, policies, procedures, and guidelines in regards to regulations, taxation, community outreach services, agricultural subsidies and aid, social policies, human rights issues, marriage customs, election law, the court system, legal remedies, and so on. Today, cultural and traditional Hmong leaders do not have the political power to organize such a ritual. However, family groups hold an annual dinner to strengthen their social ties. In some cities, Hmong community-based organizations organize and hold annual social gatherings to celebrate Hmong socioeconomic progress and successes.

Another old practice is the clan blessing ceremony (*thov vaj-tsab-xeem-lis pab txhawb*). The clan blessing is known as *huam xeem*. In the old days, a sick or frail individual might need the support of clan blessings to speed up a slow recovery from a spiritually related illness. Usually, the sick person or his or her parents went to the houses of different clan members in town and asked for their blessings. Clan members might just tie a string to the wrist of the sick or frail person to wish him or her good health and a fast recovery, so the sick person accumulated a collection of cloth strings from various clan members. Later the cloth strings were sewn on a shirt as spiritual symbols to protect the person. Today, Hmong no longer practice this tradition. However, Hmong can request similar blessings during any ritual or ceremony. Hmong still honor visits from different clan members (*vaj-tsab-xeem-lis*) because they still believe the spiritual support and power of clan members can make a difference in their health. In other words, Hmong believe that the united clan is stronger than the single entity of the family, so having a number of clan members bless the sick and frail individual strengthens them spiritually. In some instances, the spiritual psychology works very well, but in other cases the clan blessing may serve little or no purpose at all.

Hmong used to practice a ritual called the bridging spirit ritual (*tuam choj*). This ritual is derived from Laotian religious practices. It helps the sick and frail find their guardian parents who will spiritually adopt and help them get well. The parents of the sick person build a small bridge across a small creek, ditch, or canal and wait there for a passerby. The parents wave at the very first person who walks by and asks that person to perform the bridging spirit ritual to obtain a spiritual remedy for the sick. Not everyone can perform the ritual. Once a passerby agrees to help, he or she performs a short ritual by chanting and taking the sick child across the bridge to his or her biological parents. The soul calling ritual (*hu plig*) is then performed to affirm the finding of the guardian parents of the sick child and a string is tied to his or her wrist to wish that he or she will get well.

New Crop Rituals

The new crop rituals may not be relevant to today's life, but they are part of Hmong culture. For centuries the seasonal harvest played a major role in Hmong life. The Hmong depended on the spirits of the Heaven and Earth for the survival of their harvest and the cultivation of their crops. Hmong have strong ties to the animals and crops they grow. Hmong folktales tell of a time long ago when rice and corn could walk home from the field. The crops were growing near the homes of the Hmong, but because Hmong were lazy and did not tend the crops, the crops decided to return to live on the farm. The main staples of the diet were rice, corn, vegetables, poultry, beef, and fish. The Hmong also ate a variety of wild fruits and berries. They raised draft animals such as horses, cows, and water buffalo as well as pigs, goats, ducks, and chickens. During the fifth and sixth month of the Hmong lunar calendar, the early harvest and cultivation season began.

By July and August, most crops were ready to be harvested. Before Hmong parents consumed their very first crop, they made offerings (*laig dab qoob*) to the spirits of Heaven and Earth and their ancestors, thanking them for giving them food to eat for the rest of the season. Typically, the first crop harvested was the vineyard cucumber that grew along the edge of the rice field. The father picked some fresh vineyard cucumbers, put them into a pile, and made an offering to the spirits. The chanting could take up to a few minutes, depending on the individual parents. The ritual was short but succinct. When it was over, the father let others know they could eat the crop.

Following the vineyard cucumbers, the early corn was ready for harvesting. The Hmong grew two types of corn. The early sweet corn (*poj kws cauj*) grew in patches scattered throughout the rice field. The field corn, or dent corn, grew in large amounts in a full field. Hmong refer to this corn as slow growing corn (*poj kws taj*). Normally, the sweet corn became ripe first and was harvested for the new crop ritual. The father of the family would pick a bundle of sweet corn and boil it. Taking a little from the pot, he would place it in a bowl or on the table and make an offering to the spirits of Heaven and Earth and family ancestors, thanking them for giving the family food to eat for the rest of the season. Hmong offer to both the spirits of Heaven and Earth and the ancestors because the Hmong crop is protected by the *dab roog*, meaning the natural spirits of protection. The purpose of the offering made to the ancestors was to invite them to join the family in eating the new crop. The large corn field was left to be harvested for multiple uses throughout the year. The dent corn was stored in a makeshift barn (*txhab poj kws*).

In some bad seasons, Hmong ground the dent corn and consumed it as a rice substitute. Hmong also used dent corn for chicken feed and pig feed. A few baskets of dent corn was reserved for seed for the next planting season. On rare occasions, dent corn was a cash crop for Hmong.

Next in line was the celebration of the first rice in the field. As with corn, Hmong farmers grew two rice crops, one (*plej caug*) ripening before the other. The early-ripening rice was usually grown in smaller patches. Typically it had shorter stalks than the normal rice, a coarser grain, and a blander taste. It was rich in sappy liquid and had a pleasant aroma. The Hmong farmers separated the grains from the stalks by hand and cooked and roasted the grains in a giant wok until the husk and grain were dry enough for dehusking in a wooden mortar (*qhov ncho*) or a portable mortar with a pestle. Once the separation was done, the celebration of the new rice feast began (*noj mov plej tshiab*).

The first meal with the new rice was very important for all family members and close relatives. Throughout the year, a rooster was reserved for this meal. The rooster was castrated at a very young age and was a fat, juicy, tender capon (*lau qaib sam*) by the time of the new rice meal. The rooster was killed and steam cooked with Hmong herbs. Before dining, the father of the family would make an offering to the ancestors, deceased parents, and dead close family relatives so they would join the family in celebrating the first meal of the season. Poor families that did not have the castrated rooster would substitute a pig, a regular chicken, a duck, or a wild hog. This family feast is still held in the old country but not in the West because Hmong in the West do not have rice fields.

It is sad that Hmong crop rituals have faded because Hmong no longer grow their own food and raise their own animals. Today, small Hmong farmers grow a variety of vegetables for a cash crop but they no longer celebrate these traditions. Hmong in the West have abundant food so the rituals would probably have little meaning for them. Western Hmong might replace the crop rituals with the new traditions, such as celebrating Thanksgiving, Christmas, Mother's Day, Father's Day, and so on. Nevertheless, the memory of the crop rituals will always be part of Hmong culture.

Name Changing Ritual

Human beings generally receive an official, legal name from their biological parents at birth. Prior to the birthday, parents usually search for a name for their unborn. Hmong do the same except they do not reveal the name prior to the child's birth. Selecting a name for a baby is spiritually sensitive because the baby might not like the name. Hmong parents secretly pick a few names and keep them in their hearts until the baby is about to be born. Normally, both parents agree to a name prior to labor and delivery. When the baby is born, the mother gives the name chosen by both parents to the nurse and doctor. Once the name is recorded on the birth certificate, Hmong parents usually keep it quiet until a month later unless it is an American name.

When the baby is one full month old (*puv hli*), Hmong parents hold the soul calling (*hu plig*) ritual to welcome the baby, his or her soul, and his or her name to the family. The soul calling ritual is usually conducted by a shaman or an elder who knows how to perform soul calling chanting for newborns. During this ritual, the real test is to determine if the baby actually likes the given name. A pair of split animal horn pointers (*kuam*) is used by the conductor of the ceremony to tell whether the soul of the baby likes the name given by his or her parents. If for some reason the conductor feels the name may not be to the liking of the baby, the parents will be advised secretly to rename the baby after the soul calling ritual. In some cases, the baby may show signs of disapproving of the name, such as getting sick before or right after the soul calling ritual. Again, a shaman can determine if the name is spiritually incompatible with the soul of the baby. If so, a new name will be chosen. A baby may go through two, three, or more names because of the soul's disapproval. However, the Hmong parents cannot change the legal name on the baby's birth certificate. Therefore, many Hmong babies have one or more Hmong names in addition to their legal original names. The new name ensures the baby's spiritual wellbeing only, no matter what name is on the birth certificate.

Many Hmong parents give their babies American names, and whether the child likes it or not, that is the legal name. However, Hmong parents still can give their baby a Hmong name if the legal name meets with the soul's disapproval as determined by the soul calling ritual. For male children, the given name is the name by which he will be called until he receives his social courtesy name (*npe laus*) from his in-laws at the name changing ceremony (*ti npe laus losi daws npe laus*).

Social courtesy names are only for Hmong males. Hmong females do not have social courtesy names of their own, but they are recognized by the name, social courtesy name, social status, or title of their husbands. Social courtesy names are given only to married Hmong males who have children. When a married Hmong man has one or two children, his in-laws rename him with a social courtesy name in recognition of his mature manhood and fatherhood.

The Hmong name changing ritual can take place in three different ways. The most common is for the in-laws, the wife's parents, to select or approve the social courtesy name. Hmong call the courtesy name ritual the mini wedding ceremony because it is similar to the Hmong traditional wedding ceremony minus the best man, bridesmaid, bride price, and marital vow. The in-laws do not necessarily choose the social courtesy name; rather, they approve the name chosen by the son-in-law, his wife, and his family members. In rare cases, the in-laws choose the courtesy name for their son-in-law. Their approval means that they must tell all the in-law relatives about the new courtesy name in order for the in-law relatives to recognize and remember the son-in-law by the new name from that point on.

Part of the ritual is a gift exchange between the son-in-law and his in-laws. The son-in-law is required to give traditional burial costumes (*ris tsho laus*) to the in-laws as a gift in return for their approval. In some families, the traditional burial costumes have to include the burial shrouds (*teem kiam*) for the in-laws. Because his name is being changed from the original child name to a mature and courtesy name, the in-laws give him a gift, usually money, a silver bar, or traditional costumes, for inviting them to be part of the ritual and ceremony and for the blessing of his new, mature name.

Sometimes a new name is given without the approval of the in-laws. This method is not preferred but is unavoidable if the in-laws are dead or are living in another country. In that case, the man and his family select a new name and have close relatives approve the name change or social courtesy name. Choosing a name without the involvement of in-laws may also be necessary if the man has spiritual sicknesses or has been cursed and the name changing needs to proceed in order to protect the soul and spirits of the son-in-law. The son-in-law may have been sick for several days, the family calls the shaman to perform a ritual to determine the cause, and the shaman finds out that his name needs to be changed in order for him to recuperate from the illness. In such a case, there may not be time to involve the in-laws.

Another example is the son-in-law who is a Christian. Christian individuals may not necessarily involve the in-laws in name changing or selecting a social courtesy name. The Christian man, together with his family members, selects a new name and organizes a gathering with a pastor or priest to honor the new name before God. At the family feast, the family and guests pray and approve the name without the in-laws unless the in-laws are also Christians. The new name will be announced to other family members and church members. Christian in-laws may not want to follow the traditional name changing ritual in honoring non–Christian sons-in-law unless the sons-in-law insist.

The third name-changing method is self-name changing for personal convenience. Some individuals simply rename themselves. Some even have two or three social courtesy names. This type of name changing is common among divorced, separated, and remarried men and those who are often sick. They rename themselves because they believe a courtesy name that no longer seems appropriate might have given them bad luck or because they have new wives. In some instances, the new wife may not like the current social courtesy name, so she initiates the name changing. Most Hmong prefer the traditional method because it shows respect to both sides of the family. Today, however, name changing and social courtesy names may not be necessary because they are not legally recognized and are used only for cultural purposes.

The formal name changing ritual lasts about one full day for both families. The steps that are followed are as follows:

1. The son-in-law and his family initiate the changing of the son-in-law's original name to a social courtesy name.
2. The son-in-law's family selects two messengers to notify the in-laws of the date and time for the ritual because they want to make sure the in-laws are available on that particular day.
3. The son-in-law's family plans and prepares for the ceremony according to Hmong traditions.
4. Two chickens and two pigs are secured.
5. A person is selected to conduct the soul calling ritual.
6. The son-in-law selects two messengers for the event.
7. The in-laws select their own messengers.
8. Immediate family members, close relatives, friends, guests, and neighbors are invited.
9. Gifts are prepared for exchange at the ritual.
10. Some elders are invited.
11. The in-laws prepare a meal for all close family relatives to formally inform them of the new name.
12. Later in life the in-laws conduct a soul calling ritual for the first child of the family to fulfill the marital obligation of both families. Hmong usually refer to this last step as the ending marital ritual (xaus tshoob).

On the day of the name changing ritual, when the in-laws arrive, the family welcomes and greets them with honor. The in-laws bring their own messengers along because it is humble and courteous to have the messengers communicate with the other family's messengers on their behalf in regard to the ritual and ceremony. All messengers are spokespersons for both sides. Shortly after his arrival, the father-in-law is invited to sit at the table where toasting and drinking are taking place. There, the family spokespersons ask the father-in-law to help select a new name or social courtesy name for his son-in-law in order to start the ritual and ceremony. The sacrificial animal, usually a pig, is shown to the father-in-law, who begins his selection and approval of the name change. Sometimes the father-in-law asks the son-in-law and his family members to give him some names. At other times he simply agrees with the name preselected by the son-in-law and his wife. The father-in-law rarely has to choose a name out of the blue. Sometimes the in-laws will not comply with the name changing, usually because of personal animosities between the son-in-law and the in-laws or between the two families. Such incidents are rare but they have happened.

Once the father-in-law selects a name, the spokesperson calls the son-in-law to the table. There, the father-in-law may ask him if he likes the selected name. In most cases, the son-in-law accepts it without question. With his approval of the name, the toasts and drinking cease and the ritual gets started. The pig and two chickens are brought to the main door for the soul calling ritual (hu plig). When the first round of the soul calling is done, the animals are slaughtered and cooked.

A second pig is used in honor of the in-laws. Both pigs are cooked for the feast and a hindquarter of the bigger pig is saved for the in-laws for later use at their house to entertain their relatives in recognition of the social courtesy name of the son-in-law. During this time, family members sit, enjoy social time, and chat while waiting for the main meal. This feast can include any dish without restrictions. For the wedding ceremony, certain dishes are excluded, but for the courtesy name ritual every dish is acceptable. The purpose of the soul calling ritual is to validate the appropriateness and acceptance of the new social courtesy name in place of the original name. In some instances, the spirits and soul of the son-in-law may not like the new name or may reject it; however, such disapproval is rare. Reading the split animal horn pointers and the different parts of the cooked chicken can reveal acceptance or rejection.

When the two chickens and the tail of the first pig are cooked, the second round of the soul calling ritual takes place. Meanwhile, members of both families prepare and cook the dishes for the feast. When everything is ready, the table is set and the food placed on the table. The elders are called first to sit on one side of the table because it is time for the string-tying ceremony (*khi te*) and for honoring the spirits of the house, in-laws, immediate family members, close relatives, friends, guests, and other invitees with kneeling down or kowtowing (*pe*). One elder is selected from among the group to do the soul sweeping and soul blessing (*cheb plig thiab txhawb plig*) before tying the strings on the son-in-law. After the sweeping and blessing, everyone lines up to tie strings to the wrists of the son-in-law to give their personal blessings and to wish him the best of luck, good health, love, romance, and fortune. The string-tying ceremony takes about 20 minutes, then the kneeling-down custom takes place to thank everyone for coming. The meal is served and the feast begins.

During the feasting time, several rounds of drinking take place in honoring the soul calling, the in-laws for coming, the name changing, the courtesy name, and all the guests. Typically, the drinking protocol goes like this: The first round goes to the soul calling and its conductor, the second round to the name changing and the new social courtesy name, the third round to the string-tying, the fourth round to the in-laws, and the fifth round to all guests from near and afar. This formality is done with beer and hard liquor. Some people get drunk because of the many rounds of drinking and some drink beyond the rounds required for the event. Once everybody has finished dining, the in-laws return home because they have another family feast at home with their relatives. The ceremony ends with lots of thanks and good-byes.

Usually the in-laws have notified family members and close relatives about the event and instructed some family members to prepare a meal at home to be ready at their return. When they reach home the meal is pretty much ready and most of the relatives have arrived. The meal is served and the relatives are informed of the new name given to the son-in-law. The in-laws ask all to eat and drink in recognition and honor of the son-in-law, calling him by his new name from this day forward. The name changing ritual is actually two celebrations, with meals in the homes of both families. Sometimes it takes the son-in-law seemingly forever to prepare for it although many sons-in-laws have chosen to abandon the tradition for sociopolitical reasons. They have decided to keep their original name forever regardless of socioeconomic status and professional title.

Household Spirits

Every part of a Hmong house has some kind of spiritual significance. Finding the right location to build a house is religiously sensitive. In the old days, Hmong looked for sites on a sloped surface because they believed the remains of animal bones washed down to places that were flat. Before building the house, Hmong would burn joss sticks or incense to summon the Heaven and Earth spirits to ask if the location was appropriate. To determine the right location, Hmong also dug a small hole in the ground and placed a few rice grains inside the hole. After covering the hole, they summoned the spirits to give them any omens by altering the rice grains. The rice grains were used as a means of communication between the spiritual world and the physical world. When the person who wanted to build a house returned the next day, if the rice grains were unchanged he would know it was a good location. If some grains are missing, the spot was not suitable; if the grains doubled in size or amount, the location was a lucky location. If the grains had germinated, the location was part of the dragon bloodline (*sawv toj losi mem toj*), and if the grains were broken, the location was bad. These omens helped Hmong determine the location for their houses. Similarly, for the deceased, Hmong are looking for a good place called *looj mem* to bury the body. Literally, *looj mem* refers to the path to the dragon, and as in Hmong, it means power, fortune, luck, and prosperity.

When they dug to make a level foundation for the house, Hmong paid close attention to any unexpected findings that were unearthed. Any object could be an omen warning of inappropriateness. If animal remains, objects that appeared to come from a gravesite, or unusual minerals and rocks were found, the family had to decide whether to continue or abandon the construction site.

Today, Hmong seldom build new houses; they purchase or rent houses that are already constructed. But Hmong are still cautious about the shape and the design of their houses. Hmong elders prefer the front door to face east because the sun rises in the east, although this orientation is not as important as it once was. Hmong families avoid houses in which the front door and the back door are perfectly aligned because this design coincides with the death ritual practices of some families.

Hmong believe the house is a sacred place for the immediate family members and the household spirits (*dab vaj dab tsev*) are there to protect and safeguard only them. The phrase "immediate family members" means all who share the same ancestral spirits (*thooj dab koom qhua*). Every part of the house is guarded by a spiritual angel or guardian. The four corners of the house, the center post of the house, the bedrooms, the front door, the back door, the north wall, the center beam, and the storage loft above the fireplace are considered spiritual locations. The altar or shrine is the most sensitive location inside the house because most protective angels and guardians live there. The center post (*ncej tas*) is also a spiritual place. Typically, a Hmong house is divided into two sections or two halves. The first half is occupied by the family and the second half belongs to the household spirits. Hmong families believe the household spirits not only safeguard them, but also give them warnings of dangers inside and around the house or away from the house. For instance, wild animals should not be inside the house for any reason but if a wild animal (snake, frog, bird, and so on) not owned by the family is found on the doorstep, Hmong take this as a sign or omen. Sometimes, warnings are revealed in the dreams of family members. The spirits of family members could be in imminent danger, so a Hmong shaman is called to perform rituals to divert the cause and to cast away the bad omens.

Home Restriction Ritual

Traditional Hmong families still practice the home ban ritual (*hnub caiv*). Sometimes this ritual is referred to as home restriction, reservation, or sacred family days. The Hmong home ban ritual can take place in a few different ways. The shaman can order a sick or frail person to stay home, in a sort of spiritual house arrest, for a few days without engaging in any dutiful activities such as using any tools, talking on the phone, driving, traveling, or performing outside work. If the restricted individual does not comply with these conditions, something bad may happen to him or her. Home banning is required when a family member has unexpectedly encountered any signs of spiritual curses toward any members of the family. For instance, having a dream of a terrible catastrophe or a death in the family may prompt parents to ban the home on a temporary basis and the family cannot receive any visitors during the ban. The parents may instruct family members to be extra careful while engaging in normal duties.

Commonly, the home ban is applied to the entire family when the shaman has determined that the family is in danger or may face imminent danger. For instance, if the mother or father of the family has been seriously sick, the Neeb Spirits (*Leej Nkaub*) may decide it is in the best interest of the family to restrict the home for a specific period until the omen has been lifted by the supernatural world or the spirits of the shaman. Home banning is set specifically by the shaman, and in most cases all family members have to comply with his orders. If his orders are ignored, bad things may happen immediately. Sometimes an omen will recur, in which case the shaman is called again to perform another shamanistic ritual to lift the bad luck, misfortune, or omen.

The purpose of the home ban is to maintain the spiritual wellbeing and health and safety of the family. Anyone who intentionally enters the house during a ban may have to pay a spiritual price to the family. If someone intentionally enters a house that is banned, violating the ban, a shaman must be called to perform a ritual to lift the violation in order to reinstate the ban; otherwise, the family or the violator may suffer unknown consequences. That is why Hmong always look for the sign of the ban on the front door before entering a Hmong house: a small branch of green leaves (*ib tshua nplooj*) or a woven bamboo mat with a branch of green leaves. Normally, visitors ask (*nej puas caiv os ... nej puas caiv los tsis caiv os...*) family members if the home is banned, restricted, or reserved before entering. They ask regardless of whether or not there is a sign on the front door because the family might have forgotten to remove the ban after it was lifted or the family may have not put the sign up yet.

Sometimes a home ban is not for spiritual and religious purposes, but it is a personal restriction for socioeconomic reasons. Some Hmong families intentionally ban their homes to keep out unexpected and unwanted visitors. Others ban their homes to avoid inconveniences during busy occasions such as preparation for the New Year, feasting times, family celebrations, working hours, weekdays, weekends, and so on. In the old days, according to Hmong legends, wealthy Hmong families banned their homes because they did not want to receive visitors, and in Hmong culture the host family has to entertain guests hospitably, with food and drinks. To avoid this responsibility, rich families put restricted and banned signs on their front doors to keep away all except invited guests. Hmong characterize such families as stingy, self-centered, and narrow-hearted, as people who live a closed-door lifestyle (*ua neej kaws qhov rooj nti*).

Hmong still practice home bans and restrictions for spiritual and religious reasons and some families ban their homes for unknown, mysterious, and superstitious reasons. Regardless of one's relationship to the home owner, one has to always ask before entering a Hmong home just to show respect for the traditional customs and rituals. Perhaps the western way of life will increase Hmong home bans as Hmong attempt to avoid legal liability.

Maternity and Postpartum Practices

Culturally, childbirth entails restrictions and prohibitions. In the old days, a midwife was often called to help deliver the baby at home and some mothers-in-law were available to help if they lived nearby. Traditionally, childbirth occurred with the mother lying on her back although some women preferred the squatting position or kneeling down position. Normally, a midwife handled the delivery and the husband cut the umbilical cord and washed the newborn right after birth. Natural birth frequently caused some tearing and bleeding, and Hmong women were told to expect such pain.

Today Hmong women have different delivery options, and medical doctors and western medicine have made labor more bearable. In some cases, such as a baby in the breach position, a woman may decide to have a Caesarean section (C-Section) instead of a natural birth. Most Hmong are sensitive about any surgery or incision made to the body. However, they are getting used to medical incisions under general anesthesia even though they feel the mother's soul and spirits are being shaken down during child birth. In a natural birth, Hmong women prefer tearing and natural healing to clinical episiotomies.

Hmong believe the placenta of a newborn has to be buried inside the house because it has connection to soul reincarnation after death. The placenta is referred to as *lub tsho txhuj tsho npuag* in the Hmong death ritual "Showing the Way," meaning the silk coat or shirt, or the cloth the baby wore at birth.

Postpartum, the mother is kept warm for several days. She is instructed by the midwife or elder women not to bathe or wash her feet and hands with cold water. In the old days, a new mother was required to lie down by the fireplace for most of the day to keep warm and keep her newborn warm. In the western nations, Hmong mothers can keep themselves comfortable by wearing warm clothes and using an electric heater. New mothers are still advised to drink hot or warm water frequently after birth to ease the biological and physical adjustments taking place in their bodies. Hmong elders believe that drinking cold water or failing to eat warm foods with herbal medicine can lead to cold symptoms associated with the feet and hands, chronic headaches, irregular pains, seasonal agonies, facial wrinkles, skin rashes, and fragile bones. Some mothers who do not protect themselves with a proper diet suffer poor body posture later in life.

These days, Hmong mothers recuperating in the hospital are instructed not to eat the hospital diet because it lacks proper nutrients, especially Hmong herbs. Traditionally, the husband or other family member, usually the mother-in-law, cooks a warm meal for the mother to eat following the birth. The new mother eats hot rice and chicken soup with special herbs for 30 days postpartum to properly nourish her body before she can return to a regular diet. Some new mothers are allowed to eat fish, chicken eggs, pork, and pheasant after several days. Beef is prohibited because Hmong believe beef contributes to improper healing of the tearing that occurs during birth. A new mother is told not to eat fruits and vegetables during the postpartum period. She cannot drink soda or cold water until the 30-day reservation and restriction is over. New Hmong mothers are not supposed to do household chores soon after giving birth. To prevent potential ailments and complications, physical activity postpartum is restricted because Hmong believe the mother's spirits and soul are not well enough to engage in such tasks.

During the first 30 days postpartum, a new mother is banned from visiting relatives, is not allowed to enter anyone's house, and is not permitted to travel. If she violates these restrictions, she may have to compensate for her actions. For instance, if she enters someone's home during the banned period, her family may have to call a shaman to perform a ritual to wash away or lift her sinful spirits in order to spare the family members from potential religious calamities or in order to spare her from pain and suffering. These restrictions are still enforced in Hmong families and communities unless the new mother is a Christian. Most Hmong still refuse to allow new mothers to enter their homes during the postpartum period.

Superstitions and Taboos

Like other ethnic groups, the Hmong have superstitions and taboos that have developed over time. Inappropriate behaviors of past generations have created religious superstitions and taboos. The purpose of the superstitions and taboos is to cause people to remember the misdeeds others committed in the past so they will not follow their examples. Hmong respect the superstitions and taboos set for them by past generations, believing they will suffer negative consequences if they violate them. Hmong superstitions and taboos are not all that difficult if one respects and complies with them. However, if one disregards the spiritual and religious commitments they entail, one has to endure whatever punishment as set by the vow of the taboo. The punishment could be mild or severe, depending on the infraction.

Most Hmong religious restrictions and bans are initiated by the sister of a dead father, who family members refer to as the aunt of the dead (*muam phauj*). In Hmong death customs and rituals, the death of a brother is more significant than the death of a sister because Hmong are patriarchal. The sister no longer retains the family root once she is married to her husband who is a member of a different clan. However, she still has the powerful religious right to correct any misdeeds and inappropriate behaviors associated with the death of her brother.

Therefore, at the funeral and death ritual of her dead brother, she has the powerful religious right to impose bans and restrictions on his family to prevent them from repeating the misdeeds and to protect the living family members. The bans and restrictions are uttered to the dead brother; therefore, his souls and spirits are the guardian angels that protect and prevent family members from repeating the bad acts associated with his death. If anyone fails to comply with the bans and restrictions, the dead father's souls and spirits will punish them. These bans and restrictions are not written down; the living family members have to remember them in their hearts and minds forever and have to follow them from that point on. These requirements are incorporated into the parental spirits and soul ritual (*ua nyuj dab*) because someone died as the result of some egregious behavior. Each Hmong family determines its own religious bans and restrictions, and only members of the same clan of the same family ancestry are subjected to the restrictions.

Traditional Hmong families still adhere to their religious bans and restrictions unless family members have converted to other religious beliefs, especially Christianity. Here are some examples of Hmong religious bans, taboos, and restrictions that are still in everyday practice:

- No Hmong woman should sit at the head of the table or at the tail of the table at any social event.
- Most Lo clan families and some Vang clan families are banned from mixing fruits and food together.
- Most Lo clan families and some Vang clan families cannot carry fruits and food together in a back basket.
- Most Lo clan families and some Vang clan families cannot eat fruits with rice.
- Daughters-in-law in some Vang clan families and most Cha clan families cannot climb a ladder into dry storage above the fireplace inside a house.
- Daughters-in-law in some Vang clan families cannot dine at a table along with the father-in-law.
- Fathers-in-law in some Vang clan families cannot enter the bedroom of their daughters-in-law.
- Some Vang clan families cannot eat meat during the funeral and death rituals of a family member.
- Some Vang clan families and some Xiong clan families cannot wear the color red.
- Most Yang clan families cannot eat the heart of any animal.
- Most Lee clan families cannot eat the spleen of any animal.
- Most Cha clan families cannot use bows and arrows.
- Some Thao clan families cannot play with fire.
- Members of the Fang clan and the Vang clan cannot marry each other.
- Members of the Thao clan and the Kue clan cannot marry each other.
- Some Vue clan families (daughter's side) restrict the prosperity and longevity of the son-in-law.
- Most Hmong women are banned from eating the sacrificial chicken offered at the household shrine or altar.

- All Hmong women are banned from seeing the Npua Tais ritual.
- All Hmong women are banned from kowtowing.
- All Hmong women on maternity are banned from entering the house of others during the first 30 days postpartum.
- All Hmong women are banned from taking charge of funeral rituals.
- Offering to the dead can be given in odd numbers only.

In addition to these, there are hidden taboos in Hmong culture that cannot be revealed. Some still cannot be explained clearly to Hmong children. Usually, children just have to follow what their parents tell them. For instance, Vang children are told not to eat fruits with rice, but they are not told why. Yang children are restricted from eating animal hearts but no clear rationale for the restriction is given to the children. For each taboo, there are confusing tales and conflicting stories about the origin that sometimes seems like nonsense. For example, why are Cha families not allowed to use bows and arrows but cross bows are allowed? Children are pressured to comply with these taboos without being taught the reasons behind them. For some of the taboos, no one really knows the whole truth behind them.

Nonetheless, the consequences of breaking these taboos are very real. Vang fathers-in-law who violate the ban about entering the bedroom of a daughter-in-law will suffer blindness or vision impairment. Members of Yang families who eat animal hearts will vomit, become sick, or lose their vision. Members of Lo and Vang families who carry food with fruits in a back basket will see a snake inside the basket. Those who deliberately use these taboos to trap their friends who are restricted will suffer even more disastrous consequences. Therefore, everyone has to honor and respect these taboos.

Like any other ethnic groups, Hmong also have cultural superstitions. A few of them are:

- Unwedded mother cannot give birth in her biological parents' home.
- Children cannot spend money for three days during the Hmong New Year's ritual.
- Looking down on disabled, handicapped, and poor people is a curse.
- Being cruel to cats and dogs may result in curse.
- An wild animal enters the house.
- A snake crosses one's path on the way to a wedding.
- Seeing maggots crawling in the house.
- Children are told not to point their fingers at the moon.
- Children cannot eat egg yolks.
- Babies should not be complimented directly and truthfully with comments about being cute or adorable or they will become sick.
- Dreams mean the opposite of what they portray.
- Children and adults cannot ingest breast milk or they will be struck by lightning.
- The reed bamboo piper instrument player cannot look at the dead.
- The reed bamboo piper instrument player cannot play for a dead person who has the same name as his even their last names are different.
- Present life is predetermined by past life.
- The reincarnated soul returns only to the same family.
- Souls and spirits of the dead stay with the family forever.
- One's present sex or gender is the opposite of one's past sex or gender.
- The soul of a person has many spirits.

These superstitions are not jokes. Those who defy or ignore them experience real consequences. It is imperative that Hmong families teach these superstitions and taboos to their children because the intricacies can be difficult to understand when inter-clan marriage enters the picture. For example, a female Yang who marries a Vang is not subject to the ban of eating animal hearts anymore because she has become a Vang. On the other hand, a Vang female who marries a Yang is subject to the ban because she has become a Yang. Furthermore, a Vang female who marries a Lee is released from the ban of eating fruits and food together because she is no longer a Vang; however, now she is banned from eating the spleen of animal. These things are deeply rooted in Hmong culture and traditions, and all Hmong should learn them culturally and religiously; otherwise, Hmong offspring would have to learn them in illogical ways.

Summing Up

This chapter described Hmong cultural traditions and practices and discussed many religious rituals and practices that traditional Hmong families still honor and respect. Hmong culture and traditions are old and have evolved over time. Some practices are now obsolete and impractical and others are intact. Hmong New Year is the biggest Hmong sociocultural event and is celebrated worldwide. However, Hmong face a dilemma in celebrating the New Year because Hmong in different locations observe the occasion at different times and there are many New Year's observations throughout the year. Hmong New Year's celebrations are held from July until December each year, and each event lasts three to seven days. The celebrations are large and costly, and Hmong need to find a place where they can celebrate the New Year comfortably.

Hmong worship spirits, guardian angels, and benevolent spirits. Traditional religious practices include opening rituals, soul calling, the ceiling sweeping ritual, the household shrine ritual, the shaman spirits release ritual, shamanistic rituals, the herbal ritual, the Heaven and Earth Spirits ritual, the parental spirits protection ritual, npua tai, npua dab roog, the totem pole ritual, new crop rituals, the name changing ritual, the home ban and restriction ritual, and superstitions and taboos. These are the most common rituals and there are other, less common ones. Hmong retain many of these religious practices even though some are costly. However, Hmong do not teach the traditional beliefs and rituals to their people. Some Hmong are converting to other religions, especially Christianity, which better accommodates western lifestyles. If Hmong culture and traditions are to be preserved for another century, it is imperative that Hmong teach rather than preach their traditional practices.

SEVEN

Hmong Marriage and Wedding Practices

Cheb qab vab kom to...
Ntxuav qab yia kom qawj...
Ua lub neej sib hlub kom txog hnub kawg...
Hmong wedding riddle

Introduction

Hmong wedding traditions began thousands of years ago in the ancient world and have continued to the present day. Even though Hmong wedding chants have evolved and transformed over time, Hmong wedding practices remain much the same as they have been for centuries regardless of the years Hmong have been resettled in the western nations. Hmong still believe that weddings should be based on cultural and religious values. In the old days, young couples maintained deep connections with their families, often tapping kin for assistance, sharing living space with the paternal family, and depending on the immediate family for childcare and guidance. In the western nations, socioeconomic factors are beginning to alter Hmong wedding practices because Hmong children, becoming accustomed to the western way of life, are not learning the importance of preserving Hmong marital and matrimonial customs. This chapter describes Hmong traditional marriage and wedding practices: common formalities, protocols, procedures, and processes.

Origins

The Hmong approach to marriage and weddings is different from the western view. In the West, the terms marriage and wedding are used interchangeably; if there is any differentiation between the two it is blurred by the fact that they occur together as one event. In Hmong culture, the marriage and the wedding are two distinct events. The marriage is the union of a man and a woman and their families; the wedding is a ceremony that celebrates that union. The wedding takes place after the marriage, usually weeks and sometimes months later. There are customs and rituals for both.

The Hmong practice of intertribal marriage is characterized as mutual cultural reciprocity in the Hmong language: "*koj qaib pws kuv cooj, kuv o pws koj nkuaj,*" meaning "your daughter is in my house and my daughter is in your home. The Hmong words *qaib* (chicken) and *o* (duck) are symbolic and mean "daughter" or "sister" and the Hmong words *cooj* (chicken shack) and *nkuaj* (duck house) are locus words meaning "house or home." The matrimonial phrase can be said in reverse order, depending on the speaker's position. Hmong usually close the wedding ceremony with a mutual reciprocity phrase called *nkawg lus* to remind both sides of the marital kinship and seal the marriage: "*niam txiv thiab kwvtij tog ntxhais muab hauv hlua rau nej, los kom niam txiv kwvtij tog tub nco paub tias qab hlua niam txiv tog ntxhais tseem tuav, no mog….*" This phrase means that the bride's parents have allowed their daughter to marry the groom, like giving one end of a rope to the groom and his family to hold, but the bride's parents still hang on to the other end of the rope to make sure the marriage works out. If the marriage does not last, the bride's parents have a matrimonial obligation to redress the marital vow.

The true history of Hmong marital traditions and matrimonial customs remains unknown. However, there are two possible historical roots. The first matrimonial root started with two brothers or two sons who survived the great flood. Many Hmong who practice the traditional wedding chants and traditional ceremonies believe that the Hmong way of commemorating the marriage of two people started with the odyssey of the two sons, *Liag Lwm* and *Rhwv Mis*, or as pronounced in English, Lia Lou and Tru Me. According to the legends, the two sons not only survived the great flood, but also created the Hmong wedding formalities that have been used for thousands of years. The two brothers invented the ceremonial practices, including the ceremonial symbols, wedding chants, customary rules, guiding protocols, drinking formalities, dining patterns and processes, social etiquette, and ways of showing familial respect and honor for all involved family members.

The second possible matrimonial root of Hmong marital traditions has to do with the marriage of a brother and a sister who survived the great flood. Since there were no other survivors, the Heaven and Earthly God (*yawm saub*) instructed the two siblings to marry in order to repopulate the barren world. Because there was no one to assist them in their wedding ceremony, God advised them to go to the kingdom of an old dragon to learn the arts of marriage from the old dragon (*zaj tswg zaj laug*). The siblings followed the old dragon's advice. Once they learned the arts

of marriage and mastered the wedding songs, the old dragon gave two ceremonial symbols to the siblings. The brother received the black umbrella (*lub kaus tshoob*) and the sister received the black and white striped cloth headband or turban (*tsoj siv ceeb*), which was from the underbelly of the dragon. The ceremonial symbols were given to spiritually and religiously safeguard the marriage in order for the newlywed couple to receive marital blessings from God. When they returned from the kingdom of the old dragon, the brother insisted on marrying his sister as God had instructed. At first she refused, but because there was no one else she finally agreed and the two were married in accordance with God's plan to repopulate the empty world.

According to Hmong legends, the bride gave birth to an oval shaped fetus without limbs, face, or head. The guiding God instructed them to cut the fetus, divide it into several pieces representing human flesh, and put the piece in different locations. The cut pieces became the 12 family clans or tribes that form the Hmong nation.

Hmong elders say the two brothers of the first-root story wanted Hmong descendants to pay great respect to the benevolent spirits and living family members of the two families involved in the marriage during the wedding to stress the importance of knowing the roots of Hmong marital traditions, marital bloodlines, family kinship, and lineages. Most Hmong today believe the two brothers, Lia Lou and Tru Me, were the creators of Hmong wedding traditions. Some firmly believe Hmong wedding customs originated in the marriage of the two siblings. Whichever story is accepted—and both accounts are sketchy—most Hmong, regardless of socioeconomic status, profession, or religious background, highly respect and honor the old traditions.

Variations in Marital Practices

Although most Hmong follow the same wedding traditions, there are wide variations in practice of those traditions. The groom's family and the bride's family may have different practices, and there may be some variations between the two clans. The type of marriage affects the specifics of the practices as do the socioeconomic status of the groom and the bride and the size and cost of the ceremony. Any history or issues involving the two families and their leaders can also influence the practices. The personalities and behaviors of all involved parties make for variations. As succinctly expressed in Hmong, *ib rab tej ib tsa txuj*, meaning "it is not the same way in every family or location." In other words, different people living in different regions practice Hmong marital traditions in different ways. Therefore, Hmong do not have a one-size-fits-all model for Hmong weddings. Hmong do have flexibility that enables them to accommodate differences in practices. As Hmong say, "*Tsoob kos yoog tau luag, tabsi dab qhuas mas yoog tsis tau luag.*" Hmong can embrace and accommodate differences in traditional wedding practices, but Hmong cannot accommodate differences in religious rituals and practices. In other words, Hmong have diversity in their traditional practices, but they can reconcile their differences through cordial understanding, compromise, and mutual respect except when it comes to the practices of Hmong familial religious beliefs and taboos.

Marital Restrictions and Taboos

Hmong cannot marry a member of the same clan, or someone who has the same last name. Such a marriage is a cultural taboo because Hmong believe all who have the same last name belong to the same tribe with the same family ancestry. In the past, same clan marriages did occur, but the practice was abandoned for good because it met with severe public disapproval. In addition to the intra-clan restriction, some Hmong clans prohibit members from marrying members of specific other clans regardless of their different last names because they share the same ancestry. For instance, no one in the Vang clan can marry someone of the Fang clan because they are actually the same clan with the same family ancestry. Intermarriage between the Lo and Pha clans is likewise forbidden for the same reason. If a prohibited marriage were to take place, the elders of both families would have to sort things out before it is too late. Normally, such a marriage would not be made public.

In the old days, marriages between first cousins were highly controversial. Such marriages are not prohibited by Hmong traditions. Today, Hmong first cousins do marry and some of those marriages are quite successful. However, Hmong are cautious about such marriages because they led to everlasting marital conflict and warfare in the past.

Traditionally, Hmong allow only one marriage per family per year although this custom is not strictly enforced. Hmong believe having two or more marriages in a family within a year does not allow the family to properly honor its spirits to ensure a good quality of life for the new couple. Hmong want to spare the couple the grave consequences that may come from not properly honoring the spirits, such as misery, hardships, misfortunes, poverty, and premature death of parents. Hmong also prefer that siblings, especially girls, marry in accordance with their birth order; the older should get married before the younger. If a girl should marry before her older sister, the younger sister's husband is penalized by a fine. The fine is called *nyiaj qhwv niam laus hauv caug*, meaning, "a small fine is collected to cover the knees of her older sister." Covering her knees, symbolically, means to pay respect to her birth order because she has the familial right to get married first.

Best friends, regardless of gender, are discouraged from marrying at the same time on the same day of the same week in the same month of the same year. Hmong believe that such a practice will bring bad luck and misfortune. It may bring unhappiness and poverty to one couple and not the other or to both couples.

Any issues between families and clans emerge at marriages. If the history of the relationship between families has been peaceful and pleasant, that will show; if there have been conflicts, those too will be evident. Hmong do not use marriages as battle grounds for seeking revenge, but the marriage customs are used to keep both families in check. For instance, at the very first marriage between two families, a special oath or agreement is made to bridge the marriage and wedding traditions between the two families. Hmong refer to the first marital bridge as *tuam choj tshoob*, meaning, a connection or tie between the two families for the very first time. Sometimes, the marital bridge is required only for repeated weddings between the same two families. At the next marriage and thereafter, all the family members have to honor the agreement that was made. This is especially important for the bride's side. If the agreement is disregarded, the offended side of the family may begin a mild controversy. To remedy the dishonor, a fine is imposed on the violating party unless some mutual agreement is reached. The matter is brought up again at all future marriages involving the families.

Minor issues are usually resolved quickly without fines, but verbal agreements and promises to act differently in the future may not be reliable. Some of the biggest issues have to do with an unpaid bride price, a high bride price, an abusive relationship, divorce, polygamy, raucous family issues, marital disputes, and the death of individuals in the marital bloodline. There are two sides to every story, and this way of reconciling differences has a dark side and a bright side. For the dark side, past issues should be abandoned because the new couple has nothing to do with them. It is not fair for one family member to be held responsible for the action of a different family member. For the bright side, this method is a way of showing mutual respect that Hmong families have been practicing for thousands of years. Sometimes cultural respect is more important than money. It is important to understand that the purpose of Hmong marital restrictions and taboos is to bring honor and respect to the families involved.

Honoring Traditions Honors Families

Hmong place high value on saving face. Some Hmong children who are accustomed to western culture and values have dishonored their parents through their courtship practices. Those who live together before getting married bring disgrace to their parents. Most Hmong children today do not adhere to traditional Hmong values and customs. However, the fault is not all theirs because their parents have failed to teach them proper expectations before their teenage years. This does not mean that all western attitudes and behaviors are bad; some western values are just as worthy as Hmong values. But when Hmong children disregard the values and wishes of their parents, they bring them great dishonor and cause them to lose face.

Interracial marriages sometimes bring dishonor to Hmong families at their weddings because the non–Hmong party does not always follow the strict protocols for the ceremony. If the wedding formalities are not followed properly from beginning to end, Hmong parents and their families are insulted and feel personal humiliation. Some non–Hmong grooms follow Hmong marital traditions and pay the bride price, but for example, and others discount Hmong traditions, showing no respect for the bride's parents and family members. A non–Hmong groom in an interracial marriage may not be willing to fulfill the kneeling-down ritual to pay respect to Hmong household spirits, family relatives, and deceased ancestors. Some parents may excuse such behavior and accommodate it with a dual Hmong-American ceremony, but most Hmong families feel disrespected by the intrusion of outside cultures.

Despite the dishonor, Hmong are getting used to the idea of interracial marriages and dual ceremonies. As of now, more Hmong daughters marry people of other races than Hmong sons. However this is changing because Hmong sons have become more comfortable with interracial courtship over the last 20 years. In fact, a growing number of Hmong male professionals are married to non–Hmong wives. Remember, Hmong are more tolerant of Hmong males who marry non–Hmong wives than of Hmong females who marry non–Hmong husbands. A Hmong female in an interracial marriage is considered an outcast, and if her marriage is dissolved for any reason, even the death of her husband, she is not welcome to or has a difficult time to marry a Hmong in the community. Hopefully, this prohibition will be removed. However, as of now, there have been only one or two cases in which a Hmong daughter who married outside the race had her marriage dissolved and subsequently married a Hmong man within the Hmong community.

The traditional Hmong wedding ceremony can last up to two days because of all the ritual chants and family feasting. Preparing for a wedding takes both families a great deal of time. They have much to consider, such as invitations to family members living near and afar, organizing the event, paying for the costs involved, and securing the manpower required for a successful ceremony.

Hmong grooms are usually one or two years older than their brides. In the old days, much younger women, often teenage girls, were married to much older men. Underage marriage still exists in the Hmong community, but it is not as prevalent as it used to be. Two decades ago, many Hmong teenagers would be married by the time they were 15. Underage marriage is not as common anymore because Hmong men often wait to marry until their late teens or early 20s. Some focus on their careers and postpone marriage until they have completed their education. However, teenage marriage is acceptable in Hmong communities in different parts of the world, and it is still relatively common for girls to get married before their 18th birthday. The stigma of being called an old maid or a spinster encourages girls to marry at very young ages and also encourages interracial marriage among Hmong females in the western nations. Hmong parents want to make sure their children are ready for marriage regardless of their ages because having a family entails financial and social responsibilities.

Also, family honor or dishonor may rest partly on the size of the wedding, the expense of accessories, and the socioeconomic status of the bride and groom, all of which are affected by the age of the bride.

The Right Time for Marriage

When is the best time for Hmong to marry? Typically, Hmong children are not concerned about the timing of anything in their lives until they are planning to marry. They know that the best time for a Hmong marriage has to do with the lunar cycle. It may sound odd, but Hmong have believed this for thousands of years. Hmong ancestors have passed down to their descendants for centuries that the best time to get married is during a waxing moon phase (*hli xiab*). No one really knows why, but many believe that the moon is the guiding light for all living objects on earth and it is therefore logical to marry on a moonlit night. Traditionally Hmong marriages take place at night.

In selecting the night a couple has to consider every event that may have any association with the fate of the marriage. During the process of bringing a wife home after the two parties have agreed to the marriage, one has to watch for any unusual or extraordinary situations along the way. For instance, if the couple encounters certain animal calls, an accident, a snake crossing the path, or strange noises, these could be omens warning of some danger to their marriage. These sights and sounds may not have meaning to a casual onlooker, but for a Hmong, such things could be warnings of luck, fortune, struggle, hardships, or accidents in the future. If any omens appear, the time for the wedding has to be altered, the wedding must be postponed or even delayed indefinitely.

Hmong today do not pay attention to the phase of the moon when they plan to marry. They are getting married throughout the year during a waxing moon phase (*hli xiab*) or a waning moon phase (*hli nqig*). So far, no case of either good luck or misfortune has been clearly linked to timing of marriages in relation to the phases of the moon. However,

Hmong legends say that couples who follow Hmong traditions appear to fare better in life than those who fail to honor the traditional timing for getting married. The timing does not apply to the marriages of those who believe in other faiths, values, and customs. Christian Hmong generally disregard the tradition of marrying under the waxing moon and the possible omens warning of a marriage.

Types of Marriages

In Hmong matrimonial thinking, the union of a man and a woman in marriage brings two distinct families together in a formal, everlasting relationship. The kinship of the two families is held together by marital bloodlines. The union can occur by mutual consent, through elopement, by force, by bride-capture, through engagement, or by parental arrangement. Marriages by force and bride-capture were common in the old days, but they are rare today in the western nations.

Mutual Consent

Normally, marriage between two people takes place through their mutual consent (*sib yeem*). In the old days, a Hmong girl as young as 12 could marry by her own choice, but this practice is illegal in the West. In the West, a minor cannot legally give consent to marry someone, and adult males over the age of 18 who marry underage girls are subject to legal prosecution. In some U.S. states, minors can get married legally at the age of 16, but in most states the legal age is 18. If minors marry, their families are legally and culturally responsible for the marriage. When Hmong adults marry, their mutual consent should be validated and approved by both families. One cautionary note: mutual consent does not mean the marriage is legal in the western nations; it is not legal until a marriage license is issued to the couple. Most Hmong marriages today are based on mutual consent, and Hmong marital common law is still in practice.

Elopement

The adult children of Hmong parents do not need parental permission to get married. However, their parents have the right and the traditional obligation to know who their children are marrying. Elopement is quite common today. In elopement (*sib raws, tug pom tug qab*), two people forgo the marriage traditions and get married without parental permission. The type of elopement that is totally foreign to Hmong parents is the type that occurs when a son or daughter takes off to marry a person he or she met online. Keep in mind that marrying someone the family disapproves of can bring hard feelings, shame, and a bad reputation not just to the individuals marrying, but also to members of both families involved. Families are dishonored when a good daughter marries an unemployed high school dropout, a gangster, a drug addict, or an alcoholic or when a good son marries a lazy, out of control, rebellious, and defiant girl.

Hmong elopement is not unheard of but it is very rare in traditional Hmong families. Two Hmong seldom take off to get married without involving their family members because Hmong fear marrying without parental approval. Nevertheless, there have been cases in which two people elope to live together without the marital customs. Although such cases are rare among traditional Hmong, they are becoming quite common among westernized individuals who dishonor and disrespect Hmong culture and traditions.

Forced Marriage

In the old days, Hmong practiced forced marriages (*muab yuam rau yuav*) for several reasons. If the girl was pregnant with the would-be groom's child, the two were caught sleeping together, or both had violated the family curfew and other rules while courting, a forced marriage followed. If the daughter's parents liked the man for socioeconomic reasons, or the son's parents liked the girl, they could be forced to marry. Forced marriages are ways for some parents to honor family ties and to repay debts. Sometimes parents are pressured by leaders and other family members to give up their daughters, and sometimes parents of both families agree to force the marriage. Today forced marriages are rare but they still happen. Most Hmong will force a marriage when possible if the girl is pregnant because it is not acceptable in Hmong culture for an unwed daughter to give birth to a child in the home or because parents do not want the child to be born out of wedlock.

According to Hmong legends, songs, and folktales, forced marriages usually are unhappy. Some brides have committed suicide with opium after being forced to marry someone they did not like, and some parents in forced marriages divorce later in life. One example is that of a beautiful Hmong girl whose parents forced her to marry an older man who intentionally carried her to his home to marry her. In Hmong culture, his intent warranted a marriage. She begged her parents to take her home because she did not like the man. She adamantly refused to let go of the post she was holding until her hands bled. Her parents left her after the relatives of his family agreed to the marriage. Ultimately, she had no choice but to marry him. Years later, after they had four children together, she divorced him because she had no intention to live with him forever. This and similar heartbreaking stories have changed Hmong attitudes toward forced marriages. Forced marriage can be abusive, violent, and sometimes deadly because the bride is forced to get married against her will.

Bride Capture

Bride-capture (*zij poj niam*), or bride kidnapping (*kwv poj niam*), is probably obsolete in the western nations, but in the old days any man could kidnap any girl with the intent to marry her without her approval and even without her knowing him well. This practice would be met with legal roadblocks in the western nations. In the past bride capture involved physical force and beating because the girl's mother and her female relatives fought off the men who accompanied the groom to help him if they refused to let the girl go. As

with some forced marriages, some girls who were captured committed suicide and others ran away. In some cases, the groom's parents ended up paying more for the bride price than if he had the parents' consent in addition to fines and penalties. If the girl killed herself before the wedding ceremony, the groom's family would be charged double for her death plus more for the emotional distress, pain, and suffering that resulted from the kidnapping. Perhaps worse, many kidnapped girls were raped by the grooms to obtain their consent to marry. Hmong legends tell of incidents in which girls were held down physically by family members if she refused to sleep with the groom. The fact that Hmong have stopped this practice for good is a relief.

Hmong have also abandoned the catch-hand practice (*tuav te*) because it is somewhat controversial and strange in the U.S. In the old days, any man who had given a gift to any girl could hold the girl's hands with the intent to marry her. If this happened, Hmong elders would be called to judge the validity of the hold on her. The elders would ask the girl if she had received any gift from him willingly or unwillingly, knowingly or unknowingly. If he had not given her anything, she was free to go. If he had given her something as marital collateral, the hold was culturally appropriate and the girl was bound to marry him. Even if she did not receive the item directly but found it in her back basket or under her pillow, she was still subject to his marital interest. The strength of the hold depended on the value of the gift. The collateral objects can be likened to gifts that today would be signs of romance and heartfelt feelings: a dozen roses, earrings, a ring, a cell phone, a car, or clothing. Sometimes the situation was resolved peacefully, but at other times the girl ended up marrying the man. Some holds became public fiascos when the girl's parents showed up to take her home.

Engagement and Arranged Marriages

Hmong marriage can be preceded by an engagement (*qhaib*) based on specific marital conditions and terms such as bride price, timeline, age, health, and life circumstances. In the old days, the engagement was arranged through a strict protocol of negotiations between both families. Some parents made blind marital engagements for their children. That is, prior to their children's conceptions and births families promised each other to allow their sons and daughters to marry each another. Such engagements were not permanent contracts and the terms and conditions could be breached by either side. Children often refused to honor their parents' wishes, and such a breach required that both families renegotiate all the costs involved. Sometimes restitution was difficult and force was used to make the marriage happen without the bride's or groom's approval. For these reasons, Hmong stopped this ineffective practice.

Sometimes the engagement arranged by the parents is honored with great respect and the terms fulfilled as planned. Before the marriage date is set, some tedious negotiations are conducted at the bride's home, as in another traditional Hmong ceremony. The purpose is to bring the two families to agreement in arranging the wedding. Typically, when an engagement has been made, children are expected to follow their parents' wishes about who they should marry.

An arranged marriage can be the final part of a prior marital engagement or it is a marriage arrived at through negotiations and bargaining between two families. Usually, parental arrangement means both sides have come to an agreement with the approval and consent of the bride and groom. However, if the arrangement took place early in the children's lives, it might not directly involve the bride and groom until closer to the marriage. Arranged marriage is more practical and viable then engagement, but it has its ups and downs as well because the arrangement may not work out as planned. Therefore, Hmong parents rarely arrange marriages unless they have promised their children to someone through religious vows. Even this is rare today because such promises have deadly dangerous consequences when unfulfilled by the children.

In-Person Negotiation

In Hmong culture, second to the mutual consent model, in-person negotiation (*nqis tsev hais or mus zawj yuav*) is a type of marital arrangement Hmong parents like because it shows honor and respect to the girl's family. There are three common types of in-person negotiations. The first is one in which two people are in love, they have reached mutual consent to marry, and the girl will not get married until the boy's family talks to her parents in person; she will not violate the wishes of her parents, who want an in-person negotiation. In such a case, the in-person negotiation is smooth because the girl has agreed to the marriage.

The second type of in-person negotiation is one in which the boy and the girl know each other but their courtship has been distant because of their personal shyness or family ties. There is no mutual consent to marry, but the boy feels the girl may marry him if his family goes in person to negotiate the marriage and wedding with her parents. In such a case, the boy's family initiates the proceedings with the girl's parents to negotiate the possible marriage. The girl may consent to marry him or she may reject his request. If there is a marital bloodline relationship between the two families, her parents will pressure her to marry him because of the honor and respect received from his family; however, attempts to force her to marry him are unlikely to succeed because she does not love him. The negotiations may end up empty because in-person negotiations are voluntary acts.

The third situation involves a perfect stranger who sees the girl as a potential mate and seizes the opportunity to initiate an in-person negotiation because of his family status, wealth, reputation, or standing in the community. In this case, the girl and the boy had no courtship. Her parents honor and respect his family's approach to the negotiation; however, the decision often rests with the girl. If she thinks the boy is a good potential husband, she may agree to marry him regardless of their lack of personal relationship. If she feels she needs time to think about the marriage, her request is likely to be granted. In some cases, the girl's decision may not matter because her parents approve the marriage because of his family's socioeconomic status and the urging of well-known Hmong elders and leaders. In such a case, the girl may be pressured and somewhat forced to get married against her will. If the boy is well-established, her life might be better socially and economically, and she may come to love him over time.

In-person negotiation can be costly and tedious, depending on the girl's family situation and religious faith. The process is shorter for Hmong Christian families than for traditional Hmong families. Most Christian families have modernized and streamlined Hmong customs to accommodate their religious practices. As for traditional Hmong families, the process has to follow Hmong customs. In-person proceedings may end up with nothing, so the boy's family takes a big financial risk in initiating the negotiations. Some negotiations wind up in an engagement and arranged marriage after a period of time because the two families reach an agreement to permit courtship before finalizing the marriage arrangement or because the girl asked for time to get to know the boy. In such instances, the in-person negotiation is worthwhile. Hmong parents often ask their sons to make sure the girls are interested in them before they begin in-person proceedings in order to save time, money, and energy.

Types of Weddings

No two Hmong weddings are exactly the same because each Hmong family expects different things to be included in the marital celebration. Not only are the formalities different, but so are the family situations and the histories of marital bloodlines between the two families and clans. Also, the persons in charge of the ceremonies contribute their ideas.

Whether a civil union was made through mutual consent, elopement, force, bride capture, engagement and arrangement, or in-person negotiation, it is generally followed by a series of events that culminate in a wedding ceremony. These events (*tshoob tog qws*) have four major components. Step one: the bride and the groom are married according to Hmong culture and traditions.

Step two: the groom's family inducts her religiously and spiritually into his family through the first marital ritual (*lwm qaib losi lwm sub*). The word *lwm* means waving or spinning over, and the word *qaib* means chicken. The word *sub* means evil spirits, devil, demons, or bad omens. Taken together, the phrase means waving a live chicken over their heads to ward off evil. This step is done differently for Hmong Christian families. Usually, the pastor or priest inducts them into the family with religious blessings instead of waving a live rooster in a circular motion over their heads to cast away bad luck, misfortunes, and bad omens. On the third day, the groom's family holds a formal induction proceeding and soul calling ritual (*hu plig*) to formally welcome her and her soul into the family. The word *hu* means calling and the word *plig* means benevolent spirits. Again, Hmong Christian families do this differently. Instead of using soul calling, the groom's family is blessed with God's grace given by the pastor or priest and church members during the family gathering. In this formal induction the bride is converted religiously and spiritually into the groom's family's religious faith without objections. In traditional Hmong families, this formal induction involves formalities and religious protocols such as family feasting, drinking, respecting, honoring, kneeling-down customs, and offerings. Christian Hmong follow the same formalities except the kneeling-down customs and they add blessings and prayer.

Step three is the actual wedding ceremony. A time is set on a specific day, usually on a weekend, for the groom and bride to return to the bride's family for the ceremony. Christian families may hold the wedding ceremony at the bride's family's home, at church, or at another designated location, and their proceedings are different. The wedding ceremony lasts one or two days. It is a tedious affair, similar to the formal induction held at the groom's family's home, but with more intense formalities and protocols. It involves feasting, drinking, dining, kneeling-down customs, respecting, honoring, offering, blessing, and negotiating.

In the fourth and final step, another celebration takes place at the groom's family's home with the groom's relatives and clan members. This ceremony may be short with basic formalities and a light meal. However, the report back to the groom's parents about the wedding ceremony could be lengthy and detailed. For Hmong Christian families, this celebration might be held at a church without a meal or at home with a blessing and prayer.

Because U.S. Hmong live in two cultures, all the components of a traditional wedding are not always seen as necessary or are not carried out meticulously because weddings are frequently done in the western way. The formalities and protocols may be administered differently. The dining, drinking, and feasting may be more formal and less intense as compared to the old-fashioned ceremony. The ceremony may be costlier, but the meals are often more varied and healthier because they are not limited to traditional dishes.

In addition to the traditional wedding ceremony, Hmong have other ceremonies classified according to the nature of the marriage: *tshoob zawj* (in-person proceedings), *tshoob zij* (kidnapping, forced, catch-hand, or bride-capture), *tshoob yuam* (forced), *tshoob coj* (mutual consent or elopement), *tshoob raws* (follow-him-home), *tshoob niam yau* (second wife), *tshoob poj ntsuam* (widow marriage), *tshoob nkauj fas* (separated marriage), *tshoob nkauj thim* (returnee marriage), and *tshoob poj nrauj* (divorced marriage). According to Hmong marital legends, these classifications determine the nature of the ceremonial proceedings, formalities, and protocols. Each type of wedding is slightly different in approaches, negotiations, processes, and bride price.

Of all the types of weddings, the follow-him-home marriage (*tshoob raws*) is prob-ably the most unusual, but is a critical ceremony that is still used today. In the old days, a follow-him-home marriage took place if she was pregnant with his child, he raped her, her parents forced her to marry him, she was caught in an inappropriate act with him, she learned that he was going to marry someone else, he told her to follow him home, she was just crazy about marrying him, or she just wanted him to pay her money for something he did to her. In these situations, the groom could agree to marry her or he could refuse. If he agreed to marry her, the traditional marriage and wedding proceedings would follow. If he refused, his family members would have to sort out why she followed him home. If it turned out that he fooled her, raped her, or she was pregnant with his child, the family would determine that he should marry her in accordance with Hmong traditions. If he still refused to marry her, his family would have to return her to her parents with detailed information about his refusal plus fines and penalties in order for him to be free of his marital burden. Otherwise, his family and he would be held responsible for her wellbeing. Hmong elders usually resolve this kind of dispute with mutual respect and binding principles in accordance with Hmong customs. Today Hmong girls follow their loved ones home or live with their boyfriends and their families as married couples without honoring Hmong traditions, and some Hmong boys are living with their girlfriends. Culturally, this is not acceptable; however, some Hmong parents do not care as long as their children are responsible adults.

Despite the variations, the basic traditional Hmong wedding customs are intact. The level of feasting and dining may differ depending on the socioeconomic status of the bride and groom and their families, but all Hmong weddings involve feasting and dining. Whether the families of the bride and groom follow traditional religions, Christianity, or another faith, they follow the traditional wedding formalities so they do not disrespect the bride's family and its clan members.

Marital Notification

In Hmong culture, when two people get married, a notification of the marriage has to be sent right away except in remarriages of divorcees and widowed people. First, however, the groom takes the bride to his parents' doorstep and a marital ritual (*lwm qaib losi lwm sub*) is performed to culturally and spiritually induct the girl into the groom's family. Culturally, this religious induction initiates the process of spiritual conversion of the bride in order for the household spirits of the groom's family to accept her unconditionally. An elder or the groom's father can perform the ritual to cast away any bad omens, bad luck, or misfortunes before the bride and groom enter the house. At the doorstep, as the couple stands together facing the inside, the conductor takes a live rooster and waves it in a circular motion over their heads as he intones a special chant. The first round of waving is done in a clockwise direction and the second round in a counter clockwise direction. The second round ties the two together as husband and wife, wishing them blessings, fortune, luck, and children. When this ritual is completed, the couple can enter the house. Right away, the groom has to kneel to pay spiritual and religious respect and honor to the house spirits, older siblings, family relatives, and ancestors because he has brought a bride into the family. This is not required of Hmong Christian families. In some cases, the groom may also need to pay respect to his parents and ask them for help and support in his marriage.

The next step is to immediately find two messengers who are family members or close relatives to notify the bride's parents. In some families, one messenger is sufficient, but a pair is preferred. The sooner this is done the better because late notification may incur a penalty. The purpose of the notification is to properly inform the bride's parents that their daughter has gotten married to the groom so they do not need to look for her. If the bride is underage, her parents may insist on talking with her before accepting the message. If she is 18 or over, the parents may also wish to verify the messenger's announcement. In rare cases, parents may disapprove of the marriage and insist on going to the groom's house to retrieve their daughter regardless of her legal age.

Before the messengers make the announcement, they give strokes to members of the bride's family. Strokes are tokens that show good faith as well as respect and honor from the groom's family. Traditionally, money was used as marital strokes (*tsab ib kab luam yeeb*) but today chopped tobacco leaves or cigarettes are used in place of money. When the messengers arrive, they ask for permission to enter the house. Inside, before saying anything, they quickly stroke every adult present, including both parents, with cigarettes. Usually, they give two cigarettes per adult male. As Table 7.1 indicates, the messengers give extra strokes to the father to honor his deceased ancestors and other close family relatives. As Table 7.2 shows, a few hundred dollars are given with the cigarette strokes to affirm the marital ties and the seriousness of the marriage.

When the messengers have stroked everyone, it is time to properly notify the parents and all relatives present about the marriage between the bride and the groom. The messengers carefully relay the message that their

Table 7.1. Marital Strokes

Bride's Family Members Present	In Hmong Language	Item Given
Ancestors	Poj yawm ntxwv txoob	Two cigarettes
Paternal uncles and their wives	Niam hlob txiv hlob niam ntxawm txiv ntxawm	Two cigarettes per couple
Maternal uncles and their husbands	Niam dab laug txiv dag laug	Two cigarettes per couple
Paternal aunts and their husbands	Muam phauj yawg laus	Two cigarettes
Bride's brothers	Nus tij nus kwv	Two cigarettes each
All adult relatives present	Kwv tij	Two cigarettes per person
Bride's father and mother	Niam thiab txiv yug	Two cigarettes per person

Table 7.2. Marital Money Given to Bride's Parents at Notification

Bride's Family Members	In Hmong	Typical Amount
Father	Txiv lub khaub tshos	$100
Mother	Niam lub khaub tshos	$100
All Relatives	Niam hlob txiv hlob niam ntxawm txiv ntxawm, nus tij nus kwv, losi ntaus tsiaj tsis paub faib hno	$ 60
Clan leader	Tus tsawb tshoob	$ 20
One Stroke of Cigarette	Ib kab luam yeeb	$ 20
Groom's Family Message	Lub xo	$ 20

daughter, whom they name, and the groom, whom they name, have gotten married; they do not have to look for their daughter because she is safe with the groom's family. Usually, the father simply accepts the notification, but traditionally the father would contact his family leaders and elders to come to the home to receive and accept the message on the family's behalf.

If the family leaders and elders (*tus coj tshoob coj kos*) come, the messengers stroke them the same way before relaying the same message to them. The leaders and elders may ask both parents if they have any objections to the marriage. If not, the leaders and elders accept the notification. If the parents express any concern, their concerns have to be addressed and resolved right away. In some cases, the parents need to speak with the bride and verify the news over the phone. Some parents ask for the names of the groom's parents and clan. The messengers can supply this information.

Once the notification has been accepted, the messengers give the father or the family leaders a traditional headband with black or navy blue stripes (*siv ceeb*) with the monetary strokes specified in Table 7.2. The final step is to ask the parents about the date and time for the Hmong traditional wedding ceremony. Usually, the bride's parents pick the date and time. Sometimes the wedding is delayed for days, weeks, months, or a year because of family matters. In most cases, the wedding is scheduled for a few weeks following the marriage. The messengers return to the groom's family to notify them that the bride's parents received the notification and the date and time for the wedding has been set.

The cigarette strokes are standard protocol but the amount of the marital money varies from family to family. The messengers do not attempt to resolve any issues between the two families during the notification. If issues arise, all the messengers have to say is that they will relay the concerns to the groom's family. The two families may have to resolve issues during the proceedings for the wedding ceremony. Also, unless an immediate family member of the groom accompanies the messengers to the bride's family, the messengers do not need to conduct the kneeling-down rituals because they are only relaying messages. An immediate family member, however, would kneel down to pay respect to the bride's family's deities and spirits. The purpose of the notification process is simply to alert the bride's parents of the marriage. The two families will negotiate other marital matters, such as bride price, feasting, drinking, dining, and expenses, later.

Bride Price and Dowry

The *bride price* is always controversial, but it is a matter of honor. In Hmong culture, the bride price is the amount of money the groom and his family give to the bride's parents in exchange for permitting her to become the wife of the groom and the daughter-in-law of the groom's parents. Collection of the bride price is a long-standing Hmong tradition. In return for the bride price and to help the newlywed couple start a new life together, the bride's parents and family members honor the marital union with a dowry, a gift to the bride to maintain their bond to her. Hmong use the term *dowry* differently from the way it is used in the West. In the U.S., a dowry is something like the bride price except it is given by the bride's family to the groom's family. For Hmong, a dowry is given by the bride's parents, but it is not given to the groom's family, but to the bride.

Historically the bride price was very high and most middle-class and poor Hmong men were not able to pay it. A bride might cost the groom seven to fifteen silver tales (Hmong silver bars). The high bride price led to polygamy because rich men could afford more wives and because unmarried daughters agreed to marry instead of continuing to live with their parents. Some poor grooms became slaves of their bride's families. Moreover, the high and often unpaid bride price became the source of marital conflicts, debts, and controversies between families and among clans.

Hmong daughters were impacted heavily by the high bride price as well. Many remained unmarried for a long time and became spinsters because suitors could not afford the bride price. Some Hmong parents were wrongfully accused of selling their daughters for profit. According to Hmong legends, the lack of contraceptives coupled with the high bride price led to out-of-wedlock births, and some promiscuous women who became pregnant gave birth in the jungle because allowing an unmarried daughter to give birth at home was unacceptable in Hmong culture. These problems led to modest reforms in Hmong marital practices in the mid–1900s.

In the 1930s, Hmong leaders condemned the high bride price and asked Hmong parents to consider lowering the price in order to accommodate the marital predicaments of so many Hmong who were facing economic hardships. The leaders warned that parents who insisted on the high bride price might not be able to receive it, and if conflicts continued as a result of the price and they should reach the Hmong tribunal court, the leaders would not resolve the disputes. Hmong elders say that the bold call for reform alleviated ̀he problem somewhat although the bride ̀ce is still controversial and is not accepted ̀l Hmong families and clans.

The rationale behind the bride price has never been clear to most Hmong, but they accept the burden because it has been part of Hmong culture for thousands of years. The Hmong are not the only ethnic group that requires a bride price. The reason for it may be to compensate the bride's parents for some of the costs of bringing up and providing for their child. Some think it secures the daughter's life and welfare. Hmong children today see it as a gift in a mutual exchange. However it is seen, Hmong daughters are not commodities for sale and families can set the bride price at anything they agree on.

Rather than complaining about the bride price, Hmong can compromise on it. Hmong daughters are neither worthless nor for sale, but human beings who deserve respect and honor. The bride price is a cultural formality based on long-standing marital traditions. If someone does not want to honor and respect Hmong culture and traditions, that person should think carefully if he really wants to marry a Hmong daughter or if his root is truly Hmong. It is not fair to hold only Hmong men accountable for paying the bride price and not the men of other races who want to marry Hmong daughters. Most Hmong parents give their daughters a dowry regardless of who they marry, and some dowries are expensive. The bride price is not a cost the groom and his family pay to the bride's family; it is something the groom and his family give to the bride's parents in honor of her marriage and their bond, just like the dowry given by the bride's family.

The standard bride price for a never married Hmong daughter today is $5,000, as shown in Table 7.3. The bride price for previously married or divorced Hmong women is lower. In addition to the bride price, the groom's family is expected to pay about $800 to cover some ceremonial expenses. For divorcees and widowers, the secondary bride price ranges from zero to a couple thousand dollars. Not all families go by this cultural standard when their daughters get married; therefore, the bride price could be lower or higher. Any man, Hmong or non–Hmong, who marries a never-married Hmong girl,

Table 7.3. Typical Expenses for a Hmong Marriage

Item	In Hmong	Estimated amount
Bride price	Nqi tshoob	$5,000
Food, drinks, & miscellaneous	Noj haus	$ 800
Paternal uncle	Txiv ntxawm, txiv cob txeeb	$ 100
Older brother	Nus tij	$ 60
First male cousin	Nus npaw	$ 60
Shirt for the father	Txiv lub khaub tshos	$ 100
Shirt for the mother	Niam lub khaub tshos	$ 100
Grandfather	Yawg, poj tsiag zov kwv	$ 100
Grandmother	Pog, poj tsiag zov kwv	$ 100
Ceremonial pig	Npua dab	$ 40
Ceremonial chicken	Qaib dab	$ 20
Clean/sweep the table fee	Cheb rooj	$ 12
First time marital tie and bond	Tuam choj tshoob	$ 60
Older sister	Qhwv niam laus hauv caug	$ 60
Gifts for wedding conductors, negotiators, or facilitators	Nyiaj sia siv	$ 100

regardless of his age and number of prior marriages, is expected to pay the full bride price plus ceremonial expenses.

Keep in mind that Hmong traditions are not under the protection of any civil or criminal law. No law prohibits Hmong parents from collecting any bride price on any Hmong daughter regardless of whether she has been married before. By the same token, no law forces the groom to pay any particular bride price. The best way for both sides to look at the bride price is to consider the value of the bond between the families because this tie is more important than any amount of money.

Moreover, remember that what is legal may not be cultural and what is cultural may not be legal in this country. When a marriage is dissolved and parents are divorced in a court of law, Hmong traditions have no role in the legal system and the parents of a divorced woman cannot recover the bride price from the courts. Return of the bride price is unlikely unless the marital dissolution takes place within Hmong cultural norms.

The average cost for a Hmong traditional marriage and wedding is between $10,000 and $12,000. A dual ceremony will cost more, but not as much as a formal wedding that is arranged by a wedding planner. Hmong parents are culturally responsible for average traditional weddings, and adding other wedding ceremonies is up to the bride and groom as long as they can pay for them. Of course, some Hmong parents are more than happy to chip in to help.

Marital Kowtowing Customs

In Hmong culture, a verbal thank you is sometimes not enough. Although Hmong do use the verbal thank you on a regular basis in a variety of social situations, the proper and formal way to really thank someone is to kowtow according to the Hmong kneeling customs (*kev pe hawm losi mom xyom*). Hmong kowtowing is not bowing; Hmong do not bow their heads to show respect. Kowtowing is kneeling on both knees to show special respect and honor. Remember, *mom xyom* is not appropriate for marital events and is only used during Hmong death rituals and rites. Moreover, *xyom* means paying respect to the deceased by kneeling down on both knees, holding joss sticks in hands, and bowing head down two times when guided by the blessing singer, death song singer, and bamboo reed pipe player during funeral service. Again, Hmong Christian families do not use kowtowing customs.

Anyone can kneel at any time to petition someone for something, but this is not kowtowing. This type of kneeling is not part of Hmong culture, but an expression common to all mankind. Other ethnic groups also have kneeling customs. For instance, Thai use specific kneeling customs to pay respect to Buddha, to show respect to a higher authority, to give honor in religious practices, and to greet the king and queen.

Hmong kneeling customs are widely used for spiritual, religious, and cultural purposes in lieu of the verbal thank you. These customs show respect and honor to persons who provide benevolent assistance to needy individuals. Two kneelings (*pe ob pes*) are required for socio-cultural purposes and only one kneeling (*mom xyom losi ib pes*) is used for funeral and death rituals. Table 7.4 gives some examples of different occasions for kneeling. At cultural and religious events, Hmong men kneel two times to thank guests for their attendance. At religious events and formal religious rituals, they kneel two times to thank the performer, conductor, negotiator, provider, facilitator, or organizer of the event. In a spiritual circumstance, Hmong men kneel two times to thank the spirits of the deceased, guardian angels, deities, and house spirits.

In Hmong marital practices, the kneeling customs are critical and must be followed regardless of one's professional career, socioeconomic status, or age. Males must pay respect to various male members of the families of the bride and groom as well as to the house spirits of the bride's parents. Usually, the groom and his best man are the ones to kneel down; however, substitutes are allowed. Table 7.5 illustrates the kneeling customs for the traditional Hmong wedding ceremony.

Table 7.4. Hmong Kneeling Customs for Selected Purposes

Person/Purpose	In Hmong	Number of kneelings
Soul caller & soul calling ritual	Tus hu plig	Two
Shaman & shamanistic ritual	Tus ua neeb	Two
Ritual assistant	Tus pab saib	Two
Guests	Tas nrho cov qhua tuaj koom	Two
Wedding go-between ambassador, conductor, negotiator, facilitator, director, and so on	Meej Koob	Two
Wedding ceremony	Tshoob kos	Two
Ask for help, assistance, support	Thov pab cuam	Two
Funeral & death ritual	Kev ruam sim	One
Funeral & death ritual assistants	Thawj lwm tub ncig	One

Table 7.5. People/Spirits Honored in Marital Kneeling Customs

Honoree	In Hmong	Number of kneelings
Bride's parents	Niam thiab txiv	Two
Bride's grandparents	Pog thiab yawg	Two
Older paternal uncle and his wife	Txiv hlob thiab niam hlob	Two
Younger paternal uncle and his wife	Txiv ntxawm thiab niam ntxawm	Two
Paternal aunt and her husband	Muam phauj thiab yij laug	Two
Maternal uncle and his wife	Dab laug thiab niam dab laug	Two
Paternal brother	Txiv cob txheeb	Two
Older brother	Nus tij	Two
Younger brother	Nus kwv	Two
Bride's parents' house spirits	Niam txiv ncej dab ncej qhua	Two
All wedding and ceremonial guests	Qhua saib tshoob	Two
Lead wedding go-between ambassador, conductor	Txum mej hauv tsev	Two
Assistant wedding conductor	Lwm mej hauv tsev	Two
All older brothers	Tas nrho cov nus tij	Two
All younger brothers	Tas nrho cov nus kwv	Two

Proper kneeling requires that the kneeler touch the ground with his knees, feet, and thumbs, but not his other fingers, palms, or fists. So at a wedding the groom and his best man stand straight, side by side, then bend their knees to touch the ground, keeping their toes on the ground. They fold their fingers into fists, leaving their thumbs extended, and plant their thumbs on the ground simultaneously with their knees and feet, keeping their upper bodies lowered by bending their elbows outward. They do this twice for each person honored. Most of the paternal males in the bride's family receive this honor from the groom, but only few of the family's maternal females are so honored. This process is physical, brutal, and raises a sweat. The total number of kneelings seems countless. Only Hmong males are required to kneel down to pay respect, not females. Some Hmong Christian families no longer require the kneeling ritual.

During the Hmong wedding ceremony, if the kneeling is done improperly, it must be repeated correctly and the conductor of the ceremony fines people for repeated mistakes. Usually the fine is a can of beer or a gulp of other alcohol. It is considered disrespectful and very unusual to ask an older person to kneel in front of a younger person. Birth order, generational order, familial rank, and age usually play roles in Hmong kneeling customs, so one has to be careful about cultural taboos.

Marital Food Basket

On the day of the beginning of the traditional wedding ceremony, the groom's crew—family members who have various roles in the ceremonies—leaves the groom's house to go to the home of the bride's parents. Traditionally, the crew brings along a food basket (*lub kawm mov su*). Usually the basket is carried by the groom, the best man, or another designated person. It has to be a Hmong back basket or something similar, but not a backpack or an athletic bag. Inside the basket are specific items required by marital customs regardless of religious beliefs:

three boiled and fully cooked chickens, two packages of rice, a small peeling knife with a sheathe or bag, a small container of cooking oil, some utensils (a few spoons), some table salt, a bottle of wine or a six pack of beer, and napkins. In the old days, a live chicken (*qaib dab*) and a live pig (*npua luam xim*) would have also been brought, but money has been substituted for these animals. A folded blanket is strapped nicely to the basket.

When the crew reaches the half-way point, it is time for lunch (*noj su*) regardless of the time of the day. Two of the three boiled chickens (*qaib su losi qaib noj sus*) and one package of cooked rice (*pob mov su*) have been designated for lunch and have to be eaten by the crew. Before they eat, the lead wedding go-between ambassador (*mej koob*) performs an offering (*laig dab su*) to the guardian angels and spirits of the land to invite them to eat along with the crew and to give the crew peaceful blessings. According to Hmong marital customs, the feet of the two eaten chickens are saved to be shown to the go-between person of the bride's family as evidence that the crew had lunch along the way. If the feet are not presented, a penalty is assessed, usually a monetary fine. The third boiled chicken and the second package of rice are kept for a later meal at the bride's family's home.

On the way back to the groom's house, the crew carries the same basket with new contents from the bride's parents: a cut hindquarter of a pig (*ib ceg npua*), six pork ribs (*sawb nqaij*) for marital gifts, and twice the original number of spoons. The hindquarter of a pig is to be used for a meal for the groom's family's relatives and the six pork ribs are to be given as gifts to the parties helping the groom, such as the two go-between ambassadors (*mej koob*), the best man (*tub phij laj*), the bridesmaid (*niam tais ntsuab*), the groom's father (*niam txiv tog vauv*), and other assistants. The Hmong marital food basket custom is spiritually and culturally sensitive and needs to be followed as carefully as any other practice related to the marriage and the wedding.

Marital Umbrella

Traditionally, a black or navy blue umbrella is given to the couple as a symbol that the bride and the groom are protected from bad luck, evil spirits, bad omens, and anything negative that may occur during the entire course of their marital journey. The umbrella must be black or navy blue and the striped cloth headband has to be black and white or navy blue and white. No other color is acceptable.

Today the umbrella represents the bride (*tus nkauj nyab*) and the black and white striped cloth headband or turban symbolizes the wedding ring (*lub nplhaib*). The umbrella and the striped cloth headband represent the core of the marital traditions, including the wedding songs and chants, the formalities and protocols, the feasting and dining, and the marital spirits. The closed umbrella is spiritually and religiously significant to the newlywed couple because fortune, good luck, wishes, romance, prosperity, health, children, dreams, and wealth are believed to be contained inside the umbrella. In some families the umbrella is opened at the groom's home and in others it remains closed. Regardless of families' religious practices, the umbrella and the striped cloth headband are still used during the traditional wedding.

Wedding Songs

The Hmong have a large number and variety of wedding songs (*nkauj tshoob*) or wedding chants (*zaj tshoob*). Different songs and chants are appropriate for the different types of marriages: mutual consent, in-person negotiation, widow marriage, and so on. The songs and chants are used in connection with various proceedings during the course of the wedding ceremony. Typically, they are sung or chanted at the following steps or for the following purposes, among others:

- Opening
- Reception
- Acknowledgement , appreciation, and recognition
- Seeking permission, pardon, and forgiveness
- Giving a general thank you
- Showing mutual respect and honor
- Bridging, forging, and connecting family ties
- Retrieving ceremonial symbols
- Expressing gratitude and manners
- Bidding farewell and closing

Table 7.6 lists nearly all the Hmong traditional wedding songs and chants that are used today. The songs are not listed in ceremonial order. Normally, several songs are sung at a wedding, but not all of them. They are selected in accordance with the nature of the marriage. If all the songs and chants were used, the wedding ceremony would be unbearably long. The Hmong traditional wedding is one of the most ceremonial events in Hmong culture.

The whole process of singing wedding songs is quite entertaining. It is also quite

Table 7.6. Traditional Hmong Wedding Songs and Chants

Song/Chant	English translation	Purpose
Ceeb toom rau niam thiab txiv paub	Alerting bride's parents	To give a courtesy notice to bride's parents
Ceeb toom rau niam thiab txiv nyob hauv tsev	Warning bride's parents	To formally tell the bride's parents
Cob qaib laig dab	Giving the spiritual chickens to the host family	To give the spiritual chickens to the host's go-between negotiators
Cob npua luam xim	Giving the spiritual pig to the host family	To give the spiritual pig to the host's go-between negotiators
Coj paj mus rau txiv hlob thiab txiv ntxawm	Introducing the older and younger paternal uncles	To introduce the ceremonial process to the older and younger paternal uncles

Song/Chant	English translation	Purpose
Dais kaus	Hanging the ceremonial umbrella	To ask for a place to hang the ceremonial umbrella
Fis tshoob	Notifying the marriage	To notify the bride's parents of the marriage
Kawm qaib kaws tsiaj	Showing the spiritual animals	To present the spiritual animals
Hais rau txiv hlob thiab txiv ntxawm	Telling the older and younger paternal uncles	To formally tell the older and younger uncles about the wedding
Hauv cawv yeeb cawv tshuaj	Drinking the ceremonial wine	To introduce drinking formalities and protocols for the wedding
Laij nyuj (hais 3 zam ua 3 zaum)	Performing the kowtowing customs on 3 different occasions	To perform the kowtowing or kneeling customs to pay respect
Raws kwvtij tuaj	Inviting all family relatives to come	To call out to all family relatives to join in the wedding celebration
Muab ntawv tshoob	Seeking the wedding formalities and protocols	To ask for the wedding formalities and protocols related to feasting, dowry, and bride price
Niam thiab txiv ntuas ntxhais	Lecturing the bride by her parents	For the bride's parents to lecture or reprimand the bride
Tus qaib dab ciaj losi qaib tshoob	Presenting the live spiritual and ceremonial chicken	To give the live spiritual and ceremonial chicken to the host's go-between negotiators
Qhib qhov rooj	Opening the door to receive	To ask the host to open the door to receive the guest
Qhib tshoob thiab tsim tshoob	Opening the wedding ceremonial processes	To ask to open the wedding ceremonial processes
Ua niam thiab txiv tsaug	Thanking the bride's parents	To thank the bride's parents for the ceremonial feast
Taij dej txuav muag	Asking for water to wash face	To ask the host to provide water so guests can wash their faces
Taij kaus	Asking for the ceremonial umbrella	To formally ask for the return of the ceremonial umbrella
Tsim kaus	Creating the ceremonial umbrella	To explain the creation of the ceremonial umbrella
Tsim rooj tshoob	Creating the wedding ceremonial processes	To explain the creation of the wedding ceremonial processes
Tso ntawv tshoob	Letting go or coming down to the wedding formalities and protocols	To let go or to come down to the wedding ceremonial processes
Tso nyiaj	Putting down money or bride price	To put down the bride price on the table
Tso qaib qhia tsiaj	Bringing the cooked chickens	To ask to bring the cooked chickens for feasting
Tua tsiaj	Butchering the ceremonial animal	To inform of the ceremonial animal for the wedding feast
Txais nyiaj	Receiving money	To accept monetary offerings related to the bride price, dowry, and feasting

Song/Chant	English translation	Purpose
Ua niam thiab ua txiv tsaug thaum kawg	Thanking bride's parents for the last time	To offer the final thank you to the bride's parents and her side of the family for the feasting
Ua raug vauv tsaug	Thanking the groom	To offer a thank you to the groom and his side of the family for the feasting
Ua theej cawv mov	Feasting and drinking formalities and protocols	To announce feasting and drinking formalities and protocols at the ceremonial table
Ua tsaug yeeb tsaug tshuaj	Thanking all feasting and drinking	To give a final thank you for the feasting and drinking at the wedding ceremony

time consuming as some of the chants are very long. Today the go-between negotiators often skip at least some of the wedding songs not only to save time, but also because many people would rather communicate directly with one another than indirectly through wedding songs. Open communication in lieu of so many wedding chants is the preferred ceremonial language today. A few wedding songs are usually sung for entertainment purposes. Hmong are finding ways to preserve their traditional wedding songs and chants while modernizing them to accommodate contemporary life. For instance, they are singing some of the wedding chants at groom's home but nowhere else.

Marital Manners and Conduct

Hmong expect perfection from both themselves and others. However, they rarely see their expectations met. That is one reason they continue to practice good and responsible manners during the wedding ceremony. Good manners honor the newlywed couple, their wedding, and their family members. Good conduct creates an atmosphere of happiness and peace. Every adult in attendance at a wedding is expected to conform to basic principles of behavior. Word choices and proper communication are part of good marital manners. The principles and behaviors can be learned by imitating well-mannered peers. Typical ground rules for what one can

and cannot do during the wedding ceremony are as follows:

- Use only positive words
- No negative talking
- No folding arms or crossing legs while sitting down
- No resting arms on the table
- Do not use the word "finish" (tas) in reference to drinking
- Only use the words "clear, complete, or done" (meej) in reference to drinking
- Pay close attention to drinking formality and protocol
- Maintain self-control if intoxicated
- Do not get up and go as you please
- Be courteous and respectful
- Be attentive and alert
- Suspend personal queries
- No interjections
- Keep with the flow, order, and proceedings
- Warn the person next to you before drinking
- Say thank you when appropriate
- Stay put and sit still
- Find a replacement before leaving the table
- Watch for misconduct and correct it
- Be careful about eating time
- Learn table etiquette and norms
- Ask for permission when necessary
- Avoid sidebar talking and unnecessary conversations

At a wedding, the drinking formality and protocol could be enforced with strict proceedings and guidelines; however, it is usually flexible enough to accommodate people who cannot consume alcohol because of health-related concerns. Listening to the go-between ambassadors who conduct the ceremony is helpful for learning the basic ground rules and avoiding mistakes. Remember, only males are permitted to sit at the table. Barring females may be biased, but it has been a long-standing tradition.

Common Marital Penalties

Penalties are imposed for infractions of traditional Hmong marriage and wedding norms (*txheej txheem tshoob kos*). Infractions might be improper conduct during courtship (*kev txhaum txheej losi kev ua tsis yog raws kev cai*), improper marital notification (*fis xov tsis raws kev cai*), problems resulting from past family marital matters (*lus txeej lus xuam losi kev sib cov nyom*), unpaid past marital fines and bride price (*tshuav nuj tshuav nqi*), or other minor infractions (*kev txhaum lwm yam*). Usually, these penalties can be resolved through negotiation, compromise, mutual agreement, family truces and promises, and small monetary fines. For instance, at the outset, the groom's family may offer $300 to pay for any improper conduct during courtship and any issues related to marital notification. His family would make the offer to keep the bride's family from bringing up anything that may stall the wedding preparation process. These kinds of infractions are normal and family representatives usually settle them through mutual agreement. In extreme cases, severe marital penalties imposed by the bride's family could delay the wedding. Such cases, however, are unlikely unless there is some bad blood between the two families. In most cases, money is the solution.

Minor infractions that occur during the wedding ceremony related to drinking, dining, talking, or improper conduct incur fines of a can of beer, two gulps of wine, kneeling down, or other such things. The nature of the infraction determines the fine, but there is no need to impose a monetary fine unless the offense was intentional. Wedding ceremonies have differing proceedings, formalities, and protocols, so the infractions are not the same from one wedding to another and the go-between negotiators cannot always keep up. In most cases, they are able to correct any mistakes they make. The go-between individuals are not responsible to pay marital fines; the groom's family is responsible for the fines imposed by the bride's family and the bride's family is responsible for fines imposed by the groom's family. The go-between negotiators can suggest ideas, but it is up to the families to resolve the matters. Both families usually work hard at settling problems because they do not want to cancel the wedding or terminate the marriage because of simple, typical conflicts.

Marital Crews

When two Hmong get married, nearly every one of their family members becomes involved directly or indirectly in the wedding. Family members include immediate family, family relatives, kinship members, clan members, and friends. In Hmong culture, clan leaders and representatives play significant roles in traditional weddings, helping forge a union that will last forever. Each family needs to have a wedding crew, a group that agrees to fill specific roles for the wedding. Table 7.7 identifies the people who typically make up the bride's and the groom's crews and the roles they play. A formal wedding ceremony could not take place without these individuals.

If the groom and bride have decided to celebrate their wedding in the American way, crew members are still needed for several functions in the wedding ceremony. In extreme cases, both families leave everything to the bride and groom because they are unhappy that their children do not want to follow Hmong customs. More commonly, significant family members play important roles in the wedding ceremony. For example, the clan leader or family leader will help resolve marital conflicts in the future, so he receives

Table 7.7. Hmong Groom's and Bride's Crew Members' Roles

Groom's Family Crew Member	In Hmong	Basic Roles	Bride's Family Crew Member	In Hmong	Basic Roles/ Responsibilities
Two messengers	Ob tug fis xov	Notifying and informing	Receiver	Tus txais lub xos	Receiving and accepting the notification
Two go-between negotiators, ambassadors, directors, conductors, or facilitators	Ob tug mej koob	Negotiating, carrying messages, communicating, spokesperson, conducting, etc....	Two go-between negotiators, ambassadors, directors, conductors, or facilitators	Ob tus mej koob	Negotiating, carrying messages, communicating, spokesperson, conducting, etc....
Bridesmaid or maid of honor	Niam tais ntsuab	Accompanying, covering, assisting, protecting, spying, etc....	Older brother	Nus tij	Accompanying, assisting, entertaining, ensuring, talking, etc....
Best man	Phij laj	Accompanying, assisting, protecting, supporting, substituting, etc....	First cousin	Nus npaw	Accompanying, assisting, entertaining, ensuring, talking, etc....
A family representative on behalf of his parents	Niam txiv lav tshoob	Surrogate parent, resolving matters, making decisions	Paternal uncle	Txiv cob txheeb	Consulting, lecturing, promoting, assisting, advising, etc....
Clan leader	Tus coj tshoob	Supporting, consulting, advising, enabling, recognizing, resolving matters, etc....	Maternal uncle	Dab laug	Consulting, lecturing, promoting, assisting, advising, ensuring, etc....
Elders	Kev txwj laus neeg	Supporting, enabling, advising, recognizing, resolving matters, consulting, etc....	Paternal aunt (a male substitute)	Muam phauj	Consulting, lecturing, promoting, assisting, advising, ensuring, etc....
Wedding director, wine pourer/ server, busboy	Kav xwm, thiaj com, tub ce cawv	Feasting, drinking, transporting, preparing, cooking, packing, etc....	A family representative on behalf of her parents	Niam txiv lav tshoob	Surrogate parent, resolving matters, making decisions, etc....
All females	Cov niam tsev	Cooking, feasting, dining, washing, cleaning, packing, preparing, transporting, etc....	Wedding director and other males	Thiaj com thiab cov kwv tij	Feasting, drinking, transporting, preparing, cooking, packing, etc....
Mother and father	Niam thiab txiv	Preparing, organizing, consulting,	All females	Cov niam tsev	Cooking, feasting, dining,

Groom's Family Crew Member	In Hmong	Basic Roles	Bride's Family Crew Member	In Hmong	Basic Roles/ Responsibilities
		advising, ensuring, transporting, spending, etc....			washing, cleaning, packing, preparing, transporting, etc....
All other males	Cov kwv tij	Assisting, helping, feasting, dining, preparing, packing, drinking, transporting, standing by, etc....	Mother and father	Niam thiab txiv	Preparing, organizing, collecting, consulting, advising, ensuring, transporting, spending, etc....

a $20 stipend from the wedding funds. However, today, most marital conflicts are dealt with by the police, lawyers, and the court system. Family representatives of both families are accountable for marital agreements, the bride price, the dowry, and promises. However, they have no legal means of enforcing the agreements if the couple should dishonor them. Today these cultural roles are still sound and desirable, but they are not legally practical.

Drinking Formalities

Weddings are occasions for excitement and enjoyment. As in many other cultures, informal drinking in and out of the home with family members, relatives, and friends takes place during weddings. Formal drinking usually starts in the groom's home beginning on the third day after the initial induction of the bride ritual (*hu nkauj nyab plig*).

This drinking is usually done in conjunction with eating, but sometimes a few rounds of drinking take place before a meal. The rounds of drinking (*xeej cawv*) are formally begun from the head table. There may be rounds with:

- The reception and welcoming of the bride (*txais tos nkauj nyab*)
- The induction and admission of the bride to the family (*nkauj nyab los txog vaj txog tsev*)
- The soul calling ritual (*tus cawv hu plig*)
- The string tying string ceremony (*tus cawv khi te*)

- The time of thanking guests (*tus cawv ua qhua tsaug*)
- The ritual for the blessing of the souls and spirits of the bride and groom (*tus cawv txhawb plig rau nyab thiab tub*).

Usually, these rounds are controlled and formal. However, overdrinking can occur if the groom, his family members, and friends indulge themselves with lots of drinking, especially toasting. After this event in the groom's home, either immediately or on another day, the groom's crew goes to the bride's house.

The drinking formalities and protocols at the bride's house are similar to those at the groom's house except that the rounds are designated for different purposes. These rounds, in order, accompany the following customs:

- Opening the ceremonial door (*tus cawv qhib roog*)
- Receiving the guests (*tus cawv tos qhua*)
- Entering the house of the bride (*tus cawv poob plag*)
- Eating rice with cold water (*tus cawv mov dej txiag*)
- The ceremonial marital trade (*tus cawv luam xim*)
- Showing respect and honor to the family relatives (*tus cawv piam thaj losi laij nyug*).

Only the bride's family partakes of the first four rounds; the groom's family joins in the last two. This drinking is facilitated by the four go-between negotiators from the two families. Besides the formal drinking, the negotiators also serve other drinks through-out the ceremony.

Once the lead negotiators have concluded the formal rounds of drinking, it is time for the crew members of both sides to get to know one another. Until this point, most crew members have acted like strangers. This is their once-in-a-lifetime opportunity to build a ceremonial relationship through a marital drinking ritual (*tus cawv sib zeem*). Crew members exchange drinks to build ceremonial bonds. This drinking is quite heavy because of the volume each has to consume on the way out of the bride's house to the cars waiting outside. The amount is the same for both sides and all crew members. This ritual marks the end of the wedding ceremony at the bride's house.

But it is not the end of the wedding. When the groom's crew returns to his house, the termination ceremony takes place. The sole purpose of this mini celebration is to allow the two negotiators to report back to the groom's parents and family members about the wedding ceremony, all expenses incurred, and if any stipulations were imposed by the bride's parents and family members. The report is referred to as the post-wedding ceremony summary (*pom sam*). A meal is waiting for the returning crew. Upon entering the house, the groom and the best man perform a kneeling-down ritual to honor and respect the family members and household sprits.

Right away, a table is set and a meal is served. All crew members are invited to sit on one side of the table and the rest of the family members sit on the other side. As is done during the soul calling ritual on the third day, two lead persons take the head table and two assistants take the tail table, participants consume four rounds of drinks to honor crew members. The first round acknowledges their return home; the second shows appreciation to the two go-between negotiators; the third gives respect and honor to family members, crew members, and all household spirits; and the fourth is a drink in unison taking place in a circular drinking pattern (*koos cawv*). The groom and his best man may be too drunk to join in these rounds,

but that does not stop family members from paying respect to the crew members. Substitutes are frequently used and a lead person conducts the kneeling ritual to pay the final respect and honor to the crew members, negotiators, family members, and household spirits. Stipends and rewards are given to each crew member to thank them for helping in the wedding. Stipends are usually money and pork ribs. The two negotiators receive $100 each for their roles and all other crew members get $20 each for their assistance. The groom's family has the choice of asking the lead negotiator to open the wedding umbrella or leave it closed. Sometimes the lead negotiator will chant while opening the umbrella to further bless the bride and groom with luck and fortune. Everyone thanks him for his generosity and blessing. That concludes the ceremonial aspects of the wedding.

Wedding Progression

A traditional Hmong wedding follows a standard progression. It starts in the groom's home when the bride and groom are married and is followed by the initial induction of the bride ritual (*lwm sub losi lwm qaib thiab hu plig*), performed on the first day of the marriage and on the third day. Next it moves all the way to the bride's family's home where the traditional wedding ceremony is held. It comes back to the groom's family's home, where the wedding concludes. Not all weddings are done the same way, but they all follow the same progression.

At the Groom's Family's Home

Normally, on the third day, a formal induction ceremony with the soul calling ritual (*hu plig*) takes place. Sometimes the soul calling is delayed for a few weeks or months because of family situations. For the ritual, two live chickens, one male and one female, are used along with a bowl of uncooked rice, two raw eggs, and a burning joss stick or incense. Remember, for Hmong Christian families this event is different. Following the soul calling, a spiritual ceremony (*khi te*) of tying strings to the bride and groom takes place. First, at a decorated table, the couple stand together with their hands stretched out, palm down. The soul caller sweeps a bundle of strings over the backs of their hands from the wrist to the finger tips as he chants to cast away bad luck, bad omens, misfortunes, and evil spirits. Then the couple turns their hands face up as he chants and sweeps from finger tips to wrist to offer them marital blessings for a lifetime. When he is finished, the family members and friends line up one by one to tie wishful and hopeful strings to the wrists of the newlywed couple and congratulate them with blessings and best of luck. The ritual director asks the elders sitting around the table to read the tongues, skulls, eyes, wings, and feet of the two boiled fully cooked chickens and give the bride and groom the spiritual and religious interpretation and meanings. Usually, the interpretation is positive and the couple is blessed by the elders.

Just before a long table is set and a meal served, the father or a representative makes an offering (*laig dab*) to the spirits and souls of ancestors and deceased family members, asking for their blessings and protection over the newlywed couple. For Christian Hmong, a family pray takes place. The Hmong word *laig* means offering or eating, and the Hmong word *dab* means spirits or benevolent spirits. In formality, the soul caller and other elders are invited to sit on one side of the table, starting in the middle, along with wedding crew members, and the rest of the people sit on the other side of the table. Two sets of shot glass–sized drinking glasses are set on plates for the rounds of drinking that will follow. Sometimes each person has his own pair of glasses and sometimes two sets are shared. Before the drinking protocols begin, two leading individuals are designated to sit at the head table to take charge of the proceedings and two assistants are asked to sit at the tail table to help monitor the drinking patterns. Before this event the groom's family assembled a wedding crew (*cov mej zeeg*), including two go-between negotiators—the lead negotiator (*tuam mej koob*) and his assistant (*lwm mej koob*)—the maid of honor,

a best man, a surrogate parent, a server, a busboy, and a representative; all these are invited to join in this event. Normally this ritual ends with the sending of the wedding crew (*tsa mej zeeg sawv kev*) to the bride's family's home.

The crew goes to the brides' family's home before sundown. As mentioned earlier, along the way, the wedding crew carries a marital basket with all required contents: a folded blanket, an umbrella with a black and white striped cloth headband tied around it, and a few packs of cigarettes. Depending on the family, other cultural items may be included, such as an apron (*sev*) or sash. In the old days, the crew walked on foot but today a designated driver transports them. The bride and maid of honor are dressed in traditional Hmong clothing (*hnav ris tsho Hmoob*). When the progression is from the groom's house to the bride's family's home, the bride and the maid of honor are dressed in traditional clothes that represent the groom's family's culture and traditions, and when the progression is from the bride's family's home to the groom's house, the bride and the maid of honor are dressed in traditional clothes that represent the bride's family's culture and traditions. Half way to the bride's family, the crew has to take a lunch break. The lead negotiator manages the lunch and conducts the marital lunch ritual (*laig dab su*). Remember, the four chicken feet are saved as evidence for the go-between negotiators of the bride's family that the crew ate as expected. The meal break with its rituals is repeated when the crew returns to the groom's house after the wedding ceremony.

At the Bride's Family's Home

When the crew arrives at the bride's parents' doorstep, the lead negotiator asks if the house is under restriction. Someone comes to the door and answers him and the crew enters the house. In the old days, the crew had to enter through the back door. Today, the crew usually enters through the front door. In rare cases, the opening door and bridging wall ritual (*qhib roog tuam ntsa*) has to be performed by the groom's negotiators to gain access into the house because the door is blocked. At the door, the host negotiators (bride's side) and the guest negotiators (groom's side) interact. The guest negotiators are now called by a new name: *plhov mej*. The guest negotiator sings a wedding chant to ask the host negotiator to open the door to allow the crew to enter the house. Sometimes the negotiators negotiate to remove the barriers and reach a mutual agreement without having to sing a wedding chant.

As soon as the crew enters the house, the groom's lead negotiator instructs the groom and his best man to perform the kneeling-down ritual (*pe*) to show respect and honor to the bride's family, ancestors, relatives, and household spirits. At the same time, the bride and her maid of honor are asked to change from their traditional clothes into regular outfits. When this is done, the lead negotiator hands the ceremonial umbrella to the host negotiator or a family representative for safeguarding throughout the wedding ceremony. Usually the ceremonial umbrella is hung on a wall near the family altar or shrine (*xwm kab losi seej khab*). If there is no altar, the best location is the north wall (*hauv plag*) or a wall in the dining room or living room area where a ceremonial table will later be placed for the wedding.

Before sitting down, the groom's lead negotiator quickly strokes every adult present in the house, including the spirits of the family ancestors, with two cigarettes. Symbolically, cigarettes are used in place of monetary gifts to show respect in honor of the bride's parents. The crew then sits and waits for the rest of the family relatives to show up, especially important representatives and negotiators. Meanwhile, the bride's family is preparing a pre-wedding ceremony meal, usually a dinner, for the crew and all family members. Traditionally, all wedding meals are simple, perhaps just cooked meat and steamed rice. Sometimes the bride's family disregards this custom and prepares s delicious dinner, especially if the family is Hmong Christian or non–Hmong. Many Hmong families depart from the traditional wedding menu and include a variety of dishes. However, the elders and most Hmong parents still prefer the old foods. Normally, the wedding formalities will not begin until after the dinner is over. By the time the ceremony gets started, it is around seven or eight o'clock in the evening.

The guest negotiators cannot start the process until the father or a family member introduces them to the host negotiators. Sometimes, the guest negotiators look for the family's representative to initiate the process. At this point, the bride's family is ready for the wedding proceedings. The guest negotiators offer two sets of glasses of wine to the host negotiators and ask them for a table and four chairs. The host negotiators arrange the table and chairs and show the furniture to the guest negotiators. The guest negotiators invite the hosts to sit at the table, and at the same time they invite other people to join the four of them at the table. Usually no one joins them because the table is reserved for the negotiators. At the table, the four negotiators introduce themselves to one another and begin the wedding formalities with a few rounds of drinking. This process may be different for Hmong Christian families, some of whom drink little or no alcohol.

The guest negotiators acknowledge their roles and responsibilities on behalf of the groom's family and assert that it is an honor and privilege for them to conduct the wedding in accordance with the groom's family's instructions and expectations. Therefore, they explain, all discussion during the proceedings, including wheeling, dealing, and sharing, will be conveyed to the grooms' family. At this point, the guest and host negotiators begin a ceremonial discourse and negotiation, opened by the guest negotiators. Normally the negotiations involve two tiers of subjects. The first tier has to do with concerns associated with the courtship between the bride and the groom:

- Concerns related to the groom's behaviors during the time of the courtship (kev txhaum txheej, kev ua siab niam siab txiv, losi kev luab lim tsis raws cai)
- Past marital issues, problems, or conflicts or unresolved and outstanding

matters between the two families (lus txeej lus xuam, kev plaub kev ntug, losi kev ua tshoob ua kos)

- Any prior marital engagement or existing arrangement for the bride that may interfere with this wedding (muam phauj dab laug cuam tshuam, kev sib qhaib, losi kev sib cov lug ua tshoob ua kos)
- Concerns related to the marital notification by the groom's messengers (fis xov raws kev cai los tsis raws, puas muaj lus siab lus qis, losi puas muaj kev sib cov nyom)
- Other issues the bride's parents may have in regard to this wedding (puas tshuav dabtsi, puas muaj datsi, losi puas muaj kev tus ncuas)

Often the guest negotiators avoid discussing the groom's courtship behavior, marital notification, and issues of the bride's parents by putting a few hundred dollars on the table as an offer to seal off any inquiry into these areas. Actually, it is good faith offer. Normally, the bride's family takes the offer without questions. There is hardly ever any past marital or prior arrangement issues, but if there are, the bride's family has to resolve them before the wedding can go on because they pertain to the bride. The families are usually able to negotiate and resolve any marital issues through discussion. The groom's family is obligated to discuss whatever issues the bride's family raises; but he does not have to put up with explaining any little or unimportant thing the bride's family thinks of. Both sides have to show respect toward each other. Stalling by bringing up petty issues may terminate the wedding proceedings.

The second tier of wedding subjects for discussion and negotiation has to do with ceremonial and collateral money. They address the bride's family's requirements related to the specific amounts of money allocated for each of the following family members and ceremonial needs:

- The grandparents of the bride (pog thiab yawg tsiag zov kwv)
- The older sister or sisters of the bride (qhwv niam laus hauv caug)
- The paternal uncle or closest relative (yaj ncos cob txheeb)
- The marital bridge between the two families (tuam choj tshoob)
- The authority fee or the clan leader fee (nyiaj khaib nom)
- The bride price (nqi mis nqi hno)
- The main wedding feast and dining expenses (nyiaj ua noj haus)

The bride price may be higher or lower than the standard $5,000 and the request for the feasting and dining expenses may be more or less than the $800 norm. Everything is negotiable, but sometimes the negotiations stall and become awkward. One way of smoothing the negotiation is to have the bride's family give an itemized list of expenses to the groom's family for review and approval. Most Hmong Christian families do this to shorten the negotiation. If the amounts requested seem too high, the groom's family might make a counteroffer. Once the negotiations settle the matter, the mutually agreed upon amounts are given to the bride's family and the wedding can proceed.

The negotiators wrap up their part in the ceremony. A live pig and chicken (*npua luam xim thiab qaib dab*) are no longer given to the brides' family, but money is given in lieu of these animals. The guest negotiators hand over the marital basket to the host negotiators. The session ends with the final ritual (*cheb rooj*). Typically, it is a money game or a friendly gift exchange between the four negotiators called the wearing belt ritual (*mej zeeg sib sia siv*). The host negotiators initiate the game by placing $2 on each of the four corners of the table and in the middle. The guest negotiators then place $4 on top of each pile. The host negotiators add $60 to each of the two piles in front of the guest negotiators and the guest negotiators place double that amount on the two piles in front of the host negotiators. Finally, each takes the pile in front of him. Thus the guest negotiators each receive $66 and each of the host negotiators pockets $126. The middle stack of $6 is left for the server and the busboy.

To conclude the wedding proceedings for the first night, the four negotiators call for four cold, boiled, fully cooked chickens (*qaib qhe tsiaj*) and order the server and busboy to chop the chickens for a late night supper. Everyone is invited to join in the meal. The four negotiators exchange chicken legs and thighs in appreciation of their services. A wedding chant used to be sung at this point in the ceremony, but today chanting is skipped. After eating, the crew is supposed to spend the night at the bride's family's home. However, usually only the groom, bride, and maid of honor do so. The rest go home and return on the next day.

The Day of the Ceremonial Feast

Normally the wedding celebration takes place the next day, although it is sometimes delayed. A sizable pig is slaughtered for the wedding feast, which is usually held at one o'clock in the afternoon. Remember, Hmong wedding dishes are traditionally simple, but the brides' family today generally prepares all kinds of dishes regardless of the longstanding tradition. Actually, the wedding feast can be prepared by either side, depending on the negotiation. It is rare to see the groom's side take over the preparation of the feast, but it does happen. Regardless, the preparation of the feast is controlled by wedding directors (*kav xwm losi thiaj com*) from both sides so people from both families help prepare the main feast. It is the females who do most of the cooking and cleaning.

By noon the wedding directors should inform the negotiators that the main feast is ready. The four negotiators meet to organize the feast in accordance with the bride's family's instructions. Traditionally, the bride's family performs a spiritual offering ritual (*laig dab*) to its ancestors, all deceased relatives, and household spirits preceding the main feast. This offering is not required by Hmong Christian families or non–Hmong families.

A long table is usually set as the main dining table (*sam tsum*). The four negotiators along with the wedding directors take the lead in inviting the guests to sit around the main table, and they seat elders, special guests, distinguished guests, leaders, and friends together. Women and children eat at a separate table (*xyuam tsum*) although the bride's parents may dine at either table. Sometimes, but not usually, alcohol is served with the meal. If the meal at the main table includes drinking, special protocols apply as explained in the Drinking Formalities section.

After the meal, a new table is set and the four negotiators start the final wedding proceedings. On the table is a special dish, usually cooked chopped meat (*phaj ntsuag*), and forks. The two lead negotiators take charge of the head table and the two assistant negotiators take charge of the tail table to monitor the drinking formalities. The negotiators organize the seating. The seating at the head table is as follows, beginning on the right side to the right of the host lead negotiator: the paternal uncle (*txiv cob txheeb*), the groom (*nraug vauv*), the maternal male cousin (*nus npaw*), the best man (*tub phij laj*), the older brother (*nus tij*), the maid of honor (*niam tais ntsuab*), the maternal uncle (*txiv dab laug*), the paternal aunt (*muam phauj*), the groom's surrogate parent (*niam txiv tog vauv*), and the bride's surrogate parent (*niam txiv tog ntxhais*). On the left side of the table, starting from the left of the guest lead negotiator, are elders, special guests, distinguished guest, friends, and relatives of both sides. In some families, the seating pattern does not matter but in others proper seating is strictly enforced.

Traditionally, the main drinking consists of 4 to 12 rounds of drinking at this table. Some of the rounds are single count (*ib xeej lus ib xeej caw*)—meaning one (*tab* in Hmong) drink for a proceeding—or a double count (*ib xeej lus ob xeej caw*)—meaning two (*txooj* in Hmong) drinks for a proceeding. As explained under Drinking Formalities, several rounds are served before the wedding ceremony is over.

During the drinking, the four negotiators do most of the thanking, talking, directing, guiding, and correcting. However, for the round of drinking called the rice and cold water ceremony (*pluas mov dej txiag*), crew members of both sides rise up to thank one another formally. The negotiators remind everyone to give thanks with the expression "*noj qhua qaib nco ntsoov ua qhua tsaug,*" meaning "eating the guest's meat, remember to thank the guest." Each crew member calls his counterpart on the other side by name and thanks him. For example, the groom, using welcoming hand gestures, says to the older brother, "Thank you, older brother, Michael. People say the parents of the other side are not well prepared to come to this ceremony, but the parents of this side are well prepared to receive at this ceremony. We have dined and drunk and have eaten all the food during the feast and leave nothing for the parents on this side to feast on, so thank you...." In Hmong, "*Ua tsaug mog, nus tij, Michael, luag hais tias niam txiv tom ub ua tsis muaj kab muaj kes tuaj, tabsi niam txiv tom no ua muaj kab muaj kes tos, peb muab nqaij muab mov noj tshau muab dej muab cawv haus meej, tsis tseg ib yam dabtsi rau niam txiv tom no noj mog ... ua tsaug....*" This pattern is repeated until all crew members have given and received thanks. The actual words may be different at different weddings, but the contents are fairly consistent. Basically, crew members thank the bride's parents and family relatives for their hospitality during the wedding ceremony.

The next round of drinking honors the marital trade (*tus cawv luam xim*) between the two families and the next one shows respect and honor to the family relatives (*tus cawv piam thaj losi laij nyug*). This time the bride's family relatives give thanks to the groom's family for the mutual trade taking place during the wedding ceremony, meaning the bride price and the expenses of the ceremony. For example, the bride's surrogate parent, making farewell hand gestures, says to the groom's surrogate parents, "Thank you, parents of the groom. People say the parents of the other side have brought money and livestock to this ceremony to prepare a feast for all members of the family on this

side so we can dine and drink. Nothing is left for the parents of the other side to feast on and that will sadden their hearts. Thank you...." In Hmong, "*Ua tsaug mog ... niam txiv, luag hais tias niam txiv tom ub npaj nyiaj npaj txiaj coj tsiaj coj txhuv tuaj ua tshoob ua kos tuaj npaj pluas noj pluas haus rau peb noj peb haus tshau rau peb noj peb haus meej, tsis tseg ib yam dabtsi rau niam txiv tom ub noj niam txiv tom ub haus yuav tu niam txiv tom ub siab mog ... ua tsaug....*" In response to this special thank you, the receiver says something similar to his counterpart on the other side. Again, the main point here is to express gratitude to the groom's family for paying the expenses involved in this wedding.

For the round to show respect and honor to the family relatives, the guest lead negotiator calls the groom and best man to pay respect to the family relatives, ancestors, and house spirits by performing the kneeling-down ritual. The groom and his best man pay two kneeling-down respects to each person, soul, and spirit listed in Table 7.5. The guest lead negotiator starts directing the kneeling then hands the direction over to the host lead negotiator to take charge. As there are many deserving of this respect, the ritual is quite demanding physically. The bride and the maid of honor prepare wet washcloths to wipe the sweat from the faces and necks of the groom and the best man. This ritual brings the drinking to an end.

Next is the marital relationship ritual (*kev sib zeem*), the last mini drink for the groom, the best man, the older brother, and the maid of honor. For this ritual, the bride and her maid have dressed in traditional Hmong costumes in preparation for going back to the groom's family's home. Remember, as said earlier, while going to the bride's family home, the bride and her maid of honor are dressed in the groom's family traditional customs; and when returning to the groom's family, the bride and her maid of honor are dressed in the bride's family traditional customs. The wedding crew members are packing and leaving the house to return to the groom's family's home.

The marital relationship ritual can be unpleasant depending on what is used to tie the relationship. Beer, fatty meat, hard liquor, and mixed drinks are commonly used. Sometimes, the groom and the best man are already drunk. To deal with the unpleasantness, the guest negotiators ask the host negotiators to be compassionate and considerate. Today, health issues are taken into consideration, so healthy food and drinks are used in place of hard liquor and fatty meats.

At the table, the negotiators move along to the next proceedings, which are the dowry report (*pom sam*), the paternal uncle's words of advice, and the start of the emotional farewells. The dowry report is read to the negotiators and prominent family members. The dowry may consist of items such as jewelry, clothes, money, gifts from all family members, or a car. It could be a sacrificial cow or the head of a bull, a set of casual clothes (*tsoos tsuj tsoos npuag*), or a set of traditional clothes (*tsoos laus losi tsoos maj tsoos ntuag*). After the report has been read and verified, the host negotiator hands it to the guest lead negotiator to take to the groom's family. At this point, the negotiators thank each other for the report.

Next, the paternal uncle addresses the bride. He reminds her of her new roles and responsibilities as a wife, a married woman, and a daughter-in-law. He directs the groom to protect, guide, support, instruct, and train her because she is now his wife who will take care of his family and his needs. More people can speak to the bride and groom, but usually only a few are designated to do so. Lastly, the paternal uncle asks the bride if she has any belongings, debts, or pictures of her male friends or former boyfriends. If so, they have to be returned, thrown away, or turned over to him. After this, the emotional farewell begins.

The final proceeding is the departure ceremony (*tus cawv sawv kev*) that sends the groom's crew home before sundown. The guest lead negotiator may sing a wedding song to ask the host lead negotiator for the marital umbrella, but often the chanting is skipped. By this time, the crew members

have loaded everything into their cars and are ready to leave. The four negotiators conclude the ceremonial formalities with the cleaning the house ritual (*cheb plag*) and bid friendly farewells (*mej koob sib faib kab*), say a final thank you to the bride's family (*ua niam ua txiv tsaug*) and the bride's crew (*ua mej zeeg tsaug*), and affirm the marital relationship between the two families (*cog ncej tsoob kos*). The final handshakes among negotiators prompt everybody to head out the door. The bride is in tears, family members are crying, and the scene is chaotic with emotions. With the marital umbrella in his hand, the guest lead negotiator makes sure no crew member is left behind. He walks behind everyone. In a sad but long-standing tradition, the bride is instructed not to look back at her house and her parents as she leaves.

Returning to the Groom's Family's Home

As the crew heads home, they stop at the half-way point to eat the last marital lunch. As with the first one, the lead negotiator manages the lunch and performs the marital lunch ritual (*laig dab sus*), making an offering to the guardian spirits and angels of the land for their blessing and protection.

When the crew arrives at the groom's parents' doorstep, the lead negotiator asks if the house is under restriction. Expecting their arrival, family members welcome the crew back into the house. If the door is blocked, the lead negotiator has to sing a wedding chant to get through the blockage; however, the crew is very unlikely to encounter a blocked door after a long day of feasting, dining, and drinking at the bride's family's home. Inside the house, the lead negotiator instructs the groom and the best man to perform the final kneeling-down ritual to show respect and honor to the family relatives, ancestors, and household spirits. Then, as explained in the Drinking Formalities section, a mini ceremony takes place that concludes all the wedding formalities. The purposes of the final ceremony are to welcome the crew back home; to thank the crew members; to hear the negotiators' report about the bride price, the expenses, and any conditions imposed by the bride's family; to show respect and honor to each individual crew member; to thank the family relatives for their assistance; and to bring the wedding ceremony to a close. The most important part of this final dining and drinking has to do with the stipends and rewards given to each of the crew members in appreciation of their vital roles and invaluable time. As mentioned earlier, the stipends consist of money (*ib nplooj ntawv ua dej siab dej ntsws losi ib lub nyuag qes rau koj*) and pork ribs (*ib tug me ntses*). The two negotiators usually receive $100 each and all other crew members get $20 each. Here is an example of one of the Hmong appreciative expressions:

> *Ua tsaug..mog, txiv tuam mej koob, luag tej laus piv txoj lus hais tias, txawj ces yog koj txawj, kab tshoob kev kos ces yog koj txuj, peb vam khom koj mus nrog peb ua tshoob ua kos ntas tshoob ntas kos, koj tso qav tso num tseg, koj mus nyiaj tshaib yoog nqis duab hnub hmo ntuj...* [In English, thank you so very much, lead go-between negotiator. As the Hmong elders say, knowing is your skill, the wedding ceremony is your art. We depended on you to master the wedding, and you left your other duties behind. You did this by starving with thirst day and night...]
>
> *Hnub no koj coj tub coj nyab los tsog vaj tsog tsev, yog peb txawj ua lub neej xws luag ces peb yuav muaj kab phaj raws ntsuag zoo los ua koj ib los tsaug, peb twb tsis txawj ua lub neej, es peb twb tsis muaj ib zoo pib dej pib cawv los ua koj ib los tsaug ... mog...*[In English, today you brought the son and daughter-in-law back home. If we lived a normal life as others do, we would have a lavish meal ready to thank you. We do not live a normal life as others do, so we do not have wonderful drinks to thank you...]
>
> *Hnub qab nram lub ntsi yog koj muaj tub muaj ntxhais qua, koj vam tsis txog peb los tseg, yog koj vam txog peb, txawm peb tsis muaj nyiaj muaj txiaj tuaj pab koj, los peb yuav coj lub dag lub zog tuaj pab nrog koj li pluas noj pluas haus kos tau raws li koj siab xav, peb yuav coj lub dag lub zog tuaj pab koj li pluas noj pluas haus kom tau raws li koj siab nyiam hos mog ... ua tsaug...* [In English, some day in the near future, if you have a wedding for your son or daughter, it

is all right if you do not want our help. If you want our help, even if we do not have money to help you, we will be there to help you perform all the duties you would like us to as you like them. We will be there to help perform all the duties according to your expectations.... Thank you...]

These are typical phrases used in expressions of thanks. With minor changes they can be worded appropriately for any individual. Once all crew members have received their stipends, rewards, and thanks and everyone has finished eating and drinking, the wedding ceremony finally comes to a close. Family relatives leave, a few designated drivers transport any intoxicated crew members home, and the newlywed couple should live happily thereafter.

Polygamy Is Not a Hmong Tradition

Where Hmong have learned the practice of polygamy from is a mystery. Polygamy is not a matrimonial norm in Hmong culture. In the old days, some men married multiple wives because having more than one wife boosted their socioeconomic standing and they could afford them, but the practice was never an accepted part of Hmong life. In fact, the high bride price of the past made the practice virtually impossible for all, but very wealthy men. Polygamy has never been a Hmong cultural practice, but a personal lifestyle choice of a few. Some Hmong women as well as men have made this choice. For example, it is culturally acceptable for a widow to marry her dead husband's younger brother regardless of his marital status. Today polygamy is a hidden socio-cultural predicament in the Hmong community.

In his 2002 article, "Hmong elders must condemn cruel polygamy," Vang explained that polygamy is not part of Hmong culture and traditions, and he encouraged Hmong leaders to condemn the practice of polygamy in the U.S.:

> The Hmong have 18 distinctive clans, each with its own distinct culture and values. In every clan, family unity and marital fidelity

are highly valued. Polygamy is considered a violation of trust and/or an act of infidelity.

In Hmong marriage customs, polygamy is unacceptable. Hmong wedding proverbs condemn marital disloyalty, adultery, and spousal treason for both sexes. Most Hmong elders would promote a household with only one husband and one wife.

[...]

Many Hmong prefer to keep silent on this subject because it is a sensitive issue. But it needs to be addressed; otherwise, it will remain an unsolved mystery and will continue to haunt Hmong future generations.

If polygamy is not condemned loudly and strongly, younger Hmong will inaccurately accept it as culturally appropriate. Their elders will not be able to stop them from bringing the humiliation and heartache of this non–Hmong practice to another generation. It will cause more harm than good to Hmong families, culture, traditions, and communities.

Last, but not least, polygamy is a part of neither Hmong religious values and beliefs nor Hmong culture and traditions. In fact, polygamy is an inventive marriage of a person who chooses to go against his own people, culture, and traditions.

Summing Up

This chapter gave details of Hmong traditional wedding ceremonies and discussed the contemporary practices that most Hmong currently use. Today, Hmong are living in a dual society and many have two wedding ceremonies. Hmong have changed the way they conduct their traditional wedding ceremonies, but for the most part, they have retained the core of Hmong marital formalities and proceedings.

Hmong marriage customs originated shortly after the Great Flood that destroyed the earth centuries ago. According to Hmong legends, the two sons who survived the flood created the traditional Hmong wedding ceremony and chants. Other legends say the wedding chants or songs were learned from an old dragon by two siblings, a brother and a sister, who survived the Great Flood. The brother and sister married and created the 12 Hmong clans to repopulate the barren world.

There are many types of Hmong marriages: *tshoob zawj* (in-person proceedings), *tshoob zij* (kidnapping, catch-hand, or bride-capture), *tshoob yuam* (forced), tshoob coj (mutual consent or elopement), *tshoob raws* (follow-him-home), *tshoob niam yau* (second wife), *tshoob poj ntsuam* (widow marriage), and *tshoob poj nrauj* (divorced marriage). Hmong marriages are made through mutual consent, elopement, force, bride-capture, engagement, or parental arrangement. Some of these practices are now obsolete.

The traditional Hmong wedding ceremony requires a lot of manpower, which is supplied by crews from both the groom's and the bride's families. The entire ceremony with its many parts usually takes at least two days. A number of ceremonial events precede the main ceremony. The proceedings begin in the groom's home, move to the bride's family's home, and return to the groom's family's home. All traditional Hmong weddings follow this progression without exception, regardless of any modifications made to the specific parts of the ceremony. The feasting part is a lot of fun, but the drinking part is heavy and can cause problems.

The bride price is not a price for purchasing a Hmong daughter. Rather it is a token of honor, an expression of the value of the bride. The Hmong dowry is a gift not to the groom, but to the bride, given by her parents. It is often costly, so the expenses of both families—the groom's for the bride price and the bride's for the dowry—may very well be the same. As contentious as financial matters associated with a wedding can be, they are not the main concern at a Hmong wedding. As Hmong elders say, "*Tus tau neeg yog tus yeej*," meaning, "The one who got the person is the winner."

Eight

Hmong Funeral Services and Practices

Ua neej nyob…
Ib leeg muaj ib daim lag zeb nplua…
Ib leeg muaj ib txoj sia…
Txoj kev muaj mob…
Txoj kev ploj txoj kev tuag…
Tsis muaj leej twg hla dhau…
A Hmong funeral ritual riddle

Introduction

The Buddhist concept of karma holds that the beauty and struggle of one's present life are pre-determined by the goodness or evil in one's previous life. Hmong picture a person's life as a walk on slippery stepping stones; one day one will slip and fall. In this metaphor, death is the final step of life in the physical world. Hmong pray for the afterlife in the spiritual world to be blissful. In another metaphor, Hmong see the physical world as a sinful city of all living beings in which no one was born perfect. Once one has descended from heaven to the earth, the existing sins are attracted to the new body, soul, and spirits. Sicknesses and death are unavoidable in the sinful city. This chapter describes some of the Hmong beliefs about death, the funeral practices of traditional Hmong families, the relationship between life in the physical world and life in the spiritual world, and the implications of that relationship.

Origins of Funeral Practices

The world's oldest person can live to the ripe old age of 110. However, in the Hmong world the ripe old age is 120 years when a person dies (*puv 120 xyoo* in Hmong). Hmong use the phrase "120 years old" to refer to death regardless of the age of a person at the time of death. This symbolic phrase has been embedded in Hmong funeral rites and rituals for thousands of years. Every Hmong knows the expression simply means death has occurred. No one knows where the phrase came from or how it was brought into Hmong funeral services and rituals. Perhaps in the ancient world the oldest Hmong lived to be 120 years old. Or perhaps the phrase was a symbolic description of the maximum life span that could be expected. Or it could be that because no one has lived to 120 years the phrase implied a ripe old age or death. Hmong also use different words and phrases, such as *tuag, qaug, tag sim neej, siav tu, ncaim lawm, tso sawv daws tseg, must tav toj tav taug, losi mus ev ntsev lawm*, to refer to death.

When asked about the origins of Hmong funeral practices, Hmong elders say their ancestors and forefathers have followed the current practices for thousands of years (*poj ua tseg yawm ua cia losi poj koob yawg koob ib txwm coj thiab ua los*). They offer no clear documentation regarding the origin of the practices or how they evolved over time. Hmong rely heavily on oral tradition for all of their rituals, rites, and ceremonies. The lack of documentation explains the variations in details of the practices among the different Hmong families or tribes.

Do Hmong have a religious book? The answer is no. Hmong have not had any religious scripture, textbook, or manuscript to guide their religious rites and ritual practices until recently. Prior to 1975, Hmong had only oral tradition and personal narratives of Hmong elders who inherited the religious rites and funeral rituals from their parents and clan leaders. No one knew how the customs started. Sadly, part of the problem is that most Hmong elders and religious leaders are illiterate in the Hmong language as well as in the other languages they speak, such as Chinese, Lao, Thai, and Vietnamese. Therefore, when and how the funeral rituals began is a mystery. However, Hmong believe their religious traditions and practices can be traced back nearly 6,000 years.

What other cultures influenced Hmong funeral practices? Although Hmong characterize their religious practices as ancestor worship and animism, they also include mixtures of different religious rites found in Confucianism, Buddhism, Hinduism, Taoism, and Islam. Hmong incorporated elements of these belief systems into the way they understand and deal with death. Buddhism had a tremendous influence on Hmong religious practices. Hmong believe in some forms of karma and nirvana, concepts found in Buddhism and Hinduism. Specifically, Hmong believe in reincarnation of the soul and the new life, the connection between the dead and the living, and the life-long worship of ancestors' spirits. Hmong death rituals and rites are similar to those in the Tibetan Book of the Dead and the Egyptian Book of Death.

What do Hmong believe about death? Hmong believe there is a heaven or nirvana, a life after death, but they believe the soul of the deceased returns to the spiritual world to meet the familial ancestors instead of going straight to heaven. Hmong believe the ancestral spirits live in the spiritual world, but not in heaven. Hmong believe that at death the soul of the deceased leaves the physical world and enters the spiritual world to restart the life cycle through the process of reincarnation. Hmong also believe that the dead person will come back to the same family, or be born again, as a new family member once his or her soul has been completely reincarnated. However, the metamorphosis of the soul during the reincarnation process is not clearly revealed in Hmong religious tenets and remains a mystery because some believe the reincarnation of the soul is only to allow the deceased to be born again into a different form of life, and that new life after death may include both human and/or animal forms. Others may strongly believe the existence of the heavenly angel or godly mother (*niam nkauj kab yeeb* in Hmong) who has the spiritual power to help the soul reincarnate into a human form again. Today, most Hmong still believe the Karma in Buddhism: *The beauty and struggle of one's present life is pre-determined and pre-destined by his goodness or evil in his previous life.* This could mean that the goodness in life may allow the deceased to be reincarnated with beauty and prosperity whereas the evil in life may curse the deceased to be reincarnated with struggle and hardship.

Why are funeral practices so important to Hmong? The sole purpose of conducting a thorough funeral service is to help the soul of the deceased navigate the long journey back in time to meet his ancestors in the spiritual world and begin the process of reincarnation. The funeral service has three mandatory stages: (1) the funeral service with the traditional death rituals (*lub ntee tuag*), (2) the after-death ritual conducted to invite the soul of the deceased to visit the home before releasing it to the spiritual world (*ua xi or puv ib tsug 13 hnub*), and (3) the final release ritual performed before releasing the soul for reincarnation or rebirth (*tsog plig*). Hmong believe that the family members left behind must complete all three stages in order for the soul of the deceased to complete the journey in the spiritual world. Failure to do so may bring spiritual harm and curses to the living family members.

How do Hmong learn their religious rituals and practices? Today Hmong have textbooks, video tapes, CDs, and audiotapes to teach them their traditions and to reinforce their learning. Cultural classes are available to those who want to learn the basic Hmong religious rites, death rituals, and funeral service protocols. Learning these rituals inside the home is prohibited because some rites are not suitable to be heard inside an occupied residence where a family lives. The best way to learn Hmong funeral practices is at a funeral home or at a location outside the home established for the purpose of religious education.

Normally, Hmong learn religious rituals through direct observation, emulation, and hands-on experience. Cultural classes teach the practice of the Hmong lushen, the bamboo reed pipe instrument (*qeej*); the death drum; death chants and songs; and marriage customs. Textbooks, CDs, audio tapes, and DVDs are widely available for practice and reinforcement. Some Hmong religious chants and rituals are not appropriate to be sung in public place or inside the occupied residence of any family.

Birth and Predestination

Understanding Hmong thoughts about death begins with an understanding of the meanings Hmong place on life and birth. Hmong believe that every birth is a gift from the highest God in the sky and every living being is born for a specific purpose in life. A birth requires the involvement of the ancestors of both biological parents and the familial ancestral spirits. Hmong believe that the children of a family come from the reincarnation of the souls of the dead ancestors, great grandparents, and grandparents.

According to Hmong legends, the time, day, month, and year of a child's birth determines the life of that child in the physical world (*ntiaj teb*) because he was sent by the spiritual world to fulfill a pre-determined life span. Hmong often seek out psychic readers (*saib yaig*), fortune tellers (*saib hmoov*), and psychotherapeutic spirits (*saib plig*) of shamans to tell them their fates as well as to explain their situations when life is difficult and seems spiritually unbalanced. For instance, symptoms of sickness may be caused by the soul wandering in search of spiritual release. If this is the case, a shaman or other person who can communicate with the spiritual world may be able to discover the cause and suggest a cure. These people can also help Hmong learn something about their predestined fates determined by their time of birth.

Hmong measure time by the Hmong zodiac cycle, which is similar to the Chinese zodiac; the Hmong lunar cycle, which is similar to the French calendar; the four seasons of the harvest and cultivation; and the position of the sun. Hmong believe the relationship of the time a child is born to all these factors directly influences the way the child is sent by the spiritual world (*yeeb ceeb*) to live in the physical world (*yaj ceeb*). However, Hmong have not been able to factor in to this religious predestination the presence or absence of opportunities and obstacles in the physical world. For instance, the various calendars may say that a child is born at a prosperous time, but without educational opportunity, the child may not be able to advance to the life predestined by his sender.

Hmong use the same 12 animal signs that are in the Chinese zodiac but their interpretations of the signs are different from those of Chinese. For example, Hmong do not see the dragon sign the same way as Chinese. The dragon has not been a symbolic part of Hmong culture. Hmong refer to the dragon as the original master of Hmong cultural and traditional rites, chants, and rituals.

According to the Hmong way of understanding birth and life, when children are born, they bring with them a few supports given to them by guardian angels in the spiritual world. The life supports include a declaration of life and living (*daim ntawv los ua neej*), a declaration of survival (*daim ntawv los ua noj ua haus*), a declaration of marriage (*daim ntawv los ua niam txiv*), and a decla-ration of reincarnation or rebirth after death (*daim ntawv thawj thiab*). Throughout life, these declarations are used to determine the child's challenges, opportunities, progress, and success. Moreover, the child's overall health may also be predestined by these dec-larations.

These declarations are pre-determined messages written on the palms prior to indi-viduals taking the long journey from the spir-itual world to the physical world—that is, prior to birth. The predestined messages are engraved on the left palms of men and on the right palms of women. Hmong read the palms of both hands. For a man, the left palm fore-tells predestined messages of life about the self and the right palm foretells the predes-tined life of a partner of the self. Palm readers have been known to misguide people, mis-interpreting the messages. Inaccurate read-ings could make people feel better or worse about themselves and their futures than is warranted.

Reading the declarations on the palms early in life may not tell the whole story. The declarations may carry hidden messages that will become clear at later times. For instance, a poor or sick child may become wealthy or healthy in adulthood and a well-off or healthy child may become poor or unhealthy in adulthood.

The declaration of life and living reveals the physical and mental capacity of the child: physical fitness, mental capability, cognitive functioning, intellectual acuity, and natural ability. These characteristics help predict life situation and life span as well as socioeco-nomic status and general health. Life situa-tion is generally not static; it has ups and downs. As Hmong see the typical progression of life, the normal life cycle has three downs and three ups: "*Kev ua neej yuav tsum qia peb zaug ntug peb zaug mas thiaj li zoo kav laus.*"

The declaration of survival pre-determines a person's luck and fortunes in farming the land, trading goods, earning an income, sav-ing money, and educating the mind. As Hmong fortune tellers explain, the first and second declarations are connected, and the

connection indicates what the person's eco-nomic future will be. Today, Hmong in the U.S. have a safety net that provides a measure of fortune to all so that no one need worry about survival. However, everyone can take advantage of opportunities before them and strive for far more than survival.

The declaration of marriage predicts the child's ability to be successful in love, ro-mance, courtship, and marriage. Hmong be-lieve that every male child is missing a rib and that missing rib was given to his future mate before his descent from the spiritual world to the physical world. While living in the physical world, the male child searches for his predestined partner who has his miss-ing rib. If he decides to marry, it must be the person who was given his missing rib. Di-vorce does not fit with this concept, but Hmong believe that life makes adjustments for social changes. The idea of the missing rib may make sense in a marriage between two Hmong, but what about an interracial marriage? The declaration of marriage has to be applied in the cultural context in which Hmong understand birth.

Hmong also believe one's fortune in life (*muaj hmoos*) is partly based on one's kind-ness in the present life rather than deter-mined solely by the past life. However, Hmong also believe that a fortunate life is partly de-termined by the declarations of life and liv-ing, survival, and marriage because one may outlive, outwit, and outscore others by one's own natural abilities. Moreover, the name given to a child at birth is spiritually and re-ligiously important. The child may accept or reject the name he is given but, as explained in a previous chapter, the child needs to be named properly so that his soul and spirits are happy to carry that name for the rest of his life. If they are not, the child may be sick often. Sometimes the diagnostic rituals of a shaman reveal that a name change is required.

Finally, *the declaration of reincarnation* is what allows the individual to be reborn after death in the physical world. Hmong believe the soul of the dead body travels back in time to retrieve its original Hmong costumes or silk coat (*lub tsho tsuj tsho npuag*) and to meet its ancestors' spirits in the spiritual world before beginning the reincarnation process. Hmong believe that sometimes the soul has been reincarnated before the physical body actually dies or even before the person gets sick and finally passes away. For this reason, Hmong believe the declaration of reincarnation should be short; if it is going to expire, the person may need an extension in order to live long enough for the soul to be brought back to the physical body so it can begin its journey in the spiritual world properly. To accomplish this, a shaman can perform a ritual to extend the reincarnation period and enable the sick person to live longer. The ritual is called "*Ua neeb ntxiv ntaub ntxiv ntawv*," meaning "adding more reincarnation time" to a living soul of a body.

Remember, in the Hmong belief system, the soul of the dead body does not go directly to heaven but goes to meet the ancestors in the spiritual world. This is contrary to the thinking of some Christian Hmong who actually believe the soul of the dead goes straight to heaven or hell.

Concepts of Heaven and Hell

According to Hmong beliefs, when a person dies, his soul returns to the spiritual world to be with his family ancestors in order to start the normal life cycle again. Hmong do not believe the soul goes to heaven (*ntuj ceeb tsheej* in Hmong) or hell (*ntuj cub tawg* in Hmong) after death. Eternity is neither expressed clearly as a religious faith in Hmong death rituals nor as a spiritual prophecy for the soul reincarnation; however, Hmong believe the soul of the deceased will remain with the family's ancestral spirits forever until reincarnation takes place in the spiritual world. The Hmong funeral rites (*txheej txheem ua ntees losi kev cai pheem tsheej*), death rituals (*kab ke pam tuag*), songs for the dead (*nkauj tuag*), and funeral blessing chants (*txiv xaiv*) do not contain the words heaven or hell. The words heaven (*ceeb tsheej*) and hell (*dej kub dej npau losi ntuj cub tawg*) were introduced to Hmong in the mid–1900s by Catholic and other Christian missionaries. Prior to that time, Hmong used the words *physical world* (*yaj ceeb*) and *spiritual world* (*yeeb ceeb*) for the places of the living and nonliving. *Yaj ceeb* is the place occupied by the living and *Yeeb ceeb* is where all nonliving belong with the spirits of the ancestors. Similarly, *Yaj ceeb* and *Yeeb ceeb* somewhat reflect the ideology of Chinese *Yan* and *Yin*; however, Hmong do not have a symbolic logo for these words. Literally, the Hmong word "*ceeb*" means being, place, location, town, city, or capital. *Yaj* refers to the physical nature and *Yeeb* means the underground world or spiritual nature. Hmong use the word *sky* to refer to the highest being (*saum ntuj*) because the sky is the highest thing the eye can see and a being in the sky can see and know everything all living beings are doing on earth. In most cases, Hmong refer to the highest God in the sky when Hmong summon Heaven and Earth Spirits for protection and guidance.

Traditional Hmong families use the *Showing the Way* chant (*zaj qhuab ke losi zaj taw kev*) to guide their loved ones from the physical world to the spiritual world on a journey back in time where they can meet with their dead ancestors and ancestral spirits. Since the mid–1900s, Christian Hmong families have abandoned this traditional belief, asserting that the soul of the dead actually goes to heaven or, if the person has committed sinful acts in the physical world, to hell. But traditional Hmong families believe the soul of the deceased travels back in time through places such as its birthplace, city of residence, fields, land, hills, mountains, snow, deserts, and thorny pastures to meet its ancestral spirits in the spiritual world.

Hmong also use the term *Yaj Teb* in place of *Yaj Ceeb* and *Yeeb Teb* in place of *Yeeb Ceeb*. However, Hmong shamans prefer *Yaj Ceeb* and *Yeeb Ceeb* to refer to the physical and spiritual worlds during their spiritual trances and rituals. Prior to the influences of western religions, Hmong usually described the northern world as *Tuam Tshoj Teb* and the southern world as *Xov Tshoj Teb*. Moreover, according to Hmong Chinese legends, Hmong referenced a heavenly place in the physical world known as *Ceeb Tsheej*, meaning present-day Beijing. When they lived in the Yellow and Yangtze River basins in the ancient world, present-day central China, Hmong believed dead persons went to rest in Beijing, a heavenly place in the physical world.

In traditional Hmong death rituals, the words heaven and hell are not used as the final destination for the soul, but these words are uttered in the physical world by western religious practitioners. For instance, the traditional Hmong religious rite called Offering to the Dead (*ntawg rau losi laig rau*), which is performed many times during funerals, says nothing about heaven and hell. It says, "If you cannot eat or consume all, put or stuff some in the gourd; if you cannot drink or swallow all, pour or stuff some in the bamboo container and take it along to share with your grandmother and grandfather." In Hmong: "*Noj tsis tag ntim nruab taub, haus tsis tag ntim nruab rag, coj mus pub pog pub yawg noj, coj mus pub pog pub yawg haus nov tos….*" The offerings that accompany these words include liquor, draft animals, chickens, pigs, and spiritual money. The idea is that the deceased takes the items offered not to heaven or hell, but to a grandmother and grandfather in the spiritual world.

The concepts of heaven and hell are relatively new to Hmong because the traditional death rituals do not reference these words or places. However, the absence of heaven and hell from Hmong rituals does not prove or disprove whether these places are real. One's faith is what convinces a person of what he practices and follows. No one really knows what life after death is like except God.

Hmong Response to Death

Death comes to every family. Everyone has a day of birth and a day of death. Death is the most devastating phenomenon that can occur in the physical world because death causes a separation in a family that lasts forever. Death also divides family members between two different worlds, the physical world and the spiritual world. Hmong take the death of any family member seriously. They often say that death means that one cannot stand up with one foot (*ib txhais taw sawv tsis ntseg*), or one cannot clap with one hand (*ib txhais te npuaj tsis nrov*). These metaphors illustrate the great loss in the family that comes with death. Symbolically, Hmong express death solemnly in this way, "*Cuag li ntuj niam tsis nqus nws te, ntuj txiv nqus nws taw,*" meaning, "like the heavenly mother does not grab his hand, the heavenly father pulls his leg." This phrase implies that he is deceased or has fallen.

A death in the family affects all family members. The family gathers immediately to comfort one another and to prepare for the funeral service. In traditional Hmong families, the house spirits may be traumatized by the loss as well if family members are crying and wailing out of control inside the home. Someone covers the altar or shrine with a piece of paper money to tell the house spirits that the family is dealing with a loss of life. In Christian Hmong families, the death of a family member is less traumatizing because family members accept the religious belief that the deceased is with God in heaven.

Traditionally, family members mourn to express their love and affection for the deceased. The wailing and crying can be very emotional and some family members might lose control as they express their grief. Sometimes sensitive information is revealed during the public wailing. Personal conduct during these times may not be considerate and polite, but this loud and deep mourning is part of Hmong tradition. A typical expression of Hmong condolences goes something like this: "There is nothing in this sinful world that is able to erase death or raise the dead to life again, and there is nothing in this sinful world that is sadder than the death of a loved one. Therefore, my final farewell is to tell the deceased to meet his ancestors in the spiritual world, to ask for a new declaration of life and living, and to return to the physical world to live one more time."

Christian Hmong families give their condolences differently because they believe the soul of the deceased goes to Heaven (*ntuj ceeb tsheej*). Traditional Hmong mourners, however, do not express their condolences in reference to heaven. Rather, they encourage the deceased to make a journey back into the spiritual world to meet with his ancestors and ask for new declarations of life so they can return to the physical world. A mourner bringing an offering gift to the deceased would say, "Giving you this flower, take it with you to the spiritual world to help you farm in the rice field to give you food, to help you work in the paddies to give you clothes. Take it to help you live in the spiritual world." In Hmong, "*Muab lub paj no rau koj, coj mus ua neej nyob yeeb teb, coj mus tam teb kom tau noj, coj mus tam liaj kom tau hnav, coj mus ua lub neej tshiab nyob lawm yeeb teb mog*." Similarly, offering paper money to the deceased is meant to help him pay for his incurred debts and fees along to way to the spiritual world or to help him build his new home to start a new life over again in the ancestral world.

Funeral Service Expenses

For Hmong, a death ritual is the final celebration of the life of the dead person and the final ceremony of the soul. Hmong believe that the funeral service is the final farewell to the soul of the dead person. They therefore make heavy sacrifices to send the dead back to the spiritual world with all the things they will need on their journey to meet with their family ancestral spirits to restart a new cycle of life through the reincarnation process. Hmong have a catchy phrase that describes the heavy sacrifices they make for the dead: "*Niam txiv tuag vaj tsev ntuag*," meaning, "The parents died; the house is torn-broken."

In the old days, at the death of a parent an expensive funeral was inevitable. An average traditional Hmong funeral lasted three to five full days, depending on the family's means. Normally, the living sons of the family were responsible for all funeral expenses and death rituals of their deceased parents. If there was no living son, the family relatives would chip in to cover the costs. The financial burden rested on the sons; they fulfilled the spiritual offering requirements in order to receive spiritual blessings after their deaths. The re-

quirements were costly. The typical offering was one or two draft animals (bulls, cows, or buffalos) or one or two pigs. Bulls or cows were the preferred offering, and families often went into debt to secure the offering. Sadly, in some cases, poor sons had to sell one of their own children in order to buy a draft animal for the spiritual offering or borrow money from rich relatives using their children, crops, or land as collateral.

Today the average Hmong funeral lasts at least three full days. As Table 8.1 illustrates, funeral expenses could amount to tens of thousands of dollars. Excluding any financial assistance from family relatives and friends, a Hmong family runs up a hefty bill for every death in the family. An average funeral costs $10,000 to $15,000; a medium-sized funeral could cost $20,000 to $40,000; and the price tag on a large funeral could be $40,000 to $70,000. In rare cases, funerals have cost $100,000. Christian Hmong families are able to keep funeral expenses to $6,000 to $10,000 per death. The amount of these expenses begs the thought-provoking question: *What is it that Hmong have not done to reduce the costs of their traditional funeral services?*

Hmong funerals are expensive in terms of time. They involve family members, friends, and members of the Hmong community. Hmong elders have a saying that describes the reciprocity entailed in supporting one another during the time of a death: "When others die, you die with them; so when you die, they will die with you." Simply, this means that when a death occurs, one should help without being asked; then when one has a death in the family, others will come to help without being asked. As expressed in Hmong, "*Luag tuag yuav tau nrog luag tuag, thaum yus tuag luag thiaj nrog yus tuag*" or, in short, "*kev sib pauv zog*." This phrase illustrates the strength of the unity in the Hmong community in the time of need, especially at a death.

Today, Hmong families do not have to sell their children to pay for the funeral expenses because they can borrow money from private lenders or use titles to their cars as collateral. However, Hmong funeral expenses are exorbitant and funeral practices need to be

Table 8.1. Expenses for Traditional Hmong Funeral Services

Item	Average Cost	Purpose
Funeral home services	$4,000	Transporting the body, preserving the body in the morgue, preparing the body, embalming the body with formaldehyde, dressing the body
Hmong funeral services and facility rental	$8,000	Renting facility or traditional Hmong funeral services and death rituals for three full days for 24 hours per day
Casket	$3,000	Container for the body
Burial plot	$4,000	Place in which to bury the body
Sacrificial draft animals	$6,000	Death of a parent or married person requires at least four draft animals (*txiv cuab tsav, muam phauj/txiv dab laug, cuas nyab, cuas ntxhais…*)
Sacrificial animals (pigs, chickens)	$2,000	Slaughter for food and ritual purposes
Traditional costumes, shrouds, shoes	$1,000	Clothing and miscellaneous items for the dead
Food for funeral	$7,000	Meals for three days of the services
Food for time prior to the funeral	$3,000	Meals served on the day of death at the home of the dead or family members
Funeral crew members	$3,000	Miscellaneous costs
Escort services	$2,000	Two to four escort officers for escort from funeral home to gravesite
Funeral decorations and miscellaneous expenses	$2,000	Seat covers, flowers, etc.
All other expenses	$2,000	Expenses not covered above

reevaluated and modernized in order to reduce unnecessary costs. If the status quo is maintained, the costly, time consuming, and tedious nature of the practices may prompt Hmong to adopt religious faiths that are less complex and demanding.

To illustrate how terribly expensive traditional Hmong funerals are, Table 8.2 shows the costs of the services of the seven most important service providers if they were paid $20 per hour. For a four-day funeral service at an average of 10 hours per day, the top

Table 8.2. Cost of Top Seven Hmong Funeral Service Participants if Paid by Hour

Participant	Hourly Wage	Friday	Saturday	Sunday	Monday	Total Cost
Master of ritual and funeral service (*cuab tsav*)	$20	10 hours	10 hours	10 hours	10 hours	$ 800
Funeral director (*kav xwm*)	$20	10 hours	10 hours	10 hours	10 hours	$ 800
Reed bamboo pipe player (*txiv qeej*)	$20	10 hours	10 hours	10 hours	10 hours	$ 800
Drummer (*txiv nruas*)	$20	10 hours	10 hours	10 hours	10 hours	$ 800
Lead singer of blessing (*txiv xaiv*)	$20	10 hours	10 hours	10 hours	10 hours	$ 800
Family representative (*thawj xyom cuab*)	$20	10 hours	10 hours	10 hours	10 hours	$ 800
Path pointer or death guide (*tus qhuab ke*)	$20	10 hours	0	0	0	$ 200
Total		70 hours	60 hours	60 hours	60 hours	$5,000

seven providers will spend a total of 250 hours, amounting to $5,000 in hourly wage costs. Most of these people are volunteers and perform their duties free of charge, and most give more than 10 hours per day. And these are only some of the people who are needed. Even though the services associated with death are very important to Hmong, Hmong may have to think of other ways to achieve the same ends in order to preserve the Hmong way of life for future centuries; otherwise, the requirements of death may eclipse the meaning of life.

Funeral Service Preparation

According to Hmong Chinese legends, Hmong practiced cliff, barrel, and cave burial in China prior to their migration to Southeast Asia. Some Hmong families practiced cremation, bone washing, and corpse preservation in China and in Southeast Asia. Today, most Hmong practice only whole-body burial with complex and rich death rituals and costly funeral services.

When a Hmong dies today in the U.S., the deceased's family makes preparations for the funeral service. Before death, the deceased may have instructed the survivors what to do in fulfilling his final wishes. In Hmong culture, children usually ask their dying parents if there is anything they can do during the funeral service to make them feel special. Dying parents usually just want a peaceful funeral where everyone is happy. A caring Hmong parent knows that the funeral service is expensive and any specific request that is made will cost the survivors more money. The parent does not want to leave his survivors with debts or have them argue with one another over expenses. In the West, the dead body is transported to the funeral home for embalming, but in the East, the body is kept at home.

In a traditional Hmong family, a family gathering takes place with immediate family relatives from near and far. Typically, family members are selected to fill different roles in planning and executing the funeral service in accordance with Hmong traditions. Because immediate family members are mourning the death, they assume a lighter role except for the financial burden. The logistics of planning and preparation varies from family to family, but the sequence of events leading to the day of the funeral service can be organized in an orderly fashion. Here are some simple steps that traditional Hmong families generally follow:

1. Immediate family members make sure the home of the deceased or a designated family member is ready for the influx of relatives. Traditionally, a ritual called Guarding the Night (zov hmo) starts right away. All the busyness and commotion takes place in the home until the funeral day. When a person dies, that person's whole family and his close relatives are considered victims (tsev xyom cuab).

2. Immediate family members and close relatives locate a funeral home or community chapel for the funeral service. Once the funeral home is reserved, the family picks a date for the funeral. Then all immediate family members and all marital kin living near and far are notified so they can accommodate their needs for traveling to the funeral.

3. Immediate family members find a burial plot for the deceased at a local cemetery. When the gravesite is purchased, immediate family members buy at least four cows for sacrificial purposes during the funeral service. The animals have to be large enough that no one of the involved parties or guests will reject them.

4. Immediate family members select a casket for the deceased. The selection is culturally and spiritually sensitive, so it is recommended that an elder person accompany the immediate family members to the funeral home to choose the right casket.

5. Immediate family members assemble a crew that will decorate the funeral home in accordance with the family traditions and customs of the death rituals. Most families practice the covered funeral rite (*Hmoob pos*) although some prefer the sun-exposed rite (*Hmoob tshwm tshav*).

6. Immediate family members hold a meeting with the relatives (*thooj dab koom*

qhua) that share the same family ancestry and religious beliefs to assemble a funeral crew (*thawj lwm tub ncig*). This crew includes, but is not limited to, the people listed in Table 8.3. Crew members need to be formally honored (*tiam thawj lwm tub ncig*) inside the funeral home on the second day of the funeral or prior to the funeral. The lead chanter of blessing (*tiam tus txiv xaiv*) is honored separately. Typically, these crew members have been informally inducted by the family members and representatives prior to the funeral. The family will need a lot of helpers (*tub qav tub num*) in order to keep the service flowing smoothly.

7. Immediate family members properly notify (*hu hauv qhua*) the required participants or summoned guests who are entitled to sit at the service table in accordance with marital kinship, as shown in Table 8.4. There are two groups of funeral guests. The first group is called the major group (*hauv qhua txooj*), meaning guests with lots of funeral responsibilities. Members of this group are obligated to slaughter a cow or tilt the umbrella (*tuaj tua nyuj losi tuaj qaij kaus*) and bid farewell to the deceased (*ua qab thu*) for the very last time.

To call these special guests, two special representatives, usually the funeral directors or chiefs of operation (*ob tug kav xwm*), go to their homes to request the honor of their presence at the funeral. Religiously, to kill a cow, the messenger has to carry an arrow (*ris xub* in Hmong) on the back to the house of the guests, and to kill a water buffalo, the messenger has to carry a small branch of green leaves (*ris nplooj* in Hmong) on the back to the house. This process could be difficult. Guests who live out of town will be honored by family relatives living near them or the notification will be made when the guests arrive at the funeral. Although some flexibility is permitted, the honor has to be done properly regardless of the situation.

The second group of guests is called the minor group (*hauv qhua tab*), meaning guests with little responsibility. Members of this group come to pay respect and offer their love and condolences to the deceased's family

because of marital relationship or friendship. Both groups come on the second day of the funeral, and members of the major group go in before members of the minor group.

Family members inform other relatives and friends via social media or telephone (*tso moo*). They also invite members of the community to come to pay respect and tribute or offer condolences for the very last time (*tuaj pab hlub ua zaum kawg*).

8. Immediate family members compile a list of all food and supplies needed for the three- to four-day funeral service, including gas tanks, cooking supplies, utensils, trash cans, drinks, coffee, etc.

9. Immediate family members arrange and coordinate the delivery of all draft animals to be offered to the deceased before transporting them to the slaughter house. The sacrificial animals have to be offered to the deceased before they are butchered.

10. Immediate family members make sure the Hmong traditional costumes, clothes, shoes, shroud, sacrificial rooster, pig, crossbow, washcloth, wine bottle, and other funeral items are ready. The deceased will need a few layers of clothing for protection during the journey (*tiv luaj tiv av*), a coat (*tsho tshaj sab*), a headband (*siv ceeb*), a pair of bird shoes (*khau noog*), a pair of hemp shoes (*khau maj khau ntuag*), a shroud (*teem kiam*), death costumes (*ris tsho laus*), and other items.

11. Immediate family member assemble a crew of family members (*tub xyom cuab*) to thank the guests for their donations. This crew may wear simple uniforms or traditional costumes. Name tags and badges are appropriate as well. Wearing a red strip of cloth or a white strip of cloth is also appropriate, depending on the family traditions.

12. Immediate family members designate two persons as recorders to record all donations made by family members, friends, and members of community during the funeral.

13. Immediate family members designate a person to be in charge of all expenses incurred before and during the funeral in order to maintain a good record of all costs involved. Usually, a family member fills this role.

14. Immediate family members prepare themselves for three or four restless days and nights because they will be physically and mentally exhausted when the burial is over.

15. Immediate family members have to depend on their family relatives and close friends for help during this time because their plate is full of things to do before and during the funeral. The family needs both emotional and physical support, and the more people who are willing to help the better the funeral is going to be because the whole funeral is laborious and intense.

These are only examples of what a traditional Hmong family does when there is a death in the family. Each family is unique and everything described above may not be required by a particular family; one has to check with the family elders to make sure of what is needed. In Christian Hmong families, church members become the crew providing the manpower for the required services, and this benevolent assistance relieves the impacted family from major duties. Moreover, Christian Hmong families have less to do because their funeral services are less complex.

There are different types of Hmong funeral rituals and services. For the death of a child or a single individual, the funeral rites are lighter and shorter than for the death of a married individual. The basic funeral service requirements for any death are a funeral crew, a bamboo reed pipe player, a drummer, a cook crew, and some family helpers. Requirements for the death of a parent are greater.

For traditional Hmong families, the success of the funeral depends on the crew members (*thawj lwm tub ncig*), the family representative (*thawj xyom cuab*), and the master

Table 8.3. Traditional Hmong Funeral Crew Members

Title	In Hmong	Roles and Responsibilities
Soul guide or path pointer	Tus qhuab ke losi tus taw kev	Perform the Showing the Way ritual to guide the soul of the deceased
Player of reed bamboo pipe	Txiv qeej	Perform the death song and play the reed pipe
Drummer	Txiv nruas	Play the drum
Family leader	Thawj xyom cuab	Represent or act on behalf of family
Master of ritual or chief of funeral	Cuab tsav	In charge of all rituals and offerings to the deceased
Funeral directors	Kav xwm losi tsav thawj	In charge of funeral operations and functions
Food preparer, arranger, or cook	Tshwj kab losi txiv thwv	Prepare, arrange, and cook food or meals
Rice preparer	Niam ua mov losi niam fam txam	Prepare and cook rice
Custodian or water carrier*	Tshaj thawj thiab siv thawj*	In charge of clean up
Busboy or dishwasher*	Kav tais kav diav*	In charge of washing utensils and cleaning tables
Lantern or lighting manager*	Ywj kab*	In charge of lighting
Casket maker*	Txiv txiag*	Make coffin for the deceased
Grinders, de-hullers, or rice pounders*	Niam diaj zeb tuav cos*	Grind corn, de-hull rice, and prepare uncooked rice
Wood cutters or firewood carriers*	Tshaj thawj*	Chop and collect firewood
War leader or lead fighter**	Tsav rog losi hau rog**	Give warning and fight warfare against enemies
Gun shooter*	Tsav phom*	Shoot the gun and warn the group
Death song chanter	Txiv nkauj	Sing and chant death song
Blessing chanter	Txiv xaiv	Sing and chant blessings

*may not be required or no longer in use
**may not be required; depends on the family's death rituals

Table 8.4. Key Players in the Traditional Hmong Funeral

Relative or Title	In Hmong	Roles and Responsibilities
Master of ritual or chief of funeral	Txiv cuab tsav	In charge of funeral and all offerings to the deceased
Oldest or youngest sister*	Maum phauj*	Manage the funeral service of her brother
Oldest brother or youngest brother*	Txiv dab laug*	Manage the funeral service of his sister
The father of the first or last daughter-in-law	Cuas nyab	Fulfill marital promise of offering the head of a cow
The father of the first or last son-in-law	Cuas ntxhais	Fulfill marital promise of offering the head of a cow
The husband of the mother-in-law**	Niam tais**	Fulfill marital promise of offering the head of a cow
The husband of wife's younger sister**	Niam tais hluas**	Fulfill marital promise of offering the head of a cow
An appointed arbitrator	Txwj laug	Debt collector and arbitrator
The brother of each daughter-in-law**	Xov txiv dab laug**	Fulfill marital obligations
Player of reed bamboo pipe***	Txiv qeej***	Play the reed bamboo pipe and drum
Food arrangers or cooks***	Tshwj kab***	Prepare and cook all meals
Oldest or youngest daughter and son-in-law	Ntxhais vauv zov qauv	Safeguard the body of the deceased

*depends on the gender of the deceased
**may not be required for all funerals
***may not be necessary

of ceremonies (*txiv cuab tsav*). As with Hmong weddings, each funeral is different and two funerals are never done exactly the same way. The functions of the crew members depend on the family's financial burden. In some cases, the crew may assume some of the financial responsibility to relieve the family. It is important to keep in mind that the funeral service is for the dead, not for the living. The deceased would not want his family to suffer financially to the point of being ruined.

In the old days, part of the preparation required finding a peaceful resting place or new home for the deceased. Hmong used to look for a burial plot (*looj mem*) on a slope or the slant of a hill where the dragon bloodline (*mem toj losi sawv toj*) is located because they believe the inner core of a mountain range has a bloodline that belongs to the dragon. If such a place were found and used, the survivors would not only prosper, but also rise to be rulers, leaders, and kings because they had buried their deceased in the right place. In the West, of course, Hmong do not look for such burial plots in cemeteries.

Sacrificial Animals

Religiously, Hmong use this symbolic phrase "coming to tilt the umbrella" to refer to sacrificial animals, as in Hmong, "*tuaj qaij kaus*." The word *tilt* implies killing, butchering, or slaughtering and the word *umbrella* means a sacrificial animal, usually a cow, a bull, a buffalo, or a pig. Culturally, if the father dies, his sister (*maum phauj*) is the primary head quest to tilt the umbrella with the accompany of his wife's brother (*txiv dab laug*) as secondary head quest; and if the mother dies, her brother (*txiv dab laug*) is the primary head quest to tilt the umbrella with the accompany of her husband's sister (*maum phauj*) as secondary head quest. The roles of these primary and secondary head guests are known as *Tuaj nia tsum* (coming to tilt the umbrella) and *tuaj phim tsum* (coming to accompany). Two other head quests who also tilt the umbrella are the father of the daughter-in-law (*cuas nyab*) and the father of the son-in-law (*cuas txhais*). The last person to tilt the most important umbrella is the master of the ceremony (*txiv cuab tsav*) in charge of the funeral service. This special sacrificial animal is the head cow or leading cow (*tus thawj nyug*) offered to the deceased to help guide the soul and spirits through the long journey from the physical world to the spiritual world.

Nobody really knows the rationale behind the use of sacrificial animals; however, it is a long-standing tradition for Hmong funeral services and death rituals. There are many versions of the spiritual tales in regard to the significance of the use of sacrificial animals during death rituals. Different families may have different traditions and different deaths may require different restitutions in the spiritual world. When asked about the use of sacrificial animals, Hmong elders give indirect explanations. Most believe that everything that is done in the physical world will help the soul of the deceased to be reincarnated successfully in the spiritual world.

The most commonly used sacrificial animals are bulls, or *koob nywj* in Hmong; cows, or *koob nywj* in Hmong; pigs, or *koob tswb* in Hmong; goats or rams, or *koob yaj* in Hmong; water buffalos, or *sij koob nywj* in Hmong; and roosters or *koob cib* in Hmong (see Figure 8.1). The sole purpose of these sacrificial animals is to help the deceased and his soul travel a long journey back in time to meet his ancestral spirits in the spiritual world. Hmong believe that the sacrificial animals play a crucial role in the journey (*coj ua luag*) and the reincarnation process (*thov ntawv thawj thiab nrog qab los ua neeg dua*). The rooster guides the soul during the long journey into the spiritual world. Even if Hmong are not sure what the journey is like, they believe the draft animals assist the soul

through the twists and turns of the journey and the reincarnation process. Without the sacrificial animals, Hmong believe, the soul of the deceased will be stranded. As the soul makes its way through the turmoil, debts are incurred along the way. When the soul finally reaches the gate leading into the spiritual world, the gate keepers ask for the sacrificial animals and spiritual money. If the soul cannot show the sacrificial animals and money to the gate keepers, the soul will be denied entrance into the spiritual world until the deceased's survivors make additional sacrificial offerings to remove the blockage.

A blockage means the soul lacks proper documentation from the physical world, and documentation means sacrificial animals and spiritual money given by the survivors. These facts are revealed through the performance of Hmong shamanistic rituals after a curse has been imposed on the survivors. If the soul of the deceased cannot enter the spiritual world, the soul will most likely return to the physical world to ask for help. The survivors will be notified of the assistance the soul needs through spiritual pain and suffering. Hmong have learned over the years that the soul of the deceased cannot travel alone; it has to be accompanied by the sacrificial animals. Otherwise, a poor soul will be rejected by the spiritual world, and in that case, the soul will not be reincarnated as expected by

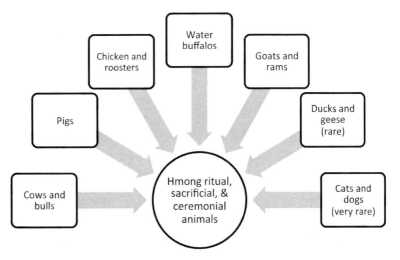

Figure 8.1. Hmong ritual, sacrificial, and ceremonial animals.

the survivors in the physical world. Hmong believe the physical body of the deceased is dead, but the soul lives on. And the soul needs the sacrificial animals for guidance and for making restitution for the sinful deeds done in the physical world in order to be granted entry into the spiritual world with the hope of being reincarnated. This hope is reiterated throughout the lyrics of the death songs sung by the chanters during the funeral service.

Currently there is controversy over the sacrificial animals because so many animals are slaughtered for the funeral but so little meat is used for food for the family. A sacrificial animal killed for a funeral is divided into three parts. The first part belongs to the purchaser, owner, or giver of the animal. The second portion goes to the funeral crew members, usually the funeral directors, lushen player, and drummer. The final third is kept for the family of the deceased. Thus for every sacrificial animal killed, most goes to stipends and less than one third of the meat is used for food for those attending the services.

Death Chants and Songs

During Hmong death rituals and funeral services (*Hmoob kev ruam sim losi kev ploj kev tu*ag), death songs (*nkauj tua*g) are chanted every day at the times of the three meals; there are the morning meal chanting (*nkauj tshais*), the noon meal chanting (*nkauj sus*), and the evening meal chanting (*nkauj hmo*). The chanting of death songs is accompanied the playing of the Hmong lushen, or reed bamboo pipe (*qeej*), and the drum. The team for the death songs consists of the chanter (*txiv nkauj*), the reed bamboo pipe player (*txiv qeej*), and the drummer (*txiv nruas*). Each chant is preceded by the playing of the reed bamboo pipe and drum beats and the words go with the time of day and the directing of the soul of the deceased. For instance, when the morning meal is ready to be served, the player of the reed bamboo pipe and the drummer perform a morning ritual to offer the morning meal to the deceased. The chanter sings the death song to accompany the morning meal offering to the deceased.

The purpose of the death song is to reinforce the offerings of the morning, noon, and evening meals to the deceased before everyone in the physical world can eat those meals. The written lyrics of each death song are utterly slightly differently in accordance with the meal and time of the day. The chants consist of repeated phrases and stanzas, and most stanzas are short with only a few words or phrases different from the previous ones. Translating the songs is difficult, but ordinary listeners and readers can understand certain words and phrases such as drinking, eating, thirsty, hungry, evil and devil, sicknesses, shamanistic rituals, death, time for meal, and put away the reed bamboo pipe and the drum. Each death song starts with a very broad introduction of the deceased to the meal at hand with a lot of entertaining lyrics and then narrows its focus to the specific meal being offered.

On the night before the burial day, another series of chanting goes from the afternoon until the early morning hours. This chanting allows the lead blessing chanter (*thawj txiv xaiv*) and his several assistants (*lwm txiv xaiv*) to perform the blessing rituals for the survivors and kinship participants and bid farewell to the deceased. This process is quite lengthy and entertaining. It is a customary ritual in all Hmong funeral services, but survivors and participants do not understand the significance of the ritual. Some believe it is helpful in a time of great sorrow because the words are touching.

The blessing ritual starts at the head guest service table (*lub rooj hais xim losi lub rooj qhau xim*), honoring all the key players (*hauv qhua txooj*) and supporters (*thawj lwm tub ncig*) of the funeral service. It ends with extensive and elaborate religious blessings for the survivors and a bidding of farewell to the deceased. Keep in mind that one of the ritual purposes of the head guest service table is to completely purge the life of the survivors and the deceased in order to separate the deceased from his survivors and to send the deceased on its way to meet the family ancestral spirits in the spiritual world. As Hmong usually put it, "*ntoj nws laus dab tu nws laus qhua*," meaning, "censoring the deceased's life, spirits, and soul." Typically, the blessing chanting event has three main parts. The first part is the acknowledgment (*qhib phiaj*) of the presence of each key player and supporter. The two assistant chanters direct questions and specific chanting to each of the individuals sitting around the service table. The second part has to do with appeasement and resolution (*cwb qhua*) for the key players and supporters. In this stage, the assistant chanters ask participants many questions to elicit their concerns and answer any questions the participants have in order to remove any hurdles for the next stage. The final part is the cast away chanting and blessings (*foom kom*) for the survivors as they bid farewell to the deceased. The last stage is the longest and most tedious part of the entire event. It is also the most enjoyable, entertaining, and appreciative moment.

Whether one believes that this kind of blessing chanting produces real blessings or not, it has been a long-standing tradition for Hmong funeral services. The positive effects of the chant may not be seen with the naked eyes because they are spiritual blessings; however, the blessing may positively affect the life of an individual survivor in a variety of ways. Today's Hmong may not see the religious chanting and blessing as important as 40 years ago because of the progress and successes they have experienced in their lives. However, they have to remember that religious practices retain their value over times and continue to be sources of strength regardless of one's socioeconomic status or educational level. Perhaps traditional Hmong families can find ways to modify some of the practices to make the funeral service and death rituals more relevant to their everyday lives.

Funeral Instruments

Several funeral instruments are used in the Hmong funeral service: the reed bamboo pipe, or lushen (*rab qeej*); the pair of split bamboo pointers (*txhib ntawg losi kuam xyoob*); the death drum (*lub nruas tuag*); the rice winnowing basket (*lub vab*); the back basket (*lub kawm*); the crossbow with arrow (*rab hneev nrog xib xub*); the knife (*riam dab*); and the death horse, or man-made gurney or stretcher (*tub nees tuag*). The reed bamboo pipe and death drum are used throughout the entire service. There are two kinds of drums. First is the domestic drum (*nruas yug*), which is a traditional drum owned by a family member (the drum master) or created by the family (the drum creator) for spiritual and religious purposes in accordance with the family traditions and beliefs. The other is a makeshift type of drum (*nruas zoj*), made for a one-time use. The two drums work the same way, but the domestic drum is usually louder. Religiously, an offering of a chicken is required for the use of a traditional drum during each funeral service, and this sacrificial offering to the spirituals and souls of the drum is called "a chicken covering the drum," or as in Hmong, means "*Tus qaib npog nruas.*"

Remember, Hmong religious instruments require careful handling and transporting. The Hmong traditional death drum has to be carried on the shoulder or back to and from the funeral home and has to be hung on a designated location on the wall inside its master's home. It cannot be dropped or placed on the ground for any reasons; otherwise, reckless handling it can be religiously sensitive and intentional violation can be resulted in spiritual curse. Similarly, for the reed bamboo pipe instrument, the owner can place it on the ground or hang it on the wall as long as it is safe and secured. Anyhow, both religious instruments do have spirits and souls that live within them and such spiritual beings require sacrificial offerings for each use.

The lushen, or reed bamboo pipe instrument (*rab qeej*), and death drum (*lub nruas tuag*) are essential for Hmong funeral services. The origin of the Hmong death instruments, especially for the reed bamboo pipe and the death drum, still remains a mystery. There are different versions about the creation of the two religious instruments; however, not all Hmong would agree because Hmong lack historical documents to support how each instrument was originated and created in the first place; therefore, Hmong continue to use them in accordance with their traditions and religious practices. Ironically, some believe that the two are nothing more than just normal death musical instruments created to entertain both the dead and living in the time of dealing with loss and sorrow, but others do believe that the two play a pivotal role in honoring and celebrating death because both are used to guide the soul of the dead back to the spiritual and ancestral world.

The *rab qeej* instrument is made of six reed bamboo pipes and is played with six fingers, three from each hand. These fingers are the thumbs, index fingers, and the middle fingers. The six reed bamboo pipes are in different sizes and lengths. Each pipe has its own metal-copper tone blade installed next to the playing hole, and therefore, the instrument has six different musical tones. One end of all pipes is inserted into the holes made on a hollow wooden barrel (looking like the shape and size of an American football, depending on the size of the lushen) with a three-foot empty shaft on top and a small solid half foot shaft on the bottom. The player inserts the tip of the long-empty shaft into his mouth without biting it with his teeth but controlling the tip with his lips. The mu-

sical sounds and notes are played by controlled inhaling and exhaling into the shaft while using his fingers of both hands to cover holes on the reed bamboo pipes for combination sounds, tones, and offerings. Each finger plays a specific spiritual tone called *ntiv* in Hmong, for example, the left thumb plays the tone of *ntiv tw*, the left index finger plays the tone of *ntiv npug*, and the left middle finger plays the tone of *ntiv puj* while the right thumb plays the tone of *ntiv luav*, the right index finger plays the tone of *ntiv raus*, and the right middle finger plays the tone of *ntiv laig*. Each of these six tones represents the specific offering, guiding, blessing, and chanting given to the deceased. At the same time, the death drum is played with two hands and each hand holds a hand-made drumstick with a round tip at one end. Both drumsticks are about twelve inches long. A rope or twine is used to tie the other end of both drumsticks to keep them together as a pair. Religiously, the two drumsticks cannot be separated or replaced and have to be the original set that comes with the drum. A replacement has to approved and justified by the owner of the drum. The rhythms and melodies of the two instruments are harmonious in most of the rituals. The two instruments are used together for a variety of purposes, as Table 8.5 illustrates.

Table 8.5. Uses of Hmong Funeral Lushen and Drum

Ritual Use	In Hmong	Purpose
Playing the death song	Qeej tu siav	To guide the soul back to the spiritual world
Playing the death horse	Qeej tsa nees	To raise the death horse with corpse
Setting up the table	Qeej rub rooj	To set up the table for rituals
Burning paper money	Qeej hlawv ntawv	To burn the paper money
Leading the way out of the house to the field	Qeej tawm nras	To guide the corpse to the field for sundry ritual
Leading the way to the cemetery	Qeej sawv kev	To guide the corpse to the cemetery and burial site
Breakfast ritual	Qeej tshais	To guide the breakfast
Lunch ritual	Qeej sus	To guide the lunch
Dinner ritual	Qeej hmo	To guide the dinner
Offering ritual	Qeej cob tsiag	To offer sacrificial animals to the deceased
Leading the fight	Qeej tsa rog	To guide the crew to fight enemies
Showing and entertaining	Qeej tiv luav	To show off for fun, entertainment, and playful purposes
Showing and entertaining	Qeej xyuas xau	To show off for fun, entertainment, and playful purposes

The reed bamboo pipe can also be used for entertainment outside the funeral home; however, the death drum may not be used for entertainment purposes because of all the spirits guarding the drum. The Hmong funeral drum is reserved for use inside the funeral home for religious purposes only.

The Days of the Funeral Service

The death of Major General Vang Pao in 2011 occasioned the longest Hmong funeral service ever in the U.S. It was a historic and honorable week-long funeral service that attracted thousands of people from around the world and included the most sophisticated rituals and religious rites. The funeral service cost hundreds of thousands of dollars. Major General Vang Pao had elevated the sociopolitical and socioeconomic status of Hmong from the early 1960s to the time of his death, and he was the longest-lived leader for the Hmong. For all he had done for the Hmong, his funeral service was not only a religious tradition, but an honorific tribute to his life, career, and leadership. As many Hmong have said, his funeral service would have been much longer if Hmong had their own independent nation. When he was alive, Major General Vang Pao was a strong advocate for inexpensive funeral services. However, for Hmong the funeral service has little to do with money; it is about the death rituals and religious proceedings that need to be done in order to guide the soul of the body through the long journey to find the ancestral spirits in the spiritual world.

In the U.S., the normal Hmong funeral service lasts a few days not counting all the days of preparation. The transition from the family home to the funeral home can be smooth or awkward depending on how extensive and elaborate a funeral is planned. Usually the facility is open for decoration a day or two ahead of the first day of the funeral. Most Hmong funeral services last three to four full days, starting on Friday and ending on the following Monday. Specific tasks, rituals, ceremonies, and services are performed on each day. The three or four days of the funeral are packed with people, rituals, and services.

Day One

The very first day of the traditional Hmong funeral service is the dressing day (*hnub tu zam*); it begins with the death costume dressing ritual (*ris tsho laus*). The body has to be dressed in a Hmong death costume. This outfit includes but is not limited to a few layers of clothing for protection during the long journey (*tiv luaj tiv av*), a coat (*tsho tshaj sab*), a headband (*siv ceeb*), a pair of bird shoes (*khau noog*), a pair of hemp shoes (*khau maj khau ntuag*), a shroud (*teem kiam*), pants (*ris Hmoob*), a long-sleeved shirt (*tsho Hmoob*), some sashes (*sev losi hlab si*), and a pair of socks (*thom khwm*). Male and female death costumes are different and each Hmong family has its own dressing customs and death costumes.

Day One is also the opening day (*hnub qhib*) and is the day of the Showing the Way ritual (*hnub qhuab ke*). For traditional Hmong, the first day is full of death rituals and tedious processes, but for Christian Hmong the day is like any other day. The goal of the first day is to accomplish two tasks: the path pointer performing the Showing the Way ritual (*qhuab ke losi taw kev*) and the reed bamboo pipe player (*tshuab qeej tu siav*) playing the death song. To prepare the deceased for these two events, formalities have to be conducted in accordance with Hmong traditions. The family members search the dead body to make sure everything is normal. They then dress the body with the death costumes. When the body is ready, the death rituals begin. Before the path pointer can start the Showing the Way ritual, all required items, illustrated in Table 8.6, have to be ready. Each Hmong family has its own customs and every family may not require all the items listed in Table 8.6.

The path pointer (*tus taw kev losi tus qhuab ke*) takes several hours to perform the Showing the Way rite, which guides the soul of the deceased through its journey through time from the present life back to the ances-

Table 8.6. Ritual Items Required for the Main Tasks of Day One

Item	In Hmong	Purpose/Use
A pair of split bamboo pointers	Ib tug txhib ntawg losi kuam xyoob	Communication between the spirits of the deceased and the living
Two empty bottles	Ob lub hwj laig dab	Contains offerings made to the deceased
One small cup or gulp	Ib lub pib laig cawv	To offer wine to the deceased
One spoon	Ib rab diav	To offer food to the deceased
A bowl of warm water	Ib taig dej sov	Washing the face of the deceased during the first task of the ritual
A washcloth	Ib daim ntaub ntxuav muag	To wash the face of the deceased
A can of cooked rice with a cooked egg	Ib co kua dis mov nrog ib lub qe	To offer food to the deceased during the first task of the ritual
One paper umbrella	Ib lub kaus ntawv	Offering to the deceased for use on rainy, sunny, windy, and stormy days during the journey
A crossbow with an arrow	Ib rab hneev nrog ib xib xub	Protect the deceased during the journey
An empty bowl or an empty gourd	Ib lub taig laig nyag	Contains offerings made to the deceased
A sacrificial rooster	Ib tug qaib npog tais losi tus qaib hauv ncoo	Guide the deceased to the spiritual world
A pair of hemp shoes	Ib nkawm khau maj khau ntuag	Flip-flops for traveling
A pair of bird shoes	Ib nkawm khau noog	For traveling
Three rings made of hemp	Peb lub cos maj cos ntuag	To pay debts along the way into the spiritual world
A piece of red cloth	Ib daim ntaub liab npog cauj	To cover the mouth of the deceased
A small board	Ib daim txiag ntoo	Platform on which other ritual items, such as the bottles, cups, spoon, etc., are placed
A bundle of money paper	Ib tum xav txheej	To pay debts along the way to the spiritual world
A cup of uncooked rice with a raw egg	Ib ntim txhuv qe	For the soul calling ritual of the pointer who performs the Showing the Way rite
A sharp knife	Ib rab riam	To divide the dead and living spirits
A bamboo flute*	Ib lub raj kub twg	To warn soldiers to get ready for war and fighting with the Chinese
A piece of bamboo board*	Ib daim txhib ntag	Used as a flag or a weapon (sword) during war and fighting with the Chinese

*may not be required for some funerals

tral world. The very first thing the path pointer has to do is check to make sure the deceased is still dead. He asks the deceased repeatedly, "Are you dead or not dead? If you are not dead, then get up, go do work, walk around the house. If you are dead, then turn your ears and listen. Turn your face around. I will chant spiritual songs for you to listen to." In Hmong: "N ... os! Koj tuag dag los tuag tiag? Tuag dag no ces sawv los ncig qav ncig num, ncig vaj ncig loog. Tuag tiag no ces tig ntsej los mloog, tig muag los nuam, kuv yuav hu nkauj dab lus taum pub koj mloog no nas...!" The pointer tosses a pair of the split bamboo pointers (tus txhib ntawg losi kuam xyoob) to determine if the deceased accepts his death. If one half is face down and the other half is face up, his acceptance is confirmed. The bamboo pointers are the only proper communication between the dead and the living. This means of communication is used repeatedly throughout the ritual.

The journey is very complex, as the elements listed in Table 8.7 indicate. The core of the Showing the Way ritual is to make sure the soul of the deceased actually accepts the death of the body and is willing to leave the physical world to journey back into the spiritual world to find his ancestral spirits and to present the soul of the deceased the hope of reincarnation. The journey is not only long, but it also has all kinds of obstacles along the way. To locate his birthplace and the ancestral spirits, the soul of the deceased must walk on foot through the mountain of caterpillars and spiky worms (*toj kab ntsuab dawm kab ntsig*), through the deadly freezing mountains (*roob tuag no*), under the dry sky on brittle earth (*ntuj qhuav teb nkig*), under the cold sky on dark earth (*ntuj no teb tsaus*), under the burning sky on scorched earth (*ntuj kub teb nkig*), under the icy sky on dark earth (*ntuj txias teb tsaus*), or through the barren land under a hot and dry sky (*ntuj qhuav teb nkig losi ntuj qhuav teb dos*).

Some of the verses may not make much sense to the living because they are not relevant to the physical life. For the deceased, however, the chanting may help the soul to understand the happenings in the physical world. The pointer tries to make the soul understand the origins of sicknesses and death, good and evil, animals, life, man-made objects, the spirits of heaven and earth, the spirits of the house, the stories of Adam and Eve, and many other mysteries. The path pointer travels with the soul of the deceased during this chanting process and at the end the pointer asks the soul to continue the journey by itself while he returns to the physical world. Some of the verses are very sad and emotional. That is why a soul calling ritual is performed following the rite—to reclaim the soul of the pointer lest it wander from his body to be with the deceased in the spiritual world.

Table 8.7. Steps in the Showing the Way Rite

Step	*In Hmong*	*Purpose*
The creation of life for all living	Tsim noob qoob noob loo	Introduce the soul of the deceased to various ritual objects such as the rooter, wine, water, coffin, clothes, drums, washcloth, and so on
Life and death	Phwb noob neej thiab kab mob kev tuag	Tell the soul of the deceased about life and death causing by sins, sicknesses, diseases, betrayal, evils, devils, demons, and so on
Thank the household spirits	Ua dab vaj dab tsev tsaug	Tell the soul of the deceased to separate from the household spirits because the body is dead and the soul is departing to the spiritual world
Ask for new declarations of life through reincarnation	Mus muab ntawv rov los thawj xeeb	Tell the soul of the deceased to take the journey back into spiritual world, where the spirits of the soul will seek new declarations of life through reincarnation and return to the earth in the new life
Retrieve the original Hmong death costumes and clothes	Mus muab lub tsho tsuj tsho npuag	Tell the soul of the deceased to find the original death costumes and clothes (the buried birth placenta, the silk coat, or the birthplace) and take it along to the spiritual world

continued on page 240

Step	In Hmong	Purpose
Locate ancestors or ancestral spirits	Mus cuag poj cuag yawm	Tell the soul of the deceased to locate the ancestors or ancestral spirits in the spiritual world, to seek reincarnation, to request new declarations of life
Pointer and deceased separate from each other, the pointer to return to the physical world, the deceased to go on to the spiritual world	Zais roj zais hneev rov qab	Tell the soul of the deceased to depart, to move on, to not return to the physical world, to continue the journey while the pointer returns to the physical world

Following the Showing the Way ritual, the player of the reed bamboo pipe and the drummer play a death song (*tshuab qeej tu siav*) to make sure the body is actually dead and the soul is traveling back to the spiritual world. The death song is quite long with many sad verses, like the verses in Showing the Way. The purpose of the death song is to send the soul away to the spiritual world. During both the ritual and the song, the soul of the deceased is questioned many times. Before and following each verse of the song, the players and chanters toss the split bamboo pointers and ask if the soul agrees with and accepts what they are chanting. If the pointers indicate that the soul does not accept, they must be tossed again until the soul is resigned to its fate. Sometimes for some parts of the ritual, the face-up or face-down position of the pointers does not give an accurate reading. When the player of the reed bamboo pipe has finished playing all the verses of the death song, the body is dead and the soul is ready to be guided to the spiritual world. Crying and wailing typically take place at this point because there is no question that the body is dead and the funeral service can now proceed.

In the old days, the deceased's body had to be lifted onto a man-made death horse (*tsa nees*) and hung on the north wall of the house. The death horse was a crude stretcher made of bamboo strips and wooden beams tied together. Today no death horse is used; the corpse is simply lifted from the floor into the casket. Therefore, the traditional death horse ritual, which lasted an hour or two, is skipped.

When the two tasks have been accomplished—Showing the Way and the death song—the first day of the funeral is over and the second day is about to begin. The second day is the busiest day, the day of many guests (*hnub qhua txws*). Christian Hmong families close the funeral home at midnight to allow the family members to rest, but in traditional families people stay up all night. The reed bamboo piper and drummers continue to entertain the deceased along with the remaining guests throughout the night.

Day Two

On the second day, the head guests (*hnub qhua txws*), those connected by marital ties, kinship, and friendship, arrive. Remember, the major group (*hauv qhua txooj*) and the minor group (*hauv qhua tab*) appear in that order on the second day, and then all the other guests come. The minor group and other guests can enter together, but the major group has to lead the way.

The lineup of the major group starts with the family leader or representative (*cuab tsav*), then come the oldest or youngest sister of the deceased (*maum phauj*), the wife's brother (*txiv dab laug*), the father of the daughter-in-law of the oldest or youngest son (*cuas nyab*), the father-in-law of the oldest or youngest daughter (*cuas nthxais*), the father-in-law of the oldest or youngest daughter (*ntxhais vauv zov quav*), and so on.

Each guest in the major group has a small crew comprised of a representative (*tus kis*), a reed bamboo pipe player (*txiv qeej*), a back basket carrier (*tus ris kawm*), a wine server (*tus ce cawv*), two cow fasteners (*ob tus khi nyuj*), two stake holders (*txhos tswg nyuj*), two cow killers (*ob tus tua nyuj losi ob tug tsav ntxuam*), and eight helpers (*8 leej tub qav tub num*). Each guest carries a bundle of specially designed paper tied to the top of a small tree branch (*ib ntshuas ntawv nrog ib rev nplooj*) with three joss sticks or incense (*peb tswm xyab*) and a ritual back basket that contains eight items: a small partially cooked pig (*ib tug menyuam npua vom siav vog*), two cooked chickens (*ob tug qaib vom*), one cooked chicken wrapped with rice (*ib tug qaib nrog ib qhov mov*), a bottle of wine (*ib hwj cawv*), a live pig or some money for a spiritual gift (*nyiaj kab tsem*), some money for a donation called a sunshine gift (*nyiaj tshav ntuj*), one yard of black fabric for a shroud (*ib daim ntaub teem kiam*), and a gun with powder or ammunition (*ib rab phom thiab tshuaj phom*). Actually, the gun and ammunition are no longer brought because western law either forbids or discourages the carrying of firearms.

At noon, the family of the deceased and the members of the major group participate in a meal ritual called the match-up and gift exchange ritual (*faj xim*) between the impacted family (*tsev xyom cuab*) and the summoned guests (*hauv qhua txooj*). The ritual involves dividing, matching, and exchanging animal parts. During the exchange, everyone shows respect and appreciation before they enjoy a lunch together (*txheeb hauv qhua, txhoov npua thiab txhoov qaib faj xim, noj hauv qhua sus, thiab xem txhwj*).

There is no lineup for members of the minor group; each guest can enter the funeral in any order. Each guest in the minor group carries a bundle of specially designed paper tied to the top of a small tree branch (*ib ntshuas ntawv nrog in rev nplooj*) and three joss sticks or incense (*peb tswm xyab*). These guests also have crews; they consist of a representative (*tus kis*), a back basket carrier (*tus ris kawm*), and a few family members (*ob peb tug txheeb zes*). The back basket contains two cooked chickens (*ob tus qaib vom siav*), one cooked baby chicken for a spiritual offering (*ib tug menyuam qaib dab*), and some money for a donation or sunshine gift (*nyiaj tshav*

ntuj). Members of the minor group also participate in a match-up and gift exchange ritual.

Traditionally, every single guest with a back basket is thanked for coming. To thank someone during the funeral service, members of the family and funeral crew utter thank you phrases and kowtow. Here is an example of a Hmong funeral thank you:

Ua tsaug os smog ... maum phauj es ... vim peb tsev xyom cuab tsev ploj tsev tuag tsev puas tsev ntsoog ... koj ho xav neej xav tsav xav ntsuab xav ze ... koj thiaj li yuav cab yaj cab ncos ... siv nyiaj txiaj qas ntsos.. dej caw qas log tuaj pab peb xyom cuab nta dab nta qhua kom tseg log puav tam ncej txawb ... nram qab nram ntsis nram qab nram qawd ... yog peb xyom cuab txawj ua lub neej xws luag ces yuav nco koj tshav ntuj mog ... yog peb xyom cuab ua lub neej tsis xws luag ces cuag li yuav nrauj koj tus txiaj ntsha txiaj ntsim rau ntsis tauj ntsis tsuag ua tshauv ua thee yaj ... ua tshau ua nag yaj no mog...! [In English, thank you, maternal aunt, because in our death and loss in the family you consider family ties and friendship. You bring food, money, and wine to help us honor the spirits and the deceased as becoming a standing pillar. In the near future, if we live a normal life like others, then we will remember your invaluable gift. If you do not live a normal life like others, then we will forget your invaluable gift as though it were on the top of a tree or a mountain, as though it were ashes gone with the wind, ashes gone with the rain.]

The response of the giver is quite short:

Sawv lauj mog..! Kuv ces twb ua lub neej tsis xws luag ces cuag li kuv tuaj los kuv tsuas coj lub qhov muag tuaj saib tuaj xyuas qhuav qhuav xwb ... kuv twb tsis muaj ib yam dabtsi tuaj pab nej xyom cuab nta dab nta qhua ... twb tuaj tauv tsis taus nej xyom cuab lub kua muag li lauj mog...! [In English, please rise! I do not live a normal life like others. I come here though I just bring my naked eyes to watch. I do not have anything to help you honor the spirits and the deceased. I cannot stop the tears of your family members at all!]

Both the giver and the receiver have to gesture (*txaum yim*) with both hands while uttering the thank you phrases and the response phrases. Only the receiver of the gift kowtows (*pe*)—kneels to the giver two times. Hmong funeral kowtowing can be done in a group as well as individually. A lead person can say the words and ask the group to kowtow in unison. Group kowtowing is appropriate for many rituals during the Hmong funeral, especially on the second day: the thank you to the guests at the lunch table (*noj hauv qhua su*), the thank you to all the guests for coming (*xem tshwj),* the thank you to the funeral crew members (*thawj lwm tub ncig*), and the thank you to all who donated (*tuaj pab tshav ntuj*). Christian Hmong families do not kowtow or kneel down; they give verbal thanks instead.

So many things need to be done on the second day. Dining and drinking are part of the day. Funeral crew members are extremely busy, but the main functions are performed by two key persons, the funeral directors or chiefs of operation (*kav xwm*) and the master of rituals or chief of the funeral (*cuab tsav*). The master of rituals is responsible for all religious rituals and offerings to the soul of the deceased. He has to make sure the cooked animals, bottles of wine, and wrapped food the guests bring to the funeral home are offered to the deceased.

The funeral director has many duties. Right after lunch he has to identify all members of the major group and return the back baskets to each one of them. He has to assign responsibilities in regard to the slaughtering of the sacrificial animals. Usually there are five cows for five different members, including the master of the ritual. Before the day is over, he has to set up a time to meet all members at the slaughter house to show them the sacrificial animals and give each an animal for slaughtering the next morning. Sometimes, he faces complications and rejections, but such things are usually resolved prior to the slaughtering of the animals. Each member is told to bring his own crew to slaughter, clean, and transport the animals to the funeral home. He meets each member at the slaughter house the next morning. Finally, he reminds each of the members to show up for the service table (*lub rooj hais xim losi lub*

rooj qhau xim) on the next day, which usually gets started in the early afternoon.

By this time, a special family dinner (*xyom cuab pluas mov*) is ready for the guests and visitors. Following the dinner, it is time for honoring the funeral crew members, including the lead singer of spiritual blessing. A special table is set and all crew members are called to take seats at the table in the order listed in Table 8.2. One by one, the family representative and other members formally acknowledge and kowtow to each crew member, thanking them for their vital roles in helping at the funeral. Usually, each receives a pack of meat, a case of soda, and a small stipend for their gas mileage and their time. Sometimes, a separate table is set for honoring the lead singer of spiritual blessing; however, this is optional as the lead singer is paid for his blessing performance (*foom kom*). Because the family of the deceased picks up all the bills, traditional Hmong families would be wise to reevaluate the whole funeral and perhaps make modest changes. Current funeral practices appear to be overkill; they require tremendous resources and manpower.

Into the night, the lushen player and the drummer keep the guests entertained. Sometimes family members take time to pay special respect and honor to the deceased. Different family members may give speeches or present a slide show in memory of the deceased or invite guests to pay special tribute to the deceased. As the third day approaches, the funeral crew gets ready for more rituals while family members work tirelessly to make sure everything is going smoothly.

Day Three

Traditionally, the third day is a day of religious and cultural exhibition involving amusement and some theatrical scenes. The head guests who make up the core of the funeral service discuss the life of the deceased as well as the funeral service held by the survivors. Actually, this day is the life purging day of the deceased and the censorship day of the survivors. At the head guest service table (*lub rooj hais xim losi lub rooj qhau xim*), several head guests who have been invited by the family to take part in the funeral ask questions, voice concerns, and probe the life of the deceased, inquiring about his wealth, children, property, and debts. Normally, the head guests are the master of the rituals (*txiv cuab tsav*), the oldest sister (*muam phauj*), the oldest brother-in-law of the wife of the deceased (*txiv dab laug*), the father of the first or last daughter-in-law (*cuas nyab*), the father of the first or last son-in-law (*cuas ntxhais*), the appointed arbitrator or judge (*txwj laug*), the reed bamboo pipe player (*txiv qeej*), and the cook (*tshwj ka*b). Remember, as shown in figure 8.2, the line up of head guests to seat at the service table starts from left to right and may be different for each funeral service, depending on the family traditions, social status of the deceased, and the age and gender of the deceased. In Hmong funeral ritual, *ncej vag* means the death of the father and *txhib vag* is the passing of the mother.The funeral directors (*ob tug kav xwm*) would take charge of all proceedings. Culturally, the head guest table is required for the purpose of checks and balances. Each guest has a specific role to play; however, all censor his survivors,

making sure the deceased has received adequate provisions and support. This is a common process, but it can raise issues that are personally and emotionally sensitive. Sometimes unexpected and serious issues emerge or shocking information is revealed. Therefore, the third day is sometimes referred to as the judgment day or doomsday for the deceased and his survivors.

On this day, an appointed debt arbitrator, judge, or collector (*txwj laug*) asks those gathered if the deceased owes anyone money or if anyone owes the deceased money, for all debts must be resolved before his departure to spiritual world. If no one comes forward to claim a debt from the deceased, the arbitrator declares all debts forfeited by default at that moment. Once the arbitrator declares the deceased debt free, an offering is made to tell the deceased that he is free to go without leaving any debts behind and without anyone in the physical world owing him money. This declaration means the soul of the deceased is free to return to the spiritual world to undergo the reincarnation process in order to return as a new birth once again to his family in the physical world.

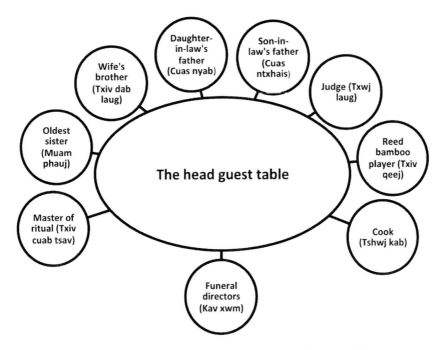

Figure 8.2. Seating arrangements at the head guest table.

Rituals are performed on the third day and morning and lunch meals are served to all guests. The funeral director and master of rituals return from the slaughter house and the slaughtered animals are divided among different parties with some delivered to the funeral home for food. Special ribs and other meats are reserved for specific crew members. Family members prepare the service table. A good sized pig is slaughtered for the table in addition to other foods and drinks. The family members compile a list of items the family has given to the deceased to be reported to the group of head guests at the table. If the deceased's wife is one of the survivors, the group will ask what the deceased has left behind for her and what she has given to him as well. These funeral queries are tedious, but culturally appropriate.

Right after lunch a service table is set and the head guests are called one by one by the funeral director to take appropriate seats at the table, as listed in Table 8.3. Once all the guests and representatives are seated at the table, the next ritual begins. The funeral director and his assistant take charge of the proceedings. Often subordinates conduct the early parts and the funeral director takes charge of the final part. The very first step is to stop the lushen player and the drummer from performing. This is not a simple matter of asking them to stop; the chanters have to chant to appease them. Once they stop playing, the formal proceedings resume at the table.

Basically, the proceeding allows head guests and family representatives to ask questions, voice concerns, and probe the family about anything regarding the deceased and his survivors. The formalities include heavy chanting by the two people in charge. Examples of the chants are given in Tables 8.8 and 8.9. The chants are of two types: recognition and acknowledgement (*qhib phiaj*) and appeasement and resolution (*cwb qhua*). There are several rounds of questioning and answering. Sometimes the guests chant and bless the family with special songs. The

Table 8.8. Hmong Funeral Recognition Chants and Songs

Name of chants/songs	In Hmong	Addressee
Guest arrivals and meals	Kev to qhua thiab noj mov	All guests
Drinking and smoking	Kab yeeb rau sawv daws haus	All guests
Set up table	Rub lub rooj hais xim	Funeral crew and family members
Kowtowing ritual	Kom xyom cuab los xyom	Family members
Warning family members not to sleep if they want to be blessed by the deceased	Txhob mus pw yog xav tau koob hmoov	Family members
Warning family members about asking to perform the chanting	Ceeb tom rau xyom cuab	Family members
Asking the lushen player and drummer to stop performing	Txwv qeej txwv nruas	Lusher player and drummer
Warning the audience not to talk during the process	Txwv tsis pub tham	All guests
Lecturing family members to behave	Qhuab qhia xyom cuab	Family members
The warm relationship given by the deceased while living	Thaum tseem ua neej nyob	All guest and the deceased
The deceased is taken by the demons and evil spirits	Ntxwg nyoog coj tus tuag lawm	All guests and the deceased
Mankind fears sickness and death	Neeg ntshai kab mob kev tuag	All guests and the deceased
The demons and evil spirits spill sicknesses into the world	Ntxwg nyoog tso kab mob kev tuag rau ntiaj teb	All guests and the deceased

Table 8.9. Hmong Funeral Appeasement and Resolution Chants and Songs

Name of chants/songs	In Hmong	Addressee
Performing all rituals and religious offerings to the deceased	Txiv cuab tsav tuaj nta dab nta qhua	Master of ritual or funeral service
Verifying and purging deceased's belongings and ownership	Maum phauj tuaj txheeb dab laug teeg tug	Sister of the deceased
Censoring all provisions for his brother-in-law	Txiv dab laug tuaj txheeb rau tus yawm yij	Wife's brother
Father of daughter-in-law	Hais rau cuas nyab	Father of daughter-in-law
Father of son-in-law	Hais rau cuas ntxhais	Father of son-in-law
Debt collector and arbitrator	Hais rau txwj laug	Appointed arbitrator
Playing the lushen or reed bamboo pipe	Hais rau txiv qeej	Lushen player or reed bamboo player
Preparing and cooking meals	Hais rau tshwj kab	Cooks
Checking all sacrificial animals	Hais rau cuab tsav	Master of rituals and funeral service
Appeasing all without sacrificial animals	Hais rau cov tsis muaj kaus qaij	All guests without sacrificial animals
To all with sacrificial animals to compensate for the chest and neck portion of the cow	Hais rau cov muaj kaus qaij kom txais lub nrob nyuj	All guests with sacrificial animals
To all with sacrificial animals with approval	Hais txog tswg nyuj	All guests with sacrificial animals
Family will remember their invaluable contributions	Xyom cuab yuav nco txiaj ntsim	All guests with sacrificial animals
Bringing and burning the death paper money for the deceased	Hais rau txiv cuab tsav kom hlawv ntawv rau tus tuag	Master of rituals and funeral service
Carrying the corpse to the gravesite for burial	Hais rau kom sawv daws sib pab kwv tus tuag	All guests and relatives of family
Making a makeshift umbrella to cover the corpse in the field	Ua kaus roos tshwm tshav	Master of rituals and funeral service
Following the spirits of the deceased to see if he has anything to leave behind for survivors	Raws tus tuag saib nws muaj lus zoo hais licas rau cov nyob tom qab	The soul of the deceased

whole process can take several hours. Keep in mind that regardless of how tedious the process may be, the goal is to get through it. Heated discussions, disagreements, and verbal exchanges between the lead persons and members of the group are normal and conflicts are usually resolved through respectful mutual agreement.

The chants and songs listed in Tables 8.8 and 8.9 are for the head guests and representatives sitting at the service table. The most powerful person is the sister of the deceased (*maum phauj*) or the brother (*txiv dab laug*)

of the deceased, depending on the gender of the deceased. Once the most powerful party has finished his or her queries about the death and the family provisions, the others follow with their queries. By the time the process is over, it is about midnight. The chanter chants a special song to signal the removal of the existing table (*tuam rooj*) and the setting up of a new table for the rest of the night. At this point, the lead singer of spiritual blessing takes charge.

The lead singer of spiritual blessing blesses the deceased and his survivors. This final phase of chanting, the blessing phase remains (*foom kom*); this is the most important part of the entire process. It consists of both positive and negative songs. First, the lead singer casts away all negative predicaments and then he blesses the survivors, as Table 8.10 illustrates. At the end, the lead singer blesses everyone with good luck, fortune, and prosperity. Then he gives blessing wine to the family members and reaffirms his wishes for their success and prosperity that he bestowed in the chants and songs. When he concludes the blessing, it is about one or two o'clock in the morning.

These chants and songs are sung in the Hmong language and some Hmong, especially young children or youth who grew up in the West, may not comprehend the content. Still, the blessing words, whether understood or not, have deep meanings.

Before dawn the master of rituals offers paper money to the deceased and instructs the family members to collect the spiritual money so it can be burned (*hlawv ntawv*) in preparation for the final day. The lushen player and the drummer perform the burning rituals preceding the burning. The burning of paper money symbolizes that the money has been given to the deceased to accompany him on his journey and help pay for his debts on the way to the spiritual world. The ashes of the paper money are bagged and placed in the casket, often under the layers of clothes worn by the deceased. In this way the deceased has possession of the money. Sometimes the paper money is burned just before leaving for the cemetery.

Day Four

The last day of the funeral service is the day of burial (*hnub sam sab*). This is usually a short and busy day because everything has to be cleaned up before going to the cemetery. Traditionally, funeral crew members and family members do not return to the funeral home after the burial. Most go straight home from the cemetery to take part in the final appreciation of all participants.

Breakfast is served early to the guests and crew members. The lushen player and the drummer begin their rituals while the master of rituals makes the final offerings to the deceased. Family and crew pack and load their belongings and the last paper money is burned (*ntshuas ntawv vam sab*). Flowers and other decorations are taken down for

Table 8.10. Hmong Funeral Blessing Chants and Songs

Name of Chant/Song	In Hmong	Addressee
Lecturing survivors to behave	Hais kom tsim txiaj ua neeg zoo	Family members
Lecturing daughters and daughters-in-law to work hard	Hais cov ntxhais thiab nyab kom rau siab ua noj	Daughters and daughters-in-law
Reminding children of the father's love for them when they were young	Hais cov menyuam kom nco txog leej txiv tej kev hlub	Children of family
He does not want to die but his soul is going to be reincarnated	Tsis xav tuag los tus plig yuav mus plis	Family members
Learning from raising chickens and pigs to live a prosperous life	Kawm ua neej raws li kev tu qaib tu npua ua neej yuav vammeej	Family members
Find the dragon bloodline in the hill and the right burial plot	Nrhiav sawv toj thiaj looj mem zoo	Family members
Bury in the right place	Txam rau lub looj thawj	Family members
Bury the corpse in the ground	Faus rau hauv av	Family members
Do not let the burial house collapse	Tsis pub lub vaj lub tsev vau	Family members

transport to the cemetery. The lushen player and drummer have to perform their final ritual (*tshuab qeej sawv kev*) before the hearse and escort officers arrive at the funeral home. The master of rituals makes the very last offerings to the deceased before taking the dead rooster and all other ritual objects away from the casket. He tells the deceased that his body is going to its new home (*looj mem*), which will be his permanent home.

Hmong prefer to bury their loved ones in the afternoon, but burials may take place in the late morning as well. The casket is usually placed in the hearse by noon. The master of rituals carries the dead rooster, pointers, cross bow, the container for the offerings, and the wine cup. The crying and wailing of family members is heard as the funeral home empties. The hearse and cars snake their way to the cemetery.

At the gravesite, the casket is set next to the burial plot that was dug a day earlier. Family members are invited to say their final farewells to the deceased. One by one, they approach the casket and say their final goodbyes. The family representative, usually an elder, and a few family members search the body one more time to make sure no foreign objects are in the casket or hidden under the layers of clothes. The elder or the master of rituals takes a knife and gently slices the clothes, telling the deceased that all his clothes have been cut in case anyone in the spiritual world should ask him to take off his clothes; this prevents other spirits from taking or stealing his clothes from him. After the cloth cutting ritual is over, an elder performs a short ritual. The elder tells the deceased his body will be living in this casket forever once the lid is closed. Then the lid is finally closed and locked. The cemetery crew slowly lowers the casket into its place while everyone watches.

Once the casket is situated perfectly in its final resting place, the elders tell family members to place dirt on top of the casket before the cemetery crew covers it with dirt. The elder warns that anyone who attempts to disturb the casket or the gravesite will suffer severely. Anyone who tries to remove the cas-

ket is cursed with life-threatening illness. When the casket is fully covered with dirt and the ground is leveled, the master of rituals makes the last offering to the deceased. The final message tells the deceased to get used to the underground spirits, the land spirits, and the new home before the family comes to invite his soul to visit them in the home. This is the verse of the final gravesite ritual:

> *Puv ib tsug 13 hnub, ib hnub 30 nyoog ... muab 10 hnub mus xib neej, 10 hnub mus xib dab ... 3 tag kis koj nyob hauv tsev tos xav tshais tuaj koj noj....* [In English, fulfill the 13-day cycle. Each day has 30 periods. Ten days to visit the living, 10 days to visit the spirits, 3 mornings you stay home and wait; we'll send you breakfast.]

The master of rituals tosses the pointers. If they land with one side facing down and the other side facing up, the deceased has accepted the terms of the ritual. This ends the four-day funeral service. In the old days, the new grave might be left bare (*ntxa suav*), decorated with stacked rocks (*txhim zeb*), or covered with bushes, limbs, and brush (*tsuab khaub*). Today, a headstone is installed permanently.

Before leaving the gravesite, elders instruct participants to kowtow to ask the spirits of all beings to protect the grave and safeguard the deceased. They also thank the participants for being there and for their help throughout the entire funeral service. Finally, they invite participants to meet at the home of the deceased for lunch before going home. Usually, only close family relatives return to the home; most participants go straight home, exhausted.

At the home, a pot of boiling water is placed on a portable gas burner on the walkway leading to the front door. All returnees have to walk over the hot water before entering the house. The purpose of this ritual is to wash the spirits of the deceased away from the participating family members. Once all family members have returned, they express their final appreciation to all participants and crew members. A discussion of sunshine money may take place, but only a very small portion of that money is distributed to family members and close relatives to thank them for their help. Most donations, including sunshine money, are kept by the sons to offset the funeral expenses. A lunch is served to the participants and family members.

When most participants have left the house, a family member has to perform the ritual to cast away all unwanted spirits from the house. This ritual is called beating or chasing the bad spirits out of the house (*nquam nkog*) for the family's sake. The spirits are chased out with three sticks with loops tied to their tips. These sticks are planted in the ground on the walkway leading away from the front door to keep the unwanted spirits away forever.

When that is done, the family members gather to discuss the funeral expenses and anything from the deceased to be divided among them. Usually, the sons of the deceased keep the sunshine money collected from the funeral after reimbursing family members for their expenses. Family members are free to take items belonging to the deceased as long as they all agree on how the items are distributed. Finally, the funeral is over. However, the guarding of the night ritual (*zov hmo*) may be performed and continued for a few days to keep the family warm and comfortable until the 13th day after death.

Soul Release Ritual

The 13th day following the burial marks a full cycle for the soul of the deceased. This cycle is called the spiritual fulfillment of the soul (*puv tsug*). It involves 30 periods of waiting (*nyoog*). On the 13th day, the soul of the deceased is waiting for family members to conduct rituals either to release the soul to the spiritual world or to invite the soul to visit the home on a temporary basis until the final soul release ritual. The family has the option of performing two rituals after burial: the Xi ritual, which is the first release of the soul for a family visit, and the final soul release (*tso plig*), which is the permanent and final release of the soul to the spiritual world for reincarnation.

The 13th-day soul ritual is called the first release of the soul with an invitation to visit the family (*Xi*). In Hmong religious practices, *Xi* means bringing the soul home, or inviting the soul home for a short visit. This process requires specific rituals and religious proceedings and involves some cooked rice, a crossbow, a cooked egg, some wine, a pair of split bamboo pointers, and some warm water. To perform the ritual, one has to go the gravesite and bring home some dirt from the grave. Along the way, one has to offer a drink to the soul, give the soul the warm water so it can wash its face, and offer food to the soul. At home, one places the dirt, in which is the soul, on a small board, walks with it around the fireplace or stove several times, and then places it next to the central post inside the house. Next, one offers a sacrificial chicken or young rooster to the soul, then slaughters and cooks it.

The cooked rooster or chicken has to be divided into five specific parts and placed on five different plates. The head and the rump make up one part, the left wing and right wing are two more parts, and the left drumstick and right drumstick are two more parts for a total of five. The five parts must be distributed with both hands, first the right hand and then the left. Once this procedure is properly done, one has to offer the wine to the soul as well. For a man, one offers nine drinks plus three drinks to go back to the grave; for a woman, one offers seven drinks plus three drinks to go back to the grave. When all offerings are made, one asks the soul to see who should take the offerings back to the grave. The pointers are tossed to discover who the right person for this task is. Once the name is revealed, that person takes the board out of the house and throws it to the ground, indicating that the soul has returned to the grave to wait for its final release.

Most Hmong traditional families skip the Xi ritual and perform the final and permanent soul release (*tso plig*) on the 13th day or after, usually some time before the New Year, releasing the soul to the spiritual world. The final and permanent soul release is referred to as a mimicking mini-funeral service for the soul. The final release of the soul ritual is similar to Xi ritual, except it involves more people and more formalities. In addition to family members, the ritual requires the master of the ritual, funeral directors, a lushen player, a drummer, cooks, a few guests, a path pointer, and other close family relatives. Ritual items are needed: a winnowing bamboo basket; some rice cakes or patties (*ncuav*); a headband (*siv ceeb*); a traditional Hmong costume, usually a shirt; a makeshift gate; two sticks; a pig or cow for sacrifice and for a meal, a gate, and paper money. The sticks are formed into a half circle and placed upright inside the winnowing basket, and the shirt is hung on the sticks with some of the sticks exposed so the headband can be wrapped around them; the whole thing resembles a head. A crossbow is placed inside the basket next to the rice cakes to symbolize the arrival and return of the soul. The lushen player and the drummer perform some religious rites before the carrier carries the basket through the makeshift gate into the house. The gate is a spiritual barrier that admits only good spirits; all bad spirits are kept out once the carrier walks the basket through the gate and into the house.

Inside the house, the carrier walks the basket around the fireplace several times before setting it on a stool or short table to be viewed for the entire day. Inside a family home, the process may be a little bit different, but today the ritual is usually done at the funeral home. There is much crying and wailing because this is the final farewell to the soul of the deceased. The lushen player, the drummer, and the master of rituals perform routine rituals and make offerings to prepare the soul for release. Family members cook and prepare a meal for all participants as well. The sacrificial animal is slaughtered and paper money is burned to make spiritual offerings to the soul for the final farewell. The process usually comes to an end by noon.

The basket is carried outside through the makeshift gate and placed on the ground while the lushen player, drummer, and master of rituals make the final offerings before releasing the soul to the spiritual world. At this point, Hmong believe, the soul is on its way to find its ancestral spirits in the spiritual world so it can be reincarnated. Remember, Hmong do not believe the soul goes to heaven. The religious items in the basket are removed and family members roll the basket forward. The rolling of the basket determines whether the soul is leaving or refuses to leave. If the basket rolls forward and falls upside down or face down, the soul is released and gone. If the basket rolls forward and falls face up, the process is repeated until it falls face down.

Once the rolling of the basket is over, the ritual crew goes back into the house and stands at the front door to wait for the bamboo reed pipe player and the drummer. At the door, the bamboo reed player and the drummer hand over all ritual instruments to the carrier and family members. Usually, the family asks the lushen player or the path pointer to chant special songs to bestow blessing, fortune, and prosperity on the survivors of the deceased for the very last time. These chants and songs are very emotional because the lyrics reflect the final farewell of the soul.

Normally, the final ritual (*xem tshwj*) to express heartfelt appreciation to all participants in the funeral should follow. The ritual is quite simple. A table is set with bottles of wine or cases of beer, the family leader call upon all guests and crew members to sit around the table and take turns thanking each one individually. This final display of gratitude releases all participants from their funeral duties.

Sometimes the release of the soul of the deceased is delayed for weeks, months, or even years. Such delays may be permissible, but they strand the soul in the spiritual world. In addition, long delays may bring unhappiness and curses and therefore require more religious rituals. The final and permanent release of the soul takes a full day and the cost is minimal. Even so, additional rituals are difficult financially and physically for some families. But once the soul release is done, the final chapter of the funeral service for the deceased is closed.

Summing Up

This chapter presented information about traditional Hmong funeral services and rituals. Hmong funerals are among the most complicated and sophisticated in the world. They are based on a concept of death framed by the religious practices of ancestor worship, animism, and Buddhism. The concepts of heaven and hell are not part of the Hmong belief system; rather, Hmong believe in a physical world and a spiritual world. Hmong believe the soul of the deceased travels in the spiritual world to find its ancestral spirits and is then reincarnated.

The traditional Hmong funeral service lasts three to four days and requires a great deal of manpower. It is very expensive, but to Hmong, the benefits far outweigh the high cost. Hmong want to do what they feel is right for the soul of the deceased because they believe caring for the dead is more important than pleasing the living. They are willing to make great sacrifices to honor the death of family members.

The Hmong way of life is closely connected with the spiritual world regardless of an individual's or a family's socioeconomic status. For instance, the soul of the deceased will be enshrined with those of the ancestral spirits and treated as a spiritual guardian of the family who one day can be called upon to provide benevolent assistance to needy family members. In Hmong belief, the soul of the deceased never dies; it will return to its living survivors when it faces hardship and is hungry.

This connection between the physical world and the spiritual world makes Hmong religious practices unique. However, the connection is not always peaceful. Imbalances and curses can come from the spiritual world to the physical world, sometimes through ignorance. Many Hmong children have not been taught the spiritual consequences of some of their actions. They do not speak Hmong so they cannot grasp the significance of their rituals.

Hmong accept the basic Buddhist and Hindu ideas of karma and nirvana that hold that one must be good in the present life in order to become better in the next. However, Hmong go beyond this narrow understanding of reincarnation. Hmong believe it is important to leave the physical world in a natural and non-sinful so as not to bring chaos and sorrow to the spiritual world. Hence the long and complex funeral practices.

• NINE •

Hmong Oral Traditions

Noj tsis taus ces yuav tuag...
Hais tsis taus ces yuav swb...
Kev plaub kev ntug ces nyob ntawm tib neeg lub xwb qwb...
A Hmong wisdom riddle

Introduction

Hmong have been called by a number of names according to different criteria. In the East they are identified by ethnicity: Miao-Hmong, Hmong Chinese, Hmong Thai, Hmong Lao or Laotian Hmong, and Hmong Vietnamese. In the West the criterion is nationality: U.S. Hmong or Hmong Americans, French Hmong, Australian Hmong, German Hmong, Argentinean Hmong, Guyanese Hmong, or Canadian Hmong. Another form of classification is by language. Hmong in the western nations can be divided into two main groups according to two broad language categories: White Hmong (*Hmoob Dawb*) and Blue Hmong (*Hmoob Lee*).

This chapter traces the etymological development of Hmong oral language and oral skills. It presents the evolution and transformation of Hmong languages through oral traditions and discusses the myths, legends, epics, and folktales that are still part of contemporary Hmong storytelling, values, beliefs, and customs.

Hmong Languages in Colors

In the Hmong world, the *white* and *blue* categories are used to classify Hmong families and languages based on the association of the color of traditional costumes and the two most commonly spoken dialects, *Hmoob Dawb* (White Hmong) and *Hmoob Lee* (Blue Hmong). The terms *white* and *blue* have nothing to do with skin color. The terms White Hmong and Blue Hmong denote two principal groups speaking two languages; each language unites a number of diverse Hmong dialects. Actually, Hmong have several dialects including White Hmong, Blue Hmong, Green Hmong, Striped Hmong, Black Hmong, Red Hmong, and Flowery Hmong. These terms refer to slightly different dialects, but regardless of the differences, most Hmong dialects are intelligible to one another.

Hmong recognize one another according to their family traditions, family last names, clan systems, and traditional family costumes. Each Hmong family has its own history, ancestry, and traditions although the traditions of the different families are very similar, often nearly identical, except for the current religious practices of Hmong Christian families. Hmong society is divided into four major dimensions: immediate family members (*cov kwvtij koom niam koom txiv yug*), clanmates (pawg *kwv tij koom ib lub xeem*), in-law relatives (cov *neej tsa*), and relatives at large (*qhua*). Hmong sometimes focus on the clanmates and the in-laws be-

251

cause they constitute the foundation of the Hmong family's marital structure.

The colors used to identify different Hmong languages and dialects have nothing to do with any differences in ethnic identity; there are no ethnic differences. The origin of the use of the white and blue colors is in the differences in the traditional costumes of two broad family groups—the designs, textures, motifs, and appliqués of their clothing. Although the two colors refer to the two languages spoken by most Hmong, linguistic variations exist among subgroups that help differentiate family clans and lineage subgroups. For instance, under the classification White Hmong there are a few family clans and subgroups that speak slightly different dialects such as *Red Hmong, Black Hmong, Flower Hmong, Striped Hmong,* and others. Among Blue Hmong there are a few family clans and subgroups that speak nearly identical dialects such as *Green Hmong, Hmong Shi, Hmong Leng,* and others. There are more dialects among White Hmong than Blue Hmong. Hmong dialects differentiate among family ancestries and identify genealogical relationships. The Hmong linguistic system is complex because it had no written form until the mid–1950s. Without the standardization of writing and with the separation of peoples resulting from a history of migration, the language was subject to variations.

History of Hmong Oral Languages

What language did most Hmong speak in ancient China? The answer is unknown to the present day because no research has been done on the history of Hmong oral languages. Over the years, Hmong oral languages were most likely mixed with other languages such as Mandarin, Cantonese, Vietnamese, Laotian, Burmese, and Thai. At one time, some Hmong read the Pollard script, which was somewhat similar to Chinese characters. The traditional Chinese writing system, which was in logographic or logogrammatic form, also played a role in the history of Hmong language development.

But as to what language Hmong spoke in ancient China, some western Hmong believe that most Hmong Chinese spoke Blue and Green Hmong dialects as opposed to White Hmong dialects. According to Hmong Chinese, most Hmong living in China identify themselves as Hmong Shi or Hmong Leng, meaning they speak Blue Hmong or Green Hmong. Interestingly, Hmong Chinese claim that White Hmong originated as a simplified version of Hmong dialects resulting from the fact that individuals in some interracial marriages could not speak Blue or Green Hmong correctly. This claim suggests that most Hmong Chinese speak Blue Hmong dialects and few speak White dialects.

However, this contention is not supported by the majority of Hmong refugees and immigrants who spoke White Hmong when they settled in Southeast Asian nations and later resettled in the western nations. Most Hmong who settled in northern Laos and in the West speak White Hmong dialects. A possible explanation for the fact that most Hmong living in China speak Blue Hmong dialects could be that most who fled China were White Hmong and most who submitted to Chinese dominance were Blue or Green Hmong. This explanation raises another possibility. Perhaps most White Hmong were raw Hmong (*Sheng Miaozu,* in Chinese) and most Blue and Green Hmong were cooked Hmong (*Shu Miaozu,* in Chinese) in accordance with the Chinese political classifications of Hmong during the Warring States periods and the Spring and Autumn eras. This would support the claim made by some western Hmong that most Hmong Chinese speak Blue Hmong or Green Hmong and are Hmong Shi and Hmong Leng, the original Hmong.

Over the last 60 years, many Blue and Green Hmong speakers have begun to speak White Hmong for sociopolitical purposes, but very few White Hmong speakers have changed to Blue or Green Hmong dialects. The practice of intertribal marriage has contributed to the dialect changes in some Hmong families. For instance, the children of a father who speaks Blue Hmong and a mother who speaks White Hmong might speak a mixed Hmong dialect of White-Blue Hmong. Or Blue and Green Hmong families, who are in the minority, may blend with the majority who speak White Hmong. Sometimes linguistic conversions are only temporary as situations make them desirable.

The origin of Hmong languages remains a mystery. As Vang (2010) noted, Hmong languages probably belong to the Sino-Tibetan language family and share linguistic variations similar to those of the several Chinese languages. However, it is also possible that Hmong languages are partially derived from the broad Austro-Asiatic language family because of its linguistic association with the Vietnamese and Cambodian languages. Some western scholars claim that Hmong languages are of the Miao-Yao language family, which is spoken by Chinese Mien, Mhu, Yao, Iu Mien, and Hmong.

Remember, the nationality classified as Miao includes several dozen racial and ethnic minorities in southern China and Southeast Asia, and Hmong is one of the groups. The history of Hmong languages is inextricably woven in with the history of the Miao-Yao or Hmong-Mien language family, but most Hmong do not speak Yao or Mien languages and Yao and Mien do not speak Hmong languages. Therefore, even though Hmong speak several dialects similar to the Miao-Yao, Miao-Mien, or Hmong-Mien linguistic families, Hmong have their own languages and dialects. Hmong may speak some of any number of languages in addition to their native tongue because most Hmong are bilingual. But very few other ethnic groups speak any Hmong dialect.

It is possible that the translations or transliteration of Asian languages has caused Hmong dialects to be misclassified as a mixture of Miao-Yao or Hmong-Mien languages. And many of these diverse ethnic languages and dialects are mutually intelligible and compatible. Spoken words and verbal expressions in the different languages have similarities although the written forms are distinct and incongruent. Similarities in languages such as modern Hmong, Mien, Vietnamese,

and Cambodian could be based on the same borrowed words and determinatives in all of them. In other words, linguistic similarities in different ethnic languages do not necessarily mean that the languages were once the same. Moreover, the claim that the Hmong language is the same as Yao, Miao, Lu Mien, or Mhu is not supported by the different histories of the ethnic groups. Conflating Hmong with other ethnic languages is based on the presumption that all these groups have some ethnic similarities and socio-cultural relationship. However, Hmong have always maintained their own languages distinct from those of other groups.

Regardless of how Hmong languages and dialects originated, today the many Hmong dialects have become unified into the two currently spoken dialects, *White Hmong* and *Blue Hmong.*

Hmong Language Learning

Hmong parents have always had the primary role in Hmong language development and maintenance. Hmong speakers learn the language primarily from their mothers through child-directed speech. Language learning takes place at home from infancy as verbal communication is used to convey information in the family circle. Hmong children are taught by Hmong parents how to listen, speak, memorize, replicate, and apply Hmong colloquial words to everyday situations. Today the majority of Hmong speakers still learn to speak Hmong casually and orally rather than through formal training by Hmong professionals. Most Hmong speakers have learned the language through emulation; very few have learned Hmong in school.

Most people who read and write Hmong as well as speak it are self-taught. In other words, the majority of adult Hmong speakers, even those who speak Hmong proficiently, cannot read or write the language. A large number of adult Hmong do not speak, read, or write Hmong fluently, and the majority of Hmong children born in the West are losing both oral and written abilities in the Hmong language. Most young Hmong parents and their native-born children have lost basic Hmong interpersonal communication skills for basic conversation in the home. Today *Hmonglish*, a mixture of Hmong and English, is quite popular in Hmong families because most Hmong children lack Hmong language skills and most Hmong parents lack English skills.

Perhaps it is time for Hmong to teach the language to their Hmong children formally and academically. Hmong language classes taught in college may help Hmong students brush up on their linguistic skills but are inadequate to enable Hmong students to become native speakers. To reinforce the oral traditions, which are so important in Hmong culture, western Hmong children need to be taught systematically and consistently early in their lives; otherwise, maintenance of the Hmong language will continue to depend on the oral teaching of Hmong parents and the Bible studies held by Christian Hmong families, both of which are wholly inadequate for the task.

Hmong Oral Tradition

Learning to speak Hmong is not the same as learning Hmong oral tradition. By instinct, Hmong children whose parents and other family members speak Hmong learn how to speak Hmong. Their fluency in Hmong oral language is the foundation for their enjoyment of Hmong myths, legends, and folktales. It is the beginning of their journey into Hmong oral tradition.

What is Hmong oral tradition? Simply put, Hmong oral tradition is a long-standing custom of storytelling. Hmong communicate their values, beliefs, customs related to their cultural norms, and events of the past through ethnic stories without written script. These stories contain expressions of ideas, thoughts, and emotions. Hmong oral history can be traced back thousands of years and has continued to the present day. Even though writing systems are available, Hmong still rely heavily on the telling of stories to convey everyday thoughts as well as formal information. Hmong use their oral tradition for ed-

ucation as well as for simple communication and entertainment. Hmong oral tradition is taught in various ways through different media, and oral mastery of the Hmong language is highly prized regardless of one's formal education or socioeconomic status.

Hmong males are expected to be proficient in Hmong oral skills. Mastery of Hmong oral language is a prerequisite for singing Hmong wedding chants (*zaj tshoob*), courtship songs (*kwv txhiaj*), funeral chants (*txiv xaiv*), death songs (*nkauj tuag*), wedding songs (*nkauj tshoob*), Hmong musical songs (*hu nkauj Hmoob losi yas suab*), social and celebration chants (*nkauj nkaum toj*), folksongs (*kwv txhiaj losi lus taum*), Hmong poems (*paj huam*), and Hmong kowtowing chants (*ua tsaug*). It is necessary for performing religious rites (*kev cai dab qhua*) such as soul calling (*hu plig*), making sacrificial offerings (*laig dab losi ntawg rau*), and summoning the benevolent spirits (*fiv yeem*). In the old days, oral arguments were part of Hmong tribunal court proceedings and leaders who had strong oral skills and etymological knowledge could speak well on behalf of their clan mates.

Remember, in the Hmong way of life, gender enters into everything. Because sons will eventually lead their own households, Hmong sons must acquire at least the minimum level of Hmong oral language proficiency required for traditional rituals, speeches, and everyday communication. By their late teen years, sons have to demonstrate adequate mastery of Hmong oral skills. They have to show that they know how to speak to adults and interact with adults in solving basic family problems and conflicts. Most importantly, they must be able to demonstrate that they can apply basic reasoning of Hmong oral arguments in accordance with Hmong cultural and traditional values, customs, and beliefs.

Hmong daughters, on the other hand, do not have to master the Hmong traditional oral rituals because they are barred from performing these religious rites. They have to develop appropriate verbal skills and learn social vocabulary, including verbal expressions that reinforce traditions. They learn from their mothers, aunts, grandmothers, and other female relatives the words and manners used in everyday situations. Hmong daughters as well as Hmong sons, having acquired the language, can participate in Hmong oral traditions.

As Hmong parents expose their families to various cultural and traditional events, they make learning Hmong oral tradition a ubiquitous part of life for their children. However, if the children are to continue the traditions and pass them on to their children, the sons must develop the language skills that enable them to repeat the verses, chants, and songs used in Hmong ceremonial and religious rituals. Developing this capability is difficult for many native-born Hmong children today because they are taught to speak English first and do not master Hmong in their early years. To preserve their oral tradition, Hmong children must be literate in Hmong; their oral proficiency should be reinforced with Hmong texts and other written materials.

The stories that make up the rich Hmong oral tradition are found in rituals, folk songs, myths, epics and legends, folktales, religious stories, and death songs and funeral chants.

Rituals

Verbal utterances are the central ingredients of Hmong rituals. Performing rituals requires observation, emulation, rote memorization, and constant practice. Verbal skills and sharp memory are valuable keys to the practice of Hmong religious and cultural rituals. Hmong males in traditional families assume the responsibility of performing simple ceremonies and religious rituals such as the soul calling ritual (*hu plig*), household altar or shrine renewal (*txi xwm kab losi seej khab*), making spiritual offerings to the deceased (*laig dab losi ntawg rau*), summoning benevolent spirits for protection and guidance (*fiv yeem*), performing New Year's rituals (*foob yeem, cheb qab nthab, losi lwm sub*), and worshiping ancestors (*coj dab qhua*). Christian Hmong families do not have to fulfill the religious ritual obligations. Good oral skills are very important in performing the rituals because failure to follow protocols ac-

curately may result in curses, bad luck, and sometimes death.

Here is an example of Hmong soul calling ritual:

> *Hos, hnub no tsuas zoo hnub, hnub no tsuas zoo nyoog. Hnub no tsuas yog hnub hu, hmo no tsuas yog hmo tos. Hnub no tsuas yog lawm zaj laug hnub, hnub no tsuas yog lawm zaj tso nyoog. Kuv tsuas hu me ntxhais Emilee no ces kom nws cia li sawv tsees rov hlo los rau os.... Niam thiab txiv muaj qaib muaj qe tos, tsis txhob tu siab mus tu saus, cia li sawv tsees rov hlo lo rau lo rau os....*

Even though plenty of pre-recorded materials and written texts on the rituals are available in Hmong, oral mastery of the traditional rituals is the key to successful performance. Hardly ever does anyone see a Hmong performer reading scripts or referring to a video while performing religious rituals. Hmong expect all performers to have fully mastered the verses, chants, and scripts before performing. Reading the words or watching a video is considered immature and inadequate. Hmong people do not go by written scripts or scripted speeches; they prefer that performers speak straight from their minds and hearts. Speeches can be out of context and irrelevant, but the ability to articulate verbally allows the speaker to say what is appropriate for the moment. A great ritual performer has excellent communication skills and wonderful logical abilities, but he may be a lousy public speaker.

Hmong shamans and magicians demonstrate great oral skills by memorizing all their songs, chants, and riddles, and they perform all the rituals without reference to any written materials. They have to study hard and practice diligently in order to commit so much to memory. The path pointer or death guide (*tus taw kev losi tus qhuab ke*) who performs the Showing the Way chants has to memorize many verses, the lushen instrument player (*txiv qeej*) must be able to play all spiritual songs, and the death song singer (*txiv nkauj*) has to remember a vast number of different chants.

Many Hmong children lack the oral skills to take on these tasks. Many Hmong children cannot sing the traditional songs during the New Year's celebration. Hmong children cannot translate or interpret the English word *jaundice* in Hmong. The word *jaundice* means "pale" or "looking pale in the face or eyes," but Hmong children typically translate the word as "yellow face" or "having a yellow appearance." Here is another example, the Hmong word for "*uterus*" is "tsev memyuam," therefore, in English, it can be translated as "the house of the baby or the baby's house." Perhaps textbooks, scripts, CDs, DVDs, Hmong-English dictionaries, and audio tapes can be used to help the younger generation. Or Hmong may need to modernize their religious rituals in order to accommodate the lower level of oral skills in future performers. Otherwise, the high oral skills requirement may hinder the traditional practices because Hmong do not have consistent reinforcement or a formalized process for training Hmong children in their oral traditions. The current minimal training may not be adequate as the Hmong population continues to grow.

Folk Songs

Singing Hmong folk songs requires rote memorization, improvisation of verses, social skills, a creative mind, and oral linguistic proficiency. During the Hmong New Year's celebration adults and teenagers sing traditional folk songs and courtship songs. In Hmong culture, singing is an indirect expression of emotion. Hmong oral tradition is rich with emotions, creativity, innovation, and symbolism. Hmong sing the traditional folk songs to express their feelings through symbolic and imaginary verses of fantasies and dreams.

Most Hmong courtship songs are based on thoughts, wishes, hopes, fantasies, and dreams. Hmong folk songs can have a wide range of themes: finding love and romance, immigration and separation, leaders and leadership, an enemy taking over the homeland, memories of childhood, misery, expectations and dreams, parental approval or disapproval, comparative beauty and fatal attraction, foolish thoughts and enticements,

poverty and orphanhood, a good life with loving parents, living with tears and a broken heart, the beauty of love and romance, a blind date, instant courtship, imaginary sexuality, the purpose of Hmong New Year, the lonely heart without a loving partner, teasing with a kind heart, or eternal love. The singers of these songs are very creative; they usually assemble and sing their verses spontaneously. They have to master the Hmong colloquial language, including registers, pragmatics, and imaginary expressions.

Here is an example of a folk song:

> *Nia yais ... me niam leej ntxhais ... xyoo no loj yog dabtsi xyoo es txiv leej tub yuav tuaj daj dees khaub plees nkauj raum zoo nyog luaj no ... cas yuav muab niam thiab txiv lub tsiab peb caug los noj tag nrho es txiv leej tub lub siab nyiam koj yuav ua cas nco....*
>
> *Nia yais ... me niam leej ntxhais ... xyoo no loj yog dabtsi xyoo es txiv leej tub yuav tuaj ntsib tau me nkauj Hmoob tus siab loj siab dav ... cas yuav muaj niam thiab txiv lub tsiab peb caug los noj tag nrho es txiv leej tub yuav ua cas mus ua noj thiab yuav ua cas xav....*
>
> *Nia yais ... me niam leej ntxhais ... xyoo no loj yog dabtsi xyoo es txiv leej tub yuav pom tau me nkauj Hmoob tus siab zoo siab ncaj ... cas yuav muaj niam thiab txiv lub tsiab peb caug los noj tag nrho es txiv leej tub lub siab yuav ua cas nroo thiab yua ua kaj....*

These three verses tell the story of a first encounter and include the New Year's spirits, emotions, and life. The rhyming words are key words and the stanzas are connected with symbolic expressions. The lyrics are similar to those of modern songs. Hmong traditional courtship folk songs can be plaintive or funny, depending on the singers. Some songs are memorized, rehearsed, and recited, but most singers are innovative artists. The purposes of this type of folk song are to initiate the courtship, express interest in one another, express emotions and mutual respect, affirm the relationship, and entertain the New Year's spirits. Once a romantic alliance has been established between two parties, the traditional courtship songs can also be expressive and detailed, and if the singers are interested in each other, their songs could be personal and serious. Sometimes, the singing ends in marriage.

In the old days, Hmong children were encouraged from a young age to create and sing simple verses. Hmong have always placed a strong emphasis on oral skills and verbal expression because they had no written works to fall back on or to support their linguistic development. The emphasis may be less today because printed materials are available. However, Hmong still prefer oral communication, whether in Hmong or in English. Hmong parents reinforce oral skills through storytelling, using fictional and nonfictional characters and events as well as fanciful plots and fantasies.

Myths

Myths are stories of gods and goddesses and imagined characters and events told to entertain and keep children interested in learning and practicing the Hmong language. They may be legends, fables, folktales, and imaginary stories, similar to animated movies and cartoons. An example of Hmong mythological events is the great flood. The story of the great flood has a few versions and has been told to Hmong children for thousands of years. Some of the details of the story match those of similar tales from other cultures, but the Hmong version is relevant to their history, religious practices, and everyday lives. Table 9.1 presents one of the Hmong versions of the great flood.

Table 9.1. An Excerpt of the Hmong Mythological Story of the Great Flood

Hmong Story *Dej Nyab Ntiaj Teb*	*English Translation* *The Great Flood*
Puag thaum ub ces, lub ntiaj teb ua voj ua vias, ntuj ntxeev ces teb nphau lau, ces dej nyab ntiaj teb. Tib neeg tuag tag, tabsi tshuav ob tug nus muag uas nkawv tau khiav mus nkaum hauv ib lub nruas tuag loj loj xwb lau.	A very long time ago, the whole world was wobbly unstable. The whole world turned upside down and water flooded the whole world. All the people perished except two siblings, a brother and a sister, who survived the flood and took refuge in a very large death drum.
Ces dej txawm nyab zuj zus tuaj lau, ces txawm nyab loj zus loj zus ntos plaws ntuj tiag lau. Ces uacas lub niag nruas ntawd txawm ntab must ntsoo ntuj lau, ces nrov ntuj ntoog, ntuj ntoog lau.	The water kept rising and rising until it reached the sky. The death drum floated and bumped the sky, making the sound "thone, thone, thone."
Nrov nrov, ces aub, qaum ntuj txawm hnov lub nruas nrov ces qaum ntuj txawm hais thiab nroos hais tias, "Ab, mus xyuas ntiaj teb saib uacas lub nruas pheej nrov li ntawd no lau." Thiab xav paub tias yog ua licas tiag no ces.	The "thone, thone, thone" sound continued. Heaven heard the sound made by the death drum and said, "Oh, go visit the underworld. Find out why the death drum is making such a sound." Heaven wanted to know what was going on.
Qaum ntuj txawm tso neeg los xyuas, ces uacas aub, dej nyab ntiaj teb puv tuaj ntos plaws ntuj lawm tiag lau, ces qaum ntuj thiaj li hais tias, "Peb yuas tau tso hmuv tooj hmuv hlau mus nkaug ntiaj teb kom tos qhov es cov dej thiaj xau, no lau.	Heaven sent people down to the underworld to inspect the sound made by the drum. Then, gosh, the water flooded the earth, reaching up to the sky. Heaven said, "We have to get copper spears and iron spears to puncture the underworld to make holes so the water can flow away."
Qaum ntuj thiaj li tso hmuv tooj hmuv hlau los nkaug ntiaj teb ces, dej thiaj li xau tag tiag lau. Ces lub nruas ntawd thiaj li maj mam poob zuj zus rov qab los txog hauv ntiaj teb, ces aub uacas, ob tug nug muag txawm hnov lub nruas ntog ntsoo av, ces nkawd txawm muab lub nruas tho qhov lau, ces knawd tawm tau rov rau sab nraud, ces aub, ntiaj teb neeg tuag tag lawm tiag lau. Thiab me tsiaj txhu, mi nas mi noog thiab mi kab mi ntsaum los tuag tag tib si lawm lau, tsis tshuav thiab seem ib tus nyob qhov twg li lau....	So Heaven hurled copper spears and iron spears, piercing the underworld, and the water flowed away. Then the death drum slowly descended back to the underworld. All of a sudden, the two siblings heard the landing thump of the death drum. The two siblings broke the death drum open to get out of it. When they were outside the drum, they realized that all the people had perished. There were no animals left, no birds, no insects. Nothing was left anywhere....

In this mythological story, the Hmong words *ntiaj teb* stand for the whole world or underworld; *qaum ntuj* means heavenly place or upper world; and *nruas* means death drum, funeral drum, or domestic drum. These terms are related to Hmong migration history; the Hmong occupation of the Yellow River basin in China; Hmong death rituals; and the Hmong world composed of *Yaj Ceeb* and *Yeeb Ceeb*, or the upper world and lower world in ancient China. *Qaum ntuj* means *Ceeb Tsheej*, a new Hmong word for heaven. The Hmong word *ntiaj teb* refers to the Hmong occupation of the Yellow River basin. The flood may not have affected the whole world, but only the Hmong kingdom in the Yellow River basin. This myth is a way for Hmong to share the events of their past.

Epics and Legends

Like other ethnic groups, Hmong have long stories of heroes and heroism. Some Hmong epics are based on fictional characters and others tell of actual leaders and heroes. For example, the great story of the Hmong icon *Vang Yee Leng*, who possessed magical power that enabled him to conquer evil and defeat his enemies, is fiction whereas true epics tell of the sacrifices and accomplishments of real-life Hmong leaders such as Major General Vang Pao, Touby Lyfong, Kiatong Lo Blia Yao, Kiatong Moua Chong Kai, Pa Chai Vue, Shong Zer Lo, Kiagtong Lo Pa See, Vue Pa Yia, and others. Hmong legends that narrate true stories include both male and female characters, but Hmong non-fictional legends are pretty much about male heroes.

Table 9.2 gives an example of a fictional legend about a wife who has a kind heart. She sacrificed to give the king a meal, and her action lifted her and her husband from their poor life to prosperity. Hmong use this kind of story to tell their children that if they are considerate and compassionate they may achieve greatness. In this story the wife may appear to be overstepping her cultural boundaries, but her act of kindness change the couple's lives and fortunes.

In their epics and legends, Hmong retell

Table 9.2. The Hmong Legend of the Woodcutter

Hmong Story *Tus Neeg Txiav Taws Lub Neej*	*English Translation* *The Life of the Woodcutter*
Puag thaum ub ces … muaj ob niam txiv ua neej txom txom nyem, tsis muaj dabtsi li. Nkawd tsuas niaj hnub mus txiav taws los muag xwb lau.	A long time ago, there was a couple who were very poor; they had nothing. They went out every day and gathered firewood to sell.
Tabsi nkawd muaj ib tug lau qaib zoo zoo nkauj. Tus txiv mas nyiam tus lau qaib heev li. Mus ris ib fij los txog mas nws yuav tsum mus xyuas tus lau qaib ib zaug mas thiaj li zoo siab.	But they had a handsome rooster. The husband loved the rooster very much. He would check the rooster every day when he came home from gathering firewood; this made him happy.
Ces aub, huab tais hnov tias nkawd txom txom nyem no lau. Ces muaj ib hnub huab tais txawm taug kev tuaj saib nkawd.	The king heard that the couple were very poor. One day the king walked by to pay them a visit.
Hnub huab tais tuaj ces tus txiv tsis nyob hauv tsev lawm lau, tshuav tus niam nyob xwb ces. Aub, tus niam tsis paub yuav nrhiav mov rau huab tais noj lau, vim hais tias nkawd txom txom nyem xwb tsis muaj dabtsi li.	When the king arrived, the husband was not home; only the wife was home. The wife did not know how to prepare a meal for the king because they were so poor and had nothing.
Ces tus niam txawm xav tau tias tshuav tus lau qaib xwb. Tabsi yog nws muab tua, tshe tus txiv yuav tsis txaus siab. Ces tus niam txawm xav tias yog tsis muab tua ua mov rau huab tais noj tshe huab tais yuav tu siab rau nkawd.	Then the wife thought of the handsome rooster. But if she killed the rooster, her husband would be unhappy. She also thought that if she did not kill the rooster to prepare a meal for the king, the king would be sad. The wife decided to butcher the rooster to

Hmong Story	*English Translation*
Tus Neeg Txiav Taws Lub Neej	*The Life of the Woodcutter*

Ces tu niam txiav txim siab muab tus lau qaib tua ua ib pluag nyuag mov meme rau huab tais noj lau. Huab tais noj tag ces huab tais tab tom yuav sawv kev los mus tsev.

Ces aub, tus txiv txawm ris taws los txog tsev lau. Nws mus saib tus lau qaib, nas has aub, uacas tsis pom lawm. Nws khiav rov los nug nws poj niam tias, "Koj niam, uacas tsis pom kuv tus lau qaib lawm?"

Ces tus poj niam teb tias, "Koj txiv, thov txim, kuv muab koj tus lau qaib tua ua ib pluag mov meme rau huab tais noj lawm vim wb tsis muaj dabtsi, thiab zaum no yog thawj thawj zaug uas txiv huab tais tuaj saib wb, no ces."

Aub tus txiv txawm chim chim rau nws tus poj niam, es tsis zoo siab rau nws tus poj niam li lau. Tus txiv ntxawm muab tus niam ntau, ces tus niam txawm quaj quaj nrov hauv txaj tuaj.

Ces huab tais hnov, ces huab tais txawm hais tais, "Uacas neb thiaj li sib ntau sib ceg?"

Tus txiv tsis paub yuav hais licas lau. Tus niam txawm teb ntuas hais tias, "Txiv huab tais, twb tsis muaj dabtsi, nws hais tias uacas kuv tsis tua ib tug npua es kuv yuav tua tus qaib meme ua mov rau koj noj xwb, vim tus qaib me dhau heev lawm."

Ces huab tais teb tias, "Zoo kawg nkaus li lawm mog, tsis txhob sib ntau sib ceg lawm. Tus qaib los leej zoo heev lawm." Ces txiv huab tais sawv kev los tsev lawm.

Cas aub twb tsis tau ntev, txiv huab tais txawm tso nws cov thawj coj thiab tub mab tub qhe tuaj tsav tus txiv ua ib tug coj saib kav peb xeem. Ces txij li hnub ntawd los mus ces tus txiv thiaj li nrog luag ua nom ua tswv, ces nkawd lub neej thiaj li zoo zuj zus los mus lawm lau.

Thaum kawg ces, nkawd tsis tau mus txiav taws los muag lawm vim tus niam lub siab zoo rau txiv huab tais, thiab vim tus niam yog ib tug neeg ntse.

prepare a very small meal for the king. The king finished dining and was about to leave for his palace.

All of sudden, the husband arrived home from gathering firewood. He went to check on the rooster, but the rooster was not there. He ran home and asked his wife, "Dear wife, why do I not see the rooster?"

The wife replied, "Dear husband, please forgive me. I have slaughtered the rooster to prepare a very small meal for the king because we did not have anything else and this was the very first time the king came to visit us."

The husband became very upset with his wife; he was not happy at all. In the bedroom the husband battered the wife for killing their only rooster.

The king heard the commotion and said, "What were you two fighting and arguing about?"

The husband did not know how to respond to the king. The wife gently replied, "Honorable king, there was nothing wrong. He asked why I did not kill a pig to prepare a meal for you, but I only killed a very small rooster; the rooster was way too small."

The king responded, "It was enough. No more fights and arguments. The rooster was good enough." The king left for home.

Not long thereafter, the king ordered his loyalists and servants to appoint the husband a ruler of people. From that day forward the husband was a leader. The couple's life grew better and better.

In the end, the couple did not have to go out and gather firewood for sale anymore because of the kind and considerate heart of the wife toward the king, and because the wife was clever and wise.

the tales of heroism, bravery, and kindness and apply the contents of stories such as this one to convey meaningful messages. The story of the woodcutter has a message of the value of modesty and benevolence. In Hmong culture, practicing benevolence and altruism has nothing to do with family wealth, but with a heart of kindness and compassion.

The story of the husband being exalted by the king reminds the wives of Hmong leaders that if they act in kindness they can elevate the social status of their husbands even if their husbands disagree with some of their actions. However, this does not suggest that Hmong wives should render their decisions without consulting with their husbands, and remember,

Hmong fathers are the primary owners and guardians of their families.

Folktales

Unlike some of the rituals, Hmong folktales do not have to be memorized. They can be told with the help of props such as felt boards, pictures, objects, videos, tapes, books, and animated characters. These props may help inspire and inflame a passion for hearing and learning Hmong stories. Hmong have so many types of folktales that incorporate a number of elements:

- cumulative stories—stories that build, that incorporate repetition, rhythm, and vivid imaginary
- humorous characters—funny figures with peculiar names or magical powers, godly persons, angels, supernatural heroes
- beasts—talking animals, characters that change into animals, dual figures, monsters
- magical stories—fairy tales and tales of magical power, enchantments, healings
- tall tales—fictional tales, exaggerated stories, imagined events
- realistic stories—using actual phenomena, nonfiction, true events, life experience, warfare, religious events
- extraterrestrial experiences—near-death experiences, dreams, power of divinity, psychic readings, palm readings, fortune telling

Some Hmong stories, fictional and nonfictional, have become common fables and many folktales have real-life implications. Hmong refer to these stories as *dab neeg* or *lus nruag*, meaning real stories of real people or imagined stories based on life circumstances and phenomena. Some Hmong folklore is more creative—stories that incorporate imagined characters such as talking animals in real-life situations that teach a moral lesson or a universal truth about life.

Hmong folktales were born out of and therefore describe the Hmong way of life. Many rekindle Hmong agricultural practices and agrarian lifestyle. For example, here is a Hmong folktale that uses as its characters animals that would have been familiar to Hmong ancestors:

Hmong Story A: The Tiger, the Fox, and the Big Ox

Once upon a time there was a herd of wild oxen living on the edge of a huge forest near Hmong villages. A huge and ferocious tiger came out of the forest every day to attack and eat the oxen, but it failed.

The herd was safe because the big ox who was the leader, protector, boss, and elder of the oxen drove the tiger away each time the tiger tried to attack the oxen. The big ox was so strong and fierce that the gigantic tiger could not get near any of the oxen. The tiger became hungry and greedy. He finally ran out of patience.

One day the tiger went to see the fox living in the same vicinity and said to him, "I need you help because there are so many oxen living in the area. Go to the big ox and tell him that soon there will not be enough grass for so many of his fellow oxen to eat. Tell him if he allows me to eat some of them, he will be able to have more grass for himself." The tiger pleaded to the fox for help and promised the fox, "The oxen can be our meal. When I kill the oxen, you, fox, can eat the meat with me." The fox was not certain but agreed to the tiger's request.

The next day the fox went to the big ox to relay the tiger's message. The fox said, "Hello, big ox. I am here to tell you something I heard from the tiger. The tiger king told me to tell you that there are so many of your folks eating the grass here and soon there will not be enough grass for you to eat. Is that right?"

The big ox snorted and ignored the fox. The fox repeated the same statement a few times. "Yes, my family is big and that is right," said the big ox. "Soon we'll have to find a new place because the grass does not grow quickly enough to feed us all. Then what should we do, fox?"

The fox said to the big ox, "Big ox, you do not have to move. But you need to reduce the size of your family. So, if you allow the tiger to eat some of your fellow oxen to make their number less, there will be enough grass for you to feed the rest of you for some time. And you can keep your family here for much longer. "

The big ox looked confused. After thinking for a while, the big ox replied to the fox, "Well, I don't want to move from this place. This is my place, but I do not care much about the rest of the oxen if we should run out of grass to eat. Do whatever you want as long as the grass is green."

The fox thanked the big ox and went back to the tiger with the news. The fox said, "Big ox says we can do whatever we want as long as the grass is green. Everything went well, Mr. Tiger. It is time for delicious meals."

On that day, the scavenger mission got started. The gigantic tiger killed an ox each day. And the fox followed the tiger and ate the leftovers. As the days, weeks, and months went by, they killed and ate nearly all of the oxen except the big ox.

The tiger became very fat. The big ox, eating all the grass by himself, became very fat too. The fox was not very happy about eating leftovers; he wanted to eat more.

The time came when there was no animal left to be hunted by the tiger and the fox. The two scavengers became hungry again. One day the fox return to the big ox and told him a lie about the tiger's hunger. The fox said, "Big ox, the tiger is saying that he has nothing left to eat since he has finished off all of your folks, and he is now so hungry that he wants to eat you as well. And he wants me to tell you that."

The big ox stared at the fox, snorted, and asked, "Is that true? You tell the tiger that I will not let him eat me."

The fox replied to deceive the big ox, "Yes, it is certainly true. That is what the tiger has told me to tell you." So, from that point on the big ox was very careful. He felt betrayed by the fox and the tiger. However, his herd was gone.

The fox went to the tiger and told him a lie about the big ox's intent to drive him away from the forest. The fox said, "Tiger, I am telling what the big ox is saying about you. The big ox is saying that because you have killed all of his folks and he has eaten all the grass by himself, he is now strong enough to drive you away. If you ever go near him, he will chase you from the forest."

The tiger was shocked to hear the news and became very careful too. "Fox, you tell the big ox that he cannot chase me away. I will fight him to death," the tiger warned. The fox had fooled both the big ox and the tiger.

Not too long after that, the tiger and the big ox met each other on the road. They immediately became enemies and engaged in a quarrel. Neither of them was afraid of the other, so they started to fight. The fox sat and watched them fight.

The battle continued for days, weeks, and months. The big ox and the tiger fought and fought until they were both physically exhausted and died on the road. Then the fox came out of the woods and ate both of them.

When the fox finished eating the big ox and the tiger, he had nothing left to eat. He became hungry and came to the nearby Hmong villages to search for food. Each night, the fox snatched and killed Hmong chickens from the chicken house. The Hmong villagers became very angry.

After many chickens had been killed and eaten by the fox, the village people wanted to catch the fox. Many said, "We have to catch that sneaky fox or more chickens will be killed."

So, the village people set traps and snares around their chicken houses to catch the fox.

The next day, when the fox came to the villages for the chickens, he was caught in a trap and died. The village people celebrated the fox's death and displayed his body to warn other foxes not to snatch and kill Hmong chickens.

Another Hmong folktale describes how a snail outwits a monkey who made fun of the snail because of its physical limitations. Hmong believe that deliberate disdain of others is not appropriate behavior but that one should show respect for others. This folktale makes that point through a story:

HMONG STORY B: THE RACE BETWEEN THE SNAIL AND THE MONKEY

A long time ago there was a monkey who went out to search for food. The monkey met a snail that was also looking for food.

The monkey saw that the snail crawled slowly. The monkey laughed and said, "Snail, I walk and move so fast and could not find food. You are crawling very slowly; in one day you cannot crawl even three feet. So how you can find food to eat?"

The snail replied, "Well, I can find food, too, even though I am slow. We can race to search for food if you'd like."

The monkey answered right away, "When can we race to find food?"

The snail answered, "How about three days from now? We will meet here and we will race. Whoever can cross the three hills and three valleys first will win the race."

"All right, it is a deal. Whenever you are ready, I am ready. I am not worried if it is only you," the monkey responded. Then the monkey and the snail went their separate ways.

The monkey returned to the forest and continued to search for food. He enjoyed his meals and did not worry about the race. Going up the three hills and down the three valleys would be easy. But the snail was concerned and returned home to call all his brothers and relatives for help.

The snail held a meeting with all his friends to discuss the plan for racing the monkey in three days. The snail asked, "What should we do?"

The snail told his brothers and relatives to crawl out to the three hills and three valleys and wait for the monkey to show up in three days. "Whenever the monkey pauses to check on the snail, any snail who hears the monkey must respond by saying, 'I am here.' Only the one in front of the monkey should respond." The snail gave these instructions to all the snails. They all agreed to help the snail win the race. As planned, they dispersed to different locations along the race's path to wait for the monkey.

When the third day came, the monkey and the snail met at the designated location to race each other. Both agreed to count to three and then race up the three hills and down the three valleys. Right away, the monkey sprang ahead of the snail and disappeared in the woods. The snail started crawling slowly.

When the monkey was half way up the hill, he paused and called to the snail, "Snail, where are you?"

The snail ahead of the monkey replied, "I am here, ahead of you."

The monkey resumed running until he reached the top of the hill. Again he called to the snail, "Snail, I am here. Where are you?"

The snail ahead of the monkey answered, "I am ahead of you. I am up here."

The monkey rushed down the hill to the valley. At the midway point, the monkey stopped and called to the snail, "Snail, I am here. Where are you?"

Again, the snail ahead of the monkey responded, "Monkey, I am ahead of you."

The monkey raced down the hill so fast that he stumbled many times. Every time he called to the snail, the snail was always ahead of him. The monkey continued to dash downhill and uphill to try to get ahead of the snail. Before the race was over, the monkey was completely exhausted and had no more energy. He panted, slipped, and walked clumsily.

The monkey kept wondering why he was not able to beat the snail, but he could not come up with an idea for how to win the race. The monkey tried and tried until he collapsed and couldn't get up. The snail was still ahead of him.

At the end, the monkey was so embarrassed because he lost the race against the snail that he crawled slowly. The monkey could not believe that he lost and he suffocated himself and died on the way back. The snail remained at the starting line and did not even run at all because his friends and relatives helped him win the race.

In Hmong culture, folktales such as these have been told for thousands of years to instruct children and keep them engaged in Hmong myths, legends, and storytelling. Of course, these stories have little meaning if one is disinclined to learn the values, beliefs, and customs related to everyday Hmong life hidden beneath the words. For instance, the story of the tiger, the fox, and the big ox is about disgruntlement, betrayal, greed, and treachery, and it ended unhappily for all those who displayed these traits. The final scene—the death of the fox—illustrates that greed, disloyalty, and reckless ambitions lead to one's demise.

Hmong apply these stories to their real-life situations. For instance, the story of the monkey and the snail illustrates that even if one is bigger, faster, smarter, and richer one should not show off with boastful attitudes and behaviors, disdaining those who may not possess the same physical and material advantages. Hmong elders use this kind of story to remind young people to refrain from unacceptable attitudes and behaviors and develop appropriate manners so they can conduct themselves properly in social settings.

Some Hmong folktales contain accounts Hmong believe explain how certain things came to be. Regardless of how many times these stories are told by different people, the content remains the same. Here is an excerpt from such a story:

HMONG STORY C:
THE GENESIS OF PEOPLE

Once upon a time, at the beginning of life on earth, only the two siblings, a brother and a sister, survived the great flood. There was no one else besides them living on this massive earth. They lived in solitude and became lonely and sad because they saw no other living beings.

When they reached their teen years, there were no other people they could court to marry. There were no friends. The two siblings decided to seek help from the highest authority; they went to seek advice from the wizard of prophecy (*saub*), who could communicate with God about their marital dilemma. The two siblings asked if they could marry each other because there was no one besides them. The prophet told them they could if they performed some feats that determined that it was suitable for them to marry because they were siblings. The prophet gave the two siblings specific instructions to follow.

According to the prophet, the two siblings had to carry two pieces of rock up the hill behind their house. Once they reached the top of the hill, they had to roll their rocky pieces downhill. If the two pieces of rock rolled down the hillside and landed on top of each other face down or the two pieces landed upside down on top of each other, they could get married. Otherwise, they would never be allowed to marry each other. The two siblings set out to perform the feat prescribed by the prophet.

The brother and sister made the two pieces of rock. They took the two pieces of rock to the top of the hill and rolled them downhill. The two pieces did not land on top of each other as described by the prophet. The two siblings tried many times, but they could not get the rock pieces to land as they wanted. Then one morning the brother rolled his piece down the hill and went after it. He rushed downhill and placed his piece over his sister's piece so they were on top of each other as the prophet had said. When his sister ran downhill to check her piece, she saw that the two pieces were on top of each other. She was convinced that

they had accomplished the feat given by God through the prophet.

The two siblings felt relieved and went to tell the prophet of their success. After listening to them, the prophet had no choice but to allow them to get married. The two siblings finally married.

Not long thereafter, the wife became pregnant with a son. The couple was extremely happy. When the son was born, he had no eyes, nose, mouth, ears, or head. The baby looked like a solid piece of meatloaf that had an oval shape. The father was very sad and very disappointed. He went to tell the prophet about the baby's deformity because the purpose of their marriage was to repopulate the earth. He asked the prophet to tell him how they could populate the world with a piece of meatloaf.

Calmly, the prophet heard his concerns and told the father to return home and chop the meatloaf into pieces. The prophet instructed the father to scatter the cut pieces in different hills, valleys, and other locations. The father was told to wait and see what would happen next. The father was reluctant to chop his son into pieces, but the prophet gave him the authority to do so and he complied.

When he returned home, he told his wife what the prophet had instructed him to do. His wife was very concerned but because the baby was so deformed she felt she had no choice but to comply with the order and see what would happen next. The very next day the parents performed the sacrifice, cutting the meatloaf into pieces and scattering the pieces in different places. The father and mother were weary after spending the whole day cutting the meatloaf and scattering the pieces. So they went to bed.

When they woke up the next morning, they saw smoke rising from all the places where they had scattered the cut pieces of the meatloaf. They were shocked by the smoke. They rushed to see what the smoke was about and they were surprised to find a group of people at each location. They checked all the places where they had placed pieces and found people living at each location.

They did not know what to call these new people. They decided to name each group in accordance with its location. They named the group living in a garden (*lub vaj*) the Vang family (*tsev neeg Vaj*). They called the group that emerged from the corn storage (*lub txhab*) the Chang family (*tsev neeg Cha*). To the group that got stuck at the top of some trees (*ntsis ntoo*) they gave the name the Li family (*tsev neeg Li*). The group coming out of the bamboo forest (*hav xyoob*) became the Xiong family (*tsev neeg Xyooj*). The group that came from the slope (*ntav toj*) they called the Thao family (*tsev neeg Thoj*), and so on.

This was how the two siblings repopulated the earth after the great flood. This is the genesis of human life on earth.

This story not only explains the genesis of people on earth, but also the origin of the

Hmong family clan system. The story describes how Hmong family last names came about. Even if this and similar stories do not portray true events, Hmong still honor these folktales as part of Hmong past because they have been told for thousands of years. Table 9.3 lists more folktales that have been part of Hmong oral tradition. The reiteration of stories helps Hmong think about their history and their evolution. Hmong storytelling ties the past generations to the present and future ones.

Table 9.3. Selected Hmong Folktales

Title of story in Hmong	English Translation	Story
Liab thiab Tsov	The Monkey and the Tiger	This story is about the playful tricks between the Monkey and the Tiger.
Tub Npluag Tau Ua Huab Tais Vauv	A Hmong Cloth Story: How a Poor Man Became the King's Son-in-law	This story is about a poor man who fulfills the King's wish that someone would get his daughter to talk.
Dab Neeg Hais Txog Ib Tug Tub Kawm Ntawv Hmoob	Story About a Hmong Student	This is a nonfiction story about a Hmong refugee child who achieved his dream in America.
Liab thiab Tsov Sib Tso Dag Uasi	A Prank Between the Monkey and the Tiger	The big and slow tiger and the smaller and faster monkey engage in a mischievous act.
Hmoob Lub Neej Thaum Ub Nyob Teb Chaws Nplog	Hmong Way of Life in Laos: Life Before America	This is a nonfiction story about the Hmong agrarian lifestyle before coming to America.
Ntuj Tsim Teb Raug-Neeg, Noob Qoob, Nqaij, Hnub thiab Hli	The Beginning of the World: People, Grains, Meat, Sun, and Moon	A long time ago the earth was dark and people discovered light and food for survival.
Dab Neeg Niam Nkauj Zuag Paj	The Legend of Nia Ngao Zoua Pa	This is a romantic story of a very poor orphan who married a princess.
Vauv Qav Kaws	The Toad Son-in-law	This is a romantic story of a toad who is a handsome man with a camouflaged body who marries a princess.
Muam Nkauj Lia Lub Cev Cia Li Txawj Xeeb Tub	Mua Ngao Lia and Her Miraculous Conception of a Child	This is a romantic story about a virgin daughter who became pregnant before marrying an orphan.
Txiv Nraug Ntsuag Nrhiav Tau Nyiaj thiab Tau Kub	An Orphan Found Buried Treasures	A very poor boy who has nothing in life seeks help from a wizard and listens to different cave animals who know where to find buried treasures.
Nkauj Ntsuab thiab Sis Nab	Ngao Youa and Shee Na	This story is about a newlywed couple and the ruling king who took the beautiful bride away from the husband.
Vim Licas Neeg Ua Liaj Ua Teb Thiaj Tau Sau Qoob Loos Los Tsev	Why Farmers Have to Harvest and Carry Their Crops from the Field to Their Houses	This story is about the Hmong farming lifestyle and the walking and talking crops that Hmong once rejected.

Notes: Information on Hmong stories from Dab Neeg Hmong *(Myths, Legends and Fold Tales), by C. Johnson & Se Yang, 1992, St. Paul, MN: Macalester College.*

Religious Stories

Hmong have many stories that are related to the practice of Hmong death rituals and funeral rites. For instance, the story of a beautiful bride who was stolen by a tiger (*Nuj Nphlaib thiab Nkauj Ntxawm*) or the story of a tiger who courted a beautiful Hmong girl at night (*Tswv Xyas*). There are stories of messianic saviors, heroic warriors, and guardian angels; stories about healing from pain and suffering, rescuing the poor and the oppressed, fighting evil and demons; and stories that tell of karma and nirvana. These religious tales are more than stories; they have implications for life.

Traditional Hmong families believe that spiritual curses after death are real and the reincarnation of the soul in a new life is important to the everlasting connection between the physical world and the spiritual world regardless of the time of death. Hmong believe the soul of the deceased never dies but will return to the family when it has been reincarnated. Also, Hmong believe the soul cannot leave the family but will be reincarnated in a new member of the same family. Therefore, the life of the soul of the deceased will remain in the family forever. None of these beliefs can be proven, but Hmong hold fast to them.

Nevertheless, some of the beliefs that are in Hmong religious stories have been borne out in the form of spiritual curses. For instance, the shamanistic spirits of deceased parents and ancestors have appeared to return to convince a living family member to become a shaman (*dab neeb los tshoj*); family members have become shamans in response to inner urgings. It appears true that the spirits of deceased fathers have sent illnesses to family members to tell their living sons to honor their soul because the parental spirits are searching for food (*tuaj nrhiav noj*); family members have actually become ill. Such real-life incidents reinforce the value to Hmong of their religious stories.

Hmong religious stories are communicated through shamanistic practices because only Hmong shamans can communicate with the spiritual world and with the dead. Families usually accept and comply with the shaman's assessment of situations. Hmong shamanism plays a major role in Hmong religious practices; however, not all shamanistic stories are true and accurate.

But what about religious stories that have been told over and over for thousands of years, such as the stories of *Siv Yis thiab Dab Tsog-Dab Noj Nyoog Haus Txias* (Shee Yee and the Evil Spirits: Eating People and Drinking Blood) and *kev tsis sib haum xeeb ntawm Siv Yis and Ntxwg Nyoog* (The Warfare Between Shee Yee and the Ferocious Beast Churn Young)? In these stories, Shee Yee is the master of Hmong shamanism and the magician who protects the sick, raises the dead to life, and stops the demons from oppressing innocent people; Dab Tsog, or Churn Young, is the ferocious beast, demon, evil, or satanic being who does all the evil spells that make people sick and die.

According to Hmong shamanism, the legends of Shee Yee play a crucial role in Hmong religious practices, particularly those practices that have to do with herbal medicine and healing. Here is a simplified version of one of the versions of the story of Shee Yee and Churn Young:

A long long time ago, the Hmong people came down to live on earth from a very high place known as the upper world. Soon after their arrival, the ferocious beast known as Churn Young (*Ntxwg Nyoog*) sent evil spells to curse the Hmong. Many became ill with pain and suffering. Lots of people died. The Hmong had no cure and called out for help, but no one seemed to be interested in helping the sick and dying. The death toll was high and people continued to die. But the Hmong kept calling out to the sky for help.

The highest God in the upper world heard the Hmong calling for help. He sent Shee Yee (*Siv Yis*) down to check out the situation and all the commotion on earth. Shee Yee was a shaman and came down with a life-saving coat of arms, a protective shell, a sword, a crossbow, a gong, two rattling finger rings, magical power, drums, and all sorts of shamanistic tools. When he landed on earth, Shee Yee saw Hmong getting sick and dying. Shee Yee used his magical power to raise the dead, heal the blind, remove curses, relieve pain and suffering, fight the evil spells, protect the oppressed, safeguard innocent victims, overcome all the sicknesses, and train Hmong to become shamans.

When Churn Young learned of Shee Yee's magical power and healing abilities, the ferocious demon became very angry and waged a spiritual war against Shee Yee. The beast cast more evil spells and more people died. Every time Churn Young killed someone, Shee Yee raised the dead back to life again. The war continued for many years. The Hmong depended on Shee Yee for help and they honored Shee Yee for his spiritual protection from the ferocious beast. Shee Yee trained Hmong to become shamans and gave them the power to cure the sick and to protect the human soul.

One day Shee Yee had to ascend back to the upper world to fight with the beast for the last time. Shee Yee took all his tools with him. Churn Young knew that Shee Yee was on his way to the upper world to fight him. Churn Young became fearful and sent his evil spells to curse Shee Yee's son. Churn Young turned Shee Yee's son into a beautiful bull.

While traveling to the upper world to face the ferocious evil, Shee Yee came in contact with the beautiful bull, but he did not know that the bull was his own son whom Churn Young had turned into a bull. Before engaging in the spiritual fight, Churn Young told Shee Yee that the beautiful bull was a sacrificial animal that had to be killed to make a final offering to the highest God before the fight. Shee Yee had no objection and complied with the offering.

When the beautiful bull was butchered, Churn Young secretly cooked part of the meat and invited Shee Yee to dine with him before their final battle. Shee Yee agreed and ate with the ferocious beast. When they finished eating, the ferocious beast made an unusual request to Shee Yee. He told Shee Yee that if he returned to earth to help cure the sick he would not cast evil spells anymore. Churn Young reminded Shee Yee that they had been fighting for many years and he said he did not want to continue fighting. Shee Yee agreed to return to earth.

While descending to earth, Shee Yee saw the soul of his own son wandering in the opposite direction. Shee Yee called out to his son, but his son did not respond. Shee Yee called out again and again. The soul walked farther and farther away. Shee Yee knew it was his son. Shee Yee was upset. He took out his crossbow to shoot at the soul. Finally, the soul turned around to face Shee Yee and said, "Father, why are you calling me and why do I have to respond to your calling?" Shee Yee replied, "You are my son." Then the son said, "Father, you know I am already dead because you have already eaten part of my flesh. The ferocious beast, your only enemy, has fooled you. He used his evil spell to turn me into a beautiful bull and give you an illusion. The beast made me a sacrificial animal to be offered to the highest God. I am the bull that was just killed."

Shee Yee was stunned and disbelieved. The soul of the son continued walking in the opposite direction. Shee Yee called out to him not to go. The soul never turned back to face Shee Yee again. Shee Yee was devastated. He cried aloud in vain because his own son had been sacrificed by Churn Young; but worse, Shee Yee had to admit to having eating his son's flesh. When the soul disappeared from sight, Shee Yee was heartbroken, distraught over his misguided actions.

Shee Yee threw all his magical tools down to earth and ascended back to the upper world. The Hmong people called out to Shee Yee for help, but Shee Yee decided not to come down again. The Hmong made sacrifices to try to persuade Shee Yee to come down, but Shee Yee refused to descend to earth. The Hmong begged Shee Yee to come back, but Shee Yee ignored their calls. Finally, the Hmong stopped calling Shee Yee and mentioned his name only while performing the shamanistic rituals he had taught them. Shee Yee never returned to earth to overcome the evil spells and did not finish his spiritual warfare against the ferocious beast.

Hmong shamans are good, but they are not as magically strong as Shee Yee because Shee Yee did not give all his magical power to the Hmong shamans to cure all sicknesses. Hmong shamans are able to practice shamanism in honor of Shee Yee. They do so to try to counteract the evil spells in order to defend the body and to preserve the soul from being taken away by the ferocious beast and prevent the soul from suffering harm.

Hmong shamans engage in shamanistic rituals to fight the evil spirits and devils. They use Shee Yee's magical chants along with the instruments he left them: water, fire, magical dust, shields, swords, bows, and drums. When they go into trances, Hmong shamans become possessed by the *Neeb Spirits* once owned by Shee Yee and are led into the spiritual world. To foretell the future, Hmong shamans sacrifice chickens, pigs, cows, goats, and buffalos. They examine the tongues, eyes, wings, feet, and skulls of boiled chickens and the tails of cows and pigs to predict future events. However, the accuracy of their predictions is subject to different interpretation and the interpretations are sometimes symbolic.

Death Songs and Funeral Chants

Hmong rely heavily on verbal skills for conducting all their death rituals and funeral rites. Good verbal communication is the key to the successful performance of all religious ceremonies. All the death songs and funeral blessing chants are sung orally, and all singers and chanters have to memorize all the verses of all the songs and chants. Although all the proceedings are done without written materials, here is an example of a stanza of a Hmong death song:

Mog npliag mog sib saub! Saub laug saub sib lis aim, zoo li kuv txiv nkauj yuav xau nkauj lis zus lawm toj peg, neb yuav xaus neb ntiv qeej ntiv nruas tseg no tsi sub es! Mog npliaj mog sib saub! Saub laug saub sib lis aim, zoo li kuv txiv nkauj ces yuav xaus nkauj lis zus rau lawm toj mus rooj ntxhia, neb txiv qeej txiv nruas yuav xaus qeej xaus nruas lis zus cia. Ua txiav kuv txiv nkauj ces xa tsis txhua, neb nkawm txiv qeej txiv nruas xa kom txog ncua, txiv nkauj ces nkauj tsis muaj tag no tsi sub es! [In English, to the spirits of the wizard of prophecy like me, I will end my singing of the death song gradually. You, the players of the bamboo reed pipe and the death drum, will stop playing! To the spirits of the wizard of prophecy like me, I would like to end my singing of the death song gradually toward the slope of the chilly hill. You, the players of the bamboo reed pipe and the death drum, will stop to put them away. Suddenly I, the death song singer, cannot deliver it to all. You, the players of the bamboo reed piper and the death drum, will

send it with the wind. The death song singer then has no more coming!]

This stanza is the ending verse of the death song; the whole contains 11 verses. The stanzas are repeated with slightly different wording each time. Singing all 11 verses is quite impressive. Think about the fact that the death singer must memorize all 11 verses. It takes time for him to learn and practice. Imagine that a death song singer often must sing 10 to 20 different songs during the funeral service, all of which he has memorized; that is incredible! Here is an example of a stanza of a Hmong funeral blessing chant:

Hais! Txog siav tuaj lawm yuas nej tsev txoos npoj xyom cuab. Txhia niaj mus txhia xyoo, nws laus ua neej nyob ces nws laus yuav caij tau lawm nws laus tus txiv nees tsaj tsuam mus ua qhua. Xyoo no ces nws laus qaij qaug lis yeev los mus ces ntshai nws laus yuav caij tau lawm sib ntxwg nyoog tus nees txaij nees kwv nyob mus tus hlua. Txhia niaj mus txhia xyoo, nws laus ua neej nyob ces nws yuav caij tau nws laus tus txiv nees tsaj tsuam mus ua qoob. Xyoo no ces nws laus qaij qaug lis yeev los mus ces tshai nws laus yuav caij tau sib ntxwj nyoog tus nees txaij nees kwv nyob mus tus txoob. [In English, say! Here comes the wailing sound of loss to the grieving family. In the usual year, as he, the old, lives, he would ride his dancing, flying horse to become a guest. This year he, the old, has fallen. He will ride the devil striped death horse without reins. In the usual year, as he, the old, lives, he would ride his dancing, flying horse to harvest crops. This year he, the old, has fallen. He will ride the devil striped death horse without its mane.]

This stanza is the beginning verse of a funeral blessing chant; the entire chant has 42 different verses, or stanzas. The verses have a rhyming pattern and many phrases that the singer has to remember. Think of singing three or four chants, each with 42 verses during the blessing phase of the funeral—all from memory. Amazing! The singer cannot reference any book or manuscript. Remember, saving face is important to Hmong, so a singer's performance has to be exemplary. This kind of singing requires a great deal of cognitive acuity, intellectual capacity, and mental energy. It demands excellent oral skills. Singing death songs and funeral blessing chants is not for everyone.

Hidden Stories in Pa Ndau

For thousands of years Hmong arts and handcrafts have been used to convey hidden messages. Hmong women use the artistic designs, symbols, motifs, and appliqués in Hmong flowery fabric and cloth to tell stories through artistic needlework and embroidery textures.

The word *Pa Ndau*, which should be spelled *Paj Ntaub* in Hmong, refers to Hmong tapestry, a flowery cloth or fabric with a flowery design. Pa Ndau is the name given to Hmong needlework, the hand-stitched embroidery Hmong use for their traditional costumes (sashes, aprons, skirts, blouses, shirts, pants, headdresses, and headbands). Literally, Pa Ndau also refers to as Hmong tapestry scripts and is an informal writing system that contains hidden texts, messages, emotions, and expressions. The handcrafts with their elaborate designs and delicate stitching are part of the oldest writing system in Hmong history. The art tells stories in great detail. Some embroidered pieces relate ancient stories of legend and some tell recent stories of war and resettlement. The Hmong art of Pa Ndau is a form of Hmong oral history.

Hmong Pa Ndau conveys many hidden stories created and written mostly by Hmong women, as illustrated in Figures 9.1, 9.2, 9.3, 9.4 and 9.5. It can tell of shamanistic rituals; the Hmong wedding ceremony; Hmong emigration from Laos; Hmong folktales and fables; love stories; and stories of livestock and draft animals, rice and corn fields, harvest and cultivation seasons, Hmong villages, musical instruments, agricultural tools, wild

Figure 9.1. Hmong livestock, draft animals, and wild animals. From Dr. Christopher Vang's collection.

Top: **Figure 9.2. The fall of Laos in 1975 and Hmong escape from Laos to Thailand.** *Bottom:* **Figure 9.3. Hmong agrarian lifestyle and Hmong crops. Both from Dr. Christopher Vang's collection.**

games and hunting seasons, and the Hmong agrarian lifestyle.

Most Hmong Pa Ndau handcrafts are artistic characteristics and symbols designed by Hmong women. Hmong women teach their female children the art of Pa Ndau needlework early in life because they will use the knowledge and skills throughout their

Top: **Figure 9.4. Hmong cultivation and harvesting.** *Bottom:* **Figure 9.5. Hmong folktales, legends, and myths related to the great flood and the survival of the two siblings who repopulated the world by creating the Hmong family clan system. Both from Dr. Christopher Vang's collection.**

lives. Hmong Pa Ndau truly reflects the practice of storytelling using the old ideographic scripts and characters that enable Hmong women to express their thoughts through symbols and metaphors.

All the pictures, designs, and symbols in each Pa Ndau piece contain valuable information that can be narrated orally. The images are actually stories, legends, myths, and folktales. Like the oral stories, these artistic stories breathe life into Hmong history, sacrifices, struggles, and search for freedom. For example, the art in one of these tells the story of the fall of Laos in 1975, the final evacuation at Long Cheng, the conflict between communist soldiers and Hmong Chao Fa guerrillas, the exodus of Hmong refugees, the escape from Laos to Thailand, the crossing of the Mekong River, an ambush and attack by Laotian and Thai pirates, and the arrival in refugee camps in Thailand. Such art keeps Hmong history alive. Today Hmong Pa Ndau handcrafts with words and pictures that tell stories about the Hmong way of life are sold worldwide and are displayed in museums and art galleries in many places around the world.

History of Wars

Hmong war stories are tales of courage and survival. Most U.S. Hmong are war-displaced refugees; only a few are immigrants. Hmong refugees have retained many incredible war stories from the three latest Chinese dynasties (Yuan, Ming, and Qing) to the settlement in Southeast Asian nations (Burma, Vietnam, Laos, and Thailand). After settlement in Southeast Asia, from the early 1900s to the mid–2000s, Hmong were involved in more warfare. They revolted and fought against French colonial policy in Indochina, fought against Japanese invasion, joined the Royal Laotian Army to help stabilize civil conflicts in Laos, fought the invasion of the Pathet Lao and Vietminh from North Vietnam, struggled to protect the Ho Chi Minh Trail, became abandoned war refugees in May 1975, fled Laos into Thailand to save themselves from political oppression and persecution,

formed the reactionary Chao Fa force to fight against the brutal communist reeducation policy and inhumane imprisonment, were hunted down for their political ties with the U.S., resettled in the western nations, and have been persecuted harshly to the present day. Their cooperation in the U.S. CIA's Secret War in Laos not only decimated the Hmong, but changed their lives forever.

War History from China

Each Hmong family has its own accounts of its great grandparents' escape and migration from China to Southeast Asia, but all the Hmong war stories of the China period tell of thousands of years long, bloody struggles with the Chinese. Together with the loss of the Hmong kingdom in the Yellow River basin and the death of the mighty ruler ChiYou, the war history from China still lives in Hmong hearts and souls through oral history. Hmong funeral rites include a ritual called *Leading the War Against the Chinese* (*tsa rog*) to protect the soul of the deceased. Reciting this ritual story is a long-standing tradition in many Hmong families because the Chinese exterminated family members and desecrated Hmong graves. The soul of the Hmong is still haunted by the brutality and atrocities. The Chinese crackdowns on Hmong revolts and the brutal land encroachment are long-remembered in Hmong traditions. Table 9.4 gives an excerpt of 3 of the 10 stanzas from the ceremonial chant used for the Hmong traditional totem pole celebration that contains references to the Chinese invasion of Hmong land (as cited in Cha, 2013).

Table 9.4. Excerpt of Chant for Hmong Totem Pole Celebration

Verses of Hmong Chant	English Translation
Ntoj ntig rov thaum ntxuv	In the early time of life
Moob txwj Moob laug nyob rov Nam Ntuj	Hmong ancestors lived in the mother world
Dlej dlaag tej taj nraag	The land field of the Yellow River Basin
Peb Moob yog Moob txiv yawg lug coj ntuj	We Hmong were Hmong rulers to rule the world
Un neej tshaav ntuj lug	Lived life happily
Tsis paub tug tsaav naj tug tsaav dlaab tsi hu ua ncej paag	Did not know what was the rise called the totem pole
Ntoj ntig rov thaum ntxuv	In the early time of life
Moob txwj Moob laug nyob rov Dlaim Ntuj	Hmong ancestors lived in the world

continued on page 271

Verses of Hmong Chant	English Translation
Dlej dlaag nam teb	The Yellow River Basin of motherland
Peb Moob yog Moob txiv yawg lug coj ntuj	We Hmong were Hmong rulers to rule the land
Ua neej tshaav ntuj lug	Lived life happily
Tsis paub tug tsaav naj tug tsaav dlaab tsi hu ua ncej ntxheb	Did not know what was the rise called the totem pole
Tug tsaav naj dlaab tsi coj nrug tsis vim	The rise of what not taken with is not because of spirit
Yeeb vim nam maab miv shuav lub sab tsis zoo	Is the result of enemy Chinese's insincere hearts
Nam mab mi shuav tug Huamtij nom tswv txeeb tag peb Moob tej laj teb	Enemy Chinese's yellow ruler took over Hmong rice fields
Yuav txeeb zog lawm tej tag nraag	Encroached on the land fields
Peb Moob txiv yawg le coj tau Moob txwj Moob laug tej tub rog	Our ruler led Hmong ancestors' soldiers
Nrug Huamtij nom tswv rov ntaus tag cuaj lub kab yim lub zog	With the yellow ruler we fought all nine villages eight cities
Tug tsaav naj tug dlaab tsi coj nrug tsis vim...	The rise of what not taken with is not because of spirit...

The beginning verses of this chant clearly reflect the Hmong struggle to keep their fertile land from being taken by the Chinese; they describe how the Hmong fought the Chinese to stop their encroachment on Hmong land. The chant describes Hmong civilization in the Yellow River basin and how it was destroyed by the Chinese invasion.

The oral story illustrated in Table 9.5 is an account Hmong elders share about Hmong great grandparents' sacrifices that led to the Hmong migration from China.

Table 9.5. Oral Story of Hmong Great Grandparents' Sacrifices and Migration from China

Hmong Story	English Translation
Hmoob nyob tsis taus	Hmong could not live
Hmoob khiav tawm Suav teb los vim hais tias	Hmong fled China because
Suav tsim Hmoob phem heev li	Chinese persecuted Hmong badly
Thaum Hmong swb rog,	When Hmong were defeated
Ces Suav tuaj muab Hmoob cov coj noj coj ua ntes coj mus kaw	Chinese arrested and imprisoned Hmong rulers and leaders
Suav rau txim nyav heev	Chinese punished cruelly
Muab ntau, muab khi, muab yoog tshaib, muab xauv caj dab, thiab muab hlais ciaj	Beaten, tied up, starved, locked by the neck, and butchered alive
Tej tug ces Suav muab tua pov tseg li tsiaj,	Some were killed like animals by the Chinese
Tej tug ces Suav muab hlawv kub nyhiab tag	Some were burned to death by the Chinese
Hos tej tug ces Suav muab faus ciaj,	Some were buried alive by the Chinese
thiab Suav muab coj txawj thiab ntse tua kom tu noob	And Chinese exterminated all intellectual individuals
Tsis tag li xwb, Suav muab Hmoob cov txiv neej ntes khi	Moreover, Chinese arrested Hmong males
Tus muaj lub noob luaj li lub taum daj	Anyone with testicles of the size of a yellow pea
Ces Suav yeej muab tua kom tu noob li	Chinese extirpated all
Hmoob thiaj li ntshai	Hmong became terrorized
Ces Hmoob khiav nkaum nyob hav zeb hav tsua xwb	Hmong hid in the rocky mountains
Cov txiv neej ces tsis tau luag li	All Hmong males were in constant fear
Hos cov poj niam ces tus zoo nkauj thiab tseem hluas	As for the Hmong women, the ones who were young and pretty
Ces Suav muab cov mus yuav ua poj niam tag	Chinese took all of them as wives

Hmong Story	English Translation
Cov menyuam tseem yau ces Suav muab yuam ua qhev	Young children were forced to be slaves
Yog Hmoob tsis khiav mas Hmoob yeej yuav tu noob tiag tiag	If Hmong did not flee Hmong would be wiped out for real
Vim hais tias Suav kom Hmoob los nyoo Suav thiab ua li Suav hais	Because Chinese forced Hmong to follow the Chinese way of life
Yog Hmoob tsis kam ua raws li Suav nyiam ces	If Hmong refused to comply
Suav muab Hmoob rau txim nyav heev	Chinese punished them cruelly
Tsis tag li xwb, Suav txeeb Hmoob av ua noj thiab liaj teb tag	Also, Chinese took Hmong land and rice fields
	Hmong had no land and field to farm
Hmoob tsis muaj chaw ua noj ua haus	Chinese even imposed heavy tax on Hmong
Suav tseem kom Hmoob them se nyav heev thiab	Chinese levied heavy taxation
Suav sau se loj heev	If not paid, Chinese confiscated land and rice fields
Yog tsis them, Suav txeeb teb txeeb liaj yuav mus li	Going to dispute would never win over Chinese
Mus hais los yeej tsis yeej Suav li	More complaints led to arrest
Hais ntau tseem mag ntes kaw	
Yog lino Hmoob lub neej thiaj puas ntsoog...	That was why Hmong life was ruined...

It is sad to listen to this kind of story. The events occurred during a time of warfare between Chinese states, and political persecution and oppression could have happened to anyone at such a time. As Fadiman (1997) wrote about Hmong history in China, the Hmong often rebelled because they wanted independence, but the Chinese came down heavily on them; the Hmong retreated and rebelled again and the Chinese came down on them again. The Hmong kept revolting but after centuries of unsuccessful rebellions and imperialist persecutions, the Hmong retreated from their fertile rice field in the Yellow River and Yangtze River basins to barren land and desolate mountains.

Besides the struggle to be free, Hmong had to integrate into the host culture or face severe mistreatment. Table 9.6 shows an oral story about Hmong division during a time of forced social integration in China.

Table 9.6. Oral Story of Hmong Adopting Chinese Culture and Traditions

Hmong Story	English Translation
Peb Hmoob tawg ua ob pab	Hmong divided into two groups
Vim hais tais Suav muab Hmoob faib	Because the Chinese separated Hmong
Pab ib ces yog cov Hmoob tsis tawm tsam Suav	The first group was the group that did not rebel against the Chinese
Suav hais licas ces lawv ua li ntawd	Whatever the Chinese wanted, they followed
Cov no yog cov Hmoob Suav hu ua Hmoob Siav	These people were the Hmong Chinese called cooked Hmong
Pab ob ces yog cov Hmoob tsis nyiam Suav txoj kev cai	The second group was the group that did not like Chinese rule
Thiab tsis nyiam yoog Suav kav	And did not submit to Chinese dominance
Cov no yog cov Hmoob Suav hu ua Hmoob Nyoos	These people were the Hmong Chinese called raw Hmong
Suav xav kom Hmoob xyaum Suav	Chinese wanted Hmong to adopt
Ua li Suav nyiam thiab hais lus Suav	To follow the Chinese way and speak Chinese
Cov Hmoob Siav ua tau	Cooked Hmong could adopt
Tabsi cov Hmoob Nyoos ua tsis tau	But raw Hmong could not

continued on page 274

Hmong Story	English Translation
Feem ntau cov Hmoob siav xyaum Suav Chais	Most cooked Hmong adopted Chinese ways
taub hau ua mag qos li Suav	Shaved their heads looking like Chinese yam style
Hnav ris tsho Suav thiab coj li SuavTsis tag li,	Wore Chinese clothes and acted like Chinese
Hmoob mus tuaj Suav tog rov qab tua Hmoob	Yet, Hmong sided with Chinese against other Hmong
Hos cov tsis hloov raws Suav feem coob yog cov Hmoob nyoos	Those who refused to adopt most were raw Hmong
Yog Suav hais	If Chinese demanded
Lawm khiav losi tawm tsam Suav	Hmong ran or rebelled against Chinese
Txawm Suav tseem muab lawm rau txim	Even if Chinese arrested them
Los Hmoob tsis ntshai	Hmong were not intimidated
Tabsi Hmoob khiav mus nyob kom deb	But Hmong retreated to live far away
Es kom Suav tuaj tsis txog lawm zos	So Chinese could not trek to their villages
Yog Suav tuaj nrhiav, Hmoob khiav lawm	If Chinese came looking for them, Hmong took off
Ua mus ua los	Ran back and forth
Ces Hmoob khiav deb zus deb zus	Hmong ran farther and farther away
Ces khiav khiav ntau xyoo	They ran for many years
Ces Hmoob cia li mus nyob toj roob hauv pes lawm li	Hmong retreated to live in barren and desolate areas
Kom Suav tsis tuaj raws lawm xwb...	So Chinese would not go after them...

This story reflects accounts in Hmong oral history that the Hmong once lived in desolate and barren locations and had little fertile land to farm. The climate was bad, either too cold or too hot. The Hmong had no firewood and used cornstalks and ricestalks for firewood. They ate corn instead of rice because the poor conditions for harvest and cultivation led to famine. The Hmong were constantly on the move in search of fertile land. Table 9.7 displays an oral story of a Hmong great grandparent who fled China into Southeast Asia.

Table 9.7. Oral Story of Migration from China

Hmong Story	English Translation
Peb yawg suab piav hais tias	Our great grandfather told that
Thaum tseem nyob Suav teb	While living in China
Lawv muaj 5 tug kwv tij ob tug muam	They had five brothers and two sisters
Ces muaj ib hnub	Then one day
Suav tuaj raws lawv tua	Chinese came to hunt them down
Nws txiv thiab niam mas txawj te taw	His father and mother knew martial arts
Nws peb tug tij laug hlob hlob puav leej txawj tetaw thiab	His three oldest brothers knew martial arts, too
Ob tug muam puav leej txawj	The two sisters also knew
Hos nws thiab tus tij laug hlob nws tsis tau txawj	But he and his older brother did not know
Vim nkawv tseem yau	Because they were still young
Suav tuaj ces lawv sib tua	Chinese came and they fought
Nws niam thiab txiv coj nkawv thiab ob tug muam mus khiav nkaum	His parents took them and the two sisters into hiding
Hos peb tug tij laug hlob tiv thaiv Suav	The three oldest brothers fended off the Chinese
Sib tua tau muaj li 10 hnub	Fighting lasted about 10 days

Hmong Story	*English Translation*
Ces uacas tsis pom cov tij laug tshwm los	The three brothers failed to show up
Tos ob peb hnub ntxiv los tsis pom los thiab	They waited two, three more days. Still they did not show up
Ces nws txiv thiaj li rov qab mus nrhiav lawv	Then his father went back to look for them
Nws txiv nrhiav tau ob tug tij laug hlob ob lub cev	His father found the two oldest brothers' bodies
Tabsi tsis pom tus tij laug thij peb lub cev	But he could not locate the third brother's
Ces nws txiv rov qab los hais qhia lawv tias	Then his father came to tell them
Cov tij laug raug Suav tua tuag tag lawm	All three oldest brothers were killed
Nws niam thiab txiv chim siab heev	His parents became so angry
Nkawv tu siab heev	They were heartbroken
Tabsi tsis pom qab yuav ua tau licas	But there was nothing they could do
Ces nws txiv thiaj li coj lawv khiav	Then his father led them to migrate
Lawv khiav los nyob ntau lub zos	They migrated to live in many villages
Ua liaj ua teb noj ces mam khiav dua	They farmed and harvested, then migrated again
Ib xyoo khiav mentsi	Each year they migrated a bit
Ces khiav tau 10 lub xyoos nkaus	Then migrated for 10 years
Ces muaj ib hnub nws txiv txawm hais rau nkawv ob tug kwv tij tias	One day his father told the two brothers that
Nkawv yuav tsum khiav los mus rau xov tshoj teb	They had to migrate to Southeast Asia
Vim nws niam thiab txiv laus lawm khiav tsis taus lawm	Because his parents were old and could not migrate anymore
Cias ob tug muam nrog niam thiab txiv nyob	Let the two sisters stay with the parents
Ces niam thiab txiv ntim ris tsho thiab muaj mentsi nyiaj rau nkawv	Then his parents packed their clothes and gave them some money
Ces nkawv khiav los mus lawm tseg niam thiab txiv nyob tom qab	So they migrated and left his parents behind
Nkawv khiav los ces tsis muaj txoj hmoov	They migrated, but they lacked fortune
Tus tij laug hlob muaj mob los tsis taus	His brother became sick and could not migrate
Ces muab tus tij laug tso cia rau Suav teb	Then he left his brother behind in China
Nws mam li khiav los tshwm rau teb chaws nplog	He migrated to Laos
Thaum ntawd nws muaj li 25 xyoo	That time he was about 25 years old
Ces nws mam los nrog Hmoob nyob	Then he came to live among other Hmong
Los yuav poj niam Hmoob	He married a Hmong wife
Los tsim neej tshiab	Started a new life
Nyob tsis muaj kwv muaj tij uas yog niam txiv ib plab	Lived without biological siblings
Mam los zeem kwv zeem tij tshiab	Found and became part of a new family
Ces nws mam li los nyug tau 4 tug tub	Then he had four sons
Peb tug ntxhais	Two daughters
Ces mam li maj mam ua neej los mus zuj zus	They gradually lived a new life
Yeej tsis hnov thiab paub tias niam thiab txiv	Never heard from or knew about his parents
Nyob Suav teb ua licas lawm	How they lived in China
Tsis muaj leej twg paub...	No one knew...

The trail of Hmong migration from China to Southeast Asia echoes today in Hmong history and daily life because family members and relatives were left behind. Today, western Hmong are able to make some family connections, but they cannot prove their ancestry because it has been so many generations since the migration of Hmong great grandparents who made the sacrifice to free themselves from the Chinese. More details of Hmong history from China will emerge as more research is conducted on Hmong history. Meanwhile, the few hundred years in Southeast Asia changed the course of Hmong life for the better, but Hmong had to pay a high price for their freedom.

War History from Laos

Reading *Sky Is Falling: An Oral History of the CIA's Evacuation of the Hmong from Laos* by G. Morrison is heartbreaking because it reminds the reader that Hmong life in Laos came to a sudden end. The Hmong in Laos faced an uncertain future because there had been no planning for what would happen to them after they spent 15 long years fighting the CIA-financed Secret War in Laos. Hmong refugees suffered insurmountable pain as the result of disingenuous betrayal by the U.S. government. The final rescue and evacuation that took place at the air base in Long Cheng was a doomsday for Hmong. Morrison's book contains stories from many individuals who were part of the final evacuation and who had roles in the Secret War—military officials, civic leaders, pilots, soldiers, and members of the Hmong Guerrilla Unit (SGU). Table 9.8 gives a story of the sudden shock that struck many when Laos fell into the hands of the communist regime.

Table 9.8. Hmong Story of Sudden Shock

Hmong Story	*English Translation*
Lub 5 hli ntuj xyoo 1975	May 1975
Yog lub hli uas Hmoob poob siab loj tshaj plaws	Was the month of sudden shock for Hmong
Vim hais tias lub teb nplog tau nchuav	Because Laos fell
Thaum Hmoob hnov tias nyab laj kag tuaj	When Hmoob heard the communist regime invading
Hmoob tsis paub yuav ua licas	Hmong did not know what to do
Hmoob tsuas tos Nai Phoo Vaj Pov xwb	Hmong only waited for Major General Vang Pao
Ces thaum Hmoob hnov tias Nai Phoo Vaj Pov	Then when Hmong heard Major General Vang Pao was airlifted to Thailand
Caij dav hlau mus rau Thaib teb lawm	
Ces Hmoob quaj ntsuag cia	Hmong wept and cried
Tsis pom qab yuav ua licas	They did not know what to do
Yuav khiav los nyuab	They wanted to flee but flight was difficult
Tsis khiav los ntshai	To not flee was fearful
Thaum Hmoob hnov tias Asmesliskas yuav coj dav hlau tuaj thauj Hmoob tim Looj Ceeb	When Hmong heard Americans brought the planes to evacuate Hmong in Long Cheng
Ces Hmoob vuag ntuj vuab teb	Then Hmong were in turmoil
Tias yuav ua licas	What to do?
Cov nyob deb mus tsis tau	Those who lived far could not make it
Cov nyob ze mus tag lawm	Those who lived near had gone
Cov laus tsis kav khiav	The old refused to flee
Cov hluas yuav khiav	The young wanted to flee
Ces thaum nyab laj tuaj nyob hauv zej zog	Then when communist soldiers came to live in town
Hmoob pib txhawj thiab ntshai	Wanting to flee was fearful
Yuav khiav ntshai	Wanting to stay was fearful
Yuav nyob ntshai	
Tsis qab siab mus ua noj ua haus li	They had no desire to farm and harvest crops
Thaum nyab laj pib ntes neeg	When communist soldiers started arresting people
Hmoob rov ceeb dua ib zaug	Hmong became terrorized again
Cov txawj thiab ntse khiav nkaum	Those who were intellectual took off to hide
Cov mag nte mus lawm tsis pom los	Those who were arrested failed to return

Hmong Story	*English Translation*
Ces ua rau Hmoob sib huas kev khiav raws Nai Phoo Vaj Pov qab...	Then Hmong fled following Major General Vang Pao...

Thousands of Hmong refugees experienced this sudden shock when Laos fell and Major General Vang Pao left for Thailand. Not only was the sky falling on them, but Hmong life was turned upside down because Hmong knew they had reached a dead end. The communist regime was merciless and would not spare their lives. The only choice left was to fight or flee; however, they did not know what to do without Major General Vang Pao. The exodus of Hmong refugees began and the Chao Fa was established to protect Hmong families and loved ones. Table 9.9 presents a story of a child who survived the massacre at the Hin Her Bridge in 1975.

Table 9.9. Story of Massacre at the Hin Her Bridge

Hmong Story	*English Translation*
Raws li kuv nco	As I can remember
Kuv muaj li 7 xyoo	I was about 7 years old
Kuv tsev neeg muaj 6 leej	My family had 6 people
Kuv niam, kuv txiv, kuv ob tug muam, thiab kuv tus tij laug hlob	My mom, my dad, my two sisters, and my older brother
Peb khiav uake nrog ob peb yim Hmoob	We fled with other Hmong families
Ces thaum peb tuaj yuav txog Heem Hawj	When we approached Hin Her
Peb mus poo nrog ib pab Hmoob	We blended with other marching Hmong families
Tag nrho muaj ze li 400 to 500 leej	The total was about 400 to 500 people
Raws li kuv nco	As I recall
Peb tuaj txog ntawm tus daj thaiv kev	We reached the security check point (fortress)
Cog neeg nre rau qhov tus daj kaws lawm	All people stopped because the gate was closed
Thiab tsis muaj neeg zov kev	And there was no guard on duty
Ces muaj ob peb tug txiv neej mus muab tus daj tsa kom neeg mus tau	Then a few men lifted the gate to allow passing
Tos nco xwb ces, nyab laj qws zom zws tom ntug kev tuaj	All of sudden, communist soldiers yelled at the crowd from the side of the road
Tsis pub neeg hla mus	Did not allow people to cross the security check point
Nyab laj tawm tuaj coob zuj zus	More soldiers appeared
Cov Hmoob ntshai thiab poob siab	Hmong became frightened and terrorized
Hmoob txawm mus kom dlau tus daj	Hmong walked past the fortress
Tabsi nyab laj muab Hmoob thawb rov qab	But communist soldiers pushed them back
Ces Hmoob txawm mus coob zuj zus	Then more Hmong crossed the fortress
Nyab laj qws tias kom txhob mus	Communist soldiers hollered at them to stop moving
Hmoob tsis mloog	
Ces uacas phom nrov pha! pha! pha!	Suddenly, gunfire exploded, pha! pha! pha!
Hmoob sib tws khiav	Hmong dispersed from the scene
Poj niam thiab menyuam mas quaj ntsuag qee	Women and children wailed and screamed hysterically
Ib cov vaus tag rau hauv av	Some collapsed to the ground
Ib cov khiav rov qab	Some ran backward
Ib cov khiav mus hla tus choj	Some ran to the bridge ahead
Ib cov khiav mus tom ntug kev lawm	Some ran into the bushes on the roadside

continued on page 278

Hmong Story	English Translation
Ib cov raug tsuj nyob hauv av	Some were killed
Ib cov tuag	Some were wounded
Ib cov rau mob	Some were stepped over
Nyab laj coj tau ob peb lub tsheb loj loj tuaj thaiv kev	Communist soldiers brought a few big vehicles to block the road
Yuav muab luam Hmoob	Tried to run people over
Kom Hmoob ntshai	To scare them
Cov nyob ram tub choj tsis pom qab yuav ua licas	Those on the bridge didn't know what to do
Nyab laj muab lawv ntau	Communist soldiers beat them up
Thawb pov hauv dej	Pushed them over into the water below
Ib cov dhia rau hauv dej	Some jumped into the river
Ib cov khiav hla tus choj	Some ran across the bridge
Ib cov khiav rov qab los	Some ran back toward the crowd
Ces nyab laj luaj phom ntxiv	Then communist soldiers fired more shots
Raug neeg coob	Shot many people
Peb muaj hmoov tsis raug leej twg	We were lucky, none of us was hurt
Kuv niam thiab kuv txiv coj peb khiav mus nkaum tom Hmoob tsev	My father and my mom took us to hide in the Hmong house
Ces peb mam li khiav lug kev tuaj rau Vientiane	Then we detoured to make it to Vientiane
Ob tug txheeb ze raug tua tuag lawm	Two relatives were killed
Hos ib tug txiv ntxawm poob dej tuag lawm	One uncle was drowned
Kuv tseem nco thiab ntshai txog niaj hnub no...	I still remember and am still afraid today...

This kind of childhood story not only resonants with the past of Hmong refugees' struggle but retells how Hmong refugees made risky life sacrifices to save themselves and to escape from the communist regime. The few thousands who were airlifted to safe haven in Thailand were lucky, but the hundreds of thousands of Hmong refugees who were left behind were subjected to political persecution and oppression. Many were taken to reeducation camps where they disappeared. Many joined the Chao Fa to fight for their freedom, and many are still in hiding. Table 9.10 gives a story of a Chao Fa family that made its final sacrifice for freedom after years in hiding in the jungles of Laos.

Table 9.10. Oral Story of a Chao Fa Family's Final Sacrifice

Hmong Story	English Translation
Thaum teb chaws nplog nchuav xyoo 1975	When Laos fell in 1975
Nws tsev neeg txiav txim siab tsis khiav	His family decided not to flee
Ib lub xyoo tom qab	One year later
Lawv nyob tsis taus lawm	They could not live anymore
Vim nyab laj nrhiav ntes cov txiv tsev	Because communist soldiers searched to arrest all males of the household
Coj mus xam mas nas nyob nyab laj teb	To be sent to a reeducation camp in Vietnam
Nws tsev neeg khiav mus ua Chao Fa xyoo 1977	His family decided to join Chao Fa in 1977
Nyob nkaum tim hav zoov txog xyoo 1985	They lived and hid in the jungle until 1985
Qab xyoo 1985	Late 1985
Lawv txiav txim siab khiav los mus rau Thaib Teb	They decided to leave for Thailand

Hmong Story	*English Translation*
Vim tshaib plab heev	Because of starvation
Nws tsev neeg muaj 4 leeg, ob tug menyuam	His family had 4 people
Ib tug tub ib tug ntxhais	One son and one daughter
Lawv sib yaum khiav nrog cov kwv tij neej tsa Hmoob	They fled along with other family relatives
Tag nrho muaj ze li 200 leej	Together there were about 200 people
Lawv khiav tau ib lub hli	They trekked through the jungle for about a month
Ces cov neeg muaj mob khiav tsis ntau ntxiv lawm	The sick individuals could not take it anymore
Cov tshaib plab los muaj	There were many hungry people
Cov laus los ces los tsis taus	The old couldn't trek along
Cov menyuam yoo tshaib tsis taus	The young couldn't bear the starvation
Ib cov muab tso pov tseg ib taug kev	Some left along the way
Ib cov rov qab mus thawj nyab laj lawm	Some returned to surrender to the communist regime
Ib cov yoo tsis taus tshaib ces tuag lawm	Some died of starvation and malnutrition
Txog ib nrab ke xwb	At midway
Cov neeg tshuav ze li 100 leej	The group had about 100 people
Ces lawv maj mam khiav los mus	They trekked slowly
Muaj ib zaum	One time
Nyab laj caum lawv qab	Communist soldiers followed them
Muaj lawv tua	Shot at them
Raug ib cov menyuam thiab poj niam tuag	Wounded some children and women
Nws tus tub kuj raug tua tuag lawm	His son was killed
Tshuav tug ntxhais	His daughter survived
Lub sij hawm khiav	During the trek
Tsis muaj mov noj	They had no rice
Noj nplooj hmab nplooj ntoo, nkau ntoo nkau xyoob, qos hav zoov, thiab txi ntoo cawm siav xwb	They ate leaves, tree and bamboo sprouts, wild yams, and berries to save their lives
Tus ntxhais mob mob plab	The daughter suffered a severe stomach ache
Noj tsis taus ces tus ntxhais xiam lawm	She couldn't eat and died
Thaum lawv los txog nram ntug dej nab qoom	When they reached the bank of the Mekong River
Ces cov neeg tshuav li 50 tus	The group had 50
Tsis muaj dabtsi hla dej	They had nothing with which to cross the river
Lawv mam xeem los ua phuaj xyoob	They made makeshift bamboo rafts
Es mam li hla dej thaum yuav kaj ntug	And then crossed the river before dawn
Hla dhau dej rau sab Thaib Teb	Crossing the river to Thailand
Thaib muab lawv khuj nyiaj tag	Thai robbed them of all their money
Thaib muab lawv coj mus kaw tau ob hnub	Thai locked them up for 2 days
Mam li muab lawv xav mus rau xum Ban Vinai	And then transported them to the Ban Vinai Camp
Ces nkawv ob niam txiv mam li tuaj nyug tau 4 tug menyuam, ob tug tub ob tug ntxhais	Then they had 4 children Two sons and two daughters
Nyob Vinai txog xyoo 1990	They lived in Ban Vinai until 1990
Mam li tuaj nyob rau Mekas	And then they came to the U.S.
Tuaj lub neej tshiab dua	To start a new life all over
Hais txog lub neej ua Chao Fa mam ua rau lub kua muag los…	Talking about Chao Fa life makes tears come down…

Most Hmong families can talk about their war stories all day long. Table 9.11 presents a short story from an eyewitness to fighting between the communist regime and the Chao Fa guerrilla group in late 1975.

These stories are only examples of the

Table 9.11. Oral Story of Fighting with the Communist Regime

Hmong Story	English Translation
Lub 10 hli ntuj xyoo 1975	In October 1975
Kuv muaj li 6 xyoo	I was about 6 years old
Thaum ib tag hmo	In the middle of the night
Phom rov	The gunfight broke out
Kuv niam thiab kuv txiv tsa peb sawv	My parents woke up everyone
Qhia kom peb kag tawm qhov rooj tag	Told all to crawl on our knees through the back door
Nkawv coj peb mus zaum hauv lub qhov taub nyob nram qab tsev	They led us to a tunnel behind the house
	We sat inside
Phom nrov ib hmo	The gunfight continued through the night
Kuv cov tij laug thiab kuv pom mos txwv yam liab vog sau peb qaum tsev	My brothers and I saw flaming bullets flying over our house
Phom loj nrov doog diaj	The cannon roared
Suab nrov thoob ntuj	The sound filled the sky
Pas kub nyhiab ncho tshwm sau ntuj	Smoke appeared in the sky
Peb hnov tshuaj phom tsws	We smelled the burning of gunpowder
Peb hnov luj tem tawg ze tsev	We heard a grenade explosion near our house
Kuv niam thiab kuv txiv kom peb nyob twj ywm hauv qhov taub	My parents told us to remain in the tunnel
Thaum pom kev dawb vog	When dawn appeared
Suab phom ntsiag	The gunfight stopped
Thaum hnub tawm tuaj	When the sun rose
Hnov suab nyooj hoom yas tuaj	The sound of a helicopter was heard
Nyooj hoom yas tuaj tshaw ntawm lub tiaj nyob tsis deb	Airplanes landed in the nearby field
Kuv niam thiab kuv txiv kom peb nyob twj ywm	My parents told us to stay calm
Nkawv mus hauv tsev	They went inside the house
Nqa tau zaub mov tuaj	They came back with some food
Thaum sawv ntxov yuav dua	By late morning
Kuv txiv kom peb tawm	My father told us to get out of the tunnel
Thaum kuv txiv qhib lub qhov rooj tawm mus	When my father opened the door to go outside
Ib tug txheeb ze khiav tuaj qhia nws tias	A relative came by to report to him
Coob tus nyab laj raug tua lawm	Many communist soldiers were killed
Thiab coob tus Chao Fa kuj raug tua thiab	And many Chao Fa soldiers were killed or captured, too
Tav su, kuv txiv coj wb mus tom yawg hlob lub tsev	At noon, my father took us to the chiefs' house
Wb pom 10 tus tub rog lub cev tuag nyob hauv av	We witnessed 10 dead bodies laid on the ground waiting for transportation
Tab tom to dav hlau tuaj thauj	
No yog ib yam uas ib tug menyuam tsis xav pom ... tsis yog npaus suav, tabsi yog thaj chaw tso cov tub rog tau tag sim neej...	That was an unexpected encounter for a child ... not a dream, but a scene of dead soldiers....

many, many Hmong war histories. These war stories are an integral part of Hmong oral history. Hmong children and adults can narrate these and other events they have lived through. This story was an actual event told by an adult who lived the event when he was six years old. It is not a dream, but he tells it like a dream because he was so young to have been an eyewitness to such a traumatic event.

Emphasis on Oral Language Skills

Oral skills are among the most desirable of personal attributes to Hmong. Hmong have always placed a greater emphasis on oral language and verbal competency than on writing skills or written language. The stress on oral speech over writing has had adverse effects on writing competency in the Hmong language and has contributed to a low Hmong language literacy rate. Fewer than half of Hmong professionals can read and write in the Hmong Romanized Popular Alphabet (HRPA, *ntawv Hmoob La Tee*) and fewer than 2 percent of all Hmong professionals are literate in Hmong messianic writing, or Pa Hawh (*ntawv Hmoob Phaj Hauj*). Approximately 40 percent of U.S. Hmong adults are learning to be literate in HRPA and barely 10 percent of Hmong adults have learned to read and write the Pa Hawh ideographic characters.

No known Hmong writing system was used for the Hmong language in China or elsewhere prior to the 1950s. In ancient China, Hmong could have been able to read Chinese characters and scripts such as logographic characters, idiosyncratic characters, logogrammatic scripts, and the oracle bone scripts. During the Warring States period and the Spring and Autumn era, Hmong were literate in some forms of Chinese writing, such as the *Xiaozi, Kiashi, Dazi,* and Chinese traditional logographic scripts; however, there is no evidence suggesting that these writings were created by Hmong or that the Hmong-Chinese language was written in these scripts.

The literacy rates for both the HRPA and Pa Hawh writing systems are astonishing low; Hmong adults and children still struggle to learn either system. Prior to the fall of Laos in 1975, only about 5 percent of Hmong adults who had gone to school could read and write HRPA, and even fewer could read and write Pa Hawh. Nearly 40 years later, the literacy rate for HRPA has increased substantially for a number of reasons. HRPA is easy to learn, read, and write; it is widely used and promoted by Hmong; it is the main form of written communication for both White and Blue Hmong dialects; it was used by Catholic and other Christian missionaries to translate the Bible into Hmong; its alphabet is similar to those of western languages; tons of materials have been written in HRPA; and HRPA is flexible and compatible with technological and computer applications and software. Knowing HRPA can enhance one's learning of English because the two written languages use the same alphabet. Despite the advantages of learning and using HRPA, the overall literacy in HRPA is still low.

Literacy is even lower for Pa Hawh. Nearly 10 percent of Hmong in the U.S. have mastered the scripts. Most are not inclined to learn Pa Hawh because it is complex. Interestingly, most who can read and write Pa Hawh scripts are males. Nonetheless, those who have mastered the Pa Hawh writing praise it because of its linguistic authenticity despite its linguistic intricacies. Hmong language literacy is likely to remain low in both writing systems because there is no formalized process for consistently promoting the teaching of either system. Christian Hmong families learn to read and write HRPA in churches because it is required for their Bible studies but nowhere else is writing in Hmong encouraged. Where either writing system is taught, it is taught by private tutors. Both systems are useful and each has its advantages. The majority of Hmong who do read their language favor the HRPA over the Pa Hawh because it is simpler and more materials in HRPA are available.

In a study of nearly 400 Hmong high school students, Vang (2001) found that 80 percent of the Hmong secondary school students were illiterate in HRPA and none were literate in Pa Hawh. Of the 20 percent who were literate in HRPA, 60 percent could only read the writing and 40 percent could read and write it to some degree. Of the total number of students, only 60 percent could speak Hmong, and they could not speak it proficiently. This means that Hmong secondary students lack Hmong basic interpersonal communication skills. Interestingly, among the parents of the students in the study, 35 percent were literate in HRPA and only a few could read some Pa Hawh characters; that meant nearly 65 percent of the parents were illiterate in the Hmong language even though all could speak Hmong proficiently.

The findings of this study confirm the fact that Hmong literacy is barely growing. The slow pace of the growth is due to three factors: (1) English is the common and daily language of many Hmong, (2) Hmong literacy is not promoted either at home or in school, and (3) there are no formalized settings for learning the Hmong language. If this trend continues, Hmong literacy will decline even further because native-born Hmong children will not learn how to read and write the Hmong language and Hmong parents are using Hmonglish to communicate with their children.

At the very least, Hmong should learn their language well to retain their oral traditions. They should develop not only oral skills in Hmong, but also reading and writing skills or literacy in Hmong. The oral skills—and thus the preservation of all the oral history and traditions—cannot survive long in a society where the language is not used without the backbone support of a Hmong writing system. Literacy is the support Hmong parents and children need for linguistic reinforcement.

Oral Language Competency

The Hmong language is intricate and complex. Most Hmong speakers learn how to communicate verbally without learning the grammatical structure of their language. Furthermore, the Hmong language lacks some linguistic and lexical terminologies needed for communicative competence; speakers must create their own phrases to fill the needs.

Hmong speakers today are accustomed to the use of *Hmonglish,* a modern Hmong language that is a mixture of Hmong and English. For instance, the English phrase "I don't care" has been adopted as a loan word for Hmong communicative purposes: Hmong Americans say "*Kuv tsis care*" instead of using the proper Hmong phrases, "*kav liam, kav chawj, sij peem, tsis ua licas, tau kawg mas, ywb siab,* or *tsis txhob quav ntsej.* Despite the fact that "I don't care" can have different meanings to native English speakers depending on the context, Hmong speakers probably assume it means the same thing in all social contexts. This is one example of why Hmong speakers often use code switching when speaking Hmong; that is, they alternate between English and Hmong in the same conversation. Sometimes Hmong speakers have no choice but to use English words because there are no Hmong words for what they want to say or because the loan words are easier and convenient. Common loan words are computer, TV, DVD, CD, truck, pickup, ice cream, bread, cereal, milk, key, and smog. Hmong speakers also use words and phrases from languages other than English, such as Lao, Thai, and Chinese. For instance, the English word "go" in Hmong is "*mus,*" but most Hmong speakers use "*pai*" instead; the word "*pai*" is a loan word from Lao and Thai.

Communicative competence has to do with one's oral language abilities and skills. Oral language abilities include knowledge and skills in grammar (syntax, semantics, vocabulary, and structure) and in matching speech to social and cultural settings (forms, registers, styles, expressions, emotions, and appropriateness). For Hmong, matching speech to social and cultural settings means giving attention to colloquial and discourse manners (utterance, expression, meaning, modesty, humbleness, and consideration) and to tactical and strategic occasions (asserting, interjecting, arguing, deciding, solving, resolving, cross-examining, cross-complaining, addressing, persuading, convincing, ordering, and analyzing). For instance, communicative competence is required for Hmong actors, actresses, radio-talk-show hosts, local television anchors, singers, journalists, entertainers, cultural leaders, and religious healers and chanters.

Language competence is assessed in three areas: speaking ability (oral and verbal skills), reading ability (sociolinguistic skills), and writing ability (grammatical skills). One may be fluent in Hmong poetry, rap, idioms, slang, proverbs, chanting, and singing, but fluency in these areas does not necessarily mean that one is competent in the delivery of a public speech or making a detailed argument to resolve a civil matter. In other words, Hmong oral language competency requires the linguistic ability that enables the speaker to actually articulate and use the language in ways that achieve its main objective of effective communication in multiple settings.

The multiple settings requiring Hmong oral language competency are basic interpersonal communication, religious rituals and cultural ceremonies (chanting, singing, and offering), and leadership (making public speeches, addressing audiences, articulating platforms, and engaging in discussions). Many Hmong elders and parents are fluent in Hmong verbiage, including technical linguistic terminologies, but giving a well organized speech is quite challenging for them because such a task requires some academic background and sociolinguistic competence. Despite the limitations, most Hmong elders and parents can perform the verbal religious rituals and rites without many linguistic challenges.

For Hmong, language competence is complicated by the fact that Hmong speak a number of dialects and many of the words in the different dialects are used interchangeably. Even though Hmong commonly understand the different vocabularies, the mixture of words from different dialects can affect the communicative fluency of a speaker in a specific Hmong dialect. For instance, the word "future" in White Hmong is *yam tom ntej* but in Blue Hmong is *yam pem suab.* A fluent White Hmong speaker will use *yam tom ntej* and a fluent Blue Hmong speaker will use *yam pem suab*; however, a mixed speaker will use either one.

Dialect variations influence oral competency in specific dialects. For example, the word "broken" or "out of order" can be expressed by a number of different words in White Hmong dialects: *puas, piam, dam, tawg, ntsoog, tsis zoo lawm,* or *tsis ua hauj lwm lawm.* These words are understood by all White Hmong, but the word *piam* is used only by certain White Hmong families. Also, some basic words are completely different in White Hmong and Blue Hmong dialects. For instance, the word "blanket" in White Hmong is *daim pam,* but in Blue Hmong is *dlaim choj.*

Hmong use many political terms borrowed from Lao. For instance, *Chao Muong, Chao Khoueng, Tasseng, Nai Kong, Nai Ban, Phuteng, Phutong, Chongkone, Chongcha,* and *Xaophay* are all Laotian words. The word *Kiatong,* which many believe is a Hmong word for ruler or ruling family, is actually a loan word from French, *canton*; however, some Hmong believe Kiatong is actually a Hmong word originated in China prior to Hmong resettlement in Southeast Asian countries.

Hmong idioms, slang, proverbs, and riddles (*piv txoj lus, paj lug, txhiaj txhais, losi paj huam*) play another complex role in Hmong oral language competency. Table 9.12 presents examples of Hmong idioms, slang, proverbs, and riddles, most of which were created by Hmong speakers for entertainment purposes. In recent years, these expressions have become embedded in Hmong customs. Similarly, Hmong have created new verses and phrases for Hmong kowtowing customs, death rituals, funeral rites, death songs, blessing chants, and wedding chants. Since 1975, Pa Hawh readers and writers have actually contributed to the development of more Hmong idioms, slang, riddles, and proverbs because of their use in religious chants and rituals.

Interestingly, the use of Hmong *oxymorons* is on the rise. For instance, "*muab yus roj kib yus txha,*" in Hmong means "use my fat to fry my bone." The transliteration implies that one is taking advantage of the situation by tweaking, twisting, coercing, or bending the truth to get one's way. Here is another common Hmong oxymoronic expression, "*npua tshom dev noj*," meaning "the pig digs out the dog eats it." Culturally, Hmong use this expression to explain sociopolitical events that one may work hard for nothing, or one is opening up a golden opportunity for other people to achieve successes. Even if Hmong oxymoronic expressions are used in situational colloquium, the verbiage used in such verbatim expressions affirms the communicative competency of an individual who can apply Hmong linguistics subtly.

Like Hmong culture and traditions, Hmong languages and dialects have evolved over time; therefore Hmong oral language is dynamic. For instance, the use of Hmong *onomatopoeia*, or Hmong words that sound like their meanings is quite common, like *ntsiantsiantsia*,

hlubhlubhlub, nconconco, kuvkuvkuv, or *losloslos.* Hmong need to give some thought to language maintenance in order to preserve the language, continue its development, and maintain linguistic authenticity, particularly during this time of enculturation. Forty years from now, Hmong oral skills and oral language may be significantly degraded or lost altogether if nothing is done at the present time because the majority of Hmong children will be fluent in English but not in Hmong. The Hmong language, and with it Hmong culture, will struggle for survival unless Hmong start searching for a systematic way to learn, share, and preserve their long-standing oral traditions. Most importantly, Hmong oral skills and oral language development need to be supported by a formalized process of teaching and learning. In other words, Hmong need to be intentional about teaching Hmong languages and dialects to Hmong children.

Table 9.12. Examples of Hmong Idioms, Slang, Riddles, and Proverbs

Proverb/piv txoj lus	Slang/paj lug	Idiom/txhiaj txhais	Riddle/paj huam	Symbolic and Metaphorical Words/lus sib twv
Txhuag zam ces zam tshiab, txhuag siav ces siav ntev	Puv 120 xyoo	Ob lub ncuav pias, ib lub sov ib lub txias, yog dabtsi?	Ntawm no mus yog lus qhuab ntuas	Tuaj qaij kaus
	Niam txiv tuag, vaj tsev ntuag			Ib txoj hmab soo tag ib lub zoov
Nplooj yoog kav, noob yoog tsav	Lus nyiaj lus kub	Tsuj dev tw dev quaj qw quaj qw, yog dabtsi?	Thov muab nquas hais rau peb Hmoob	Muaj paj los yeej meem thawg, muaj txiv los yeej meem txi
Ua lub neej kom tawg paj txi txiv	Tsis pom dej dag ces siab tsis nqig			
Pub laus noj, laus nco tshav ntuj, pub menyuam noj, menyuam zov ruj	Siab phem tsis tau ntuj ntoo

Sov los yoj, koob los yoj | Hnov nyuj qov tim dawm, mus txog tsis pom lawm, yog dabtsi? | Uas nyob thoob rau lub ntiaj teb, qhia rau peb txog Hmoob keeb kwm | Peb paim kua tsis tso saib

Nyuj ciab nyuj kaus |
| Cuaj lub hli tsis zoo npaum li ib lub hnub, cuaj leeg ntxhais tsis zoo npaum ib leeg tub | Rov taw tuam ntuj

Cuaj plua sib nte yim plua sib luag | Qaum ntuj tso qe hlaus, ntiaj teb khiav

dos haus, yob dabtsi? | Saib Hmoob tshwm qhov twg los tiag, tsam ib pliag tas peb cov laus, Hmoob hauv paus peb tsis paub lawm… | Kom ntseg log puav tam ncej txawb

Nej tuaj pem hauv dej tuaj, los nej tuaj qab deg tuaj |

Summing Up

This chapter described Hmong language development and the essential place of oral language and oral language skills in Hmong culture and traditions. The many Hmong dialects have been unified into two mutually intelligible languages: White Hmong and Blue Hmong. The colors have nothing to do with the linguistics of the dialects; they reflect the colors of the traditional costumes that distinguish the two groups that speak the two languages. There are several subgroups of the White Hmong language and only a few subgroups of the Blue Hmong language.

Hmong today use the Hmong Romanized Practical Alphabet (HRPA) created by western missionaries in the early 1950s as their writing system but the literacy rate is considerably low among Hmong adults. Oral skills continue to be strong because Hmong place great emphasis on oral skills, but literacy in Hmong languages remains low because written language is not seen as important. The majority of Hmong children are both illiterate in Hmong languages and unable to speak Hmong languages fluently. A very small number of native-born Hmong children speak Hmong languages proficiently; most are unable to read and write Hmong. Hmonglish is used in most Hmong families because it is the common language for children and parents.

Hmong adults continue to practice their oral skills in their religious rituals and traditional ceremonies. Despite the availability of written materials in Hmong languages, Hmong oral skills are used exclusively in Hmong folksongs, storytelling, chanting, and singing. Developing the oral skills required for these traditions comes through firsthand experience, emulation, rote memorization, linguistic creativity, and ongoing practice. Hmong children are encouraged to develop Hmong oral skills very early in life, before starting their elementary education. Traditionally, Hmong male children are expected to master Hmong oral skills for religious purposes and Hmong female children are expected to learn Hmong oral skills for social and colloquial purposes. However, today, Hmong children learn English and many lack Hmong oral skills.

Hmong handcrafts are a form of storytelling very similar to oral narration. Hmong Pa Ndau, the Hmong flowery fabric adorned with embroidery and appliqués, contains stories of Hmong myths, legends, and folktales. The detailed artistic designs reveal hidden messages that tell tales of Hmong migration, struggles, and search for freedom.

Nearly 40 years in the western nations, Hmong oral skills remain strong. However, they will not continue to be strong unless Hmong find a systematic way of helping Hmong children learn Hmong languages and dialects in a formalized process. Without formal instruction, the literacy rate in Hmong languages will fall precipitously and Hmong languages will be replaced by English in the next 40 years. All Hmong living in America need to give careful attention to current language trends.

• TEN •

Hmong Linguistics
and Writing Systems

Tus neeg tsis txawj ntawv ces
zoo ib yam li tus neeg uas nws ob lub qhov muag tsis pom kev...
A Hmong educational thought

Introduction

Was there a Hmong writing system in the past? According to Hmong Chinese legends, there were a few writing systems used by Hmong during the Warring States period and the Spring and Autumn era in ancient China. Some of the early writing systems were known as *Kaishu, Kaizi, Hanzi, Dazi,* or *Xiaozi.* It is possible that Hmong also practiced *Mongshu* writing, the inscriptions of Chinese logographic characters in stones and/or platforms. They were early logographic characters and pictographic scripts for the Chinese language. Scholars do not know whether the graphics in these systems were those found in the old oracle bone scripts or more like the current logographic scripts. In the Chinese logographic script, the graphemes—the units of the system—represent words or sounds. Different scripts were used at different times in Chinese history. It is plausible that some Hmong were literate in the early Chinese scripts. This chapter discusses the contemporary linguistics and writing systems for the Hmong languages focusing on aspects of Hmong everyday language.

Origin of Hmong Languages

The Hmong are an ancient people group of families, clans, and tribes that speak mul-tiple languages and dialects, including Green Hmong, White Hmong, Black Hmong, Red Hmong, Flower Hmong, and others. Hmong lived in central China prior to their settlement in Southeast Asia and later resettlement in the West. Their languages were influenced by their residence in these different parts of the world.

Most studies of the languages of ancient China mix Miao and Hmong languages and dialects because some western historians believe the two groups were the same people and spoke the same languages and dialects. This mischaracterization persists partly because the Chinese classified many ethnic groups, including the Hmong, under the Miao nationality, calling them Miao-Yao, Hmong-Mien, or Mien-Yao. However, Hmong know that Miao and Hmong are two distinct ethnic groups with different cultures, traditions, and languages. According to researchers and historians, Hmong has at least 18 different languages or dialects whereas Mien-Yao has only 6 different languages or dialects.

Some linguistics scholars place the Hmong languages and dialects in the broad Sino-Tibetan language family, which includes several Chinese languages spoken by the Tibetan tribes and other ethnic groups. Others link Hmong languages to the Austro-Tai or Austronesian language family, which includes Thai, Lao, and the languages of Pacific Islanders, Hawaiians, and other indigenous islanders. Some associate Hmong languages with the Austro-Asiatic language group that includes Vietnamese and Cambodian (Khmer). All these possible linkages indicate that the Hmong are an ancient people with linguistic relationships with many tribes and ethnic groups that once lived in central and southwestern China.

The connections are supported by Hmong oral history. According to Hmong legends, the Hmong lived at various times in their history among many aboriginal ethnic groups: the Chinese, Haw, Miao, Yao, Mien, Kha, Khamu, Mhu, Man, Lao, Thai, Vietnamese, Cambodian, Puyi, Lue, Lahu, and others. Many Hmong spoke Chinese (Cantonese and Mandarin), Khamu, Lao, Thai, Mien, Miao, Yao, and Vietnamese because of their trade relationships and ethnic associations. These associations explain some of the shared vocabularies; however, the Hmong languages, like the Hmong culture, are distinct from those of any ethnic group with which they were associated.

Despite the linkages, there is no direct linguistic connection between Miao, Mien, or Yao and Hmong languages or words. However, the Hmong language does have some words from the cultures among whom the Hmong lived—Hmong-Chinese words such as x*ib fwb-shiƒu* (teacher or master) and *niam-niang* (mother) and French words such as *Fabkis-Faguo.* In the late 1900s, Hmong added Lao and Thai words such as *kuv* (I or me), *keej* (smart, clever, shrewd, or intelligent), *foob* (accuse or sue), and *pai* (go, leave, depart, take off). However, loan words are not evidence of the derivation of the language. The most reasonable conclusion is that Hmong belongs to the Sino-Tibetan language family because Hmong lived in central and southwestern China for thousands of years and millions of Hmong still live in China today.

In central China, the Hmong were an ethnic minority. The Chinese were the dominant culture, and the development of Hmong languages was influenced by the evolution of Chinese language and culture. What we know of the evolution of the Chinese language can be divided into *four* periods. As noted in Cha (2013), according to Chinese historical accounts and Hmong Chinese legends, the earliest period is known as the *Gudai,* or "ancient," period, known in Hmong as the *Qub Tiam losi Tiam Qub.* This is the time from the Spring and Autumn era (770–476 BC) through the Warring States period (475–221 BC) to about AD 1800. During this long period of time the Chinese language went through many changes as wars displaced populations and states fought one another for dominance. There was no unified language as many ethnic groups lived and fought throughout the vast country, each speaking its own language. The migration of peoples fleeing war and seeking land, the rise and fall of dynasties, and the influx of foreigners brought changes to languages as well as to governments.

The second stage of language transformation is known as the *Jindai* period (from the early 1800s to the early 1900s), known in Hmong as the *Ze Tiam losi Tiam Ze.* The northerners conquered the south and moved southward to occupy the land. The northern tribes formed dynasties and established an official language, forcing all in the conquered territories to adopt the new language. The official language contained terminology and vocabulary from diverse languages and dialects of the south.

The third change in language came in the *Xiandai* period (from the early 1900s to the mid–1950s), known in Hmong as the *Xam Tiam losi Tiam Xam.* This period is sometimes called the national curricular period because China took bold steps to reform its national language. The government undertook to grammatically organize, modernize, consolidate, and unify local languages and dialects systematically in order to enhance and advance the Chinese national language. Northerners and southerners were made to share common terminologies and grammatical rules to improve the use of phonetics, phonemics, morphemics, writing systems (pictographic, logographic, logosyllabic, and ideogramic) and, most importantly, intonation and pronunciation.

The fourth major stage of change in the Chinese national language occurred in the *Dangdai* period (from the 1950s to the present time), known in Hmong as the *Tam Tiam losi Tiam Tam Sim No*. In this current period, the Chinese national language, Mandarin, is undergoing constant reforms and enhancements as contemporary Chinese are learning to adapt to the socioeconomic influences coming from the western nations. The language is changing in response to developments in music, sports, social media, technology, education, science, lifestyles, human rights, social policies, trade, laws, and international politics. China faces major ongoing changes because it has the largest labor market in the world.

This picture of Chinese linguistic history sheds some light on Hmong language history. Hmong legends say that Hmong once had a writing system for their language, but it became extinct in the ancient world. It is easy to see how a Hmong writing system and literacy in that system could have been lost in the many times the Chinese conquered their land, in the multiple revolts and wars, in the oppression of ethnic minorities, in the forced compliance with a dominant system, and in the many migrations to myriad places.

Roots of Hmong Written Language

Despite the likely loss of a writing system, Hmong retained their unique oral languages.

But those languages remained unwritten until the 20th century, when several writing systems were created in different countries. These *White* and *Blue* Hmong writing systems include a *Hmong-Chinese version* (1906–1909, or Hmong-Chinese othrography), a *Hmong-Thai version* (1932, or Hmong-Thai orthography), the *Romanized Practical Alphabet version* (1951–1953), *Hmong Pa Hawh version* (1959), a *Hmong-Vietnamese version* (1960, or Hmong-Vietnamese orthography), a *Hmong-Lao version* (1970, or Hmong-Lao orthography), and *Hmong Embroidery and Texture scripts* (1988). Of all the writing systems, the Hmong Romanized Practical Alphabet (HRPA) system, known in Hmong as the *Ntawv Hmoob LaTee*, has become the most prominent, popular, and widely adopted. Practically, HRPA is also recognized as Romanized Popular Alphabet system.

Comparatively, Cha (2013) linked Hmong words written in HRPA with Chinese words written in Mandarin Pinyin, the system for writing Chinese words with Roman letters. Table 10.1 lists some of the words that Chinese, Hmong-Chinese, and western Hmong use with similar meanings. The transliteration of these words may make them appear phonetically different, but most of the words with the same meaning are verbally articulated in the same way. The Hmong writing system is relatively new and may lack some features that would enable it to represent the sounds more precisely.

Linguistically, Cha (2013) also noted that the HRPA writing system has 17 vowels and eight tones whereas the Chinese Mandarin Pinyin has 8 vowels and 6 tones although

Table 10.1. Selected Hmong Words Written in HRPA with Chinese Words Written in Mandarin Pinyin

Mandarin Word	Hmong Chinese Word	Hmong RPA	Meaning
Ai	Ai	Aiv	Tiny, short, small, brief, little
Bang	Bang	Pab	Help, assist, support, give a hand
Baohu	Baohu	Pov hwm	Guard, safeguard, protect, help
Cai	Cai	Txhais	Translate, interpret, guess, imply, mean
Che	Chei	Tsheb	Car, auto, vehicle, mobile
Chong	Chong	Tshooj	Add more, layer, pile up, put on top

Mandarin Word	Hmong Chinese Word	Hmong RPA	Meaning
Deng	Deng	Teeb	Lamp, light, lantern, bulb
Di tai	Di tai	Tiv thaiv	Defend, protect, resist, guard
Du	Du	Ntuj	Sky, capital, big city, metropolitan
Fu	Fu	Fwm or Fwv	Leader, ruler, authority, respect, build up, high position
Gong ming	Gong ming	Koob meej	Fame, reputation, celebrity, honor, reverence
Gu niang	Go niang	Poj niam	Wife, female, girl
Hu	Hu	Hu	Call, holler, yell, shout
Hua	Hua	Huam	Become bigger, become more, grow, increase, expand, swell up
Ji	Jing	Ceev	Fast, hurry, swift, quick, rush, speed, run, hasty move
Kang	Kang	Qha	Hang, dry, bake, in mid air
Kong	Kong	Khoom	Free, not busy, have time, not working
Lang	Lang	Laj	Cool down, breeze, cool wind, satisfy, cool air
Luo	Luo	Luaj	Cut down, chop down, slash
Man	Man	Mab	Wood people, wild people, barbaric people, foreigner, jungle people
Meng	Mong	Hmoob losi Moob	Hmong people
Nang	Nang	Hnab	Bag, sack, pocket, carry bag
Pao	Po	Pov	Throw, cast, toss, hurl, discard
Qi	Qi	Chim	Angry, upset, mad, rage, outburst
Rang kai	Rang gei	Zam kev	Move out of the way, make way for, forgive, spare, pardon, excuse
Rong yi	Yong yi	Yooj Yim	Convenient, easy, no brainer, not hard
Shang liang	Shang lang	Sab laj	Meeting, discussing, brainstorming, sharing, planning
Shi fu	Si fu	Xib fwb	Teacher, master, pastor, preacher, coach
Tong	Tong	Thoob	All, entire, everywhere, throughout
Tu	Duo	Tua	Kill, shoot, slaughter, cut, butcher, extinguish, turn off, put out, murder
Wang	Wang	Vaj	Family name, king, yard, ruler, power, supreme
Wu	Wu	Vov	Cover up, seal, conceal, hide, muffle
Xiang lai xiang qu	Xiang mong xiang luh	Xav mus xav los	Think back and forth, contemplate, procrastinate, and preoccupy
Xiao xin	Xuo xi	Xyuam xim	Careful, cautious, weary, watchful, not reckless

Note: The transliteration of Chinese and Hmong Chinese words may not have the same phonetics or phonemics.

only four tones are used for academic teaching in Mandarin. The linguistic similarities are significant because the two writing systems appear to use the same tone markers even though each writing system was designed for its language. Table 10.2 compares the consonants in the two systems, and Table 10.3 correlates the vowels used in Chinese Mandarin with the vowels in the HRPA writing systems. Even though some of the consonants and vowels are not phonetically matched in spelling, phonemes, and graphemes, the emphasis, tones, intonations, accents, and pronunciations appear to be linguistically compatible and intelligible. As Table 10.1 shows, some of the Mandarin words do not require tone markers for intonation whereas the same words written in HRPA might require tone markers. For example, the word *Ai* (tiny, short, small, brief, little) in Mandarin has no tone marker, but as written in HRPA, it is spelled *Aiv*, with the "v" serving as a tone marker.

Table 10.2. Comparison of HRPA and Mandarin Consonants

Consonant	Mandarin	Hmong RPA
B	B	P
C	C	Tx
Ch	Ch	Ts
D	D	T
F	F	F
G	G	K
H	H	H
J	J	C
K	K	Kh
L	L	L
M	M	M
N	N	N, Nc , Ny
P	P	P, Ph
Q	Q	Q, C
R	R	R, Z
S	S	S, X, Sh
T	T	T, th
W	W	V
X	X	X, Xy
Y	Y	Y
Z	Z , Zh	Z,Tx, Ts

Table 10.3. Comparison of HRPA and Mandarin Vowels

Vowel	Mandarin	Hmong RPA
A	A	A
Ai	Ai	Ai
Ao	Ao	Au
An	An	Aa (Blue Hmong only)
Ang	Ang	Aa (Blue Hmong only)
E	E	Aw
Ei	E	E
I	I	I
Ia	Ia	Ia
Ie	Ie	Ia
Ia	Iao	Au
Ian	Ian	Ii (Blue Hmong only)
In	In	Ii (Blue Hmong only)
Ing	Ing	Ee
Iong	Iong	Oo
O	O	Ua
Ua	Ua	Ua
Uo	Uo	Ua
U	U	W

Amazingly, the Mandarin system is very similar to the new version of HRPA, which includes all 26 letters of the Roman alphabet (A–Z). HRPA has a total of 63 segmental phonemes or tonal consonants, each represented by one to four letters. The HRPA has approximately ninety (19) single consonants, twenty-four (24) double consonantal blends, sixteen (16) triple consonantal blends, and four (4) quadruple consonantal blends. In the newest version, 10 simple consonants were replaced with 10 complex consonant (NP = B, NPL = BL, NK = G, NTS = J, NTX = DX, NPH = BH, NPLH = BLD, NKH = GH, NTSH = JH, and NTXH = DXH). The new version added eight new consonants (HXY, NG, NGH, OH, PR, RR, WH, and ZZ), introduced five new vowels (AA, AE, AWE, EW, and OI), created one new tone marker (R = cim pa), and eliminated one old tone marker (S = cim mus). The old version is less complex and easier to learn, but the two versions are equally valuable. Most Hmong prefer the old version over the new one because of its simplicity in vowels and word structure (prefixes, roots, and suffixes, or tone markers). Perhaps the new version can be improved in the academic arena. Meanwhile, both White Hmong and Blue Hmong adhere to the old HRPA system.

Hmong Written Languages Today

According to Hmong-Chinese legends, Hmong were literate in Chinese official writings; however, after the first written forms of their language, known as *Kiashu, Hmongshi, Dazi, Xiaozi,* or *Hmongshu,* were lost, Hmong had no writing system until French missionaries created the Hmong Romanized Popular Alphabet (HRPA) for them in the early 1950s. Thereafter, as mentioned earlier, other less known and less prominent forms of Hmong writing were developed, such as the Lao version, Thai version, Pa Ndau scripts, Vietnamese version, Pa Hawh version (*Phaj Hauj Hmoob*), and Chao Fa scripts.

A separate system of religious scripts and characters (*ntawv neeb losi ntawv dab neeb*) has been developed for Hmong shamans and magicians. The spiritual writing system, or magical scripts, is similar to the Chinese logographic characters and pictographic scripts. However, the religious writing system is only known and understood by the shamans and magicians; other Hmong cannot learn it.

In Southeast Asia, Hmong tried to create their own writing system, but the lack of schooling and linguistics training prevented them. They did not have a workable system until the American missionary linguists J. Linwood Barney and William Smalley, in association with French Catholic missionaries, invented the Hmong Romanized Practical Alphabet (*Ntawv Hmoob La Tee*). The missionaries had spent years researching Hmong history, languages, dialects, and oral language development.

At about the same time, a Hmong peasant named *Song Lue Yang,* mother of writing, came up with a Hmong writing system called Pa Hawh (*ntawv Hmoob Phaj Hauj*). It is based on the logographic scripts and logosyllabic characters in Vietnamese, Chinese, Lao, Thai, and Khmer (Cambodian). At first, Pa Hawh was an indigenous messianic writing system for any Hmong who was inclined to learn it from his master. After the fall of Laos in 1975, the Pa Hawh system was used for spiritual and religious worship and offering rites made by the Disciples of God in association with the Chao Fa movement.

HRPA, on the other hand, was widely adopted by Hmong people and taught in village schools and religious institutions prior to the fall of Laos and thereafter. As noted in Ly (2013), the first Hmong language class taught in HRPA by Yang Dao was offered in 1958. Thus the HRPA system became widely used and was formally taught to Hmong students in the 1960s and early 1970s in Laos. Table 10.4 compares HRPA and Pa Hawh. In the past up to the present day, the HRPA writing system, *ntawv Hmoob La Tee,* is the Hmong written language or writing system for both White and Blue Hmong dialects. Table 10.5 compares the phonemes and graphemes used in White Hmong and Blue Hmong, or the basic consonants used in both dialects. Blue Hmong and White Hmong have different phonetics, intonations, inflections, and pronunciations. Table 10.6 illustrates some basic differences of phonemic spellings between the two dialects. Despite the differences in sounds listed in Table 10.4, both Hmong languages are monosyllabic in verbal and written forms; however, Hmong do use bisyllabic and polysyllabic words that are made up of monosyllabic words—for example, *xovtooj, menyuam, vammeej, xovtshoj, kasnoos, koslosnees, tuamtshoj, vajtimhuabtaim, Asmesliskas, Kasnasdas,* and *Khalisfausnias.*

Like other languages, Hmong dialects contain simple and complex etymologies and linguistic phrases that require the speaker to develop in-depth mastery of Hmong oral skills and written knowledge in order for him or her to articulate Hmong dialects proficiently and fluently in different contexts, especially singing, chanting, offering, blessing, and writing poems.

Table 10.4. Comparison of Pa Hawh and HRPA Consonants and Vowels

HRPA characters	Hmong Pa Hawh (symbols and characters)

Consonants:
C: cas coj cib cij;
D: das doj dib dij;
F: fas foj fib fij;
H: has hoj hib hij;
K: kas koj kib kij;
L: las loj lib lij;
M: mas moj mib mij;
N: nas noj nib nij;
P: pas poj pib pij;
Q: qas qoj qib qij;
R: ras roj rib rij;
S: sas soj sib sij;
T: tas toj tib tij;
V: vas vaj vib vij;

X: xas xoj xib xij;
Y: yas, yoj, yib, yij
Z: zas zoj zib zij
W: Was waj wib wij;

Vowels:
A E I O U W
ai ia au ee aw oo aa (aa used in Blue Hmong only)

Tone markers:
B = cim siab (heart);
M = cim niam (mom);
D = cim tod (there);
J = cim ntuj (sky);
V = cim kuv (me);
UA = cim ua (do);
S = cim mus (go);
G = cim neeg (people)

Number system:
1 2 3 4 5 6 7 8 9 10 11 12 13...
Ib, ob, peb, plaub, tsib, rau, xyas, yim, cuab, kaum, ...

Consonants:

vau	nrau	fau	nkau	ntxau	rhau	nau	nqau	gau	yau	ncau	sau
[v]	[nʈ]	[f]	[ŋk]	[nts]	[tʰ]	[n]	[ɴq]	[ŋ]	[j]	[ɲc]	[ʃ]
lau	dau	dhau	hnau	khau	ntau	chau	xyau	tau	nchau	nrhau	npau
[l]	[ʔd]	[ʔdʰ]	[ʰn]	[kʰ]	[nt]	[cʰ]	[ç]	[t]	[ɲcʰ]	[ɳʈʰ]	[mp]
ntsau	tsau	phau	rau	nphau	nphlau	hlau	zau	ntxhau	nthau	nplau	nkhau
[nʈʂ]	[tʂ]	[pʰ]	[t]	[mpʰ]	[mpʰl]	[ʰl]	[ʒ]	[ntsʰ]	[ntʰ]	[mpl]	[ŋkʰ]
qhau	nyhau	hmau	mlau	hnlau	nqhau	hau	thau	plau	cau	ntshau	txau
[qʰ]	[ʰɲ]	[ʰm]	[ml]	[ʰml]	[ɴqʰ]	[h]	[tʰ]	[pl]	[c]	[ntʂʰ]	[ts]
xau	au	nyau	plhau	tshau	pau	mau	txhau	qau	dlau	ndlau	ndlhau
[s]	[ʔ]	[ɲ]	[pʰl]	[tʂʰ]	[p]	[m]	[tsʰ]	[q]		[ndl]	[ndʰl]
										dlhau	
										[dʰl]	

Vowels:

keeb	kib	kaub	kub	keb	kaib	koob	kawb	kuab	kob	kiab	kab	kwb
[εŋ]	[i]	[au]	[u]	[e]	[ai]	[ɔŋ]	[aɨ]	[ua]	[ɔ]	[ia]	[a]	[ɨ]

Tone markers:

Table 10.5. Phonemes and Graphemes of Consonant Sounds Used in Hmong Dialects

One Sound	Two Sounds	Three Sounds	Four Sounds
A, C, D, F, H, I, K, L, M, N, P, O, Q, R, S, T, U, V, X, Y, Z	Ch, D, Dh, Dl, Hl, Hm, Hn, Kh, Ml, Nc, Nk, Np, Nq, Nr, Nt, Ny, Ph, Pl, Qh, Rh, Th, Ts, Tx, Xy	Hml, Hny, Nch, Nkh, Nph, Npl, Nqh, Nrh, Nth, Nts, Ntx, Plh, Tsh, Txh, hn, ndl	Nplh, Ntsh, Ntxh,
Examples: Cas, Das, Fas, Kas, Las, Mas, Nas, Pas, Qas, Ras, Sas, Tas, Vas, Xas, Yas, Zas	Examples: Chas, Dhas, Hlas, Hmas, Hnas, Khas, Mlas, Ncas, Nkas, Npas, Nqas, Nras, Ntas, Nyas, Phas, Plas, Qhas, Rhas, Thas, Tsas, Txas, Xyas	Examples: Hmlas, Hnyas, Nkhas, Nphas, Nplas, Nqhas, Nrhas, Nthas, Ntsas, Ntxas, Plhas, Tshas, Txhas	Examples: Nplhas, Ntshas, Ntxhas

Table 10.6. Phonemic Spelling Differences in White Hmong and Blue Hmong

Basic Word	White Hmong	Blue Hmong	Meaning
Co	Co	Cu	Shake, tremble, vibrate
Paj	Paj	Paaj	Flower
Tiab	Tiab	Tab	Skirt
Diav	Diav	Dlav	Spoon
Hais	Hais	Has	Speak, talk, say, tell
Kub	Kub	Kub	Hot, gold
Qaib	Qaib	Qab	Chicken
Phiab	Phiab	Phab	Bowl
Thawb	Thawb	Thawb	Push, Thrust
Dhia	Dhia	Dlha	Jump, spring, gallop
Khub	Khub	Khub	Dirty, stained, fifthy
Qhia	Qhia	Qha	Teach, instruct, preach
Hmong	Hmoob	Moob	Hmong
Liab	Liab	Lab	Monkey, red, hot
Mus	Mus	Moog	Go, leave, take off, depart
Niam	Niam	Nam	Mother, mom, mommy
Nyiaj	Nyiaj	Nyaj	Money, currency
Txiv	Txiv	Txwv	Father
Vaj	Vaj	Vaaj	Garden, yard
Xovtooj	Xovtooj	Xuvtooj	Telephone, cell phone
Yaj	Yaj	Yaaj	Sheep, disappear, vanish, melt

The Pa Hawh writing system is used by specific families and groups of Hmong who have mastered its complex logographic scripts, symbols, and characters. Linguists are unsure if Blue Hmong dialects can be written in the Pa Hawh system. In the West, both writing systems have been technologically enhanced over the last 20 years. In fact, as stated earlier, there is a second version of HRPA that uses all the letters of the Romanized alphabet (A–Z); however, the new version seems to have some linguistic complications that will cause difficulties unless it is taught formally. On the other hand, Pa Hawh is making slow progress. It is not widely used by Hmong people for everyday written communication, but only for special occasions and social purposes. As Table 10.4 illustrates, learning Hmong Pa Hawh requires visual acuity and memorization of many logographic characters and symbols. Additionally, learning the Pa Hawh system is difficult without first learning the HRPA writing system. For most Hmong learners and writers, learning Pa Hawh without first mastering HRPA will take a long time because of Pa Hawh's linguistic complexity and logographic structure. There is an example of Pa Hawh writing on the Omni lot website: http://www.omniglot.com/writing/pahawh hmong.htm.

cle, religious rituals, and community settings has not changed much in the last 40 years. However, in the sociopolitical arena, the way

ᘱᔌ ᗷᕿᗯᴼ ᘚᗞ ᘾᗞ ᗐ ᗟᕟ ᗯᗞ ᗐᕿᴼ ᗷᘲᘘ ᘚᔌᕀ ᗟᕟ ᘾᘲᕀ ᘶᕿᴾ ᘶᔀᕀ ᗷᘶᴼ ᗟᕀᗯ. ᘶᔀᕟ ᘱᘚᗞ ᗟᔌᕀ ᗷᘶᴼ ᗟᕀᗯ

ᗐᕟᕼ ᘶᕀᕿᴾ ᘔᗞ ᘱᗟᕿᴾ ᗷᘷᴾ ᘶᗟᕿ ᗯᗞᗞ ᘚᔌᘘ ᗟᔌᕀ, ᗟᗞᗞ ᗷᗞᕀ: ᗟᗞ ᘙᗞ, ᘔᗯᕿᴾ ᘔᗞᕀ, ᘔᗞ ᗷᘔᕀ ᘙᗞᕀ, ᘱᗷᴾ ᗷᘔᗞ ᗟᗷᘲᴾ

ᗷᗞᕀ ᗷᗞ. ᘔᗷᴾ ᗟᕟ ᘱᔌ ᗷᕿᗯᴼ ᗷᕿᗯᴼ ᗷᘲᘘᴾ ᗷᗞᕀ ᘔᕟᗐ ᗟᕟ ᘔᗞ ᗟᘲᔀ ᗟᗞ ᘙᗞ. ᗐᘘ ᗷᘶᴾ ᗟᕀᗗ ᘶᕀᕿᴾ ᗟᕀᗗ ᗟᗷᔌ

ᗐᕟᕼ ᗐᗗᕼ ᘔᗗᕼ, ᘱᕀᕟ ᗷᗞ, ᗷᗟᗞ ᗷᕀᗐ, ᗷᘲᴾ ᗷ ᘱᕀᕟ ᘘᗞᕀ, ᘱᗷᴾ ᗟᗷᕿᴾ ᗟᕿᴾ ᗷᘲᴾ ᗟᕿᴾ ᗐᔌ ᘱᗞ ᗟᕼᗯ ᗟᗐ ᗷᗞᕀ ᗟᗞᕀ

ᗐᕟᴾ ᗟᕟ. ᗷᘱᘲᘘ ᗷᕿᗯᴼ ᘱᗞ ᘔᕟᕟ ᗟᕟ ᗷᕿᗯᴼ ᗟᗞᕀ ᘔᕀᗐ ᕼ ᗟᕿᘘ ᗟᘲᔀ, ᗟᗞᕀ ᕼ ᗯᘱᴾ ᗐᗗ, ᗟᗞᕀ ᗷᗐ ᗟᕼᕿᴾ, ᘔᕿᴾ ᕼ

ᗟᗐ ᗯᕟᴾ, ᘔᕿᴾ ᗟᗞᕀ ᕼ ᘔᕟᴾ ᗷᕼ, ᘔᕟᴾ ᗟᗷᘘ ᗷᘲᴾ ᘔᕟᴾ ᗯᗷᔀ ᗷᗐᕀ.

Changing Usage and Unified Language

Over the last 100 years, the many Hmong languages and dialects have become unified into the current two spoken languages known as *White Hmong* and *Blue Hmong*. As previously stated, the colors used to name Hmong languages have nothing to do with the languages themselves, but with the colors of the traditional clothing and handcrafts associated with the speakers of the languages. The colors help Hmong identify the linguistic roots, cultural similarities, and traditional commonalities among different families, clans, and tribes. All the families, clans, and tribes that share similar family traditions and embroidery styles and that speak similar dialects are classified with a larger group, either the White Hmong group (*Hmoob Dawb*) or the Blue Hmong group (*Hmoob Lee*). Linguistic variations as well as variations in family traditions exist in each group, but there are similarities within each group and some differences between the two groups.

There is no official Hmong language; however, most Hmong prefer to use the White Hmong in both formal and colloquial communication, and this preference has nothing to do with the quality of either language. Hmong still use the various dialects for everyday communication regardless of their country of residence and often for formal communication as well. In other words, Hmong use of the Hmong languages in the family cir-

Hmong dialects and languages are used has changed dramatically. For instance, nearly all Hmong singers sing songs in White Hmong rather than in Blue Hmong because audiences of White and Blue Hmong fans prefer the musical tones and lyrics of White Hmong. However, most Hmong Christians songs are written and sung in Blue Hmong because the majority of Christian Hmong are Blue Hmong.

One of the changes in language usage has to do with the new fields of learning and employment that have opened up to Hmong. The new contexts require new words and new syntactical structures. Different professions have their own vocabularies, semantics, pragmatics, slang, registers, and idioms. Hmong employed in various occupations have to adjust their use of the Hmong languages to accommodate the specific needs of their fields, just as English speakers do. They have to be careful about their word choices. For example, they cannot use religious words and phrases in formal conversation. As in English, the same Hmong word may be used in different fields and have different meanings in the different professions. For example, the legal and medical professions may use the same word but the word may not have the same meaning in the two fields. To demonstrate different uses of the Hmong languages for different fields of endeavor, Table 10.7 presents the basic purposes, linguistic approaches, and some examples for six professions.

Table 10.7. Hmong Language Differences by Profession

Education	*Medicine*	*Law*	*Religion*	*Leadership*	*Shamanism*	*Chanting/ Singing*
Basic purpose: Teach, learn, read, write, and do math	Basic purpose: Treat, cure, heal, and diagnose	Basic purpose: Debate, hear, argue, cross-examine, resolve, decide, and sue	Basic purpose: Preach, perform rites, chant, sing, read scriptures, conduct rituals, offer, and sermonize	Basic purpose: Give speeches, use rhetoric, make decisions, resolve civil issues, make rules, and lead	Basic purpose: Chant, heal, perform rites, conduct rituals, fall in trance, and use magical power	Basic purpose: Chant; sing; write phrases, verses, stanzas; perform; conduct; create lyrics; and entertain
Linguistic approach: Academic teaching and learning (kev qhia txuj thiab kev kawm txuj ci)	Linguistic approach: Diagnose, treat, and care (tshuaj xyuas kev kho mob kho nkeeg)	Linguistic approach: Cross-examination and decision making (kev hais plaub hais ntug)	Linguistic approach: Preaching and conducting sermons (cob qhia kev cai dab qhua thiab kev teev hawm kev ntseeg)	Linguistic approach: Leading the way (kev coj noj coj ua)	Linguistic approach: Performing magical power to heal (kev ua neeb ua yaig)	Linguistic approach: Chanting, singing, and writing songs (kev sau nkauj thiab hu nkauj)
Explain (piav)	Explain (qhia)	Explain (piav qhia)	Explain (txhais tau tias)	Explain (qhia tau tias)	Explain (piv tau tias)	Explain (txhais tau tias)
Think (xav)	Think (xav)	Think (rhiav tswv yim)	Think (xam pom)	Think (xav tau)	Think (xam pom)	Think (xav)
Feel (paub)	Feel (mloog tau)	Feel (xav)	Feel (mloog tau)	Feel (paub)	Feel (sim)	Feel (xav losi mloog)
Understand (to taub)	Understand (nkag siab)	Understand (paub)	Understand (nkag siab)	Understand (to tsib)	Understand (paub)	Understand (nkag siab)
Sue (tom, nug)	Sue (nug kom tseeb)	Sue (foob)	Sue (nug kom tseeb)	Sue (taug qhov tseeb)	Sue (nug kom tseeb)	Sue (nug qhov tseeb)

Another change in usage resulted from the introduction of writing systems. When the HRPA writing system became available in the early 1950s, Hmong were eager to learn how to write and read Hmong. Because the writing system was devised by Christian missionaries, some of the first texts to be written in HRPA were translations of Biblical passages. Translation and written transcription of the Gospels was first available in Blue Hmong because a large number of Blue Hmong had converted to Christianity in 1957; large-scale conversion of White Hmong came in subsequent years. So even though the Bible has been translated and written in both Hmong languages, more Biblical texts are still printed in Blue Hmong than White Hmong. Nevertheless, HRPA was available in both White Hmong and Blue Hmong and writing for both dialects was taught to Hmong students in public schools in the late 1950s. Because White Hmong was spoken by the majority of Hmong, it was the language used for instruction in HRPA in the public schools in Hmong towns and villages. In the academic arena, this meant that literate Hmong tended to gravitate toward White Hmong, which grew in common usage while Blue Hmong faded further into the background. Thus the invention of HRPA changed Hmong language usage at the same time as it made literacy in the Hmong languages possible. In the U.S., nearly all Hmong language and culture courses in college are taught in White Hmong; very few are taught in Blue Hmong.

In the public schools of the western nations, teachers notify Hmong parents of various matters in writing using both White Hmong and Blue Hmong dialects. The linguistic complexity of Hmong dialects has caused some misinterpretations and miscommunications among parents in the Hmong community. Most White Hmong parents cannot understand some of the Blue Hmong dialects and therefore cannot read Blue Hmong writing well whereas most Blue Hmong parents can read and understand White Hmong dialects. Moreover, the majority of Hmong students are White Hmong. This dilemma has prompted most school districts to use White Hmong only in formal communication with Hmong parents. This decision does not mean that White Hmong is easier, better, or clearer than Blue Hmong. Some Hmong believe that both dialects should be used for formal communication for both groups. However, just as Spanish is used in formal communication for all groups who come from different Spanish-speaking countries, Hmong have to accept school administrators' policies. Many schools have both White Hmong and Blue Hmong translators and interpreters to help with communication issues. Ironically, many White Hmong speakers cannot speak fluently in Blue Hmong and their verbal interpretation and translation of Blue Hmong could be linguistically sensitive and inaccurate whereas most Blue Hmong speakers can articulate White Hmong fluently.

The use of White Hmong for most formal communications is not a put-down of Blue Hmong; it is based on public perception. Both Hmong languages are used in the Hmong movie industry and Hmong social media, but as previously stated, almost all Hmong songs are written and sung in White Hmong. Music in White Hmong is more lucrative and most Hmong music fans prefer White Hmong lyrics. In recent years, the Hmong community has gotten into a dispute about the spelling of the name *Hmong*, which is White Hmong, or *Mong*, which is Blue Hmong. Some contend that the word *Hmong* represents only the White Hmong group and the word *Mong* should be added to all formal documents and communications to recognize the Blue Hmong group. This controversy had not only damaged Hmong pride and dignity, but it has also created a sociopolitical nightmare that has shocked Hmong and non–Hmong who hear it. Vang (2003) discussed the dispute in the Valley Voices of the *Fresno Bee*:

"HMONG RESOLVE THEIR DIFFERENCES THE DIFFICULT WAY"

At just the time a new education bill is poised to be passed into law, many in the Hmong-American community are bewildered by the public debate over a morphological distinction in a name. Some are arguing about their ethnic designation: "Hmong" or "Mong." The controversy over a Hmong Education Bill (AB78) introduced by Sarah Reyes, D–Fresno, mystifies a few Mong-Americans. Some strongly feel that the bill should contain both names, and others believe the dispute is an old political maneuver to sabotage the bill.

[...]

The suffixes Daw, Leng and Njua were added to denote colors and are used only to identify clans, families, dialects, costumes, customs, and linguistic variations among groups. These suffixes are not used to communicate disdain, condemnation, inferiority, or humiliation.

Today's Hmong Americans belong to one of two distinct groups—White Hmong and Blue Hmong—recognized by the dialect spoken at home. Many Hmong families now mix two or more languages and cultures in their homes. If the fractionalization should continue, how would such a Hmong American classify its children? Are they White Hmong, Blue Mong, Green Mong, Hmong-American, Mong-American, Hmong-Mong American, or Southeast Asian-American?

Eventually, AB 78 became law in California. It required 7–12 schools to include in their social studies curricula Hmong history related to the Secret War in Laos. Keep in mind that *Hmoob* and *Moob* are both Hmong. The variations in Hmong linguistics will remain somewhat controversial among some Hmong individuals who want to safeguard the equality of their unique dialects, and the use by school districts, social media, and government agencies of one Hmong dialect over the other for formal communication will continue to arouse hurt and animosities. Concerned individuals should feel free to advocate for their dialects and inform the general public about their concerns. Finding a balance between the different dialects used in private and the need for a single voice in public is challenging. Hmong should keep practicing their family dialects at home to preserve their culture and traditions but at the same time accept the usage of one Hmong language in public communications. Perhaps all Hmong should become bilingual in Hmong languages because having the ability to speak both languages is socially and culturally advantageous.

Hmong Grammar and Subsystems

As mentioned previously, Hmong languages have some commonalities and share a number of linguistic phonemes, graphemes, and structural properties with other languages of eastern and southeast Asia, namely Chinese, Vietnamese, Lao, Thai, Khmer, Mien, Yao, Haw, Khamu, Lu, Lahu, and Miao. Of all these languages, Hmong is most closely related phonetically to Chinese, especially Mandarin Chinese. The various languages have similar monosyllabic terminologies, tone markers, inflections, word tenses, masculine and feminine classifiers, descriptive noun classifiers, and serial usage of constructions and conjugations. Even with the similarities with other Asian languages, the Hmong language is unique, distinct from other Asian languages. As a newly developed written language, HRPA has linguistic limitations and restrictions. Perhaps examination of the subsystems of the language can provide grammatical foundations for learning and understanding the grammar of Hmong languages and dialects.

Monosyllabic Words

Hmong is spoken and written in single-syllable words that are phonologically identical to words in Chinese, Vietnamese, Miao, Yao, Mien, Khamu, and other Asian languages. Hmong languages do not have polysyllabic words such as are used in English, French, and Spanish. Consider the sentence: You (*koj*) go (*mus*) to (*tom*) the market (*kiab*). Hmong has no article or adjective equivalent to the English word "the." Now look at the sentence: You (*koj*) explain (*piav*) it (*nws*) to (*rau*) me (*kuv*) with (*nrog*) information (*lus qhia losi lus paub*). One monosyllabic Hmong word is used for the English word "explain" and two to five monosyllabic words are needed for explaining the English word "information." Thus some Hmong words are, in essence, polysyllabic words formed by combining monosyllabic words that can stand alone independently. For example, the words "student" (*tub ntxhais kawm ntawv*), "teacher" (*xib fwb losi xib hwb*), "school" (*tsev kawm ntawv*), "paper" (*daim ntawv*), "teaching" (*qhia ntawv*), and "playing" (*ua si*) all require more than one monosyllabic word. Here is another set of Hmong polysyllabic words: "heaven" (*ceebtsheej losi ceeb tsheej*), "Jesus Christ" (*vajtswv losi vaj tswv*), "God" (*yawmsaub losi yawm saub*), "Minnesota" (*Misnisxaustas losi Mis Nis Xaus Tas*), and "America" (*Asmesliskas losi As Mes Lis Kas*).

Hmong monosyllabic words have no ending inflections such as *ing, ed, s, th, ch, ies, er, or,* and so on. Hmong languages do not have inflectional endings that make a singular word plural. The English "dog" (*dev*) is made plural by adding an *s,* "dogs," but in Hmong the plural is the polysyllabic word *cov dev losi ntau tus dev*). Similarly, the plurals of "sheep" (*pab yaj losi cov yaj*) and of "children" (*cov menyuam losi pab menyuam*) are polysyllabic. Hmong use descriptive monosyllabic words in compound forms to describe objects and natural occurrences: *laimtxias, tsigtsuag, zigzuag, ntxheesyees, dawbpaug, ntsuabxiab, and dubnciab*.

The use of monosyllabic words in Hmong languages is somewhat of a hindrance to Hmong children in learning to speak English correctly in the early stage of their second-language acquisition. Hmong children may need to break the English polysyllabic words into phonological syllables that resemble Hmong monosyllabic words before trying to decode the inflections of the words. This linguistic issue may not be a challenge for native-born Hmong children who have been exposed to the English language on a daily basis since birth, but it is quite difficult for foreign-born and older Hmong children who immigrated to the U.S. as well as for Hmong adults who want to learn English. Once the basic morphemes and phonemes of accented and unaccented syllables of English words are learned (e.g., "a" as in man, "ie" and "e" as in pilot (pie+let), "o" as in lot, "oo" as in school and cool, and so on), the English polysyllabic words can be learned.

Linguistic Tones

In western languages, intonation (pitch variation) and inflection (word endings) are used to indicate the meanings of words in a sentence. Hmong languages, like Chinese, are tonal. Tonal languages do not use intonation to indicate what words mean according to how they are used in the sentence; rather they use tones (pitches) to distinguish one word from another. The same base word can be pronounced in different tones and the meanings are different depending on the tone. So, for example, the White Hmong word *pa*, when uttered in different tones (as indicated by the final consonant), has different meanings: *pa* (breath), *pab* (help), *paj* (flower), *pav* (tie or wrap), *pag* (gun sound), *pas* (stick), and *pam* (blanket).

In HRPA, the tone of a word is indicated by the final consonant, called a tone marker. The tone marker tells the reader how to pronounce the word in terms of pitch and therefore determines the word's meaning. Table 10.8 lists the tone markers used in HRPA together with their pitches and gives examples of Hmong words for each tone marker. As the table shows, Hmong use at least eight different tone markers to indicate the tone, pitch, or sound of Hmong monosyllabic words. The *D* and *M* tone markers indicate the same tonal phoneme with only slight differences.

Table 10.8 HRPA Tone Markers

Marker	*Tone, Pitch, or Sound*	*Example of Hmong Word*	*English Translation*
B = cim siab	High tone	Tob	Deep
J = cim ntuj	High falling tone	Toj	Hillside or slope
V = cim kuv	Mild or mid rising tone	Tov	Mix or dilute
Cim ua = no tone marker, only based on sound of the word with a vowel	Mid or mid flat tone	To	Puncture, rapture, or has a hole
D = cim ntawv, cim tod	Low falling with creaky pitch or voice	Tod	There, over there, at, or in
G = cim neeg	Mild or mid low tone with breathy pitch or voice	Tog	Sink, end, or side
S = cim mus	Low tone	Tos	Wait, sponsor, or halt
M = cim niam	Low falling with creaky pitch or voice	Tom	Bite or to

Notes: Tone markers M and D are used interchangeably with a slight difference.

Hmong tones may sound different from one speaker to another; speakers may raise or drop the pitch differently and articulate the sounds differently. The quality of pitch can depend on the speaker's plain, breathy, or creaky voice quality; aspiration; lips and tongue placement; and nasal or throaty voice.

As in English, the speaker may use some intonation not to differentiate between word meanings, but to express questioning, emphasis, or some other attitude of the speaker about the message. Such meanings are conveyed in Hmong not through tone markers but through similar ending particles such as *uali, yog ma, lov, li los, aw, nes, li ntawd, hos, mog, haus yaus*, and so on. Just as in English prefixes and suffixes added to words often change the words' meanings, so in Hmong the ending particles are important to meaning. Therefore, Hmong speakers must pay attention to voice pitch and intonation of words and phrases to be sure the listener understands what the speaker intends to communicate.

No Inflection and Tenses

In Hmong languages, a number in front of a noun indicates the quantity or plural form of the noun. For example, Hmong say *ob lub tsev* to indicate "two houses," *peb tug dev* for "three dogs," and *plaub lub tseb* for "four cars." Hmong do not use inflection (word endings) such as *ing, ed, s, es, ies, en, y, ch, th, ism, or ics* to indicate the plural, possessive, or tense of words. In English, inflection is used, for example, to make the word *move* present tense (moves), past tense (moved), progressive tense (moving), or to change it to a noun (mover). Verb tenses do not exist in Hmong languages. Hmong do not use possessive nouns or pronouns such as the English words "his, hers, mine, theirs, its, girls', boys', cats', dogs'," and so on. Moreover, Hmong languages do not have masculine and feminine forms of nouns that require corresponding forms of verbs and adjectives, like in French and Spanish.

The absence of inflection makes Hmong languages flexible and easy to use in reference to any situation. Instead of verb tenses, Hmong add monosyllabic words to the present-tense form of the verb to classify an action as past, present, future, present progressive, or future progressive, as shown in Table 10.9. For example, the word "go" (*mus*) is used with support words to form the expressions *kuv tab tom mus* (I am going), *kuv mus los lawm* (I went), *kuv mam li mus* (I will go), *kuv tau mus los lawm* (I have gone), *kuv tseem yuav mus* (I will go), and *kuv twb tau mus* (I had gone). The expressions can be further modified to add the element of time: *tav sus kuv mam mus* (I will go at noon), *tsau ntuj kuv mam mus* (I will go at dusk), *tag kis kuv mam mus* (I will go tomorrow), *nag kis kuv mam mus* (I will go the day after tomorrow), and *pug nraus kuv mam mus* (I will go two days after tomorrow). Hmong words have only one form; for example, the verb *mus* (go) remains unchanged regardless of tense.

Table 10.9. Examples of Hmong Verb Tenses

Present English/Hmong	Present Progressive English/Hmong	Past English/Hmong	Future English/Hmong	Future Progressive English/Hmong
Take/nqa	Taking/tab tom nqa	Took/tau nqa	Will take/yuav nqa, mam nqa	Will be taking/ tseem yuav nqa
Go/mus	Going/tab tom mus	Went/tau mus, mus lawm	Will go/yuav mus, mam mus	Will be going/ tseem yuav mus
Eat/noj	Eating/tab tom noj	Ate/noj tag lawm, tau noj	Will eat/yuav noj, mam noj	Will be eating/ tseem yuav noj
Talk/hais lus	Talking/tab tom hais lus	Talked/tau hais lus, hais lus tag lawm	Will talk/yuav hais lus, mam hais lus	Will be talking/ tseem yuav hais lus
Be, is, are/yog	Being/tab tom yog	Was, were/tau yog, yog lawm	Will be/yuav yog, mam yog	Will be being/ tseem yuav yog

As Table 10.9 illustrates, it is difficult to express the past progressive tense in Hmong, such as "I was going" or "I have been gone" because of linguistic limitations. To indicate possession, Hmong use classifiers; for example, *nws li* or *nws cov* (his or belong to him, its or belong to it, hers or belong to her); *kuv li* or *kuv cov* (mine or belong to me); *tus tswv yog* (the owner is), and *leej twg li* or *leej twg cov* (whose or belonging to whom). The same Hmong possessive pronoun or noun could be translated in different ways; for example, *kuv* means "I, my," or "mine"; *koj* means "you," "your," or "yours," and so on. However, Hmong possessive pronouns require classifiers such as *li* or *cov*, as in *kuv li* (mine), *kuv cov* (mine), *koj li* (yours), or *koj cov* (yours). Similarly, Hmong use pronoun as classifiers; for example, *kuv lub tsev* (my house), *koj tus dev* (your dog), or *nws daim nyiaj* (its money, his money, or her money). Hmong also use sexist classifiers to indicate gender: female (*poj, maum, xyuas, nkauj*) and male (*txiv, la, taw, lau, heev*). Thus an unmarried woman is *hluas nkauj*, a married woman is *poj niam*, an unmarried man is *hluas nraug*, a married man is *leej txiv or txiv tsev*; wearing a skirt is *poj niam losi ntxhais* and wearing pants is *txiv neej losi tub*. Also the word "fruit" (*txiv*) is used for male and "flower" (*paj*) is used for female.

The lack of inflection does not keep Hmong languages from being used correctly in verbal or written forms. As long as speakers express themselves in complete thoughts, the meaning of their expressions can be understood. In writing, however, misapplication of tone markers will change the meaning of words. For instance, the verb in the sentence *kuv tos koj* (I wait for you) is *tos*; however, the sentence is completely changed if the tone marker "s" is replaced with "m, " changing the verb from *tos* to *tom*; the sentence becomes *kuv tom koj* (I bite you). Proper use of tone markers for Hmong languages is the key to good written and verbal expression.

Limited Classifiers

Hmong does not have adverbs to classify monosyllabic adjectives, adverbs, and nouns as English does. For example, the phrase "thank you so very much" can be expressed in Hmong as *ua tsaug ntau ntau heev*. In this context, the Hmong words *ntau ntau* and *heev* express the same meaning as the English words "so very much." To get this expression, the word *ntau* has to be repeated because there is no Hmong word for the English intensifier "so." The Hmong phrase *ua tsaug ntau ntau heev* is more directly equivalent to the English phrase "thanks very, very much."

Hmong languages lack inflected adjectives and adverbs that indicate temporal action and comparatives and superlatives such as *early, earlier, earliest* and *fast, faster,* and *fastest*. Hmong use monosyllabic words in place of these descriptive adjectives and adverbs. For example, with the addition of other words, early (*ntxov*) becomes earlier (*ntxov zog, ntxov dua, ntxov heev, ntxov tshaj*) or earliest (*ntxov tshaj plaws*) and good (*zoo*) becomes better (*zoo zog, zoo dua, zoo heev, zoo tshaj*) or best (*zoo tshaj plaws*). Hmong use double adjectives in place of comparatives and superlatives: *heev* (very), *heev heev* (very very); *ntau* (many), *ntau ntau* (many many); *loj* (*big*), *loj heev* or *loj loj* (very big); *me* (small), *me me* or *me heev* (very small); and *maj* (hurry), *maj maj* or *maj heev* (in a big hurry).

In English, classifiers are generally placed before the adverbs, adjectives, and nouns; this is not always the case in Hmong languages. For instance, article classifiers (a, an, the) appear before the words they modify, as in "the car" (*lub tsheb*), "the house" (*lub tsev*), "the plate" (*lub phaj*), and "the book" (*phau ntawv*) whereas adjectival classifiers come after the noun, as in "red car" (*tsheb liab*), "old house" (*tsev qub*), "clean plate" (*phaj huv*), and "good book" (*phau ntawv zoo*). This placement means that direct transliteration from Hmong to English does not make sense; transliterated, *tsheb liab* would be "house red," *tsev qub* would be "house old," *phaj huv* would be "plate clean," and *phau ntawv zoo* would be "book good." Table 10.10 presents some common classifiers used in Hmong languages.

In Hmong, nouns may have different

Table 10.10. Selected Common Hmong Classifiers

Classifier	Example of Use	Use
Tus	Tus tub (the son), tus nyuj (the cow), tus nab (the snake), tus tsov (the tiger)	Before objects, nouns, and animals
Rab	Rab rauj (the hammer), rab riam (the knife), rab phom (the gun), rab hneev (the crossbow), rab qeej (the bamboo reed pipe), rab qws (the stick)	Before objects, tools, instruments, and nouns
Lub	Lub raj (the flute), lub tsev (the house), lub txiv (the fruit), lub khob (the glass)	Before objects, fruits, things, tools, instruments, shapes, and nouns
Daim	Daim ntawv (the paper), daim duab (the picture), daim pam (the blanket), daim nyiaj (the money)	Before objects, things, nouns, and shapes
Leej	Leej txiv (the father), leej niam (the mother), leej tub (the son), leej muam (the sister), leej tij (the brother)	Before people, persons, parents, brothers, sisters, and relatives
Cov	Cov nyiaj (monies), cov txiv (fruits), cov neeg (people), cov dej (water), cov memyuam (children)	Before nouns to indicate quantity, number, scale, and group
Ib, ob, peb, plaub, tsib, rau, etc...	Ib daim (one piece), ob daim (two pieces), peb daim (four pieces), etc...	Number can be used before classifiers, nouns, things, and objects
Lawm, xwb, nawb, mam, na, mog, aw, etc...	Puas lawm (broken), tag lawm (gone), poob lawm (fallen down), yog lawm (correct)	After any action verb or at the end of a sentence

meanings depending on the classifier placed in front of the noun. For example, classifiers can change *duab* (picture) into *daim duab* (a picture), *phau duab* (picture album), *dais duab* (hang picture), or *kos duab* (draw picture). Similarly, *ntawv* (book) can become *daim ntawv* (piece of paper), *phau ntawv* (a book), *ntshua ntawv* (bundle of paper), or *tsab ntawv* (a written letter). Hmong classifiers can go after action verbs, as indicated in table 10.10. The Hmong language lacks classifiers for certain specific descriptions such as secondary colors (cream, tan, beige, gray, metal silver, metal green, metallic charcoal, and so on) and social formalities (ladies and gentlemen, Mrs., Ms., Miss., Mr., Dr., honorable, Maiden, Madam, Sir, lieutenant, and so on).

Double Verbs

Another interesting aspect of Hmong linguistics is its treatment of two verbs in a single sentence. English also has some double verb constructions: "I'll go see him" (*kuv mam mus ntsib nws*), "I'll go ride a bike" (*kuv mam mus caij tsheb kauj vab*), and "you'll come talk to me" (*koj mam tuaj nrog kuv tham*)." These sentences are similar to some Hmong structures: *kuv mus txog tom tsev kawm ntawv* (I go arrive at the school); *kuv tuaj tos koj ntev lawm* (I came wait for you for a long time); *kuv khiav mus nyob hauv Fresno* (I run move live in Fresno, or I move live in Fresno); and *kuv mus yuav khoom noj* (I go buy groceries)." However, Hmong languages have no way of conjugating double verbs in a sentence in the past or the future tense (I went arrived at the school; I came waited for you; I went rode my bike). An adverbial classifier has to be placed before each verb to indicate past tense or future tense. For example, "*kuv tau tuaj ntsib koj* (I came see you), *kuv tau mus caij tsheb kauj vab* (I went ride a bike), and *kuv yuav mus yuav khoom noj* (I will go buy groceries)." In these sentences, the Hmong words *tau* and *yuav* change the tense of the verb. "Tau" indicates past tense and *yuav* expresses future tense.

Phonology

Phonology deals with the sounds (phonemes) of a language. Hmong language have consonant sounds, vowel sounds, and tone markers; for the most part, Hmong languages use monosyllabic tonal words. The old HRPA system has 13 vowels and 56 consonants, as shown in Tables 10.11 and 10.12. Of the 13 mono-vowels, 6 are written as single Roman letters and 7 are written as double Roman letters, or bi-vowels. Of the 56 consonants, 17 are written as single Roman letters, 22 are double Roman letters (bi-consonants), 14 are triple Roman letters (tri-consonants), and 3 are quadruple Roman letters (quadra-consonants). The tri-consonants and quadra-consonants are called consonant clusters because a few letters are clustered together to make sounds. The new HRPA system has a total of 63 consonants and 18 mono-vowels.

Hmong consonants are ordinary Roman

Table 10.11. Hmong Mono-Vowels

Mono-vowels	Oral front	Oral Central	Oral Back	Sound Equivalent	Sample of Monosyllabic Word
A		Low tone		As "A" in French	Tas (finish)
E	Middle tone			As "A" in English	Es (and)
I	Middle tone			As "E" in English	Ib (one)
U			High tone	As "Uh" in English	Ub (uh sound)
O			Middle tone	As "Of" in English	Os (swell)
W		High tone		As "EEw" in English	Wb (we, us)

Note: Oral front, central, and back are indications of the sound of each mono-vowel and of where in the mouth the sound is made.

Table 10.12. Hmong Mono-, Bi-, and Tri-Consonants

Hmong mono-vowels	Nasal front	Nasal central	Nasal back	Diphthongs	Sound Equivalent	Sample of Monosyllabic Word
Au				xx	As "Australia" in English	Aub (dog)
Ai				xx	As "I" in English	Pai (go)
Aw				xx	As "Aw" in English	Aws (response)
Ee	Middle tone				As "Ing" in English	Tee (as in latee, latin)
Oo		Middle tone			As "Own" in English	Ntoo (tree)
Ia				xx	As "Ear" in English	Tias (that in a sentence, hais tias)
Ua				xx	As "Dual' in English	Tua (kill)
Aa		Low tone			As "A" in French	Aav (soil, in Blue Hmong)

Note: Nasal front, central, and back are indications of the sound of each consonant and of where in the mouth the sound is made.

letters; however, not all the Roman consonants are used as Hmong consonants in the HRPA writing system. The HRPA left out those consonants that had a sound in the Roman alphabet but no equivalent sound in Hmong, for example, the letters B, G, and J. The letters G and J are used as tone markers and the letter B is replaced with the P consonant. In Hmong writing, a syllable has three components: a consonant, a vowel, and a tone marker. The consonant is optional in some situations, such as when the mono-vowel is used as a word, but a syllable must contain a vowel or it cannot have a tone marker. In other words, the vowel has to be pronounced on one of the tone levels. Each consonant is a sound, and this means that each consonant marks a syllable of a monosyllabic word ending with a vowel or diphthong. An example of a typical monosyllabic Hmong word made up of a consonant, a vowel, and a tone marker is *tsib*; *tsib* consists of the consonant cluster "*ts*" plus the vowel "I" pronounced in the high tone indicated by the tone marker "b." As illustrated in Tables 10.13 and 10.14, syllables are articulated from the lips to the glottis.

Table 10.13. HRPA Consonants and Vowels

Consonant or Vowel	Manner of Release and Articulation
A	Bilabial
B	Bilabial with lateral release
C	Labio-dental
D	Apico-dental
E	Apico-dental affricate
F	Lamino-dental with palatal offglide
G	Apico-alveolar
H	Lamino-alveolar
I	Apico-post-alveolar with rhotic release
J	Palatal
K	Velar
L	Uvular
M	Glottal

As Table 10.14 shows, there are a total of 11 groups of consonant clusters: four of stopped consonants; two of voiced and voiceless affricatives; and five consonant clusters that require nasals, liquids, and a mono-voice glide. These consonant clusters can be grouped into three main series, as indicated in Table 10.15, and the three main series can be broken down further to better understand the phonemes and graphemes of Hmong languages, as presented in Tables 10.16 and 10.17. Of all the stops and affricates, some consonants have no aspiration, such as *p*, *t*, *k*, and *d*, and

Table 10.14. Sounds of Hmong Consonants

Consonant	Manner of Release and Articulation	Manner of Articulation in Hmong
T, th, nt, nth n, hn, x, z	Dental	Hais ntawm nhiav
Tx, txh, ntx, ntxh	Dental, affricated, affricative release	Ruas hniav hais
H, hxy	Glottal	Hais tom qas
D, dh	Glottalized	Ruas qas
F, m, hm, p, v, np, nph	Labial	Hais ntawm dis ncauj
L, hl, hml, ml, pl, plh, npl, nplh	Labial release	Tso tom kom ncauj
C, ch, nc, nch, ny, hny, xy, y	Palatal	Hais saum ruv qhov ncauj
Ts, tsh, j, ntsh, ng	Palatal affricated, affricative release	Ruas saum ruv hais
R, rh, rr,nr, nrh, s, z	Retroflexed	Quav plaig hais
K, kh, nk, nkh,	Velar	Hais ntawm plaig
Q, qh, nq, nqh	Back velar	Hais hauv qab plaig

some have aspiration as in English. In this particular cluster, the aspiration notation belongs to the letter *"h"* because it is preceded by the stopped consonant or consonants. Some consonants require both aspiration and pre-nasalization articulation. All together, there are approximately 38 stops and affricates; however, the new HRPA version may have more stopped consonants than the old version.

Table 10.15. Three Main Series of Hmong Stopped Consonants

Stops and Affricates	*Fricatives*	*Nasals, Liquids, and Glides*
P, pl, ph, phl, np, npl, nph, nplh		V, z M, ml, hm, hml
T, th, nt, nth, tx txh, ntx, ntxh	F, x, s, xy, h	N, hn, ny, hny
C, ch, nc, nch		g
D, dh		L, hl
Ts, tsh, nts, ntsh		Y
R, rh, nr, nrh		
K, kh, nk, nkh		
Q, qh, nq, nqh		

Table 10.16. Hmong Phonemes and Graphemes

Two Lips	*Teeth/ Lips*	*Tongue/ Teeth*	*Tongue/ Ridge*	*Tongue Tip/ Roof*	*Tongue Mid/ Roof*	*Tongue Curled*	*Tongue Back/ Soft Palate*	*Throat*
P			T	D			K	q
Paj			Tiab	Diav			Kub	Qaib
Ph			Th	Dh			Kh	Qh
phiab			Thawb	Dhia			Khub	Qhia
Np			Nt				Nk	Nq
Npua			Ntawv				Nkoj	Nqaij
Nph			Nth				Nkhaus	Nqh
Nphob								
	F		X		S		Xy	H
	Fuab		Xauv		Sov		Xyoob	Huab
	V		Y		Z			
	Vaj		Yaj		Zos			
			L					
			Liab					
Hm			Hl				Hny	
Hmoob			Hlis				hnyav	
			Hn					
			Hnub					
M			N				Ny	
Me			Niam				Nyiaj	
			Tx	C	Ts	R		
			Txiv	Co	Tsev	Riam		
			Txh	Cho	Tsh	Rh		
			Txhob	choj	Tsheb	Rho		
			Ntx	Nc	Nts			
			Ntxiv	Nceb	Ntses	Nruas		
			Ntxh	Nch	Ntsh	Nrh		
			ntxhw	ncho	Ntshav	Nrhiav		

Table 10.17. Hmong Articulation and Pronunciation with Flow of Air and Aspiration

Stop/Voiceless	*Stop/Voiceless/ Aspirated with Air*	*Stop/Voiced/ Vocal Cord Vibrate*	*Stop/Voiced Aspirated*	*Cont/Voiceless*
P paj	Ph phiab	Np npua	Nph	F fuab
T tiab	Th thawb	Nt ntawv	nphob	X xauv
D diav	Dh dhia	Nk nkoj	Nth	S sov
K kub	Kh khub	Nq nqaij	nthuav	Xy xyoob
Q qaib	Qh qhia		Nkhaus	H huab
			Nqh	
			nqhis	

Cont/Voiced/ VCV	*Cont/Aspirated with Air*	*Cont/Nasal Air Thru Nose*	*Affricate/Voiceless Aspirate*	*Affricate/Voiced/ Aspirate*
V vaj	Hm	M me	Tx txiv	Ntx ntxiv
Y yaj	Hmoob	N niam	Txh	NTxh
L liab	Hl hlis	Nyiaj	txhob	ntxhw
Z zos	Hny		C co	Nc nceb
	hnyav		Cho choj	Nch ncho
			Ts tsev	Nts ntses
			Tsh tsheb	Ntsh
			R riam	ntshav
			Rh rho	Nr nruas
				Nrh
				nrhiav

Notes: Cont = continuation, VCV = vocal cord vibrate

Furthermore, some fricative consonants are either voiced or voiceless and others require nasals, liquids, and glides for articulation and pronunciation. Of the 38 different stopped consonants, many stops and fricative consonants have different pronunciations or articulations in different manners depending on the phonemic emphasis at the time of utterance by the speaker. Some non-aspirated and voiceless consonants could be the first letters of monosyllabic words, as in *Hmong, hnov, hmo,* and *hnav.* In these words, the "*h*" is voiceless, as in *Hmab, Hmub, Hmaj,* and *Hmoob.* These spellings are related to the vowels used in HRPA and the way each vowel and tone marker produces the sound for articulation and pronunciation. Finally, the sounds of

Hmong vowels are summarized in Table 10.18 for quick reference, and Tables 10.16 and 10.17 also provide clear guidelines for articulation and pronunciation of Hmong vowels and consonants. The stops, affricates, fricatives, nasals, liquids, glides, and diphthongs play major roles in the process of learning how to speak, write, and read Hmong languages.

Morphology

Morphology is concerned with the way words are built in a language in both oral and written forms. In English, morphology involves root words, prefixes, and suffixes. In Hmong, consonants, vowels, and tones are the linguistic elements in building monosyllabic words. The building blocks are 56 con-

Table 10.18. Quick View of Hmong Vowels with English Vowel Sounds

Monophthong Vowels	*Nasalized Vowels*	*Diphthongs*
I /i/, e /e/, a /a/, o /o/, u /u/, w /t̕/	Ee /ē/, aa /ā/, oo /ō/	Ai /ai/, aw /at̕/, au /au/, ua /ue/

sonants, 13 vowels, and 8 tones. For example, the elements in the word *tas* are the consonant *t*, the vowel *a*, and the tone marker *s*. The speaker sounds every element in the morphological structure in order to produce the word. To learn to read and write Hmong, a person needs to learn three things: how to read each tone marker correctly, how to read each vowel phonetically, and how to read each consonant accurately. For instance, *x + au + v = xauv*, the word for a Hmong necklace design, or *s+au = sau*, the word for write.

The Hmong morphological system has four different levels. The first is the single-vowel or single-consonant structure; for example, *e+s = es*, *t+e+s = tes*, or *c+e+s = ces*. The second is the double-vowel or double-consonant structure; for example, *aw+s = aws*, *au+b = aub*, *ph+au = phau*, *nt+au = ntau*, or *nk+o+j = nkoj*. The words *phau* and *ntau* do not have tone markers at the end because they are sounded correctly without using a tone. The third morphological level is the triple consonant structure; for example, *tsh+e+b = tsheb*, *ntx+i+v = ntxiv*, *nrh+o = nrho*, *nqh+i+s = nqhis*, or *hny+a+v = hnyav*. Again, the word *nrho* has no tone marker at the end because it is phonetically correct without using a tone to modify the sound of the word. The fourth level is the quadruple

consonant structure; for example, *ntsh+ai = ntshai*, *ntxh+w = ntxhw*, *nplh+ai+b = nplhaib*, or *ntxh+ai+s = ntxhais*. The word *ntxhw* has no need of a tone marker. Some Hmong words are toneless and end with a Hmong vowel instead of a tone marker.

All the elements of Hmong morphology, everything necessary to build words, are listed in Table 10.19. The words are put together to form phrases, sentences, and various forms of oral and written communication according to the rules of Hmong syntax.

Syntax

Phonology describes the sounds (phonemes) of a language and morphology explains how the morphemes, the meaningful elements of the language—in Hmong, consonants, vowels, and tones—are structured to create words. Syntax defines the structure and grammatical architecture of sentences or statements used in a language for communication. Hmong syntax is not greatly different from English syntax, but there are some differences. Hmong languages do not use inflection, verb conjugation, plurals, or contractions. Also, Hmong do not intonate and words do not have ending consonants. The use of ending consonants in written Hmong explains why written Hmong appears odd to English readers. In addition, written Hmong

Table 10.19. Elements of the Hmong Morphological System

Tone Markers (tsiaj ntawv cim)	Vowels (tsiaj ntawv niam)	Consonants (tsiaj ntawv txiv)
B = cim siab	*Single vowels:*	*Simple consonants:*
M = cim niam	A, E, I, O, U, W	C (cos) = cws, shrimp
D = cim tod		D (dos) = dev, dog
J = cim ntuj	*Samples of sound:*	K (kos) = kub, hot
V = cim kuv	Ab, am, ad, aj, av, a, as, ag	T (tos) = twm, buffalo
Ua = cim ua	Ib, im, id, ij, iv, I, is, ig	N (nos) = noog, bird
S = cim mus	Wb, wm, wd, wj, wv, w, ws, wg	P (pos) = paj, flower
G = cim neeg		
	Double vowels:	*Complex consonants:*
	Aa, ai, au, ee, ia, oo, ua, aw	Ntx (nos, tos, xos) = ntxiv, add
		Nko (nos, kos, os) = nkoj, boat
	Samples of sound:	
	Aab, aub, aum, aud, auj, auv, au, aus, aug	Tsh (tos, sos, hos) = tsheb, car
	Eeb, eem, eed, eej, eev, ee, ees, eeg	Ntxh (nos, tos, xos, hos) = ntxhw, elephant
	Iab, iam, iad, iaj, iav, ia, ias, iag	Nplh (nos, pos, los, hos) = nplhaib

does not have punctuation although Hmong sometimes use western punctuation marks.

A syntax system is a set of grammatical rules that govern a language. Hmong languages have basic rules, but not as many as in English. Table 10.20 presents some of the parts of speech that form the foundation of the Hmong syntax system.

Hmong languages have simple sentence structures as well as complex writing in narrative and expository forms. As in English, Hmong have different kinds of speech and writing: poetry, song lyrics, stories, letters, reports, official memoranda, chants, riddles, slang, idioms, and so on. Here are examples of simple and complex Hmong sentences.

1. Simple form: Kuv mus tom tsev kawm ntawv. I go to school.

2. Complex form: Kuv mus kawm ntawv thiab kuv rau siab ua kuv cov ntaub ntawv kom tias vim hais tias yog tsis tiam ces kuv niam thiab kuv txiv yuav hais tias kuv tsis rau siab kawm ntawv. I go to school and I work hard to finish my schoolwork because if it is not finished my mother and my father will say that I do not study hard enough.

3. High level of complex writing: Tus xib hwb nug Maiv hais tias ua cas tsis pom koj daim ntawv uas kuv kom nej muab coj mus rau nej niam nej txiv sau lawv lub npe es kuv yuav coj nej mus ncig xyua lub tsev ua mis nyuj thiab lub tsev ua suab thaj tag kis; Maiv hais tias kuv txiv twb sau nws lub npe lawm, tab sis kuv tsis nco qab nqa tuaj, tseem nyob saum rooj noj mov. The teacher asked May why did not see the letter that I told you to give to your mother and your father for them to sign and I will take you to tour the milk factory and the sugar process plant tomorrow; May said that my father signed his name, but I forgot to bring it, still on top of the dining table.

The syntactic structures of these three sentences are different. The first sentence is a simple expression of a complete thought that follows basic grammatical rules. The second sentence has complex structures with compound sentences. It does not use punctuation to tell the reader when and where to pause or stop, but in Hmong it does not need punctuation; it is a functional sentence based on Hmong oral and written syntax structures.

Table 10.20. Hmong Parts of Speech

Pronouns English/ Hmong	Objects English/ Hmong	Possessive Adjectives English/ Hmong	Possessive Pronouns English/ Hmong	Adjectives English/ Hmong	Adverbs English/ Hmong
I	kuv	Me/kuv	My/kuv li, kuv cov	Mine/kuv li, kuv cov	Good/zoo	Well/zoo heev
You	koj, neb	You/koj, neb	Your/koj li, neb li, neb cov	Yours/koj li, neb li, neb cov	Bad/phem	Badly/phem heev
He	nws	Him/nws	His/nws li, nws cov	His/nws li, nws cov	Small/me	Very/heev, tshaj
She	nws	Her/nws	Her/nws li, nws cov	Hers/nws li, nws cov	Big/loj	Slowly/qeeb heev
It	nws	It/nws	Its/nws li, nws cov	Its/nws li, nws cov	Cold/txia	Kindly/siab zoo heev, txawj xav heev
We	peb, wb	Us/peb, wb	Our/peb li, wb li, peb cov, wb cov	Ours/peb li, wb li, peb cov, wb cov	Hot/kub	
They	lawv, nkawv	Them/lawv, nkawv	Their/lawv li, nkawv li, lawv cov, nkawv cov	Theirs/lawv li, nkawv li, lawv cov, nkawv cov	Early/ntxov	
					Late/lig, qeeb Slow/lig, qeeb Fast/ceev	

The third sentence is not only complex, but the English transliteration has several grammatical errors. First, the English is grammatically awkward because English syntax is different from Hmong syntax. Second, the word *kuv* is used in place of both "he" and "she" in the sentence; however, in Hmong languages, that is grammatically correct. Third, the reader assumes that the letter is still on the dining table, but there is no subject with a verb to actually say that the letter is still on the dining table. Again, for Hmong colloquial communication, this is grammatically appropriate. As for syntax in the Hmong writing system, all three sentences are linguistically appropriate, comprehensible, and functional.

Even though Hmong languages do not have verb tenses, Hmong syntax structures use classifiers to indicate different times. Here are basic examples of Hmong expressions in present, past, and future tenses:

1. Present tense: *Kuv mus uasi tom tsev kawm ntawv.* I go play at the school.

2. Past tense: *Kuv tau mus uasi tom tsev kawm ntawv. Kuv mus uasi tom tsev kawm ntawv los lawm. Kuv twb mus uasi tom tsev kawm ntawv tag lawm.* I went play at the school.

3. Future tense: *Kuv yuav mus uasi tom tsev kawm ntawv. Kuv mam li mus uasi tom tsev kawm ntawv. Kuv tseem yuav mus uasi tom tsev kawm ntawv.* I will go play at the school.

As for progressive tenses, the words "now" or "going" (*tab tom* or *tam simno*) can be used to place the verbs in any sentence into a progressive mode. For example, for present tense, *kuv tab tom mus uasi tom tsev kawm ntawv* or *kuv mus uasi tom tsev kawm ntawv tam simno*; for past tense, *thaum kuv tab tom mus uasi tom tsev kawm ntawv*; and for future tense, *kuv tseem tab tom yuav mus uasi tom tsev kawm ntawv* or *kuv yuav mus uasi tom tsev kawm ntawv tam simno.* For past tense, a preposition, adjective, or article is needed. Other words that signal future tense progressive include *tseem yuav mus tam simno, sawv kev mus tam simno,* and *yuav mus tib pliag no, tab tom yuav mus.*

As in English grammar, Hmong use conjunctions such as *tabsi, vim licas, thiab, ces, and vim hais tias* to combine thoughts and expressions. Here are examples of phrases that can be combined by placing one of these conjunctions in the blank:

1. *Leej xib hwb tsis tuaj qhia ntawv _____ nws mob lawm.*

2. *Sawv daws tshaib plab _____ nqhis dej heev.*

3. *_____ wb tus me nyuam thiaj quaj?*

4. *Pov tsis tau noj tshais _____ nws thiaj nkees heev.*

5. *Maiv Yeeb nyiam ua paj ntaub kawg _____ nws tsis nyiam saib ntawv.*

As mentioned earlier, Hmong sentences contain articles and classifiers. These descriptive words are placed either before or after the nouns they modify depending on the specific articles or adjectives used in a sentence. For example, *lub tsev* (the house) but tsev liab (red house), *ib lub tsev* (one house) but *lub tsev qub* (the old house). Here are some examples of sentences that need proper classifiers (*tug, daim, txog, tus, nplooj, sau, saib, nyeem*) and prepositions (*saum, tom, ntawm, zes, tim*):

1. Nws leej niam yuav tau ib _____ chij rau nws.

2. Koj _____ txiv noj su tom tsev ua mov noj.

3. Muab ib _____ ntawv dawb rau kuv sau.

4. Peb kawm _____ ntawv hu ua "Keeb kwm ntawv Hmoob.

5. Daim pib mov su nyob _____ lub rooj.

6. Tus tub mus _____ tsev kawm ntawv.

7. Tus miv zaum _____ tsob ntoo.

Hmong languages do not use interrogative and negative syntax structures in the same way as English. Hmong languages insert the word "*tsis*" as a negative where English would use words such as "not, do not, does not, is not, are not, were not, was not, will not, no," and so on. For example, I do not have money (*Kuv tsis muaj nyiaj*) and I have no money (*Kuv tsis muaj nyiaj*) are identical constructions. The word "*tsis*" is used in all these sentences: I do not call (*Kuv tsis hu*), I am not

(*Kuv tsis yog*), I will not or won't go (*Kuv tsis mus*), and I was not there (K*uv tsis nyob tom*). "*Tsis*" can also be used in interrogative form; for example, *tsis yog koj xav noj mov lawm los?* (Isn't right that you want to eat already?), *tsis yog koj vwm lawm los?* (Isn't right that you are crazy?), *tsis yog kuv xav tau yuam kev lawm los?* (Isn't right that I've thought the wrong way?). However, Hmong use the word "*puas*" for most interrogative forms. For example, *Koj puas mus?* (Will you go?), *Koj puas tau noj mov?* (Have you eaten? Did you eat?), *Puas yog koj quaj?* (Did you cry? Do you cry?), *Puas zoo los tsis zoo?* (Good or bad?), and *Puas zoo siab* (happy?). Other forms of Hmong interrogatives include sentences such as *Koj noj?* (You eat?), K*oj nyob qhov twg?* (Where are you?), *Koj hais kuv puas yog?* (You talk about me, right?), *Yog vim licas?* (Because why?), *Vim licas* (Why?), *Dabtsi ua rau koj quab* (What makes you cry?), *Leej twg hais koj?* (Who talks about you?). Similar to English, the tone of voice conveys the interrogative nature of the sentences.

Hmong sentences have subjects and predicates just as English does. They have articles, adjectives, adverbs, and prepositions, but these elements are not in the same position in the sentence as in English. Here is an example of a Hmong sentence: *Maiv hais lus Hmoob tau npliag lias* (May speaks very good Hmong). The subject is *Maiv* (May), the predicate is *hais lus* (speaks), the object is *Hmoob* (Hmong). There are two classifiers, *npliag* (good) and *lias* (very). *Npliag* is an adjective modifying the noun *Hmoob* and *lias* is an adverb modifying the adjective. In English, the intensifier *lias* would be in front of *npliag*, but in Hmong the adverb follows the adjective and, moreover, both classifiers (adjective and adverb) come after the noun *Hmoob*. The Hmong names for the parts of the sentence are as follows: the subject is *tswv*, which means owner; the verb is *qhia*, which means tell or reveal, and the predicate object as *qhia tshwm*, meaning result.

Linguistic Semantics

Semantics is the study of the meaning of words as used in particular syntactic structures, including oral and written forms of communication. Meaning and structure are inextricably connected; it is the connection that creates the need for semantics. Hmong languages are diverse and contain words that can be misinterpreted, especially when transliterated. Hmong semantics can give clearer understanding of phrases and sentences and clear up ambiguities that arise in chanting, singing, and religious rituals. The meanings of Hmong words and phrases depend on the type of vocabulary—whether the expression is intended to be taken literally or symbolically or as a proverb, idiom, riddle, or slang. Some examples of different forms of expression that affect the semantics of the words are shown in Table 10.21.

Table 10.21. Examples of Hmong Idioms, Slang, Riddles, and Proverbs

Proverbs/ *piv txoj lus*	Slang/ *paj lug*	Idioms/ *txhiaj txhais*	Riddles/ *paj huam*	Symbolic and Metaphorical Words/ *lus sib twv*
Txuag zam ces zam tshiab, txuag siav ces siav ntev	Puv 120 xyoo	Ob lub ncuav pias, ib lub sov ib lub txias, yog dabtsi?	Ntawm no mus yog lus qhuab ntuas	Tuaj qaij kaus
	Niam txiv tuag, vaj tsev ntuag			Ib txoj hmab soo tag ib lub zoov
Nplooj yoog kav, noob yoog tsav	Lus nyiaj lus kub	Tsuj dev tws dev quaj qw quaj qw, yog dabtsi?	Thov muab nquas hais rau peb Hmoob	Muaj paj los yeej meem tawg, muaj txiv los yeej meem txi
Ua lub neej kom tawg paj txi txiv	Tsis pom dej dag ces siab tsis nqig			

continued on page 310

Proverbs/ piv txoj lus	Slang/ paj lug	Idioms/ txhiaj txhais	Riddles/ paj huam	Symbolic and Metaphorical Words/ lus sib twv
Pub laus noj, laus nco tshav ntuj, pub menyuam noj, menyuam zov ruj	Siab phem tsis tau ntuj ntoo Xov los yoj, koob los yoj	Hnov nyuj qov tim dawm, mus txog tsis pom lawm, yog dabtsi?	Uas nyob thoob rau lub ntiaj teb, qhia rau peb txog Hmoob keeb kwm	Peb paim kua tsib tso saib Nyuj ciab nyuj kaus
Cuaj lub hli tsis zoo npaum li ib lub hnub, cuaj leeg ntxhais tsis zoo npaum ib leeg tub	Rov taw tuam ntuj Cuaj plua sib luag yim plua sib ntes	Qaum ntuj tso qes hlaus, ntiaj ntej khiav dos haus, yog dabtsi?	Saib Hmoob tshwm qhov twg los tiag, tsam ib pliag tas peb cov laus, Hmoob hauv paus peb tsis paub lawm…	Kom ntseg log puav tam ncej txawb Tuaj qab deg tuaj los tuaj qaum dej tuaj

Hmong languages have simple and complex words. Simple words are used in everyday conversation; complex words are used in academic, spiritual, and professional environments. Complex words are words such as *tswv cheej* (power), *cib fim* (opportunity), *limpiam* (weekday), *cuab yeej toom txeem* (tools), *yajceeb* (physical world), *yeebceeb* (spiritual world), *yeebyam* (character), *cwjpwm* (attitude), *yamntxwv* (behavior), *xeebceem* (attitude, behavior, character, or habit), *foom kom* (blessing), *kev ruam sim* (death, loss), *cuam tshuam* (involve, interrupt, meddle, stop), and *hwj chim* (charisma, appearance, honor).

The meanings of Hmong written expressions can be determined semantically based on knowledge of the main idea, an understanding of the thesis statement, and logical analysis of the contents and context. As an example of how semantics can be used to infer meaning, consider the following paragraph:

> *Muaj ob tug kwv npawg yog npawg hlob thiab npawg yau, nkawv ua phooj ywg zoo sib hlub, nyob ib lub zos ua ke, muaj ib hnub nkawv txawm sib yaum mus tua noog nyob tom hav zoo. Thaum nkawv tab tom yos xauj saib seb puas muaj noog, ces txawm muaj ib tus dais dub loj loj tawm plaws los tom nkawv, ces tus npawg hlob uas nws muaj hnub nyoog dua txawm cia li khiav mus nce ntoo lawm, tus npawg uas muaj hnub nyoog yau txawm cia li pw khwb rwg kiag rau hauv av. Tus dais dub loj loj ntawd txawm muab*

> *tus npawg yau ntawd hnia hniu xwb, tsis tom tsis khawb tus npawg yau dab tsi, ces dais cia li khiav lawm. Tus npawg hlob nqis saum ntoo los, nws nug tus npawg yau hais tias, dais hais li cas rau koj, "ua cas dais ho tsis tom koj?" Tus npawg yau teb hais tias, "Dais hais tias txawm ua kwv tij phooj zoo npaum li cas los yog txog thaum yuav tuag, ib tug ho tsis pab ib tug, ces tsis txhob ua kwv tij kwv npawg zoo dua.*

After reading this paragraph, the reader can draw out the main idea and see a number of implications for everyday life situations. What the younger friend (*npawg yau*) said to the older friend (*npawg hlob*) might make one wonder about coincidences, friendship, survival skills, miraculous escapes from death, betrayal of trust, facing life and death situations, and hunting experiences. Semantics is not just a matter of knowledge and linguistic or analytical skills; it is about finding meaning in communications that can be applied to everyday situations.

Linguistic Pragmatics

Pragmatics refers to the functionalities of a language or dialect used in different social contexts and situational settings. For example, the language used in a courtroom is different from the language heard at a sporting event. Hmong use different vocabularies and constructions for informal and formal speech. Pragmatics are different for wedding ceremonies, funeral rituals, religious rites, formal addresses, academic teaching, and so on. Some words are restricted in Hmong religious practices and some archaic word phrases are appropriate in certain social situations and not others. For example, the Hmong words *xyom cuab* are used to describe the family of a deceased person or the family that has lost a loved one in settings dealing with the death, but the words cannot be used to describe the family in any other situation. Similarly, the Hmong words *mom xyom* are used in kowtowing when kneeling down to pay respect to others during the death ritual, but the word *pe* is used in place of these words in other social contexts because the word phrase *mom xyom* is related to death and the word *pe* is related to life.

Commonly, Hmong like to use the word phrase *tab kaum koj* to show appreciation for help received from others. This social phrase could have a variety of meanings: thank you (*ua tsaug*); appreciation for your help (*ua tsaug rau koj lub sij hawm thiab kev pab cuam*); your kindness and heartfelt assistance (*kev pab cuam dawb paug tsis yuav nqi*); your sympathy and empathy (*kev pab cuam vim kev txom nyem*); or your love, support, and guidance (*kev sib pab sib hlub*). The appropriate response to the word phrase is "*tsis tab kaum dabtsi, hos…*" or "*tsis ua licas.*"

Here is another example of Hmong pragmatics. The Hmong word *tag* is used to mean "finished" or "done" in everyday life; however, this word cannot be used during the feasting at a Hmong wedding ceremony because it is culturally unacceptable. The right word to use is "clear" or "gone," which in Hmong is *meej*. The two words *tag* and *meej* mean exactly the same thing, but at a ceremony the word *tag* carries the negative connotation that "no more" is coming. At the Hmong wedding ceremony, it is presumed that the drinking and feasting have not ended until the wedding is over. The Hmong word *tag* is appropriate at home and during funeral rituals, and the word *meej* is seldom used in daily life and is prohibited at funeral services. However, in Hmong colloquial instructions, *meej* means clear, understood, and learned.

An aspect of pragmatics, register, is im-

portant in the Hmong languages. Linguistically, *register* refers to the situational use of appropriate forms of a language or dialect. Register matters in Hmong languages because archaic word phrases commonly used in Hmong religious practices, chants, traditional songs, and hidden expressions can cause difficulty in certain situations. For instance, some of the archaic words or word phrases sound like Chinese words, spiritual words, ghost phrases, or Godly phrases. Hmong magicians have their own etymological register. Here is an example:

> *Txheev com txheev leej vam com vam leej*
> *Txheev tom txheev nyeej cuab tsoob*
> *Txhawm tom laj fab laj fab mas txhij fam*
> *Theeb fab mas txhij fam…*
>
> *Txheev com txheev puj tsi*
> *Tim puj tsi twm ho*
> *Tim txhooj tim xyab tim puab looj*
> *Thej fam yeej tim fam fam*
> *Yuj puav tsov pej lov lov…*
>
> *Txheev com txheev puj tsi*
> *Tim puj tsi twm ho*
> *Tim txhooj tim nyab tim puab looj*
> *Zej ceem mas tseev ceem*
> *Tim ceem puab tseev ceem*
> *Tiam sij mas leeb txhaj…*

English transliteration of these archaic words and phrases is impossible. Even in Hmong languages, they sound like nonsense. Only the magician knows what he is saying. These words and phrases are used strictly for magical purposes. Similarly, the chants during death rituals contain archaic words and phrases that are pragmatically appropriate for religious purposes and religious purposes only. Here is an example:

> *Nyem no, koj mus txog pem Ntxwg Nyoog toj kab ntsig dawm kab hno, kab ntsig kab hno dhia luaj thav yaj, ces koj tes lauj muab koj khau maj, niaj kab ntsig kab hno dhia rhees luaj thav npua, ces koj tes lauj yuav muab koj khau ntuag … koj li tau kev mus cuag poj cuag yawm…*
> *Teg lum teg lum tum lum liv lo rog lob, tom lom looj lug lees rum, teg lum los rum qeev suj tug lum, rum lum geev gum lum loo, tom lom liv qeev rug, qeej rug qeej teg lum, tum lum liv lo rog lob…*

The register of Hmong traditional songs (*kwv txhiaj*) contains rhyming phrases that are appropriate for their purposes. These traditional songs can be sung all year long except for some songs that are designated for use only during the death rituals. Here is example of a traditional song:

> *Chim lub laj xeeb los yuav tuag, ua nyab zoj tas nrho txhooj tsis zoo ces muab txoj siav khuam lis nkaus rua lawm txoj mus hlua ntuag...*
>
> *Tsiag luj tsis tsiag lias, yuav tsiaj lawm luj lias rau daim nplooj ciab, ua nyab zoj los tsis zoo ces cia cev ntaj xib lis tsuj mus tua lis nthi rau lub zoov mus nuj xiab.*
>
> *Tsiag luj tsis tsiaj lias, yuav tsiag lawm luj lias rau daim nplooj awv, ua nyab zoj los tsis zoo ces cia cev ntaj xib lis tsug mus tuag lis nthi rau lub zoov nuj txeeg doog lis nkawv...*

These archaic and rhyming words and phrases can be transliterated into English, but the result would be confusing. However, for Hmong traditions and customs, the language is appropriate and makes sense.

As a final point on Hmong linguistics, it must be remembered that there is no single standard Hmong language. Although White Hmong is spoken by more Hmong than Blue Hmong, both languages and several dialects of both are spoken. HRPA has become the standard written language because it is used by nearly all Hmong people worldwide. Still, regardless of the consolidation into two languages, the Hmong people remain linguistically diverse. Table 10.22 presents some of the differences between White Hmong and Blue Hmong. As briefly mentioned earlier, Hmong languages and dialects are for the most part mutually intelligible. However, not all Hmong words and word phrase mean the same thing in all dialects and not all are spelled the same way.

Hmong slang and idioms continue to evolve as Hmong are learning Hmonglish terms along with archaic Hmong word phrases. Moreover, the continuity in Hmong religious practices and other traditions will keep the Hmong languages and dialects alive and well.

Table 10.22. Comparison of Selected White Hmong and Blue Hmong Words

English	White Hmong	Blue Hmong
Hmong	Hmoob	Moob
Go	Mus	Moog
See	Pom	Pum
Grandmother	Pog	Puj
Water	Dej	Dlej
Jump	Dhia	Dlha
Knife	Riam	Rag, tsag
Garden	Vaj	Vaaj
Sheep	Yaj	Yaaj
Mother	Niam	Nam
Itch	Khaus	Txob
Sit down	Zaum	Nyob txawg
Scold	Cem	Tshev
Story	Zaj	Zaaj

Summing Up

This chapter presented a comprehensive overview of the diverse Hmong languages and dialects. Hmong languages have a complex background with deep roots that go back to ancient China. There are some linguistic similarities between contemporary Hmong languages and Chinese Mandarin. The morphological systems of the two languages are different in some ways, but the phonological systems are nearly identical in syntax structures, pronunciations, and use of tones.

Despite the claim, which may very well be true, that Hmong had their own writing system in the distant past, Hmong languages and dialects existed only in oral form for thousands of years until the early 1950s when western linguists and Christian missionaries invented the Hmong Romanized Practical Alphabet (HRPA). At about the same time, the Hmong Pa Hawh was developed by a Hmong messianic leader. Since the introduction of HRPA, Hmong languages and dialects have evolved to the point where they were consolidated under two main languages known as White Hmong and Blue Hmong.

The Hmong writing system, because it is relatively new, is fairly simple as compared with systems that have been in use for thousands of years. Despite some deficiencies, the HRPA writing system is functional with appropriate representations for the phonemes, morphemes, and syntax structures of the languages. A newer HRPA version adds more complexities to the current writing system, which remains the system of choice for the majority of Hmong worldwide.

Hmong languages are tonal, words are monosyllabic, and grammatical rules are few. These facts should make academic instruc-tion for learning the language relatively easy. Because Hmonglish is replacing true Hmong in many homes and many Hmong children are growing up speaking English rather than Hmong, educating children in Hmong languages is essential. Transmitting Hmong history and culture to future generations depends on it.

• ELEVEN •

Hmong in Public Education

Paub tsis tau txawj...
Kev kawm yog kev txawj...
Kev xyaum yog kev ntse...
Kawm txawj thiaj yog txoj hau ke...
Hmong Educational Wisdom

Introduction

Today's Hmong-American students face a variety of challenges in public schools. Their academic needs must be dealt with if they are to succeed in the K–12 system and higher educational institutions. Although much research has been conducted on bilingual students from a variety of backgrounds, little research has focused specifically on the needs of Hmong K–12 students and Hmong students in higher education.

Hmong students are refugees and children of refugees who immigrated to the United States since 1975, leaving their home country of Laos to save themselves from certain death and to start life over again. Since the 1990s, California public schools have had one of the largest K–12 Hmong-American student populations in the West. The total number of Hmong students with English language deficiencies and other special needs in California was estimated at approximately 36,000 in 2010. Nationally, a total of 75,000 Hmong students is enrolled in K–12 schools, with the majority in California, followed by Minnesota and Wisconsin. Of all K–12 Hmong students in California, 80 percent are classified as limited English proficient (LEP) and 20 percent are identified as fluent English proficient (FEP) students. In some schools,

80 percent of Hmong-American students in grades K–6 are LEP students. Nationally, nearly 60 percent of the estimated 75,000 Hmong K–12 students are classified as English language learners (ELLs) or LEP students. Hmong students comprise the third largest LEP group in California's public schools, with Vietnamese students constituting the second largest group and Hispanic pupils the largest. The number of Hmong-American students in U.S. public schools continues to grow at a rapid rate, and many have language impediments that need attention if they are to succeed academically.

The emergence of first-generation Hmong-American educators in different fields of study is encouraging as is the increasing number of Hmong-American college graduates, but overall, the number of second-generation Hmong-American students in graduate and doctoral programs is still relatively low. This chapter examines the opportunities, challenges, progress, and successes of Hmong Americans, based on recent research, that provide some insights into the contemporary factors that affect academic success and/or failure of Hmong-American students.

Hmong Perceptions of U.S. Education

What are Hmong attitudes toward U.S. education? One of the main reasons Hmong refugees wanted to come to the U.S. was public education. Hmong parents wanted their children to receive a formal education because few of the children or their parents had formal schooling in the old country. Hmong refugees had and still have positive attitudes toward schooling and toward the opportunities provided by the U.S. educational system. Prior to their arrival in the West, Hmong refugees had very limited educational opportunities. Back in war-torn Laos, very few Hmong children were able to attend any school; only the affluent could afford education. Most Hmong children were hungry for what was available through public education in the U.S. American-Hmong refugees have a great respect for public education as a means to a better life and socioeconomic stability. As noted in Vang (2001), most Hmong high school students are more concerned about future stability than their present-life situation, and this attitude is also true for Hmong parents, who made many sacrifices to bring their children to the U.S. They brought them not only to save them from disaster, but also to enable them to begin new lives. Western education gave them the strength, hope, and motivation to fulfill their quest not just for freedom, but for better opportunities.

Here is one of the most popular and eloquent public statements Major General Vang Pao said about the value of education for all Hmong refugees:

Peb lub neej Hmoob txom txom nyem. Muaj txoj hmoo peb tuaj txog rau lub tebchaw Asmeslikas no ... nws yog ib lub tebchaw vammeej. Nej cov tub cov ntxhais Hmoob yeej meem mob siab ntso nrog luag lwm haiv neeg kawm ntaub kawm ntawv kom txawj kom ntse thiab kom paub luag tej txuj ci es thiaj li muaj lub peev xwm los nrhiav tau laj tau kam zoo ua, los khwv nyiaj khwv txiaj pab yus thiab yus tsev neeg. Thaum txawj lawm, yus thiaj li tig rov los pab thiab rub yus tsev neeg Hmoob kom muaj noj muaj

haus thiab muaj lub neej ua zoo xws teb xws chaw kom vammeej li luag lwm haiv neeg es luag thiaj li saib taus yus cov Hmoob. [In English, our Hmong life is very poor. Fortunately we have come to America ... it is a developed nation. You Hmong sons and Hmong daughters must motivate to study with other people to sharpen and to earn their academic skills and to have the ability to find good job, to earn money to help yourself and your families. When educated, you can return to help and lift your Hmong family to become socioeconomically sufficient and to have a good life like the general public to become prosperous like other people and others can value our Hmong people.]

Like many other minorities, Hmong refugees value public education for a variety of reasons. They experienced social injustice, mistreatment, and the absence of opportunity in the old country. Hmong parents have a strong desire for schooling in the U.S. because they want their children to learn how to read and write English. Most of the Hmong adults who came to America were illiterate in Lao, Thai, French, and English as well as Hmong. Back in Laos, Hmong elders valued education highly and considered literacy among the most important of all possessions, but they were denied the opportunity to achieve it. Hmong call those who can read and write "persons with seeing eyes" and those who cannot read and write "persons with blind eyes." These expressions indicate how much Hmong refugees value public education and how much educational opportunity means to them.

Hmong parents respect teachers highly as authority figures. However, some parents had bad experiences with teachers who punished them harshly when they were students in other countries. They may worry that U.S. teachers might do the same to their children. Therefore, they tell their children to behave in the classroom and not question the teacher's teaching. At first, Hmong parents thought parent/teacher conferences were disciplinary actions, like meetings teachers in the old country arranged to admonish a problem child who lagged behind in class.

Therefore, being asked to meet with the child's teacher made them feel inferior. Teachers need to communicate clearly with Hmong parents that the purpose of parent/teacher conferences is to discuss the academic needs and progress of the student. Today, Hmong parents understand that the purpose of the meetings is to provide meaningful information about their children's academic performance and progress in order to enhance the children's learning experience.

Moreover, Hmong refugees have positive views on bilingual education because nearly all Hmong refugee adults grew up bilingual and speak two or more languages despite their limited schooling. Lee and Shin (1996) found that most Hmong parents support bilingual education because they feel it results in greater knowledge and it facilitates the learning of various subjects. Hmong parents tend to favor complete immersion programs versus pullout programs and two-way immersion programs. In their experiences in other countries, they found that children immersed in another language learned that language rapidly. They feel that most children will swim rather than sink when immersed in an English-speaking classroom because they will acquire language skills faster than those in a two-way immersion model.

As time went by, Hmong refugee parents learned that the U.S. bilingual education programs are quite different from bilingual programs in other countries such as Japan, Canada, Thailand, and France. Hmong parents also realized that the goal of U.S. bilingual education programs is to enable a bilingual student to become English proficient, not to become bilingual in two or more languages. Hmong refugee parents want their children to learn English.

Despite their positive attitudes toward education and their gratitude for the educational opportunities in America, many Hmong refugee parents fear their children will lose their Hmong language and heritage when they are acculturated into the mainstream culture. That perception and fear is still alive today, years after their arrival in the U.S.

U.S. Educators' Perceptions of Hmong Students

How do public schools perceive Hmong students' academic needs? When refugees first began arriving from Southeast Asia, the U.S. public schools were underprepared to deal with Hmong children. Many public school teachers and administrators had no idea how to place, teach, and accommodate Hmong students. At the start, almost no public school had trained staff or qualified bilingual teachers to teach Hmong children. Some schools employed priests, pastors, Hmong paraprofessionals, and substitutes to provide daily instructions without properly informing Hmong parents. Even though Hmong children were not much different from migrant and newcomer students from other countries, most public school personnel considered Hmong students' learning styles and academic needs odd.

In the mid–1970s, when Hmong students first arrived in America, they lacked academic backgrounds, English skills, and learning styles needed for success in American schools. These students were refugees who were born in foreign countries and immigrated to the U.S. with their families. Public schools had no appropriate placement or instructional methods in place to meet the assessment and learning needs of Hmong students. Therefore, the academic performance of the students was understandably poor initially, and school personnel felt Hmong students were not college material. Schools identified language deficiency as the students' biggest handicap in school (Golstein, 1985).

Right away, the American educational system identified Hmong children as ELLs or LEP students and placed them in English as a Second Language (ESL) classes. At that time, few Hmong bilingual teachers were available. Although some schools offered academic programs designed to integrate Hmong students into the mainstream of the school, many Hmong students were socially and academically segregated from mainstream students and taught with capricious and watered down curricula. Hmong students were placed in classes based on an expectation that they could not succeed in college, regardless of whether they desired to pursue higher education. Public school administrators felt that since Hmong students were not college bound, the best course for them was to receive a high school diploma so they could enter the workforce. The surest way to see that they would earn the diploma was to place the Hmong students in classes in which they would fulfill only minimum graduation requirements (Golstein, 1985). At least 90 percent of the first-generation Hmong students in K–12 were LEP students and remained LEP students throughout their educational tenure.

The situation has changed very little since Hmong children first entered American schools. As shown in Tables 11.1 and 11.2, the ratio of Hmong LEP students to Hmong FEP students has remained very high in selected counties in California whereas in most other Southeast Asian groups the number of FEP students is considerably higher than the number of LEP students.

On a positive note, after the passage of Proposition 227 in California, the number of LEP students decreased, probably due to a number of developments:

1. Public schools slowed down the identification, classification, and designation of Hmong students' English language proficiency after the passage of Proposition 227, which effectively eliminated most bilingual education classes taught in Hmong in K–6 classrooms.

2. Hmong parents learned about the bogus English Language Development (ELD) programs and decided not to answer questions about the primary languages spoken at home on the home language survey form in order to keep their children from being designated ELL for little or no academic purpose.

3. A very small number of Hmong students got out of the ELD programs after being redesignated from LEP to FEP.

4. Native-born Hmong students easily acquired the basic interpersonal communication skills required for passing the initial assessment needed for LEP designation.

5. Public schools implemented ELD programs poorly and inconsistently, failing to carefully and accurately document Hmong LEP and FEP students.

Table 11.2. Total Numbers of LEP and FEP Students of Selected Ethnicities in California

Ethnic Group	LEP	FEP
Vietnamese	29,046	40,987
Hmong	13,175	9,606
Khmer (Cambodian)	4,152	5,636

Table 11.1. Numbers of LEP and FEP Students of Selected Ethnicities in Selected California Counties

Ethnic Group	Fresno County LEP/FEP	Madera County LEP/FEP	Merced County LEP/FEP	Stanislaus County LEP/FEP	Sacramento County LEP/FEP
Hmong	4,666/3,839	18/19	603/784	61/64	4,686/2,653
Vietnamese	131/329	5/7	5/12	119/139	1,609/2,784
Khmer(Cambodian)	361/439	2/8	11/6	312/289	138/147
Lao	373/541	0/1	13/36	130/149	386/323
Mien (Yao)	13/32	0/0	45/95	0/5	449/607
Thai	15/35	0/3	1/0	11/6	51/52
Lahu	2/1	0/0	0/0	0/0	0/0
Khmu	10/15	0/0	0/0	0/0	2/1
Punjabi	914/1,322	44/85	107/233	433/501	984/1,163
Hindi	27/63	2/1	8/8	211/289	727/996
Urdu	19/61	4/16	2/5	32/42	301/326

Note: Information from California Department of Education, http://www.cde.ca.gov/re/pn/fb/index.asp

Ethnic Group	LEP	FEP
Lao	1,984	2,525
Mien (Yao)	1,022	1,644
Thai	1,014	1,412
Lahu	277	157
Khmu	83	85
Punjabi	7,633	9,913
Hindi	3,378	7,076
Urdu	2,346	3,883

Note: Information from California Department of Education, http://www.cde.ca.gov/re/pn/fb/index.asp

Vang (2001) found that most Hmong LEP high school students are lumped together at ELD V and are not re-designated as required by state and federal mandates because they do not meet all hidden criteria used for re-designation. Vang further explained that public schools use five sources of data as the bases for making decisions about re-designation to a new language proficiency level:

- data from an objective assessment of the student's English oral language proficiency
- a teacher's evaluation of the student's English language proficiency and academic grades of "C" or better on the student's report card
- a written sample appropriate for grade level
- a record of the student's academic achievement on a standardized achievement test (at or above the 36th percentile in all tested areas)
- a record of approval from parents or guardians for re-designation.

The ways public schools designate Hmong students as LEP or FEP is practically identical in districts throughout the U.S. Nearly 80 percent of Hmong students in Grades K–6 have been identified as ELL, LEP, or special-needs and roughly the same proportion of Hmong students in Grades 7–12 have also been labeled as such. These students generally retain their designations throughout their school tenures.

Today as in the 1970s, few Hmong bilingual teachers are available to teach Bilingual Cross-cultural Language and Academic Development (BCLAD) curricula because of the enactment of Proposition 227. Known as the Unz initiative, the English-only Instruction initiative, and the Abolition of Bilingual Education initiative, Proposition 227 was passed in California in 1998 to ban bilingual education programs and curricular activities that support the second-language development of language-minority students. However, since the 1990s, the number of Hmong BCLAD and CLAD teachers in California has grown from a few to a few hundred. Currently the number of Hmong-American teachers in California is estimated to be approximately 350, including full-time teachers, part-time teachers, and paraprofessionals who provide daily instruction. Of that number, very few are teaching Hmong BCLAD curricula. In 2013, the California Department of Education reported that the ratio of Hmong bilingual teachers and aides to Hmong students from 2006 to 2010 was approximately 1 to 8,223 (teacher to student) and 1 to 92 (aide to student).

As Table 11.3 illustrates, in 2013, Hmong families were among the top ethnic groups in California with populations 5 years of age and older who were limited English proficient. Nationally, 60 percent of Hmong K–12 students are classified as LEP. This suggests that more than half of Hmong parents and children are not verbally proficient in English and that the English language skills of Hmong students are insufficient for academic tasks. Moreover, Hmong K–12 students constitute the third largest LEP student group in the country. In some states, namely California, Minnesota, and Wisconsin, Hmong students are over-represented in the LEP population as compared with students with similar cultural and linguistic backgrounds.

As of now, Hmong students still lack academic language and language skills, putting them at a disadvantage in the traditional American classroom with structured English instruction and mainstream English instruction classes. In fact, these classes are often available on paper only and Hmong students continue to be placed in non-academic classes. Giving lip service instead of genuine

Table 11.3. Percent of Limited English Proficient and English Proficient Families of Selected Ethnicities in California

Ethnic Group Dialect Other	Limited English Proficient	Proficient (Partially Fluent)	Total Speakers of a Than English at Home
Burmese	52%	48%	15,000
Vietnamese	52%	48%	486,500
Korean	48%	52%	368,600
Taiwanese	47%	53%	51,000
Hmong	46%	54%	67,800
Cambodian	44%	56%	73,000
Chinese	43%	57%	954,700
Laotian	43%	58%	36,600
Thai	41%	59%	47,900
Latino	38%	62%	532,000

Note: Information from U.S. Census Bureau, 2006–2010 American Community Survey 5-Year Estimates, table B16004.

education to Hmong students is detrimental to their academic progress. Hmong students may have difficulty keeping up with the school material, but that difficulty may be the result of misunderstanding on the part of teachers. Teachers may overlook Hmong students because they are reserved by culture. Teachers may assume that the students understand when they don't or teachers may think the students are not working hard when they simply have not understood the assignment. The truth is that Hmong students frequently do not receive the assistance they need to survive academically, much less to thrive (Lee, 2001). Their English deficiencies still contribute to low scholastic achievement, low test scores, insufficient credits, and, most importantly, an inability to go beyond secondary education.

Most U.S. Hmong parents are concerned about their children's education, but many are refugees who have not had any formal education and lack the educational background to provide necessary support at home and outside the home. The first and second generations of Hmong refugee children are now parents of K–12 Hmong students. Most of these U.S.-grown parents are no different from their refugee parents because they did not learn the hidden practices of the U.S. educational system during their schooling. Therefore, the pattern of receiving unequal, unfair, and segregated education is now being repeated in their children. At the very

least, Hmong parents have to understand the hegemonic and institutional barriers their children face each and every day in school in order to minimize the barriers to educational success and advancement; otherwise, the current covert school curricula will impede their children's academic opportunities.

Believe it or not, some parents are still locked into the old belief system that school personnel have sole authority over their children's education. They do not realize that some teachers and administrators do not truly care about Hmong children's education; they are interested only in their program compliance. Modern education is still relatively new to most U.S. Hmong refugees. Public schools continue to place them in ESL, English Language Development (ELD), Specifically Designed Academic Instruction in English (SDAIE), and other language programs based on surface assessments. Some administrators do so believing that bilingual programs such as these are safe places for Hmong students in the large and intimidating school. Others feel that grouping students based on perceived ability is dangerous and placing students in groups may result in a form of school segregation based on socioeconomic status and cultural factors. It is very important that teachers and administrators perceive students objectively, regardless of cultural, ethnic, racial, social class, or religious differences, in order to accommodate different abilities and learning styles. At the very least, public schools need to stop victimizing Hmong children and offer them the academic opportunity they, as well as non–Hmong students, really deserve.

Socioeconomic Disadvantage and Academic Performance

Are Hmong-American students socioeconomically disadvantaged in schools? In the early years nearly all Hmong students needed public assistance and many still receive aid; they could be considered socioeconomically disadvantaged because they receive this very meager help. Indeed, Hmong families are among the poorest in California, as illustrated in Table 11.4. However, from the Hmong perspective, receiving public assistance does not mean that Hmong students are socioeconomically disadvantaged because they are entitled to services from local, state, and federal government agencies. Some might say Hmong students' inability to speak English well or their status as refugees makes them socioeconomically disadvantaged, but schools have used that disadvantage to garner more funds for themselves. Public schools classify Hmong students as at-risk of academic failure because of their refugee status, not because of their academic performance.

Educators typically define students as at-risk if they are limited in English proficiency, financially poor, of an ethnic minority, economically disadvantaged, and underachieving (Siu, 1996; U.S. Department of Education, 1998; Wright, 1997). Generally, Hmong students fit the at-risk definition because of language limitations, low socioeconomic status, immigrant status, and an environment that limits their ability to perform in school. Siu found that at-risk students lacked adequate academic competencies, failed to develop academic skills, and were under-prepared for school. These characteristics are prevalent in Hmong students. However, rather than dealing with these issues, public schools seem to take advantage of Hmong students' vulnerability, exacerbating their fragile status so they fall into the at-risk category, becoming likely to fail in all academic subjects. The reason? Schools receive additional money for at-risk students. In other words, public schools are keeping these students in the nonsense academic designation for income, not for results.

Actually, Hmong students, most of whom come from economically disadvantaged home environments and a culturally unique background, are among the poorest students in the American educational system, poorer than other immigrant and refugee students (Siu, 1996; Vang, 1999; Vang, 2001). Yang (1995) described Hmong students as living in poverty and isolation, lacking privacy in overcrowded dwellings, lacking healthcare services, vulnerable to abuse and mistreatment, neglected or malnourished, and emotionally unstable. Ima and Rumbaut (1989) found that socioeconomic status and the

Table 11.4. Family Income and Income Status of Selected Ethnic Groups in California

Ethnic Group	Low-Income	Poverty	Per Capita Income	Total Population
Hmong	66%	34%	$ 9,800	91,200
Mongolian	58%	37%	$14,300	4,990
Cambodian	53%	25%	$14,400	102,300
Latino	49%	20%	$15,600	14,013,700
Tongan	47%	20%	$12,500	22,800
Laotian	46%	17%	$14,400	69,300
African American	40%	20%	$22,000	2,683,900
Vietnamese	34%	15%	$23,000	647,500
Thai	28%	14%	$23,300	67,700
White	20%	8%	$42,000	14,956,200

Note: Information from U.S. Census Bureau, 2006–2010 American Community Survey 5-Year Estimates, tables B17001, c17002, and B19301.

level of poverty of the family affected the academic achievement of Hmong children. The academic problems of LEP students are not due entirely to difficulties with English. LEP students frequently suffer from the effects of poverty, mobility, and the limited capacity of their parents to support their success in school (August and Hakuta, 1997; Vang, 1999; Vang 2001).

However, socioeconomic disadvantage is only part of the picture. Another part is the educational system's fiscal dependency on at-risk, LEP, and vulnerable students of diverse backgrounds. Because the impact of socioeconomic factors on academic performance has been given so much attention, educational researchers have not adequately studied the effect of the practices of school systems on the academic performance of Hmong students. By placing some students in academic programs for which they are not equipped and in which they are not supported, schools are telling them to sink or swim in academia without even throwing them the thinnest of ropes. By placing others in substandard programs with impoverished curricula and mediocre instructors, schools are not even letting them in the water.

School Practices and Academic Performance

Although illegal segregation died years ago, legal segregation is still practiced and is actually on the rise; in some schools, it is common. As public schools continue to legally segregate Hmong students as well as other students of similar backgrounds, refugee students socialize almost exclusively among themselves as they progress from elementary school to high school (Wehlry & Nelson, 1987). Generally, Hmong students who are thus alienated from the majority of the school population tend to have negative self-perceptions, seeing themselves as different from mainstream students. It is possible that their lower socioeconomic status is a factor that leads to alienation and a greater separation from language-majority students and host nation natives, but a close examination of school practices suggests that the hidden and null curricula have contributed greatly to the emotional and academic suffering of Hmong students.

Currently, many school districts designate special classrooms for Hmong students and other ethnic students with similar linguistic backgrounds, clustering them in groups for nonacademic purposes. Hmong students who complained about this practice to their middle and high school counselors were told that the schools have to house them in such a nonacademic environment because the of law. The counselors failed to tell these students the truth about what the law requires schools to provide for them during the time they are relegated these classrooms and ELD programs.

School districts require classroom teachers to complete ELD forms for ethnic minority students who speak a primary language other than English at home. Parents must sign the forms in order for the district to be in compliance with state mandates and continue receiving state and federal monies. However, many schools then receive the funds for services the schools and classroom teachers cannot and do not provide the students. Vang (2001) found that most Hmong secondary students who were about to graduate, many of whom had very high GPAs, did not know they were still classified as ELLs or LEP students. Vang also found that most Hmong secondary students accumulated more than the required units or credits needed for graduation because they were required to take ELD classes in addition to the core courses required for graduation.

The mismatch between the culture of the students and the culture of the schools could be a factor in teaching and learning. Heath (1982) saw the difference between the cultural background of the teacher and the cultures of some or all of the students in the classroom as a problem. Heath said the absence of cultural congruence affects instruction because teachers tend to assume inaccurately that culturally different students in their classes will respond to language routines and the use of language in building knowledge, skills, and dispositions just as other children do.

Even more important in teaching and learning than cultural differences are teachers' personalities and attitudes. Many teachers are not properly trained to handle the learning needs of diverse learners and cannot compensate for the lack of training. Most teachers are not competent multicultural educators. They claim they are "colorblind," but in reality this assertion is an excuse to overlook needs of students that might be associated with culture.

Keller, Deneen, and Magallan (1991) found that the interplay of culture and language in cognitive performance influenced second-language learners' academic achievement and language acquisition. For instance, LEP students process test information more slowly in a second language than native-speaker students. The slow speed could be the result of the LEP students' incomplete understanding of the given instructions or content. Most teachers who teach Hmong students and other minority students lack proper academic training and teaching methodologies to assist their students with second-language learning. How many teachers know anything about critical pedagogy for differentiating instruction that will benefit all learners? In fact, most teachers use a one-model-fits-all approach to instruction, not considering the different learning styles of their students. Public schools lack sufficient teaching modalities and pedagogical applications needed for instructional practices that would enhance the teaching of ethnic students who are learning English as secondary language.

At first, many believed that the cultural mismatches between Hmong refugee students and the schools created conflicting environments that led to inferior instruction for minorities and discrimination in the classroom. Many Hmong-American students entered American schools preliterate and without school experiences. They had spoken language fluency in their native language but little or no academic language or experience with a school system or expository text in their first language. For them, use of cul-turally unfamiliar materials may have had an adverse effect on their academic performance. But that cannot be true anymore after years in the U.S. Yet today's Hmong children face the same problems in the classroom as the first Hmong students faced 40 years ago. Many Hmong students continue to be the innocent victims of a school system that fiscally erodes their academic opportunities by making them recipients of state and federal programs. Hmong students may not have middle-class values and learning styles but do have the passion and motivation to learn.

Hvitfeldt (1982) described the learning style of most Hmong students as follows:

{ext}Achievement as the result of cooperative group activity is ... very much in line with Hmong social life outside the classroom. Cooking, gardening, shopping, fishing, car repair and many other daily activities are carried out by the Hmong in small groups rather than individually. Group activity appears to result in a high degree of achievement, perhaps because the Hmong exhibit greater self-confidence when working together [127].

This description of Hmong students reveals that cooperative learning works well for them. Teachers frequently use cooperative learning with Hmong students for social purposes and to promote cultural assimilation, but few know how to implement it to achieve academic ends. What Hmong students really need is academic instruction and academic engaged time, not just social and cultural survival skills.

Having a support system at home is important, but it is not a sufficient condition to assure academic achievement and success if there is discontinuity between home and school. Discontinuity between home and school hinders students from sharing ideas and/or developing new language skills. In contrast, continuity allows students to negotiate and share decision making because it permits both teachers and students to be part of the decision-making process. A study of discontinuity and continuity between community and school found that students' home experiences were not included in the school's curriculum and/or classroom activities (Delgado-Gaitain, 1987).

Perhaps Hmong parents are partly to blame for their children's poor education. However, how many public schools honestly follow legal mandates to serve the needs of Hmong students and tell Hmong parents the truth about their children's education? Most teachers in public schools have failed to comply with English language development (ELD) guidelines and mandates in serving Hmong students. Many have falsified ELD paperwork in order to receive state and federal funding. For these teachers, the ELD guidelines are about compliance with mandatory fiscal reporting responsibilities, not about teaching responsibilities.

Delgado-Gaitain (1987) noted another cultural problem for language-minority students in school. Classroom tasks normally "demand students to think mostly in abstract, linear ways, and often in English," which is difficult for students who are limited in English proficiency (p. 358). In reality, students must have multifaceted knowledge (cognitive, physical, emotional, and social competence) to perform academic tasks. Most teachers are not trained to teach students to think abstractly, so how can they expect students to think that way, especially students from cultures that have more concrete, less linear ways of thinking? The current Common Core standards require teachers to teach academic subjects cognitively and critically, but most teachers dread this requirement because they know children do not think that way. And how many teachers have any idea how Hmong children think and learn? Perhaps a very small number of teachers understand how Hmong children think; do they know how Hmong children learn?

Every child has dreams, including Hmong children. Lee (2001) and Ogbu (1993) observed that Hmong students have acquired a myth about education. It is a folk theory that links success to social mobility. Both Hmong parents and students strongly believe that education is the key that opens doors of opportunity; they hope education will enable them to ascend the socioeconomic ladder of American society. Most Hmong students dream of going to college regardless of their current social status. But, public schools do not encourage Hmong students' dreams when placing them in nonacademic classrooms, wasting their time and energy, keeping them trapped in ELD programs for years, requiring them to take additional ELD classes to retain their eligibility for the ELD programs, and assigning unqualified teachers to teach them survival English skills. Hmong students have basic interpersonal communication skills. They want to develop cognitive academic language proficiency so they can compete to achieve their dreams. Therefore, the fallacy of current practices needs to be evaluated academically and fiscally by both the law and minority parents. Otherwise, ethnic students of diverse backgrounds will continue to be the bait used by the school system to procure monies for nonacademic purposes.

Hmong Parents and Children's Academic Performance

Do parenting styles and cultural values affect students' school progress? Hmong have strong family values; Hmong parents are caring providers for their families. However, Hmong parents have a variety of parenting styles. Those styles have changed somewhat since Hmong came to America because of legal concerns. In most Hmong families, the father is the main disciplinarian and the mother manages the family. As in any group, Hmong parenting styles include authoritarian, authoritative, permissive, supportive, democratic, and egalitarian. Traditionally, Hmong parents appear to be firmer with their daughters than their sons; however, they expect more from their sons than their daughters because sons are the family roots.

Most Hmong families are two-parent households; the rate of Hmong marital dissolution is still low although divorce has become more common over the last 20 years. For example, tables 11.5 and 11.6 present the marital status of Hmong Americans 15 years and older liv-

Table 11.5. Marital Status of U.S. Hmong 15 Years and Older in Three States, 2010

State	Total Population	Never Married (%)	Married (%)	Divorced (%)	Separated (%)	Widowed (%)
California	62,120	49.4	43.2	2.8	0.9	3.7
Minnesota	40,486	49.6	40.2	4.3	2.3	3.6
Wisconsin	30,933	45.1	46.9	3.0	2.1	3.0

Note: Information from The State of the Hmong American Community, *by M. E. Pfeifer & B. K. Thao (eds.), 2013, Washington, D.C.: Hmong National Development.*

ing in the three states with the largest Hmong populations: California, Minnesota, and Wisconsin. The statistics for all categories are very similar for all three states. Slightly more than half of Hmong Americans 15 years and older are unmarried, with almost half never married.

Table 11.6. Comparison of Marital Status of Male and Female U.S. Hmong 15 Years and Older

Marital Status	Total	Male	Female
Total Population	166,900	83,200	83,700
Never married	48%	52%	44%
Married	44%	44%	45%
Divorced	3%	2%	4%
Separated	2%	1%	2%
Widowed	3%	1%	5%

Note: Information from The State of the Hmong American Community, *by M. E. Pfeifer & B. K. Thao (eds.), 2013, Washington, D.C.: Hmong National Development.*

Hmong parents are protective of their children. Ima and Rumbaut (1989) found that family structure, disciplinary methods, family composition, and the size of the family were related to low academic achievement of refugee children. Parenting styles have a strong influence on academic achievement, affecting the development of autonomy and maturity in children (Hess, 2000; Rumberger, 1991). An authoritative parenting style is the most conducive to academic success because it cultivates better social attitudes and behaviors through mutual agreement (Hess, 2000).

The Hmong socialization process, having undergone acculturation and integration without assimilation, has now come to the maintenance stage. As a result, most Hmong parents speak *Hmonglish* to support their children's first- and second-language devel-

opment. Hmong parents have always been concerned about losing their children to the host culture; now, Hmong children are losing their Hmong parents because most children are Americanized and speak English whereas their parents speak Hmong. The Hmong 1.5-generation children—adults who were born in Laos and Thailand and came to America as refugee children—are pretty much gone or have become first-generation parents of native Hmong students.

Siu (1993) reported that the following family factors contribute to academic success:

- demonstration of support, interest, and encouragement toward children's education
- placement of high value on education, success, respect for instructors, and motivation to learn
- a strong work ethic
- positive role models
- authoritative parenting

Other researchers attributed the academic success of refugee children to hard work, discipline, parental pressure to maintain family pride and honor, and family expectations (Abramson & Lindberg, 1985). The most successful refugee children appear to be those who retain their traditions and values (Caplan, Choy, & Whitmore, 1992).

In Asian-American families in general, approximately 82 percent of children are under the age of 18 and are living in two-parent households. A higher percentage of families live at or below the poverty level than in White and African American families (Siu, 1996). Yang (1995) reported that the average Hmong-American family size is 6, as compared to an average size of 12 in the older, traditional Hmong family. These demographics affect the academic performance of Hmong-American children.

Family size does not seem to be a deterrent to academic achievement for Hmong and other language-minority students; however, it is a hindrance for students from most other minority cultures (Abramson & Lindberg, 1985; Caplan et al., 1992). Perhaps family size does not hold Hmong students back because the cultural values of work and education are strong in Hmong families. Hmong traditional families seem to have stronger core family values than Americanized Hmong families. In other words, Hmong parents who adhere to the Hmong communal way of life appear to have stronger family ties and a better support system than families who are not part of the traditional communal lifestyle.

However, family obligations remain a critical issue for Hmong families. Although Hmong students rarely complain about domestic chores, family responsibilities affect students' grades and interfere with their educational pursuits. Family chores are sometimes a source of conflict between Hmong parents and their children, especially Hmong daughters and daughters-in-law.

Other sources of intergenerational conflict in Hmong families include strict curfews, tension between traditional and American ways of doing things, parental expectations, gender roles, early marriage, courtship, and gang affiliation. Many Hmong parents appear to be culturally stagnant and not acculturating at the same rate as their children. The drastic changes in children have led to role reversals in the family. Sometimes these kinds of changes bring more intergenerational tension as parents feel they are losing control of their children, family members move apart, and both parents and children experience social embarrassment. One recent study indicated that Hmong parents are willing to make compromises to help their children reconcile cultural norms and American values if those compromises will help them maintain parental authority (Lee, 2001).

Maintaining parental authority is essential for Hmong students' academic success. Many parents try to strengthen the bonds that tie their children to them and to their cultural foundations. As Yang (1982) succinctly put it, "Just as a tree torn from its roots and replanted cannot survive, so the child cannot truly blossom without the ability to relate to its sources, to its origin." So children have difficulty thriving in school without a solid cultural foundation and strong family connections. Preserving those foundations and connections requires maintenance of parental authority. Portes and Rumbaut (1996) explained how Hmong families maintain parental authority:

> Parental authority is maintained in those admittedly rare instances where little acculturation takes place in either generation. More commonly, that authority is preserved where sufficient resources exist to guide second-generation acculturation. These resources are of two kinds: first, parental education, allowing the first generation to keep up with their children's learning and to monitor its course; second, ethnic bonds, creating incentives for youth to comply with community norms and to combine them with American cultural patterns [241].

Today, Hmong parents allow flexibility to accommodate their children's academic needs. For instance, they give permission to their daughters to attend colleges and universities far from home. In the past, parents had serious concerns for the welfare of any Hmong daughter who went away to college. Moreover, some Hmong parents permit their sons and daughters to court and date while attending college, allowing them time to finish their education before building families. These family flexibilities and cultural understandings have contributed to the educational attainment of Hmong children.

Gender and Educational Opportunity

Do Hmong sons and daughters have equal chances to pursue higher education? Prior to 1975, Hmong boys and girls did not have equal opportunities to attend school. Hmong families would send their sons to schools if they could afford it and keep their daughters at home. However, this traditional practice changed in 1975. In the U.S., Hmong sons and daughters have equal opportunity to pursue higher education, but fewer Hmong females attended college than males in the U.S. until recently. Now, the numbers of Hmong sons and daughters in college are nearly equal because Hmong daughters have made cultural and social adjustments. Most married Hmong daughters continue their education in college and most Hmong female college students are single. Despite family obligations, Hmong parents are encouraging their daughters to pursue higher education. But they want their daughters to attend college near home.

The gender roles of Hmong women and men in traditional Hmong society are extremely important to the family system. The patriarchal structure of the family plays a significant role in the ways Hmong women and men are viewed in their society. Hmong men are considered the heads of their households and Hmong women are expected to marry and become homemakers and mothers. In the U.S., most Hmong women are still not expected to be economic producers for the family. They remain close to the home, providing childcare and domestic support. As Vang (1999) observed, "Men become involved in the outer or public sphere, which brings them social prestige and power. Women are involved in the inner or home sphere, which is giving them less prestige and power," (p. 223).

Some young Hmong-American girls have difficulty dealing with the differences in Hmong and American cultures with regard to gender role expectations. Vang (1999) described the conflict as follows:

> If they are unable to complete their high school due to early marriage and pregnancy, they may find themselves in poverty. If they will eventually acculturate to American society, the traditional division of labor in the home will erode. If Hmong girls are expected to do household chores and duties and work outside the home, the traditional division of labor will be a major problem among Hmong in the future [223–224].

Culturally, Hmong have come a long way. However, gender inequity continues to negatively impact Hmong women academically and socially. Some Hmong parents may not totally support their daughters' college educations for fear that the daughters may be "too old" to marry after earning a college degree (Vang, 1999). Many young Hmong girls also fear this for themselves. However, U.S.-born Hmong girls challenge the traditional concepts and seek college educations and employment outside the traditional female roles (Park, 1998). Lee (2001) wrote that female Hmong students are more likely to participate in after-school tutorial programs and work exceptionally hard to become academically successful students. According to Lee, the Hmong students with the highest educational aspiration and the highest levels of academic achievement are females.

Although Hmong females have high educational aspirations and achievements, in recent years fewer Hmong females than males actually pursued a college education: 5 percent of females versus 12 percent of males. However, approximately one third of Hmong-American educators are women. This is a strong indication that Hmong women are considering education as the key to economic stability as well as the key to achieving social status in the community. Perhaps education will be the key that enables Hmong women to gain respect inside and outside the home.

Parental Support and Academic Performance

Can Hmong parents provide adequate support at home for their children's education? Absolutely! Hmong families have incredible support systems that not only provide educational assistance, but sustain their children emotionally, physically, medically, psychologically, culturally, and socially. However, the amount of support parents can provide for their children's schooling depends largely on the parents' own level of education. Students whose parents are illiterate in English or their primary language are more likely to be underachievers in school. Ima and Rum-baut (1989) found that immigrant or refugee parents' pre-arrival education from refugee camps or their native countries together with their perceptions of the American educational system played roles in their children's academic achievement. Because many Hmong parents have little education, a large number of Hmong parents are unable to provide adequate academic support at home.

Prior to 1975 and shortly after the Hmong's arrival in the U.S., the Hmong home support system mostly depended on the father's socioeconomic status and education from the old country and what he acquired in the new homeland. Nearly four decades later, the Hmong home support system has changed. In most Hmong homes, mothers have become the academic backbones of their children's education and they can fill a caring and supportive role at home when their children need academic assistance. Hmong fathers are still the main enforcers of good behavior, including school attendance and studying, but the major support burden has shifted to Hmong mothers.

Hmong refugees had very limited schooling. Most mothers had no schooling when they came to the U.S. Reder (1982) surveyed Hmong adult refugees and found that approximately 73 percent had never attended public schools in Laos, 12 percent had 1 to 3 years of school, 7 percent had 4 to 6 years, 5 percent had 7 to 8 years, and only 3 percent had 9 or more years. This means that approximately 10 percent of Hmong adults had any elementary or secondary education prior to immigrating to America. Yang (1993) reported that Hmong people in some regions of Laos were 90 percent illiterate. Those who lived in high mountain areas had the highest illiteracy rate and those who lived in urban regions had the lowest. Siu (1996) found that only 8 percent of Hmong refugees had had school experience and were literate in either Hmong or Lao prior to their arrival in America.

In a cross-sectional survey of bilingualism among Hmong families with school-age children, approximately 37 percent of men and 83 percent of women reported no formal education in their native country (Reder, 1985). One fourth of the men in the study and approximately 37 percent of the women were illiterate in both Hmong and Lao. Furthermore, Reder (1982) found that approximately 92 percent of Hmong women had no formal education as compared to 46 percent of men. Of the individuals who had had some education in Laos, approximately 82 percent were illiterate in Lao and 70 percent were illiterate in Hmong.

Another study reported that Hmong refugees who landed in America were approximately 75 percent illiterate with no educational background (Ranard, 1988). This finding supports those of other studies that show that Hmong refugees had little or no formal education in Laos or anywhere else, including the refugee camps in Thailand, prior to their resettlement in America. Most studies concluded that Hmong refugees must face many new challenges in America due to a lack of basic skills and formal education. Lee (1993) found that nearly half of his Hmong refugee sample had no educational background. Some researchers concluded that the absence of an educational background hindered the assimilation process as well as the acquisition of a second language (Ranard, 1988; Reder, 1982).

The effect of parental deficits in education on Hmong parents' ability to support their children academically was reported by Golstein (1985). Golstein demonstrated that because Hmong parents lacked school experience and had language barriers, they were unlikely to participate in school events. Hmong parents often naively presumed school would provide their children with employment skills necessary for entering the labor force and the academic and cultural skills necessary for survival in American society. They found reality harsh when their children could not enter college or find employment after high school. Hmong parents do not seem to understand the differences in academic challenges for their foreign-born and their native-born children (Hmong Issues 2000 Conference, Fresno, CA).

Today, approximately 30 percent of middle-aged Hmong parents have some kind of formal education. Some young parents were raised in America and went through the American educational system. In the next 20 years, two out of every three Hmong parents will have a formal education at least through Grade 8. And based on the current rates of Hmong students' graduation from high schools, nearly 80 percent of Hmong parents now have some formal K–12 educational experiences. However, that does not mean the home support system is now stronger than ever. Perhaps both Hmong parents need post-secondary education to provide sound academic support at home.

Socioeconomic Status and Academic Performance

Does a family's socioeconomic status impact children's education? Perhaps, it is because family income is the primary predictor of SAT scores, which are measures of academic achievement. However, whether family income is an indicator of SAT scores for Hmong students has not yet been established because Hmong students are still relatively new to the U.S. educational system and other indicators may have more weight for Hmong students.

However, because of the socio-academic system in the U.S., Hmong family socioeconomic status may have some impact on Hmong children's education. In the U.S., the public school a child attends is determined by the child's place of residence, and schools in wealthier neighborhoods are generally better schools—better resourced and with better teachers—and the schools in the lower-income areas are lower quality. In other words, the rich get richer schools and the poor get poorer schools. Thus socioeconomic status impacts the quality of education available to students.

When Hmong first arrived in the U.S., they had no jobs. Unaccustomed to the American economy and untrained for employment in the U.S., they remained poor for years as they worked to equip themselves for the opportunities of their new homeland. But training a largely illiterate population still recovering from the trauma of war and refugee status is a long and difficult process. As Table 11.4 shows, Hmong families are still among the poorest groups in America. Therefore many still live in low-income areas and have access to only poorer schools.

Socioeconomic status, however, can change. Hmong Americans have made slow but remarkable socioeconomic progress. Hmong home ownership and employment in the U.S., shown in Table 11.7, are strong indications of Hmong's rising socioeconomic status. The states with the highest Hmong employment in 2010 were Colorado, Georgia, Arkansas, North Carolina, and Wisconsin, and the states with the highest Hmong home ownership were Arizona, Michigan, Georgia, Oklahoma, and North Carolina.

According to the 2000 census, poverty among Hmong Americans dropped from 67 percent to 38 percent during the previous 10-

Table 11.7. U.S. Hmong Home Ownership and Employment in Selected States, 2010

State	Total Hmong Population	Employed (%)	Home Ownership (%)
Arkansas	2,143	68.2	45.1
Arizona	229	59.7	80.7
California	91,224	49.6	33.4
Colorado	3,859	75.2	51.6
Georgia	3,623	71.4	71.2
Michigan	5,924	54.9	76.4
Minnesota	66,181	57.3	49.2
North Carolina	10,864	66.9	63.5
Oklahoma	3,369	55.8	65.5
Oregon	2,920	52.8	32.4
Washington	2,404	53.1	37.6
Wisconsin	49,240	62.5	54.9

Note: Information from The State of the Hmong American Community, *by M. E. Pfeifer & B. K. Thao (eds.), 2013, Washington, D.C.: Hmong National Development.*

year period. However, the poverty rate varied from state to state and city to city. Due to language barriers and lack of education, Hmong adults in California have a higher unemployment rate, approximately 60 percent, than other recent immigrant groups: Vietnamese (30 percent), Laotian (43 percent), and Cambodian (55 percent) (Hmong Issues 2000 Conference in Fresno, CA). Although Hmong refugees are still poor by American standards, they are 10 times better off in the U.S. than they were in Southeast Asia.

Studies of Hmong family socioeconomic status and family income since coming to the U.S. show some improvement. Pulaski (1994) reported that at one point approximately two thirds of Hmong refugees in California were welfare recipients. But that number dropped significantly in 1999 as a result of the Welfare Reform Act of 1996. It appears that many Hmong families left California to seek employment in other states. In California's Central Valley, some Hmong became self-employed, many as small farmers. In contrast, Ranard (1988) reported that some Hmong communities in America had an employment rate as high as 80 percent. In Fresno, the Hmong employment rate in 1999 was 35 percent as compared to 20 percent in the previous year (Hmong Issues 2000 Conference, Fresno, CA).

The incomes and socioeconomic status of Hmong families has improved as Hmong children pursue educations that help them obtain good, high-pay jobs and permanent employment in the public and private sectors. Yang (1995) noted that Hmong in Fresno are employed in a variety of occupations: as fast food servers, assembly line workers, small farmers, entrepreneurs, engineers, teachers, social workers, psychologists, pharmacists, dentists, medical doctors, college instructors, and medical interpreters.

Many Hmong working families remain financially poor because they have large families and their wages are low. Some have not been able to get out of the welfare system. Less educated parents are unable to secure long-term employment that would enable them to get and stay off welfare. Hmong parents are concerned about their inability to provide financial support for their children's education and feel that their level of family poverty directly impacts their children's futures (Hmong Issues 2000 Conference, Fresno, CA). Nevertheless, Hmong-American families are leaning toward self-sufficiency, entering the business world to become entrepreneurs and small business owners. In California, many Hmong families have become independent small farmers. As the socioeconomic status of Hmong-American adults improves, so will the academic performance of their children.

Today, the overall Hmong socioeconomic status has improved substantially compared to what it was 30 years ago. Many Hmong are employed in various professions and have good paying jobs that enable them to provide financially for their families. Many Hmong families live in homes they own located in good neighborhoods, and many Hmong children are attending good schools.

Place of Birth and Academic Performance

How do American-born and foreign-born Hmong students compare in schools? The difference in educational aspirations and attainments between Hmong foreign-born and native-born children is quiet interesting. Generally speaking, foreign-born children tend to pursue and succeed at higher education more frequently than do Hmong native-born children. Sociologists offer a number of intriguing explanations for the disparity, but the general feeling is that foreign-born Hmong children, who are usually poorer than native-born, wish to do better and are willing to work hard at getting an education in order to advance whereas Hmong native-born children appear satisfied with the status quo. Hmong parents describe children born in countries other than the U.S. as conforming children who hold traditional attitudes and exhibit traditional behaviors. They see children born in the U.S. as Americanized with odd western attitudes and behaviors that are somewhat contradictory to Hmong culture and traditions. Another way to compare the academic success of Hmong foreign- and native-born children is to look at Hmong Americans who have earned doctorate degrees in various fields; nearly all of them are first-generation Hmong refugee children who were born outside the U.S.

In 2013, approximately 59 percent of Asian Americans in California were foreign-born. In the Hmong population, 42 percent were foreign-born and 58 percent native-born, as Table 11.8 illustrates. As Table 11.9 indicates, the ratios of foreign-born to native-born Hmong are similar in all three of the states with the largest Hmong populations. These figures indicate that Hmong Americans are moving from predominantly refugee status to status as ordinary American citizens.

A large number of Hmong children were born overseas and emigrated with their parents to the U.S. In 1996, the National Center for Education Statistics reported that approximately 52 percent of Asian-American students were U.S. born and 48 percent were foreign born; three out of four came from bilingual homes. Native-born Hmong students fall into two distinct groups: the 1.5 generation, who are traditional children of foreign-born parents, and the second-generation, children who are Americanized (Lee, 2001).

Foreign born students are twice as likely as U.S. born students to be identified as at risk for school failure because they lack English skills needed for basic academic tasks. Public schools usually categorize Hmong students who struggle with English as at risk regardless of their educational aspirations or motivation to learn. Typically, foreign born students in the at-risk category are from non English language backgrounds, live at or below the poverty level, go to urban schools, and entered the U.S. in their late teens.

These individuals are over represented among under-edu-

Table 11.8. Percent of Foreign-Born and Native-Born of Selected Asian Groups in California

Ethnic Group	Foreign-Born	Native-Born	Total Population
Nepalese	83%	17%	6,200
Burmese	78%	12%	17,900
Taiwanese	70%	30%	109,900
Mongolian	69%	31%	5,000
Indian	68%	32%	590,400
Korean	68%	32%	505,200
Vietnamese	66%	34%	647,500
Thai	62%	38%	67,700
Cambodian	54%	46%	102,300
Laotian	40%	60%	69,300
Hmong	42%	58%	91,200
Latino	40%	60%	14,013,700
Japanese	27%	73%	428,000
White	9%	91%	14,956,200
African American	6%	94%	2,683,900

Note: Information from U.S. Census Bureau, 2006–2010 American Community Survey 5-Year Estimates, table B05003.

Table 11.9. U.S. Hmong Foreign-Born and Native-Born Populations in Selected States, by Gender

Native- or Foreign-Born & Gender	U.S.	Minnesota	Wisconsin	California
Population	256,400	63,400	48,100	95,100
Native born	149,300	36,200	27,500	55,700
1. Male	51%	53%	50%	51%
2. Female	49%	47%	50%	49%
Foreign born	107,000	27,100	20,600	39,300
1. Male	50%	48%	50%	51%
2. Female	50%	52%	50%	49%

Note: Numbers are rounded. Information and data from The State of the Hmong American Community, by M. E. Pfeifer & B. K. Thao (eds.), 2013, Washington, D.C.: Hmong National Development.

cated students. Siu (1996) found that foreign born Asian-American students who came from poor families were 1.6 times more likely to be under educated than those from more advantaged homes. Hess (2000) pointed out that foreign born Latino students were far more likely than their at risk peers to under-achieve in school, having a failure rate of 43 percent as compared to 24 percent for sec-ond-generation Latinos. The second-gener-ation Latinos were "presumed to be English proficient" (p. 268). Hmong students who were born in the U.S. have some mastery of English and the American culture, but Hmong LEP students from immigrant and refugee families usually do not possess much knowledge or skill in English or American culture.

In their first decades in America, Hmong foreign-born children flocked into the U.S. public schools with hopes and dreams for a better future in the new homeland. In 1989, the *Hmong California Times* reported that ap-proximately 80 percent of the Hmong stu-dents in the American public schools were born in other countries: Thailand, Laos, Philippines, and France ("Hmong Children in American Public Schools," 1989). How-ever, Vang (1992) reported that the propor-tion of foreign-born Hmong Americans dropped to approximately 60 percent in the early 1990s, when more Hmong students born in America enrolled in public schools than a few years earlier. At the present time, approximately 50 percent of K–12 Hmong students in California are foreign-born but were raised mostly in America. In the next 20 years, there will be more native-born Hmong students in public schools, and per-haps Hmong will be their second language.

Ironically, Americanized Hmong children seem to have more problems in school than traditional Hmong children (Hmong Issues 2000 Conference, Fresno, CA). However, studies indicate that Hmong students born in America appear to fare better in school because they are familiar with the structure of the English language and have been ex-posed to academics at an early age (Hmong Issues 2000 Conference; Vang, 1999).

Whatever their birthplace, external and in-ternal forces are important in Hmong stu-dents' academic success or failure. Internal forces that push toward failure include the lack of motivation, primary language defi-ciency, insufficient academic ability, and slow acculturation. Negative external forces in-clude the lack of support at home, status as newcomers, lack of learning experiences, in-adequate preparation, negative peer pressure, family poverty, and capricious academic ped-agogy. Moreover, both foreign-born and na-tive-born Hmong children have suffered ac-ademically not only because of these internal and external factors, but also because they lack middle-class values needed for social-ization (Lee, 2001).

The 1.5 generation of Hmong children have contributed to the socioeconomic changes in Hmong families during the first 20 years after the Hmong's arrival in the U.S. These children worked hard to support their fami-lies even though most had only limited edu-cations. Some of the 1.5 generation earned higher education degrees and have become successful wage earners and role models in their families. As for native-born Hmong children, they still lag behind foreign-born Hmong children in educational attainment.

Hmong Primary Language Issues

Does primary-language literacy predict En-glish acquisition in Hmong children? In the case of Hmong students, primary-language literacy may not have a large effect on sec-ond-language acquisition because Hmong languages have not been taught formally. Ac-ademically, there is no direct transference of Hmong literacy into English. As McGinn (1989) noted, the Hmong language was not written until 1952, when French and Ameri-can missionaries created the Hmong Roman-ized Practical Alphabet writing system (HRPA, *Ntawv Hmoob La Tee*).

As presented previously, Hmong students have trouble speaking English proficiently. Table 11.10 indicates that Hmong students have improved in their English speaking abil-

Table 11.10. Percentages of U.S. Hmong Students and Other U.S. Students Who Speak English at Home at Selected Levels of Proficiency

Language Ability	U.S. Students	U.S. Asian Students	Hmong Students 2006–2010	Hmong Students 2000	Hmong Students 1990
Only English at home	80%	23%	8%	5%	3%
Non English at home/English spoken very well	11%	41%	49%	37%	21%
Non English at home/English spoken less than very well	9%	36%	43%	58%	76%

Note: Numbers are rounded. Information from The State of the Hmong American Community, *by M. E. Pfeifer & B. K. Thao (eds.), 2013, Washington, D.C.: Hmong National Development.*

ity since 1990, but only slightly. Hmong adults who attended school in the old country do not believe their illiteracy in the Hmong language affects their academic ability or their ability to learn Lao, French, English, or any other language in school.

Academically, there is a difference between learning a language and acquisition of a language. Learning is the process of mastering the mechanics of a language in a formalized setting; acquisition is the ability to communicate in a language. Acquisition can take place either in or outside a formalized setting. Learning focuses on the development of cognitive academic language proficiency whereas acquisition stresses basic interpersonal communication skills. Foreign-born Hmong students have acquired basic communication skills in the Hmong language but have not learned Hmong academic language because Hmong languages are not taught to them in a formalized setting.

Native language literacy level influences refugee students' cognitive development in second-language acquisition (Morrow, 1989). Robson (1982) found that among Hmong youth acquiring English as a second language, those who could read their native Hmong did better than those who could not. Robson suggested that being able to read the Hmong language helped students learn a second language. Robson compared Hmong students without an educational background who could read Hmong to those with an educational background who could read it and found very little difference between the two groups in English language acquisition. Reder (1982) reported that those who could not read the Hmong language made less progress in acquiring English than those who were literate in Hmong. These studies strongly imply that educational background is a predictor in second-language acquisition for Hmong students. These findings support the premise that primary-language literacy plays a limited role in second-language acquisition. Although literacy in Hmong languages cannot be transferred to the learning and acquisition of English as a second language, the academic skills developed in learning to read the primary language help Hmong students in learning a second language in school.

Moreover, Reder (1982) studied newly arrived Hmong refugee children and found that the process of acquiring English was a slow one. The ability to read a primary language was a key factor in school performance and second-language acquisition. This finding supports Robson's conclusion that Hmong students who were proficient in their primary language acquired English more easily. Cummins (1991) studied the processes of second-language acquisition and first-language attrition among minority students and found that fluency in the primary language strongly related to the development of a second language. Again, these studies suggest that literacy and competency in the native language facilitates the acquisition of English because of the academic skills involved, not the language skills.

In regard to primary-language literacy, McGinn studied the native-language literacy of Hmong adolescents in California in 1989 and found that half had a minimum ability to read and write Hmong. This means that a large number of Hmong adolescents were illiterate in their native tongue while attending American public schools. If the same study were done today, the result would most likely be that most Hmong native-born children do not speak, read, or write Hmong languages (White Hmong or Blue Hmong) because Hmong languages are not taught to these children formally. In other words, the Hmong literacy rate of Hmong native-born children is three times lower than that of Hmong foreign-born children.

Similarly, Weslander and Stephany (1983) found that approximately 63 percent of Hmong students could not read their first language as compared to 30 percent of Vietnamese students. Vang (1999) observed that many Hmong students were proficient in neither their native language nor English, and approximately 85 percent of elementary and secondary Hmong students were illiterate in Hmong. However, Sonsalla (1984) found that school personnel had not explored the role of Hmong literacy as it relates to student progress. Although educators believe that primary-language literacy and age at time of arrival in America are important factors in second-language acquisition (Ima & Rumbaut, 1989; Weslander & Stephany, 1983), primary-language literacy is absent in most Hmong children.

Most American-born Hmong students currently use Hmonglish, a mix of Hmong and English, as a verbal form of communication with their parents at home. Sometimes this new dialect leads to disagreements, misunderstandings, and intergenerational conflicts between parents and children.

Age and English Language Learning

Does the age of Hmong children matter in learning English as a second language? Generally speaking, younger Hmong students learn and speak English better and faster with less of an accent than older students. Some older Hmong children learn quickly and well because they have learning experiences from the old country; other older children struggle in learning the language because they lack the academic background. Younger Hmong children have the advantages of starting their schooling early in life, but many struggle because they are enrolled in poor schools that provide poor educations. Therefore, the age factor is not as simple as it may seem.

Researchers have found that age is a factor in learning a second language (Collier, 1987; Cummins, 1981; Lenneberg, 1967). Ima and Rumbaut (1989) reported that age at time of arrival in the U.S. predicts how well Hmong children acquire English and perform in school. It is generally assumed that children learn a second language more easily than adults do. Lenneberg (1967) proposed that a second language was best learned in the critical period between the age of 2 years and the onset of puberty. He stated that the ability to learn languages is debilitated by the completion of a process of lateralization in the brain, during which each side of the brain develops its own specialized functions. Children who learn a second language before puberty do, in fact, acquire native-like pronunciation, unlike adults, who usually speak a second language with an accent.

Similarly, Bialystok and Hakuta (1994) felt that younger was indeed better, and children acquiring a second language might not be considered typical second-language learners at all if they learn the second language before the age of 5 or so years.

Furthermore, Collier (1987) found that children between the ages of 8 and 12 years acquired a second language faster than did children between the ages of 4 and 7. This could be related to cognitive maturity and first-language development and competence. Children past the age of 12 seem to slow down in learning a second language, probably because the demands made of them in school are beyond the level of language they can bring to bear on the learning process.

Hernandez (1994) cautioned that interference between two languages could have some effects on the order of acquisition of specific aspects of language, such as learning the phonological processes. Hernandez noted that transfer from the first language does not help second-language acquisition when the primary language is a completely different language from the language being learned, without any similarities in phonological forms. This explains why Hmong LEP students cannot transfer Hmong vocabulary cognates to English. They can, however, transfer the basic skills learned in their first language development. As Lessow-Hurley (2000) stated, "Using first language knowledge and skills may produce errors that resemble interference, but which are in fact evidence of a creative cognitive strategy for solving the new language puzzle" (p. 45). This suggests that academic background facilitates second-language acquisition.

Hmong parents have learned over the years that English speaking ability or verbal proficiency in English may not be sufficient to ensure academic achievement and success. They have noticed that many native-born Hmong children who speak English well do not fare better in school than foreign-born Hmong students who came here as refugees and have limited English speaking ability. Perhaps, this observation supports the contention of western scholars and researchers that proficiency in English is not a sufficient condition for academic achievement because every child has to learn how develop academic language needed for academic tasks and performance. Hmong children have to develop cognitive academic language proficiency in addition to basic interpersonal communication skills in order to be academically competent.

Residency and Academic Achievement

Does length of time living the U.S. play a role in academic achievement? Length of residency could be a short-term factor, but it is not academically significant to long-time academic progress of Hmong children. Length of time living in the U.S. is not as important to the academic performance of Hmong children as length of time in public schools.

The exodus of Hmong refugees from Southeast Asia started in the mid–1970s. This was actually a second wave of immigration from Southeast Asia. The first wave was mostly from Vietnam prior to 1975. When the Hmong came to the U.S., they were in a transitional process called "adaptation and conflict" (Hmong Issues 2000 Conference, Fresno, CA). Warfare, refugee status, and poor health disrupted Hmong students' schooling (Bliatout et al., 1988; Siu, 1996; Vang, 1999).

Length of time living in America, and more importantly, length of time in U.S. schools plays a key role in how students perform in American public schools. Caplan (1985) found that after 3 years in the U.S. some refugee children did extremely well in public schools. Walker (1988) suggested that, since Hmong students came to this country with very little or no school experience, the longer they stayed in the U.S., the better they would perform in school. Similarly, Yang (1995) and Weslander and Stephany (1983) found length of time residing in the U.S. to be an important factor influencing educational performance of Southeast Asian students, including Hmong students. These authors suggested that the longer Hmong students resided in the U.S., the better they performed in school. This assumption must be taken with some caution because no recent study has been done on Hmong native-born students as compared to Hmong foreign-born students, who were the subjects in the early studies.

U.S. residency could be a factor, but Hmong children still face multiple challenges and academic barriers after four decades living in the U.S. The majority of Hmong students have been living in the U.S. for quite some time and are still not doing well in school. Many have poor language skills, helpful only for survival. They still lack academic language needed to perform academic tasks.

Most Hmong students in grades 7–12 have superficial academic skills and lack cognitive skills needed for academic tasks. Researchers suggest that the majority of Hmong-American students are unlikely to succeed beyond secondary school. One of the issues that many K–8 Hmong students born in America still face in school is their inability to read, write, and understand English well regardless of the length of time residing in the U.S. In other words, the majority of Hmong students still lack academic language. This situation is likely to remain unsolved in the next 20 years unless public schools implement intervention programs specifically designed to help Hmong students in the earlier grades.

In the past, length of time living the U.S. and length of time enrolled in U.S. schools might have had something to do with Hmong children's academic progress, but these variables may not be important factors anymore because speaking English and going to school are parts of everyday Hmong life. What Hmong children need is quality education with quality instruction and equity of instruction. The watered down, capricious, and impoverished curricula currently given to Hmong does more harm to Hmong students than good. It is time to scrutinize the school curricula, programs, and instructional practices received by Hmong students and change them so Hmong students can thrive academically.

Hmong Academic Progress in the U.S.

What are some academic successes of Hmong in America? Hmong-Americans are emerging in every field of study. Over the four decades since 1975, many Hmong children have transformed themselves with remarkable academic progress. Some Hmong children and adults seized the op-

portunities given to them to achieve academically, to overcome socioeconomic barriers and challenges, to change the status quo by working diligently, and to aim high and achieve success in life. Hmong refugees are firm believers that education is not only the key to open doors, but is the right path to equality and a better future in their new homeland.

Generally, it is true that Hmong Americans have made remarkable progress in public education for only four decades in the U.S., but much more remains to be accomplished. As Table 11.11 indicates, Hmong Americans in California had the lowest educational attainment for the population 25 years and older of all Asian groups in 2013. Tables 11.12 and 11.13 give the figures for national educational attainment for Hmong and educational attainment in specific states. Despite numerous challenges, many Hmong children take the educational opportunities seriously, earning academic degrees and becoming professionals. Earning college degrees enables Hmong Americans to enjoy good careers and advance socioeconomically. As Aristotle once said, "The roots of education are bitter, but the fruit is sweet." Hmong Americans believe this and have demonstrated it.

Table 11.11. Educational Attainment of Selected Asian Groups in California, 2013

Ethnic Group	High School or Higher	Bachelor's Degree or Higher
Mongolian	97%	60%
Japanese	95%	49%
Taiwanese	95%	70%
Korean	93%	55%
Indian	90%	68%
Thai	86%	44%
Burmese	84%	51%
Chinese	82%	51%
Laotian	61%	12%
Cambodian	60%	14%
Hmong	58%	15%
Total population in CA	81%	30%

Note: Information from U.S. Census Bureau, 2006–2010 American Community Survey 5-Year Estimates, table B15002.

Table 11.12. Educational Attainment of U.S. Hmong in U.S. and in Selected States

Population, Degree, & Gender	U.S.	Minnesota	Wisconsin	California
Population of 25 years and older	98,000	23,900	17,500	36,600
Less than high school diploma	38%	36%	36%	43%
High school diploma	22%	23%	25%	18%
Associate's degree	26%	26%	23%	25%
Bachelor's degree	11%	12%	13%	11%
Graduate or professional degree	3%	3%	3%	3%
High school graduate or higher				
1. Male	70%	73%	74%	64%
2. Female	55%	56%	53%	50%
Bachelor's degree or higher				
1. Male	16%	17%	20%	14%
2. Female	13%	13%	13%	14%

Note: Information from The State of the Hmong American Community, *by M. E. Pfeifer & B. K. Thao (eds.), 2013, Washington, D.C.: Hmong National Development.*

Today thousands of Hmong children are enrolled in colleges and tens of thousands of Hmong graduates have successfully earned their high school diplomas, four-year college degrees, graduate degrees, and doctoral degrees in a variety of fields. As Table 11.14 shows, 495 Hmong Americans earned doctorates and 6,500 graduated from master's programs as of 2013. Of the 495 U.S. Hmong doctors, 81 are Doctors of Philosophy (PhD) and Doctors of Education (Ed.D); 78 are in law (JD); 70 in pharmacy (Pharm. D); 64 in medical fields (MD); 27 in chiropractic (DC); 16 in dental surgery (DDS); 15 in ministry (D Min); 8 in podiatric medicine (DPM); 7 in psychology (D. Psych.); 4 in optometry (OD); 3 in osteopathy (DO); 1 each in dental medicine (DDM), theology (D. Theo.), and psychiatric medicine (DPM); and 6 in unspecific fields. A number of additional doctorates have not yet been verified.

Table 11.13. Hmong Educational Attainment in Selected States, 2010

State	Total Hmong Population	High School or Higher	Bachelor's or Higher
Arkansas	2,143	37.0	00.0
Arizona	229	50.4	12.4
California	91,224	57.5	14.9
Colorado	3,859	73.4	8.4
Georgia	3,623	85.7	18.5
Michigan	5,924	65.5	19.1
Minnesota	66,181	63.1	14.7
North Carolina	10,864	59.7	9.8
Oklahoma	3,369	79.2	10.7
Oregon	2,920	72.6	10.5
Washington	2,404	64.9	14.0
Wisconsin	49,240	62.4	12.8

Note: Information from The State of the Hmong American Community, *by M. E. Pfeifer & B. K. Thao (eds.), 2013, Washington, D.C.: Hmong National Development.*

Table 11.14. Number of U.S. Hmong Earning Specific Educational Awards

High School Diploma	Four-year College Degree (BA/BS)	Master's Degree (MA/MS)	Doctorate Degree (Ph.D/Ed.D)
185,000	9,500	6,500	495

Note: Information from The State of the Hmong American Community, *by M. E. Pfeifer & B. K. Thao (eds.), 2013, Washington, D.C.: Hmong National Development and Christopher Vang's estimated data of Hmong educational attainments from 2000 to 2014.*

This level of success, starting from zero and growing to over 6,000 with postgraduate degrees in just four decades, is remarkable, especially compared to where Hmong were after hundreds of years in Laos and thousands of years in China. If the current trend holds, Hmong academic attainment will be three times this level 20 years from now. In 2014, The Hmong Tribute reported stories of some emerging Hmong American scholars who achieved significant educational goals, and their brief profiles of successes illustrate the variety of the educational achievements of Hmong Americans:

- *Ma Vang* is the first Hmong-American female professor to obtain a University of California tenure–track faculty position. Vang earned her Ph. D. in ethnic studies from UC, San Diego and spent 2 years as a UC President's Postdoctoral Fellow at UC Riverside. As an assistant professor of ethnic studies, Vang teaches in the Humanities and World Cultures program in the School of Social Sciences, Humanities, and Arts at UC, Merced.
- *Bao Lor* is a tenure-track assistant professor in the Department of Anthropology, Geography, and Ethnic Studies at California State University, Stanislaus. Lor earned her Ph. D. in ethnic studies at UC, Berkeley. She is the first Hmong-American female professor to teach ethnic studies.
- *Yang Sao Xiong* earned his Ph. D. in sociology at UC, Los Angeles in 2012 and is the first Hmong-American male professor to obtain a tenure-track position teaching Hmong-American Studies in the Department of Asian American Studies and School of Social Work at the University of Wisconsin, Madison.
- *Leena Her* is the first Hmong-American female professor to earn a Ph. D. in linguistics from Stanford University. She has been hired as a tenure-track assistant professor in the Department of TESOL and Global Learning at Kennesaw State University in Georgia.

Historically, *Yang Dao* is the first Hmong to receive a doctoral degree, which he earned in Social Science at the Sorbonne University of Paris in 1972. His educational attainment was a historic moment for all Hmong in the world, a groundbreaking academic breakthrough for all Hmong refugees prior to their coming to the West. Yang is a historic figure in education, a towering symbol of academic success and an icon in education.

To date, in 2013, Governor Jerry Brown in California appointed *Mr. Paul Lo*, a Hmong lawyer, of Merced to become the first ever Hmong-American Superior Court Judge in the County of Merced. On April 18, 2014, Lo was sworn in as a judge in front of hundreds of Hmong-Americans and non–Hmong Americans. For the Hmong community, this is another groundbreaking moment that marks the milestone of Hmong-American successes in the U.S.

Furthermore, in 2014 election in California, *Mr. Steve Ly*, an elected school board member of Elk Grove School Unified District, was elected the first ever Hmong-American City Councilmember to serve on the Elk Grove City Council. Ly's victorious city race is not new to Hmong-Americans; however, it is still new to the Hmong living in the Elk Grove metropolitan area. Hmong Americans continue to strive to meet their political challenges and socioeconomic progresses and will take any socioeconomic opportunities to achieve successes. Socioeconomically, keep in mind that education is the key to all socioeconomic successes of western Hmong.

Back in Laos, from the early 1960s to the early 1970s, the expansion of public education for all Hmong in Laos came from the strategic innovation of two individuals, an educator and a military leader, who worked together to promote public education for the Hmong and established public schools in many Hmong villages throughout northern Laos. These two men were Mr. Moua Lia, the first Hmong provincial school inspector, aka superintendent of public education, and Major General Vang Pao, the first and only Hmong general in the Royal Lao Army. Together, they devised a master plan to expand public education for all Hmong children, and Major General Vang Pao allocated funds and manpower to build public schools in many Hmong villages. Both men should be commended for their promotion of public education for all Hmong children in northern Laos.

In the West, despites these academic successes, many Hmong college students still face serious academic challenges in association with socioeconomic factors in higher education. These academic impediments include, but are not limited to lack of financial aid assistance, lack of peer advising and mentoring, lack of academic advising, poor study habits and skills, poor time management, lack of time for study, lack of motivation, lack of self-confidence, lack of direction in obtaining career information and guidance, and inadequate personal finances (Xiong & Lee, 2011). It is difficult to believe, but some Hmong college students still lack role models, mentors, and guidance. And many lack academic motivation and financial resources.

When Hmong refugees first arrived in the U.S., academic success for Hmong students was defined as achieving a high grade point averages (GPA), scoring well on standardized achievement tests, and graduating on time (Caplan et al., 1992; Ima & Rumbaut, 1989; Purdham, 1988; Wheeler, Schroeder, & Tafoya, 1982). By these measures, academic achievement among Hmong secondary students in America is lower than achievement of Hmong students in Grades K–8. The academic achievement of Hmong students appears to be declining more steeply in secondary school than in the primary grades. Yang (1995) reported that the average GPA of Hmong students, on a four-point scale, declined from 9th grade to 12th grade. The average GPA of Hmong 9th graders is 3.75; of 10th graders, 3.07; of 11th graders, 2.96; and of 12th graders, 3.05.

Similarly, O'Reilly (1998) observed that whereas U.S. Hmong students have excelled academically at different times, their academic performance changes dramatically as they go through the process of assimilation and integration. The author noted that at one time Hmong students refused to settle for any grade lower than an "A." Now, however, Hmong secondary students are failing at a higher rate than the rest of the student body. O'Reilly listed several academic problems among Hmong students: poor attendance, failing grades, poor behaviors, credit deficiencies, violations of school rules, extensive disciplinary records, suspensions, and adjudications. Basically, many Hmong students lack study skills and coping skills needed in Grades 7–12.

Hmong secondary students face a new set of values when entering the mainstream culture. In some communities, the academic trends among today's Hmong children differ from those of the first generation that came to America 40 years ago. Hmong children are becoming more Americanized every day, adopting many behaviors of mainstream American youth. Some Hmong children have undergone rapid changes in their lifestyles, social and economic development, and educational status. These drastic changes sometimes lead to academic failure and culture clashes inside the family. As mentioned earlier, Hmong children fall into two categories: the 1.5 generation, most of whom are traditional and are referred to by older Hmong as good kids, and the second-generation, who are Americanized and many of whom are thought of as bad kids in the Hmong community. Lee (2001) suggested that the academic success of Hmong students comes from accommodation and acculturation without assimilation, which is the result of both cultural transformation and cultural preservation. However, environmental factors appear to have greater effect on academics than cognitive factors.

Similar to O'Reilly (1998), in a study of successful and unsuccessful Hmong secondary students, Vang (2001) found that successful Hmong students have at least one of seven characteristics:

- a good relationship with their parents
- the ability to discuss educational situations with parents who listen to their stories

- parents who advise and guide them
- a goal and a plan for their immediate future after graduation from high school
- access to resources such as technology, teachers/counselors, extra ¬activities, school programs, and role models
- coping skills for dealing with academic, social, and economic problems
- positive self esteem

Perhaps these characteristics could be used as indicators of the potential academic success or failure of U.S. Hmong students. They certainly demonstrate that family, culture, and environment all play roles in how Hmong students perform in school.

As an illustration of the interplay of some of these characteristics, Vang (2001) described the struggle behind a Hmong secondary student's successful graduation from high school:

This student shared his story of fulfillment in life. He wanted to fulfill his father's dream. His family had been on public assistance ever since the first day they arrived in America in 1980. They were still poor and lived in an overcrowded dwelling. He shared a room with his four brothers. He believed college education is the key to a better economic opportunity in America. His goal is to have a better life. He said, "My dad told everyone to earn good education to have a better life.... My dad means we should not live in the past life... 'Cause today's action is tomorrow's success." He quoted a Hmong proverb, "Tomorrow is longer than yesterday and I believe in it. I need to prepare for my future. I have seen my present life situation … and I need a better one. To have one is to get college education" [74].

Abramson and Lindberg (1985) found that Hmong students in Grades K–12 in California have socio emotional traits that facilitate learning and school adjustment, grasping academic concepts, and making cross-cultural adjustments. However, in order to capitalize on those traits, the students required more instruction in the oral and written language of the host culture. Similarly, Reder (1985) found that Hmong adolescents have a great level of educational need because they lack language ability and study skills. Students who demonstrate deficiencies and/or differences in language, behaviors, or emotional competencies are at risk of school failure (Hess, 2000).

Academic success leads to occupational success. As the profiles given previously demonstrate, several Hmong-American professors are working at various colleges and universities across the nation. California alone has at least 10 Hmong-American professors and several adjunct Hmong instructors. Many Hmong Americans are employed as part-time instructors at the college level. Hmong-American professionals such as medical doctors, lawyers, business owners, pharmacists, judges, and politicians are becoming prominent across the nation. As Table 11.15 illustrates, Hmong Americans work in a variety of professions. Many are self-employed and own their own businesses. A small number of Hmong-American students are attending prestigious colleges and universities. And many Hmong-American students are valedictorians and recipients of

Table 11.15. Distribution of U.S. Hmong in the Workforce

Profession/Occupation	Percentage
Agriculture, forestry, fishing, mining, hunting	1.5%
Arts, entertainment, recreation, accommodation, food services	11.9%
Construction	1.2%
Educational services, health care, social assistance	19.4%
Finance, insurance, real estate, rental, leasing	4.4%
Information	1.9%
Manufacturing	28.7%
Other services	3.6%
Professional managers, science, management and administration and waste management	6.3%
Public administration	2.8 %
Retail sales	12.6%
Transportation, warehousing, utilities	3.5%
Wholesale trade	2.3%

Note: Information and data from The State of the Hmong American Community, by M. E. Pfeifer & B. K. Thao (eds.), 2013, Washington, D.C.: Hmong National Development.

distinguished honor awards. Education is the golden key that has placed many Hmong Americans on the track toward prosperity.

Below are just a few brief stories of Hmong Americans who have become successful professionals, business owners, role models, and productive citizens in the community. Their profiles were collected from stories featured in the Txhawb, a California Hmong directory. These Hmong Americans are first-generation Hmong refugees who worked diligently to overcome obstacles to get to where they are today.

- *FengLaly Lee*, a Hmong-American medical doctor, as featured in *Txhawb*, a Hmong California directory, 2014. Lee has a passion and aspiration right from the start. She always knew and decided early in life that she wanted to become a medical doctor. Lee is the only Hmong-American woman who is a medical doctor in Obstetrics and Gynocology (OB/GYN) in Fresno County and is the new owner of Omni Women's Health Medical Group in Fresno.

    After graduating from McLane High School in Fresno, Lee attended the University of California, Davis for four years and graduated with a degree in Physiology. Lee was admitted to the UC, Davis Medical School. After completion of her medical training at UC, Davis, Lee returned to Fresno to do her medical residency at the University of California, San Francisco (UCSF) Fresno Center.

    Lee is the oldest daughter and the middle child of nine children in her family. Lee's challenges and obstacles in life include (1) family responsibilities of caring for her siblings; (2) fear of not finishing school; (3) getting married before finishing her college education; (4) raising a family of her own while pursuing her goal and dream; (5) working and going to school at the same time to achieve both an educational goal and a professional career;

(5) being a Hmong daughter, a Hmong mother, and now a Hmong medical doctor.

- *Jamie Xiong-Vang*, a Hmong-American attorney, as featured in *Txhawb*, a Hmong California directory, 2014.

    Ms. Xiong-Vang decided in the third grade that she wanted to be a lawyer. Ms. Xiong-Vang is a general practice lawyer focusing on criminal, immigration, bankruptcy, and personal injury cases and has been practicing law in the Fresno area since 2006. Ms. Xiong-Vang graduated from Edison High School in 1999 in Fresno and completed her undergraduate studies at the University of California, Los Angeles; and she earned her Juris Doctorate degree at the Whittier School of Law.

    Ms. Xiong-Vang is the oldest child of 12 children in her family. Her challenges and obstacles in life include (1) growing up in poverty; (2) getting married very young; (3) raising a family during high school and college; (4) being a Hmong daughter, mother, wife, daughter-in-law, and college student; (5) making life sacrifices to pursue her educational goal; and (6) now, being a woman, young, and Hmong American.

- *Bee Yang*, a Hmong-American chiropractor, as featured in *Txhawb*, a Hmong California directory, 2014.

    Yang has passion and aspiration to pursue his professional career because he believes in the idea of healing people without the use of drugs. Yang is owner of Best Care Chiropractic in Fresno.

    Yang graduated from Edison High School in 1987 in Fresno and attended the University of California, Santa Cruz. He completed his undergraduate studies in 1991. Yang earned his Doctorate of Chiropractic from Life Chiropractic College in 1995.

- *Xengxue Yang* and *Pang X. Yang*, Hmong-American pharmacists, as featured in *Txhawb*, a Hmong California directory, 2012.

The Yangs are a Hmong-American couple, pharmacists, and owners of Pillbox Pharmacy in Fresno and Visalia, California.

They were high school sweethearts, got married young, raised a family while going to school, and pursued their American dreams. Both attended the University of Wisconsin–Milwaukee for their undergraduate studies and earned pharmaceutical doctorates from the University of Missouri, Kansas City School of Pharmacy in 2005.

Their aspirations came from their real-life experiences. As she recalls, "going to the garden with my parents, picking strawberries, raspberries, and cucumbers," which she describes as "back breaking jobs and I knew that I had to go to college if I wanted to have a better life." He said he "worked as a stockboy for a warehouse and found myself working ginseng fields, planting, weeding, picking berries, and harvesting the roots."

• *Tou Vue*, a Hmong-American naturopathic physician, as featured in *Txhawb*, a Hmong California directory, 2012.

Vue is the owner of Crossroads Naturopathic Health Clinic in Sacramento, California. Vue graduated from Lindhurst High School in Marysville and completed his undergraduate studies at the University of California, Davis. Vue did his graduate studies at Jacksonville State University in Alabama and attended the National College of Naturopathic Medicine in Portland, Oregon and earned his Doctorate of Naturopathic Medicine. Vue is the only child in his family to go to college.

• *Michael Vang*, a Hmong-American pharmacist, as featured in Txhawb, a Hmong California directory, 2012.

Vang is the owner of Vang Pharmacy in Sacramento, California. Vang attended the University of California, Davis and earned his Doctorate of Pharmacy from Chicago College of Pharmacy.

Vang's aspiration and motivation came from his own experience. As he recalls, "You are who you surround yourself with." He believes that by surrounding oneself with ambitious and successful individuals, one too will have a chance to be successful.

• *Mr. Lee Yang*, Director III of the Multilingual Literacy Department of Sacramento City Unified School District, and *Mrs. Bao Moua*, principal of Clayton B. Wire Elementary School, a Hmong-American couple in public education, as featured in *Txhawb*, a Hmong California directory, 2011.

As husband and wife, they believe that "what doesn't break you will make you." They also believe "It is how you finish that matters."

How they dealt with their hard times was remarkable. As they recall, "We had gotten married right after high school. We were living in a one-bedroom apartment across from my parents and my nine siblings, who all lived in a two-bedroom." How they overcame their dilemma was similar to many Hmong refugee children who grew up in the West. As he explains, "Bao and I, being the oldest children, had to be responsible for my extended family." Financially, they struggled to survive. As they remember, "As students we had to worry financially about our schooling as well as whatever my extended family members needed. We suffered. All of us lived off of $600 a month."

As educators and leaders, this couple handles their work with great passion, diligence, and confidence. This is how they can describe their professional careers: "We have been through a lot of obstacles. Our past experiences have prepared us well for the responsibilities we now have in our careers. What we currently do cannot compare to what we had to do in order to survive those harsh years of poverty and raising a large family." Their successes are incredible.

These stories of the struggles of successful Hmong Americans are heartfelt and amazing. None of these professionals could have gotten where they are without education. The remarkable achievements of many Hmong Americans have led some sociologists to call the Hmong a model minority for other immigrants and refugees. Despite the challenges that still confront the Hmong-American community, educators fully expect Hmong Americans to continue their exceptional progress.

Hmong School Dropout

Having their children attend school is a top priority for most Hmong parents. Is school dropout an issue for Hmong-American students? Recent data show that the national high school dropout rate for Hmong-American students is 6 percent. The highest rate is in Michigan (8 percent); followed by North Carolina (7 percent); and Minnesota, Wisconsin, and California, each with dropout rates of 6 percent. These figures mean that the overall high school graduate rate for all Hmong students in K–12 schools in these states, although at an all-time low, is still high.

Hmong high school graduates are not well prepared for college and many have met college entrance requirements. In California, only the top 10 percent of Hmong high school graduates are eligible to go to a 4-year college, the next 30 percent meet the entry requirements for admission to community colleges, 40 percent seek admission to private colleges, and the last 20 percent either go to vocational schools or seek temporary employment without going to school. Some Hmong graduates attend college part-time and work full-time or vice versa.

The biggest reason Hmong Americans are unprepared for college is that they are enrolled in public schools that offer capricious curricula that do not meet their academic needs and offer little to help them go beyond secondary education. The long-term effects of such curricula are insidious, ultimately decreasing Hmong students' chances for suc-cess in pursuing higher education. Besides rigorous curricula, Hmong students need to be placed in good classrooms with good teachers who can provide them with pedagogy conducive to academic excellence and the kind of support that will minimize their academic barriers.

Many Hmong students still exhibit serious adjustment problems and their academic skills are far below grade level (Ima & Rumbaut, 1989; O'Reilly, 1998; Siu, 1996; Vang, 1999). Adjustment difficulties and lack of academic skills result in low scholastic achievement. This is important because poor academic achievement is the most common predictor of school failure (O'Reilly, 1998). The poor academic achievement of Hmong students is a crisis in high schools as well as in the community (O'Reilly, 1998). Again, this suggests that although today's Hmong students are fluent in English, they lack the academic language needed for academic tasks. In other words, having basic interpersonal communication skills will not help Hmong students achieve academically unless they also have cognitive academic language proficiency, meaning strong skills in reading, writing, and math.

The research regarding school dropout among U.S. Hmong students is conflicting. Some studies suggest that Hmong students have a lower dropout rate than other immigrant and refugee students, and other studies report higher dropout rates for Hmong students in high school. As with students in other Asian groups such as Vietnamese, Chinese, Japanese, Koreans, and Cambodians, Hmong have a lower dropout rate than Caucasian, African American, and Hispanic students.

Generally speaking, immigrant and refugee children are at highest risk of dropping out in their first few years of schooling because this is normally a difficult time with tremendous emotional stress. If they lack support at home, these students are even more likely to drift away from school. Olsen (1988) reported that the national dropout rate for Filipinos in 1988 was 46 percent; for Pacific Islanders, 17 percent; for Latinos, 14 percent; for Cambodians, 14 percent; for Vietnamese, 11 percent, for Hmong and other Southeast-Asian sub groups (Lao, Mien, Yao, and Lahu), 5 percent, and for Whites, 10 percent.

In a narrow study, Reder found in 1982 that male Hmong adolescents dropped out of school at a rate of 60 percent whereas the dropout rate for female Hmong adolescents was 95 percent. The discrepancy between this finding and later research can be explained by the fact that Hmong teenagers were getting married in high school in the late 1970s and the early 1980s. Many male Hmong teenagers left school to find employment following marriage and the majority of married Hmong teenage girls did not return to school after marriage. The reduction in teen pregnancy and teenage marriage increased the high school enrollment rate for both male and female Hmong students in the late 1980s (Vang, 1992). A large number of female Hmong adolescents still get married during high school (Golstein, 1985; Vang, 1992).

Vang (2001) captured the story of a Hmong secondary student who dropped out of school:

> This student shared her story of disappointment. She was married at the age of fifteen and a half. She had no clue about having a family or being a married person. In Hmong culture, she had many roles and responsibilities at home. Her husband dropped out to look for a job. Things were difficult for her when she conceived her first child. She said, "All of sudden, things are falling apart on me." She added, "My mind is at home while my body is someplace else. Sometimes I do not know what I am doing in school." She said, "I cannot blame anyone for my own mistakes after I have refused to listen to my parents. I should endure my own regret." She was disappointed over her own failure. She also said, "No girl should go through what I have gone through in life. It is terrible and painful for young people. Listen to your parents if you are stuck with a problem or ask your teacher for directions. Don't try it the wrong way"[69].

Statistically, the reduction in adolescent pregnancy and marriage is still insufficient to prevent female Hmong students from leaving high school early. Vang (2001) found that 95 percent of Hmong secondary students graduate on time but only 10 to 15 percent of Hmong high school graduates are qualified to enter public universities because they still lack the academic skills needed for success. As Lee (2001) observed, "The school success or failure of 1.5 generation and second-generation Hmong students does not hinge on any one thing, but rather on a marriage of both external and internal forces" (p. 526).

Today the social and environmental factors are greater than the Hmong traditional issues, such as early marriage and childrearing. Many Hmong students fail to graduate or to achieve their educational goals because they failed to resist social temptations; they had poor study and coping skills; they became Americanized and adopted the behaviors that contradict their Hmong values; they engaged in substance abuse and gang related activities that landed them in jail; they lacked educational and career aspirations; they grew accustomed to the easy, temporary survival lifestyle; or they lost their pride in Hmong values and traditions. Quite frankly, some Hmong children these days misunderstand the American material culture and make drastic changes in their behaviors and attitudes that they will regret later in life.

Future Trends

What does the future look like for Hmong students' education? Based on the current educational attainment data, Hmong Americans should have a bright future. If Hmong carefully evaluate the current progress, successes, and pressing issues related to Hmong children's education, Hmong would be able to predict the outcome for the next 20 years. As mentioned earlier, the number of Hmong college students should triple in size. However, what should happen may not; if it does not, it will be because the aspirations and motivation to pursue higher education of today's Hmong students is not the same as of students 20 years ago. Second- and third-generation Hmong Americans may view the benefits of education differently from Hmong Americans of the first generation.

Today approximately 25 percent of U.S. Hmong high school graduates are enrolled in college. That number is considerably low because the high school graduation rate for Hmong students is at an all-time high. The low number means that Hmong students are not adequately prepared to enter college even if they have accrued enough credits to fulfill the graduation requirements. No doubt more attention needs to be given to Hmong students' academic preparation in K–12 in order for them to be prepared for college; otherwise, many Hmong students will not be on track to go beyond high school.

Today, some Hmong children do not see themselves as potential successes; rather than consider the future, they focus on their present situations. Their desire for material possessions will sabotage their academic potential because they will have difficulty withstanding the hardships that are almost certain to accompany the pursuit of a college education. These Hmong students blindfold themselves in the land of opportunity by concentrating on their daily needs and wants instead of setting up long-term goals to achieve something great in life. To pursue the American dream, Hmong students have to be willing to make personal and financial sacrifices to invest in their education. They have to appreciate all the pain and suffering their parents endured to bring them to the Promised Land where so much is available to them. The best of all the opportunities of America is education, the most precious commodity that will outlast wealth, health, and social comfort. As an article in the July 2014 *Hmong Tribune* encouraged, "The path of higher education is one way we can collectively move the Hmong American community forward" (p. 3). Actually, higher education has become the most promising path for all Hmong Americans to improve their lives and socioeconomic status, and no western country provides better educational opportunities for Hmong refugees than the U.S.

Of course, Hmong children do not need to have higher education to survive in this country because there is a safety net of services and allocations. But why should they not take the opportunity available right in front of them to make life better? Education is the foundation for the future; why let it slip away?

All Hmong children have the potential to become successful in life, and for Hmong refugees, life begins with education. Hmong children have come a long way and still have a myriad of issues and concerns to deal with, but if they think and choose wisely, they can achieve just like any other Americans can. The old saying is true: Where there is a will, there is a way. There is a way for Hmong Americans to achieve greatness and success in life, and that way is education.

The problem is that the academic skills of Hmong-American students remain superficial; therefore many students are far from achieving their potential. Generally, the public stereotypes categorize Hmong students as either high achieving members of a model minority or as low achieving delinquents. The academic path for Hmong students is clouded by poor preparation in grade school. Hmong-American adults must help the children of their communities. Hmong-American students need more positive role models to guide them through and beyond the American traditional education system. Moreover, public schools have a big responsibility to help Hmong students succeed. Schools should try to make Hmong students full citizens by showing respect for their culture and understanding of the difficulties they face as they try to straddle the gulf between their culture and the larger American society. Schools should introduce academic curricula that reflect Hmong history and provide a sense of inclusion in the school community at large (Lee, 2001).

America is the land of opportunity, but opportunity does not come without competition. Hmong students should take the academic opportunities that are available to them seriously. These opportunities are golden dreams and promises that Hmong students should take advantage of to help them enter the mainstream culture in America. As one researcher reported, "the U.S. Hmong secondary students learned that schooling did not necessarily lead to social acceptance into American society, but they continued to believe that it holds the key to economic success" (Golstein, 1985, p. 276).

Hmong-American students need not ponder what is best for them at the present time; instead they need to ponder what they can do in the present that will matter in the future. As Vang (2001) pointed out, successful Hmong students tend to think more about the future than their present situation. Hmong college students are more focused on long-term careers than short-term jobs because they have learned from past experience that long-term careers give greater stability. Vang (2001) interviewed a high school student who had dreams and recognized that he also had opportunities:

> This student shared his story of a dream of a better opportunity in America. He came from France about eight years ago. He said, "Hmong had limited opportunities in France, as compared to this country, but America gives you the opportunity after high school, not French." He added, "In France, you have to be one of the best students. Not in America. Here you can choose a future goal. I like this kind of freedom." His dream is to become a businessman. He said, "Motivation is the key and long-term goal is for future stability. Short-term goal is for today and long-term goal is for tomorrow. It is good to have both, but concentrate on the best goal." He added, "As refugee, Hmong students need to have a long-term plan, like a social security plan. I have seen people work so hard for little money and other people work so little for a lot of money. This is something they ought to think about their careers. We cannot continue to be the working poor.... The poor people become poorer every day and the rich people become richer every day" [75–76].

To go beyond the status quo, Hmong students need to understand and appreciate the sacrifices and the aspirations of their parents and find ways to achieve the goals their parents have for them. Otherwise, they will lack the motivation to do the hard work necessary to pursue the American dream, including taking advantage of every academic opportunity. Hmong children cannot afford to make excuses for their lack of effort; excuses will come back to haunt them later in life. Building themselves into strong individuals now is far better than trying to fix themselves as broken men or women later in life.

Many capable Hmong students leave school due to personal reasons such as early marriage, odd jobs, credit card debts, family obligations, and social temptations. These impediments are preventable if the students receive assistance early enough. Small problems become large problems if they are not dealt with in a timely manner. Parents and public schools often fail to detect them until they have become huge roadblocks. Hmong parents must get involved in their children's education if they want to see their children achieve. Whether Hmong parents are culturally bound to certain beliefs and cultural norms or not, they should have to think outside the box in order to advocate educational equality for their children. When parents neglect their children's education, the schools often neglect it as well. Parents and public schools have responsibilities and legal obligations to make sure that each child receives a quality education. The power to make a difference in a child's education lies in the hands of parents. Today's action is tomorrow's success. It is time for Hmong-American students to think seriously and creatively about ways to raise their self-esteem, to succeed in school, and to attain good academic and life goals.

One last thing: Hmong children have to take responsibility for their lives. Achieving educational success does not benefit their parents as much as it secures their future, the future of their children, and the future of their children's children. Once they have an education, no one can ever take it away from them.

Suggestions for Future Studies on Hmong Students

Hmong Americans still face tough problems in higher education and systematic approaches are needed to alleviate the social and cultural pressures that hold them back. Xiong and Lee (2011) found that Hmong students consider basic socio-cultural factors to be obstacles for them in higher education, as shown in Table 11.16. The authors identified some academic services the students found helpful in dealing with the obstacles; they are listed in Table 11.17. The barriers Hmong students in K–12 schools are currently facing are not entirely related to their cultural and linguistic background; some have to do with hidden institutional barriers to educational success and advancement. In other words, Hmong students in K–12 schools are victims of academic malpractice based on a hegemonic socio-academic paradigm.

This section presents some suggestions for research on Hmong-American students in K–12 public schools and in college. The academic problems of Hmong K–12 students are now their impediments in college. At the very least, research should examine Hmong students' academic impediments in relation to the constraints placed on the students by the state-mandated system of ongoing language classification, English skills testing, ELD programs, and tracking for fiscal and empirical purposes. Unless changes are made in these practices, they will continue to sabotage Hmong students' opportunities to receive a quality education in K–12 schools and to be well prepared for college. Past and current studies have provided information on the challenges that Hmong-American students face in the classroom, but they are insufficient to provide a comprehensive understanding of all the factors that affect Hmong-American students. In order to address the contemporary situation, future studies might focus on the following areas:

1. An intense study must examine the segregated academic curricula targeting Hmong-American students who are classified as limited English proficient and/or newcomers. The study should

Table 11.16. Socio-Cultural Factors Identified as Life Obstacles by Hmong College Students

Factor	Students Identifying Factor as Obstacle	
	Number (N = 55)	%
Lack of money	39	71
Poor study habits and skills	38	69
Poor time management	31	56
Lack of time to study	33	60
Lack of self-confidence	24	44
Lack of motivation	29	53
Lack of mentors	25	46
Lack of parental support	12	22
Lack of support from ASPs	14	26
Lack of interest in college	7	13
Lack of direction to obtain career goals	30	56
Influence of friends	14	26
Need to care for younger siblings	14	26
Health problems	5	9
Others	5	9

Table 11.17. Academic Services Identified as Helpful by Hmong College Students

Services	Students Identifying Service as Helpful	
	Number (N = 22)	%
Financial assistance	14	64
Peer advising and mentoring	13	59
Academic advising	12	55
Tutoring	8	36
Career advising	4	19
Personal development	4	18
Leadership development	3	14
Orientation to the university	2	9
Internship information	2	9
Scholarship information	1	5
Job search	0	0

compare language acquisition and learning in Hmong students receiving this curriculum with language acquisition and learning in mainstream Hmong students and/or fluent English proficient students enrolled in the regular course of study. The study will provide insight into the quality of this form of education and equity of instruction.

2. A comprehensive study should measure the impact of Hmong-American bilingual teachers on Hmong-American students' academic success as compared to the impact of monolingual teachers on mainstream Hmong students.

3. An intense national study should identify the academic barriers that prevent Hmong-American students from entering mainstream classrooms and other competitive courses of study.

4. An ethnographic study should examine peer pressure and gender equity issues relative to academic success and/or failure of Hmong-American students, especially female Hmong students.

5. An intense study must expose the ELD programs that put Hmong students in classrooms that only offer capricious curricula and are taught by unqualified school personnel and substitute teachers who have not been properly trained to teach LEP, ELL, and special-needs students.

Summing Up

This chapter gave some highlights of Hmong Americans' education in the U.S. When Hmong first arrived, the U.S. public school system was unprepared to deal with Hmong children's special academic needs. Nearly all Hmong refugee children were classified as LEP and placed with unqualified, untrained, and unlicensed teachers for years. Public schools overlooked Hmong students' aspirations and motivations to achieve in school, requiring them to take easy classes to simply acquire the GPA required for graduation. Such hidden and null curricula stunted Hmong children's education for years.

Numerous studies have been conducted on Hmong students to discover their academic needs and challenges. Many factors and issues have emerged; however, none of the research addressed the school programs in which Hmong children are placed as obstacles to academic performance. Most ESL curricula are not based on obligatory content, but on compatible content, which is basically watered-down instruction that is nonacademic. A large number of Hmong children are placed in ESL classes that provide daily drills on survival English skills. In the early 1980s, large ESL classes were designated for Hmong children, and today, ELD classes are filled with Hmong students as well. Most schools use perceived ability, surface assessment, and cosmetic education to determine the needs of these children without determining their potential. Some teachers and administrators do not consider Hmong children to be college bound.

Despite many challenges, Hmong Americans are emerging in every corner of education, from different fields of study. Many Hmong children have taken the opportunities in front of them seriously and pursued worthy educational goals and dreams. For nearly four decades, hundreds of thousands of Hmong Americans have graduated from high school, tens of thousands have graduated from college, several thousands have earned graduate degrees, and hundreds of Hmong have earned doctorates. The overall educational attainment has been remarkable, especially in light of many life obstacles and serious language barriers.

Based on the current data, the future for Hmong Americans is bright. More Hmong children will graduate from college and more Hmong American professionals will emerge in a variety of fields as the result of their educational successes. Hmong Americans' continuous investment in education will benefit not only the Hmong community, but the larger community as well.

TWELVE

The State of the Hmong Community

Kaum txhais te tsis zoo npaum li ob txhais npab...
Kev huam vam yog los ntawm kev sib pab...
A Hmong proverb about collectivism

Introduction

Since 1975, Hmong refugees have reestablished themselves and started their lives over again in the western nations. U.S. Hmong refugees are the fastest growing Hmong refugee population in the West and they are one of the most advanced Hmong groups in the world. Over four decades, Hmong refugees have become naturalized citizens of many western nations: the U.S., Canada, France, French Guyana, Australia, Argentina, and Germany. The socialization processes and cultural adjustments were different in the different countries, but in every western nation Hmong experienced culture shock and other challenges. Some remained in the countries where they first resettled and some relocated their families in other western nations. Hmong refugees have become transformed over time through the resettlement process. They have become more and more westernized while undergoing lifestyle changes and achieving some level of economic prosperity. Many continue to struggle with difficult obstacles as they seek freedom, better economic opportunities, and social stability in the western nations. This chapter examines the general social welfare of Hmong and the state of the Hmong community in the U.S. It explores challenges, opportunities, progress, and successes as it paints a picture of how Hmong refugees have fared socioeconomically in the western world.

Hmong Community Structure Prior to Living in the West

For thousands of years back in China, Hmong lived in groups in small villages and farmed fertile fields before suffering political oppression and encroachment on their land. Hmong engaged in many wars throughout their long history in ancient China and became victims of centuries of mistreatment, discrimination, persecution, and political brutality. Hmong were forced to live on barren land where farming was nearly impossible. They struggled for survival for hundreds of years before migrating to Southeast Asia in search of freedom, independence, and fertile land.

By the mid–1800s, Hmong migrants and refugees had reached the northern region of Laos and settled in the Nong Het (*Looj Hej*) vicinity. There a Hmong community grew as Hmong refugees and immigrants arrived from the southern regions of China. Hmong usually were called by the names of their family clans or tribes, and Hmong family groups were recognized by their clan or tribal leaders. As told in Hmong oral history, each Hmong family group settling in the Nong Het area was distinct. The pioneer clans were the Lo, Ly, Moua, Yang, Vang, and Vue families, and each tribe was led by distinguished leaders known as clan leaders, chieftains, or kiatongs. Some of the prominent kiatongs and leaders were Lo Cher Ly Cha (*Txawj Lis Tsav Lauj*), Lo Pa See (*Paj Txhim Lo*), Lo Nhia Her (*Nyiaj Hawj Lauj*), Lo Zong Cher (*Zoov Tsawb Lauj*), Ly Nhia Vue (*Nyiaj Vws Lis*), Ly Chai Zia (*Nchaiv Siab Lis*), Moua Chong Kai (*Ntxoov Kaim Muas*), Cheu Lau Yang (*Tswv Lauv Yaj*), Lo Blia Yao (*Npliaj Yob Lauj*), Chia Fong Ly (*Txhiaj Foom Lis*), and Pa Chai Vue (*Paj Cai Vwj*). Hmong referred to each clan or tribe as *cuab*, meaning family group or tribe. Hmong respected and recognized each family group or tribe by referring to each one by its family name: *Lo Cuab, Ly Cuab, Yang Cuab, Vang Cuab, Vue Cuab, Thao Cuab, Xiong Cuab, Moua Cuab*, and so on.

Traditionally, within the Hmong tribal leadership council, Hmong established a social hierarchy based on traditional structures and certain personal qualities:

- embodying words and fulfilling actions (*noj tau hais tau thiab hais tau ua tau tiag*)
- generously kind and socially considerate (*siab loj siab dav hlub taus kwv tij neej tsa sawv daws*)
- impartial, honest, sincere, fair, humble, with knowledge and skills for resolving conflicts and problems (*coj ncaj thiab coj zoo*)
- having great manners, attitudes, and behaviors; composed; diplomatic; and possessing leadership skills (*coj lus taug thiab paub qhov siab qhov qis*)
- publicly sociable, compatible, and likeable (*nyiam pab kwv tij neej tsa thiab tej phooj ywg sawv daws*)
- possessing in-depth knowledge of and skills in Hmong cultural and traditional rules, customs, norms, and tribal tranquility (*paub kev cai Hmoob*)
- being a good role model for all (*ua ib tug qauv zoo rau sawv daws*)
- having a normal life and a supportive family (*muaj lub neej nrog luag ua thiab muaj lub cuab lub yig*)

- married (*muaj poj niam tub se*)
- having great respect for other Hmong leaders and elders within the Hmong leadership structure (*muaj kev sib hwm sib raug zoo nrog cov coj noj coj ua sawv daws*)

Not all Hmong leaders have all these qualities, but most Hmong leaders possess most of them. In the Hmong world, these are basic cultural elements used to determine leadership quality. However, people with these qualities do not automatically become Hmong leaders.

In China and Southeast Asia, Hmong families lived among other Hmong families, but each family belonged to its tribal group. For instance, a Lo family could live next to a Ly family, or a Yang family and a Vang family could be next-door neighbors. In some places, Hmong referred to a Hmong village by the name of the tribe predominant there, such as Yang Village, Lo Village, Ly Village, or Moua Village. Each Hmong village had a leadership structure appointed by the central tribal administration leaders. For instance, a Hmong kiatong (*kiab toom*) or tasseng (*toj xeem*) could appoint regional representatives or village chiefs to govern a village.

The social and political organization of Hmong community and village life was based on the trinity of Hmong family structure, the Hmong clan structure, and the Hmong clan system of leadership. The basic Hmong social structure has a five-level system of shared leadership and governance, as shown in Figure 12.1. Even though Hmong leadership and social structures may seem complex, Hmong leaders know how to sort things out culturally. They understand how the system works, and they embrace its foundations of consultation, respect, compromise, pardon, leniency, and mutual reciprocity. The Hmong community is made of all family members of all clans. The clan systems distinguish families by family name and each family clan has its own leaders and clan representatives. Subclans belong to the family groups that share a common lineage and genealogy. Family systems are made up of extended and nuclear families of the sub-clan systems and individual families of the family systems.

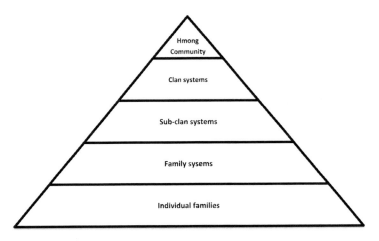

Figure 12.1. Hmong social structure of shared leadership and governance.

In the early 1900s, the Hmong practice of kiatong leadership became obsolete because Laotian officials started to not recognize the position of kiatong as an official representing the Laotian government. The Laotian officials replaced the Hmong kiatong with a tasseng appointed by the Laotian government as the only recognized representative of the village. By the mid–1900s, the kingdom of Laos had adopted a new constitution that integrated all minorities, including the Hmong, Khamu, Mien, Yao, Lue, Lahu, and other indigenous groups, into an independent sovereignty. The kingdom implemented a decentralization policy organized by geographical configuration that included the highland mountain regions and secluded villages where the Hmong lived. The new Laotian policy called for the establishment of tribal and ethnic leadership in provinces, districts, subdistricts, village, and communities. The different

ranks of Laotian-Hmong leaders were chao khoueng (*cob kheem*), chao muong (*cob moos*), nai kong (*nais koo*), tasseng (*toj xeem*), and nai ban (*nais npab*). Other appointed community leaders and representatives such as *phub toom, phes toom, phias toom, tsav toom, toom mas, thoob lis, lis teem, xov phiam,* and *xov phov* served on an advisory council and performed minor leadership roles. Figure 12.2 depicts this Laotian hierarchy. Each level of government belonged to the regional administration that represented the central administration of the Laotian government.

The decentralized structure in Laos is comparable to the western system of local government. The *chao khoueng* of the province is like a county supervisor, in charge of cities or districts in the province; the *chao muong* of the city or district is similar to a city mayor and is in charge of designated districts and cities. The *nai kong* is a metropolitan official comparable to a city council member, in charge of subdivided districts

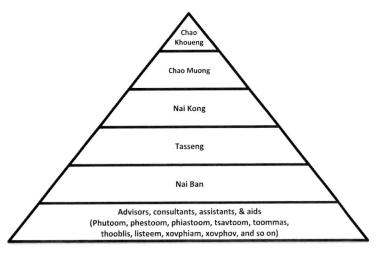

Figure 12.2. Laotian regional structure and leadership.

within the city or district. The *tasseng* of the regional township is similar to a sheriff, in charge of many towns and villages. Finally, the *nai ban* of the local village is a group leader or tribal leader in charge of a specific village or town.

Hmong were given the privilege of electing their regional leaders and representatives to rule only Hmong people without direct involvement of Laotian officials. However, the leaders and representatives they chose had to be approved by the regional Laotian officials and central administration. The special district was known as the *Chao Muong Hmong district* and had no political boundary in the Xieng Khouang and Sam Neu provinces. The elected Hmong *Chao Muong* ruled all Hmong living in the land.

From the mid–1900s to the early 1970s, Hmong had risen to the ranks of *nai kong*, sub-divided district leaders; *tasseng*, sub-district leaders; and *nai ban*, village chiefs under Laotian *chao muong* and *chao khoueng*. There were approximately 24 Hmong *tassengs* and *several nai kongs* throughout the Xieng Khouang and Sam Neu provinces in northern Laos; however, only a few Hmong *chao muong* were appointed for political purposes. In the 1960s, there were only two Hmong *chao muong*, in the Houa Phanh and Sayaboury provinces. In the decentralized government, Hmong served mostly as leaders in the rural areas; very few were appointed as sub-divided district leaders or sub-district leaders. Nevertheless, when and where there were Hmong chao muong, they appeared to have broad control and authority over Hmong villages in the designated provinces. The role of the Hmong leaders was to collect taxes for the French and Laotian officials. In these and other ways, Hmong in Laos served their Laotian masters and French imperialists well for many years.

When Hmong refugees came to the western nations, they brought this social structure and political organization with them. Their way of living is still based on the delegation of power and authority through the patriarchal hierarchical system they learned in the old country. Moreover, the organization of Hmong refugee communities in the western nations is similar to the structure the Hmong lived under for hundreds of years prior to 1975. The social and political influences from the old country are still evident in Hmong communities across the U.S.

Western Hmong Community Establishment

In the early years of resettlement, the Hmong community was in disarray because the western policy was to disperse the refugees across different regions of the various nations. The expectation was that the refugees would quickly assimilate and integrate into the mainstream culture. In some areas, notably France and Canada, dispersion worked quite well, but in most cases, particularly in the U.S., the policy failed. Hmong refugees were caught off guard when they found that Hmong families were being scattered all over the place. Hmong resettlement in the U.S. was a difficult ordeal for most families, and Hmong refugees found their own ways to counter the dispersion policy.

First, the pioneer Hmong refugees who were scattered became sponsors for relatives to bring more extended family members to the U.S. Sponsorship reunited some Hmong families and increased the likelihood that Hmong could live in community. However, the relatively few incidents of family reunification were insufficient for Hmong refugees to adjust culturally and survive socio-economically in the U.S. because Hmong refugees needed a larger community in order to have a sense of belonging.

To function well, the Hmong community must have certain basic elements:

- clan leaders and a leadership structure
- extended family members
- religious practices and cohesiveness
- inter-family and intra-family co-dependency on capable, able, knowledgeable, and skilled family members
- employable economic opportunities for adults with little or no English skills
- practice of Hmong culture and traditions

These elements are fundamental to Hmong refugees' survival. However, the resettlement policy that dispersed the population and the family leaders disrupted hopes of reestablishing a communal way of life. As the influx of refugees continued, most Hmong refugees' living situations became temporary and unstable.

The second way Hmong attempted to counter the dispersion policy was to relocate to reunify families with extended family relatives and clan members. This movement of Hmong refugees occurred in the U.S. in the early 1980s. Some of the factors pushing Hmong to move were:

- the desire to reestablish a Hmong community
- the desire to reunite families with clan leaders
- the belief that living in community would give them a greater chance of survival in the US
- the desire to maintain and preserve Hmong culture and traditions
- the desire for easy access to prominent family members in the event of need
- the desire to maintain continuity in Hmong religious and cultural values, beliefs, and practices
- the need to provide family support for one another
- the need to unite to resist immediate assimilation and integration
- the fear of losing Hmong identity and dignity
- the need for help in coping with the traumatic and drastic changes in life

In short, the need for support in their socioeconomic struggles and fears about survival prompted Hmong refugees to make great sacrifices to relocate their families to certain U.S. metropolitan areas. Moreover, Hmong refugees felt that their life in diaspora was only temporary.

Third, a call from former Hmong leaders ignited a second migration, bringing many Hmong refugees scattered among several nations to North America. Wherever they were, Hmong refugees maintained the dream that they could return to their homeland. The call from the former leaders was important because most Hmong families were immobilized by shock; the call gave them direction from leaders they trusted. During their first few years as refugees, Hmong encountered tremendous stresses and family crises, and relocation offered the hope that Hmong refugee families would survive the resettlement process. Some of the family and personal crises that made initial resettlement traumatic were the following:

- unexpected need for Hmong parents to become employed at occupations for which they were not equipped
- inability to speak English
- absence of opportunity to acquire English skills
- episodes of sudden death syndrome
- severe culture shock
- lack of everyday life skills for the new environment
- cold weather conditions
- lack of medical care, knowledge of western medicine, and interpreters and translators
- poor neighborhoods with congested housing
- absence of a Hmong community with patriarchal establishments to deal with cultural and family matters
- Hmong sociopolitical fantasies and dreams
- Living in solitude and isolated metropolitan areas
- Fear of drastic and traumatic integration and assimilation

Additional factors beyond those mentioned above also drove Hmong refugee families into the second migration. Relocation to the U.S. opened the possibilities of public education for their children, economic opportunities for their uneducated parents, and family clan reunification. The call from Hmong leaders triggered worldwide actions that brought Hmong refugee families from France, Canada, Australia, and elsewhere to the U.S.

As the result of an outcry from Hmong refugees, Hmong leaders began to establish

Hmong community-based organizations (CBOs) to meet the critical needs of Hmong refugees in the U.S. and elsewhere. In mid–1977, the first Hmong CBO was founded under the leadership of Major General Vang Pao and Hmong loyal to him in southern California. The first *Lao Family Community, Inc.* was established in the city of Long Beach, California; it has since branched out to all major metropolitan areas where there is a Hmong community. By the mid–1980s, nearly all Hmong communities across the U.S. had some type of CBO to provide social services and critical resources to help Hmong refugee families, and many Hmong mutual assistance associations still exist today. Some of the prominent Hmong CBOs and non-profit organizations, just to mention a few, are Hmong National Development, Inc.; United Hmong Council, Inc.; Hmong International New Year, Inc.; World Hmong People's Congress; Hmong International Human Rights Watch; Hmong Heritage Preservation Coalition Committee; Hmong Nationalities Organization, Inc.; Lao Family Social Services, Inc.; Hmong Women's Association, Inc.; Lao Veterans of America; and Lao-Hmong American Coalition. Hmong refugees have also established many family and tribal organizations to help immediate family members and extended relatives.

One of the most well recognized, vibrant, and viable national Hmong non-profit organization is the Hmong National Development, Inc. (HND). This organization was founded in 1987 by many Hmong leaders and was first known as the Hmong-American National Development, Inc. The name was changed to HND in 1993 when a new group of young Hmong leaders, including females, took over the leadership of the organization. The HND's present vision is to have a united and thriving Hmong community, and its overall mission is to empower the Hmong community to achieve prosperity and equality through education, research, policy advocacy, and leadership development. Since 1993, HND has become a strong voice for the Hmong people and community at national, state, and local levels, advocating for sociopolitical policies that impact the Hmong community as a whole.

The fourth factor in overcoming the dispersion policy was transnational interest in Hmong sociopolitical rejuvenation. The Hmong refugees held on to the dream that one day they would return to their native country and start all over there. This messianic fantasy misled Hmong refugees to follow a transnational political movement from the early 1980s to the late 1990s known as the *Neo-Hom movement* aka the United Lao National Liberation Front (ULNF) and Lao National Liberation Movement (LNLM). The movement involved a number of disorganized and disorderly political activities and became a double-edged sword that disrupted Hmong socialization in the U.S. for decades. The movement also contributed to brutal treatment of Hmong left behind in Laos. The fantasy grew vague as time went by and Hmong's hopes of returning home eventually faded. However, the insidious effects of the impossible Hmong transnationalism still linger in the minds of many Hmong refugees.

Today, as a result of the second Hmong migration and earlier relocations, a number of major cities across the U.S. have vibrant Hmong communities. These cities are Fresno, Sacramento, Merced, and Stockton, California; St. Paul, Minnesota; Madison, Milwaukee, and Wausau, Wisconsin; Denver, Colorado; and Hickory-Lenoir-Morganton, North Carolina. The majority of Hmong people still believe in collectivism, and the Hmong community plays a major role in Hmong sociopolitical structures and the general welfare of Hmong people.

Hmong Community Social Structure

Besides the three-tier stratum, western Hmong communities are socially and politically complex because of the way Hmong structure and operate the sociopolitical functions of the Hmong community. Western Hmong communities have factions, cliques, and special interest groups and often exhibit tribal conflict, infighting, public bickering, and personal grudges as well as a long history of betrayal, dishonesty, and rivalry for leadership. Tribal disputes are common in the Hmong community. Centuries-old tribal politics remain an unhealed scar in Hmong communal life. Major General Vang Pao warned Hmong refugees many times, "Hmong have to stop for good the vindictive attitudes and vicious behaviors that produce toxins in the Hmong way of life." He always believed that all Hmong are one big family with different family names.

Hmong communities do not operate in identical ways, but most Hmong communities in the western world face similar issues and problems. For instance, the right, left, and middle groups are frequently engaged in disputes over Hmong New Year's celebrations. Some communities are relatively small and others are big; the size of Hmong communities determines the complexity of the Hmong cultural structure, social organization, and socioeconomic operation. Moreover, some communities are divisive and others are cohesive. Some Hmong communities are not as powerful as they appear to be because of futile sociopolitical antagonisms and internal conflicts. However, many communities provide the foundations for the everyday Hmong communal way of life.

Hmong people depend on the leadership of the community for guidance. Without a community voice, Hmong people are insecure, feeling threatened by external forces. Hmong have a number of external threats to fear, some real and some carryovers from Laos: police brutality, unreasonable search and seizure during traffic stops, conflicts with the law over culture, gang activities, drugs and substance abuse, unnecessary arrests, racial discrimination, and lack of public safety and protection. For these reasons the establishment of a Hmong community is vital to meeting the critical needs of Hmong refugees. A Hmong community provides socioeconomic benefits that enhance the general welfare of Hmong people.

Prior to 1975, Hmong women had hardly any role in Hmong traditional leadership. In the late 1970s to the early 1980s, the structure of Hmong leadership revolved around former military officials, clan leaders, and spiritual healers. Distinguished clan members were often board members of Hmong CBOs. However, most of these leaders were unable to read and write, so leadership responsibilities fell to the executive directors of the CBOs. Therefore, for the first two decades in the U.S., the leadership in most Hmong communities was heavily dependent on the knowledge and skills of CBO executives.

In the early 1990s, the executive directors and the board members of Hmong CBOs clashed head-on because they had different points of view on Hmong community issues. The internal conflicts persisted until the structure of the Hmong community reverted to the old form of clan system representation. At the same time as the leadership crisis, the larger structure of the Hmong community was in turmoil because of generational conflicts between the old and the young. "The old" refers to former military officials, clan leaders, and family representatives; "the young" denotes the working class, including the CBO executives and ordinary people who advocated for change. Figures 12.3 and 12.4 illustrate the different approaches of these two groups toward Hmong community social structure. The old generation wanted to maintain the traditional structure whereas the young generation wanted to completely reverse that structure. Simply, the overall conflict of Hmong leadership has always been the power struggle between traditional leaders and professional leaders.

The squabble between the Hmong professionals and Hmong traditional leaders over community leadership structure has become an ongoing conflict that has divided Hmong communities for years. In some communities, the detachment between the young and old generations has become a permanent division. In the majority of communities, the old approach has overpowered the new for five reasons:

1. The majority of the Hmong communities support the traditional model of leadership and social structure.

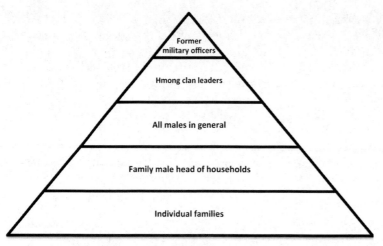

Figure 12.3. Old-generation traditional leadership model.

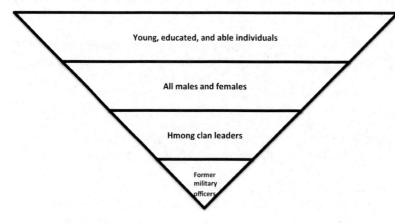

Figure 12.4. Young-generation professional leadership model.

still play vital roles in Hmong leadership and everyday life.

Despite sociopolitical polarization, young and educated Hmong refugees who grew up with the American culture have learned American ideals and values, including civic participation, and they are now emerging in the political arena. Over the last 20 years, a dozen Hmong refugee politicians have been elected to public offices at different levels of local and state government. In Minnesota, State Senators Mee Moua and Fong Her; State Representative Cy Thao; City Council member Dai Thao; school board members Ka Zoua Kong-Thao, Choua Lee, and Neal Thao, and others are good examples of Hmong-American politicians. In California, school board members Paul Lo, Steve Ly, and Tony Vang and City Council members Steve Ly, Noah Lo, and Blong Xiong are further examples of emerging Hmong-American politicians. So is school board member Soua Vang in Wisconsin. In the 1990s, LaMong Lo became the first Hmong refugee elected to public office when elected to a City Council in the State of Nebraska. Other Hmong refugees have run for public office but did not achieve victory: Vong Mouanoutoua, Chue Charles Vang, Blong Yang, and a few others. Hmong refugees have already made history in winning public office, and perhaps more Hmong-American candidates will emerge in the future.

2. Hmong professionals lack the time, commitment, and public engagement required for leadership.

3. Most traditional leaders are actively involved in Hmong everyday life.

4. Hmong professionals want drastic changes that make people of the older generation uncomfortable.

5. Both groups lack clear mission statements and goals for the Hmong community.

The old-fashioned social structure is the one in practice at the present time. In the Hmong world, seniority, elders, generational orders, social ranks, birth orders, and familial roles

Typically, the Hmong community social structure is based on Hmong cultural beliefs and the patriarchal system, a long-standing tradition of male dominance illustrated in Figure 12.5. The Hmong patriarchal system is a loose pyramid with very little formal structure. It is learned by emulation, imitation, and duplication of rank by peer appointment, favoritism, nepotism, and volunteer service.

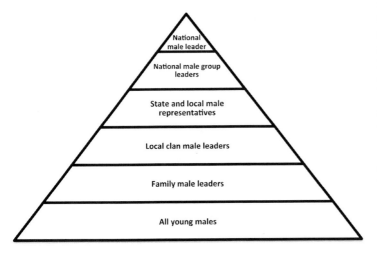

Figure 12.5. Hmong community structure.

For Hmong, leadership, whether in the family or the community, is a male responsibility. Within the Hmong traditional leadership structure, every Hmong male has a limited, designated, and natural role to play regardless of his ability. Hmong women, on the other hand, have very limited opportunity for any type of leadership. Hmong females today are being asked to serve in different capacities along with Hmong male leaders, but they do so reluctantly. Outside the family structure, Hmong women are now serving in various capacities to provide services to the Hmong community. As of now, very few Hmong communities have recruited Hmong females to serve as representatives in leadership positions in the Hmong community, and clan representatives are predominantly males. Gender inequity is very obvious in the Hmong community structure. A very few Hmong women are serving as board members, consultants, or advisors of Hmong CBOs and some are in charge of CBOs and private organizations in Hmong communities. Vocal Hmong women have provided a strong voice for Hmong people and the Hmong community at the local, state, and national levels. However, in the Hmong world, male leadership is still preferred regardless of personal qualities.

Three groups form the foundation of Hmong community social structure: the young (children and students of all ages), the old (parents, leaders, and all ordinary people), and the educated (professionals, business owners, leaders, and private citizens). As Major General Vang Pao said publicly many times in his life, Hmong community structure needs these three groups to work together in order to have a fair and democratic public process for all Hmong. Hmong have to think outside the traditional box, stretching their comfort zones, to include different individuals who can contribute to the greater good of the people instead of relying on the old-fashioned mentality of strict male dominance.

Hmong males who admit that the Hmong community social structure needs restructuring to include members of the three groups legitimately fear such a representative structure may be unstable and short-lived. They worry that potential struggles for power and control, gender and age incompatibilities, and role changes and leadership reversal could be catastrophic. A 2014 City Council race between two Hmong-American candidates in Minnesota, one male and one female, confirmed this fear. In the public arena, most Hmong males did not voice their choice but quietly voted for the male candidate regardless of political affiliation because they believed in male leadership over female leadership. Vocal Hmong-American women strongly believed in female leadership and campaigned in support of the female candidate. However, older Hmong women sided with their male partners regardless of the gender issue. Culturally, in a choice between a male and a female for a leadership position, odds are still in the favor of the male unless other very strong factors are involved.

Rightly or wrongly, Hmong males have learned from old proverbs and Laotian adages that women leaders can be meek, emotional, irrational, and indecisive under severe duress and when faced with life-and-death situations such as riots and wars. Laotians differentiated between male and female leaders with catchy phrases such as "*Nab phab caub cais mam*" for a female and "*Nab mam cais phab caub*" for a male. In the context of leadership, these phrases say that a female leader may have a change of heart easily as opposed to a male leader, who has a strong heart and can face all kinds of problems. Perhaps this old mentality will fade away in time.

The one and only national Hmong leader in modern times was Major General Vang Pao. Even though he was not a perfect leader, no Hmong was higher than he in the Hmong community social structure. No Hmong has the charisma and military power that he had, no Hmong could lead the way as he did, and no Hmong can duplicate all that he did for the Hmong people in his 67 years. Since the death of Major General Vang Pao in 2011, the U.S. Hmong refugees have lived with no active national leader who can provide social, cultural, spiritual, and political guidance to the Hmong people. As a Hmong hero and messianic leader, Major General Vang Pao urged all Hmong to love one another and work collaboratively to find the next leader through a democratic process. So far, the U.S. Hmong refugees have been unable to find common ground on which to initiate the process of reestablishing national Hmong leadership. It may take many more years for Hmong refugees to restore trust in one another so they can move ahead in unity and solidarity.

In two articles in 2012, Vang shared the implications to U.S. Hmong refugees of the loss of Hmong leadership after the death of Major Genera Vang Pao:

Article One: "Why Hmong live in the state of apostasy"

Are Hmong Americans sheep without a shepherd? Or Are Hmong Americans shepherds without the sheep? I have received emails and phone calls from people around the world about avoiding cultural apostasy. Who will Hmong Americans follow next? No one knows the answer to this question. It is time for some kind of cultural revolution because apostasy has occurred from the beginning of Hmong civilization to the present time.

After the death of the honorable General Vang Pao, many Hmong Americans have no one to turn to or follow. Everyone is left to fend for themselves. So, apparently, they are sheep without a shepherd.

Hmong leadership is now in a state of apostasy. This is the time when most Hmong Americans are living without celestial and divine direction from a living leader or prophet that can lead them to the Promised Land. It is a time of great struggle for power, a time of cultural tribulations. No one listens to anyone, and everybody has to wait for a messianic miracle to happen. Many Hmong Americans are turning from the hopes and dreams that General Vang Pao left behind for them. Some Hmong Americans are renouncing his leadership and are beginning to apostatize themselves to become wicked individuals because many Hmong Americans are left alone to struggle for new leadership in darkness.

Since some Hmong Americans have been practicing self-made and self-proclaimed leadership for hundreds of years without a democratic process, many are now shepherds without sheep. Some leaders are waiting for people to come to them, while others are claiming leadership yet lead no one. Why are Hmong doing this to hurt themselves? And why can Hmong not see what other racial groups in America have done to help their own communities? Should the fish come to find the water, or should the water come to find the fish?

Everyone appears to be selfish in promoting democracy for the greater good of the Hmong people as General Vang Pao proposed upon his death. He foretold Hmong future and leadership as a time when everyone has to be united to withstand apostate influences in order to find a democratic process to elect new leaders Hmong would respect and follow. So far, all most Hmong Americans have witnessed is the familial group apostasy that is deeply rooted in individual apostasy, and this kind of immorality will continue to haunt Hmong unity until the individual apostasy comes through the sins of omission or sins of commission. When this time arrives, these individuals will repent to redeem their lost souls and spirits for good.

In the time of apostasy, people neglect personal responsibility to enhance life, fail to keep their good hearts to do what is right for the people, become disobedient toward each other, commit corruption to protect what is wrong instead of what is right, use crooked tongues to mislead people and the community for personal gain, and become traitors to betray their own people. Yet some people do not repent for what they have done to others and continue to practice immorality with the guilt of sins. Therefore, when all is considered, how could Hmong Americans overcome apostasy when they have failed to recognize the individual apostasy that lives inside their hearts? Perhaps it is time for change; it is time for disapostatizing the self to do what is right for the people. And it is time for modernizing the Hmong way of life.

Right now, many people falter in finding their own peace, happiness, and freedom because of their loss of hopes and dreams. Perhaps the pressures begin to build upon their conscience, responsibility, immorality, and disobedience. There are social and political pressures used to frighten off them. There are personal appetites and greed involved. There are false ambitions to lure others. There is a weakening of the will to do what is right. There is lack of personal discipline and management to deal with apostasy. There is capitulation to improve life or to degrade life, and admittedly, there is personal remorse, self-gratification, self-accusation, bitter tears, and regret for wrongful acts.

Finally, together, Hmong Americans can redeem their wicked mindsets, disobedient attitudes, and anarchical behaviors by doing what is right for the betterment of their people. Apostasy could be overcome if Hmong Americans realize their weakening of the will to do great things for a common purpose. Perhaps General Vang Pao's spirit will lift Hmong Americans from being apostatized to the state of democracy in order for Hmong to become civilized individuals with kind, caring hearts that show love, forgiveness, compassion, and sympathy for one another. That is the cultural uptopia Hmong should have had for years.

ARTICLE TWO: "HMONG HAVE SEEN THE FIRST AND LAST MESSIAH"

Nearly one and a half years after the death of General Vang Pao, Hmong Americans are culturally nebulous and have been unable to find common ground to reestablish Hmong leadership for the greater good of the people. Everyone still wanders in thoughts and hopes for new direction, but many are puzzled with the status quo. It is unlikely that Hmong Americans will see any new leaders anytime soon. Perhaps General Vang Pao was the only—the first and last—Hmong messiah given by God.

Hmong Americans need to find a new beginning to help them write the next chapter of Hmong leadership. Nevertheless, looking for a turning point is quite challenging when all clans, groups, factions, and cliques are not singing the same notes in harmony. As perceived by some, Hmong leadership is dead and buried. There is no defining moment for Hmong Americans to see change as their fear over hope grows. However, many still have hopes that one day in the near future Hmong Americans will have a change of heart and reestablish Hmong leadership. Only time will tell.

As for right now, Hmong Americans will not be able to find a successor to take leadership anytime soon for a variety of reasons. First of all, Hmong Americans were left to fend for themselves when General Vang Pao passed away. His tape-recorded messages urged Hmong Americans to find a democratic process to elect the next leader(s). General Vang Pao did not name anyone to take his place or to continue his reign, and he gave no reins to anyone. Basically, he took his leadership given to him by the CIA with him and left Hmong in limbo.

At the present time, his sons are playing a pivotal role in engaging the community. However, their roles are considered insignificant by many Hmong Americans due to the fact that his familial hierarchy is in shambles and sibling conflicts within the family are evolving without any structural foundations to elicit political gravitas needed for the continued reestablishment of his reign. In other words, many Hmong Americans do not believe that his reign can continue without having a democratic process. Familial role is only for the purpose of preserving his legacy.

Second, for centuries, Hmong people have been ruled and governed with oral traditions and principles. There are no written rules, policies, or laws in place to show how Hmong people should be governed culturally and politically. For the 36 years in the US, Hmong people have practiced pretty much the same social values under General Vang Pao. His leadership has always been the best and has dominated all aspects of Hmong life for nearly 67 years. However, his leadership gives Hmong little hope or no structure to organize Hmong leadership, and the shoddy establishment of Hmong leadership is unstably controversial and spiteful in some areas of life.

Third, inheritance of leadership is considered to be an unearned asset and is not the right way of life Hmong Americans want to have anymore. General Vang Pao was right when he chose not to name anyone to be his successor(s) because he foresaw that the ripple effects of civil warfare among Hmong Americans could be deadly poisonous and the everlasting rift among the 18 family clan systems could be life-long infighting. In other words, giving his leadership to one person or one clan would do more harm than good, and moreover, he seemed not to trust anyone in his lifetime. No one really deserves to be his successor, and most importantly, he wanted to end the century-old cultural corruption and dishonesty once and for all.

Fourth, General Vang Pao asked Hmong Americans so many times to discard their personal spats, spites, curses, grudges, and menaces toward one another in order to live in harmony. However, most failed to do so while he was still alive. For instance, many Hmong Americans destroyed trust and bonds by concocting foolish tactics to gain personal favoritism from him. At the same time, some Hmong Americans devoured General Vang Pao's reputation and leadership with greed, scams, dishonesty, and corruption. In other words, the bad and the ugly ones tried to eat General Van Pao's leadership alive to steal his love, caring, and

blessing that he has had for his Hmong people. Of course, General Vang Pao was right when he said no one loves Hmong people more than he.

And, fifth, in the hearts of some Hmong Americans, there are serious problems with mistrust, greed, dishonesty, scams, bribery, treachery, treason, espionage, an enemy mindset, and corruption. For years, General Vang Pao warned Hmong people that they are their own worst enemies on the battle field, especially in socio-cultural politics. He foretold that no one would look out for them after him, and no one would be able to lead Hmong people if these acts of evil are not destroyed with fire and water for the sake of Hmong leadership.

Furthermore, he said publicly that Hmong people have lived with these problems for centuries and it is time for the eradication of the roots of evil; otherwise, there is not much hope for Hmong for the future. In other words, General Vang Pao prophesized before his death that Hmong's fate would be everlasting difficult, especially for Hmong leaders. He warned against Hmong incivility, foretelling of the coming doomsday in which Hmong cultural tribulations are about to begin.

Hmong Americans have achieved great successes in life to become self-sufficient in America. What is still missing in Hmong's life is finding good leaders for the Hmong race and community after the death of General Vang Pao. Finding a successor to replace General Vang Pao could be impossible because he was created and established by the CIA in the old days for military purposes. Today, Hmong Americans are living in a different world, with freedom, choice, and democracy. However, for a race to be part of the American fabric, Hmong Americans must be able to identify leaders in order to be respected and recognized by other communities or races in America.

Keep this in mind: there is no known human race on earth that has no leadership. Perhaps Hmong Americans are the only group of people that has no leader after the passing of General Vang Pao. Hmong Americans should considering fixing or changing themselves to do what is right for their people and must come together to set good examples for young generations to come. Or try to answer this question: Where is Hmong leadership?

Besides the lack of Hmong women in the traditional Hmong leadership sphere, Hmong educators, intellectuals, business owners, and paraprofessionals are not usually part of the leadership structure either because they lack the time and dedication to serve in voluntary capacities. A community role requires countless hours of volunteer work with unpaid responsibilities, and many working people are unable to take on such tasks. Over the years, Hmong professionals have volunteered to serve; however, the demanding responsibilities of their professional careers do not allow them enough time to dedicate quality service to public functions. Their absence leaves the community structure open for those who have the time, energy, and little or no professional responsibilities to take charge of community responsibilities. Most of the individuals who step into the leadership void are caring and dedicated people who want to serve their community. They may not have the professional attributes and personal qualities to be in such positions, but that is the way of Hmong communal life.

The U.S. Hmong Population

The U.S. Hmong refugee population is increasingly growing despite the decline in family and household sizes. In the 2010 national census, the U.S. Hmong population was listed at nearly 260,000. However, the actual number of Hmong-Americans could be much higher because some Hmong-Americans identified themselves as Laotian Hmong or Laotians, some Hmong-Americans did not take part in the national census, some native Hmong-Americans considered themselves to be normal and ordinary Americans and dropped their ethnic identification, and some naturalized Hmong-Americans and Hmong refugees living in isolated cities might have not been added to the total. These factors may not change the figures substantially, but they may increase the size of the U.S. Hmong population just a bit. Some believe the total number of U.S. Hmong is nearly 300,000, double what it was four decades ago. This best rough estimate comes from the belief that over 130,000 Hmong refugees were brought to the U.S. during the 1980s and 1990s and logically that number would have at least doubled in 40 years. Others use the size of Hmong families to predict the rough total; the average Hmong family has six people. By any measure used for prediction, the U.S. Hmong population is likely to be higher than the census number.

Moreover, the growth of the U.S. Hmong population has been steady because Hmong refugees have benefited from the basic services available to all Americans and safety net and social entitlement programs. Based on the current census number of 260,000 and a population of 186,000 in the 2000 census, the Hmong population in the U.S. has grown at least 40 percent in a 10-year period. In 1990, the national census showed that the U.S. Hmong population was approximately 90,000; the jump to 186,000 was an increase of more than 100 percent.

The Hmong population has grown at different rates in different parts of the country. In some states, the total number of U.S. Hmong has doubled or tripled in size, as shown in Table 12.1. In 2010, California had the largest Hmong population (91,000), followed

Table 12.1. U.S. Hmong Population by Geographic Area, 1990 to 2010

Area	1990	2000	2010	Increase 1990–2010
North and northeast states	1,900	3,700	3,800	100%
South and southwest states	1,200	11,600	24,200	191%
Midwest states	38,700	91,000	126,700	227%
West states	52,400	79,800	105,200	100%
Total U.S.	94,400	186,300	260,000	175%

Note: Numbers are rounded. Information from U.S. Census Bureau, 1990, 2000, 2010 and The State of the Hmong American Community, *by M. E. Pfeifer & B. K. Thao (eds.), 2013, Washington, D.C.: Hmong National Development.*

by Minnesota (66,000) and Wisconsin (49,000). During the 1980s, the size of the Hmong population in these and other states varied because of the big wave of family relocation; from the mid–1990s the number of Hmong in these states remained fairly constant.

In 2010, fifteen U.S. states had sizable U.S. Hmong populations, as indicated in Table 12.2. If the trends continue, the U.S. Hmong population will double its current size in 20 years or sooner. If U.S. Hmong families continue to maintain a household size of six, the total population size could triple in 20 years.

Table 12.3 shows the U.S. Hmong population according to the four geographic regions of the Northeast, South, Midwest, and West. In the 2010 census, the Midwest region had the largest Hmong population (126,000), following by the West (105,000), the South

(24,200), and the Northeast (3,800). At each 10-year increment, the population in each region grew but growth in the northeast region has trailed the other three regions because of Hmong refugees' disinclination to live in an area with such cold weather conditions.

In all regions the Hmong population is concentrated in certain metropolitan areas or counties, some with larger concentrations than others. The cities of Minneapolis, St. Paul, and Bloomington, Minnesota are home to approximately 64,400 Hmong as compared to the metropolitan area of Fresno, California, where nearly 31,700 Hmong live. Other metropolitan areas with sizable Hmong population are Sacramento and Yolo, California (26,900); Milwaukee, Waukesha, West Allis, and Racine, Wisconsin (11,900); Merced, California (7,200); Stockton, California (6,900); Hickory, Morganton, and Lenoir,

Table 12.2. Hmong Population in Selected States, 1990 to 2010

State	2010	2000	1990	Increase 1990–2010
Michigan	5,900	5,900	2,300	157%
Kansas	1,700	1,100	540	219%
Missouri	1,300	26	0	338%
Colorado	3,800	3,300	1,200	220%
Oregon	2,900	2,200	590	391%
Washington	2,400	1,400	850	182%
Alaska	3,500	321	0	NA
Georgia	3,600	1,600	380	839%
Oklahoma	3,300	580	166	1,930%
South Carolina	1,200	570	40	290%
Florida	1,200	163	6	1990%
Arkansas	2,100	33	0	NA
Massachusetts	1,000	1,300	134	706%
Rhode Island	1,000	1,100	1,180	–14%
Pennsylvania	1,000	800	450	123%

Note: Numbers are rounded. Information from U.S. Census Bureau, 1990, 2000, 2010 and The State of the Hmong American Community, by M. E. Pfeifer & B. K. Thao (eds.), 2013, Washington, D.C.: Hmong National Development.

Table 12.3. U.S. Hmong Population Growth by Geographic Region, 1990–2010

Region	1990	2000	2010	Increase 1990–2010
Midwest	38,700	91,000	126,700	227%
West	52,400	79,800	105,200	101%
South	1,200	11,600	24,200	1,805%
Northeast	1,900	3,700	3,800	99%

Note: Numbers are rounded. Information from The State of the Hmong American Community, by M. E. Pfeifer & B. K. Thao (eds.), 2013, Washington, D.C.: Hmong National Development.

North Carolina (5,900); Wausau, Wisconsin (5,900); Chico, California (4,300); Madison, Wisconsin (4,200); Detroit, Warren, and Livonia, Michigan (4,100), Sheboygan, Wisconsin (4,100); Green Bay, Wisconsin (4,100); Appleton, Wisconsin (4,000); and La Crosse, Wisconsin (3,100). Of all 50 states, Vermont had the lowest Hmong population in 2010 (only one person), followed by Delaware (3 people), West Virginia (5 people), Maine (7 people), and Wyoming (8 people). Table 12.4 lists the states with the highest numbers of Hmong residents in alphabetical order. California has the largest number followed by Minnesota and Wisconsin. Some Hmong communities are relatively new and much smaller.

Table 12.4. Hmong Populations in Twelve States, 2010

State	Population	Percent Employed
Arkansas	2,143	68.2
Arizona	229	59.7
California	91,224	49.6
Colorado	3,859	75.2
Georgia	3,623	71.4
Michigan	5,924	54.9
Minnesota	66,181	57.3
North Carolina	10,864	66.9
Oklahoma	3,369	55.8
Oregon	2,920	52.8
Washington	2,404	53.1
Wisconsin	49,240	62.5

Note: Information from The State of the Hmong American Community, *by M. E. Pfeifer & B. K. Thao (eds.), 2013, Washington, D.C.: Hmong National Development.*

It is difficult to predict trends regarding size and locations of Hmong communities. It is possible that small, isolated Hmong communities will spring up in the near future as young Hmong-Americans move away from their large communities to attend school or to search for employment. Older Hmong-Americans entering retirement may move to cities that suit their socioeconomic needs and accommodate their lifestyle change; these may be smaller, less expensive cities or larger metropolises where family relatives are located. Any trend in residency may shape the future of the Hmong-American community

in the U.S. As Hmong-Americans are becoming more Americanized and more native-born Hmong Americans are enculturated, living in a Hmong community may become less important.

Hmong Citizenship and Naturalization

Today, Hmong refugees are becoming naturalized. Prior to coming to the West, every Hmong refugee was a native of a foreign country; most were Laotian citizens and some were Thai citizens. Most Hmong refugees were born in Laos and lived in refugee camps in Thailand, and some Hmong children were born in the refugee camps. From late 1975 to 1980, nearly all Hmong refugees were citizens of a foreign country. Beginning in 1980, U.S. Hmong refugees applied to become U.S. citizens. Each year hundreds of foreign-born U.S. Hmong become naturalized, and at the same time, thousands of Hmong children were born in the U.S.

Today, the U.S. Hmong population consists of foreigners, native-born citizens, and naturalized citizens. As Tables 12.5, 12.6, and 12.7 show, 58 percent of the U.S. Hmong were citizens in 2010. Of these, two thirds were native born and one third were naturalized. National data indicate that the number of U.S. Hmong who are foreigners dropped from 69 percent to 28 percent in a 10-year period. If this trend continues, in 10 more years, 80 percent of U.S. Hmong will be U.S. citizens, both native born and naturalized. Moreover, by 2030, an estimated 95 percent of U.S. Hmong will be U.S. citizens, predominantly native born. As a relatively young refugee group, the U.S. Hmong citizen population is growing faster than expected. This means that the U.S. Hmong population has a lot of young, native-born citizens.

Ages of Hmong Americans

Western Hmong population is still relatively young, as shown in tables 12.8 and 12.9. Hmong refugees started coming to the western nations in late 1975. The Hmong refugees

Table 12.5. Comparison of Numbers of U.S. Hmong Foreigners and Citizens in Selected States

Citizenship Status & Gender	U.S.	Minnesota	Wisconsin	California
Population	256,400	63,400	48,100	95,100
Citizen	149,300	36,200	27,500	55,700
3. Male	51%	53%	50%	51%
4. Female	49%	47%	50%	49%
Noncitizen	107,000	27,100	20,600	39,300
3. Male	50%	48%	50%	51%
4. Female	50%	52%	50%	49%

Note: Numbers are rounded. Information from The State of the Hmong American Community, by M. E. Pfeifer & B. K. Thao (eds.), 2013, Washington, D.C.: Hmong National Development and U.S. Census Bureau, 2006–2010 American Community Survey 3-Year Estimates.

Table 12.6. Comparison of Numbers of U.S. Hmong Foreigners and Naturalized Citizens in Selected States

Citizenship Status	U.S.	Minnesota	Wisconsin	California
Population	63,700	17,400	12,900	22,000
Naturalized				
1. Male	50%	48%	50%	51%
2. Female	50%	52%	50%	49%
Foreign	43,300	9,600	7,600	17,300
1. Male	51%	51%	51%	50%
2. Female	49%	49%	49%	50%

Note: Numbers are rounded. Information from The State of the Hmong American Community, by M. E. Pfeifer & B. K. Thao (eds.), 2013, Washington, D.C.: Hmong National Development and U.S. Census Bureau, 2006–2010 American Community Survey 3-Year Estimates.

Table 12.7. Date of Entry of Hmong to U.S. and Selected States

Date	U.S.	Minnesota	Wisconsin	California
Total population	107,000	27,100	20,600	39,300
2000 and later	19%	21%	18%	18%
1990 to 1999	29%	27%	32%	32%
Before 1990	53%	52%	50%	50%

Note: Numbers are rounded. Information from U.S. Census Bureau, 1990, 2000, 2010 and The State of the Hmong American Community, by M. E. Pfeifer & B. K. Thao (eds.), 2013, Washington, D.C.: Hmong National Development and U.S. Census Bureau, 2006–2010 American Community Survey 3-Year Estimates.

who came to the West between 1975 and 1980 was mostly Laotian natives or foreign-born residents of Laos. The second wave of Hmong refugees was a mixture of Laotian and Thai residents. Most Hmong refugees were young because they came with their families and most Hmong families had children under the age of 18. Only a small portion of Hmong refugees were over the age of 18 at the time of their arrival in the western nations. This older group consisted of Hmong parents and young Hmong adults who came to the West by themselves or accompanying family relatives. In the 1990s, nearly 70 percent of U.S. Hmong Americans were under the age of 18; the median age was 14 (Hmong Issues 2000 Conference). In the 2000s, the portion of the U.S. Hmong population younger than 18 years of age dropped to 56 percent and the median age was 16.

This significant rise in median age can be explained in a few ways. One, a sizable number of Hmong refugee children turned 18 or older after time in the U.S. Two, the working class lifestyle decreased the Hmong fertility rate and household size over the years. Three, more Hmong Americans participated in the national census in 2000 than in 1990. Four, underage marriage among Hmong-American children slowed. And five, Hmong Americans adjusted to the host culture socioeconomically, meaning more Hmong children remained single while attending college to more easily pursue their educational goals and professional careers.

In 2010, the national census data indicated that 43 percent of all Hmong Americans were under the age of 18 and the median age was 17. The continued decline in the portion of Hmong Americans under the age of 18 indicates that Hmong Americans are changing their early marriage practice. Hmong children are delaying the decision to have children while pursuing their education, working, and planning for parenthood. At the same time, current Hmong Americans are having fewer children than their refugee parents.

As Table 12.8 shows, in percent of the population age 18 and older, U.S. Hmong at 57 percent trails the U.S. population (76 percent) and the Asian population (74 percent). However, current age trends strongly suggest that the portion of Hmong Americans younger than 18 is on the decline, and in the next national census Hmong may have numbers closer to those of other ethnic groups. Table 12.9 presents the age distribution of all Hmong Americans in the states with the largest concentrations of Hmong. These figures would be more accurate if more resources were designated for census activities that captured data from all Hmong-American families.

Another way to look at the ages of Hmong Americans is to examine the Hmong children born in the U.S. in various decades, as presented in Table 12.10. The oldest U.S.

Table 12.8. Percentages of Select Populations in Specific Age Groups, 2010

Age Group	U.S. Population	U.S. Asian Population	Hmong in the U.S.	Hmong in Minnesota	Hmong in Wisconsin	Hmong in California
18 and over	76	74	57	55	56	57
21 and over	71	70	48	47	47	48
62 and over	16	11	4	4	3	5
65 and over	13	9	3	3	3	4
Total population	306,700,400	16,700,800	256,400	63,400	48,100	95,100

Note: Numbers are rounded. Information from The State of the Hmong American Community, *by M. E. Pfeifer & B. K. Thao (eds.), 2013, Washington, D.C.: Hmong National Development and U.S. Census Bureau, 2006–2010 American Community Survey 3-Year Estimates.*

Table 12.9. Age Distribution of Hmong in Selected States

Age	All Hmong in the U.S.	Hmong in Minnesota	Hmong in Wisconsin	Hmong in California
Under 5 years	12%	13%	13%	12%
5 to 17	31%	32%	31%	31%
18 to 24	19%	17%	20%	18%
25 to 34	16%	16%	16%	17%
35 to 44	9%	9%	10%	8%
45 to 54	6%	6%	5%	6%
55 to 64	4%	3%	3%	5%
65 to 74	2%	2%	2%	2%
75 and over	1%	1%	.8%	2%
Total population	256,400	63,400	48,100	95,100

Note: Numbers are rounded. Information from U.S. Census Bureau, 1990, 2000, 2010 and The State of the Hmong American Community, *by M. E. Pfeifer & B. K. Thao (eds.), 2013, Washington, D.C.: Hmong National Development and U.S. Census Bureau, 2006–2010 American Community Survey 3-Year Estimates.*

Hmong native-born children are nearly 40 years old and the youngest are infants. This indicates that the majority of U.S. Hmong native-born parents are relatively young. The ages of Hmong native-born parents range from about 18 to 39. The years of birth show that all the native-born Hmong children have or will spend all 13 years of their K–12 educations in the U.S. if they do not drop out.

Table 12.10. Ages, Years in the U.S., and Years in K–12 School of U.S. Native-Born Hmong

Year of birth	Age Range	Year in the U.S.	Year in K–12 School
1975 to 1979	35 to 39 years old	35 to 39 years	13 years
1980 to 1989	25 to 34 years old	25 to 34 years	13 years
1990 to 1999	15 to 24 years old	15 to 24 years	9 to 13 years
2000 to 2009	5 to 14 years old	5 to 14 years	1 to 8 years
2010 to now	0 to 4 years old	0 to 4 years	0 year

Hmong Refugees with Disabilities

Initially, physical disability was a public shame and mental health issues were regarded as social humiliation and biological deficiency. In general, 70 percent of U.S. adult Hmong's disabilities are related to post-traumatic stress disorders (PTSD) in association with some kind of mental and psychological ailments, and the other 30 percent may have to do with medical, physiological, biological, and genetic abnormalities. Some disabilities are mental conditions; however, Hmong refugees have barely begun to learn about mental illnesses and the toll they can take without proper treatment.

Before coming to America, Hmong refugees were in poor health due to chronic malnutrition and lack of medical care. As noted by various volunteer health organizations, anemia, parasitic diseases (plasmodium, giardia lambia, clonorchis sinensis, paragoniumus westernani, and so on), scabies, respiratory conditions (pneumocystis carinii pneumonia-fungal infection, coughing, emphysema, bronchitis, and so on), tuberculosis, hepatitis, and malaria were prevalent among the refugees, including Hmong refugees. A lack of preventive medicine intensi-

fied these conditions. Prior to entering the western nations, every Hmong refugee had to undergo a health screening and several medical examinations in the refugee camps in Thailand. All had to meet medical requirements before being considered for resettlement in the U.S. By the time they resettled in their new homelands, Hmong refugees appeared to be in fairly good general health.

Hmong refugees had been exposed to western medicine prior to the fall of Laos in 1975. However, very few had access to modern medical treatments and medications. Hmong refugees often perceived medical conditions and illnesses in terms of symptomology. Most relied on their traditional practices and herbal medicine for basic medical remedies. Hmong shamanism is one of the common practices. Hmong refugees knew much about natural processes and spiritual balance in treating symptoms and sicknesses but had little knowledge about infections, diseases, birth defects, and pandemic conditions. When western medical doctors told them about these things, Hmong refugees had difficulty believing them.

Hmong refugees retained their traditional beliefs about pregnancy and childbirth. Hmong mothers traditionally adhere to special diets during pregnancy and maternity. During the 30-day reservation—the period following giving birth—the mother has to eat boiled chicken with herbs and newly cooked rice for every meal during the day. She may not consume fatty meat, spicy foods, or vegetables and she can drink only warm sauces, juice, and water to help heal and nourish her body. After giving birth, the mother is not allowed to perform chores such as cleaning the house, washing clothes, or fetching water. A band is wrapped around her waist every day for 30 days to keep her stomach and abdominal area intact. Her feet and head have to be kept warm to prevent development of ailments.

Perhaps because of these traditional practices, most Hmong children are born healthy. In the 1980s, 1990s, and early 2000s, medical personnel in Fresno County, California, considered Hmong babies among the healthiest newborns of all ethnic groups because pregnant Hmong mothers followed Hmong traditions regarding eating and drinking. Traditionally, Hmong mothers do not drink alcohol or smoke cigarettes before, during, or after pregnancy. That cultural tradition has changed somewhat since 1975; Americanized Hmong parents do not always follow Hmong maternal customs.

Today more than before 1975, some Hmong children are born with medical conditions, congenital diseases, and defects such as autism, down syndrome, heart defects, leukemia, diabetes, internal defects, facial abnormalities, Werdnig Hoffman syndrome, and others. Such disabilities are conditions Hmong refugees have to learn to accept because they are not matters of public shame. In some cases, they may be the result of a spiritual curse imposed by the spirits of the deceased and ancestors. Perhaps Hmong experienced these medical conditions prior to coming to the West but had no way of identifying them without doctors who could properly diagnose them.

Hmong expect all babies to be born healthy without any biological or genetic defects. Hmong consider any defect to be a curse, punishment, or unacceptable consequences of some action of theirs. They lack understanding of genetic disorders, heredity, and biological mutation. Thus Hmong view disabilities as a threat rather than a fact of life. A Hmong family that has a child with a genetic disorder such as down syndrome or Werdnig Hoffman syndrome may not understand that if they have more children those children may also inherit the disorder; they may take their chances and have additional children regardless of the likelihood that those children may be born with the disability.

Another cultural misunderstanding has to do with premature birth. Hmong do not believe that premature birth can be caused by environmental, psychological, physiological, and medical factors. To many Hmong, premature birth is caused by spiritual imbalance and a soul wondering off. Many still believe that holy water and shamanistic offerings can prevent miscarriage and premature birth. However, over the years, Hmong have learned that medical illnesses, genetics, and other factors can contribute to such conditions.

After nearly four decades in the U.S., Hmong refugees have learned how to cope with diseases, cancers, infections, and other medical conditions such as diabetes, hypertension, stroke, renal failure, hepatitis, gout, and cardiac dysfunction; but disabilities are more difficult. In general, nearly 8 percent of Hmong refugees who are 64 years old and younger have some kind of disability. This number is low when compared to the 12 percent rate for the general U.S. population of the same age. Despite the low rate of disability for young Hmong Americans, national data show that 51 percent of Hmong refugees who are 65 years and older have some kind of disability as compared to 37 percent of the general U.S. population and 33 percent of the U.S. Asian population of the same age (see Table 12.11). However, Hmong Americans make up a relatively small population, so such a broad comparison may not be meaningful. Comparing a small group to a population that is 10 times its size is not statistically sound.

Table 12.11. U.S. Total, U.S. Asian, and U.S. Hmong Populations with Disability, by Age

Age	U.S.	U.S. Asian	U.S. Hmong
Total	301,500,000 (12%)	16,600,000 (6%)	255,200 (8%)
Under 18	73,900,900 (4%)	4,300,200 (2%)	110,500 (3%)
18 to 64	189,200,900 (10%)	10,800,300 (5%)	136,700 (9%)
65 and over	38,300,900 (37%)	1,400,500 (33%)	7,900 (51%)

Note: Numbers are rounded. Information from The State of the Hmong American Community, *by M. E. Pfeifer & B. K. Thao (eds.), 2013, Washington, D.C.: Hmong National Development and U.S. Census Bureau, 2006–2010 American Community Survey 3-Year Estimates.*

Table 12.12 displays the numbers of U.S. Hmong with disabilities in the three states with the greatest Hmong populations. California has the highest number of Hmong 65 years and older with disability, followed by Minnesota and Wisconsin. This comparison offers some explanation for the difference in socioeconomic status of Hmong in these states and also raises some interesting thoughts about Hmong Americans' access to affordable health care and their ability to afford health insurance for the elderly in these states.

6. Some former soldiers sustained injuries during the Secret War.

7. Many suffered severe malnutrition before, during, and after the Secret War in Laos.

8. Most were true victims of warfare, violence, and turbulence.

9. Most suffered social and political brutality, oppression, and persecution.

10. Many witnessed the death, murder, destruction, and butchering of family members, loved ones, and relatives during and after the war.

Table 12.12. Numbers of U.S. Hmong with Disability in Selected States, by Age

Age	U.S.	Minnesota	Wisconsin	California
Total	255,200 (8%)	63,100 (7%)	48,000 (6%)	94,500 (10%)
Under 18	110,500 (3%)	28,300 (2%)	21,000 (2%)	41,000 (4%)
18 to 64	136,700 (9%)	32,900 (8%)	25,700 (7%)	50,100 (12%)
65 and over	7,900 (51%)	1,800 (58%)	1,200 (30%)	3,400 (60%)

Note: Numbers are rounded. Information from The State of the Hmong American Community, by M. E. Pfeifer & B. K. Thao (eds.), 2013, Washington, D.C.: Hmong National Development and U.S. Census Bureau, 2006–2010 American Community Survey 3-Year Estimates.

The fact that older U.S. Hmong have a greater rate of disability than younger people as well as older people of other groups is understandable when considering that elderly disabled Hmong Americans have suffered traumatic experiences that make them prone to mental ailments:

1. Many are former soldiers who served in the Special Guerrilla Unit during the Secret War in Laos.

2. Most if not all are displaced war refugees who suffer chronic post-traumatic stress disorder, depression, and mental illnesses associated with war.

3. Some are former prisoners of war who were arrested, tortured, humiliated, insulted, and hunted down by enemies.

4. Some are war escapees or survivors who lived in hiding for years and trekked through jungle to escape ethnic cleansing, oppression, and persecution.

5. Many lived for years in refugee camps in Thailand and were displaced by the closure of the camps.

Any one of these experiences could lead to mental disorders, and many of the Hmong refugees who came to the western nations experienced multiple traumatic events. It is clear that Hmong refugees still lack understanding of the difference between medical problems and mental health disorders. The elderly disabled U.S. Hmong are now exhibiting both medical and mental problems that are disabling.

In the U.S., Hmong refugees' reluctance to seek mental health treatment for their disabilities has resulted in domestic disturbance and violence, and even uxoricide (spouse killing) has happened in the Hmong communities. Not all spouse killing cases involving Hmong refugee families are directly linked to mental health problems, but it is fair to say that socio-cultural issues contribute to a state of mind that may develop into a mental health disorder. In other words, prolonged family and social pressures and conflicts may lead to severe anxiety, chronic ailments, and mental incapacitation that can contribute to development of severe and chronic mental health problems. Psychiatric and psychological problems are relatively new to Hmong refugees because they are incompatible with their religious values and spiritual beliefs. Access to healthcare and overcoming resistance to seeking professional assistance will help Hmong refugees deal with their PTSD and other mental health problems.

Hmong Healthcare

Medically, today, Hmong are living in two different worlds, the medical world and the spiritual world. Hmong refugees had no idea about the need for healthcare and health insurance to protect their families and loved ones when they first arrived in the western nations because these life-saving services were not available in their native country. Upon their arrival, nearly all Hmong refugees were automatically eligible for public health coverage provided Medicare and Medicaid programs. Prior to resettling in the West, Hmong refugees were introduced to humanitarian aid medical supplies during the Secret War in Laos, and they had received limited services such as immunizations, first aid applications, over-the-counter medications, and antibiotics. These services were generally scarce and available only to Hmong soldiers and their families in limited locations. Only a few Hmong had been trained as nurses and pharmaceutical assistants who could distribute the medical supplies. Most Hmong lived in remote villages and had little or no access to these services. However, some Christian Hmong families had gained access to western medicine with the help of western missionaries and religious leaders.

In the West, Hmong refugees were entitled to the medical benefits provided by public health agencies to the poor, indigent, and needy. However, Hmong refugees were reluctant to use these healthcare services because they lacked trust, language skills, understanding, and medical knowledge. Most Hmong refugees continued to rely on their traditional healing practices—shamanism, magicians, soul calling, cupping, coin rubbing, herbal medicine, spiritual healing, and religious offerings. Right after arrival, Hmong refugee families submitted to routine medical checks for preventive purposes and to treat immediate medical needs. Local sponsors and social service agencies provided trans-

portation for Hmong refugees, and bilingual medical interpreters were available to assist them. However, language was a big issue in receiving proper medical care because Hmong languages and dialects do not have words for medical terminologies, illnesses, disorders, and conditions. Terms such as post-traumatic stress disorder, delusional episodes, psychosis, stress, and depression could not be directly translated into Hmong. Interpreters used word phrases to describe these conditions.

Moreover, examining different body parts was a super sensitive matter culturally, especially for Hmong women. Allowing doctors and nurses to examine private parts such as the genital area, breasts, thighs, and the anus was uncomfortable. Just asking Hmong refugees to undress and put on a hospital gown was embarrassing and culturally inappropriate. Medically, a language barrier is one thing, but a cultural barrier is another, and because both were present, Hmong refugees avoid routine medical care altogether.

In California, the leading causes of death for Hmong refugees in 2013 were heart diseases (19 percent), cancer (16 percent), stroke (10 percent), and accidents and diabetes (6 percent each). The causes of death with the greatest growth were influenza/pneumonia and hypertension (200 percent growth). Because Hmong refugees had not had diagnoses of hidden illnesses prior to coming to the West, they understood and accepted diagnoses of medical conditions that were visible to the naked eyes but were suspicious of diagnoses of internal problems and illnesses with no visible symptoms. Calling unseen problems "illnesses" is not consistent with Hmong refugees' religious beliefs.

Due to the lack of experience in medical treatment, Hmong refugees at first were reluctant to consent to medical procedures, including drawing blood, taking a biopsy, and making minor incisions. For example, a Hmong mother who is giving birth prefers to have a small tear around her vaginal opening instead of allowing a doctor to cut the opening. However, once doctors explained that an incision heals faster and better than a tearing, Hmong refugees accepted the procedure.

Preventive medical care has become acceptable to most Hmong refugees although some routine preventive procedures are still considered culturally insensitive and inappropriate and unnecessary unless the refugee is sick. Periodic pap smears, routine physical exams, mammograms, and gastroscopic exams are all in the unnecessary category unless the patient has been diagnosed with a condition that warrants such intrusion. Hmong refugees have heard about medical malpractice and medical experimentation in hospitals operated by local, state, and federal governments. Fears of these have driven Hmong refugees further from seeking medical treatments. In 2002, Vang wrote to the editorial board of the *Fresno Bee* newspaper about medical treatment involving Hmong refugees:

"HMONG, DOCTORS NEED TO TEACH AND SHARE IDEAS"

A recent Bee article, "Hmong in Fresno reportedly suffer increased illness" [comparing the health of the Hmong in Fresno to that of Hmong in other countries] provides insights into the misperceptions that hinder the quality of medical care for Hmong. Language is an obstacle, but it is only part of the equation. The willingness to receive medical treatment is another part.

[...]

In the past, Hmong adults resisted seeking medical care unless the condition was life-threatening. Instead, they nursed most medical problems at home. The same attitude persists today.

[...]

Education can help Western doctors understand Hmong culture and Hmong patients accept Western medical treatment.

In the early 1990s, Hmong refugees suffered a medical setback due to the welfare reform law. The work re-quirements for Hmong adults who receive public assistance caused many Hmong to forfeit public health coverage because the requirements included job training that was worthless to Hmong and Hmong refused to participate in the training programs. In the mid–1990s, California's Hmong refugees revolted against the unfair, biased, and discriminatory work requirements that did not help Hmong gain employment. Many Hmong left the state, giving up public health coverage. Some were able to purchase private health insurance, but most were uncovered and remain so today. That means that many Hmong refugees have not had health insurance since the early 1990s. As shown in Table 12.13, 15 percent of U.S. Hmong refugees did not have health insurance in 2010 and 42 percent of U.S. Hmong still depend on public health coverage. Hmong in California appear to have a higher rate of dependency on public health coverage than Hmong in the other two states with the largest Hmong populations. This may help explain why Hmong refugees in other states are doing better socioeconomically than Hmong in California, and perhaps also why California has a lower employment rate for Hmong than Minnesota and Wisconsin. The good news is that nearly half of the U.S. Hmong are now covered by private insurance as compared to the 95 percent dependency on public health coverage in the mid–1970s to the early 1990s.

As illustrated in Table 12.10, 60 percent of Hmong living in Wisconsin are covered by private insurance, followed by 53 percent in Minnesota and 37 percent in California. Despite having coverage, the U.S. Hmong have

Table 12.13. Percentages of Hmong with Health Insurance Coverage in U.S. and Selected States

Type of Coverage	U.S.	Minnesota	Wisconsin	California
Estimated population	255,200	63,100	48,000	94,500
Private	49%	53%	60%	37%
Public	42%	40%	36%	52%
None	15%	12%	13%	16%

Note: Numbers are rounded. Information from The State of the Hmong American Community, *by M. E. Pfeifer & B. K. Thao (eds.), 2013, Washington, D.C.: Hmong National Development and U.S. Census Bureau, 2006–2010 American Community Survey 3-Year Estimates.*

to understand that having basic health insurance does not necessarily mean they have access to quality medical care and treatment or to all the treatments and procedures they might need. Like other citizens, Hmong Americans need to learn *what* their health insurance plans cover, *how* the coverage works, and what they can expect from the plans in order to understand the full benefits of both private and public health insurance coverage. Otherwise, Hmong will continue to face health disparities in the U.S.

Hmong Employment and Occupations

There are more Hmong professionals today than twenty years ago. When Hmong refugees first arrived in the western world, most able and employable Hmong adults were placed in jobs as blue-collar workers. Only a few Hmong refugees had any education from Laos and could therefore work in white-collar jobs. The U.S. resettlement policy that dispersed Hmong refugee families across the 50 states anticipated that Hmong adults would find temporary employment right away and not need to draw public assistance benefits. So shortly after arrival, Hmong went to work in factories as assembly line workers and/or production workers because they did not have the language skills and educational background to do otherwise. Hmong who were elderly and unemployable applied for public assistance because it was their only means of survival. Hmong refugees who had some English skills were able to get white-collar jobs as medical interpreters, office translators, teachers' assistants, social service workers, cultural brokers, and community outreach workers. For the first 10 years after arrival, most Hmong refugee families depended on some kind of public assistance while Hmong parents worked outside the home and looked for employment. But even Hmong parents who were employed full time did not have sufficient incomes to support their large families. Hmong refugees realized that the safety net benefits helped them to survive but their socioeconomic situations

and family lifestyles would not improve if they continued to depend on public assistance. By the early 1980s, Hmong refugees made some changes to seek better socioeconomic opportunities.

First, Hmong refugees stressed the importance of public education and invested more in their children's educations. Hmong parents told their children often to study hard, get a college degree, and find better jobs because minimum-wage jobs would not pay enough to cover their monthly bills. They also told their children that public assistance benefits were temporary, not for life.

Second, Hmong refugees relocated their families to areas with better employment opportunities and safety net benefits for their families, especially self-employment. In the early 1980s, Hmong refugees moved to California's Central San Joaquin Valley cities— Merced, Fresno, Madera, Atwater, and Visalia—in search of farming opportunities because of the valley's weather conditions and large agricultural community.

Third, Hmong refugees moved from small cities to big cities to find blue-collar jobs with bigger, better paying companies. Many found better employment opportunities in St. Paul, Minnesota; Milwaukee and Madison, Wisconsin; Sacramento, Long Beach, and Santa Ana, California; and Denver, Colorado.

Fourth, Hmong refugees in California, Minnesota, and Wisconsin explored new venues for farming, such as small family farming businesses. This kind of independent lifestyle attracted other Hmong refugee families, and more Hmong refugees moved to places where they found self-employment opportunities. A large number of Hmong refugee families became small farmers in Fresno, California and elsewhere in the U.S.

And fifth, a small number of Hmong refugees rose from being blue-collar workers to become self-employed entrepreneurs. While receiving what amounted to a pittance in public assistance benefits, some Hmong adults, for example, became flea market merchants, selling clothing, merchandise imported from overseas, and other goods. Such entrepreneurship enabled many Hmong refugees to become successful business owners.

By the late 1980s, the number of white-collar Hmong refugees increased for a number of reasons:

1. Hmong refugee communities across the nation founded community-based organizations that helped Hmong refugees deal with critical needs.

2. Younger Hmong refugee adults were able to get permanent employment with local, state, and federal government agencies.

3. The first wave of Hmong bilingual assistants and bilingual teachers was found to be critical in public schools.

4. Local law enforcement agencies started recruiting Hmong refugees to become community liaison officers and patrol officers.

5. A few Hmong refugees were hired as academic counselors because the number of Hmong refugee students was booming in K–12 schools, community colleges, and universities.

By the early 1990s, the numbers of Hmong refugees in blue-collar jobs and in white-collar jobs were about the same. However, Hmong refugees still faced a high unemployment rate, and a large portion of Hmong refugees were still on the public assistance rolls. In addition, the welfare reform law had tremendous impact on Hmong refugee families because many could not find employment within the time limit allotted and were therefore denied assistance. Sadly, many unemployed Hmong adults became indigent because they were no longer eligible to receive public benefits. By this time, Hmong refugee children who graduated from high schools and colleges were able to find white-collar jobs in the public and private sectors. In Fresno, California, a large number of Hmong refugees were employed by the county Department of Social Services, the Fresno Unified School District, agencies of the city of Fresno, and private companies.

In the mid–1990s, many Hmong refugees across the U.S. moved to the Midwest to explore chicken farm enterprises. Some eventually became chicken farm owners and some found other employment. Hmong chicken farming had a number of short successes, but also a number of pitfalls:

1. Most Hmong refugees who ventured into the business had little or no background knowledge about such a demanding venture.

2. Misunderstandings between landowners, chicken suppliers, and buyers caused some irregularities that dismayed Hmong refugees.

3. Hmong refugees not only lacked basic knowledge of the business operations but also had little or no education about the costs involved and the requirements for beginning a chicken farm.

4. The lifestyle of chicken farming families, detached from a community, was detrimental to Hmong refugee children, who needed good educations.

5. Most Hmong refugees who were interested in chicken farm enterprises were uneducated Hmong parents who were in their 50s or older.

Chicken farming was a lucrative business for those Hmong refugees who could tolerate the long hours of work, keep up with the burdensome tasks, and enjoy the rather solitary lifestyle. As of today, a few Hmong chicken farms are quite successful. Every business has challenges, advantages, and disadvantages.

From the mid–1990s to the present time, employment among U.S. Hmong refugees changed drastically because the educational attainment of Hmong refugees increased substantially. Hmong have made educational gains in a variety of fields, and they have found employment in a wide range of occupations. Today, Hmong refugee are university professors, college instructors, K–12 teachers, lawyers, judges, peace officers, business owners, elected officials, school counselors, school principals, academic advisors, therapists, dentists, medical doctors, psychiatrists, psychologists, chiropractors, optometrists, and in many other professions. In four decades in the U.S., Hmong refugees have made remarkable progress, elevating their socioeconomic status. If the current trends of educational attainment continue, the number of

Hmong refugees in professional occupations will double in 20 years.

However, the unemployment rate among Hmong refugees is still high. Table 12.14 presents the 2010 employment data for U.S. Hmong refugees in selected states and compares the number employed with the number in the civilian labor force, that is, the number over age 16 who are employed and unemployed. Table 12.15 gives the breakdown of U.S. Hmong refugees' employment by occupation and specialization, and Table 12.16 shows employment of U.S. Hmong refugees in occupational categories by gender. As Table 12.13 illustrates, Hmong refugee women are climbing the career ladder as

quickly as most Hmong men; in some fields, such as sales and office and K–12 teaching,

Table 12.14. U.S. Hmong Employed and in Civilian Labor Force, 2010

State	Total Hmong Population	Employed	In Civilian Labor Force
Arkansas	2,143	68	74
Arkansas	229	60	67
California	91,224	50	58
Colorado	3,859	75	78
Georgia	3,623	71	79
Michigan	5,924	55	66
Minnesota	66,181	57	65
North Carolina	10,864	67	74
Oklahoma	3,369	56	64
Oregon	2,920	53	57
Washington	2,404	53	60
Wisconsin	49,240	63	70

Note: Numbers are rounded. Information from The State of the Hmong American Community, *by M. E. Pfeifer & B. K. Thao (eds.), 2013, Washington, D.C.: Hmong National Development.*

Table 12.15. Distribution of U.S. Hmong in Selected Occupations/Specializations, 2010

Occupation/Specialization	Percent Employed
Public administration	3
Other services	4
Arts, entertainment, recreation, accommodation, food services	12
Educational services, healthcare, social assistance	19
Professional managers, science, management, administration, waste management, services	6
Finance, insurance, real estate, rental, leasing	4
Information	2
Transportation, warehousing, utilities	4
Retail trade	13
Wholesale trade	2
Manufacturing	29
Construction	1
Agriculture, forestry, fishing, hunting, mining	2

Note: Numbers are rounded. Information from The State of the Hmong American Community, *by M. E. Pfeifer & B. K. Thao (eds.), 2013, Washington, D.C.: Hmong National Development.*

Table 12.16. Distribution of U.S. Hmong in Selected Occupational Categories, by Gender

Occupational Category	Males	Females
Production, transportation, and material moving	38%	22%
Natural resources, construction, and maintenance	7%	2%
Sales and office	20%	32%
Service	16%	23%
Management, business, science, and arts	19%	21%

Note: Numbers are rounded. Information from The State of the Hmong American Community, *by M. E. Pfeifer & B. K. Thao (eds.), 2013, Washington, D.C.: Hmong National Development.*

Hmong refugee women have surpassed Hmong refugee men.

No data are available on the employment of U.S. Hmong refugees in each state. Hmong refugees living in different states choose occupations or specializations available in their places of residence. Even if Hmong refugees living in different states had the same job, the pay for that job may be different in the different states. Overall, the employment and occupations of Hmong refugees are impressive.

Hmong Family Income

Financially, Hmong are better off today than twenty years ago. Although white-collar employment among Hmong refugees has risen over the last two decades, there is still a disparity throughout the 50 states in Hmong refugees' household income, family income, and per capita income. The income differences are due to differences in employment opportunities and occupations available in the different geographic locations. Hmong in the three states with the largest Hmong refugee populations do not have the highest household or family incomes. In California, the median household income for Hmong refugees in 2010 was $42,000 and the median family income was $40,900. These figures lag behind those for Minnesota, where the median household income was $48,700 and the median family income was $46,700, and Wisconsin, with a median household income of $48,000 and a median family income of 50,500. As Table 12.17 illustrates, of the dozen states, Hmong refugees in Colorado had the highest median household income ($65,100) and median family income ($73,300), followed by the Hmong refugees in Georgia ($54,000 and $58,600) and Arkansas ($55,200 and $56,700). The lowest incomes were in Alaska, Oklahoma, and Washington.

Comparison of per capita income of Hmong refugees in these states shows that Hmong refugees living in Georgia had the highest ($16,000), followed by Hmong refugees living in Oregon ($15,600) and Colorado ($15,200). Hmong refugees living in Alaska had the lowest per capita income ($5,400), followed by those in Oklahoma ($8,200) and Washington ($8,700). Hmong refugees' household, family, and per capita incomes are far better than they were the late 1970s and the early 1990s; Hmong refugees have made significant progress in just 40 years in the new homeland.

Vang (2005) described some of that progress as he praised the Hmong people in the Central San Joaquin Valley of California:

"HMONG DESERVE PRAISE FOR THEIR QUICK PROGRESS"

On March 11, the *Bee* reported that Hmong Americans are among the poorest

Table 12.17. Hmong Median Household, Family, and Per Capita Incomes in Selected States, 2010

State	Median Household Income	Median Family Income	Per Capita Income
Alaska	$23,700	$23,100	$5,400
Arkansas	$55,200	$56,700	$13,000
California	$41,500	$40,900	$9,800
Colorado	$65,100	$73,300	$15,200
Georgia	$54,000	$58,600	$16,000
Michigan	$47,500	$47,500	$11,600
Minnesota	$48,700	$46,700	$11,200
North Carolina	$45,500	$44,500	$10,800
Oklahoma	$39,000	$52,600	$8,200
Oregon	$52,700	$54,200	$15,600
Washington	$40,300	$33,700	$8,700
Wisconsin	$48,000	$50,500	$11,400

Note: Numbers are rounded. Information from The State of the Hmong American Community, *by M. E. Pfeifer & B. K. Thao (eds.), 2013, Washington, D.C.: Hmong National Development.*

people in California and perhaps in the world. This is no surprise to the many who know and work in the Hmong community.

[...]

The report focuses on a very small segment of the entire community. The Hmong community has progressed financially and professionally. Many Hmong have moved from one-bedroom apartments to five-bedroom homes, from ethnic ghettos to affluent neighborhoods. They have gone from welfare recipients to small farming or business operators. These transitions are remarkable and should not be overlooked.

Hmong small-business entrepreneurs are flourishing in Fresno and elsewhere. Hmong children are graduating from colleges and universities and entering professions. The Hmong community is rising in the political arena as a significant voting bloc, and Hmong people are emerging as a sizable minority group in metropolitan economics. A good example of progress is the Hmong National Development 10th Annual Conference in Fresno next month.

Furthermore, the individual incomes of Hmong refugees have increased substantially over the last 10 years, and the income gap between Hmong males and Hmong females is narrowing. In some cases, Hmong women are earning more than Hmong men. In some Hmong refugee families, the wives are the primary wage earners because they have educations and professional careers. Nationally, the annual median earning of an average Hmong male is approximately $31,000 as compared to $28,000 for Hmong females. Based on current socioeconomic trends, the increased number of employed Hmong females has helped Hmong refugee families financially and economically; however, a segment of Hmong refugees is still living in poverty because of low education, low-paying jobs, and the high cost of living.

Hmong Refugees Living in Poverty

Socially, most Hmong refugees in America do not feel they are socioeconomically poor, but they may have difficulty paying their monthly bills. Most would not call their current living situation poverty because they are eligible to receive public assistance. According to Hmong refugees' values, living in poverty means having no car for transportation, no food to eat, no place to sleep, and no money to pay bills. To Hmong, poverty means going hungry every day because they cannot afford to buy food. Most Hmong refugees have at least the minimum necessities of life; those who receive public assistance feel it is at least somewhat adequate. Vang (2005) contrasted what most Americans consider poverty—ghettos, substandard housing, overcrowding—with how Hmong define poverty: absence of extended family, loss of cultural traditions, life without community.

By American standards, 25 percent of Hmong refugees live below the federal poverty line. Most poor Hmong refugee households are female-headed with children under the age of five. Some two-parent households also have insufficient income to rise above the poverty line because the two parents do not earn enough to support the whole family, and sometimes because the families are large with several children. In 2010, 31 percent of Hmong refugees in California were living in poverty, 26 percent in Minnesota, and 19 percent in Wisconsin. Of all the states listed in Table 12.18, Alaska had the highest portion of Hmong refugees living in poverty (59 percent), followed by Oklahoma (42 percent) and Washington (34 percent). The three states with the lowest portion of Hmong refugees living in poverty were Colorado (2 percent), Georgia (5 percent), and Michigan (16 percent). In general, large Hmong communities appear to have a higher percentage of their populations living in poverty; however, Alaska has a small Hmong community with the highest percentage of poverty because of the lack of employment opportunities, its remote geographic location, and the high public assistance and safety net benefits it provides.

Hmong Home Ownership

Socioeconomically, family poverty levels determine whether Hmong refugees can af-

Table 12.18. Percentages of Hmong Refugees Living in Poverty in Selected States, 2010

State	Total Families	Families with Children Under 18 Years of Age
Colorado	2%	3%
Georgia	5%	15%
Michigan	16%	18%
North Carolina	20%	22%
Wisconsin	20%	21%
Arkansas	21%	31%
Oregon	22%	20%
Minnesota	26%	35%
California	31%	42%
Washington	34%	50%
Oklahoma	42%	59%
Alaska	59%	52%

Note: Numbers are rounded. Information from The State of the Hmong American Community, *by M. E. Pfeifer & B. K. Thao (eds.), 2013, Washington, D.C.: Hmong National Development.*

ford to rent, lease, or buy their homes. Most Hmong refugees did not buy homes until the 1990s. Before then, most Hmong refugees did not have good jobs that paid enough for them to qualify for mortgage loans. By the early 1990s the 1.5 generation Hmong children had become primary wage earners in their families; they held good paying jobs and could qualify for loans. They or their parents had saved enough capital to use as down payment for purchasing homes. Prior to the 1990s, most Hmong refugees were tenants in apartment complexes. Some had applied for and qualified for low-income housing assistance. Others rented houses and shared them with extended family members.

Hmong home ownership increased substantially during the 1990s and 2000s. Many Hmong refugee families bought their first homes in those decades because rents skyrocketed, they wanted to move from crime-ridden areas to good neighborhoods, they wanted to live where their children had better schools that would prepare them for college, and working Hmong families wanted the tax advantages of owning a home. Also, in the Fresno area, the number of Hmong small farmers grew significantly and many Hmong farmers bought real estate as an investment. Before the meltdown of the housing mar-

ket in 2008, a significant number of Hmong refugees lived in owner-occupied housing units. The housing crisis impacted Hmong refugee home ownership negatively and immensely. For instance, in the City of Merced, 70 percent of Hmong refugees who bought homes before 2008 lost their homes during the meltdown, and nearly 60 percent of all houses in Merced were repossessed by banks and federal agencies. Similarly, 40 percent of Hmong refugees living in Fresno County lost their homes at the same time.

After the losses during the meltdown, home ownership of Hmong refugees is on the rise in different parts of the country. Over the last 10 years, the numbers of Hmong owner-occupied housing units have increased in Arizona, Georgia, Michigan, North Carolina, and Oklahoma. As illustrated in Table 12.19, approximately 55 percent of Hmong refugees living in Wisconsin owned their homes or lived in owner-occupied housing units in 2010, followed by Minnesota with 49 percent and California with 33 percent. The five states with the highest percentage of Hmong home ownership or housing tenure were Arkansas (81 percent), Michigan (76 percent), Georgia (71 percent), Oklahoma (66 percent), and North Carolina (64 percent). The three states with the lowest percentage of Hmong home ownership were Washington (38 percent), California (33 percent), and Oregon (32 percent). One of the reasons for the low numbers in these three states may be that many Hmong refugees there lost their homes during the meltdown. Also, regulations disqualified many Hmong refugee home owners who lacked sufficient family income during the housing crisis from refinancing to keep their homes.

Most Hmong refugees took two decades to earn a good family income, establish a line of credit, and accumulate enough financial resources to purchase their first homes. Fam-

Table 12.19. Hmong Refugee Home Ownership in Selected States, 2010

State	Hmong Owning Homes	Hmong Families Living in Poverty
Arkansas	81%	21%
Michigan	76%	16%
Georgia	71%	5%
Oklahoma	66%	42%
North Carolina	64%	20%
Wisconsin	55%	20%
Colorado	52%	2%
Minnesota	49%	26%
Alaska	45%	59%
Washington	38%	34%
California	33%	31%
Oregon	32%	22%

Note: Numbers are rounded. Information from The State of the Hmong American Community, by M. E. Pfeifer & B. K. Thao (eds.), 2013, Washington, D.C.: Hmong National Development.

ily income is the primary qualifier for mortgage loans, and job security and financial resources are based on employment history and family income status. Family structure also plays a role in Hmong home ownership; Hmong in two-parent households are more likely to be able to afford to purchase homes than Hmong in single-parent households.

Hmong Household and Marital Status

Culturally, Hmong households are bound together on solid foundations with firm marital and matrimonial beliefs. Hmong marriage is a trinity: the bride and the groom are one part, the in-laws (both the families of the bride and the families of the groom) are a part, and family clan leaders and relatives from both sides are another part. The civil union between a man and a woman forms the foundation of a household. Traditionally, a Hmong household consists of a father, a mother, and their child or children. A household is the foundation of a family unit in which all family members co-habitate and co-depend for survival, tranquility, love, sharing, celebration, joy, health, and prosperity. Maintaining the traditional marriage is extremely important in the Hmong world.

However, as Table 12.20 indicates, the

characteristics of Hmong refugee households have changed gradually since 1975. The significant increase in the number of female-led households is not only a result of divorce but also of other events such as the death of a spouse, domestic disputes and violence, Hmong-American feminism and an increase in the number of unmarried single mothers, the illegal practice of bigamy and polygamy, and the incarceration of Hmong males as a result of substance abuse and criminal activities.

Table 12.20. Characteristics of Hmong Refugee Households in 2000 and 2008–2010

Characteristic	2000	2008–2010
Total Number	29,725	46,986
Family	93%	90%
Married couple	75%	62%
Female head without spouse	12%	15%
Non-family	7%	10%
Male head	4%	6%
Male living alone	2%	3%
Female head	3%	4%
Female living alone	2%	2%
Household size	6 people	5 people
Family size	7 people	6 people

Note: Numbers are rounded. Information from The State of the Hmong American Community, by M. E. Pfeifer & B. K. Thao (eds.), 2013, Washington, D.C.: Hmong National Development and U.S. Census Bureau, 2006–2010 American Community Survey 3-Year Estimates.

Under a patriarchal hierarchical structure, Hmong men own and protect their households. Hmong fathers make decisions for their families and family members. Hmong mothers support and affirm the decisions. A family root begins with the father who owns the family name. However, the root cannot germinate without the wife, who provides critical nurturing for the root and its offspring. Hmong people expect a marriage to last forever regardless of ups and downs. Typically, Hmong mothers have little or nothing to say about their marital satisfaction or dissatisfaction publicly. In the old days, dissolution of a marriage was nearly impossible for Hmong women. Hmong elders and leaders strongly advocated for the preservation of marriages for the sake of Hmong children, who would face hardship in life as the result of marital divorce. However, divorces have been taking place in Hmong communities ever since Hmong refugees arrived in the western world, especially in the U.S.

Hmong refugees are now living in a world in which the law provides equal protection for all people, regardless of gender or socioeconomic status. Whether all men and women are created equal or not, Hmong refugees have learned that what is culturally right may not be legal and what is legal may not be culturally acceptable in the land that fosters egalitarian principles and provides protection for fundamental human rights. After four decades in the U.S., Hmong refugees still have strong households and most maintain their marital commitments.

However, the divorce rate among Hmong refugees, shown in Tables 12.21 and 12.22, has risen in the last 20 years, although the rate is still quite low compared to other ethnic groups with similar cultural backgrounds. The divorce rate for Hmong refugees in the U.S. is 3 percent, lower than the rates for the general U.S. population (11 percent) and for U.S. Asians (5 percent). Of the three states with the largest Hmong populations, Minnesota has the highest divorce rate (4.3 percent), followed by Wisconsin (3 percent) and California (2.8 percent). The portion of the Hmong population widowed is almost the same in all three states. For the percent separated, Minnesota and Wisconsin led California by nearly two points, and all states have similar proportions of married people.

The number of Hmong interracial marriages has increased significantly over the last 10 years, as illustrated in Table 12.23. Today, some Hmong families have mixtures of two or more family value systems, and Hmong children are not only changing as a result, but they too are bringing new sets of values into their families. Some Hmong refugees are married to people of other ethnicities and their children are partly White, Black, Mexican, Chinese, Korean, Vietnamese, Laotian, Cambodian, Hawaiian, and Pacific Islander. The trend toward interracial marriages appears to be growing as more second- and

Table 12.21. Marital Status of Hmong 15 Years and Older in Selected States, 2010

State	Total Population 15 Years and Older	Never Married (%)	Married (%)	Divorced (%)	Separated (%)	Widowed (%)
California	62,120	49.4	43.2	2.8	0.9	3.7
Minnesota	40,486	49.6	40.2	4.3	2.3	3.6
Wisconsin	30,933	45.1	46.9	3.0	2.1	3.0

Note: Numbers are rounded. Information from The State of the Hmong American Community, by M. E. Pfeifer & B. K. Thao (eds.), 2013, Washington, D.C.: Hmong National Development and U.S. Census Bureau, 2006–2010 American Community Survey 3-Year Estimates.

Table 12.22. Marital Status of Hmong 15 Years and Older in Selected States by Gender, 2010

Gender	Never Married	Married	Divorced	Separated	Widowed
Male (83,249)	52%	44%	2%	1%	1%
Female (83,657)	44%	45%	4%	2%	6%

Note: Numbers are rounded. Information from The State of the Hmong American Community, by M. E. Pfeifer & B. K. Thao (eds.), 2013, Washington, D.C.: Hmong National Development and U.S. Census Bureau, 2006–2010 American Community Survey 3-Year Estimates.

third-generation Hmong children graduate from high schools and attend colleges.

Table 12.23. Numbers of Hmong in Fresno County Married to People of Selected Races, by Gender

Race/Nationality	Males	Females
White	3	7
Hispanic	2	4
French	1	2
Canadian	0	1
Pacific Islanders or Samoa	0	3
Chinese	3	3
Hmong Chinese	4	0
Vietnamese	2	3
East Indian or Hindi	0	2
Black	0	3
Laotian	3	3
Thai	1	3
Cambodian	0	4

Note: Data compiled by Christopher Vang from 2000 to 2013.

Hmong refugees who are married to people outside their own race appear to be self-sufficient and well educated. Interracial marriage is no longer considered taboo by some Hmong refugees. This means that the more Americanized Hmong children become, the more interracial marriages will take place in the Hmong community.

The state of the Hmong community continues to evolve over time as Hmong people continue to undergo sociopolitical changes throughout the socialization process. Meanwhile, the overall progress and successes of Hmong Americans are substantive and remarkable.

Hmong Social Media

Prior to coming to the West, Hmong had very little access to social media, such as newspaper, movie, radio, television, computer, telephone, and cell phone. Since 1975, Hmong life has been surrounded by mainstream social media on a daily basis; however, Hmong refugees still have limited access to Hmong social media, especially Hmong radio and television programs in Hmong languages. Hmong media infrastructure is still at its early stage of development.

In the late 1980s to the mid–1990s, Hmong community was relatively new and still very small. Hmong social media, the means of communication, was not a demand until the early 1990s. Hmong refugees wanted to have Hmong social media, such as newspaper, magazine, radio, and television; however, Hmong could not afford the financial burden to operate mass media communications. To get started, Hmong private individuals tried to rent and/or lease some airtime from privately owned radio and television stations to broadcast basic local programs. Such trials and efforts were short lived because of the lack of strong financial supporters. Hmong newspaper also emerged but went away because most Hmong would prefer listening to radio and watching television over reading the newspaper. It is still true today that Hmong would rather listen and talk than read.

From the mid–1990s to the mid–2000s, Hmong community grew steadily, but Hmong businesses flourished slowly. The desire for Hmong social media was somewhat high. Hmong social media was only available in some large Hmong communities, such Fresno, CA; Sacramento, CA; St. Paul, MN; and Milwaukee, WI. Hmong individuals leased some airtime to broadcast basic programs for the Hmong community. Leasing airtime required big money. Hmong media executives struggled financially to pay the monthly bills. Financial hardship and constraint stalled the growth of Hmong social media. In Fresno, after years of leasing airtime, three Hmong businessmen launched a joint venture to lease a privately owned radio station to broadcast Hmong programs for the Hmong community; however, their plan faced serious financial hardship right from the start because of the lack of business sponsors. As of now, Hmong in Fresno have access to an evening Hmong radio program operated by a private radio station. Luckily, in Fresno, there is a Hmong newspaper, *The Hmong Tribune.*

Then from the mid–2000s to the late 2010, Hmong social media grew nationally, so did Hmong people and their businesses. Hmong were desperate for not having Hmong social media in their languages. Some Hmong individuals went into media businesses. Hmong music and movie industries also flourished in the U.S. They introduced Hmong people to the cable boxes and special satellite dish networks. During this time, Hmong had limited access to different Hmong radio and television programs telecasted from different Hmong communities in the U.S. Also, Hmong had access to internet services. Large Hmong communities owned and operated syndicated Hmong radio and televisions stations on a weekly basis; however, financial constraint was always the number one challenge because the market was very limited. A national Hmong social media group launched a worldwide Hmong television enterprise in early 2011 but went bankrupt after just only a few months in business. The group lacked capital and could not generate enough revenues to pay the monthly bills. At present, most Hmong social media, especially radio and television, are locally owned and operated by Hmong entrepreuners who lease the airtime from private owners. Hmong monthly and weekly newspapers are now available online, and there is no known Hmong daily newspaper to date.

Since early 2011 to the present time, Hmong social media has improved and Hmong have access to Hmong radio and television programs in Hmong languages worldwide, but the means of communication is still limited. Most depend on the internet services and/or the World Wide Web, such as YouTube, Facebook, Twitter, and Google for their immediate social media needs. Large Hmong communities are now owned and operated more local Hmong television stations than radio programs. Hmong are progressively moving from radio and newspaper to television and cyberspace communications. In Fresno, there are three Hmong television stations and only one evening Hmong radio program. Similarly, Hmong social media is growing in other large Hmong communities in the U.S. The current trend of Hmong social media appears to be encouraging, and Hmong still have a lot to improve.

As a community, Hmong definitely need to have a means of communication to keep their people informed of what is happening at home and abroad. Hmong and their community also need to have a team of quality-bilingual-professional Hmong journalists who can devote their professional careers to Hmong media. Meanwhile, most Hmong media executives and personalities have little or no academic background in journalism. More importantly, Hmong media infrastructure needs to be expanded from local to national and beyond. To achieve that goal, Hmong would need to have capital and strong financial support from Hmong and non–Hmong businesses, people, and communities; otherwise, without financial backbone, current Hmong social media enterprises will face difficult plight and uncertain future.

Summing Up

This chapter covered a broad range of topical issues related to the state of the Hmong community. The topics have direct impact on the lives of Hmong refugees. In the old days, Hmong community social structure was different from what it is today. Hmong communities were organized according to a five-level structure. The first level was the Hmong community made up of all families of all clans. The second level was the clan systems that separated families by their last names. The third level was the family sub-clan systems that identified families with the same ancestry or genealogical lineage. The fourth level was the family systems that included extended and nuclear families. The fifth level consisted of the individual families within the family systems. This social structure appears complex, but Hmong knew how to work things out with one another through mutual respect and reciprocity.

In the western nations, especially in the U.S., the Hmong community social structure is still based heavily on the patriarchal hierarchy of male dominance. However, Hmong communities in different metropolitan areas are different. Sociopolitical polarization of the old and the young Hmong refugees has caused cultural rifts in Hmong leadership and resulted in two social structures in the

Hmong community. The old system is run by former military officials and clan leaders who organize communities according to Hmong culture and traditions whereas the young system is dominated by Hmong refugees who grew up in the U.S. The dual system of leadership has not been effective in helping Hmong refugees advance socially and politically in the mainstream arena, but it has been part of Hmong social life for a long time. The death of Major General Vang Pao left the door wide open for reform and restructuring, but Hmong refugees have not done anything to improve the Hmong community social structure.

Hmong refugees depend on the Hmong community for socioeconomic opportunities and prosperity. The flourishing of Hmong businesses helps redistribute wealth within the Hmong communities and in the larger community, producing economic opportunities. Large Hmong communities appear to have more social and cultural conflicts than small Hmong communities. For instance, ongoing public bickering in regard to the multiple celebrations of Hmong New Year has somewhat tarnished Hmong's public image and damaged their cultural identity and dignity.

Hmong refugees have made remarkable progress in many areas of life but still have deficiencies in other areas. Hmong refugees have participated in civic affairs and many Hmong refugees have been elected to public office at different levels of government. Hmong refugees have remarkable educational attainment in just four decades. Tens of thousands of Hmong refugees have earned bachelor's degrees, several thousands have obtained master's degrees, and a hundred have earned doctoral degrees in various academic disciplines and vocational specializations. Hmong home ownership has increased significantly since the mid–1990s, and in some states, the unemployment rate for Hmong refugees is as low as 5 percent. Best of all, Hmong refugees are emerging as educated, competent, successful professionals.

Hmong refugees still have high unemployment rates in some states and many Hmong families are still living in poverty based on federal standards. Many Hmong parents still do not have access to adequate healthcare. Hmong children represent the second largest group of ELL and LEP students in some states, notably California, Minnesota, and Wisconsin. In addition, Hmong refugees are living in a state of apostasy after the death of Major General Vang Pao. As of now, Hmong refugees lack a national symbol of leadership. National leadership is an urgent need for continued progress. Hmong refugees should seek and exploit any viable opportunities to restore Hmong leadership for the greater good of the people.

• THIRTEEN •

Hmong Leaders and Leadership

Txhawb liab nce ntoo ces liab tsis tom...
Tabsi txhawb dev nce ntoo ces dev yuav tom...
Kev sib txeeb tswv cheej fwb chim yog kev sib cov nyom...
A Hmong proverb of leadership

Introduction

Hmong culture and traditions can be traced back 6,000 years, and the history of Hmong civilization has been recorded from as early as 3,000 BC. But the history of Hmong leaders had been lost for thousands of years prior to the mid–1800s. Hmong have sketchy accounts of their leaders from the ancient world and they kept little or no record of Hmong kings or royal families. Hmong remember their history only through the recitation of oral traditions in myths, folktales, proverbs, legends, and parables. Hmong oral history is rich with stories from the ancient world, but the stories are subject to different accounts, interpretations, and meanings based on creative, imagined, and speculative narratives of the past.

Hmong folktales reveal that Hmong once lived in ancient China, had their own kingdom, and farmed fertile land. Hmong kings fought the imperial Chinese dictators who wanted to conquer the Hmong and confiscate their fertile land. Wars raged for thousands of years before the Hmong lost their land to the Ma people (*Mab*) and the Chinese (*Suav Liab*) and became subjected to political oppression and persecution. Many Hmong clans still practice "*The Rise of the Army to Fight the War*" rite (*tsa rog* in Hmong) during death rituals; it speaks of fending off an in-vasion of Chinese soldiers. In the verses of chant used for the annual Hmong Totem Pole Celebration, Hmong still sing of the bloody wars between the Hmong and the Chinese, Chinese encroachment onto Hmong land, the loss of the Hmong kingdom, and the rebellions attempting to retake Hmong territory from the Chinese. This chapter takes a journey back in time to revisit the history of Hmong leaders from the ancient world to the present day. It examines cultural factors in association with the complexity and intricacy of the roles of contemporary Hmong leaders and discusses the prospect of finding new pathfinders and cultural leaders after the death of Major General Vang Pao.

Hmong Leaders in China

According to Hmong oral history, a long, long time ago, the Hmong had kings and royal families and lived independently in their own kingdoms, enjoying peace and freedom. Hmong refer to a king, or leader, as *huab tais or vaj ntswv*. The word *huab tais* or *fuab tais* can be translated in different ways, but it literally means "the highest position" or "place above all people." The word *vaj ntswv* has a similar meaning except vaj ntswv has additional connotations of protection, oversight, and greatest in power. In Hmong, *vaj* means king, leader, ruler, protector, or controller of a land, state, or country. Similarly, the Chinese word *wang* (王, *Wáng*) means king, leader, ruler, protector, or guardian of the land, state, or country. The spellings of *vaj* and *wang* are different but the *v* and *w* phonemes are linguistically compatible because the last consonants or tone markers (*j* and *g*) are silent, so there is no inflection in these words. Interestingly, both Hmong and Chinese use the last names *Vang* and *Wang*, and coincidentally, they sound exactly the same. Hmong also use the phrase *vaj tim huab tais ntuj*, meaning the lord of the sky, protector in the highest place, or almighty in the sky. The word *ntuj* means "the heavenly place, the Godly sky, or the highest place above all." The word *huab* literally means the same thing because *huab* means "the cloud" high in the sky, or the royal group. However, when *huab* is used in reference to a high class of people and a leader, it really means a group of people, such as *ib cuab, ib cov, ib pab, ib pawg*, or *ib huab*; it is used to refer to prestigious and honorable clan groups: *Vang huab, Ly huab, Lo huab, Yang huab*, and so on. The phrase *huab tais* literally means the leader, protector, or ruler of a land, state, or country. Therefore, *huab tais* and *vaj ntswv* have the same meaning and are used interchangeably to refer to Hmong rulers, leaders, protectors, and kings. Normally, Hmong would rather use the word *cuab* (group or clan), as in Vang Cuab, Ly Cuab, Lo Cuab, Yang Cuab, Vue Cuab, Thao Cuab, and so on to refer to an ordinary family, clan, tribe, or group.

In Hmong folktales, the word phrase *huab tais teb* or *huab tais ntuj* refers to the land, state, or country ruled by Hmong leaders, protectors, and kings. Hmong use the phrase *huabhwm* or *fuabhwm* to refer to a group of people, such as *peej xeem, neeg zej zog*, or *laj meej pej xeem*, meaning civilians, followers, believers, or inhabitants of a territory. To describe leadership roles, Hmong use words like *kav, tswj, saib, tswj fwm, saibxyuas, coj*, and *povhwm* to indicate the leaders' rule, protection, oversight, supervision, governing, leading, and control. Putting some of

these words together, Hmong use the word phrase *kev coj noj coj ua* to describe leadership roles, literally, as leading, guiding, showing, telling, and doing.

Hmong oral tradition uses these names and phrases, but Hmong did not keep records of the names of their ancient leaders. However, Hmong forefathers who escaped the Chinese brutally narrated stories of Hmong leaders and passed the tales down from one generation to the next. After many years of reiteration, the stories have become myths, epics, fables, folktales, and legends. Hmong do not know the real Hmong names of their past leaders or royal families; most leaders and kings in the legends had Hmong Chinese names or Chinese names. Cha (2013) listed some of these names: ChiYou (*Txiv Yawg*), Toghun Temur (*Tuam Ham Thawj Mum*), Biligtu Khan (*Blia Tub Qas Haj*), Ku Blai (*Khu Nplaim*), Arib Buke (*AZib Pujkhawv*), Mong Temu (*Mooj Thawj Mum*), and Chigkis Han (*Tseem Kws Has*). Hmong folktales and legends tell of Hmong kings who ruled Hmong kingdoms in ancient China, but the folktales and legends do not have their real names in Hmong or Chinese. Hmong remember the accounts of ethnic cleansing that took place from the 1300s to the late 1800s in which the Chinese tried to wipe out Hmong males, but they do not remember the actual names of the Hmong leaders who fought against the Chinese attempts at genocide. Table 13.1 lists names the legends and myths give to some of the Hmong leaders. The names have been transliterated into Hmong, but the spellings may not correspond phonetically to the names as they would appear in Chinese logographic characters.

The absence of all but folktale accounts of Hmong past leaders leave a big gap in Hmong history prior to their arrival in Southeast Asia. Major General Vang Pao referred numerous times to the 32 Hmong kings who reigned for thousands of years in China, but he gave neither specific names nor a timeline for the historical events that occurred under each king. Major General Vang Pao, however, did say that these Hmong

Table 13.1. Names of Hmong Leaders in Ancient China According to Legend

In Roman Alphabet	In Hmong Romanized Popular Alphabet
Zhang Shi Chen	Tsab Sim Tsheej
Chen You Liang	Tsheej Yum Liag
Han Shan Tong	Ham Sab Thoos
Temujin	Thawj Mum Tseeb
Jian Cheng	Cav Tsheej
Yuan Ji	Yawb Cim
Tai Zong	Thaiv Txoob
Dou Jian De	To Caj Daw
Zhi Shi Chong	Tswb Sim Ntxoov

kings were known as Hmong *vaj ntswv*. More research on Hmong past leaders is needed or western Hmong will think Chinese king, emperors, and traitors were Hmong leaders.

As an example of the confusion between Hmong and Chinese leaders, consider ChiYou, who was called by a variety of names—Ferocious Beast, the Red Cloud, sagacious mythical king, and magical warrior—ChiYou was unknown to western Hmong until the early 1990s. Since their discovery of this legendary figure of the third millennium BC, Hmong nationalists in the West have claimed that ChiYou was a Hmong king, not Chinese. They base the claim on five "facts" from their legends:

1. Some Hmong Chinese worship and honor ChiYou as a deity.
2. ChiYou was said to rule the Jiuli Kingdom, and Hmong lived there under his reign.
3. ChiYou was a well-known icon to the Miao nationalities, who revered him as a mythical ruler.
4. ChiYou was said to be king of 80 tribes.
5. ChiYou had a large number of followers from many different ethnic groups, tribes, and sub-groups.

Although these "facts" may suggest that Hmong once were followers of ChiYou, they do not demonstrate that ChiYou was necessarily a Hmong king or even of Hmong ethnicity. Some western scholars have made the wholly unsubstantiated assertion that ChiYou was actually a descendant of the Hmong *Yang*

clan. Some researchers have concluded that ChiYou's ancestors were Hmong, but even if that were shown to be true, that is not conclusive evidence that ChiYou was the forefather of Hmong tribes only. According to Hmong Chinese accounts, other people describe ChiYou's mythical past differently. In some of those stories, ChiYou was not a king, but a human-like creature with multiple limbs and eyes and a head like that of a draft animal with horns. This description may have arisen from the stories that ChiYou wore an iron helmet and an iron mask to protect his body in battle. The point is that multiple ethnic groups have multiple stories making multiple claims about the same person.

Western Hmong have little or no record of Hmong leaders beyond the brutal and atrocious Qing Dynasty (1644–1911). There were approximately 12 Hmong leaders who revolted against Qing rule from the 1700s through the 1800s (Cha, 2013). They had numerous charges against the emperors: heavy taxation, oppression and persecution, encroachment on their land, imprisonment and enslavement of their people, ethnic cleansing, repressive policies, executions and assassinations, and exploitation and humiliation. Hmong Chinese accounts describe some of the Hmong leaders during that time and tell of their exploits:

- Wu Ba Yue (*Vwj Paj Yias*) led a series of rebellions against the brutal treatment of the Qing.
- Yan Dawu and Bao Da Du led Hmong rebels against Chinese oppression and killed many Chinese soldiers in combat.
- Zhang Xiu Mei (*Tsav Xyooj Mem*) was a Hmong protector similar to ChiYou and led Hmong forces against Chinese oppressions.
- Yin Hua led the Crazy Miao rebellion.
- Xu Ting Jie led the Red Turban rebellion.
- Huang Hao June led the Yellow Soldiers rebellion.
- He De Sheng led the Yellow Turban rebels.

Other Hmong leaders who fought valiantly for freedom in China include *Tao Xin Chun*, who led a Hmong rebellion; *Zhang Ling Xiang*, who commanded the White Flag soldiers; *Yang Jiu*, who led a group of Hmong rebels; *Li Wen Mao*, whose troops attacked Chinese forces in battle; and *Hong Xiu Quan*, who led a rebellion against a Chinese invasion. Tragically, most of these brave Hmong leaders were arrested, tortured, incarcerated, hung, sliced to death, burned to death, or murdered in other brutal ways by the Chinese. They were either betrayed by some of their own people or hunted down like animals by mercenary soldiers. Most Hmong leaders were eventually captured and killed by the Chinese, who tried to extirpate Hmong leadership down to its roots because they feared the continual rebellions of the Hmong against their inhumane policies and practices.

History is not clear whether these rebel leaders were necessarily Hmong. They could have come from many ethnic backgrounds and belonged to different ethnic groups. The names they are given in the oral tradition do not conclusively prove that they were actually Hmong. However, Cha (2013) and other scholars believe these leaders were ancestors of today's Hmong because of their ethnic roots.

In the ancient world, the Hmong and the Chinese were at times uneasy allies, like gasoline and fire. Peace might pervade for a short time, then the Chinese would crack down on the Hmong with repressive rule and the Hmong would rebel against the Chinese suppression. There is an old saying about the Miao during the period of the Chinese dynasties; and remember, the Chinese erroneously classified the Hmong as Miao. The saying is: "A Miao riot will happen every 30 years and a major Miao rebellion will happen every 60 years." Some western researchers have claimed that in the ongoing rebellions during the Qing Dynasty, the Chinese beheaded 10,000 Miao to stop the advance of rebel groups and starved 400,000 Miao to death to crush the ethnic insurgency. There is no doubt that Hmong leaders and civilians made up a large portion of those who were brutally murdered by their Chinese oppressors.

Hmong Chinese legends describe the vows between Hmong leaders as very strong. Hmong brothers who were soldiers usually affirmed their loyalty through the use of justice water—aka holy water—blood oaths, and the summoning of Earth and Heaven Spirits for protection during battles. However, the Hmong rebel groups and the influence of their leaders were short lived. The groups frequently disintegrated and the leaders faded from prominence as the result of disunity, betrayal, dishonesty, greed, economic hardship, casualties, arrests, executions, and brutal persecution. Sooner or later, the Chinese, and later the French, learned that the way to destroy Hmong military power and group solidarity was to recruit Hmong to fight on both sides. This heinous exploitation earned Hmong the characterization of being either "raw" or "cooked"—unwilling to bend to political enticements or soft and therefore open to political or economic inducements. Hmong Chinese refugees took their patterns of leadership with them as they migrated to Southeast Asia.

Hmong Leaders in Laos

According to legends, Hmong Chinese refugees resettled in the northern regions of Vietnam, Laos, and Thailand in the early 1700s and searched for fertile land so they could resume their agrarian lifestyle in these new countries. In the early 1800s, Hmong leaders and Chinese merchants ventured into a new frontier, exploring the northern region of Laos for permanent settlement. As a result, a large group of Hmong refugees resettled in the Nong Het (*Looj Hej* in Hmong) area and its vicinity, including Tran Ninh (*xeev Tras Nees* in Hmong) and Annam (*As Nas Teb* in Hmong), bordering Laos and Vietnam. Some of the well-known Chinese Hmong refugee leaders were Lo Pa See, Cher Ly Chang Lo, Moua Tong Zer aka Moua Chong Kai, Lo Xia Vue, Lo Sai Sue, Ly Nhia Vue, Sai Kue Vue, Chao Quang Lo, and Pa Chai Vue, just to mention a few. As tribal people, Hmong families came to the area with their family leaders who led them out of southern China.

Based on Hmong oral accounts, the first group of families in Southeast Asia consisted of the Moua, Ly, Lo, and Yang clans. Subsequently, other Hmong families, such as the Vue, Vang, Xiong, and Thao clans, came to settle in the same vicinity at different times. At that time, the Hmong consisted of 12 distinct families or tribes with different last names; later 6 new families were formed and their names added to the existing 12. The new families were created as the result of marriages that occurred through family taboos, religious superstition, and incorrigible misdeeds. Culturally, each family leader, or clan leader, played a vital role in the Hmong way of life in the new homeland. The leaders were responsible for dealing with religious practices, warfare, tribal conflicts, marital customs, death rituals, and everyday life situations.

In one historical account, once Hmong refugees resettled and established communities in Laos, Hmong leaders fought against the inhabitants of the land who were there before the Hmong arrived—the Puyi, Lue, Lahue, Yao, Mien, Kha, Khamu, and other indigenous people. The worst and toughest enemies the Hmong had to face were the imperial French and the British, especially the French and their colonial policy. When Hmong leaders clashed with the French on colonial tax policy, the dispute led to a short war. French and Hmong leaders tried to reach an accord through intense diplomatic negotiation and compromise so they would avoid bloodshed. Hmong leaders, called *kiatongs*, joined together to circumvent the French control and taxation.

The position of kiatong, according to Hmong legends, originated in China; the term was not derived from the French word *canton* (*kas too*), as some western scholars claim. Although the word is not French, the French appointed Hmong leaders to be chieftains, village chiefs, and tax collectors. The word kiatong was eventually replaced with other words for leadership positions such as *chao khuoeng* (*governor*), *chao muoeng* (*mayor*), *tasseng* (*councilmember*), *nai kong* (*sub-district leader*), and *nai ban* (*village chief*). As mentioned before, in Laos, Hmong leaders were tax collectors who served their imperial French officials and local Laotian masters who relied heavily on the brutal colonial tax policy imposed on the Hmong and other ethnic groups. Historically, as explained in *Thao* (1999), the imperial Chinese way of governing land and people influenced Hmong way of life and leadership, for example, to encroach on land or to annex provinces, the Chinese employed division of power by creating *Fu* for three prefectures, *Zhou* for four-sub-prefectures, and *Zhangkwang-si* for many cantons. Some Hmong prefects became tax collectors (*tukwan* or *tusho* in Chinese, *tus sau se* in Hmong), officers (*tusi* or *tuxi* in Chinese, *tus tub siv* or *tus tub txib* in Hmong), and village chiefs (*canton* in Chinese, *kiabtoom* or *kiatong* in Hmong). Literally, *canton* can also imply leader and leadership, and in Hmong sociocultural politics, *canton* simply means the leader, meaning *tus kav, tus saib, tus thawj, losi tus coj* in Hmong.

To resolve the taxation issue, secure a reduction in the heavy taxes imposed on the Hmong who dwelled in the highland mountains, and end the civil war, Hmong leaders selected Moua Tong Zer as a Hmong representative to negotiate with the French. The two sides reached an agreement to end the civil war, but the French retained the power to impose heavy taxes on the Hmong and all other ethnic tribes living in the land. Thus, the Hmong suffered more than any other group under French rule in Laos.

In return for his part in ending the civil war, according to Hmong legends, Moua Tong Zer was promoted by the French to the position of first tasseng (*toj xeem*), the chief among all Hmong leaders. The title of *tasseng* was similar to that of kiatong, but Moua Tong Zer's official appointment by the French gave him authority over all the kiatongs, who were not officially appointed but were self-declared. Not all Hmong leaders welcomed Moua Tong Zer's new role as an imperial kiatong, or tasseng. Tasseng Moua Tong Zer is not well-known among the Hmong, and some misidentify him as Moua Chong Kai, who came later. Both Moua Tong Zer and Moua Chong Kai appear to have come from the same family and clan, and they may have actually been the same person. Based on Hmong historical accounts, Tasseng Moua Tong Zer led Hmong in the Nong Het area from the late 1800s to the early 1900s until he officially retired from office. His assistant from the Lo clan, Lo Blia Yao, took over the position of kiatong and continued the tax collection duties imposed by the French. However, according to Hmong accounts, there were other Hmong kiatongs such as Lo Pa See, Ly Nhia Vue, Lo Sai Sue, and Chue Lau Yang (see table 13.2).

All historical records of Hmong leaders and leadership prior to the mid–1800s have been lost, but Hmong oral history traces Hmong leadership in Laos from the mid–1800s to the mid–1970s. The names, titles, and achievements of the most prominent are listed in Table 13.2 and described below (Ly, 2013).

Table 13.2. Hmong Leaders from 1845 to the Mid-1900s

Name in Hmong	Name in English	Years of Service	Title/Achievement in Hmong	Title/Achievement in English
Txawj Lis Tsav Lauj	Cher Ly Chang Lo	1845 to 1850	Tus tuam thawj coj Hmoob khiav tawm Suab Teb los rau xov tshoj teb	Led Hmong migration from China to Southeast Asia
Kiab Toom Paj Txhim Lauj	Kiatong Pa See Lo	1850 to 1870	Siv kev tuav xov xeeb tiv thaiv Hmoob zej zog	Issued civic ordinances, decrees, and edicts that protected Hmong
KiabToom Nyiaj Vws Lis	Kiatong Nhia Vue Ly	1870 to 1895	Caum cov tub rog chij daj chij dub tawm tebchaws thiab nyom tsis pub Hmong them se rau Fabkis thiab Nplog	Led effort to oust the Yellow and Black Flag Bandits and rebelled against French tax policy
Kiab Toom Xaiv Xwm Lauj	Kiatong Sai Sue Lo	1880 to 1895	Nyom tsis pub Hmoob them se rau Fabkis	Supported Hmong rebellion against French tax policy
Kiab Toom Tswv Lauv Yaj	Kiatong Chue Lau Yang	1880 to 1885	Coj Hmoob mus nyob rau av loj kom muaj kev ua noj ua haus	Led Hmong refugees to find fertile land for agriculture
Toj Xeem Ntxoov Kaim Muas	Tasseng Chong Kai Moua	1895 to 1915	Thawj tug toj xeem Hmoob	First Hmong tasseng
Kiab Toom Npliaj Yob Lauj	Kiatong Blia Yao Lo	1910 to 1935	Coj Hmoob kom muaj kev sib haum xeeb nrog Nplog thiab Fabkis	Led Hmong to diplomatic relationships with Laotians and French allies
Toj Xeem Txoov Tub Lauj	Tasseng Chong Tou Lo	1915 to 1939	Tus toj xeem thib ob ntawm Hmoob tom qab toj xeem Ntxoov Kaim Muas	Second Hmong tasseng
Paj Cai Vwj	Pa Chai Vue	1918 to 1921	Nyom tsis pub Hmoob them se rau Nplog thiab Fabkis	Rebelled against French tax policy

Name in Hmong	Name in English	Years of Service	Title/Achievement in Hmong	Title/Achievement in English
Soob Ntxawg Lauj	Song Ger Lo	1918 to 1921	Nrog Paj Cai Vwj nyom tsis pub Hmoob them se rau Nplog thiab Fabkis	Supported rebellion against French tax policy
Nais Koo Paj Zeb Lis Foom	Nai Kong Pa Ge Lyfong	1938 to 1940	Kawm tiav kev cai lis choj thiab ua ib tug nai koo nyob Looj Hej	Graduated from Laos and held Nai Kong post in Nong Het
Cob Moos PhasNyas Tub Npis Lis Foom	Pragna Touby Lyfong	1947 to 1957	Yog tus Cob Moos Hmoob nyob tom xeev	Hmong Chao Muong in Xieng Khoueng province
Cob Moos Tub Liab Lis Foom	Chao Muong Hmong Tou Lia Lyfong	1957 to 1958	Yog tus Cob Moos Hmoob nyob tom xeev	Hmong Chao Muong in Xieng Khoueng province
Cob Moos Txiaj Xab Muas Nyiaj Nus	Chao Muong Chia Xang Moua Nhia Nu	1958 to 1959	Yog tus Cob Moos Hmong nyob tom xeev	Hmong Chao Muong in Xieng Khoueng province
Cob Moos Lis Tooj Pov	Chao Muong Ly Tong Pao	1960 to 1966	Yog tus Cob Moos Hmoob nyob tom xeev	Hmong Chao Muong in Xieng Khoueng province
Nais Phoo Vaj Pov	Major General Vang Pao	1960 to 1975	Yog tus Nais Phug Hmoob nyob Looj Ceeb	Hmong Major General in Long Cheng

According to Hmong legends, a well-known Hmong leader in China named Cher Ly Chang Lo (*Txawj Lis Tsav Lauj*) led a group of Hmong refugees that included five prominent Hmong warriors out of the southern region of China to resettle in the Nong Het area. Cher Ly Chang Lo and his force fought against the Manchu and the Han Chinese but lost the war because they could not fend off the enemy forces, which had modern weapons. The combined forces of the Manchu and Han Chinese drove the Hmong forces out of the area. Cher Ly Chang Lo brought with him four supreme soldiers and one religious leader. The four brave soldiers were Pa See Lo (*Paj Txhim Lauj*), Nhia Her Lo (*Nyiaj Hawj Lauj*), Young Cher Lo (*Zoov Tsawb Lauj*), and Nhia Vue Ly (*Nyiaj Vws Lis*); the religious leader was Chai Zia Ly (*Nchaiv Siab Lis*).

Hmong legends tell that Chai Zia Ly was the Hmong religious leader (*txiv muam* in Hmong) who reformed the Hmong religious ritual called *Nyuj Dab*, a cow offering ritual. In this ritual, a cow is offered to deceased parents whose souls and spirits have returned to family members to ask for this blessing, or a cow is offered to deceased parents by living family members to ask the deceased parents' benevolent spirits for protection during life-threatening situations. Chai Zia Ly changed the ritual from requiring 33 piles of offering plus 3 special piles of blessing (*33 ntxig thiab 3 ntsau*) to needing 13 piles of offering plus 3 special piles of blessing (*13 ntxig thiab 3 ntsau*). Later his brother, Blia Mee Ly (*Npliaj Mim Ly*) reduced the 13 piles plus 3 special piles of blessing to 10 piles of offering and 3 special plies of blessing (*10 ntsig thiab 3 ntsau*) because death offerings have to be an odd number. As a result of these changes, Hmong people practice three different rituals for the same offering.

For Hmong who stayed behind in China, the ritual remained the same as it always had been: 33 piles of offering plus 3 special piles of blessing for a total of 36 piles. Those who followed Chai Zia Ly practiced the 13 piles of offering plus 3 special piles of blessing, for a total of 16 piles. Hmong who migrated later with Blia Mee Ly used the new ritual, which called for 10 piles of offering plus 3 special piles of blessing, for a total of 13 piles. According to Hmong tradition, all Hmong practice the same religious rituals but the different migration histories of different families created variations in the practices. Today, Hmong can identify part of their history by revealing the number of offerings they use for this special ritual. However, the ritual has more variations than these three; some Hmong families use five, seven, or nine offerings. These further variations have resulted from religious clan leaders making additional changes.

While living in Nong Het, the leaders of Hmong Chinese refugees were able to compromise on their differences and select their own leader to protect their lives, strengthen their solidarity, and ensure their sovereignty. Pa See Lo was selected to be the first Hmong kiatong to lead all Hmong refugees living in the area; he served in this capacity for 20 years. Kiatong Pa See Lo was the father of later kiatong Lo Blia Yao. Among all his accomplishments, Kiatong Pa See Lo issued civic ordinances, decrees, and edicts that protected Hmong from foreigners, intruders, and invaders.

After Kiatong Pa See Lo's term, Nhia Vue Ly was selected the second Hmong kiatong in Nong Het. He ruled the Chinese Hmong refugees for 25 years. Like Hmong leaders of the past, Kiatong Nhia Vue Ly worked for peace, justice, freedom, and independence for his people. He joined the French and Laotian soldiers in putting down the insurgency of the Yellow and Black Flag Bandits and organized and led Hmong refugees in an unsuccessful effort to overthrow local Laotian tax collectors and overturn the French colonial tax policy. While fighting the French colonial policy on taxation that brutally oppressed the Hmong, he came into conflict with corrupt local Laotian tax collectors, who lured some traitorous Hmong to hunt him down for a reward. With little other choice, Kiagtong Nhia Vue Ly fled for his life to escape the Hmong mercenaries who worked for the corrupt Laotian officials. After plot-

ting to get rid of the local Laotian officials, he lost his kiatong post to the Moua clan.

The position did not go immediately to the Moua clan. This is what happened…. When Kiatong Nhia Vue Ly was still in charge of the north side of the Mouang Kham district, the French commissioner, after receiving a pair of rhinoceros horns from the Lo family, appointed Sai Sue Lo kiatong to oversee the south side of the district. The two kiatongs reigned alongside each other until Kiatong Nhia Vue Ly was forced into hiding after launching an unsuccessful attempt to get rid of the Laotian chao muoeng who wanted to collect taxes from the Hmong. Following that incident, the local chao muoeng ordered the Hmong kiatong to meet with him. Kiatong Sai Sue Lo feared for his life and after consulting with his relatives and family members, he decided to send an in-law to meet the Chao Muoeng on his behalf. This turned out to be a politically bad decision for him. The relatives chose to send his brother-in-law, Moua Chong Kai, to meet with the chao muoeng.

According to Hmong legends, Moua Chong Kai risked his life to save his brother-in-law. He went to see the Laotian chao muoeng without knowing what his fate would be, with no idea that the purpose of the order was to make an official appointment. So because Sai Sue Lo failed to come to the meeting, the chao muoeng gave the appointment to his brother-in-law instead. Moua Chong Kai received the official seal from the chao muoeng, making him the first ever Hmong tasseng (*Toj xeem*) in the Mouang Kham district. This was a blow to the Lo clan.

When Sai Sue Lo began his rule in the Mouang Kham district, the French appointed another Hmong kiatong, Yang Chue Lau (*Tswv Lauv Yaj*), to take control of an area known as Tran Ninh because a number of Hmong Chinese refugees were migrating there. Kiatong Yang Chue Lau led the Hmong to fertile land for their agricultural pursuits and helped them solve many complex social and cultural problems. Altogether, three Hmong tassengs ruled different territories or sub-districts under the French; the territories under Hmong kiatongs were areas where Hmong refugees resided.

Before Tasseng Moua Chong Kai's reign ended, he delegated all his official duties and responsibilities to Lo Blia Yao, who was his assistant. When he died, Lo Blia Yao should have assumed his tasseng post immediately, but Lo Blia Yao did not want to serve under the local Laotian officials and the French. He was willing to oversee his Hmong people, but only if he could be a kiatong like his father, Lo Pa See, had been. Lo Pa See, the first kiatong, had been selected not by the French or Laotians, but by Hmong. Lo Blia Yao believed an appointed tasseng was responsible to serve those who had appointed him, and he did not want to serve the Laotian officials or the French. He asked the local officials and the French to appoint his son, Chong Tou Lo (*Txoov Tub Lauj*) as the new tasseng because he was literate. At that time, most Hmong leaders were illiterate in French and Lao, only Chong Tou Lo and Sai Kao Lo (*Xaiv Kaub Lauj*) were literate in those languages. The local Laotian officials and the French honored Lo Blia Yao's request and named his son the new tasseng, overseeing Hmong people in the entire district; thus Chong Tou Lo became the second Hmong tasseng in Laos. Lo Blia Yao continued unofficially in the role of kiatong, the last Hmong kiatong in Laos. The local Laotian officials had stopped appointing Hmong kiatongs as tax collectors ever since the official appointment of Moua Chong Kai as tasseng. Nevertheless, Lo Blia Yao remained as a powerful Hmong kiatong until the mid–1930s.

Of all the Hmong leaders in the early days in Laos, Kiatong Lo Blia Yao was the most prominent, the most well-known. He was not the best leader in Hmong history because all he wanted to do was assume the role of kiatong and nothing else. He turned down the offer of the tasseng post, giving it to his son. But he ruled over all Hmong living in the land as had his father, Kiatong Pa See Lo.

The harsh French taxation placed the Hmong kiatongs and tassengs in a difficult position because they had to collect the taxes. Many poor Hmong had to sell their children to pay their taxes and other debts. Hmong were required to perform physical labor for the government, such as paving roadways and cultivating crops, in compensation for the unpaid taxes. According to Hmong legends, some Hmong children taken from Hmong families as payment of taxes became slaves in rich Hmong families. Most Hmong were poor to the bone and had no way to fight the inhumane French taxation policy.

The tax burden infuriated Hmong civilians and leaders. The abuse of power and the unbearable pressure put on Hmong leaders intensified, leaving them no choice but to revolt. Around 1918, Pa Chai Vue, a mysterious Hmong individual and messianic leader, rose to the occasion, organizing a rebellion to overturn the French colonial tax policy against the Hmong. His mythical and sagacious power and magical abilities attracted Hmong from all over to join the cause. Song Ger Lo (*Soob Ntxawg Lauj*) was one of the many leaders who supported the revolt. However, there were some pro–French Hmong who did not like the anti–French movement. The rebellion became known as Pa Chai's war, also known as the "madman's war" or the "crazy war." The uprising was short lived. The French and pro–French Hmong went after Pa Chai and his forces and completely crushed the rebellion.

As the result of Pa Chai's rebellion, in early 1920, the imperialist French enacted a new set of colonial policies and guidelines to control the Hmong refugees living in northern Vietnam (Tonkin region) and northern Laos (Xieng Khouang and Sam New Provinces) and ordered all Hmong to comply with French ruling during and after the rebellion. As cited in Cha (2013), the new imperialist French policies contained eight specific clauses:

1. Hmong shall not ever create war, if any Hmong intended to up rise, there would be severe punishment. Hmong revolt would not intimidate the French government; it only creates chaos among the country and the punishment will not be pardoned.

2. Hmong are prohibited from creating

wars, and the French government agrees for Hmong not to be managed by other nationality. The will manage their own people just like Laotian and Vietnamese under the sovereignty of the French.

3. Under such government structure, French government requires that all Vietnamese Hmong be documented into communities, and well documented for administration work. New jurisdiction, whether under new clan leaders or village leaders, everyone shall be able to dwell at their original land as they have been. The jurisdiction of different counties and cities must be clearly and properly defined.

4. Soon, all Hmong in northern Vietnam and Laos will be allowed to come and elect their own leaders under a democratic government system as follows: One county will elect one Hmong county leader. One clan region will elect one clan leader. Under a clan region, every village will elect a village leader. The electoral office would not just be stationed in major cities or counties, but they will be made available in all Hmong villages as well. Those nominated for positions would be decided by the voice of the people, and the place for nomination would be handled by a French official or French General in the same manner as when they elected the Kiatongs at Xieng Khouang province.

5. Tax collections are as follows: Villagers are to give the tax directly to their village leaders, who will hand over the tax money to their clan leaders aka Daoxing. Clan leaders and their village leaders shall go together to deposit the tax funds to the main county leader. Together, the Daoxing and the county leader then would take the funds to the French government in Vietnam.

6. Law and order, Hmong will need to put together their by-law and submitted to the French to be certified for the Hmong. Since the Hmong's by-law and norms do not fit French laws, every Hmong person still retains the right to use the French courts. All law and litigations, disputes between two ethnic nationalities have to be resolved through the French courts.

7. Hmong leaders (county leaders, Daox-

ing, and village leaders) have the right to resolve and fined individuals as always been done; however, must be based on witness system. All court fees must be sent to the French with the names of leader, the parties involved and witnesses.

8. Hmong leaders will manage and govern their own people. On an annual basis, they will maintain a census of all families, newborn, deceased, marriages, new immigrants, or move out the village to report to the French government.

Indeed, these new colonial policies and guidelines had influenced Hmong leaders and leadership positively and negatively throughout the mid–1900s. Similarly, nearly two decades prior to Pa Chai's rebellion, Chao Quang Lo was a Hmong warrior who was recruited by the French to help fight in the war between the communist Vietminh and the French. In the end, the French left the hero they called the "Terrestrial Dragon" to defend himself. While hiding in a grotto, he was assassinated by mercenary soldiers who worked for the Vietminh and the communist Chinese.

Other Hmong past leaders worth mentioning include Lo Chong Vue (*Phutoom Lauj Txooj Vws*), Sai Kao Lo (*Xaiv Kaub Lauj*), Chia Long Vang (*Txiaj Looj Vaj*), Neng Chue Vang (*Phutoom Neej Tswb Vaj*), Ly Tong Pao (*Listeem Lis Tooj Pov Thab Kub*), Chong Toua Moua (*Nai Koo Txoov Tuam Muas*), Song Lue Muas (*Nai Koo Soob Lwj Muas*), Youa Pao Yang (*Nai Koo Ntsuab Pov Yaj*), Pa Cha Ly Nhia Vue (*Nai Koo Paj Tsab Lis Nyiaj Vws*), Va Sai Pa Cha Ly Nhia Vue (*Nai Koo Vas Xais Lis Nyiaj Vws*), Moua Sue (*Phub thees Muas Xwm*), Ly Tou Yia (*Phub Thees Lis Tub Yias*), and Lau Chue Cha (*Phub Thees Los Tswb Tsab*).

Politically, the pro–French stance of Hmong kiatongs like Lo Blia Yao brought improvements to Hmong's lives, and the leadership of the kiatongs elevated the Hmong's sociopolitical status in Laos somewhat. Without these leaders, Hmong were subjected to insults, humiliation, and disregard from the Laotian officials who controlled the implementation of the tax policy imposed by the French. The French installed kiatongs like Lo Blia Yao, Moua Chong Kai, and others in accordance with a western political philosophy, establishing bureaucratic leadership that changed the course of Hmong leadership history. Even though Hmong kiatongs and tassengs struggled under the harsh and chaotic French colonial policy, they developed leadership skills that made them real models for all Hmong leaders who came after them.

A political feud between two Hmong clans, the Lo and Ly families, had many twists and turns that would weave their way throughout the history of the Hmong. Western scholars have portrayed Kiatong Lo Blia Yao (of the Lo family) as the official Hmong kiatong in the early 20th century. However, as explained above, Lo Blia Yao, was an unofficial Hmong kiatong who continued in power because his son was the tasseng appointed to rule all Hmong living in the province. Then Ly Fong, aka Ly Chia Fong (*Lis Txhiaj Foom*), a nephew of Lo Blia Yao and a member of the Ly clan, who was married to Lo Blia Yao's daughter, joined the reign. Ly Fong came to work for Chong Tou Lo, Lo Blia Yao's son and the official tasseng, to carry out some government responsibilities, including the responsibility of collecting taxes. According to Hmong legends, Lo Blia Yao, who wielded the real power, dismissed Ly Fong from his post after he took a second wife following the death of his first wife, Lo Blia Yao's daughter.

Ly Fong's dismissal created a rift between the two families. When Tasseng Chong Tou Lo failed to fulfill his duty as a tax collector and could not account for a shortage in the taxes required by the local Laotian officials and the imperial French, Ly Fong seized the opportunity. He personally made up for the loss in uncollected taxes. In return, the French revoked Chong Tou Lo's tasseng post and gave it to Ly Fong. Ly Fong immediately appointed his son, Li Bi (*Ly Bee*, or *Touby*) as tasseng of a sub-district. The revocation of Chong Tou Lo's title and authority infuriated the Lo family. One of the family members, Fay Dang Lo, filed an official complaint and petitioned the king of Laos for remediation. The only reply was a promise to return the tasseng post to the Lo family upon Ly Fong's death. A few years later, when Ly Fong died unexpectedly, the promise proved to be meaningless lip service. Laos was under French occupation and the French, not the Laotian king, controlled the appointment of Hmong leaders.

After Ly Fong's death, the French made his son Touby the new tasseng of the district. That action deepened the rift between the two families. The humiliation became unbearable for the Lo family and most of its family members moved to Vietnam. Touby continued to work for the French and his Laotian masters. After he sent his Hmong soldiers to help the reigning Laotian king successfully defend the Xieng Khoueng and Sam Neu provinces from takeover by rebel groups, he became the first Hmong chao muoeng in those provinces.

Touby Lyfong and his brothers, Tou Lia and Tou Geu Lyfong, were the most educated Hmong leaders at that time. Their father, Tasseng Ly Chia Fong, had invested in their education and foresaw their promising future as Hmong leaders. He had realized that without proper education Hmong would not be able to compete with Laotians for positions of power. Touby served the king and the French well as special chao muoeng Hmong from 1947 to 1957. He left that position to serve as an official representative (*phub thees, pwm-tsav*) and later became phagna in the Laotian government under the Laotian king. Tou Lia filled his post of special chao muoeng Hmong in 1957 and 1958 and also left to serve as one of the 47 official representatives (*phub thees*) in the Laotian government under the Laotian king. In 1958, Moua Chia Xang became the third special chao muoeng Hmong and was assassinated by an unknown assailant in 1959. In 1960, Ly Tong Pao was appointed the fourth special chao muoeng Hmong; he held the post until 1966, when Laotian officials appointed him Lieutenant Chao Khuoeng Xieng Khouang. This appointment marked the end of the special chao muoeng post. Tou Geu Lyfong served as one of the 12 advisors in the Laotian king's council. Prior to that assignment, he served in other leadership positions in the Nong Het district.

The position of special chao muoeng Hmong was created specifically for the Hmong people. The appointed chao muoeng Hmong ruled over all territories where Hmong resided in the Xieng Khoueng province and its surrounding areas. According to legends, the special chao muoeng Hmong post was eliminated because of sociopolitical corruption and nepotism; the reform of Laotian government policies; fighting among Hmong people to hold the post; fear that Hmong leaders, tassengs, and kiatongs would have more political clout if the post should continue; and lack of educated Hmong individuals who could serve as chao muoeng. As some Hmong leaders eloquently explained in Hmong, "*Nom tswv nplog thiab Fab Kis muab pob txha pom rau dev noj kom dev sib tog, xwb*," meaning the special chao muoeng Hmong post was used as a prop to pit Hmong against one another. Nevertheless, the official tasseng post shaped Hmong leadership throughout the 1900s until the fall of Laos in 1975.

Throughout Hmong history in Laos, many Hmong leaders contributed to the betterment of the Hmong refugees. The three Hmong leaders who had the most positive impact on Hmong refugees' lives were Kiatong Lo Blia Yao, Phagna Touby Lyfong, and Major General Vang Pao.

Lo Blia Yao

One of the most influential Hmong traditional leaders ever governed Hmong people in the Nong Het District (*Looj Hej*) was Kiatong Lo Blia Yao (*Kiab Toom Lauj Npliaj Yob* in Hmong). Despite not wanting to become a tasseng, Kiatong Lo Blia Yao held his kiatong post in the Nong Het area for many years. In this unofficial position, Kiatong Lo Blia Yao was not only a powerful and influential leader of all the Hmong living in the Xieng Khoueng and Sam Neu provinces but was a charismatic leader who safeguarded the Hmong under the imperial French and Lao-

Lo Blia Yao.

tian government. He exercised authority over Hmong leaders and continued to execute a leadership role to help shape, organize, structure, and unify Hmong leaders. In his administration, Kiatong Lo Blia Yao structured the bureaucracy of Hmong leaders by distributing authority and power as follows:

1. The leader (*tus tuam thawj coj*) of all was the unofficial Kiatong Lo Blia Yao, who oversaw all Hmong leaders and all people living in the Xieng Khoueng province.

2. The vice-leader (*tus lwm thawj coj*) was Phutoom Lo Chong Vue (*Lauj Txooj Vws*), who supervised all functions of the leaders.

3. The official tasseng (*tus toj xeem Hmoob*) working as a tax collector for the local Laotian officials and the French was Tasseng Chong Tou Lo, Lo Blia Yao's son. His official role was to collect taxes from Hmong civilians living in the province and deliver them to the local Laotian officials and the French.

4. The secretary of records (*tus tuav ntaub ntawv losi tus xab veem*) was Sai Kao Lo (*Xaiv Kaub Lauj*). His role was to maintain all official records of taxes and expenses related to all functions of the administration.

5. The advisory council of consultants

(*cov sablaj kev coj noj coj ua*) included *phub toom* Chia Long Vang (*Txiaj Looj Vaj*), *phub toom* Neng Chue Vang (*Neej Tswb Vaj*), and *phub toom* Fai Yia Cha (*Faiv Yias Tsab*).

6. The delivery man or messenger (tus xov phov losi tus xav ntaub xav ntawv) was Ly Tong Pao (Lis Tooj Pov). His role was to deliver mail and messages to the village chiefs and responsible leaders living in the province.

7. The appointed village chieftains or chiefs (*cov txoov kav losi nais npab*) were responsible for their villages and towns. Each village chieftain could appoint two assistants: a secretary (*tus xov phiam*) and a delivery person or messenger (*tus xov phov*) to help carry out the official roles and responsibilities on behalf of the tasseng.

8. A group of prominent community leaders was appointed to assume and oversee minor leadership roles and responsibilities to help the tasseng. These included *phub toom, phes toom, phias toom, tsav toom, toom mas, thoob lis,* and *Lis teem.*

Under the unofficial Kiatong Lo Blia Yao, there were approximately eight levels of shared governance, and all levels were mainly responsible to help the appointed tasseng, Chong Tou Lo, collect the taxes imposed on Hmong civilians by the local Laotian officials and the French. Many Hmong families struggled to pay their personal taxes. As mentioned before, poor Hmong families sold their children to wealthy Hmong families to pay for tax and some Hmong children were collected by Hmong leaders as tax collateral when their parents failed to pay. According to Vang (2008), in 1940, the imperialist French and Laotian officials imposed new tax pol-

icy and required all Laotians to pay exorbitant taxes as follows:

1. Those paying 20 piastres of personal tax, 25 piastres of more of land tax and 355 or more for commercial license. There were nine categories of exempt persons, including the royal family, district chiefs, heads of villages, bonzes and military personnel. The poor were not excused from paying personal tax.

2. Those paying at least 10 piastres of personal tax, 10 to 25 piastres of land tax and over 15 piastres for commercial license fees.

3. Those paying at least 5 piastres of personal tax, those urban landholders paying land tax of 5 to 15 piastres and those paying commercial license fees from 5 to 15 piastres per annum.

4. Those Lao, Vietnamese and evolved montagnards such as the Hmong, Man, Lu, Yao, and Kha who paid 2.5 piastres a year of personal tax.

5. Those primitive montagnards such as the Kha and Phoutheng who paid 1.5 piastres a year of personal tax.

This model of administration, as depicted in Figure 13.1, is a pyramid hierarchy. As father and mentor to his son, Tasseng Chong Tou Lo, Kiatong Lo Blia Yao did all he could to help the Laotian officials, the French, and

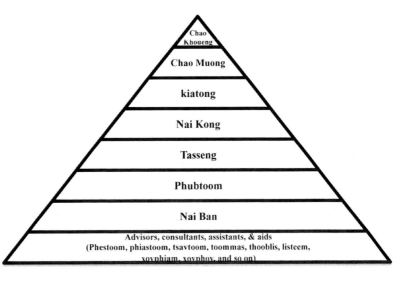

Figure 13.1. The hierarchy of Hmong leadership under Kiatong Lo Blia Yao.

Hmong civilians. Like any other Hmong leader of that time, Kiatong Lo Blia Yao experienced ups and downs in his leadership. His reign was historic; it altered the course of Hmong leadership forever.

Touby Lyfong

As a charismatic Hmong educator, leader, tasseng, chao muoeng Hmong, phub thees, and phagna serving in different government posts in the Laotian government, Phagna Touby Lyfong was well–known and well-recognized for all his public service. He earned his honorific title "phagna" from the Laotian officials and the king of Laos, under whom he served. When he became the first ever special chao muoeng Hmong in the Xieng Khoueng and Sam Neu provinces, Phagna Touby Lyfong seized the opportunity to promote his fellow Hmong to positions of official leaders in his administration. He appointed five nai kongs (*nais koo* in Hmong) Hmong to oversee five sub-districts: the Nong Het (*Hooj Hej*) district located in the Muong Kham district, the Phou Doom (*Phuv Dum*

Touby Lyfong.

or *Vias Fab*) district located in the Muong Pek district, the Muong Nyan (*Moos Nyaj*) district located in the Muong Mok district, the Muong Van Xai (*Moos Vasxais*) district located in the Muong Mok-Muong Pek district, and the Muong Khoune (*Moos khus*) district located in the Muong Khoune district. The five Hmong nai kongs were Moua Chia Xang (*Muas Txiaj Xab*) for the Muong Nyan district, Ly Tong Pao (*Lis Tooj Pov*) for the Nong Het district, Moua Chong Toua (*Muas Txoov Tuam*) for the Muong Pek district, Youa Pao Yang (*Ntsuab Pov Yaj*) for the Muong Khoune district, and Ly Pa Cha (*Lis Pab Tsab*) for the Muong Pham district. These Hmong nai kongs were appointed to oversee Hmong people only, not Laotian people or any other tribal people living in these districts. Phagan Touby Lyfong was a special chao muoeng Hmong who ruled all Hmong people living in the northern region of Laos, including Xieng Khouang and Sam Neu provinces.

Later, Phagna Touby Lyfong officially appointed more Hmong tassengs (*toj xeem*) to help govern all the districts located in the Xieng Khoueng and Sam Neu Provinces and their environs. The 10 new Hmong tassengs were Moua Nao Lue (*Muas Nom Lwm*) for the Khas Hoos district, Yang Chia Chue (*Yaj Txiaj Tswb*) for the Moos Ros district, Ly Soua Toua (*Lis Suav Tuam*) for the Keeb Khuais district, Pha Chong Toua (*Phab Txoov Tuam*) for the Pham Pheeb district, Ly Blia Tria (*Lis Npliaj Riam*) for the Pham district, Xiong Youa Chao (*Xyooj Ntsuab Txos*) for the Vas Xais district, Vang Chai Pao (*Vaj Nchaiv Pov*) for the Nas Vas district, Vue Chia Ying (*Vwj Txhiaj Yeeb*) for the Xas Thoos district, Ly Xiong Ga Xao (*Lis Xyooj Nkaj Xauv*) for the Xam Luam district, and Yang Nou Yee (*Yaj Nou Yig*) for the Phuv Fab district. In addition to the district officials, Phagna Touby Lyfong appointed his two brothers, who were well educated, to serve in government posts. His brother, Tou Geu Lyfong, was appointed as one of the 12 advisors serving on the king's council, and his other brother, Tou Lia Lyfong, was appointed as one of the 47 representatives working for the Laotian government under the Laotian king.

A few years after making these appointments, Phagna Touby Lyfong left his position as special chao muoeng Hmong to work for the Laotian government under the Laotian king. Pragna Touby Lyfong was the only Hmong leader who both won public election and was officially appointed to Laotian government posts under the king. In 1958, he was elected in Xieng Khouang province as vice-president of the National Assembly, and two years later he was appointed to serve as Minister of Justice and Social Welfare.

Prior to these major accomplishments, his political career included appointment by his father, Tasseng Ly Chia Fong, as tasseng of a sub-district in the Nong Het district and, several years later, appointment by the French as Chief of Nong Het district. Following his tasseng posts, his involvement in the political turmoil in northern Laos and his successful intervention to rescue the king of Laos from communist takeover earned him an appointment as deputy governor of Xieng Khoueng and Sam Neu provinces and as the first ever special chao muong Hmong. Phagna Touby Lyfong was an influential Hmong leader and politician who successfully penetrated the ethnic barriers to serve high profile posts in the Laotian government.

Learning from his father, Tasseng Ly Chia Fong, Phagna Touby Lyfong became one of the most well reputed, decorated, and honorable Hmong leaders of all time in Laos. In 1974, Pragna Touby Lyfong took part in the peace process known as the Laotian National Reconciliation to restore a positive political climate in Laos. Unfortunately, his passion for serving in government cost him his political life following the fall of Laos in 1975. Shortly after the communist Pathet Lao took over Laos, Phagna Touby was arrested along with other high ranking Laotian officials and Laotian royal family members and was sent to a reeducation camp along the Vietnamese border. He died in captivity in 1979. Hmong lost a great leader who had devoted his entire life to public service.

Under Touby Lyfong's reign, Hmong leaders followed the traditional model of shared governance presented in Figure 13.1. Hmong

civilians were still required to pay the exorbitant taxes demanded under Touby's predecessors. Phagna Touby Lyfong set a monumental example for all Hmong leaders who came after him.

General Vang Pao

Unlike any other Hmong leaders, Major General Vang Pao was predestined to become a military leader. He was commended for his bravery and heroism because of his military prowess, multiple intelligence, natural wisdom, astute leadership, prudence, and charisma. His birth name, "Pov (*Pao* in English)," in Hmong means protection, safeguarding, supervision, overseeing, or security. His last name, "Vang," in Hmong can be translated as a leader, protector, ruler, guardian, or king. Thus his full name "Vang Pov" actually means "the protector of all." No Hmong leader in history has had a name that suited him more perfectly. As a young child, Vang Pao was ambitious because of his extraordinary skills and natural abilities. He was quick, agile, patient, persevering, intel-

General Vang Pao.

ligent, compassionate, tireless, eager, and astute. In his early teen years, he worked as a messenger, courier, and interpreter for Hmong leaders such as Phagna Touby Lyfong and the French in the Xieng Khoueng province. He launched his military career during World War II, joining the French Military Training Academy to be trained as a combat soldier. He fought the invasion and occupation of Japanese forces in order to help safeguard his fellow Hmong. A brief timeline of his military career is given in Table 13.3. While taking part in the "Meo Maquis," or Hmong resistance forces, and the Groupement de Commandos Mixtes Aéroportés (GCMA), working for the French against the Japanese forces, his military prowess, shrewdness, intelligence, leadership skills, and personal qualities enabled him to advance quickly in his military career. The French recruited him to take part in the first Indochina war with the Vietminh, and even though the French lost the war in 1954 and left Laos, Major General Vang Pao remained active in the army of the newly formed independent Kingdom of Laos.

Table 13.3. Brief Timeline of Career of Major General Vang Pao

Year	Military Accomplishment
1942	Worked for Touby Lyfong as a messenger, courier, and interpreter for the French
1942–1952	Enrolled in the French Military Academy
1947	Received Corporal rank and joined the French GCMA Laos
1949	Became leader of all Corporal officers
1949–1950	Received sergeant-major rank
1954	Led Hmong soldiers in Nong Het
1955	Received captain rank
1960	Received his lieutenant colonel rank
1959	Approached by CIA operatives
1961	Received colonel rank
1961–1975	Commanded Special Guerilla Unit (SGU) for the Secret War in Laos
1962	Became the first Hmong general in the Royal Lao Army
1975	Left Laos for Thailand

Major General Vang Pao was a natural and charismatic military leader. He received an honorific title from the kings of Laos for his stellar military service and he was recognized as *Phagna Norapamok General Vang Pao*, meaning *Lord Protector of the Land*. For his entire military career and political life, he was a true patriotic leader who showed political allegiance to the French in Indochina, the Kingdom of Laos, and the United States of America. After graduating from the French Military Training Academy, Major General Vang Pao joined the Royal Lao Army and served during the Second Sino-Japanese War, the First Indochina War, the Laotian Civil War, and the Second Indochina War, known as the Secret War supported by the Central Intelligence Agency of the U.S. He was the only Hmong military leader to earn the highest rank of General in the Royal Lao Army, which he received during the Secret War fought from 1960 to 1975. His brilliant work and outstanding military service for the imperial French and Laotian Kings earned him several distinguished honors and prestigious awards: (1) Grand Officer of the Order of the Million Elephants and the White Parasol, (2) Commander of the U.S. Legion of Merit, (3) Knight of the French Legion d'Honneur, (4) Grand Officer of the Thai Order of the White Elephant, (5) Medal for Combatants from King Sisavang Vong, (6) Medal of the Reign of King Sisavang Vathana, (7) French Croix de la Guerre Des Operations Exterieures—four bronze stars and one bronze palm, (8) French Foreign Legion Indochina Vietnam Colonial Medal, (9) French Foreign Legion Indochina Campaign Dien Bien Phu, and (10) more than a dozen of leadership and life achievement awards from Hmong leaders, private and non-profit organizations, and elected officials. His honorific title, *Lord Protector of the Land*, also gave him exalted fame, reputation, and leadership that automatically elevated him to become the Father of the Hmong people.

The turning point in Major General Vang Pao's military career came in 1959 as the Kingdom of Laos underwent political turmoil because of rivalries between three groups seeking to seize control of the whole country. These factious groups were a neutral group (located in Vientiane), a rightwing group (located in Savanhnakhet), and a leftwing group (located in the Sam Neu province). The neutral group belonged to Laotian Prince Souvannaphouma. The rightwing group, calling itself a "pure and free democratic group," was led by Laotian Prince Boun Oum Nachampasak. The leftwing group was known as "the red" and was a coalition organized by members of the communist party who supported the Pathet Lao. At this point in time, Hmong leaders and civilians were in a catch–22 situation because they did not know what group to join. Most Hmong leaders in the Xieng Khouang and Sam Neu provinces were loyal to the reigning Laotian king, but the Thai government and western nations supported the pure and free democratic leaders of the southern region.

When western countries, especially the United States, learned of the political plight in Laos, they became concerned that Laos could be the next domino to fall to communism in Southeast Asia after South Vietnam and Cambodia. Therefore, the U.S. Central Intelligence Agency (CIA) decided to approach any well-known Hmong military leader who had proper training for help in containing the expansion of communism from North Vietnam over the Ho Chi Minh Trail into South Vietnam.

The CIA operatives came to Laos seeking Hmong military leaders living in the Xieng Khoueng and Sam Neu provinces to carry out covert operations. Initially, the CIA operatives approached a particular Hmong military leader who had been properly trained, but that individual lacked civilian followers and ready military support. On the day of a final meeting with the CIA, the individual could not make up his mind to take the job. His wife, who was Vang Pao's sister, directed the CIA operatives to Vang Pao, who had the capabilities they sought. Hmong elders say that the CIA operatives were eager to meet with Vang Pao and asked the wife to fly with them to meet with Vang Pao in Xieng Khoueng

province. That was how Vang Pao came in contact with the CIA personnel.

In January 1961, the CIA's Captain James W. (Bill) Lair came to meet with Vang Pao at the Tha Vieng airfield near Xieng Khouang. No one knows the terms and conditions Vang Pao and the CIA operatives discussed. Hmong elders say that Vang Pao requested military equipment and training for his fellow Hmong soldiers, and the CIA operatives promised to deliver whatever he needed for the job. When he met with his fellow Hmong leaders and soldiers about the CIA operation, Vang Pao told them that weapons and equipment were on the way to them. However, the U.S. was looking for bravery soldiers who were determined defense to sabotage the advance of communism, and Captain Bill Lair knew that Hmong disliked communist invasion and would fight to protect their land, families, and country. For that, giving Hmong civilians the arms-support, medical assistance, and food supply would do the job.

Vang Pao took the initiative, collaborating with his other Hmong leaders to orchestrate the operation. The expansion of communism, if it took place, would impact their lives, land, and future. At first, Vang Pao had neither Hmong soldiers nor military equipment. Other Hmong leaders, such as Chao Muong Hmong Ly Tong Pao, Ly Nao Ko Lyfong, Nai Ban Ly Blia Chong, Phub toom Nao Tou Lo, Nai Khu Ly Xang Tong Pao, and Cas Xam Ly Tou Pao served as his advisors and supporters, helping him recruit and organize a Hmong civilian soldier force. Chao Muong Hmong Ly Tong Pao recruited 300 soldiers and Ly Blia Chue brought in another 120 soldiers. Vang Pao was the grassroots military leader who was eager to protect the land and country he loved dearly.

The guns, ammunition, grenades, and military equipment promised by the CIA were late in coming. Because of the delay, Hmong civilians started to leave Xieng Khoueng province in fear of a communist invasion. In late December 1960, the arms finally arrived and were distributed among the Hmong civilian soldiers to use in safeguarding their villages and the rest of the land. By this time, the enemy had captured the Plain of Jar from the Laotian forces. Vang Pao retreated, regrouped his forces, and recruited more Hmong soldiers. Major General Vang Pao could not have done this without assistance from all the Hmong leaders who called out their civilians to take up arms and join his special guerrilla unit (SGU) to protect their villages. This is how Major General Vang Pao and the Hmong soldiers got involved in the Secret War from 1960 to 1975.

As one of the most powerful military leaders in Laos, Major General Vang Pao restructured Hmong leadership through his military and political appointments. With special permission from the king of Laos, Major General Vang Pao organized the Hmong leadership infrastructure in a way no other Hmong leader had done in Hmong history. With only a third-grade education, he had become one of the most influential, powerful, respected, esteemed, decorated, and revered Hmong leaders of all time. He appointed four new lieutenants (*hnub qub ob*), 21 sergeants and captains (*hnub qub ib*), and 22 assistants for the sergeants and captains. The Hmong lieutenants were Ly Nao Kao Lyfong, Ly Tou Pao, Ly Xang, Tong Seng Lo, Neng Chue Thao, Ly Chao Nhia Long, Ly Sue Blong Lyfong, and Ly Fue Sai Her.

The appointments and promotions inspired more Hmong civilians to join his force. Within two years, the SGU had grown from hundreds of soldiers to thousands. However, the Hmong civilian soldiers lacked proper military training and education. While the CIA operatives continued to train new recruits, Vang Pao and his lieutenants were on the frontlines leading Hmong civilian soldiers in sabotaging the advancement of communist forces from North Vietnam.

Because of Vang Pao's military genius, he brought Military Region II (MR II) under his control. He wasted no time expanding his military mission. He created five new divisions of military operation, known as departmental offices (*hoob kam*), which were similar to the five branches of the U.S. Pentagon. The first department (*hoob kam 1*) was responsible for gathering intelligence in support of military operations and personnel on the frontlines. The second department (*hoob kam 2*) was in charge of national security matters and gathered intelligence in support of the operations of Department 1. The third department (*hoob kam 3*) was to coordinate military equipment, food supplies, and recruitment and delivery of humanitarian aid for military operations and civilian needs. The fourth department (*hoob kam 4*) was to distribute military equipment, food supplies, new recruits, and humanitarian aid to military bases, operations, and villages. And the fifth department (*hoob kam 5*) was to provide military supportive services and financial compensation to military families, survivors, and deceased. In addition, to orchestrating his military mission, Major General Vang Pao recruited Hmong to be trained as pilots for transportation, fighting and bombing, and spying. The first group of Hmong pilots included Moua Va Chia Xang (transportation), Xiong Kou (transportation), Vang Toua ka Ge (fighting and bombing), Ly Lue Chong Ger (fighting and bombing), Vang Chou Pa Yia (spying), and Vang Ge Chue Cheng (spying).

To strengthen the military mission, Major General Vang Pao reformed and restructured Hmong civilian leadership by promoting the chao muong to position of lieutenant chao khuoeng, raising the nai kong to chao muong, and elevating other low profile positions such as tasseng (*toj xeem*), nai kong (*nai koo*), village chiefs (*nais npab*), and advisory council members (*phub toom, phes toom, xov phov, lis toom*. Under his leadership, the newly appointed Hmong leaders included Ly Neng Thong Pa Yia, chao muong of Nong Het district; Moua Ger Mouanoutoua, chao muong of Vian Fa in Muang Pek and Phou Doom districts; Youa Tong Yang, chao muong of Muang Van Sai district; Ta Cau Ly Xiong Ka Xao, chao muong of Muang Mok district; and Saw Chia Chou Leng Thao, chao muong of Muang Xiang Hong district. Vang Pao's reorganization of Hmong leadership gave Hmong soldiers and civilians more opportunities to become civil leaders. Many tassengs and phub tooms became nai kongs and a series of new nai ban emerged under Major General Vang Pao's leadership. Some nai kongs performed civil duties and organized civilian soldiers. Best of all, all Hmong leaders at all levels received monthly paychecks from Major General Vang Pao's general fund for the military operation in Laos.

Besides restructuring civil leadership, Major General Vang Pao worked tirelessly to promote public education for Hmong civilians throughout the country. He collaborated with the Hmong school inspector, aka Hmong superintendent, Lia Moua, to build public schools in many Hmong villages where Hmong children could have access to public education. Major General Vang Pao also advocated for distribution of medical supplies to Hmong villages to treat basic medical conditions. He made sure Hmong civilians did not go hungry by asking the U.S. to provide humanitarian aid, especially food supplies (rice and canned foods), to all Hmong living in MR II.

In the mid–1960s, Major General Vang Pao brilliantly created the Hmong tribunal court system to mediate, resolve, and decide Hmong criminal and civil matters in accordance with Hmong cultural and traditional values and beliefs. The tribunal court system had *three tiers* of justice and the first two court levels had 12 judges appointed from different parts of MR II. Most were Hmong leaders with supreme knowledge, exceptional skills, superb logical and intuitive abilities, and remarkable intelligence. The system was similar to the U.S. state supreme courts and appellate courts. Major General Vang Pao oversaw the tribunal court system and issued monetary stipends to all presiding judges. However, he neither presided over its proceeding nor was directly involved in its decisions, appeals, or remediation process. Appearing before the Hmong tribunal court was the final step of all Hmong criminal and civil litigations, prosecutions, and appeals in MR II. The low level Hmong appellate court was called *Xam Khab Dis* and the high level Hmong appellate court was named *Xam Phuaj Phais*. The highest level was the *Hmong Supreme Court* with a single supreme justice

and that was Major General Vang Pao's court. According to Hmong judges, very few decisions had to be reviewed by Major General Vang Pao, and very few cases had to be brought to his personal attention. Hmong criminal and civil matters were resolved by the 12 judges based on the merit of the individual case. Prior to establishment of the tribunal court system, a criminal or civil matter could go from the local level to the very highest level of government; the typical process was from the nai ban to the tasseng, from the tasseng to the chao muong, from the chao muong to the kiatong, from the kiatong to the chao khoueng, from the chao khoueng to the Laotian king or to the imperial French.

As a leader, Major General Vang Pao restructured the Hmong tribunal justice system not to make it more modern, but because he wanted to make sure Hmong matters were handled by Hmong leaders. Hmong have a saying: "*Hmoob tshuaj Hmoob rhaub, Suav tshuaj Suav rhaub,*" which means: Hmong resolve Hmong problems and Chinese resolve Chinese problems. The saying implies that Hmong should handle Hmong criminal and civil matters in accordance with Hmong traditions and the Hmong way of life rather than letting other people (Chinese, Laotian, and French) decide Hmong matters according to their customs and values.

The nearly 14 years of war under Major General Vang Pao's military leadership changed Hmong life forever. Although war is never pleasant, the lives of Hmong were actually better than they had been during thousands of years of struggle in China and hundreds of years in Laos. From 1960 to 1975, Hmong made tremendous progress in education, politics, economics, and civil leadership. Major General Vang Pao appointed more Hmong civil leaders than any other Hmong before him and he elevated the sociopolitical status of Hmong and the Hmong way of life far above where they had been before 1960. He was a leader in many spheres: military, spiritual life, politics, society, and education. World history may remember Major General Vang Pao as a major general in the Royal Lao Army, but Hmong refugees will remember him as the people's leader and the messianic war hero who brought Hmong civilians to the Promised Land, saving them and giving them the ability to begin their lives over again.

Hmong Leaders in the West

Since no Hmong refugee leader has held a title or a leadership position higher than that of Major General Vang Pao from Laos, he continued to be the sole traditional leader of most Hmong refugees in the West for another 36 years. Many Hmong refugees looked up to him for guidance and encouragement. Most Hmong still respect and honor his leadership.

In late 1975, Major General Vang Pao departed Southeast Asia for the U.S., leaving Hmong refugees behind in Thailand. As a leader, he designated his former military officers to take charge of the Hmong refugees, but most felt insecure and uncertain without his leadership. Many followed him to the U.S., and others chose to resettle in other western nations such as France, Canada, Australia, and French Guyana. In the U.S., the U.S. government provided Major General Vang Pao with a luxurious home; he lived on nearly 500 acres in the state of Montana with some close family relatives nearby. However, nearly all his former military officers, the civic leaders, and Hmong civilians who followed him to the U.S. were dispersed throughout the 50 states.

Back in Laos, the soldiers and Hmong civilians who had been left behind were subjected to brutal atrocities. In Thailand, many Hmong languished in refugee camps. All the Hmong suffering in Southeast Asia looked to their hero for guidance and support. As Major General Vang Pao later explained, "My telephone started to ring off the hook every five minutes and every caller was asking me pretty much the same thing about the life situations in the US, Thailand, and Laos. And each wanted to know what I was going to do about these things because everyone was waiting for me." He recalled, "I could not sleep through the night, could not eat well,

and could not stop thinking about those situations; I wanted to do something about them."

Major General Vang Pao travelled to visit the Hmong communities throughout the U.S. to find out what critical needs they had and to listen to what Hmong refugees had to say about their lives in the new homeland. He also travelled oversea to different countries to learn more about the international politics related to the political plight in Laos. Back in the U.S., he met with former military officers, civil leaders, community leaders, and Hmong educators to find solutions to the urgent social and cultural adjustment problems faced by Hmong refugees. He was interested not only in helping his fellow Hmong refugees, but he also had serious concerns about the lives of Hmong and the political situations in Laos and Thailand.

In 1977, Major General Vang Pao travelled to Orange County in California to meet with former Hmong educators from Laos, military officers, civil leaders, and social service agency representatives to address the Hmong refugee matters. Together with them, he helped found the Lao Family Community, Inc. (LFC), a community-based organization and mutual assistance association to provide for the critical needs of Laotian Hmong refugees living in that county. It was a successful start. The first LFC was established in Long Beach, California and later moved to the City of Santa Ana. Shortly thereafter, the non-profit LFC established branches in many cities with large Hmong refugee population: Fresno, Merced, Stockton, and Sacramento, California; St. Paul, Minnesota; Denver, Colorado; Milwaukee, Wisconsin; and others. By the mid–1980s, there were approximately 32 LFCs in the U.S.; many still exist today.

At the same time, Major General Vang Pao wanted to address the brutal atrocities in Laos. He organized an international leadership group of many former allies (former Laotian military officers, Laotian royal family members, Hmong military officers, Hmong civic leaders, educators, and civilians) to create the United Lao National Liberation Front, also known as the Lao National Liberation

Movement, best known as the rightwing pro-royalist political movement *Neo Hom* aka United Lao National Liberation Front (ULNF) and Lao National Liberation Movement (LNLM). This was a political organization with a transnational political platform to advocate for the return to freedom and democracy in Laos. It was strong in the mid–1980s but fell in the late 1980s when the U.S. government became concerned about its intention to carry out transnational political activities. Today, only the skeletal structure is left among a few loyal followers of the pro-loyalist political movement. However, this is still an undying dream for those Hmong who fought the "Secret War" in Laos.

Major General Vang Pao eventually decided to relocate his family to Orange County to be closer to the Hmong communities in Southern California. His relocation sparked the second Hmong migration in the U.S. As a result, larger Hmong communities are concentrated in three states: California, Minnesota, and Wisconsin. Some of his former military officers moved from France to join him in the U.S.

In the U.S., Major General Vang Pao was the supreme national leader of most Hmong refugees and he has always been the international leader. No Hmong has risen to a higher sociopolitical status than he and no other Hmong has been able to claim to be the leader of all Hmong. Throughout his 36 years in the U.S. before his death in 2011, Major General Vang Pao was a national symbol of which Hmong refugees have always been proud.

Despite his immense popularity, some Hmong refugees living in the U.S. have not embraced his traditional leadership and vision. Their reluctance to follow his lead wholeheartedly is due to a number of factors:

- Many western Hmong refugees do not support the platform of his international political movement.
- His approach to solving community and cultural issues, such as the multiple Hmong New Year's celebrations, was always static and stalling.

- His creation of several social organizations caused conflicts of interest and social turmoil in the Hmong community.
- The supremacy of his leadership caused young Hmong leaders to leave his camp and joining opposing groups.
- His style of leadership appeared to lack systematic structure that his followers could duplicate.

Overall, Major General Vang Pao's 67 years as a Hmong leader have had a tremendous positive impact on all aspects of Hmong refugees' lives in the U.S. and abroad. While living in the U.S., Major General Vang Pao strongly advocated for measures that would meet the critical needs of Hmong refugees in the U.S. He was actively involved in the everyday lives of Hmong refugees in the U.S. and abroad, founding non-profit organizations to help them adjust and make smooth transitions to the host culture. He kept Hmong refugees united and organized, helping them maintain Hmong culture and traditions and promoting Hmong clan leaders and leadership. Major General Vang Pao played a vital role in the national and international political arena, decrying human rights violations against former Laotian soldiers. He encouraged Hmong refugees to love one another and come together as a big family. No Hmong leader in Hmong history has done more than Major General Vang Pao to promote Hmong sociopolitical well-being. He dedicated his entire life to serving Hmong in Laos and Hmong refugees worldwide. Even Hmong who may disagree with some of his actions have to remember and honor this: if it had not been for his military genius and sacrificial leadership in rescuing downed U.S. pilots along the Ho Chi Minh Trail and fighting the covert Secret War financed by the CIA, Hmong refugees would not have been brought to the U.S. and other western nations to start over in places with such great opportunities.

Incredibly, just as the Chinese predicted thousands of years ago, wars, battles, and leaders rise and fall like the spring and autumn seasons. In this, Major General Vang

Pao was no exception. He fell many times throughout his life, but he always rose, always conquered obstacles and political enemies. In Laos, he was ambushed and shot, but he survived. A plane carrying him crashed, but he survived. In the U.S., he was wrongfully arrested along with other Hmong civic leaders and unjustly accused of crimes, but the charges were dropped and he was vindicated. No Hmong leader dealt with the rises and falls better than he. A fellow Hmong said to him, "Phagna Norapramok General Vang Pao, you were born to be a leader to safeguard the Hmong people and you are God's gift to the Hmong because you have survived when other people ambushed and shot you, when the plane you were in crashed to the ground, and when the US government wrongfully accused you of plotting to overthrow the Laotian government." These words are so true.

Also true is the American saying: "Freedom is not worth having if it does not include the freedom to make mistakes." Every leader stirs some controversy, and no leader is perfect. Leaders in violent circumstances such as war-torn Laos cannot please everyone or do everything right. In 2003, Major General Vang Pao agreed to a secret meeting in Amsterdam with some Vietnamese government officials who sought his support for normalized U.S. trade relations with Laos. His decision to meet such people raised suspicions among his fellow Hmong loyalists and followers. However, in exchange for his support, he simply requested that the Vietnamese government exert pressure on Laos to get the Laotian government to stop persecuting Hmong. No one really knows if the deal had any effect on halting the ethnic cleansing in Laos, but for Major General Vang Pao, it was a step toward potential reconciliation.

On June 4, 2007, the arrest of Major General Vang Pao and 10 other Hmong civic leaders shocked the world. It was a very dark moment in Hmong history. Vang (2007) wrote about the impact of the arrests on Hmong communities across the U.S.:

"HMONG ARRESTS REVIVE PAINFUL MEMORIES"

Like so many other Hmong, I am saddened by the arrests of prominent Hmong leaders in California. The shock I felt when I heard the news took me back more than 30 years. It recalled memories and feelings etched painfully in my head and heart in 1975, when the Communists invaded my country, Laos.

[...]

I remember how hard it was for me to leave my country, even as a child. I feel the sting of that loss again today. Today is another dark moment in Hmong history.

But in that earlier dark moment, 30 years ago, we fought through the pain and suffering and made new lives for ourselves. We will do the same today. In 1975, our leaders left only to show us the way out. In 2007, we will do what we can for them. For the moment, together as a community, let us pray for the best for our leaders, remember their great contributions, and continue to give them our loyal support.

A few days after the arrest, Major General Vang Pao and the other Hmong civic leaders, along with an American who was a West Point graduate and retired army infantry officer, were indicted by the federal government under the federal "Operation Tarnished Eagle," investigation. Initially, Major General Vang Pao was denied bail but after Hmong people gathered to demonstrate in support of his release, the court set his bail at $1.5 million and family members combined resources to make the bail. On July 12, 2007, Major General Vang Pao was released from Sacramento County Jail on bail. The case dragged on for nearly two years before all charges were completed dropped on September 18, 2009. Major General Vang Pao was vindicated. When asked about his involvement in the plot, he simply responded, "It is all about the old politics. I have done nothing wrong."

A month later, Major General Vang Pao made another stunning announcement to the Hmong refugees: he planned to return to Laos to pursue the Reconciliation Project, an initiative to restore peace, democracy, and freedom to the Laotian people. His announcement sparked national and international interest. However, a few weeks prior to his scheduled departure, the Lao Democratic Republic of People issued a firm diplomatic statement denouncing his desire to return and threatening a death sentence for the exiled war general.

At the age of 81, Major General Vang Pao had been battling diabetes, heart disease, cataracts, and other minor medical conditions. In 2010 he was sick often and hospitalized a couple of times. Nevertheless, as the supreme chair and the only Hmong national leader, he had wanted for years to restructure the leadership of the Hmong International New Year's celebration organization and the United Hmong International Council, Inc. in order to restore public trust and support. However, his attempts had failed because of conflicts and division in the Hmong community. He released a DVD describing his new vision for the Hmong and urged them to reconcile, make changes, cooperate, and, most importantly, love one another. He did not want to see two New Year's celebrations divide the people and he made a final request in December 2010 for immediate reconciliation, but this effort was also unsuccessful.

On December 26, 2010, he became ill after attending the Hmong International New Year's celebration in Fresno and was hospitalized the same day. On January 6, 2011, Major General Vang Pao died from cardiac complications and pneumonia. His death marked another dark moment in Hmong history; Hmong refugees lost their greatest leader and a beloved father.

Many Hmong refugees called Major General Vang Pao "king," or in Hmong, "*Huab Tais*" or "*Hmong Tus Vaj*." However, he had never proclaimed himself to be a Hmong king, and he had never been honored with such a title officially with investiture. Many times he had said publicly that he was the leader of the Hmong people and the one who brought the Hmong people to the U.S., but he had never wanted to be called "Hmong King." Regardless, Major General Vang Pao was suited to be recognized as a Hmong King because of his longest reign and all his mon-

umental contributions to the betterment of all Hmong people.

Shortly after his death, the federal government announced that all charges against the other 10 defendants were being dropped and the whole case was dismissed. Mystery still surrounds the charges and their dismissal. Hmong refugees believed Major General Vang Pao was the prime target of the action and without him the entire case was meritless.

The funeral service for the honorable leader and beloved father was held on February 4 to February 9, 2011. The six-day ritual attracted thousands of Hmong and non–Hmong. The lavish funeral service and the magnitude of attendance made history. Hmong communities across the world also held funeral rites to pay respect to the greatest Hmong leader of all time. For his loyal followers, Major General Vang Pao, beloved father and military genius, had died but his life-long legacy lives forever. Vang (2012) expressed the grief so many Hmong felt at the death of Major General Vang Pao:

"Hmong need to move from grief to find solace"

In January 2011, Hmong entered the most difficult grieving process of the century when General Vang Pao died unexpectedly. Everyone was emotionally and psychologically tormented and depressed internally regardless of their physical appearance and facial expression, realizing what is next for Hmong without him. The passing of General Vang Pao was unbearable to so many people around the world, especially for Hmong.

Each has grief in life at different times and some grieves go away swiftly while others stay with the person for a long time. Grieving is part of the loss process and remembering the departed is part of the healing process. Today, most Hmong still grieve and remember.

In the beginning many grieved in deep sorrow over the death of this great warrior and mighty leader who loved his people dearly for so many years. People wished that anyone, including God, would restore life to this departed Hmong leader; however, their wishes and hopes were pure fantasies since no one is able to rise from death. The time of sorrow slowly passed and finally most returned to their normal lives, but the grief never stops bothering them because Hmong are still living in peril without a leader who can show the way.

Most Hmong went through phases of grieving. Some experienced relief while others suffered psychologically and emotionally traumatic episodes. Of course, normally, individuals' attitudes, personality, life circumstances, depth of testimony, and accepting understanding might help them cope with the depression, anxiety, and despair of these phases. Hmong did understand the cause of death by old age and lingering medical conditions, but the suddenness of the death of such a great leader and the fact that it was unexpected intensified their grief over the loss. Both young and old suffered insurmountable sorrow through shock and denial, suffering and anger, disbelief and dismay, and love and acceptance.

Hmong remember this time of the year as part of their sorrow and loss since General Vang Pao was the spiritual leader who always opened the New Year celebrations held throughout the nation for Hmong people and the Hmong community. Many gather to pray, to pay respect, to honor his legacy, and to pay tribute to his life-long achievements for humanity. A few statues were built to honor him in different cities and towns. Most have overcome the loss somewhat and will move on. But many are still in shock mode and the chill feelings in hearts, souls, and spirits are so real during this time of the year. Hmong need to find solace; however, they have no way of finding it. Perhaps, solace will come from the Godly angels to console them in their sorrow and comfort them in their painful memories.

Remember, in times of need Hmong are more inclined to be teachable with condolences and respect and to put aside influences such as cultural imperialism, blackmailing tactics, and religious mania. These harmful activities may have been barriers to receiving solace between the living souls and spiritual living during the healing process. Whether Hmong can find solace through other sources or not, they need to overcome negative attitudes and feelings developed during the grieving process by understanding the nature of death and accepting the great loss and replacing personal internal suffering with faith, humility,

forgiveness, respect, and gratitude. Hmong need to keep praying hard until solace comes to live in their hearts and souls.

Prior to Major General Vang Pao's arrest, a brand new elementary school in Madison, Wisconsin, was supposed to be named in his honor; however, in light of the federal indictment, his name was dropped from consideration. In 2012, nearly a year after his death, a new elementary school in Fresno, California was named in his honor: *Vang Pao Elementary School*. Several monuments and statues have been crafted in his honor in different cities throughout the U.S. In Fresno, the old Vang Pao Foundation has been revitalized to keep his legacy alive.

As unexpected, some western researchers who had been in Laos made erroneous allegations, accusing the Hmong general of involvement in opium trafficking during the Secret War. Many Hmong educators, former military officers, and scholars who worked with and knew Major General Vang Pao refuted such bazaar claims, testifying that Major General Vang Pao had never been involved with the opium trade. Because the general controlled MR II during the war, he had knowledge of those who took advantage of the war to transport opium from MR II to the West, but he neither participated in nor approved of the practice. Those who made the false allegations never interviewed Major General Vang Pao about the matter but gathered information from those who disliked him and Laotian leaders who did not work for the Hmong general in MR II. When the allegations were made, Major General Vang Pao adamantly denied them and held private meetings with Hmong educators and scholars to launch a national campaign to clear his good name. Unfortunately, no campaign was begun before his death. Perhaps U.S. Hmong refugees should research this very important topic and investigate opium trafficking in Laos, especially during the Secret War period. It would be good to identify those who actually participated in the drug trade and provide more details that would prove or disapprove Major General Vang Pao's role. The

Hmong general should be presumed innocent unless proven otherwise. This research could be a new investigation—"Operation Untarnished Eagle"—that would restore the image of the late Hmong general who is currently resting in peace.

It will take some time for U.S. Hmong refugees to fill the vacuum left by Major General Vang Pao. In his farewell speech, he urged all Hmong to come together to find common ground on which to elect the leader that would come after him, using the democratic process. He asked Hmong to love one another. If they didn't, he warned, they would be like positive and negative terminals on a car battery that spark and burn each other. Perhaps, the U.S. Hmong refugees will heed his messages in the near future and find their next leaders. Major General Vang Pao had left Hmong leadership in the hands of all Hmong to find a new beginning to start a new life cycle of Hmong leadership all over again.

Why No Successor Named

When Major General Vang Pao died, no successor was named and Hmong were left in limbo. For many Hmong people, it was a shocking moment. They felt like the sky was falling; they were mystified as to why they were left leaderless.

While he was alive, Major General Vang Pao asked his followers on several occasions about their personal sacrifices for replacing him; however, no one would dare to answer him, and more importantly, no one seemed to have sincere commitment and personal conviction to carry out his leadership mission. He also mentioned numerous times that he would choose someone to take the leadership post before his time was over, but he did not fulfill his promise prior to his death. Whether his followers and loyalists were disappointed in his decision or not, he was absolutely right not to appoint his successor. He knew Hmong would disrespect, condemn, denounce, and disapprove of anyone he named. More importantly, his designation of a new leader would drive Hmong clans

into unending tribal warfare. To be fair and to avoid inevitable conflict and infighting, Major General Vang Pao decided not to name his successor. He acted for the sake of the Hmong people.

Evidently, he had denied several people who had approached him privately and made personal requests that he abdicates and transfers his leadership to them or name them the new leaders before he died. While he was sick and hospitalized, an individual made an unexpected personal plea to Major General Vang Pao, asking him to officially relinquish his leadership and name him as the new Hmong leader. Here is the crux of his request: "*Yog koj kam no koj kuj muab Hmoob tus coj rau kuv.*" In English: "If you were allowed, please, relinquish Hmong leadership to me."

Major General Vang Pao simply replied, "I cannot make you the Hmong leader. Hmong leadership has to be approved by the people." In Hmong, "*Kuv muab tsis tau Hmoob tus coj rau koj. Yuav tsum yog pej xeem pom zoo.*"

Similarly, prior to this incident, other people had asked Major General Vang Pao indirectly for the same thing, but he had refused to give up his leadership or to name anyone to follow him or to become his successors, including his own biological sons.

Here is an excerpt of the transcript from Major General Vang Pao's final recorded messages for all Hmong refugees living in the western nations:

HMONG STRUGGLES

Hais rau tsoom Hmoob sawv daws, yug los ua Hmoob tiam no kuv yeej hlub hlub sawv daws. Rub sawv daws lub neej tawm qhov txom txom nyem, pluag pluag ntsev twb tsis muaj noj. Coj los kom txawj ntaub txawj ntawv, kom muaj noj muaj haus. Peb tuaj txog teb chaws no 35 xyoos, peb sawv daws yeej tuaj noj sib pab haus sib ce. Yeej coj cov Hmoob ua neej zoo los lawm ib theem es hais rau cov kwj tij neej tsa Hmoob hais tias kawg nkaus sawv daws sib hlub. Khiav tawm lub npe Hmoob tsis tau. Sawv daws yuav tsum sib hlub es sawv daws thiaj li muaj neej ua… [In English, *to all fellow Hmong, born to be Hmong in this life I love all very much, elevate all from the life* in *poverty, so poor without having any salt to consume. Bring up to be educated, to become sufficient in life. We have been in this country for 35 years, we all have come to love one another. Have improved Hmong life one increment, and tell all fellow Hmong that all have to love one another. Cannot depart from the name Hmong ... all have to love and all will have a life to live...]*

Hmong next leader

Sawv daws pom zoo tus twg ua tus coj, sawv daws txhawb tus ntawd, es ho los ua tsis tau los yuav hloov dua. Qhov no yog qhov tseem ceeb... [In English, *all agree whoever to lead, all support that individual, and if cannot lead then will replace. This is the importance...*]

His funeral service

Kuv lub ntees mas tsis pub cov kwv tij sib txeeb nawb. Yeej yuav as xaim cov kwv tij nyob pem Fresno yog cov coj dab coj qhuas mas lawv thiaj li ua tau ... tej me tub me nyuam sawv daws yuav tsum mloog lus es yog tias dua kuv lawm es tej nyiaj tshav ntuj liam li cas los kom sawv daws txhob sib txeeb. Kuv dua lawm los kuv yuav tso kuv cov koob cov hmoov tseg rau cov kwv tij neej tsa sawv daws tag nrho huv tib si. Kuv yeej tsis coj ib yam dab tsi mus nawb... [In English, *my funeral shouldn't allow fellow Hmong to topple one another. Will depend on all relatives living in Fresno to be in charge of rituals and rites and they can manage ... all descendants must listen and if I am gone and all sunshine donations they should not topple one another. I have departed I will leave behind all my blessings for all fellow Hmong. I will not take anything with me...*]

A Quest to Return

Kom lwm tiam peb rov qab ua txiv tub ua kwv ua tij dua.... Kuv twb coj nej mus thaum hauv paus mus txog ntsis ... kuv muab lub neej rau nej ua, muab kev txawj kev ntse rau nej. Nej tsis xav txog los cia li, nej xav txog nej txhob tso kuv tseg.... Kuv hais rau nej tias dua kuv hnub twg lawm los kuv yuav tso kuv tej koob tej hmoov rau sawvdaws tib si. Cov tsis hlub kuv ces kuv kuj tsis tu siab. Cov twg hlub hlub kuv, nco txog kuv txiaj kuv ntsig lawm, kuv yuav tso koob tso hmoov rau sawv daws tib si ... cia kuv rov los yug ua Hmoob dua tshiab es peb mam li sib hlub ib yam li peb tau sib hlub rau tiam no... [In English, *predestining for*

next life we will return to be fellow Hmong again.... I have lead you from the beginning to the end.... I give a life to you, give you education. You don't think about it, it is fine, you think about it, you don't abandon me.... I tell you all when I am gone I will leave all my blessings for all. Those who don't love me, I am not sadden in heart. Those who love me very much, remember my legacy and contributions, I will leave blessings for all ... let me reborn to be Hmong again and we will love one another as we have been in this life...]

One of the reasons Major General Vang Pao decided not to name his successor was simple: He knew no Hmong would love Hmong people as much as he did. Therefore, he reasoned, Hmong leadership belonged to the people, not to him. The people should be the ones to select their next leader. He announced his decision in his recorded messages as he encouraged all Hmong to love, embrace, and respect one another individually and as a group of people. He asked Hmong to work collaboratively to establish a democratic process for electing the next leader and, once he is elected, to follow, respect, and support him. So, who is next?

Hmong Need New Leaders

From the 1800s to the 2000s, Hmong refugees had generations of Hmong leaders who made sacrifices, underwent tribulations, fought brutal and inhumane persecution, searched for freedom and independence, overcame political oppression, elevated Hmong sociopolitical status, and brought Hmong to the Promised Land. Historically, the civilization of Hmong leaders and leadership underwent the cycle of transformation that involved the rise and fall of Hmong rulers for many centuries, and the timeline of Hmong leadership emergence could be divided into three major periods: The convergent period, the divergent period, and the parallel period. The convergent period refers to those times Hmong had a nation, lived under a ruling king, came together in great numbers to do something for the greater good of the people, and demonstrated their ethnic unity in the time of need to fight for their freedom and independence. The divergent period explains Hmong struggles for survival and those times Hmong faced political turmoil and tribulation, suffered great loss of their land, and lived miserable life because they were politically oppressed and brutally persecuted, and at the same time, they became victims of extirpation and exploitation under imperial control. The parallel period reveals Hmong co-existence in society and those times Hmong had peace, freedom, and independence; and most importantly, Hmong achieved some successes in life and were able to maintain their group solidarity and ethnic sovereignty.

It appears that the Western Hmong are now undergoing these periods ever since the death of Major General Vang Pao. Who will become the next Hmong leaders to take Hmong through and beyond the present time? The time to search for a new generation of Hmong leaders is now. It is time to plant a new seed.

Hmong refugees need to look for traditional leaders who can be pathfinders who will keep the Hmong people and the Hmong community together. Since the death of Major General Vang Pao in 2011, U.S. Hmong refugees have been looking for a way to find a new beginning to reestablish Hmong leadership. Most are unsure how to start and how they should approach one another when the latest Hmong leader left them in limbo. So far, U.S. Hmong have not been able to find any credible, viable, and vibrant candidates to fill the traditional leadership roles. Vang (2013) wrote about the prospect of finding the new Hmong national leader in the U.S.:

"WHO SHOULD HMONG FOLLOW NOW?"

Hmong are in dire need of answers to leadership that is in peril. Hmong face a tough fate when talking about who will become the next cultural leader(s) and healer(s) for Hmong people in the United States. Since the death of General Vang Pao, many groups have emerged from the darkness to claim leadership roles; however, as of now, no group seems to be credible or successful because all appear to be egocentric individuals.

On Christmas Day a public forum is open for Hmong to gather to listen to the messages General Vang Pao left behind in attempting to bring all diverse groups within the Hmong community together and to aim high at a common goal-restoring leadership role to embody trust, bonds, unity, and past sacrifices. Hmong are living in a state of apostasy and need to find common ground to refurbish Hmong leadership for the people. There is no quick fix to this complex issue; it is no easy task for anyone to embody his messages after years of unresolved tribal infighting over cultural incompatibilities and disingenuous practices of leadership.

No doubt General Vang Pao was the last messiah given to Hmong by God and he warned Hmong for years that doomsday will come to them when his reign is over since no one will be able to take his place as the result of disloyalty, dishonesty, disrespect, and disorganized familial structures. So now that day has arrived and Hmong are hearing and following whom? Can Hmong hear his voice and follow his words this time? Perhaps listening to his recorded messages will wake up Hmong to think about how to fulfill their hopes and dreams in a time of great tribulations through cultural revelations. Yet Hmong have no cultural doctrine and covenants to bind them together. However, Hmong have familial ties to inextricably live together as a big family in separate communities.

In light of all the cultural complexities, General Vang Pao did have the doctrine and covenants for Hmong people when he said Hmong need to let go of their century-old grudges, spats, and machinations and learn how to follow him as the guide to live a better life. Moreover, he repeated his words orally so many times that many felt discouraged and frustrated. Most importantly, he knew that he could not write his doctrine and covenants on paper but chose to record his words for his people to follow upon his death if they want to see change.

Now, his tape recorded messages are being used as scriptures of the Hmong doctrine and covenants. Hmong are moved by his words but still face tremendous internal struggles to overcome the egocentric attitudes and behaviors that have kept them blackmailing one another for years. As some westerners foretold, "Hmong are their own worst enemies in the political arena." For centuries, Hmong could not find their own leaders without imperialism. However, Hmong strongly believe in divine power and messianic saviors. As of today, many still believe that righteousness will descend from heaven to give them the truth of leadership. In other words, Hmong have learned to distrust one another more than building honest, lasting bonds as the result of thousands of years of imperialistic indoctrination. Therefore, Hmong truly lack religious scriptures and cultural doctrine and covenants that bind Hmong life, values, beliefs and leadership roles together.

Today, Hmong are doing soul and spirit searching. Perhaps General Vang Pao's messages will rekindle their hearts and minds to redeem their spiritual lives by hearing his voice and following his words to forgive and embrace one another before finding the righteous path of leadership that will bring a cultural democratic process to reunite the Hmong people.

The U.S. Hmong are somewhat divided when it comes to Hmong leadership. Some U.S. Hmong refugees feel there is no need to find a new leader to take Major General Vang Pao's place because there is no viable candidate of the older generation and most former military officers are inactive and aged. But most Hmong refugees still believe that Hmong need a national symbol or a leader who can speak on their behalf and can advocate for their needs. As an ethnic group, Hmong refugees are a community full of people and therefore a leader or a group of leaders is needed. Vang (2012) explained the complexity of Hmong leadership and encouraged all Hmong to continue the search for viable candidates with cultural gravitas:

"Hmong face a sense of gloomy leadership"

At the present time Hmong people are scouring the 18 familial groups and diverse individuals in the large community to find new ideas for reestablishing Hmong leadership roles. Searching for answers is not easy, and perhaps it will take months or years to find credible, believable, knowledgeable, electable, charismatic, honest, and trustworthy individuals. As of today, Hmong leadership is in peril due to the lack of viable candidates with cultural gravitas.

Many are waiting for a new group of leaders to emerge and to give them new direction after the death of General Vang Pao. So far, there are too many heads with titles but no one seems to have a clear sociopolitical mission and vision for the people. As seen and heard at most Hmong New Year celebrations held from July to December, most heads and speakers brag about General Vang Pao's achievements and accomplishments but no one has offered any new and fresh ideas that embody his beliefs and values and enable Hmong people to carry their hopes and dreams into the future. The so-called incipient leaders of most events go into hibernation after the celebrations are over and emerge again to court Hmong people when the New Year season comes again.

Without hearing and seeing a clear and tangible direction, Hmong people continue to face a sense of gloomy leadership and keep hoping for a new direction during the Hmong New Year season. Those who have titles given by General Vang Pao or by self-establishment still believe they can be anointed to claim the throne; however, their wishes are unrecognized by the people since they are shepherds without sheep at the present time. The message General Vang Pao left behind is crystal clear: Hmong need to find a democratic process for electing the next leader(s).

Sadly, most could not convey themselves and their messages to the people truly as leaders, and most of the time, they give speeches filled with counterpoints of their own underprepared leadership skills. In the public spotlight, these people lock themselves in circles of cultural rhetoric. In other words, their rhetoric reveals that they are passive individuals incompetent for leadership. For instance, they blame Hmong as having bad hearts in history for committing treason while trying to lead Hmong in the present time; this is counter-productive. Self-blaming does not help at all.

Hmong are good, quality people with a track record dating back to mainland China, and they want to have visionary, responsible leaders who may under-promise but over-deliver. For 37 long years, most self-made leaders have over-promised and under-delivered. It seems that these individuals are likely to continue their futile leadership for another long decade before Hmong people see any real changes. Most of these individuals, with the exception of a few, do not have solid foundations for becoming people leaders. Most are seriously lacking leadership qualities, such as compassion, empathy, integrity, character, charisma, and most importantly, a global education. Their speeches are given in incoherent formats and styles that reveal them as disingenuous individuals who cannot deliver what the people are expecting of them.

What Hmong people need to see now is someone who has an honest heart and can understand and convey their values, beliefs, broken hopes, shattered dreams, and plans for prosperity and posterity. They do not need someone who wants to promote his or her egocentric ideology and egotistical propaganda. Hmong have witnessed enough foolish mindsets, futile leaders, inactive principles, cultural fabrications, and rhetorical platitudes. General Vang Pao left the door wide open for Hmong to make changes, and now is the time.

As a civilized group of people, Hmong need to stop following those individuals who cannot lead but pretend to be leading Hmong; they are leading them in the wrong direction. It is time to sequester the impostors, egomaniacs, self-made leaders, cheaters, and title seekers. Let Hmong people welcome and install the visionary, inspirational, charismatic, law-abiding, educated, honest, and people-oriented individuals who can share, forgive, forget, trust, respect, support, promote, collaborate, and cooperate. As a large family, Hmong need someone who can bind them together, not someone who wants to focus on familial oligarchy to continue the reign of cultural tribulation, oppression, imperialism, and corruption.

Finally, of course, Hmong people have to have leaders in power in order to protect and preserve their best interests, their community, and their cultural values. Hmong need to grow their own leaders whom they can elect, trust, respect, follow, and honor as prophesized by General Vang Pao upon his death. And that is the right message!

The call to find new leaders is a challenge to come together to engage in formal dialogue, to exchange ideas and find meaningful purpose and common ground, to reinvigorate new directions in a reestablished Hmong leadership. So far, different groups are emerging from different backgrounds, and each group has its own propaganda that politicizes the process. Each group is after personal gain and discourages other groups from being part of the process. What Hmong really need to do now is to put the community and people ahead of themselves instead of putting themselves in front of the people. In other words, Hmong need to do what is right for the people and the community instead of focusing on what is best for their own groups, clans, and families. Vang (2013) explained the importance of finding a national symbol for all Hmong:

"HMONG LOOK FOR LEADERSHIP SYMBOL"

In today's world, Hmong Americans are facing an uncertain plight when it comes to finding a symbol of leadership to guide the Hmong community. Everyone is searching for answers and no one has yet been able to find the right approach to attract the public to call for national reform to restore and structure Hmong leadership. General Vang Pao's hopes and dreams will go cold if Hmong Americans cannot put their heads together to do what is right for the greater good of the people.

Hmong are loving, caring, social, cordial, respectful and well-liked people. However, when it comes to sociopolitical matters, Hmong have difficulty finding the right mindset, gravitas, and approach. Even though Hmong are in dire need of reforming Hmong leadership, their mistrust and distrust overshadow their hopes and become barriers that block them from achieving what they need in life. For over two years, Hmong leadership has seemingly been dead or lost in the dark. A few groups of individuals started to revive the leadership for personal gain to satisfy their hungry appetites, but they failed to reach the goal. They are now stumbling in the process of finding their roles in leadership. Their hasty quests are now hanging in mid-air.

Here are some thought-provoking questions Hmong Americans need to answer while searching for a national symbol: What is missing in this leadership quest? Are Hmong capable of doing good things for their own people? What is preventing them from creating their own national symbol? And why are Hmong their own worst enemies when it comes to finding leaders?

What is missing in the leadership quest is

an honest heart. For years, Hmong have not been able to use their honest hearts to do good things for themselves. Most of what Hmong have experienced is related to leaders' hearts of dishonesty, disloyalty, corruption, disrespect, and betrayal. This is what is missing in Hmong leadership today.

Hmong are capable of doing anything to help their own people. When it comes to leaders and leadership, Hmong are torn and scarred by past imperialism, indoctrination, communism, and selfishness. The old mentality serves little or no purpose; however, the pain and suffering endured over the years of brutal domination still linger in Hmong minds and impede their ability to do great things for their own kind. In other words, Hmong are living with toxins in their blood politically and culturally. Nonetheless, Hmong are praying, begging, and searching for messianic relief from the Almighty to cure their wounds, pain, suffering, scars, and despair. Remember, Hmong say they have seen bloody tears so many times, but Hmong have failed to change themselves to stop the tears from running down their cheeks and boiling up in their hearts.

Nothing need prevent Hmong from creating their own national symbol or national organization. In fact, Hmong themselves are the real hindrance that limits their opportunity and prevents them from achieving what they need in life. Hmong constantly blame other Hmong for any failures. They have very low tolerance toward Hmong when it comes to making mistakes or helping one another. Today, some Hmong are blaming and criticizing General Vang Pao for their personal dilemmas after his death. That is like Hmong bludgeoning Hmong to death without any compassion.

As told by non–Hmong viewers, Hmong are their own worst enemies when it comes to politics. At first, this statement appears to be false, but after examining it closely, it seems to be quite correct that Hmong create their own roadblocks and sabotage their own advancement while non–Hmong open the door wide to accept Hmong. The selfishness of Hmong has become chronic, especially in the political arena. Hmong tortured Hmong politically when Hmong took leadership positions and were employed by their imperial masters. Hmong imposed heavy taxes on Hmong when Hmong worked for the imperial government. Hmong betray Hmong when Hmong disagree with one

another. And Hmong destroy Hmong trust when Hmong are stroked by others. These coincidences have been spoken of in Hmong fairy tales, folklore, and oral traditions for hundreds of years. Even General Vang Pao reminded Hmong so many times before his death that Hmong have to overcome such evil deeds in order to find peace and harmony in their hearts and lives.

Hmong leadership is still far from Hmong's reach if Hmong ignore General Vang Pao's messages. No Hmong leader in history knows Hmong better than did General Vang Pao. He led Hmong for nearly 67 years before his death, and most importantly, he was one who rose from a poor life to become the mighty leader who brought Hmong to the Promised Land and helped Hmong seek freedom and become free at last.

Hopefully, Hmong will look at themselves in the mirror to see who they really are. Will they see a reflection of betrayal or a true Hmong image? Perhaps Hmong will learn to treat their own kind with unconditional love, respect, and kindness before Hmong can find the leaders they need. Hmong have to value their own abilities to fulfill what is missing in Hmong life; that is the symbol of Hmong leadership.

Since General Vang Pao's death, different groups of Hmong people have tried to bring people around the country together to engage in discussion about finding common ground to initiate the process of choosing a leader. However, the response to this kind of call has been slow and most people appear to be disinterested or disinclined to participate in the dialogue. If bringing different people together is hard, how will Hmong ever begin the democratic process? To have a democratic process Hmong must be willing to come together and make personal sacrifices for the cause. Otherwise, the democratic process will not work and Hmong will go back to the old-fashioned corrupt process for selecting their leaders. This is what Major General Vang Pao discouraged Hmong from doing. Because of past conflicts and squabbles, General Vang Pao wanted Hmong to avoid the centuries-old problems and urged all Hmong to believe in and use democracy. Vang (2012) explained the need for finding cultural gravitas to attract Hmong leaders to initiate the process of selecting a new leader:

"Hmong need to find cultural gravitas"

Is it time to suspend one's attitudes? Or is it time to show kindness to Hmong people? Everyone has a part in answering these two questions.

In this time of a quest for leadership, Hmong need to clearly define the cause and effect of Hmong apostasy prior to discussing the mission, vision, and goals and before calling on the general public to hold a national conference to share with everyone about the Hmong leadership movement and what is going to happen next. Hmong are searching for new ideas to engage Hmong individuals to elicit the right pathways to reestablish Hmong leadership. But the current approach lacks cultural gravitas.

Admittedly, Hmong are hungry for leadership. However, publicly, Hmong are too narrow-minded when it comes to having open discussion and sharing concrete thoughts. Many are trapped in the familial corner in which they can only see what is best for their tribal family rather than advocating for the greater good of the people. In other words, Hmong put the family's best interest first and leadership second, or Hmong put the wagon before the bull. This has been a real dilemma in dealing with Hmong leadership discourse. At the very least, Hmong need to separate themselves from the centuries-old familial politics that only promotes oligarchic mindsets, and they have to get out of the box in order to promote the democratic approach and inspire one another.

Hmong are living in a state of cultural apostasy since General Vang Pao left the door wide open for Hmong to search for new leaders and leadership. His hopes and dreams are cultural solutions to end Hmong centuries-old familial politics based on tribal envies and personal jealousies. General Vang Pao predestined Hmong's plight by giving Hmong a quest to start all over again after his death. If Hmong should fail to honor his messages, then Hmong will never come close to finding new leaders and leadership because Hmong are lacking fundamental common sense to do what is right for Hmong people.

Today's Hmong have to have leadership collaboration and professional diplomacy to engage Hmong in compromising tactics to do great things for Hmong people. Most discourses are centered on old-fashioned ideologies, perspectives, modalities, and approaches—good old boy attitudes without clear directions. Even though Hmong are living in the 21st century, Hmong individuals are not up-to-date on leadership issues. Some are asleep while others are drifting in the dark. In most cases, today's Hmong individuals are under-prepared to undertake leadership roles and responsibilities. This lack has stalled the process of reform. Leadership collaborations and diplomatic relationships can help Hmong compromise so they can cooperate on their basic principles; they desperately need cooperation to ignite the passion for restructuring Hmong leadership. So far, no one has been able to inflame such passion to fulfill General Vang Pao's hopes and dreams.

If this trend continues, Hmong will have a difficult time finding the cultural gravitas needed to restore trust, bonds, respect, and relationships toward achieving group solidarity and unity. In other words, Hmong will remain divided as prophesized by General Vang Pao until Hmong are able to overcome their differences, or Hmong will face an uncertain future without a national symbol.

Finally, the missions, visions, and goals of Hmong leadership are not foreseeable at this time until Hmong bring their honest hearts to the table to discuss what is best for all Hmong. As predicted by General Vang Pao, Hmong have to cast away the evil spirits living in their hearts and souls before they can achieve a prosperous life without being afraid of cultural espionage or being cursed by satanic, centuries-old demons. And of course, being willing to change one's attitudes by coming together, Hmong can join hands to do more for their people. That is cultural gravitas.

Historically, Hmong are tribal; they live in independent groups. However, the groups live among one another and depend on one another for survival. When it comes to political matters, Hmong often separate themselves by brotherhood, familial ties, clanship, and ancestry, but they come together on issues that affect them all. As the Chinese described Hmong unity during times when they joined together in rebelling against Chinese oppression, Hmong used blood oaths, holy water, justice water, and religious solemnization to bind themselves together to fight battles and wars. At other times, Hmong political unity was fragile because they lacked trust as the result of a history of betrayal, dishonesty, treason, espionage, and treachery.

Major General Vang Pao knew Hmong history well. He purposely left a leadership vacuum so Hmong would make changes— changing themselves before changing others. The founding fathers of the U.S. used a phrase to describe the bond that tied the American people together: "One nation, under God, indivisible, with liberty and justice for all." Hmong people need to find a similar motto that embodies their identity to keep them united. As Major General Vang Pao said many times when he lectured his soldiers on the battle field, "United we stand, divided we perish."

The problem has little to do with unity but has a lot to do with trust and betrayal. Throughout history, Hmong often mistrusted one another because of personal greed and egocentric attitudes, and personal egos led Hmong to betray one another. Today, the symptoms of mistrust and betrayal are living inside Hmong souls and spirits. Hmong need to overcome such political toxins in order to develop lasting relationships. Frankly, Vang (2012) shared his concerns about Hmong unity issues:

"Why Hmong still face unity issues"

At a time when they face a dire plight in Hmong leadership, Hmong individuals are asking for Hmong unity in order to establish cordial working relationships with one another. That is the approach most want to see taken before showing their commitment to the cause. Without agreeing on some fundamental values and theoretical principles, Hmong will miss the target because, as seen today, Hmong still have problems trusting one another, and at the same time, Hmong individuals have not changed much since 1975. Perhaps the imperial indoctrination is living deeply in Hmong hearts and souls.

Over the 37 years living in the US, the quest for unity has always failed to serve the best interest of Hmong people since unity itself comprises a myriad of issues and concerns that cannot be resolved culturally and professionally. However, if the focus now should be on unity, then the discussion will drive Hmong individuals off task.

Unity simply means coming together for a common purpose, or unity means agreement that binds all together for a common purpose. The individual's pledge for unity is not that easy if there is nothing that interests the person. First, coming together is easy, but the real challenge is what will tie the group together for a common purpose. For instance, people often get bored or become less interested after days, months, or years of having tedious discussions with one another. Yet, people make sacrifices to spend time away from family to be in this group. For that very reason, coming together is not the same as staying together until the very end.

Second, having an agreement is a good thing for all to feel secure, trusted, bonded together, and inclusive; however, the conditions and terms included in the agreement have to be spelled out clearly and have to be enforced accordingly in order to keep all members staying together, not leaving the group. Most importantly, there should be logical consequences for leaving or violating the agreement; otherwise, signing an agreement does not mean much to the individual if there is no disciplinary policy in place. So, the terms and conditions have to be laid out for everyone to agree to. That is a real challenge.

Third, social and cultural unity is often based on voluntary conditions and terms. There is not much anyone can do to enforce or reinforce the agreement if someone should decide to leave. For instance, the past leaders used simple tactics (spiritual binding and/or life-long devotion) to bind Hmong leaders together while organizing social and political movements; however, the lack of equality and of a democratic process caused members to depart the party for personal reasons. In other words, subordinates cannot question higher authority figures when things are abnormal, or when they disagree with the plan. Quite often, members are to follow orders from the top only. Moreover, the complexity of unity will exhaust the efforts needed for the mission.

What Hmong individuals ought to think about now is their self-modification, self-regulating, and self-compassion for the mission. Unity will exist if the individual sees the needs of the people, comes to the group with an open heart, uses his or her honest heart to do what is best for the people, changes oneself to follow the mission, talks about what is best for the people, advocates for the people, focuses on "We the People," and leaves personal baggage at home. In other words, the individual has to cleanse his or her spirits and souls prior to joining the group in order to do what is right for the mission instead of joining the group and asking the people in the group to cleanse themselves. If Hmong individuals come to the group clean, then seeking unity is not necessary, or is not that difficult.

Hopefully, Hmong individuals will leave their personal vendettas, anger, frustrations, and animosities aside while engaging in dialogues. At the same time, they will abandon the past to focus on the present and future to do what is right for the Hmong people. That is unity!

Furthermore, as prophesized by Major General Vang Pao, after his time no Hmong will be able to unite Hmong people unless Hmong people themselves are willing to leave their past behind. Finding a new leader is possible, but finding an exact duplicate as a replacement is totally impossible. It is time for Hmong to ponder finding a leader who can fill the traditional roles. Can educated individuals or Hmong elected officials fill the roles for the Hmong people?

Educated and Elected Hmong Individuals

Hmong educated and elected officials are emerging around the U.S. This is a sign of change in Hmong leadership. However, as a community, Hmong people need a group of leaders who understand the Hmong way of life. Most Hmong educated and elected officials have little or no involvement in Hmong traditional and cultural leadership; they are elected by the general public to serve as public servants not for Hmong only. As for the educated, they have little or no time to do volunteer work for the Hmong. Of course, they can help initiate the process of find new

beginnings, but they cannot fill the role of Hmong leaders themselves for a number of reasons:

- Hmong traditional leaders receive no monthly salary or fringe benefits.
- Hmong leaders must spend countless hours dealing with clan issues and community problems.
- Hmong clan systems are complex and the Hmong way of life is different from that of other Americans.
- Americanized leaders and individuals lack cultural gravitas and the proper foundations to serve as Hmong leaders in traditional leadership positions.
- Most elected officials may be unfit to serve as Hmong leaders for a variety of reasons, and Hmong people are not prepared to be led by leaders who may prefer the western way of life as opposed to the Hmong way of life.

Moreover, most of the U.S. Hmong refugees still have great respect for the latest Hmong leader regardless of his shortcomings as a traditional leader in the West. The new generation of young Hmong leaders may need to build trust and bonds with Hmong people in order to earn their respect in the community. In most cases, the new leaders and elected officials may not feel the need of trust and bonds because they are well-known and well-recognized by the general public in the political arena, but public service does not last forever. Also, the emerging young and educated Hmong leaders and elected officials may not be able to fill the role of Hmong leader because they have professional careers that leave them no time to volunteer in such capacities. They may look for other ways to perform public service. Some young Hmong may not see the role of Hmong leader as a vibrant responsibility in today's society as it once was. Furthermore, they may not have the cultural capability of devoting themselves to serving in the role.

However, educated individuals and Hmong elected officials can play an important role in Hmong leadership by mobilizing Hmong people to help organize and structure Hmong communities for social and political purposes. They can also help Hmong people and the Hmong community to find a sensible pathway for reforming the role of Hmong leadership by bringing different groups and clans together to engage in a democratic process of eliciting new ideas and directions for reestablishing the traditional role of Hmong leaders for the sake of the people and the community. Simply, both elected officials and traditional leaders need to have the Hmong community and people around them; otherwise, they will be shepherds without sheep and Hmong people will be sheep without a shepherd.

Meanwhile, Hmong elected officials (educated, professional, and westernized individuals) and Hmong traditional leaders (clan leaders, former military officers, and family heads of household) need to work together to restore the Hmong leadership role. If possible, they should come together as pathfinders and collaborate to organize and unite Hmong people to advocate for the greater good of the people. For instance, the multiple Hmong New Year's celebrations taking place around the U.S. need to be organized and reformed to conform to other ethnic groups' way of celebrating their cultures and traditions. As of now, the Hmong way of celebrating Hmong culture and traditions is out of control. Moreover, Hmong people and the Hmong community need to reexamine Hmong traditional customs, especially the Hmong funeral service and rituals, because the cost for such an important event has skyrocketed. These basic socio-cultural changes require visionary leaders with strong leadership to find the right pathway for Hmong's future. Without strong leaders making changes, the status quo will be perpetuated.

Prior to his death, Major General Vang Pao strongly advocated for reform in these areas. One leader cannot make the drastic changes that are needed in the thinking of so many. But perhaps many leaders can collaborate to initiate gradual changes and reforms. That is the challenge for the next traditional Hmong leaders.

The Next Hmong Leaders

Are Hmong forbearing people? Based on current conditions, Hmong are facing difficult plight and are dealing with uncertain fate. Together, Hmong have to forge alliances among themselves and need to have pathfinders to lead the way. Any Hmong can become a pathfinder; however, these pathfinders have to be honest in heart. Otherwise, finding the next Hmong leaders to fill the traditional roles for the Hmong community and the Hmong people will not be easy because Hmong appear to have a myriad of cultural issues to overcome before they can find a sensible way to embrace one another for the greater good of the people. Despite cultural conflicts, at the very least, the U.S. Hmong should show some respect for all Hmong leaders, past, present, and future, in order to bring up a new generation of leaders. Hmong traditional leadership will continue to be in peril until Hmong learn to treat their leaders with respect. Because some Hmong publicly complained about General Vang Pao, Vang (2013) wrote to criticize those who chose not to lead but to scold, reprove, and berate Hmong past leaders, especially Major General Vang Pao, for no reason other than to vent personal feelings:

> ### "WHY SOME HMONG CRITICIZE GENERAL VANG PAO PUBLICLY"
>
> From December to now, I have watched video clips on YouTube, listened to cassette tapes given to me by a friend, and had conversations with college students who were appalled while some Hmong college professors who teach Hmong cultural classes berated General Vang Pao bitterly in class. It is time to get the facts straight.
>
> As a Hmong myself, I have a very difficult time seeing some Hmong people rebuking General Vang Pao by holding public forums, recording personal vendettas, making public speeches, or lecturing college students. I was disheartened to know that these individuals are the real cultists who will continue to haunt the Hmong way of life. Also, these personal attacks are not only malicious, but culturally bizarre and intolerable.
>
> In fact, these individuals do not have to agree with General Vang Pao or like him,

but at least they have to pay respect to General Vang Pao for his military leadership that brought these cold-hearted people to the Promised Land.

In fact, the educated Hmong who berate General Vang Pao have no cultural values to offer to Hmong students in college classes, and more importantly, these individuals have not read the history book correctly while going to school. Therefore, at least, these people have to accept the truth that Hmong are free at last because of General Vang Pao's leadership.

In fact, these people can use their freedom of speech to reprove General Vang Pao, but at least they have to accept the truth that their reproofs are meritless and unnecessary after his death. Attacking a deceased leader is purely cruel and evil in heart.

In fact, these people appear to know General Vang Pao better than he knew himself, but at least they have to accept the truth that they followed General Vang Pao to the West, and most importantly, the American government would not accept them or could not have known them if it was not for the leadership of this great leader.

In fact, these people are arrogant to condemn General Vang Pao after his death. But at least they have to accept the truth that there is no Hmong person holding a military rank, leadership role, or position of honor and respect higher than did General Vang Pao.

In fact, these people are envious of General Vang Pao's reign. But at least they have to accept the truth that they are not Hmong leaders whom Hmong people will follow, respect, honor, and pray for like General Vang Pao.

In fact, these people can vent their cancerous anger, frustration, anxiety, and insanity for self-gratification, but at least they have to accept the truth that there is no cure for their century-old cancer and heartache. At the same time, they have to redeem their own debacles instead of blaming General Vang Pao for their personal demise.

In fact, these people can read the history books, but at least they have to accept the truth that General Vang Pao made history for them to read about and to learn Hmong history.

In fact, these people can claim to be smarter than General Vang Pao, but at least they have to accept the truth that General Vang Pao was a heroic messiah, Godly gift, warrior, commander-in-chief, and mighty leader no other Hmong man can be compared to.

In fact, these people appear to have anarchical mindsets, but at least they have to accept the truth that they were once followers of General Vang Pao, and many times they sought the opportunity to elevate their social status in his shadow.

In fact, some of these people are former military leaders who are more educated than General Vang Pao. But at least they have to accept the truth that General Vang Pao was the only leader who promoted them without questioning their lack of military prowess and war experience.

In fact, some of these people can read and write better than did General Vang Pao. But at least they have to accept the truth that General Vang Pao outwitted them all naturally.

In fact, these people have tried to discredit General Vang Pao for personal gain. But at least they have to accept the truth that nearly 90 percent of Hmong people around the world still respect General Vang Pao as an all-time great Hmong leader regardless of their claims. Moreover, other non–Hmong friends also respect General Vang Pao and his people for their role in the Secret War in Laos.

Finally, in fact, these people might rise to the occasion to seek leadership roles. But at least they have to accept the truth that they do not have the charismatic quality of General Vang Pao to lead, and moreover, they have not earned enough respect to claim the throne of Hmong leadership. All they have done so far is to spill the evil spirits over Hmong people to make them their victims of cultic mania.

Overall, General Vang Pao was the like the Golden Gate bridge that all Hmong refugees walked on to cross the Atlantic Ocean to make it to the Promised Land. And that is the truth; these people have to know that they did not come here by themselves in the first place.

As a Hmong, I do hope that we will continue to pay great respect to all past, present, and future Hmong leaders and stop slandering past leaders maliciously. I find it hard to believe that some Hmong people are not real Hmong people at heart at all when they scold a deceased leader such as General Vang Pao in seeking leadership roles for themselves.

At the moment, there are plenty of young, promising, educated, and well-liked Hmong Americans who can rise to the occasion to become the new pathfinders who are able to assume leadership roles, but Hmong people are still waiting patiently for someone who has a kind and honest heart and can embody Hmong values and beliefs. The character traits required of Hmong leaders have to include civility and humility. For that very reason, Hmong need to work hard to find the next leaders; otherwise, Major General Vang Pao could very well be the first and last messianic leader in the 21st century.

Summing Up

This chapter focused on Hmong leadership from the past to the present and for the future. It gave a comprehensive overview of Hmong leaders who made sacrifices to elevate Hmong in socio-political status in Laos and elsewhere.

Hmong have lost their history of Hmong leaders in ancient China and have only sketchy accounts of who their leaders were in the ancient world. Today Hmong claim people who may have been Chinese or other non–Hmong as their past leaders, such as ChiYou, Zhang Xiu Mei, and some others. Hmong nationalists identify as Hmong past leaders people who were heroic, iconic, and powerful and made great contributions but refuse to accept as Hmong those who had less than stellar records in history. Hmong need to do more research on their leaders of the past before claiming these heroic leaders to be their past saviors, rulers, protectors, and kings.

In Indochina, Hmong resettled in the Nong Het area and reestablished Hmong life under Hmong leaders who were known as phagna, kiatongs, village chiefs, chieftains, tassengs, nai kongs, chao muongs, chao khuoengs, nai bans, phub tooms, phes tooms, and so on. Hmong refugees underwent tribulations and endured hardships, especially unreasonable taxation, under the French occu-

pation and the brutal colonial policy. Hmong fought and made great sacrifices for their freedom and independence in Laos.

Hmong leaders such as Moua Chong Kai, Lo Blia Yao, Ly Chia Fong, Touby Lyfong, and Major General Vang Pao transformed the Hmong way of life through battles, wars, and political action. Moreover, they led the Hmong through the transition from unrecognized and marginalized people to patriotic freedom fighters during the first and second Indochina wars and especially the Secret War financed by the CIA of the U.S. from 1960 to 1975. If had not been for the bravery of these leaders, Hmong would not have been known to the western world, and most importantly, Hmong could not have come to the western nations to start over again after the fall of Laos in 1975.

In the western nations, especially in the U.S., Hmong have made remarkable progress. Hmong receive educational opportunities as well as economic opportunities that can elevate their way of life and socioeconomic status. Over 40 years, Hmong have become like other Americans. Many Hmong refugees continue to struggle with changes in the new homeland and others are acculturated and integrated into the host culture.

Hmong leadership is now in disarray after the death of Major General Van Pao in 2011, and Hmong people and the Hmong community are in a state of apostasy. Hmong are working hard to seek a new beginning to reestablish Hmong leadership. However, the prospect of finding new leaders is dim and uncertain based on the current situation.

Many Hmong hope that Hmong will come together to find leaders who will revitalize the Hmong way of life and work together to do what is right for the greatest good of the people. Together, Hmong leaders can help Hmong refugees move beyond the state of apostasy by gradually and consistently changing the status quo. Meanwhile, Hmong leadership is in peril and Hmong refugees are desperately in need of new leaders for a new beginning.

FOURTEEN

The Hmong Journey Forward

Lub neej dhau los thiab lub neej tam simno...
Kuv yog tus coj nej...
Tabsi lub neej no lawm yam tom ntej...
Nws yuav yog nej thiab nej cov menyuam li...
Hmoob yuav tsum sib hlub, sib pab, sib txhawb...
Kom Hmoob vam nkaus li xub ntab, nroo ntws li xub mu...
The words of Major General Vang Pao, 2010

Introduction

Perhaps U.S. Hmong should ponder this question: *Where do we go from here?* For those who do not need other Hmong people, the Hmong community, and traditional Hmong leaders, the answer is simple: Nowhere. However, those who are concerned about the prospect of a Hmong future and leadership after the death of Major General Vang Pao and the overall socioeconomic status of the U.S. Hmong think differently. They believe the Hmong, as a race, have come to a turning point and need to reestablish Hmong traditional leadership roles and mobilize the Hmong people and the Hmong community to preserve Hmong culture and traditions and, most importantly, maintain Hmong identity while living in a pluralistic society.

U.S. Hmong are getting used to a dual lifestyle, remaining traditional at home while becoming integrated and assimilated into the host culture. Many think that whenever possible they should let go of beliefs and practices that are antiquated because survival in a different world requires a different body of knowledge and different behaviors (as expressed in Hmong, *ib rab teb ib tsa txuj*). Throughout history, Hmong people and their leaders have fought against brutal invaders, oppressors, and dictators who wanted Hmong to submit to their ways of life. They have endured much to keep Hmong culture and traditions alive and to save Hmong from being extirpated down to their roots. When Hmong were oppressed to near ethnic extinction, they demonstrated cultural resiliency, often having to retreat to save themselves from being wiped off the face of the earth. Today's Hmong should think about all the challenges faced by all the past generations and ask how they are going to preserve Hmong customs, values, beliefs, and norms for their children. How are they going to share with the young and future generations what it really means to be Hmong?

This chapter discusses a variety of issues related to the formidable challenges facing U.S. Hmong refugees as they consider the future. Its purpose is to help Hmong think in terms of society as a whole and encourage them to study the past carefully and examine the present critically. Understanding and appreciating the past and dealing with the issues of the present will give Hmong insight that will prepare them to face the new challenges of tomorrow.

Hmong and Their Community

Today, Hmong refugees belong to a close-knit community. Ethnically, Hmong have one of the most complex social systems in the world. The patriarchal structure leaves many in limbo, especially Hmong females and native-born Hmong-Americans. At present, many Hmong-Americans are living on the edge because Hmong lack a national leader who can provide sociocultural leadership and guidance for the community. Hmong should find sociocultural gravitas to help them develop and organize their community systematically for collective sociopolitical purposes if they want to advance and improve the status quo. Simply, Hmong people and their community need to be empowered and inspired from the ground up. Since Major General Vang Pao's death, Hmong Americans have faced pandemonium in their daily lives. Here are some critical sociocultural factors that Hmong refugees should ponder regarding their life prospects in the western world:

- Their college education and academic degrees will empower their socioeconomic opportunities, including career paths, professional occupations, socioeconomic status, wealth, prosperity, job security, and self-actualization.
- Their religious reform, modernization, and conversion will empower their religious practices and funeral services, including having common faiths and values, group solidarity, cultural unity, religious tolerance, and support system.
- Their social media infrastructure will empower their social capital, including social networks, advocacy, reform, communication, movement, radicalism, sociocultural mobility, and community reorganization and development.
- Their integration, assimilation, and en-

culturation processes will empower their cross-cultural competencies and functionalities needed in a pluralistic society, including embracing diversity, having different family lifestyles, having different childrearing practices, and accepting western values and ideals.
- Their cultural preservation and New Year's celebration will empower their ethnic identity, including safeguarding their dialects, cultures, traditions, values, beliefs, norms, and customs.
- Their lack of national leaders and Hmong leadership in peril will empower their dire quest for a new beginning, including coping with the rise and fall of anarchic reforms, dealing with cultural tribulations, transforming the state of apostasy, coming together for a common purpose, joining hands in efforts needed for a great cause, seeking cultural gravitas, dealing with sociocultural complexities, reviving and restoring leadership, and rebuilding and restructuring the community as a whole.

Hmong definitely need to develop a macrocosm of leadership to forge alliance among Hmong factions, cliques, and social groups. As Major General Vang Pao envisioned, Hmong have to have a system that can unite Hmong as a large group; otherwise, the microcosm of leadership is fragile and will further divide and separate Hmong into disorder, fragmented, and isolated unitary groups. Without collaborative and unified efforts to revive the structure of Hmong national leadership, Hmong will soon face difficult plight and uncertain future. The current Hmong sociocultural structure is not working collectively and is moving gradually toward the formation of anarchical communities because of the ongoing tribal infighting and leadership in peril.

It is a high time for Hmong refugees to think about the reconstruction of their communities in order for them to develop tactical approaches and strategic actions to deal with the overall complexities of Hmong sociocultural challenges. If little or nothing is done to improve the current leadership in peril, western Hmong will enter another decade of chaotic sociocultural dilemma. Radicalism may help Hmong-Americans exercise their American values and ideals; however, such approaches may not be the best course of action that most Hmong refugees would expect to see. For instance, Hmong radical movement may include drastic reform and propagandistic activities, such as uprising, unrest, uproar, and lawsuit. Also, without taking bold steps toward sociocultural reform, Hmong tribal bickering over cultural norms and traditional values will lead Hmong toward sociopolitical instability. At present, Hmong traditional leadership and sociocultural organizations may be at stake for radical reform because of futility, corruption, extortion, and tribal conflict. Hmong-Americans are likely to gear toward adopting democratic views in order to restore trust, bond, power, and leadership. However, such approaches may work but will drive Hmong and their community into more sociocultural upheavals. For instance, Hmong are suing one another in court to take control of the Hmong New Year's celebration in California and elsewhere in the U.S. More importantly, Hmong solitary behaviors and attitudes will erode Hmong sociopolitical power, for example, the lack of collaborative leadership, cooperative collaborations, and unity. That is why Hmong need to find sensible ways to help them reconstruct Hmong leadership for the greater good of the people.

The life of Hmong refugees will continue to evolve, transform, and change as long as they are living in the U.S. and elsewhere in the West. As a community, Hmong refugees need to have leaders who can lead the way and can act on their behalf to advocate for their best interests in the sociopolitical arena. As a group of people, Hmong refugees will continue to have sociopolitical issues and problems related to their cross-cultural adjustments. To deal with Hmong complex issues, Hmong and their community would need to have strong leaders and leadership in order to find sensible solutions. Keep in mind that Hmong may not need to have cultural managers because Hmong can manage their own lives, but Hmong definitely need to have leaders who can lead and can intervene in solving Hmong complex problems. When needed, these leaders can provide them with quality leadership to bring together a body of Hmong and non–Hmong representatives to deal with Hmong sociopolitical needs and wants; otherwise, Hmong and their community will continue to be in the state of apostasy. Here is one pressing issue: Hmong are holding multiple New Year's celebrations each year and no one can tell Hmong to change. Such solitary leadership and defiant behaviors will not only divide Hmong and their community but will continue to tarnish the true meaning of Hmong New Year and traditions.

When it comes to community leadership, Hmong have to produce their own leaders who can govern them and who can give them the respect, trust, vision, and leadership. As an appointed imperial leader, Major General Vang Pao was not a perfect leader for all Hmong but was the most influential icon, honorable war hero, and powerful traditional leader most Hmong look up to for guidance. Now, it is time for Hmong refugees to learn from their past history in order for them to grow new leaders to lead them to the future.

Since the mid–1970s the western Hmong population has grown exponentially from a hundred thousand to nearly three hundred thousand and is increasingly growing despite the decrease in family and household sizes. It is true today that Hmong people in the West do not live in a patriarchal world. However, most Hmong people still have a patriarchal mindset; their philosophy, culture, and community are all patriarchal. From the 1700s to the 2000s, Hmong have seen a generation of Hmong leaders who made great sacrifices for the betterment of the Hmong people and helped pave the way for Hmong to walk in search of freedom, independence, and socioeconomic opportunities. Without Hmong leaders, Hmong would not have been in the western nations in the first place. Hmong history is remarkable, with the fortunes of the people rising and falling over the centuries. More than a story of struggle, it is a story of progress and successes.

All Hmong should have learned from their history as well as their present life circumstances about who they really are as a people; that is, where they have come from and how they got here in the first place. Although they are one group of people living in the same community and coming from the same country, Hmong are not only linguistically and socioeconomically diverse but are also religiously and politically incompatible in some ways. Typically, Hmong people are good, decent, loving beings and have so much to cherish with one another, but individually, Hmong people and families must admit that they are territorial, tribal, clannish, and solitary people who share a common culture and common traditions, customs, values, beliefs, languages, histories, and ancestries. As with other ethnic groups, Hmong people face challenges, suffer tribulations, transform over time, make progress, achieve successes, and seek prosperity.

Nonetheless, Hmong as a group of people have difficulties with one another when it comes to the establishment of their own leadership. Hmong people are not a vibrant and significant political force without Hmong leaders. For Hmong, there is a trinity of life that consists of the people, the community, and the leaders, as illustrated in Figure 14.1. Life as a people is not viable without these three inseparable components. As Hmong used to say in the old days, the burner of a cooking pit has to have a tripods, each of three legs is needed for something to stand straight and strong, as in Hmong, *ib lub kos yuav tsum muaj peb tug ceg thiaj yuav ua tau noj, ib pab neeg yuav tsum muaj peb tug zoo coj thiaj li ciaj haiv.* Similarly, Hmong use a symbolic phrase to explain the importance of group collectivism, "*ib tug xyoob yuav ua laj kab xov tsis thoob ib lub vaj, ib haiv neeg yuav tsum muaj kev sib koom sib pab thiaj li yuav tau txais kev muaj yeej*," meaning, "one bamboo tree cannot fence around the whole garden, one ethnic group has to have collective cooperation and support in order to achieve triumph."

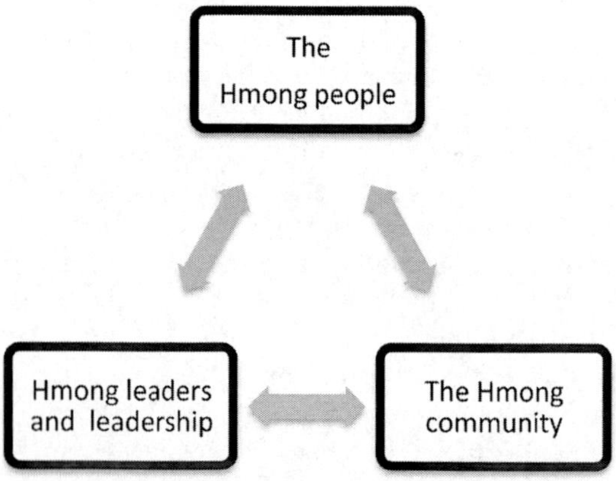

Throughout history, for the most part, Hmong leaders have been Hmong who were appointed by imperial governments that ruled them; Laos, France, and the U.S. chose leaders for the Hmong. Perhaps that is why Major General Vang Pao urged Hmong today to cleanse themselves of their sinful and ingrained attitudes about leadership and develop a democratic process whereby Hmong can establish a new generation of Hmong leaders for themselves.

Hmong must work through a number of cultural dilemmas in order to establish a process for selecting leaders who can be pathfinders for the Hmong people and their community. Some of the dilemmas are as follows:

- Some Hmong clan clubs and clan leaders have to learn how to compromise to advance the Hmong people and community as a whole. For the time being, clan clubs need to think outside the box and get out of their comfort zones.
- Hmong still have serious trust and unity issues and problems among themselves. They need to find sensible ways of restoring confidence, humility, and civility.
- Some Hmong individuals and groups may have leadership capabilities but are interested in themselves rather than

Figure 14.1. Hmong trinity of life.

The Hmong people

Hmong leaders and leadership ⟷ The Hmong community

in the betterment of the Hmong people. Hmong need leaders who will provide pathways, guidance, and advocacy for all Hmong and for the Hmong community.

- Hmong do not understand that there is power in numbers. They need to join hands in efforts that can improve the Hmong communal way of life. Hmong need to produce their own cultural leaders who can represent the interests of all US Hmong in the larger society.

Tribal Trust and Mistrust

Culturally, Hmong have a strong bond of cordial relationship because of their matrimonial and marital kinship; however, in politics, most still have lots of sociopolitical mistrusts because of bad past experiences with their imperial masters, warlords, dictators, and oppressors who forced them to betray and exploit Hmong. For instance, Hmong were negatively affected and influenced by the *guanxi culture*, a long Chinese history of bribes and extortions in China, the French colonial tax policy, and the communist indoctrination. However, now is different and Hmong have the opportunity to build and restore trust and bond among one another. Western Hmong should have to find a common ground to forge alliances among different clan leaders, tribes, and social groups in order for them to reestablish sensible cultural gravitas needed for the revival and restoration of Hmong leaders and leadership.

Throughout Hmong history, Hmong leaders used blood oaths, justice water, shamanistic vow, and animal blood to bind themselves together to fight against oppressors, invaders, dictators, brutal policies, and political persecution. The brotherhood formed in this way made the leaders who had pledged their loyalty to one another staunch allies as they stood up for their freedom and independence. In great numbers, the Hmong were powerful forces. However, enemies of the Hmong who wanted to destroy their group solidarity exploited their tendency to become self-centered when it came to power and status. Political greed led some Hmong to develop treacherous behaviors that made Hmong leaders vulnerable to outsiders. The outsiders found Hmong who were willing to betray their own people; these Hmong defectors became the Hmong's worst adversaries. For instance, in China, where Hmong frequently rebelled against imperial oppression, Hmong fought on both sides. Some Hmong joined the imperial Chinese dictators who went after Hmong rebel groups. In Laos, one group of Hmong joined the U.S. and the Royal Lao Army and another group teamed up with the communist regime. Hmong fought Hmong on the battlefield. What is true in the bigger picture is also true in the smaller communities; treachery has occurred in the past so tribes still do not fully trust one another. Hmong still fear enemies from within their own community, having a sense of insecurity among themselves.

In the mid–1960s, some Hmong defectors plotted to take over leadership from Major General Vang Pao when he was wounded and hospitalized in another country. Although the coup did not take place, the memory of it remains in Hmong hearts and souls to the present day. In the West, Hmong often squabble with one another and form cliques and factions to sabotage one another in the Hmong community. For instance, the infighting over the Hmong New Year's celebration still divides Hmong people and communities, which is why multiple celebrations take place each year. For the betterment of the Hmong people and the Hmong community, Hmong have to stop the mistrust and eradicate these behaviors. Otherwise, Hmong are going to see another four decades of turmoil, tribulation, and sociopolitical instability before change begins.

Some of the behaviors of past leaders that have given rise to mistrust and divisions because whoever was in power:

- Rules as a dictator and tyrant, controlling every aspect of Hmong life.
- Plays favorites and uses nepotism for personal reasons.
- Lacks a democratic mission and vision for the Hmong people.

- Tries to topple other leaders.
- Rules through tribal and clan manpower and fails to act according to cultural norms.
- Becomes corrupt because of bribery, extortion, greed, and exploitation.
- Fails to fulfill his civil responsibilities and maintains the position merely for self-gratification.
- Lacks leadership structure and foundations to guide the Hmong people and their community.
- Duplicates what his predecessor did, maintaining the status quo and not advancing the people.
- Dislikes and mistrusts those who question and criticize his actions and decisions.
- Tries to keep power in the family or clan by passing down his position as an inheritance.
- Lacks basic education and training needed for quality leadership.
- Wants to reign forever without any term limit.
- Misuses the privileges and authority given by the Hmong people.
- Supersedes written rules, policies, and procedures in place.
- Becomes a life-long appointee without the approval of the general public.
- Reigns as long as he lives.
- Preys on the poor and less fortunate and isolates capable and able people.
- Fails to develop democratic collaborations, shared governance, cooperation, and transparency.
- Monopolizes the Hmong people and the Hmong community for personal gain.

Furthermore, Hmong people tend to have covetous behaviors and attitudes that drive them to blind opposition to their own leaders. Some Hmong defectors have had personal vendettas against Hmong leaders who expelled them from positions of power. As Major General Vang Pao said many times, Hmong need to stop these evil and sinful acts in order to become a unified group of people; they need to let go of the vindictive attitudes.

If they don't, the jealousy and toxins in Hmong blood will continue to destroy Hmong trust, bonds, values, unity, and most importantly, leadership. To pave the way, Major General Vang Pao left behind a vacuum of leadership for Hmong people to fill by searching for their next leaders whom they can trust and follow.

The Need for Pathfinders and Personal Sacrifice

Hmong are now living on the edge and need to find new pathfinders to lead the way. To be a powerful group of people, Hmong need a pathfinder who can envision a long-term future for Hmong that is greater than the present. He needs to believe fully in that vision. He must be willing to show sincere commitment to embark on a mission that requires personal sacrifice. Throughout history, Hmong people and leaders have shown courage as they revolted against oppressors who invaded their kingdom and tried to take their agricultural land. Hmong have also made great sacrifices to overcome adversaries and imperial suppressions and relocate to find freedom and independence.

Today, Hmong people lack pathfinders who understand the need for personal sacrifice for the betterment of their people and their community. Most Hmong today who would be leaders are more concerned with their personal needs and wants than those of the people. Their egos lead them into corruption and exploitation of others. If they consider the needs of the people, they focus on urgent needs and short-term goals and act for the benefit of a few rather than the majority. Their mission statements are unsustainable and their goals are unclear. Those who want to be leaders are clan-centered and want their clan to dominate other groups forever.

This has been a problem throughout Hmong history. From the mid–1800s to the late 1800s, the Lo clan, Moua clan, and Ly clan dominated the Hmong people. From the early 1900s to the mid–1900s, the Lo clan and Ly clan vied for dominance and from the 1940s to the mid–1970s, the Ly clan and Vang clan dominated. From 1975 to 2011, the Vang clan dominated Hmong people in the West. These examples of familial dominance and clan rule indicate that Hmong leadership is clan-centered. At present, since the death of Major General Vang Pao, U.S. Hmong are living in a state of apostasy, abandoning their loyalty to any leader, and are therefore undergoing cultural tribulations and turmoil.

Major General Vang Pao said numerous times that without sincere personal commitment and sacrifice a leader cannot change the course of history or make a difference in the lives of many. Whether Hmong leaders are born or made, he encouraged Hmong people to do for others before doing for themselves, to advocate for others before asking for themselves, to protect others before protecting themselves, and to stand for others before standing up for themselves. These actions of a true leader require personal sacrifice. Major General Vang Pao pictured a good leader as a horse who lets the people ride on his back day and night. Great leaders, like Phagna Touby Lyfong, Major General Vang Pao, Lo Blia Yao, Moua Chong Kai, and some other historical heroes, made personal sacrifices in standing up for what they believed for the betterment of their people, their community, and their country.

Contemporary Hmong lack personal sacrifice but seek social status for self-gratification. Before the death of Major General Vang Pao, many Hmong criticized his leadership and tried to usurp it. Based on what they considered solid political credentials but which were nothing more than book smarts, they tried to assert western political ideologies. They did not remember their personal histories, how they got here in the first place, and so they divided the Hmong people and the Hmong community. After Major General Vang Pao's death, more Hmong individuals appeared in the public spotlight with their personal cultural propaganda to seek public support for their personal pursuits. Hmong people know these types of leaders are working to fill their own pockets, and Hmong are wary of following them.

Emerging Hmong leaders have to have personal commitments and be willing to make sacrifices to undertake the responsibilities of a traditional leader, which is what is needed for the advancement of the Hmong people as a whole. At the same time, Hmong followers have to abandon their vindictive attitudes and eliminate adversarial infighting. Otherwise, the Hmong tendency to betray one another, to pit one against another, and to sabotage one another will continue to frustrate Hmong leaders. These attitudes will continue to erode Hmong trust, bonds, unity, and solidarity because such demeanors will sell Hmong leadership and Hmong people for personal gain and the security of social status, as has happened throughout Hmong history.

At this defining moment, it is crucial for Hmong to develop true leaders with attainable and sustainable missions and goals for the Hmong people. They must be able to inspire others to contribute to the cause and sacrifice for the success of all the people. Hmong need to set up a leadership structure that will be a blueprint that enables Hmong leaders to navigate the past, the present, and the future. A democratic process for establishing a solid leadership structure might follow steps such as the following:

1. Have open minds and positive attitudes.
2. Foster and embrace Hmong diversity and adversaries for a common purpose.
3. Invite Hmong who have sincere commitments to work together to establish the structure.
4. Form a national entity to draft a declaration or referendum of Hmong leadership structure.
5. Organize and hold a national convention to engage in discourse on leadership.
6. Draft a preliminary set of principles and a preliminary framework for the structure.
7. Hold debates and public meetings to gather public input.
8. Draft a revised set of principles and a revised framework for discussion and debate.
9. Consolidate and synthesize a first draft of the Hmong leadership structure.

10. Develop policies, procedures, and guidelines for implementation.

11. Pilot the structure and ask for public input.

12. Restructure and reorganize the leadership structure.

13. Draft the final version of the Hmong leadership structure.

14. Seek resources for promoting the leadership structure.

15. Develop a national campaign and platform to publicize the structure.

16. Strategize a national platform to elect the first Hmong national leadership group.

17. Install the new leadership group in power.

18. Craft the mission and goals for the national entity.

19. Construct and develop an implementation plan.

20. Modernize and consolidate Hmong leaders under the structure.

21. Promote democratic processes.

22. Establish and follow clear and transparent policies, procedures, and guidelines.

The overall result of such a democratic process will be a renaissance of Hmong leadership and the rebirth of quality Hmong leaders. The steps suggested above do not have to follow the order listed, but can flow in whatever way Hmong want to structure their process for defining and selecting leaders. The point is that a process has to be developed and it must involve all Hmong who are committed to reviving effective Hmong leadership. Good Hmong leaders cannot and will not emerge without a willingness to engage in a group process that includes collaboration, cooperation, compromises, and shared governance. Here is the question for Hmong to ponder: *How can Hmong plant a new seed of leaders and leadership together?*

The process may seem tedious, but anything worthwhile takes time and careful work. The new group of Hmong leaders will not be able to correct all the mistakes of the past, but together they can prevent the same or similar mistakes from recurring. Most importantly, the new leaders should be willing to put themselves at risk to save others and to stand up for others. Sometimes dangerous and risky actions can result in gains in the sociopolitical arena that justify the personal sacrifices.

Hmong Strength in Numbers

As a community, Hmong must work together to achieve what is right and best for their people. Hmong have demonstrated an ability to cooperate and support one another and large causes: they do so in their death rituals and funeral services, family feasting, and cultural events and celebrations (New Year), and they have done so in the past in revolts against oppression, in migrations, and in participation in transnational politics. Hmong come together in large numbers when they face great difficulty, but they often fail to show up en masse when life is peaceful. For instance, when a Hmong candidate organizes a fundraising event for his political campaign, the turnout of Hmong people is generally low. Hmong are willing to make contributions to people who have suffered loss but do not see making contributions to a living person as valuable. Even if they did, they think their small contribution will not make a difference. Some do not show up because they are still locked into the mindset of tribal-centered isolation. Those who do give expect something of equal value in return. Culturally, these reasons for failure to support a Hmong candidate are perfectly logical, but politically, they are unrealistic.

Hillary Rodham Clinton once quoted an African proverb: "It takes a village to raise a child." The proverb can be applied to the need for Hmong to combine resources to help a Hmong candidate. Hmong elders have a similar saying: "It is hard for one person to feed the many, but it is easy for the many to feed the one." In other words, large numbers give strength, and coming together as a large group will make a difference.

In 2007, following the arrests of Hmong leaders in California, Hmong communities in the U.S. held public rallies and demonstrations in support of the release from jail of Major General Vang Pao and those who were arrested with him. Hmong combined their resources to voice their concerns and the entire case against the men was eventually dismissed. The unity evident in the public outcry was historic. One Hmong educator described it as *"the power of the people versus the power of the law."* It was the first and greatest set of Hmong demonstrations in U.S. history. Regardless of the legal merits of the federal indictments, the whole ordeal was not only about Hmong knowing and exercising their first-amendment rights, but it was also about saving the leader who had been their savior and had brought them to the Promised Land. In reality, all Hmong know that there is great strength in large numbers. If they fail to exhibit themselves en masse, they are as good as invisible.

One area in which Hmong have an opportunity to show their strength in numbers and at the same time raise the standing of Hmong in the larger community is the election of Hmong individuals to public office. In an article in the *Fresno Bee* newspaper, Vang (2002) congratulated Hmong on the victorious election of the first Hmong to serve on the board of the Fresno Unified School District:

"DR. TONY VANG'S ELECTION PROVES HMONG POWER"

After 22 years in Fresno, the Hmong made history recently. With the help of many non–Hmong friends, they elected Tony Vang to the governing board of the Fresno Unified School District.

Vang was one of the "Four Voices for Children," a slate of reform candidates for the school board. He was the second Hmong-American ever to seek public office in Fresno; the first was Charles C. Vang, who ran for a city council seat.

The Hmong people and the Hmong community will be in a different place if Hmong have more leaders who will make personal sacrifices, run for public office, and become bridge-builders for Hmong Americans. Coming together in large numbers will make the Hmong people and the Hmong community stronger and, best of all, will make Hmong people visible in the political process. For instance, in 2014, the Hmong community in St. Paul, Minnesota, helped elect two Hmong: city council member Dai Thao and state legislator Fong Her. These elections are great examples of Hmong unity and of what coming together in great numbers can accomplish.

Hmong Adversaries and Conflicts

Hmong should learn how to compromise their differences professionally and must show respect for one another in order for them to forge tribal alliances among them. In the family circle, Hmong have marital kinship and family ties that reinforce their social and cultural unity. In the political arena, however, Hmong still lack unity. As James Emery once wrote, Hmong are their own worst enemies in political matters. In the past, Hmong feared creating adversaries because of traitors in their midst, so they used blood oaths, justice water, and religious practice to enforce their unity. In many cases, even the trust supposedly cemented by such solemn means was broken. Hmong have stopped using these antiquated measures because they live in a different world. Today Hmong are politically divided along clan lines. Each clan has its own leaders. Clan leadership is very political and controversial, and sometimes it is very personal.

For example, amid the controversial reform of a Hmong community-based organization (the new Lao Family Foundation, Inc.) in July 2014, new information about an old incident came to light. During the early part of the Secret War in Laos, some Hmong had attempted unsuccessfully to assassinate Major General Vang Pao, who later founded Lao Family Community, Inc., a non-profit organization. In the squabbles among Hmong leaders in St. Paul, Minnesota, the fact was revealed that the leaders who wanted to reform the Lao Family Community, Inc. had been among the culprits who had taken part in the plot. This political tidbit was used to undermine and derail the reform process and opened a can of worms of Hmong past politics between two rival groups. The revelation inflamed Hmong community educators, leaders, and civilians.

Hmong people have become adversaries and some are becoming disrespectful toward other Hmong in the political arena. Some show little or no respect for Hmong leaders who tell them what to do but have great respect for leaders who are non–Hmong who issue the same commands. When Hmong people are disobedient or disrespectful toward non–Hmong leaders, they are reprimanded and scolded severely, but when they are disobedient or disrespectful toward Hmong leaders, the Hmong leaders harbor resentment against them and plan for future retaliation. These patterns of behavior contribute to Hmong disunity, mistrust, and betrayal.

One example is the public criticism of Major General Vang Pao after his death. Before his death, a group of Hmong hooligans had attempted to oust him from chairmanship of an organization he had founded and led for years. After his death, these Hmong held public forums to disparage his leadership. To Hmong, attacking a deceased person's integrity is not only disrespectful, but pure evil.

Hmong disunity stems from a long past during which Hmong used to pit one against the other for personal security and gain when Hmong were oppressed and persecuted severely under Chinese rulers and a communist regime. Hmong often fought on both sides, in some cases serving as political mercenaries to go after Hmong rebels. This type of political exploitation has eroded Hmong brotherhood, trust, and unity as well as Hmong leadership. Vang (2013) pointed out how the distrust and incivility that are still quite prevalent have contributed to the failure of Hmong to develop a process for choosing a new leader:

"Hmong failed leadership quest"

In the early months of 2013, many Hmong individuals made personal sacrifices to help restructure Hmong leadership but failed to carry out such a development as planned. The process is now stalled and the future of such propaganda faces an uncertain fate.

The so-called Hmong tribal and traditional leaders have failed to meet such a quest to give Hmong people and their community a sense of hope.

Last May, a town hall meeting was held in Minnesota to engage various Hmong individuals in leadership discussions. However, only a fraction of Hmong traditional and tribal leaders showed up at the meeting. The discourse went nowhere and the crowd dispersed before the meeting ended. This kind of inpatient and futile leadership attitudes and behaviors indicates how divisive Hmong people really are and how poisonous their relationships really are. If so, why have Hmong come together for such discourse anyway?

Furthermore, many Hmong continue to live in the spiritual shadow of General Vang Pao while others distance themselves from such myths and organize their own groups to seek out the opportunity to dethrone the left-behind legacy in order to claim the leadership role. But so far, such oppositions also face a stone wall since the tripartite of Hmong factions has caused perplexing cultural disarray and disorder in the Hmong leadership movement. In other words, the quest seems to be a cultural platitude, and no one seems to be credible and believable. If so, whom are Hmong waiting for? Perhaps, Hmong are awaiting a newborn divine creature which speaks Hmong and understands Hmong. For today's tribulations, Hmong leaders are made, not born.

The so-called community leaders are passive but stubborn, and at the same time, serve no role different from those who are forming factions and tribal coups to derail leadership restructuring. The current situation is not new and is based on a centuries-old mindset, a toxin in Hmong leadership. Hmong people deserve better. However, Hmong factions are deploying destructive schemes to break up new talks and negotiations among some prominent and promising individuals. If so, why do Hmong distrust and mistrust themselves but continue to live together as a big family with all familial ties, lineages, and/or bloodlines?

Nearly two and half years after the death of General Vang Pao, the so-called leaders have failed to put together a plan to restore Hmong leadership for the greater good of the people, and at the same time, continue to hold personal grudges and familial conflicts by concocting exploitation schemes to distort Hmong values, beliefs, and advancement. If so, how much longer can Hmong people tolerate such actions?

There is no doubt in mind that Hmong people are facing a difficult and uncertain plight while seeking new directions. But at least it is time for these individuals to put their raucous and spiteful cold-hearted interests aside in order to advocate for the Hmong race. Today, keep in mind that tribal conflicts are wars without bloodshed, and personal wars are conflicts with everlasting internal bloodshed. At least Hmong people have to end their own warfare in order to reach a cultural accord to start all over again. Otherwise, the so-called Hmong leaders will continue to fail at the quest for a new beginning.

To overcome Hmong sociopolitical unity issues, Hmong people need to consider taking several steps:

- Learn how to forgive and forget things that occurred in the past.
- Learn how to reconcile their differences peacefully and diplomatically.
- Decide whether they are friends or foes; they rely on one another for survival.
- Separate the bad from the good and hold each person responsible for his own actions.
- Learn how not to tattle on one another based on unfounded and unproven information.
- Take responsibility for their actions.
- Stop using the "saving face" mentality to evade their misdeeds.
- Learn how to issue appropriate apologies for personal misdeeds.
- Show remorse for improper actions and ask for forgiveness.
- Respect written policies, procedures, and guidelines.
- Stop despising one another because of differences in opinions.
- Stop taunting one another.
- Stop tantalizing one another.
- Stop using tattletales.
- Go beyond their personal comfort zones to do what is right for the people.
- Be considerate of others.
- Make these changes in themselves be-

fore asking others to change for the purpose of unity.

One of the most prevalent leadership problems in the Hmong community is taunting. Hmong leaders use taunts to frame others and create their own adversaries. Then they form small cliques and factions. This jeering of others arises from covetous attitudes, lack of cooperation, insubordination, impatient and impulsive behaviors, and personal egos.

Remember, Hmong unity issues are always the leaders' problems; unity in the community rests on the shoulders of Hmong leaders. Hmong can come together in great numbers, but they do so only when a leader unites them in a common cause.

Need for Cooperative Collaborations

Hmong should learn how to build a vibrant community with trustworthiness, honesty, integrity, and responsibility. Once Hmong people make personal sacrifices and demonstrate political unity in large numbers, the Hmong people will be a strong, healthy community. Lack of cooperation among Hmong cultural leaders has stifled Hmong potential for socioeconomic development in some metropolitan areas. In the past, Hmong cooperative collaborations failed as due to the lack of proper education; however, today, Hmong are better prepared for such an operation. Of the three states with the largest Hmong populations, Minnesota has the most sophisticated Hmong community infrastructure, which includes political involvement, economic gain, civic participation, leadership, and cultural centers.

The lack of trust and unity has kept Hmong communities from forming cooperatives for Hmong economic development. If Hmong united, Hmong businesses could expand greatly. Currently, most Hmong community chapels (funeral homes) work under non–Hmong funeral directors who are licensed morticians and own most of the properties. If Hmong who operated Hmong community chapels located in Fresno and Sacramento cooperated, they could form a major

Hmong-American chapel enterprise. At present, most Hmong-American farmers sell their special crops through Vietnamese and Chinese cooperatives. Owners of Hmong mini-markets contract with Vietnamese, Chinese, Thai, and other major cooperatives such as Sun-Fat, Sun Lee, Dragonfly Jasmine Rice, Producer Rice Mill, and so on. If Hmong small farmers throughout California collaborated, they could form a Hmong-American farmers' union and explore greater opportunities for selling their produce. If Hmong mini-markets located in Fresno and Sacramento cooperated, they could create a giant corporation that could build supermarkets in other Hmong communities. Together, Hmong-Americans should be able to have a distribution warehouse owned and operated by Hmong business owners in every major city with a large Hmong population.

Of course, Hmong vendors can be independent business owners; however, Hmong business owners could learn from their Chinese, Vietnamese, Cambodian, and Thai counterparts how to control the wealth distribution in their own communities. Each year, Hmong people contribute billions of dollars to local, national, and international economies. For instance, in Fresno, California, the Hmong International New Year is a million-dollar celebration, but most of the revenues generated from the event go to pay incurred debts, the city, police, and county because Hmong leaders lack a clear vision for making the event lucrative and thus returning economic benefits to the Hmong people and the Hmong community. Similarly, the July 4 event in St. Paul, Minnesota, is a million-dollar event, but again, most of the revenues generated go to pay incurred debts, the owner of the park where the event is held, and private vendors.

As a community, Hmong people need to find Hmong leaders who are true pathfinders who will reexamine the Hmong economic infrastructure inside Hmong-American communities across the U.S. for potential economic development. If Hmong leaders fail to think economically, they should at least try to answer this question: *How much longer do Hmong people have to rent or lease private land, city parks, and county facilities to celebrate Hmong New Year?* This question should provoke some action toward Hmong community growth and development. However, nothing can be done if no qualified Hmong leaders emerge to lead the way in the type of action needed.

Cooperatively, western Hmong would not be able to find or build a perfect socioeconomic system to please every Hmong; however, they can learn how to improve and to be honest with one another. In the Hmong world, unity may be an important matter but honesty is the most spicy and delicious ingredient of trust, bond, unity, collaboration, and cooperation.

The Emergence of New Hmong Leaders

Hmong are now experiencing the rise and fall of leaders and leadership and there is no doubt in mind that a new set of leaders will emerge. First and foremost, new Hmong leaders need to develop a blueprint for the Hmong community to help the people navigate the process of everyday life; otherwise, the futility of leadership will continue. Also, new leaders are bridge-community-builders and must be able to foster Hmong values and culture. From the past to the present, many Hmong leaders lack clear vision and have been largely inactive and therefore unproductive. In other words, they have followed in the steps of their predecessors who over-promised and under-delivered. Very few Hmong leaders even attempted to change or improve the status quo. From the present to the future, Hmong need at least three groups of new leaders who are pathfinders. As Figure 14.2 illustrates, the three groups are cultural and traditional leaders, community leaders, and mainstream leaders. Leaders in each of these groups may be young and new to leadership; they may need to build cultural gravitas.

Currently, two of these groups—cultural and traditional leaders and community leaders—are dominated by males, but there are more female leaders in the mainstream lead-

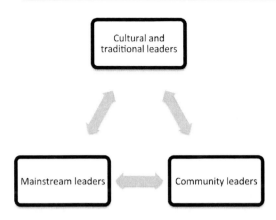

Figure 14.2. New Hmong leadership groups.

ership group. To unite and stand together, the Hmong people and the Hmong community need leaders from both sexes. Moreover, both traditional and more modern leaders are essential; they are equally important to the advancement of the Hmong people and their community.

The cultural and traditional leaders could include former military officers, clan leaders, family representatives, cultural brokers and religious leaders, and designated speakers and spokespersons. This group should work collaboratively to strengthen Hmong cultural and traditional values, customs, rituals, beliefs, and norms. They should find ways to improve and modernize the Hmong communal way of life. For instance, these leaders need to develop a pathway for establishing a community center for Hmong cultural preservation. They should also tackle issues related to Hmong funeral services, marriage customs, oral history, and language maintenance.

The second group of leaders is known as the community leaders who are bridge-builders to engage Hmong people with the mainstream culture. They have specific roles to play, including:

- Building the economic infrastructure of the Hmong community.
- Improving the education of Hmong students in K–12 schools and higher educational institutions.
- Procuring private, local, state, or federal

funding for the development of community-based organizations, mutual assistance associations, and private organizations to help Hmong deal with critical needs and socialization adjustment issues.
- Advocating for the needs and interests of Hmong at local, state, and federal levels.
- Mobilizing Hmong through the sociopolitical process to help them make the changes necessary to accommodate Hmong culture and traditions in the western nations.

The community leaders are prime resources for the Hmong people and the Hmong community. They will deal with various facets of Hmong life to help Hmong learn to work, cooperate, and support one another in large numbers. Their goal should be not only to make Hmong communities visible, but also to make them financially and politically vibrant.

The final group of leaders consists of Hmong-Americans who are mainstream-oriented. Mainstream leaders should include Hmong educators, professionals, and business owners who can work with both Hmong-American communities and non–Hmong communities. These Hmong professionals act as representatives of Hmong people and candidates who are seeking public offices at all levels of government. They should be visible in the political arena to advocate for the betterment of Hmong people and the Hmong community as a whole.

All three groups of leaders play vital roles in politics, but the mainstream leaders have the primary responsibility of recruiting Hmong leaders who would consider seeking public positions. The Hmong community needs these mainstream leaders because currently very few if any Hmong people are willing to run for public office. The reasons are many:

- Hmong candidates lack resources and information about the political process.
- Most Hmong candidates who do run are loners and appear "out of the blue."

- Hmong candidates lack foundations and support from the community.
- Even Hmong candidates who are highly qualified lack confidence to run for public offices.
- Hmong candidates believe their political careers will be short-lived because of the lack of solid political foundations in the community.

These are the primary factors that deter Hmong candidates from seeking public office. Therefore, Hmong people need mainstream leaders who can facilitate the recruitment, resourcing, encouragement, and support base of potential candidates.

In 2006, voters in Fresno, California, elected two Hmong Americans to public office. In the *Fresno Bee* newspaper, Vang (2006) described the importance of those victories to Hmong unity:

> ### "UNITED HMONG SCORE BIG IN THE ELECTION"
>
> The 2006 election was groundbreaking. For the first time in Fresno's history, and in the history of America, two Hmong-American candidates were elected to public offices.
>
> [...]
>
> In this election, the Hmong, as the underdog community, worked diligently, willingly, and tirelessly to triumph in what seemed an impossible quest. They learned American politics at the grassroots level. They also showed that money couldn't buy their votes. They knew that what they wanted was more important than what other politicians could offer them. They wanted to be a part of shaping their future and their country.
>
> And they did.

As this article emphasizes, Hmong Americans have achieved some successes in local politics, but they still have work to do to advance Hmong politics to the next level. The creation of Hmong leadership groups will help Hmong people reach that goal in the near future. Needless to say, without these groups of leaders in place, the Hmong community will continue to function the same way it has for the last 40 years. That would mean little or no improvement in the current situation, living in the state of apostasy and seeing Hmong leadership in peril.

Hmong Civic Participation and Leadership Development

All Hmong must learn to be Hmong and American at the same time. As a growing community, Hmong people need to have strong leaders who can guide them as they participate in the political process. Hmong leaders have to be the pathfinders to show the way. Vang (2003) wrote an article to motivate Hmong people to get involved in western politics because America needs to hear their voice:

> ### "LET'S TALK ABOUT CIVIC PARTICIPATION"
>
> Why should Americans—European, African, Asian, or Hmong Americans—get involved in the politics of their country? Is civic participation important for Americans, specifically for Hmong Americans?
>
> Let's look at the current situation. Hmong Americans have been living in this country for at least 27 years, since the fall of Laos in 1975. Migrating to America was a long and hard journey, and Hmong Americans living here still face great challenges simply to survive. Many struggle with American ways of life, including American politics. Nevertheless, Hmong Americans have become part of the mainstream society. America is their homeland.
>
> Why Get Involved in Politics?
>
> Because America is their homeland, America needs their voices. Despite being cast as a minority, the Hmong American community is a fast growing segment of the American population. Hmong are patriotic citizens, proud of their past and the sacrifices they and their fathers made in fighting for freedom and democracy. They have much to contribute to the social and political fabric of their country.
>
> And they have much to gain. America is the land of equal opportunities, and Hmong Americans should be thinking about sharing the American "pie." They came here to save themselves and to plan for the future of their younger generations. Civic participation will allow them rather than others to shape that future.
>
> It is time for Hmong Americans to move from autocracy to democracy. They can

decide what they would like to have from their government and their leaders and who will have authority over them. Getting involved in politics will permit them to advocate for social-political platforms that serve public interests.

Because life in America is complex and difficult for many Hmong Americans, the importance of their role in politics is obscured and uncertain. Some may shy away from this responsibility because public service demands self-sacrifice and the results are often unpredictable. As Mao Tse Tong said, "Politics is war without bloodshed, while war is politics with bloodshed." But Hmong leadership in government is essential in helping their people understand, predict, and influence civic matters.

Why Are Hmong-Americans Not Involved?

What keeps Hmong Americans out of the political arena? For one thing, the political process is relatively new to most Hmong Americans. Western politics is complex and intricate; it is intimidating to many newcomers.

Leveling the playing field of politics is difficult for Hmong Americans. Because their communities are scattered throughout the United States, and because their political participation is still weak, Hmong Americans' presence in politics seems small and ineffective. It may take additional decades before Hmong Americans feel included and welcomed in the political arena. But they should not wait for others to include them. Paving the road to the future for their children is too important. Hmong Americans need to assert themselves to learn and at least be visible in the political process. Success in politics requires a life-long commitment to public service. It is not as difficult as it may seem. Woody Allen once said, "Success is 20 percent timing and 80 percent just showing up." Hmong Americans need to show up—just become involved in the affairs of their government.

One reason Hmong Americans tend to avoid politics is that it can be very expensive. Every politician knows that money is the milk of politics. Office seekers spend millions of dollars each year on political campaigns. Most Hmong Americans feel poor, powerless, oppressed, and perhaps hopeless in politics because of their low socioeconomic status. They may not realize that other minority groups face the same challenge. They need to know that voters are more valuable than money. If they would stop procrastinating about money and just get their feet in, they may discover that they have greater power than they thought.

Power comes through leadership. Some bad experiences with corrupt leaders have kept Hmong Americans out of politics for years. In the past, some political crooks led Hmong Americans on a pursuit of social-political justice, but they were merely using the people for personal gain. These leaders were, as Paul Hersey explained, "successful in the short term but ineffective in the long term." They scarred many Hmong deeply, souring them against involvement in politics. Establishing trust in their leaders will be an essential and challenging prerequisite for Hmong American success in politics.

The internal turmoil among Hmong Americans can hinder their civic actions, but it also deprives them of political clout. It gives the appearance of no leadership or social control in the community. The only solution is active engagement in the political process.

How to Become Involved

There are many ways that Hmong can get involved in American politics. To make their voices heard, both individuals and the community as a whole need to be proactive, mobilizing to take action. Activism and civic participation are basic political endeavors, and at the very least these should be established in the community. Civic participation involves organizing the community, developing leadership, and forming collaborative coalitions. Hmong Americans need all these.

At the same time, intense education about civic participation and civic governance is needed. Education is key for civic participation. Once they are educated about the political process, Hmong leaders, educators, and college students can act proactively on behalf of their communities and people to raise social-political concern for education, economy, justice, foreign policy, and domestic tranquility. Educated people are ready for action.

Some are already ready. There are Hmong Americans who are politically-oriented and have charisma and integrity. They should be encouraged to participate in the political process. Hopefully, some will be able to take charge in leading their communities and helping others learn about and take advantage of the power of politics.

Although Hmong Americans are still considered by many to be incipient citizens, not quite ready to successfully merge into mainstream politics, Hmong leaders have begun to become active players in government. The emergence of Hmong-American politicians is a breakthrough and marks the beginning of a new political challenge.

The first challenge is to enroll Hmong voters. In American politics, everyone is counted, and one way they count is by voting. However, a great number of Hmong Americans stay away from the polls. Of the 250,000 Hmong living in America, only several thousand adults vote. Hundreds of thousands of young Hmong over the age of 18 are qualified to vote. But voter registration drives are absent in most Hmong-American communities. If every qualified Hmong voted, together, Hmong Americans would constitute a significant force in local politics, perhaps an essential bloc for mainstream politicians.

Not only must Hmong voters be enrolled, but they must also be empowered. In order to vote effectively, voters must have access to election materials and information. Hmong Americans need to find ways to disseminate information to the people. If going to the voting booths poses a challenge for minority voters, community activists can advocate to have voting booths installed in their community. If younger Hmong Americans do not care about voting, leaders and educators must make elections important community events and explain to young people the privilege, responsibility, and power involved in casting their ballots.

And Hmong Americans must be encouraged to enter their own names on those ballots. Hmong are conservative and reserved; they usually set high expectations for their leaders. They also have a long memory and a strong oral tradition that etches into their minds any time a leader misleads or takes advantage of them. This mindset sometimes discourages intelligent Hmong Americans from running for public office. Hmong Americans must become more flexible, encouraging their members to participate in government without fear of community repercussions and social humiliation. They need to practice greater forgiveness and tolerate human imperfection if they are to produce dedicated public leaders.

On the other hand, when elected politicians are corrupt, Hmong-Americans must adamantly denounce and condemn them. The emerging Hmong-American politicians must be law-biding citizens who can restore public trust and a positive image. Leadership is all about character and influence. It is imperative that capable Hmong Americans learn to lead well so they can, as Henry Kissinger said of great leaders, "enable [their] society to follow the path [they] have selected."

Now the question is: Are Hmong Americans ready to play politics?

We're Making Progress

Recent events have demonstrated that Hmong Americans are ready to exercise their political responsibility. With little background in politics, Hmong Americans are making good progress in America. Several have been elected to political office: Tony Vang (Fresno, California), Mr. Paul Lo (Merced, California), Mr. Charles C. Vang (Fresno, California), Mr. Cy Thao (St. Paul, Minnesota), Mrs. Mee Moua (St. Paul, Minnesota), Mr. Lamong Lo (Omaha, Nebraska), Mr. Steve Ly (Sacramento, California), and others elsewhere. These are Hmong-American heroes and political role models. Yet more are needed.

Moreover, many financially successful Hmong Americans have contributed their time, energy, and money to support their political comrades in the political process. This is a welcome exercise of civic responsibility, and one that must continue.

Civic participation is taking action today to ensure success tomorrow. Hmong Americans cannot afford to wait another decade before getting involved. They cannot wait until they are rich or better educated. They must get ready for action now. As Abraham Lincoln once said, "I will get ready and then perhaps my chance will come." Twenty-seven years is a long time for Hmong Americans to prepare for politics. The political landscape today is favorable for people of all ethnicities. It is high time for Hmong Americans to join their ranks. America needs their voice.

Civic participation is a valuable right that this country offers to all its citizens. It enables all citizens express their opinions and advocate for their interests as they vote for people who will best serve their needs. As long as Hmong continue to live in this nation, they cannot afford not to participate in this part of life in America.

Hmong and Their Cultural Heritage

After 40 years in the U.S., Hmong have made significant progress in many areas. They still need to make modest adjustments in their everyday lives so they can co-exist with people of many other ethnicities in the pluralistic American society. Hmong live a dual lifestyle in a dual society; they follow the practices of the dominant culture while retaining Hmong customs and traditions. To do this, they must be culturally sensitive, learn about other customs and traditions, embrace cultural diversity, and accept other people's diverse views. Like any other ethnic group, Hmong have to figure out how best to adapt to the ever-changing world around them in order to live in harmony with other people. Hmong must do what they can to preserve their own heritage while learning, appreciating, and respecting other people's cultural heritages.

The Hmong Clan System

Hmong clans and tribes are the integral part of Hmong social system. All Hmong should use the clan system as their strength in numbers. Major General Vang Pao believed that all Hmong belong to one big family and their family names are for the purpose of marital practices. For thousands of years, the clan system has been the backbone of Hmong existence. In the past, Hmong family clans were separated by leaders, villages, religious adherence, and political factions. Today, Hmong clans live among one another in a diverse community. In the Hmong world, Hmong clans struggle for social justice and equality, and sometimes tribal conflicts lead Hmong to tribal bickering, infighting, and long lasting squabbles. To strengthen the Hmong clan system to accommodate today's life events and realities, at the very least Hmong clan leaders must consider the following:

1. Clan leaders must collaborate and cooperate to advance the Hmong community as a whole.

2. Clan leaders must strengthen the clan system instead of dividing into groups and sub-groups.

3. Clan leaders must do whatever they can to promote Hmong cultural events and minimize the multiplication of such events to prevent interest groups from capitalizing on the events for private benefit.

4. Clan leaders must modernize Hmong customs and traditions in meaningful ways, controlling the costs and duration of festivities, rituals, and offerings.

5. Clan leaders must be good role models for ordinary Hmong people to look up to and must show respect toward other clan leaders.

Furthermore, Hmong clan leaders also need to pay close attention to the pressing issues Vang (2013) described as he wrote about the need to reform Hmong clan clubs:

"Hmong clan clubs need new focus"

Perhaps it is time for Hmong to change the clan communal way of life. Hmong are an advanced group of people who are continuing to live a primitive way of life. Change is a fear for most and most have failed to change themselves because of fear. Here are some ideas to help Hmong wonder about their tribal clubs before searching for a new turning point to start a new beginning. Some Hmong would rather listen to their non–Hmong friends to guide their unforeseeable futures, but it is time for Hmong to listen to themselves to plan their own lives and futures.

There is no doubt in mind that Hmong need a new beginning after the death of General Vang Pao. So far, two groups have secretly selected their own leaders to lead their groups; however, the rest of the people are stranded between the left and right sides. The two major groups are the Vang Pao loyal followers and the new regime of tribal reformers. No one has emerged as a national symbol for Hmong, but more and more factions are being formed each and every day. Hmong must find new directions to start all over again. To pave the way, Hmong have to think beyond their own clan clubs.

For hundreds of years, the Hmong clan clubs have been established to strengthen clan relationships to deal with intertribal clan issues, but for the most part, Hmong clan clubs have failed to enhance the Hmong way of life. Today, the clan clubs are organized in such ways that they compete with one another for members and divide Hmong people and community based on tribal sovereignty and clan issues and personal politics. For instance, some clan clubs focus on international relationships and practice imperialism to elevate their social status overseas, but such clans have not been able to bring positive results to share with Hmong people and community about life overseas, such as human rights violations, ethnic cleansing, and the military actions against Hmong civilians who have ties with the US. Other clans are focusing on privatizing and organizing Hmong New Year's celebrations to protect the status quo.

Hmong clan politics is quite popular but the platforms are meaningless to contemporary Hmong individuals and community because such politics causes more division within the clan system itself. For instance, internal conflicts among clan clubs are looming and separate the educated from the uneducated, the rich from the poor, the old from the young, and males from females. Such practices are nothing new in Hmong life, but Hmong like it because of covetous attitudes and greed. Historically, some Hmong cannot eradicate the roots of evil in their familial leadership. In other words, Hmong have failed to learn that disunity is their civil war that needs to end before unity can happen. As noted many times, Hmong suffered severe communist indoctrination and such a mindset will take them forever to show cooperation, collaboration, and commitment for the Hmong race.

It is important to note that most Hmong are committed to their clan clubs for many reasons. For instance, one is religious cohesiveness; two has to do with cultural and marital practices; three is about clan pledge of allegiance; fourth has to do with the familial name; fifth has to do with familial history and roots; and finally, it is all about familial support while living. These are great values in the Hmong way of life, but Hmong have to embody such values to enhance the Hmong way of life for the people and community as a whole. The clan clubs have not been able to promote such a quest and, in some cases, the clan clubs prevent and prohibit such advancement. As seen today, Hmong have 18 clan clubs and their leaders are chiefs who cannot get along when dealing with Hmong national issues and conflicts or communal peace and advancement. It is time for these chiefs to refocus their tribal establishments.

To go beyond the clan clubs, Hmong need to realize that they need to overcome the century-old abiding tragedies and tribulations in their families or tribes. Tribal infighting will never end, but compromises can be made. Territorial conflicts will never heal Hmong scars and wounds, but the hurts can be lessened and pardoned. Practicing clan clubbing will never enhance the Hmong way of life, but it relegates Hmong to primitive clan organizations and uncivilized leadership practices. It is time for Hmong to think outside the box of clan club and focus on a national symbol for all Hmong to cherish together as a race. Together, Hmong can do better and advance. That is not just a perspective, but is a real opportunity for all.

The power of clan clubs should be united for a common purpose instead of creating infightings to disunite Hmong families. For instance, Hmong have to consider if Hmong people and community should have to fit into the clan clubs or the clan clubs should have to fit into the Hmong people and community. For thousands of years, tribal principles have only divided the Hmong way of life, but the Hmong way of life depends on Hmong people and community. Therefore, it is time for Hmong to revisit their clan club system to craft a new visionary mission for Hmong. Otherwise, as a whole, Hmong people and community are fragile and weak even if some clan clubs are strong and powerful.

Since the early 1980s, the clan council has not worked well in accordance with its mission statement and goals. It is time for clan leaders to revisit the purpose of the Hmong council and reform its structure and mission statement to provide guidance and leadership for the Hmong people and the Hmong community. Otherwise, the Hmong council will continue with unclear roles and leave unfulfilled its responsibility to promote the overall leadership needed for community organization and structure. If nothing is changed, Hmong will consider the current council system antiquated because it does not function professionally and culturally as a leadership organization. Fewer people will depend on it for providing guidance when dealing with Hmong cultural matters. The unity of Hmong clan system requires cultural gravitas; otherwise, Hmong families will continue to practice solitary leadership to serve only the best interests of familial members.

The Hmong Funeral Service

Since 1975, Hmong communal way of life has transformed and evolved over time and Hmong cultural traditions have changed to accommodate western values and ideals. But still, Hmong have not been able to find a cost effective way to help them advance and enhance the practice of their sociocultural beliefs, values, and norms. Hmong belief systems are always meaningful and Hmong value life and death highly; however, it is a high time for Hmong to find sensible ways to modernize and consolidate Hmong funeral service. Otherwise, the exorbitant funeral cost will somewhat tarnish Hmong way of paying final respect to their loved ones. Before the death of Major General Vang Pao, many Hmong individuals had asked him to call for an overhaul of the Hmong funeral service. The Hmong funeral service has become a major burden in the Hmong community for several reasons:

- There are not enough Hmong community chapels for all the Hmong funerals and many grieving families have to wait for days or weeks before the funeral service of their loved ones can start.
- The funeral service has become a costly celebration of death for Hmong families instead of a respectful conclusion of life.
- The death rituals of the funeral service require many draft animals.
- There are general health and safety concerns associated with the Hmong funeral service in regard to food preparation, sanitation, the possible spread of communicable diseases, and the heavy drinking formalities and ritual protocols.

- The death rituals and progression that are part of the Hmong funeral service require three full days or more, depending on the socioeconomic standing of the deceased.
- Some funeral homes and chapels have refused service to Hmong families because of the way Hmong conduct funeral services and the great numbers of people who attend.
- Hmong funeral rites and rituals need reform and restructure for modernization and improvement.

Major General Vang Pao tried to reform the Hmong funeral service. He urged Hmong to limit the number of sacrificial animals and to kill only two draft animals for each death ritual and proposed that the ritual progression be reduced to one or two days instead of three or more days. He also encouraged Hmong to show love to their parents while the parents were still living instead of waiting for their deaths to celebrate and ask for blessing.

It is time for Hmong clan leaders and religious leaders to reexamine the way Hmong conduct the Hmong funeral service in order to modernize it and shorten its meaningful rituals so the service concludes the life of the dead instead of being a major end-of-life celebration. If nothing is done, the cost of the Hmong funeral service will continue to soar beyond the reach of many Hmong. Drafts animals are becoming scarce and prices are rising for burial plots, so do rental fees for funeral homes or chapels, and stipends for funeral directors and crew members. With no changes, overall expenses for the funeral service will double in the next decade. The exorbitant costs may drive more young Hmong families to change their religious practices and convert to Christianity. At present, sick and dying people are more concerned about their funeral expenses than their medical conditions. In some cases, people save for their funerals instead of for retirement.

Hmong often recite a word phrase: "*Niam txiv tuag ces vaj tsev ntuag,*" meaning the death of a parent results in debt for the surviving family members. Hmong should do all they can to prevent death from causing debt; that is necessary to preserve Hmong traditional customs.

Hmong Marriage Customs

The beauty of Hmong traditions will never fade away and the practice of Hmong traditional matrimony will continue on forever. It is time for all Hmong to help polish the arts of their customs and values in order for them to preserve the inner core of its beauty for the future generations. Remember, what is cultural may not be legal and what is legal may not be cultural. The Hmong wedding ceremony is a long-standing tradition that will continue as long as Hmong exist on this planet. Since 1975, Hmong people have made some slight changes in the feasting and drinking formalities and protocols of Hmong marriage customs. However, the traditional bridal price remains even though it is controversial among Hmong families and clans. Some clans accept a bride price cap but others do not recognize the cap as culturally appropriate. Some Hmong families collect the bride price in accordance with their family traditions and refuse to recognize any difference in custom imposed by clan leaders. This practice has caused inconsistencies in the Hmong community. Some non–Hmong misunderstand this tradition and accuse Hmong of selling their daughters when they get married. This is not at all what the bride price is about. Collecting a bride price is a traditional in-kind gift exchange between two families; the bride's family (that receives the bride price) gives the bride a dowry in return. In most cases, the bride price and dowry are equal in value.

Moreover, the Hmong marital kowtowing ritual needs to be reexamined to include some modest adjustments because it is unfair for the groom and his best man to pay two kowtows to show respect to all males, dead or living and young or old, in the bride's family and the families of all blood relatives regardless of their ages, maturity, and socioeconomic standings. Is this a little bit too much or is this a true marital respect? Perhaps, Hmong should be considerate of others' integrity, character, and status instead of lowing the son-in-law's personal values and feelings during the celebration of his wedding.

Even back in Laos, the bride price was usually high. Major General Vang Pao and other Hmong leaders tackled this issue numerous times, trying to hold the bride price at an affordable level. They could resolve the issue only in specific cases without interference and outside influences. In America, Hmong parents have the right to accept or refuse the bride price custom, and some Hmong families show little or no respect for Hmong clan leaders when it comes to collecting the bride price.

At the current cap, the Hmong bride price of $5,000 seems a bit low for some, but it is about right for the majority of Hmong. However, for some Hmong, a $5,000 bride price is a financial burden. Some Hmong teenagers have been known to resort to robbery to obtain enough money for a bride price. Vang (2005) addressed this cultural problem after two brothers were shot during a robbery in Goshen, purportedly committed so that they would have money for a dowry:

> ### "HOW HMONG DOWRIES DRIVE MEN TO CRIME"
>
> Among Hmong Americans, payment of the dowry is controversial. Some consider the practice outrageously expensive and meaningless. Others feel it is a tradition that must be preserved. Some parents are conforming to the American system; others are adamantly against dropping the requirement. In most families, neither parents nor children can afford it. Some have been forced to drop the practice because it is economically impossible. Others, like the Goshen brothers, resort to drastic measures to continue the tradition.
>
> [...]
>
> How much longer can Hmong Americans put up with this impasse? Parents and children alike need to learn how to accommodate their present circumstances without assimilation into a group identity that would compromise the values they hold dear. They need to be able to embrace both cultures.

To address this urgent issue, Hmong clan leaders need to take proactive steps to devise options for Hmong families to consider. Otherwise, the bride price controversy will continue to erode the fundamental values of Hmong customs, and if it is not resolved, more Hmong people will refuse to comply with the requirements of Hmong culture and traditions because the Hmong bride price is only required of Hmong grooms and their families. To be absolutely fair, Hmong clan leaders should not fail to impose the bride price on all grooms and their families regardless of ethnic backgrounds—just to be fair to all. Above all, the practice of marital bride price may be cultural, but not legal in the U.S. While learning what it means to be Hmong, Hmong offspring may be subjected to a double standard within their own cultural norms. For that, it is foreseeable that the practice of cohabitation will rise, so does the multi-partner family pattern. This emerging pattern will also tarnish Hmong culture and traditions when Hmong native-born children refuse to honor Hmong marriage customs. Furthermore, the legalized same-sex marriage in 2015 will have adverse effect on Hmong marital and matrimonial practices in the U.S.; however, most Hmong families religiously adhere to their traditions and marriage customs and hopefully, such a strong belief system will help them withstand the negative impact imposed by the landmark decision. Otherwise, Hmong refugees may have to set a new pride and/or groom price for the same-sex marriage of their sons and daughters in the near future.

Hmong New Year's Celebration

Celebrating Hmong New Year does not have to be multiple festivities starting in early July and ending in late December, or on January 1; however, it has to be a specific day designated in a specific month of the year that all Hmong can honor their cultural heritage. It is a high time for all Hmong to think about the true celebration of their Hmong New Year. At least Hmong should try to answer this question: *Why there are many Hmong New Year's celebrations in the U.S.?* Normally, one culture has only one New Year to celebrate. Just before his death, Major General Vang Pao proposed an overall reform to restructure the way Hmong New Year's celebrations are held in the U.S. and urged event organizers to find better ways to celebrate Hmong New Year and, at the same time, he wanted Hmong leaders and organizers to utilize the financial gain generated by these events to develop a strategic action plan to help rebuild Hmong communities. Simply, he wanted Hmong people to have a community center where Hmong can celebrate their culture and traditions with pride and unity.

The way Hmong people celebrate their New Year is different from the ways people of other ethnic groups celebrate. Hmong New Year is the longest cultural festivity in the world. The multiple celebrations held in different Hmong communities throughout the year make people wonder if Hmong are really celebrating their New Year or if they are celebrating their culture and traditions for capitalistic purposes. Because of the multiple celebrations, they are considered Hmong cultural fairs rather than celebrations of Hmong New Year. The multiple New Year celebrations distort the core values of Hmong cultural identity, especially when rival groups emerge to hold their own mini-celebrations. Simply, the status quo has led Hmong into anarchical patterns of honoring their culture and traditions.

There are no quick fixes to this four-decade-long problem. Hmong leaders should reexamine the way Hmong celebrate their New Year and make modest changes and improvements. Otherwise, Hmong people ignore the New Year's celebrations of other people and forget the real meaning of the event. If the status quo should continue, Hmong people will continue to be seen as the only ethnic group living in America that cannot cooperate and make modest adjustments to their customs in order to be compatible with so many other cultures and traditions. Remember, no ethnic group in America celebrates multiple New Year's events and holds separate celebrations for the same event; only Hmong people do this. It is time to think about the values of this Hmong tradition: one ethnic group one New Year's celebration.

Hmong Cultural Identity

What is Hmong identity? Or, what does it mean to be Hmong? These are fundamental questions some Hmong children are asking themselves today. Hmong ethnicity is *Hmong Dawb* or *Mong Leng*, not Meo, Miao, Ma, Mu, and Meng. Hmong nationality is *Hmong Dawb* or *Mong Leng*, not Lao, Thai, Chinese, Meo, Miao, Ma, Mu, and Meng. Hmong identity has to do with Hmong culture, traditions, costumes, values, customs, beliefs, and norms. For thousands of years, Hmong did not establish a true Hmong identity; they were recognized as people in the shadow of other cultures. Hmong have been labeled Meo, Miao, Miaozu, San Miao, Ma, Man, Meng, and other derogatory names throughout their history. Sometimes Hmong people were easily misidentified because of their linguistic similarity and ethnic compatibility with other groups. Hmong people have a tendency to adopt other people's values and beliefs freely; this is another reason people have identified them incorrectly. For instance, Hmong believe in karma and nirvana, both tenets of Buddhism, but Hmong are not Buddhist. Hmong true religious values are ancestor worship and animism. The mixtures of faith and values make describing true Hmong identity difficult. It is time for Hmong people to rediscover true Hmong identity. *How will they answer the young generation when it asks what it means to be Hmong?*

Hmong people have to reestablish their true identity and preserve it as a matter of Hmong pride. The true and correct Hmong identity is in the Hmong ethnic *name* (*Hmong* or *Mong*) and the Hmong languages (White and Blue dialects). Hmong people need to discard all other names (Meo, Miao, Miaozu, San Meo, Man, Ma, Meng, Laotian, Thai, and so on) and identify with the Hmong or Mong name. Some Hmong are now calling themselves Americans and Laotians, but not Hmong.

Culturally, Hmong have never called their children Meo or Miao. When someone refers to them as Meo, Hmong children are confused. Hmong parents cannot even explain to Hmong children why they are ever called Meo or Miao. Hmong people have to demystify the names Meo and Miao in order to reclaim their history and true identity. And Hmong people and their leaders have to reject derogatory and misrepresentative ethnic names for the name Hmong or Mong.

Hmong people speak a variety of dialects; however, most Hmong dialects are mutually understandable and intelligible. The Meo or Miao people speak an entirely different language and have different religious beliefs and cultural values. Hmong are not Meo or Miao, and Meo or Miao are not Hmong or Mong. Hmong people have to insist on being known as *Hmong*.

In recent years the name "*Hmong*" has been translated into English as "*free*," or Hmong means free. This definition is troublesome because Hmong people have never been free except at the cost of great sacrifice and not every Hmong is free even after a war that ended 40 years ago. Hmong people are not past criminals, prisoners of war, or illegal aliens; they are refugees and immigrants. The word "*Hmong*" or "*Hmoob*" has not been carefully studied to discover its derivation and morphological structures. Therefore it is premature to assume the name Hmong means "*free*." Even though the name "*Hmong*" has always been with Hmong people from their beginnings, the spelling of the name "Hmong" was not developed until the early 1970s. The translation as "*free*" does not match Hmong history. Hmong Chinese refugees left China to search for land for their agrarian lifestyle as much as for freedom and independence. The name "*Hmong*" could just as easily mean "brotherhood, royal group, patriotic fighters, brave warriors, fearless disciples," or "tribal group." Therefore, the idea that Hmong means free has to be used with some caution until new evidence is gathered to support this definition.

Politically, Hmong people in the U.S. are Americans and will be referred to as Americans. However, the word "American" is a national and political term, not an ethnic categorization. Ethnically, Hmong people have to identify themselves by the correct ethnic name and language; that is their true Hmong identity.

Hmong and Their Languages

The so-called *Hmonglish*, a code-switching dialect, is not a Hmong language; however, most U.S. born Hmong children are getting used to it. Losing one's native language is like losing one's cultural identity and dignity. All Hmong should do what they can to preserve Hmong primary language literacy. Hmong native dialects can be promoted and preserved through Hmong social media (radio, television, and internet services), Hmong entertainment industries (movies, DVD, Video, and performance arts), Hmong oral tradition (singing, chanting, narrating, everyday colloquiums, and the practice of religious rituals and rites), and community-based-schooling programs (adult education classes, religious teaching seminars, and private tutorial literacy services). Holistically, as a mixed ethnic group, Hmong parents and leaders should be very concerned about the high rate of illiteracy of Hmong people in Hmong languages.

When Hmong first came to America, barely 10 percent of Hmong adults could read and write Hmong or Lao languages. That figure has not been changed much since 1975. Today, a large number of Hmong adults cannot read and write Hmong languages using HRPA, and their literacy in English is even lower. There are plenty of opportunities for Hmong adults to learn how to read and write their native languages and English, but for many, education is not a priority. The 1.5 generation children are now parents and their parents are grandparents. The first-, second- and third-generation Hmong children are emerging. English and Hmonglish are now the primary sources of communication inside and outside the home. Yet Hmong children in K–12 schools constitute a large portion of ELL and LEP students; they are not academically fluent in English and are illiterate in Hmong languages.

As a community, Hmong people need to find ways to preserve their primary languages because most of the first-, second- and third-generation children are non–Hmong speakers and their literacy in Hmong languages is dismal. Most Hmong students in higher education barely speak Hmong languages and are illiterate in their native tongues. One's language is part of one's cultural identity. It is a challenge for Hmong people to teach their children Hmong languages while the children learn English in school on a daily basis and English proficiency is what they need for academic success and everyday use. However, more importantly, Hmong parents must promote bilingual education in Hmong in order for their offspring to learn Hmong primary languages in formalized settings; otherwise, the high rate of illiteracy in Hmong primary languages will continue.

Hmong oral language skills are more likely to continue than literacy skills in Hmong languages. Unless Hmong parents and leaders are serious and proactive about finding sensible solutions to raising the literacy rate in Hmong adults and children, the struggle to preserve Hmong languages and dialects could be a very difficult challenge, but worthwhile.

Hmong Faiths and Values

Hmong people are religiously diverse when it comes to ritual practices and sacrificial offerings, but nearly all are religiously compatible when it comes to honoring the death of a person. All Hmong should learn how to embrace religious diversity in a pluralistic society. Faiths and values may be practiced differently and religiously, but both are crucial part of the quality of life. Today's Hmong people and families are divided along religious lines. When a Hmong listens to Christian preaching on Hmong social media or attends the funeral service of a member of a Hmong Christian family, the clash of faiths and values is evident. Religious adherence raises controversies in Hmong traditional marriage as well. Sometimes when two people with two different religious faiths get married to each other, family members clash head-on during the marital negotiation process that is part of traditional marriage.

First and foremost, regardless of religious adherence, Hmong people can be private about their religions but should not be brutal about them. Hmong believers, non-believers, and followers of different religious faiths need to stop bashing one another. No matter what religious beliefs a person has chosen to follow, all people are imperfect beings; all are sinners. Therefore, Hmong people have to learn to embrace their difference in religion instead of creating religious adversaries among themselves.

Vang (2008) explained the importance of showing religious tolerance to people of different faiths and values when living in a pluralistic society:

"Religious tolerance is needed to embrace different faiths and values in America"

The United States of America is one of the world's most religious nations. Its first law of the land was framed based on biblical principles. The founding fathers envisioned faiths and values as part of the new life and guaranteed all citizens the freedom to practice religions. Even if there is no official religion, most Americans worship God in the form of a divine supreme being associated with theological foundations related to the scriptures in the Bible. Americans are religiously diverse but theologically similar when it comes to faiths and values.

All religions are purposeful in nature, depending on what an individual wants to believe in. Some are religious in heart while others are religious in life. Hundreds of years ago, Marx declared that religion is the opiate of the people. His assertion provides different perspectives on how one views religion today.

Whether you are a believer or nonbeliever, if you live in the Central Valley, you should listen to the KCIV radio station on FM 99.9 once in a while. There are hundreds of Christian radio programs on this station. The one that I listen to every once in a while is the Bible Answer Man broadcast, called CRI, which stands for Christian Research Institute. The host always introduces the program by emphasizing the slogan "Truth Matters." He was referring to the biblical scriptures in teaching and preaching the Gospels of Jesus Christ.

In a recent week, I read an article in the local newspaper about religious tolerance, and it is a real eye opener. The CRI radio program keeps reminding its audience that Christianity is in crisis because there are so many religious denominations and branches of believers who practice different principles of faith and values that are contrary to the truth of Christianity.

On several occasions, I heard the host and his guests discussing the Book of Mormon, Jehovah's Witnesses, LDS, and other denominations that are considered deviating from the real Christian faith and values. The intention was not to devalue other people's faiths and values; it was more of the way to find out the truth about Christianity. I was open to listening to what they had to say about other religions, but sometimes, I realized that criticizing other religions does not make Christianity better or stronger since there is no such thing like purity or 100 percent truth, faith, or values in a religion. People practice their belief systems as they live their lives and adapt to new life situations each and every day. Each religion has its own ups and downs.

In fact, I do agree with the notion that many believers and nonbelievers alike do not read the scriptures biblically and are unable to interpret its meanings theologically. Most tend to pay more attention to oral preaching, the power of the tongue, rather than learning to read what's said in the scriptures. Biblical literacy seems to be a major problem in most religions.

Several religious leaders from different denominations and churches contributed to the article by expressing their views on religious tolerance toward different faiths and values as a way to accommodate one another and to reach out to other people who may not share the same religious principles. They spoke up against religious condemnation, isolation, ignorance, and intolerance in the community and encouraged people to learn more about each other's religious values. I thought it was a relief to see these leaders breaking their religious ranks and silence to publicly express their opinions toward tolerance. Their messages should clearly encourage people to think outside the box.

In reality, ordinary believers do not have isolated views of other religions unless they have learned from the group leaders to strictly and religiously refrain themselves. Religious sermons play an important role in religious ignorance. For instance, I have heard so many times when prominent religious leaders condemned other religious on the radio, during congregational sermons, and at funeral services. Some intentionally expressed negative views toward nonbelievers and attacked the values of those who do not belong the same as their congregation. The negative preaching and sermons form false beliefs in the minds of believers and followers. As a result, they develop religious anti–Semitism and antagonistic mindsets toward other groups.

Moreover, in most religious scriptures, it is hard to find written words suggesting condemning other religions, attacking other faiths and values, destroying other ways of life, forcing indoctrination, and annihilating the nonbelievers with pressure to commit conversion. Most scriptures are righteously phrased based on the founding principles of a specific religion to guide its followers.

By reading the article and comparing my listening to different radio programs, I am often confused about the religious charisma and dogma of today's preaching and congregational sermons. Many believers do not pay close attention to the dogmatic messages that are not supported by the scriptures. Rarely, the group leaders would use charisma to preach the congregation to help members understand the faiths and values that should be embodied based on biblical scriptures. In other words, the reference of biblical teaching is weak.

Due to the fact that nonbelievers and believers are getting mixed messages, nowadays religions become biblically obscure and theologically meaningless when people question the validity and reliability of their own congregational preaching. Some shop for a congregation or a group of believers that share similar faiths and values. In other words, people are hearing too much of the same stuff, like scolding, belittling, blaming, besetting, condemnation, criticizing, putdowns, negativity, admonition, and bittersweet preaching. It is spiritually troublesome and religiously incoherent. Instead, people are anxious to learn more about religious civility and social compatibility.

In the present day, people are religiously diverse; therefore, considering religious tolerance could be a huge step to overcoming religious prejudice, stereotyping, discrimination, ignorance, hatred, bigotry, and isolation. Religious respect and tolerance could be a two-way street. To overcome religious bias, one has to be willing to change oneself to fit the world's views.

Putting oneself in the other person's shoes would help one understand the feeling of welcoming, acceptance, inclusion, sensitivity, and recognition. Valuing views other than one's own would definitely be beneficial and help one grow religiously and spiritually as well as socially and professionally.

Willingness to learn more about the religions of one's friends, co-workers, neighbors, and clients would accommodate a broader range of awareness of different faiths and values. Perhaps that would strengthen social and religious civility. Engaging in social conversations or discussions with different people would also be a polite way to learn more about others' views. Distant feelings could be embraced while isolation could be diminished through mutual understanding.

To increase the level of understanding of different religions, education plays a key role. Higher education institutions encourage students to take religious courses to learn more about world religions, cultures, traditions, faiths, and values. Studying would open one's horizon to accept, respect, accommodate, integrate, and be aware of other views in religion. Moreover, academics could help differentiate right from wrong. What is in the text could be different from what is preached, heard, or practiced. Knowledge is a powerful tool. Most hidden messages of faith and values of a religion that many lack are buried in the scriptures.

To show tolerance, one should not be judgmental when talking about different faiths and values. Experts believe that all religious paths aim at the same destination, peace and happiness. Regardless of one's belief in the number of supreme powers, there is only divine intelligence. In other words, the universe is ruled and governed by one Supreme Being, and that is GOD. With this kind of understanding, one would be more tolerant to the views of other beliefs. Religious centrism isolates people based on closed-minded attitudes and selfishness; however, well-established religion encourages unconditional love for people. Judging one faith over the other is an individual choice but should not be imposed on the universality of all believers. Quite often, people prejudge one another based on religious affiliation without having any insights into others' views.

Believe it or not, most religious groups worship differently but have similar prayers. For instance, believers use the process to pray for health, peace, love, help, and forgiveness. To increase the level of religious tolerance, one should be encouraged to visit different places of worship of different groups. While visiting, one should pay close attention to the preaching and also listen to the messages and prayers. Religious isolation is the result of fear and lack of understanding. Site or community visitation would help one to overcome fear and bias. Religious phobia could be real for some groups; however, most places of worship are holy, sacred, and religiously and spiritually respected.

In closing, despite one's faith and values, religious tolerance is a must since America is a nation of the world's religions. The US Constitution allows its people to practice religion freely; however, its people need to show that they all can get along even if they may disagree on religious principles. Tolerance would help people realize that they can come together to honor and respect diverse views, and at the same time, believers and nonbelievers could live in the same neighborhood, work in the same office, sit in the same classroom, take the same bus, dine in the same restaurant, shop at the same department store, visit the same shopping mall, share the same bathroom, and most importantly, live in the same country. Tolerance is powerful knowledge.

Hmong people should realize that no one will win the religious battle until they understand and appreciate the religious beliefs of other people. Whatever they choose to believe or not believe, Hmong have got to learn how to co-exist in America religiously and culturally.

Hmong and Their Children's Education

All Hmong should make education their top priority because education is the key to socioeconomic successes. For Hmong refugees, a good education has always been the root of their socioeconomic possibilities, including respect, integrity, honor, esteem, equality, security, stability, opportunity, and prosperity. Without it, Hmong offspring will face multiple formidable obstacles in life along with serious socioeconomic limitations. As predicted by educators and experts in the field, nearly two-thirds of all jobs will require postsecondary education by 2025 and beyond. Currently, the overall focus of public education concentrates on accessibility, affordability, and academic learning outcomes. Nationally, as reported by the mass media in 2014, the overall unemployment rate is highest for the least educate Americans. For instance, 10 percent is for those who have less than high school diploma, followed by 6 percent for those who have some college or associate degree and 3 percent for those who have a four-year degree or higher. These alarming numbers are predictors and indicators of the trend of quality education for all Americans and the importance of educational attainments.

Hmong people have learned from their past that nothing can replace what their children have received through quality education. One of the primary reasons Hmong parents made sacrifices to bring their families to the U.S. was the opportunity for public education. Education has always been a most powerful tool to not only bring great honor to Hmong families but also to help Hmong change their lifestyles and improve their socioeconomic status. Over the 40 years in America, Hmong people have made remarkable progress in education, and educational opportunities have elevated Hmong in socioeconomic status as well as provided them access to professional careers in many areas. The number of Hmong-American educators and scholars is on the rise as the number of Hmong college students is growing. However, as Xiong and Lee (2011) found, Hmong students in higher education still face some serious academic challenges and socioeconomic impediments, as shown in Tables 14.1 and 14.2. At the same time, the number of Hmong children enrolled in K–12 schools is at an all-time high as is the high school graduate rate among Hmong-American students. The dropout rate of Hmong K–12 students is low compared to that of students with similar

Table 14.1. Socioeconomic Factors Identified by Hmong College Students as Academic Obstacles

Socioeconomic Factor	Students Identifying as Obstacle Number (N = 55)	(%)
Lack of money	39	71%
Poor study habits and skills	38	69%
Poor time management	31	56%
Lack of time to study	33	60%
Lack of self-confidence	24	44%
Lack of motivation	29	53%
Lack of mentors	25	46%
Lack of parental support	12	22%
Lack of support from ASPs	14	26%
Lack of interest in college	7	13%
Lack of direction for obtaining career goals	30	56%
Influence of friends	14	26%
Need to care for younger siblings	14	26%
Health problems	5	9%
Other	5	9%

Table 14.2. Academic Services Identified by Hmong College Students as Helpful to Their Academic Success

Academic Service	Students Identifying as Helpful Number (N = 22)	%
Financial assistance	14	64%
Peer advising and mentoring	13	59%
Academic advising	12	55%
Tutoring	8	36%
Career advising	4	19%
Personal development	4	18%
Leadership development	3	14%
Orientation to the university	2	9%
Internship information	2	9%
Scholarship information	1	5%
Job search	0	0%

ethnic backgrounds. These are highlights of Hmong academic successes.

Many Hmong children still have not taken seriously the educational opportunities available to them. Some are satisfied with the status quo and so lack motivation and interest. For them, education is a low priority. Others lack academic skills and preparation or guidance and counseling. Some are socioeconomically disadvantaged or are unable to overcome cultural and language barriers. Some cannot resist social temptations or peer pressure and others become young parents. Some have social, psychological, and personal problems (substance abuse, criminal behaviors, gang involvement, and medical conditions). These are serious hindrances, but Hmong children are not alone in these challenges.

Besides, Hmong children are far better off today than 40 years ago. Their parents did not have the same opportunities to go to school in the old country. Education was very limited and available only to affluent families. Hmong children should appreciate what is offered to them regardless of their socioeconomic status and make education their number one priority. They must aim high to achieve what they want to become in life, what was denied to their parents. In America, anything can happen, but they have to choose wisely. For instance, accessibility and affordability may not include quality academia that produces positive learning outcomes.

Hmong parents and leaders should pay close attention to the national trends in the number of Hmong ELL and LEP students in K–12 schools. The over-representation of Hmong designated as LEP students is a national crisis and something needs to be done about it before these children reach the upper grades. The non-academic designation put on Hmong children is a label for failure, and public schools designate these children as such because of fiscal and financial interests, not for the best academic interests of Hmong children. In other words, Hmong children are innocent victims of the fiscal greed of school districts, used as bait to procure state and federal funds. Schools are failing to provide quality education to these victimized children whose futures are at stake. Many Hmong children are enrolled in capricious programs that bring income into the schools; they are not in quality academic programs that lead to academic success. Hmong parents and leaders need to ask themselves this question: *Are Hmong children enrolled in the current programs for the school's income or for the children's academic outcome?* For years, public schools have intentionally ignored the law and education codes that require that they provide academic services to Hmong children who need academic intervention and support. The current practices are leaving many Hmong children behind.

Hmong children are scapegoats in this system. If nothing is done, Hmong children will continue to fall through the cracks and become insufficient, underprepared, and disqualified for entering colleges and universities because of their LEP academic status. The point of all this is simple: Hmong children are not the culprits in their academic failure, but the system is because public schools set them up for failure. It is high time for Hmong parents and leaders to cut to the crux of the academic failure of their children. Otherwise, public schools will continue to give them lip service and empty promises.

Illegal segregation ended 60 years ago, but legal segregation is taking place each and every day in the school system across this diverse nation. Hmong children are academically segregated into different classroom settings to learn little or no academic skills. They are victims of state and federal programs and because of their linguistic challenges public schools fail to comply with state and federal mandates to serve them academically. Actions are needed to rescue these Hmong children or they will continue to be subjects of academic exploitation until they are completely drowned and academically ruined. Hmong children deserve better. However, without their parents' support, voices, and advocacy, their academic needs and wants will continue to be ignored by the system.

Hmong and Their Physical and Spiritual Health

All Hmong should need to learn how to find a sensible balance between physical and spiritual health in order for them to meet their medical needs and to develop healthy lifestyles, and at the same, Hmong should be knowledgeable about the quality of healthcare available to them in order for them to take advantage of western medical services. Today, when it comes to medical treatments, most Hmong are still living in two different worlds, the physical world and the spiritual world.

In Laos, Hmong lived on slopes, hills, and mountaintops and were accustomed to the weather of tropical forests. Most Hmong feared coming down to lowland cities, villages, and towns because they thought they would be vulnerable to diseases. Hmong grew their own food and vegetables and raised their own livestock to meet their dietary needs. They consumed primarily natural foods. They drank natural water from streams and rivers, and culturally, Hmong could not drink well water unless it was boiled. Hmong had very poor immunity to mosquito bites and were susceptible to malaria. Colds and hot fevers were among Hmong's worst sicknesses because Hmong did not have medicine to treat these conditions. When family members became sick, Hmong usually depended on shamanistic rituals to determine the wellbeing of their spirits and souls, or the expiration of their predestined declarations of life. Many Hmong died from high fever after coming down to towns to purchase salt. Hmong referred to such a tragic death to as "Mus ev ntsev." Generally speaking, most Hmong were fit and healthy in the highlands because of their agrarian lifestyle and blue-collar type of work.

In 1975, the Hmong way of life changed drastically with an entirely new lifestyle in the U.S. They had a high protein diet; received free medical care; and consumed meat, dairy products, and condiments. When Hmong first arrived, most could not drink cow's milk because they could not break the milk down in their stomachs. They learned to love soda with its high sugar content. Hmong had no knowledge of food calories, nutrition facts, or the ingredients in foods, and this is still true today.

U.S. Hmong are generally in good health, but they have medical needs and conditions as a group. In the early part of life in the new homeland, Hmong suffered an epidemic of sudden death syndrome, probably due to multiple factors related to PTSD and adjustment issues. In subsequent years, Hmong developed medical symptoms associated with diabetes, hypertension, renal failure, cardiac malfunctions, stroke, hepatitis, gout, cancer, influenza, pneumonia, respiratory infection, and other diseases. Today, the leading causes of death among Hmong people are heart disease, cancer, stroke, diabetes, accidents, influenza, pneumonia, and hypertension. Some Hmong still lack medical insurance coverage for basic medical care, but most Hmong are covered by private insurance or public assistance medical programs such as Medicare and Medicaid.

Hmong people, especially the elderly, should be encouraged to seek medical treatment whenever necessary because some medical problems are preventable or curable. Others are manageable with proper medical treatment plans. Even though Hmong are still suspicious about western medical treatments, there is no place better than the U.S. for Hmong to receive medical care. There is nothing wrong with combining western medicine with traditional healing practices and herbal medicine for basic medical concerns. However, Hmong need to understand that routine blood tests, medical exams, and regular doctors' visits help them avoid potentially serious medical conditions. Most importantly, Hmong people should take medical advice from their doctors seriously and follow it carefully. They should not wait until their conditions have reached critical levels before consulting a doctor. If they avoid western medical treatment until late in the disease process, doctors have to rush to make unexpected life and death decisions to save them or have to provide medical treatments that may be traumatizing.

Vang (2012) wrote to encourage Hmong people to keep their religious beliefs and practices and at the same time take advantage of western medical services:

"HMONG SHOULD PRESERVE THEIR RELIGIOUS BELIEFS AND PRACTICES"

A little over a decade ago, when I first read the book The Spirit Catches You and You Fall Down by Ann Fadiman, I was thrilled to learn more about my Hmong culture and traditions in the West. Since 1975, we, the Hmong, resettled in the western nations and brought with us to America our 6,000-year-old way of life. And we preserve and cherish what we believe to the present day.

In recent days, I read another wonderful article in the Modesto Bee newspaper on Hmong traditional healing practices and spiritual medicine titled "Soul Healer." The story detailed Hmong shamanism and the practices of ritual and spiritual medicine to heal the soul of the sick in the hospital. This article reminded me of the past struggle the Hmong faced in America. It also rekindled painful memories.

Initially, shamanistic practices became endangered when Hmong arrived in the new homeland since they felt that these practices were considered taboo in western nations, especially in America. In some Hmong families the rituals went extinct because they required animal sacrifices. Hmong shamans were intimidated by law enforcement agencies because they offered animals as part of their spiritual healing and soul incarnation to redeem the lost souls and spirits of sick or dying individuals. The inability to practice religion freely has caused some Hmong Americans to abandon their traditional beliefs.

Several years ago, there was a classic case in Fresno, California, in which a Hmong shaman was arrested for sacrificing a dog during his shamanistic rituals. The case created a rift between the Hmong American community and the local police department as well as the county court system. Prior to this case, the court system had recognized Hmong traditional medicine and spiritual healing practices. Some Hmong spiritual healers had received legal documents from the court to permit them to continue practicing their ritual and spiritual medicine. However, the court did not specifically say anything about sacrificing animals.

Moreover, most hospitals in the local area recognized the value of Hmong shamanistic practices and accommodated the wishes of the sick culturally. In that regard, Hmong shamans could enter hospitals to perform soul healing practices at any time without causing hot brushes with the laws or western medicine. As I recall, the case in Fresno was dismissed by the court because of cultural misunderstandings and legal misinterpretations involving the first-amendment rights of the Hmong shaman; however, animal activists still disagreed with the outcome. As a result, the Hmong community has somewhat changed their way of preserving traditional beliefs and healing practices to a way that is not intrusive to western philosophies, ideals, and values.

Hmong traditional healing practices are not much different from those of many other non–Hmong Americans. For instance, western medicine honors the services of a religious chaplain who offers spiritual guidance and prayer to the sick in the hospital. Most hospitals have a designated office for this kind of service. In some cases, Buddhist monks pay visits to the hospital to offer their karma blessings to the spirits and souls of the sick. Occasionally, church pastors and family members gather around the hospital bed and pray for the sick to get well. These kinds of religious offerings and healings are acceptable in most cultures and perhaps in most societies as well. Thus Hmong soul healing is not all that odd.

Nevertheless, most religious practices and offerings have changed over time to accommodate today's' societal and political views toward spiritual rites and healing practices. For instance, there are animal rights activist groups and people with anti-theist, anti–Semitic, anti-idolatry, and anti-multicultural values. Regardless of the guarantee of religious freedom in the US Constitution, Americans in general still have some problems accepting different religious faiths, values, and practices. And even if this nation is the land of free religious practices, most Americans have a strong belief that Christianity should the framework of worship since nearly 70 percent of Americans believe in the teaching of the Bible or Gospel. However, Christians are religiously and theologically diverse among themselves. As the Bible

Answer Man has always cautioned his radio listeners: Christianity is in crisis. His introductory phrase, "because truth matters," seems to explain why people do not tolerate one another's religious practices in America: they lack knowledge about the truth of all different faiths.

Not too long ago, I wrote an article on religious tolerance when I read about religious leaders who publicly acknowledged ignorance and intolerant attitudes toward other faiths. This is a good example of religious respect, sensitivity, empathy, and awareness. Most importantly, regardless of one individual's religious belief or values, we all have to respect the man-made laws that govern all beings.

Moreover, religious practices have become very political over the last three decades. Recently, the situation has gotten worse. For instance, the animal rights movement, legalizing abortion, the anti-gay and lesbian movement, civil union laws, the 9/11 attack on the World Trade Center Towers and the US Pentagon, and the controversies involving the "don't ask don't tell" federal laws. These are just a few examples of what Americans are dealing with. Perhaps, the religious dilemma and conflicts will continue to dominate the political arena in the next four decades when new refugees and immigrants arrive in America from other countries, like Iraq, Iran, Afghanistan, Pakistan, Kosovo, Kuwait, Bosnia, and Georgia.

With these in mind, Hmong Americans do not have to feel ashamed or embarrassed to preserve their religious practices in America. Hmong should learn to exercise their constitutional right to protect their religious values and interests in order to preserve the traditional medicine, ritual ceremonies, and spiritual healing practices. In the meantime, Hmong also need to learn how to modify their religious practices to show respect to non–Hmong Americans and the laws that protect all citizens. Meanwhile, Hmong Americans should not overlook the benefits of western medicine that would help them improve their quality of life. For instance, most religious practices offer prayer for healing souls and spirits but not to cure infections, diseases, viruses, stroke, heart attack, diabetes, and renal failure. Combining both treatment practices should be ideally beneficial to the sick.

In addition, Hmong Americans should have the flexibility to adapt to other forms of religious practices whenever possible and necessary to accommodate societal changes and values. For instance, in 1957, the largest group of Hmong villagers in the Northern region of Laos converted to Christianity—mainly Catholicism and CMA. Today, Hmong Christian groups are considered small in numbers but their quality of life has improved. For instance, primary language literacy among Hmong Christians is higher, Hmong Christians have more cohesive groups or denominations, they are becoming recognized in their religious practices worldwide, they engage in religious scholarship activities and join the ranks of religious leaders and pastors. Furthermore, these groups are oriented toward education in their practices rather than using rote memorization and oral traditions.

Keep in mind that all faiths are valuable regardless of religious offerings, sacrifices, prayers, and forms of worship. Hmong culture and traditions are still in transition even after 35 years in America. Hmong Americans should continue to preserve what is beneficial to their daily lives and social well-being. Whether it is a soul healing or spiritual calling, Hmong Americans possess one of the best ancient religions in the world, and what Hmong Americans are preserving and practicing right now is a mixture of Hinduism, Buddhism, Taoism, fatalism, Shintoism, animism, and ancestor worship. In other words, Hmong have been influenced by different faiths and have been considered multi-religious believers for centuries.

Shamanistic practice is just a part of Hmong religious rites and ceremonial rituals. And perhaps, shamanism is one of the core religious values that differentiates, identifies, and represents the origin of Hmong religious history dating back to China. Culturally, the traditional practices of soul healing and spiritual calling are still popular and beneficial to Hmong people today.

Hmong traditional healing and herbal medicine are used to deal with basic urgent needs; they are not good for fighting infections, defects, and diseases. Some herbs are healthy for supplementing the diet and for the treatment of basic ailments only. Hmong shamanistic rituals and soul calling are helpful in supporting the well-being of the soul

and spirits that safeguard the body of the sick, and Hmong shamans can communicate with the spiritual world to determine spiritual curses. However, they cannot determine medical conditions, diseases, viruses, and infections. Therefore, Hmong people should be knowledgeable about the benefits of both systems in order to receive complete medical care and receive it on time.

Hmong and Their Transnational Politics

It is time for Hmong to stop living in a fantasy of dream, and also, it is a high time for Hmong to focus more on the reality of life. For Hmong parents who were born oversea, the dream of returning to the native country, Laos, is long gone; and the hope that Hmong will have their own independent country to live is a fantasy of the past. To Hmong dreamers, this four-decade-old prophesized dream that still lingers in their thoughts will never come true for them—an undying quest. It is time for Hmong parents and leaders to move on. For the betterment of the Hmong people, one very critical thing that new Hmong traditional leaders have to abandon for good is Hmong transnational politics. From the early 1980s to the mid–2007, Hmong people did more harm than good to the international community and their own people, especially those who were left behind in Laos. Many Hmong refugees have been victimized by this worthless and fruitless sociopolitical movement. On June 4, 2007, the arrest of Major General Vang Pao and 10 others should have taught all Laotian-Hmong a life-long lesson that the type of transnational politics they were pursuing is illegal in the U.S. The U.S. government considers anyone who engages in this illegal transnational activity a criminal. More importantly, the arrest should have dampened Hmong interest in promoting propagandistic and senseless cold war politics and, at the same time, the death of Major General Vang Pao should have put a damper on Hmong transnational movement.

If Hmong people and their leaders want to help those who are being persecuted for their ties with the U.S., they should organize their people and their community to lobby elected officials in Washington for support. At the same time, they should work with the United Nations Security Council for Human Rights to advocate for those who are being hunted down like animals by the communist regime. Taking matters into their own hands will not help anyone abroad or at home. It is time to stop living with a fantasy. No Hmong leader will be able to vindicate them if the U.S. government arrests them. At least all Hmong who have a passion for such an impossible mission should think about the national security of this nation first.

Here is an excerpt from an article written by Vang (2011) in regard to the revival of Lao-Hmong transnational politics that sought to rekindle the fantasy:

> If these Lao-Hmong individuals really want to find peace and freedom for the people living in the native country, then they should get involved in US international politics to help change the political landscape that will provide the most benefit to the greater good of the people. Playing dirty and illegitimate politics will do more harm than good to the Lao-Hmong international community. Remember, on June 4, 2007, 11 Hmong leaders were arrested for plotting to overthrow the Laotian government. This is a lesson learned for all Lao-Hmong Americans who are addicted to the Post-Traumatic Old-Politics Disorder (PTOPD), and they have to take this lesson as a serious warning from the US government; otherwise, transnational politics is an act of terrorism.

The U.S. Hmong who are communists and defectors working for the overseas oppressors and dictators should also abandon their espionage mission because:

1. Working as a communist informant and undercover agent to betray Hmong is not only illegal and bad but is an act of a cold-blooded traitor.

2. Living with Hmong while taking advantage of Hmong is like shooting oneself in the foot.

3. Working as a mercenary Hmong citizen who lives a double life is not patriotic, but evil.

4. Selling secretive and false information to a communist country to frame western Hmong people for personal gain is treason against humanity.

5. Being a cold-blooded traitor living among Hmong is like a leech sucking blood out of Hmong veins, and that is pure evil.

As Major General Vang Pao predestined Hmong political plight, "As long as Hmong defectors and traitors are living among Hmong, Hmong people and the Hmong community will continue to be sabotaged, persecuted, extirpated, and humiliated." Therefore, it is time for Hmong to think about a way to eradicate the roots of Hmong-grown enemies who are taking advantage of other Hmong and the Hmong way of life. Otherwise, in a time of great need for new leaders, these leeches will derail Hmong people and the Hmong community. Perhaps, it is time for Hmong traitors and defectors to cleanse their sinful political souls and spirits, renounce their past treachery, and seek and receive forgiveness for all the misdeeds they have committed over the years. Mercenary Hmong individuals are communist culprits working as espionage agents for the ruthless tyrants, dictators, and oppressors who want to extirpate Hmong refugees down to their roots. Hmong put the "*red label*" on these traitors because they are cruel in heart and evil in soul when they prey on their own kind for a pittance of personal gain to elevate their social status. In the Hmong world, the "*red label*" means enemy, cold-blooded traitor, raw hearted, crooked, and heinous criminal. Hmong defectors and traitors are also known as HINO individuals, meaning, *Hmong in name only individuals* who are sold out. When completely exploited by dictators, these HINO have no place to go and would come back to live in the Hmong community. Nonetheless, the scars and excruciated pains they have caused Hmong will remain unhealed and permanent forever, so does the non-expungeable "*red label*" Hmong put on them. It is a high time for these individuals to repent their sins. As Major General Vang Pao warned many times, "Hmong have to get rid of their sins and toxins in blood to pre-pare for the future," in Hmong, it means, "*Yuav tsum muab tej nyuag vij sub vij sw no tso pov tseg mam Hmong thiaj li muaj lub neej nrog luag ua lawm tom ntej.*"

Moreover, the continuity of Hmong trans-national politics will further relegate Hmong sociopolitical leadership to the role of being disobedient citizens because their propagan-distic activities are somewhat related to the promotion of terrorism at home and abroad. At present, some Hmong traditional leaders are searching for political gravitas to start the revival of undying hopes and fantasy of dreams. This is a mission impossible that will plunge Hmong leadership into another decade of sociocultural crises, such as cor-ruption, extortion, human right violation, atrocity, imprisonment, and persecution. More importantly, the revival of Hmong transnationalism will take Hmong commu-nity back to the past, and for that Hmong people definitely need to have new visionary pathfinders and leaders who can lead them to the future.

Hmong and Their Formidable Future

All Hmong are holding the golden key to unlock their present and future, and together, everyone can play a pivotal role in the revival of Hmong leaders and leadership. Currently, Hmong people have no national cultural leader and are living in a state of apostasy. Without new pathfinders and personal sac-rifice, Hmong refugees face a difficult plight and an uncertain future. After the death of Major General Vang Pao, U.S. Hmong have not been able to join efforts to launch a na-tional campaign to restore Hmong leader-ship. Hmong leadership has died and it will take some time for Hmong people and the Hmong community to come together to so-lidify their needs and wants before the emer-gence of new leaders. Such a time is still far away. Major General Vang Pao was not a per-fect leader for all Hmong, but he was a per-fect role model who loved all Hmong in his heart and soul and left behind a vacuum of

leadership for Hmong to fill. If for some rea-son the U.S. Hmong should fail to honor his legacy and hopes, Major General Vang Pao will have been the Hmong's first and last messianic leader.

As a community, Hmong need to find sen-sible medium to empower one another to come together for a common purpose, to stand united for the greater good of the peo-ple, to energize Hmong and their commu-nity, and at the same time, to make complex decisions and personal sacrifices to enhance the present and to shape the future.

Remember, the future is not about what Major General Vang Pao left for, to, and with Hmong people; it is all about what he left in Hmong people so they could shape their fu-ture. The U.S. Hmong have to plant a new seed to start a new cycle of new leaders and leadership.

As Hmong face their formidable future, they face several deficiencies in leadership. Going forward is challenging because Hmong lack:

- existing leadership structure
- mutual respect and reciprocity
- strong leaders with visionary leadership
- pathfinders who can help Hmong search for the right pathway to restore Hmong leadership
- resources for finding cultural gravitas in Hmong leaders
- unity, trust, bond, interests, support, co-operation, collaboration, cohesiveness, and commitment to reinvigorate Hmong leaders and leadership
- basic organizational structure that em-braces the Hmong trinity of power: people, leaders, and community
- actions undertaken in great numbers
- gender equity
- common purpose, a clear mission state-ment, and attainable goals for people to rally around
- cultural gravitas for and among clan and tribal leaders

These are some of the core issues faced by Hmong people in the present time. Without finding some sensible solutions to these ongoing problems, Hmong's search for new leaders will be fruitless because there are many factions, cliques, and special interest groups. It will remain fruitless until Hmong learn to appreciate one another and treat one another with dignity and mutual respect.

While living in the state of apostasy, Hmong are rebelling against Hmong for little or nothing. They will become further divided, disorganized, and traumatized by Hmong tribal and cultural conflicts and familial politics if Hmong fail to reorganize, reestablish, restore, reunify, and restructure Hmong leadership for the greater good of the people. What would Hmong say to non–Hmong people when they ask this question: *Who is the Hmong leader after General Vang Pao?* It is time for Hmong to change themselves before advocating for change in others, and it is time for Hmong to do what is right for the Hmong people and their community as a whole. It is time for Hmong to learn what Major General Vang Pao left in them and how to utilize it to pave the way to the future.

Here is the transcript of the recorded millennium vision Major General Vang Pao left for all Hmong to do:

Yog li nos mas txij yav no mus, yuav tau nrhiav ib cov neeg coj los sau cov cai no zoo zoo, hais txog ntawm kab-tshoob kev-kos yuav ua li cas, kab mob kev tuag no yuav ua cas. Peb ua neeg nyob ntiaj teb no peb yuav pib li cas rau li cas, kev kawm ntaub kawm ntawv thaum txawj ntaub txawj ntawv lawm yuav mus nrhiav laj nrhiav kam ua, es nrhiav kom tau nyiaj tau txiaj. Thaum uas nrhiav tau nyiaj los lawm ne yuav ua li cas yus cov nyiaj thiaj li nyob. Nws kuj muaj hauv paus rau ntsis, maj-mam ua mus. Mas nws tsis nyuab nawb...

Yav tom ntej no yog muaj sij-hawm cob qhia cov Hmoob, qhia cov Hmoob mas yuav tsis nyuab, ces sawv-daws yuav tau lo zaum es sau ib phau ntawv, phau ntawv ntawd mas yog phau directives li kuv lub tswv yim thiab kuv lub qhov muag pom, mam muab phau ntawv ntawd mus qhia cov Hmoob, tsis hais qhia cov poj-niam-txiv neej laus hluas tag nrog huv tib si. Tom qab coj mus qhia lawv tas lawm mas, kuv xav hais tias cov Hmoob yuav tig rov qab los ua ib pab Hmoob khov

kho, yog los ua ib pab Hmoob kom muaj hauv paus rau ntsis mus lawm yav tom ntej...

Hmoob tsis yog ib cov neej phem nawb Hmoob yog ib cov neej zoo, vim tib qhov tsis qhia xwb, yog qhia sau phau ntawv coj mus qhuab qhia hauv tsev kawm ntawv, qhia raws kev tswj hwm, tej lub zej lub zos, tej lub state, ib xyoo xwb Hmoob yeej ras tag nrho tib-si lawm, Hmoob yuav hloov Hmoob cov siab cov ntsws, yuav los ua ib pab ib pawg, yuav los txim kho lub neej li cas. Tim qhov niam-no Hmoob twb muaj kev vam-meej dua los lawm, Hmoob ntshai ntshai plam Hmoob lub neej kawg nkaus, tiam sis tsis tau muaj sij hawm los kho tej no ces thiaj tseem nyuab...

Tiam sis txij 2010 no mus rau 2015, kuv ua txiv kuv twb xav tau cov kev tawm tas lawm ces niam-no kuv yuav tsum nrhiav cov tub txawj nthxais ntse, nrhiav cov neeg ib cov ua tij, nrhiav cov laus los nyob ua ke, es coj ib cov nrub nrab thiab cov tseem hluas niam-no coj los sau tej policy, los yog tej kev qhuab qhia kuv hais no. Tom qab sau tau lawm, mam coj los kho xyuas, yog raug, coj mus luam, mam coj mus register rau hauv Supreme Court hais tias peb cov cai nyob teb chaws no tag nrho zoo li no. Ces dhau ntawd ces yuav tsis muaj dab tsi lawm thiab.

[Note: Translating the above stanzas in English may lose the actual meanings.]

The crux of Major General Vang Pao's message provides the U.S. Hmong with allusion to the five basic needs and wants they definitely have to have: (1) using the democratic process to elect and select new visionary Hmong traditional leaders; (2) seeking innovative socioeconomic infrastructure for greater advancement; (3) forging alliance among all clans to unionize and strengthen ethnic sovereignty and solidarity; (4) searching for strategic action plan to craft a master plan for cultural revival and preservation; and (5) constructing cooperative and collaborative community for sociocultural restructure and reorganization. Together, it is a high time for all Hmong to turn to one another instead of turning one another in the time of leadership in peril. Hmong can help Hmong change the status quo and make a difference in Hmong life. Without altruism, the journey forward for Hmong may be impossible because of Hmong adversaries and tribal impediments. To stand united, at the very least, the U.S. Hmong have to show their willingness to embody and embrace Major General Vang Pao's final quest in searching for a new beginning to restore Hmong leadership for the betterment and enhancement of Hmong people and leaders.

At this very defining moment, all Hmong are created equal and should have received the call of duty to fulfill a left behind legacy that will shape their future. Hmong have to believe in themselves that they can change, can unite, can compromise, can overcome, and can achieve great successes in life. All they will ever need is joining hands to solidify their differences as the old lyrics of a classic Hmong song is calling upon all Hmong to love one another: *"Hmoob tsis sib hlub Hmoob leej twg thiaj yuav hlub Hmoob,"* meaning, "if Hmong do not love Hmong who will love Hmong." Remember, Hmong culture is always beautiful, so are Hmong people.

Summing Up

This chapter laid out the foundations Hmong need to take a journey forward and provided in-depth information on a variety of topics that are crucial to the betterment of the Hmong people and their community.

Among other concerns, finding the right leaders to guide the Hmong people and the Hmong community is the most pressing issue at hand. Hmong people should come together to find their next national leader who can become a national symbol and advocate for their cultural and traditional beliefs, values, customs, and norms. Since the death of Major General Vang Pao in 2011, Hmong people and the Hmong community have been leaderless, and his followers are living in a state of apostasy. The next group of Hmong leaders must be pathfinders who can advance and enhance Hmong people and their community.

Hmong people need to tackle their own adversaries who stall their search for the new leaders, and at the same time, find common ground on which to come together in a democratic process to rebuild their cultural trust and bonds. The 18 different clan leaders have a vital role in this process, but they must be willing to set their personal and tribal spats aside. Major General Vang Pao left a leadership vacuum, and if Hmong fail to fill that vacuum, Hmong leadership will be in peril forever.

It is high time for Hmong people to think collectively, realizing that they have to produce their own leaders who are respected and trusted. There will be no more imperial Hmong leaders who are appointed by the U.S., France, or the Laotian king. This is a golden opportunity for all Hmong to write the next chapter of Hmong leadership. In order for this to be a good chapter, all Hmong people need to chip in. Personal sacrifices are necessary for the greater good of the people, and now is the time. Together, Hmong people

Bibliography

Abramson, S., and Lindberg, G. (1985, March). *Achievement of Southeast Asian students and its relation to school resources programs.* Paper presented at the annual meeting of the American Education Research Association, Chicago, IL.

August, D., and Hakuta, K. (1997). *Improving schooling for language-minority children: A research agenda.* Washington, D.C.: National Academy Press.

Bialystok, E., and Hakuta, K. (1994). *In other words: The science and psychology of second language acquisition.* New York: Basic Books.

Bliatout, B.T., Downing, B.T., Lewis, J., and Yang, D. (1988). *Handbook for teaching Hmong-speaking students.* Folsom, CA: Folsom Cordova Unified School District.

Caplan, N. (1985). Working toward self-sufficiency. *Institute for Social Research Newsletter, 13*(1), 5, 7. (ERIC Document Reproduction Services No. ED 263253)

Caplan, N., Choy, M., and Whitmore, J. (1992, February). Indo-Chinese refugee families and academic achievement. *Scientific American,* 35–42.

Cha, T. (2013). *Mong: China history and heritage preservation.* Shenzhen, Guangdong, China: China Gold Printing Group.

Collier, V.P. (1987). Age and rate of acquisition of second language for academic purposes. *TESOL Quarterly, 4*(3), 21–30.

Cummins, J. (1991). The development of bilingual proficiency from home to school: A longitudinal study of Portuguese-speaking children. *Journal of Education, 173*(2), 342–345.

Delgado-Gaitain, C. (1987). Traditions and transitions in the learning process of Mexican children: An ethnographic view. In G. and L. Spindler (Eds.), *Interpretive ethnography of education* (pp. 332–362). Hillsdale, NJ: Lawrence Erlbaum Associates.

Emerging Hmong American scholars. *Hmong Tribune,* July, 2014, p. 3.

Golstein, B.L. (1985). *Schooling for cultural transition: Hmong girls and boys in American high schools.* Unpublished doctoral dissertation, University of Wisconsin, Madison.

Heath, S.B. (1982). *Questioning at home and at school: A comparative study.* In G. Spindle (Ed.), *Doing the ethnography of schooling* (234–236). New York: Holt, Rinehart and Winston.

Hernandez, R.D. (1994). Reducing bias in the assessment of culturally and linguistically diverse populations. *Journal of Educational Issues of Language Minority Students, 14,* 269–300.

Hess, R.S. (2000). Dropping out among Mexican American youth: Reviewing the literature through an ecological perspective. *Journal of Education for Students Placed At-Risk, 5*(3), 267–289.

Hmong children in American public schools. (1989). *Hmong California Times,* p. A5.

Hmong Issues 2000 Conference, Fresno, CA. Sponsored by Hmong Educators of Fresno.

Hmong National Development and Hmong Cultural and Resource Center. (2004). *Hmong 2000 Census Publication: Data and Analysis.* Washington, D.C., and Saint Paul, MN: Hmong National Development and Hmong Cultural and Resource Center.

Hvitfeldt, C. (1982). *Learning language and literacy: A microethnographic study of Hmong classroom behavior.* Unpublished doctoral dissertation, University of Wisconsin, Madison.

Ima, K., and Rumbaut, R. (1988). *The adaptation of Southeast Asian refugee youth: A comparative study.* Washington, D.C.: U.S. Department of Health and Human Services, Office of Refugee Resettlement.

Ima, K., and Rumbaut, R.G. (1989). Southeast Asian refugees in American schools: A comparison of fluent-English-proficient and limited-English-proficient students. *Topics in Language Disorders, 9*(3), 54–77.

Johnson, C., and Yang, Se. (1992). *Dab Neeg Hmong* (Myths, Legends and Folk Tales). St. Paul, MN: Macalester College.

Keller, G., Deneen, J., and Magallan, R. (1991). *Assessment and curriculum: Hispanics in higher education.* New York, NY: State University of New York Press.

Lee. S.J. (2001). More than "model minorities" or "delinquents": A look at Hmong American high

455

school students." *Harvard Educational Review,* *71*(3), 505–528.

Lee, B. and Shin, F. (1996, spring). Hmong parents' perceptions of bilingual education. *CAAPAE Newsletter,* 10–15.

Lee, V.W. (1993). Low literacy immigrant students pose new challenges. *New Voices,* 3(1), 1–3.

Lenneberg, E. (1967). *Biological foundations of language.* New York, NY: John Wiley and Sons.

Lessow-Hurley, J. (2000). *The foundations of dual language instruction (4th ed.).* New York, NY: Addison Wesley Longman.

Lie, G.-Y., Yang, P., Rai, K., and Vang, P.Y. (2004). Hmong children and families. In R. Fong (Ed.), *Culturally competent practice with immigrant and refugee children and families* (122–145). New York, NY: Guilford Press.

Ly, P. (2013). *Keebkwm Hmoob kev cojnoj cojua.* Fresno, CA.

MacCorrquodale, P. (1998). *Mexican-American women and mathematics: Participation, aspiration, and achievement.* Hillsdale, NJ: Lawrence Erlbaum Associates.

Martin, G. (1991). Family, gender, and social policy. In L. Kramer (Ed.), *The sociology of gender* (320–345). New York: St. Martin's Press.

McGinn, F. (1989). *Hmong literacy among adolescents and the use of Hmong literacy during resettlement.* Unpublished doctoral dissertation, University of San Francisco, San Francisco, California.

Morrison, G.L. (1999). *Sky is falling: An oral history of the CIA's evacuation of the Hmong from Laos.* Jefferson, NC: McFarland.

Morrow, R.D. (1989). Southeast Asian child-rearing practices: Implications for child and youth care workers. *Child and Youth Care Quarterly,* 18(4), 273–288.

National Center for Education Statistics. (1996). *A comparison of high school dropout rates in 1982 and 1992.* Washington, D.C.: Author.

Ogbu, J.U. (1993). *Variability in minority school performance: A problem in search of an explanation.* In E. Jacob and C. Jordon (Eds), *Minority education: An anthropological perspective* (83–107). Norwood. NJ: Ablex.

Olsen, L. (1988). *Immigrant students and the California public schools: Crossing the schoolhouse border.* San Francisco, CA: California Tomorrow.

O'Reilly, T. (1998*). An investigation of Hmong students' academic success.* Unpublished doctoral dissertation, University of Minnesota, St. Paul.

Park, C. (1998). *A comparative study of educational and occupational aspirations: Southeast Asian and Anglo students.* Paper presented at the annual conference of American Educational Research Association, April, San Diego, California.

Pfeifer, M.E., and Thao, B.K. (Eds.). (2013). *State of the Hmong American community.* Washington, D.C.: Hmong National Development.

Portes, A., and Rumbaut, R. (1996). *Immigrant America: A portrait* (2nd Ed.) Berkeley, CA: University of California Press.

Pulaski, A. (April 15, 1994). Welfare reliance among Hmong spreads to next generation. *The Fresno Bee,* Sec. A, pp. 1, 15.

Purdham, L. (1988). *Teaching English limited proficient children: PREP-preparing refugees for elementary programs.* Bataan, Philippines: World Relief Philippine Refugee Processing Center. (ERIC Document Reproduction Services, No. ED 342206)

Quincy, K. (1988). *Hmong: History of a People.* Cheney, WA: Washington University Press.

Ranard, D.A. (1988, November). The Hmong: No strangers to change. *In America: Perspectives on Refugee Resettlement, 1,* 1–3.

Reder, S. (1982). A Hmong community's acquisition of English. In B.T. Downing and D.B. Olney (Eds,), *The Hmong in the West* (268–303). Minneapolis, MN: Southeast Asian Refugee Studies Project Center for Urban and Regional Affairs, University of Minnesota.

Reder, S. (1985). *The Hmong resettlement study.* Washington, D.C.: U.S. Department of Health and Human Services, Office of Refugee Resettlement.

Robson, B. (1982). Hmong literacy, formal education and their effects on performing in an ESL class. In *The Hmong in the West* (201–225). Minneapolis, MN: Southeast Asian Refugee Studies Project, Center for Urban and Regional Affairs, University of Minnesota.

Rumberger, R.W. (1991). Chicano dropouts: A review of research and policy issues. In R.R. Valencia (Ed.), *Chicano school failure and success: Research and policy agendas for the 1990s* (64–89). New York: Falmer.

Siu, S.F. (1993). *Taking no chances: A profile of a Chinese-American family's support for school success.* Paper presented at the annual meeting of the American Educational Research Association, Atlanta, Georgia.

Siu, S.F. (1996). *Asian American students at risk: A literature review.* Report No. 8. Baltimore, MD: Center for Research on the Education of Students Placed at Risk.

Sonsalla, D. (1984). *A comparative case study of secondary school programs for Hmong refugee students in the Minneapolis and St. Paul schools.* Unpublished doctoral dissertation, Minneapolis: University of Minnesota.

Teranishi, Robert T. (2004). Yellow and brown: Emerging Asian American immigrant populations and residential segregation." *Equity and Excellence in Education* 37, 255–263.

Thao, P. (1999). *Hmong education at the crossroads.* Lanham. MD: University Press of America.

Thao, Y.J. (2003). "Empowering Mong students: Home and school factors." *Urban Review 35*(1), 25–42.

Txhawb: Hmong California Directory. (2011, 4th ed.). "Txhawb profiles." p. 32–34.

Txhawb: Hmong California Directory. (2012, 5thed.). "Txhawb profiles." p. 105, 107, 108.

Txhawb: Hmong California Directory. (2014, 7thed.). "Txhawb profiles." p. 58–60, 103, 107.

U.S. Census Bureau (2006–2010). *American Community Survey 3-year estimates.*

U.S. Census Bureau (2008–2010). *American Community Survey 3-year estimate.*

U.S. Department of Education, Office of Educational Research and Improvement, National Institute for the Education of At-Risk Students. (1998). *Facts about limited English proficient students.* Washington, D.C.: Author.

Vang, A.T. (1992). *A descriptive study of academically proficient Hmong high school girl dropouts.* Unpublished doctoral dissertation, University of San Francisco, San Francisco, California.

Vang, A.T. (1999). Hmong-American students: Challenges and opportunities. In C.C. Park and M .M. Chi (Eds.), *Asian-American education: Prospects and challenges* (218–236). Westport, CT: Bergin and Harvey.

Vang, C.T. (2001). *Histories and academic profiles of successful and unsuccessful Hmong secondary students.* Unpublished doctoral dissertation, University of California, Davis and California State University, Fresno.

Vang, C.T. (Nov. 2, 2002). Hmong, doctors need to teach and share ideas. *Fresno Bee*, p. B7.

Vang, C.T. (Nov. 23, 2002). Dr. Tony Vang's election proves Hmong power. *Fresno Bee*, p. B7.

Vang, C.T. (Dec. 21, 2002). Hmong elders must condemn cruel polygamy. *Fresno Bee*, p. B9.

Vang, C.T. (July 26, 2003). Hmong resolve their differences the difficult way. *FresnoBee.com*

Vang, C.T. (2003). Let's talk about civic participation. *Quarterly Hmong Student Journal*, p. 22–23.

Vang, C.T. (March 26, 2005). Hmong deserve praise for their quick progress. *Fresno Bee*, p. B9.

Vang, C.T. (Sept. 10, 2005). Hmong dowries drive men to crime. *Fresno Bee*, p. B11.

Vang, C.T. (Nov. 25, 2006). United Hmong scored big in the election. *Fresno Bee*, p. B9.

Vang, C.T. (June 7, 2007). Hmong arrests revive painful memories. *Fresno Bee*. p. B9.

Vang, T.S. (2008). *A history of the Hmong: From ancient time to the modern diaspora.* Lulu.com

Vang, C.T. (2008). Religious tolerance is needed to embrace different faiths and values in America. Personal online column, www.gohmong.com

Vang. C.T. (2010). *An educational psychology of methods in multicultural education.* New York: Peter Lang.

Vang, C.T. (2011). Lao-Hmong political movement. Personal online column, www.gohmong.com

Vang, C.T. (2012). Hmong face a sense of gloomy leadership. Personal online column, www.goh mong.com

Vang, C.T. (2012). Hmong have seen the first and last messiah. Personal online column, www.goh mong.com

Vang, C.T. (2013). Hmong look for leadership symbol. Personal online column, www.gohmong.com

Vang, C.T. (2013). Why some Hmong criticize General Vang Pao publicly. Personal online column, www.gohmong.com

Vang, C.T. (2012). Hmong need to move from grief to find solace. Personal online column, www.gohmong.com

Vang, C.T. (2012). Hmong should preserve their religious beliefs and practices. Personal online column, www.gohmong.com

Vang, C.T. (2012). Who should Hmong follow now? Personal online column, www.gohmong.com

Vang, C.T. (2012). Why Hmong live in the state of apostasy. Personal online column, www.goh mong.com

Vang, C.T. (2013). Hmong clan clubs need new focus. Personal online column, www.gohmong.com

Vang, C.T. (2013). Hmong failed leadership quest. Personal online column, www.gohmong.com

Vang, C.T. (2013). Hmong need to find cultural gravitas. Personal online column, www.gohmong.com

Vang, C.T. (2013).Why Hmong still face unity issues. Personal online column, www.gohmong.com

Walker,W.S. (1988). *The other side of the Asian academic success myth: The Hmong story.* Qualifying paper for the doctorate in education. Harvard University, Cambridge, MA.

Wehlry, B., and Nelson, W. (1987). *The assimilation and acculturation of Indo-Chinese refugees into Illinois schools.* Macomb, IL: Western Illinois University, Department of Counselor Education and College Student Personnel. (ERIC Document Reproduction Services No. 278741)

Weslander, D., and Stephany, G.V. (1983). Evaluation of English as a second language program for Southeast Asian students. *TESOL Quarterly, 17,* 473–480.

Wheeler, G., Schroeder, A.B., and Tafoya, C. (1982). *Evaluation of a dual bilingual program: English-Spanish and English-Southeast Asian languages.* Clovis, NM: Clovis Public Schools. (ERIC Document Reproduction No. 233651)

Wright, R. (1997). *A study of the academic language of college-bound at-risk secondary students.* Unpublished doctoral dissertation, Joint Doctoral Program in Educational Leadership, University of California, Davis and California State University, Fresno.

Xiong, S., and Lee, S.E. (2011). Hmong students in higher education and academic support programs. *Hmong Studies Journal, 12,* 1–20.

Yang, D. (1982). Why did Hmong leave Laos? In B.T. Downing and D.P. Olney (Eds.), *The Hmong in the West* (3–18). Minneapolis, MN: Center for Urban and Regional Affairs, University of Minnesota.

Yang, D., and Blake, J. (1993). *Hmong at the turning point*. Minneapolis, MN: World Bridge Associates.

Yang, K. (1995). *The Hmong in Fresno: A study of Hmong welfare participation and self-sufficiency.* Unpublished doctoral dissertation, Joint Doctoral Program in Educational Leadership, University of California, Davis and California State University, Fresno.

Index